Legends of Arthur

Legends of Arthur

RICHARD BARBER

BARNES
& NOBLE
BOOKS
NEW YORK

This edition published by Barnes & Noble, Inc.,
by arrangement with Boydell & Brewer Ltd.

2002 Barnes & Noble Books

ISBN 0-7607-3080-6

Printed and bound in the United States of America

02 03 04 05 06 MC 9 8 7 6 5 4 3 2 1

FG

CONTENTS

INTRODUCTION

THE IMAGE OF ARTHUR has haunted the poets and writers of western Europe for nearly nine centuries, and there is no sign of an end to the reign of the 'once and future king' in the world of literature. The Arthurian epic is as popular a subject now as it was when it was first fashioned, and the stories about Arthur and the heroes associated with him come in a bewildering number of guises. There has never been just one authentic version of his deeds, and new Arthurs are still being created apace. All this springs from a figure so obscure that we cannot even be sure that he existed, a shadow of a shadow in the fragments of history and poetry that survive from sixth-century Wales. His deeds have often, if not always, been those of other men; even the twelve great battles which the Welsh chronicler Nennius tells us about in the eighth century may be those involving other leaders, and his last victory over the Saxons at Mount Badon, centre of so much speculation and invention, is not attributed to him in the one contemporary record of it. What inspired the Welsh poets, however, was not the hero himself, whoever he may have been, but an idea, an idea which was a rallying-call to a people in retreat, driven by the Saxons into the western extremities of the land that had once been theirs: 'Their land they shall lose, except wild Wales.' Arthur, who had once held the Saxons at bay, would return to conquer them.

And, in a manner of speaking, he has done so. Later medieval stories about him make him emperor of much of Europe; and his story was called 'the matter of Britain'. The other great 'matters' which medieval poets celebrated were those of Troy and France, tales now long forgotten or best known in other, older versions. Arthur came to play a leading part in the literature of France and Germany, and later of England, conquering minds and imaginations if not bodies and lands. It is he, obscure and perhaps fictional, who is the archetypal medieval heroic figure, not the real and imperial Charlemagne, around whom the matter of France revolved.

Much of the credit for the creation of this figure must go to Geoffrey of Monmouth, probably of Welsh blood, but trained in the courts of the Norman kings and the schools of Paris. Seeking to record what scraps he could find of the Welsh past, he shaped a history of the British people which matched the exploits of Rome and France, in which Arthur almost conquers Rome, echoing the careers of the emperors of the later Roman period who began as British generals. It was fiction, but far from implausible, and it caught the imagination of his contemporaries; a few grumbled that there was no trace of Arthur in reliable books, but for the most part Geoffrey's work was taken up with enthusiasm, and incorporated into historical chronicles, where it filled an awkward blank in the past. From chronicles in Latin, poets retold the story in French verse; and with the advent of a new and sophisticated court literature in French and German, the Arthurian legends began to take shape.

The most remarkable thing about the stories grouped around Arthur is the extraordinary rapidity with which they were created. The first romances appear in the middle of the twelfth century, about 1160; by 1225 there was a huge and complex mass of interwoven tales, a 'cycle' of stories about the heroes of the Round Table – which itself had only appeared in the 1150s. Even more dramatic was the growth of stories about the Grail, invented in the early 1190s; within twenty years there was not just one fully developed romance, but at least three widely differing versions of its story. It seemed that the legends gathered up in their wake whatever was new and exciting: the idea of courtly love, the new enthusiasm for chivalry, the sport of tournaments, even the spiritual teachings of the Cistercian order and the debate about the real presence of Christ's body in the Mass.

Perhaps precisely because there was no real historical core to the stories, they were free to develop according to each writer's own agenda. We find a huge range of styles. There is an entrancing simplicity to some of the early Tristan poems; yet Gottfried von Strassburg tells the same story in an exceptionally sophisticated, highly philosophical style. Chrétien de Troyes explores the psychology of his characters in long monologues, while later writers prefer to plunge into lengthy descriptions of the physical violence of the tournament. Wolfram von Eschenbach envelops the Grail story in alchemical lore and eastern mysteries, ranging magpie-like through a vast store of knowledge. And the creator of Galahad draws on Cistercian theology to create a didactic story on the spiritual values of knighthood.

Yet by the mid-thirteenth century, something akin to an accepted core of stories had emerged. At the beginning of that century, an obscure writer called Robert de Boron had taken the story of the Grail and had given it a prehistory, a kind of Hollywood 'prequel', which in a stroke of astonishing boldness created a chronicle of the guardians of the Grail from Joseph of Arimathea, who had overseen the burial of Christ, to King Arthur's days. The story of Arthur, in this version, was intimately bound up with the story of man's redemption through Christ, and this overarching concept is present in the so-called 'Vulgate Cycle', which spans the period from the Crucifixion to Arthur's death, bringing in the tale of Arthur himself, the adventures of Lancelot and the quest for the Grail, before recounting the tragedy of the last days of Arthur's reign. Later writers reshaped and extended this material according to their own tastes; Lancelot's story predominates in one version, and the Grail story is drawn into this entirely secular tale of the love of Arthur's greatest knight for his queen, Guinevere. Another huge romance was centred on Tristan, and when it eventually winds its way to a conclusion, we find the death of Tristan and Iseult intertwined with the achievement of the Grail, with Arthur almost absent.

Although the stories continued to be read and adapted in the fourteenth and fifteenth centuries, and were as popular as ever, the main creative period of the romances was over. There are strange new tales such as that of Perceforest, a type of secular parallel to the prehistory of the Grail which takes the Round Table back to heathen times, before the birth of Christ; there are oddities, such as Arthur's adventures as knight-errant accompanied by a talking parrot in the tale called *The Knight with the Parrot*; and there are isolated masterpieces like *Sir Gawain and the Green Knight*, taking a single hero and a single story out of the throng. As for the vast earlier romances, their sheer length had become an obstacle to enjoyment, and we find a series of attempts to produce a more manageable version of the whole story, in Italy, in Germany, at the court of the duc de Berry in France, and, most notably, in England, where Sir Thomas Malory, drawing on a wide range of French and English sources besides the Vulgate Cycle, forged the most powerful of all the accounts of the Round Table.

Malory has achieved such a status in English literature that it is easy to forget the rich and varied past which lies behind his coherent work. When Victorian writers rediscovered the world of Arthur, it was largely through Malory's pages, and the successive printings of his work in the early nineteenth century match the progress of the Arthurian revival. Only gradually did the wider canvas of medieval romance become known again, as scholars worked on previously disregarded manuscripts, and translations were offered to the wider world. Indeed, the great Vulgate Cycle version had to wait for a complete edition until the 1890s, and the first full translation finally emerged in the 1990s.

What follows is an attempt, perhaps foolhardy, to present in a small space the variety of the legends. It mimics to some extent what Malory did with much more skill half a millennium ago, and plunders a variety of different sources to create the stories; but it also deliberately breaks away from the idea that there is a single, authentic version, by presenting two tellings of each of the stories that have been chosen. I have limited myself to the medieval romances, partly in order to give the stories a stylistic coherence and to avoid drastic changes of idiom. Equally, this is not an anthology; for so vast a mass of material, an anthology can only offer bleeding fragments of complex masterpieces. If I have succeeded in my aim, the reader will want to go on to the full versions of the originals, and a list of sources is given at the end of the book for those who wish to pursue their Arthurian quest further.

ARTHUR

WE KNOW VERY LITTLE about the real Arthur. The scraps of history about him date from centuries after his death; it is as if all that we knew about the historical Elizabeth I was two sentences written down at the beginning of the nineteenth century, and the rest was either hearsay or the work of today's novelists. The image we now have of Arthur as a great medieval king, leader of a splendid company of chivalrous knights in shining armour, is pure fantasy, imagined by poets of the Middle Ages who wanted to create a kind of ideal court. The Round Table and the Holy Grail are dream-symbols, born out of the longing for justice and grace in an imperfect, brutal world.

Instead, we have to forget all this, and hunt for an obscure ruler who may or may not have actually existed. For the real Arthur, we have to rely on evidence which is shadowy and unreliable; he lived in an age when records hardly existed, in the dark times after the Roman legions had withdrawn from Britain, unable to defend it against the invading Saxons. We do not really know what happened in the century after the legions left, from about AD 450 to 550, and we have to rely on the archaeologists to piece together some clues. We have just one book that may be contemporary, Gildas' *On the Ruin of Britain*; despite its promising title, it is a sermon on the vices of the rulers of his time, and Gildas does not mention Arthur at all. Instead, he portrays a land in the grip of warlords, petty kings who carved out territories for themselves in the vacuum left by the disappearance of the Roman imperial rule. The fact that Arthur's name survived may indicate that he achieved some great feat, such as winning a triumphant victory over the Saxons; and he may well have fallen in battle. The two earliest notes of his existence, in a very simple list of important events now known as *The Annals of Wales*, written down three hundred years after his death, tell us just this:

Year 72: The battle of Badon in which Arthur bore the cross of Jesus Christ on his shoulders for three days and three nights, and the Britons were the victors.
Year 93: Battle at Camlann in which Arthur and Medraut perished.

Medraut is of course Mordred, subsequently said to be Arthur's bastard son; he is one of the few among the ladies and heroes of later legend to appear in the early records with him. Arthur's wife Guinevere; Kay, the chief officer of his court; Bedivere, his cup-bearer, and one or two minor figures are the only others who are associated with him before the poets and romancers get to work. Merlin has his own tradition, and was not linked with Arthur until the twelfth century.

If we are right in believing that Arthur lived at the end of the fifth century, what was his existence like? It is tempting to go to the other extreme from his traditional image, and to portray him as a kind of throwback to pre-Roman times, living in huts made of boughs, and painting himself with blue woad before a battle. But even after the Romans left, the connections between England and the Continent continued, and although the order of Roman rule vanished, the trade routes remained open, Roman towns and villas were not entirely deserted, and Latin remained in everyday use. It was a gradual decline rather than a sudden catastrophe. Luxuries from Europe were still traded in return for raw materials such as British tin. The Cornish tin-mines were the most important source of tin in Europe, and whatever the risks of a voyage to Britain, the rewards for a merchant were great. So a ruler like Arthur would probably have enjoyed a lifestyle which his Roman predecessors would have found familiar. Pottery from Italy and glass from Bordeaux could have been on his table. Purple dyes, and spices such as coriander and dill, came on trading ships, along with salt and wine from western France; wine may also have come from the Mediterranean. Roman buildings were still in use. Arthur's dress would have been recognisably Roman, and it is possible that his armour and weapons were still Roman in general style. He has been portrayed as leader of a Roman cavalry force, but he is more likely to have led his men into battle on foot. The army could have travelled on horseback, but the idea of Arthur leading a cavalry charge is as romantic as the picture of him as a medieval knight.

Even if Arthur himself could not read, there would have been men at his court who could not only read and write, but still knew much about poetry and literature. St Patrick, almost a contemporary of Arthur and certainly from Britain, left letters which show a real knowledge of Latin style. Arthur would definitely have been Christian; the Celtic Church had begun to develop its own distinctive traditions and learning, as well as contacts with the Church in Gaul. For example, the inscriptions on British gravestones are similar to those found in Gaul at the same time. The picture that emerges is of a civilisation looking back to Rome, where a Briton had been one of the last emperors before the separation. But the Britons lacked the resources to live in the high Roman style. Towns and villas depended on a secure political structure, and kings like Arthur, whatever their victories on the battlefield, were unable to provide this. It was a civilised society in decline, threatened by the Saxons who had begun to establish themselves in the east of the island, and it was safer to withdraw to fortified camps than to try to revive the life of cities like Bath.

Soon after Arthur's death, the Saxons swept across the British lands, driving the Britons back into Wales. If there is one thing that is reasonably certain about Arthur, it is that he did not come from modern Wales, but from somewhere in the lands which were lost by the Welsh. His real history disappeared in the confusion, as refugees streamed westwards; for history, such as it was, was not written down but remembered and passed on by word of mouth, particularly by the court poets. With the destruction of whole dynasties and their courts, the traditions came to an abrupt end. But something of his story survived, and Arthur became the hero of Welsh dreams, the leader who would return to drive out the invaders. This belief in his return is almost as old as the first written records about him.

The stories about him associate him with different parts of England: Cumberland, Hadrian's Wall, the great earthwork at Cadbury in Somerset, and Tintagel all have a good claim. Tintagel, however, is particularly interesting, as it was not only an important trading centre for the sixth century, but it also figures very prominently in the first romantic version of Arthur's story; according to this, Tintagel is where he was conceived, when his father seduced the wife of the duke of Cornwall. None of the other places can claim such a clear connection with Arthur.

We have already seen how the first romantic version of Arthur's story is disguised as history, and was designed by its author, Geoffrey of Monmouth, to provide a historical account of the Welsh. His aim was to parallel the discoveries about the Saxon past which other historians of the period had been making; but whereas the Saxon histories existed in chronicles and books which had been preserved in English monasteries, and which could still be read by some of the monks, the Welsh past was only recorded in oral tradition and the occasional document. So Geoffrey had to piece together his story to a far greater extent than a historian writing about the Anglo-Saxons; and when his source material – which was often obscure and difficult – failed him, he used his imagination. At this distance in time, we cannot tell where research ends and fiction begins; but there is general agreement that the story of Arthur as would-be emperor of Rome is fiction, designed to give the Welsh a prestigious hero at the centre of their story. The broad outlines of Arthur's tale are familiar: his mysterious birth, engineered by Merlin; his heroic career as leader of the British; his expedition to the Continent; and his betrayal in his absence by Mordred, leading to his death in civil war.

All this is recounted by Geoffrey in sober style, as befits a chronicler, and when he comes to Arthur's death, he is confronted by a problem. We know that stories about Arthur which claimed that he had not died, but would return in person to lead the British, were in circulation in Geoffrey's time; and Geoffrey appears to acknowledge the existence of such tales by the way in which he abruptly ends his account: 'Arthur himself, our renowned king, was mortally wounded and was carried off to the Isle of Avalon, so that his wounds might be attended to.' This was too brief for his readers, and about a hundred years later a more extended version of Arthur's death was written, possibly with the intention of adding it to Geoffrey's *History of the Kings of Britain*. At all events, though it is more common as a separate account, it turns up in a manuscript, now in Paris, as a substitute for Geoffrey's ending. It fits so well that I have followed the example of the unknown scribe, and added the *True History of the Death of Arthur* in the appropriate place.

But Geoffrey's story does not include two crucial elements in Arthur's personal history: the Round Table and his betrayal by Lancelot and Guinevere. The Round Table first appears in a French verse translation of Geoffrey's book made about 1155; it arrives as Guinevere's dowry, and is less an institution for the encouragement of knighthood and noble deeds, than a democratic innovation to prevent Arthur's barons quarrelling about precedence, since all are seated equally at such a round table. Both the Round Table as we know it and the figure of Lancelot belong to the next stage in the evolution of Arthur's story: his adoption as the chivalric king *par excellence*, to whose court all knights who aspire to make a name must come. The writer who was mainly responsible for this new vision of Arthur came from northern France, where many cultural currents flowed together; his name was Chrétien de Troyes, and we have five surviving Arthurian romances by him. He worked in the period 1170–1190, when the new sport of the tournament was developing, and when chivalry was becoming all the rage with the knightly classes. One of the underlying themes of the romances was the idea of courtly love, by which a knight served a lady in affairs of love much as he served a lord in feudal matters. The interpretation of courtly love is a perennial puzzle; the one apparent surviving manual, by Andreas Capellanus, has been shown up as an intellectual *jeu d'esprit* by a scholar from the philosophy schools at Paris. It was undoubtedly controversial, because it was often depicted as involving a knight's love, platonic or otherwise, for a married lady; and Chrétien himself seems to have had qualms on this score.

At all events, Lancelot and Guinevere's love, whatever its purity in the original telling, was recognised as adulterous by the end of the Middle Ages. But it had also become a key element in the tragedy of Arthur: at his marriage, the king creates the noblest institution in the secular world, the Round Table, only to have it destroyed by his wife and the greatest of all the knights who sit at it. This story is first found in full in the last book of the so-called Vulgate Cycle, *The Death of Arthur*. This is the version I have largely used, with the more famous retelling by Sir Thomas Malory; the latter moves increasingly away from his original as the story proceeds, until in the closing pages he speaks with his own eloquent and authentic voice, matching in prose the tragic sequence of events that leads to the dispersal of the Round Table and to Arthur's death. But the tragedy is not Arthur's alone, and the story ends with the destinies of Lancelot and Guinevere, as a kind of epilogue.

ARTHUR THE EMPEROR

AFTER THE DEATH OF UTHER PENDRAGON, the leaders of the Britons gathered in the town of Silchester and there suggested to Dubricius, the archbishop of Caerleon, that he should crown Arthur, the son of Uther, as their king. Necessity urged them on, for as soon as the Saxons heard of the death of King Uther, they invited their own countrymen over from Germany, appointed Colgrin as their leader and began to do their utmost to exterminate the Britons. They had already overrun all the country which stretches from the river Humber to the sea named Caithness.

Dubricius lamented the sad state of his country. He called the other bishops to him and bestowed the crown of the kingdom upon Arthur. Arthur was a young man only fifteen years old; but he was of outstanding courage and generosity, and his inborn goodness gave him such grace that he was loved by almost all the people. Once he had been invested with the royal insignia, he observed the normal custom of giving gifts freely to everyone. Such a great crowd of soldiers flocked to him that he came to an end of what he had to distribute. However, the man to whom openhandedness and bravery both come naturally may indeed find himself momentarily in need, but poverty will never harass him for long. In Arthur courage was closely linked with generosity, and he made up his mind to harry the Saxons, so that with their wealth he might reward the retainers who served his own household. The justness of his cause encouraged him, for he had a claim by rightful inheritance to the kingship of the whole island. He therefore called together all the young men whom I have just mentioned and marched on York.

ARTHUR'S WARS AGAINST THE SAXONS

As soon as Colgrin heard this, he assembled the Saxons, Scots and Picts, and came to meet Arthur with a vast multitude. Once contact was made between the two armies, beside the river Douglas, both sides stood in grave danger for their lives. Arthur, however, was victorious. Colgrin fled, and Arthur pursued him; then Colgrin entered York and Arthur besieged him there.

When Baldulf, the brother of Colgrin, heard of the latter's flight, he came to raise the siege with six thousand troops, in the hope of freeing the beleaguered man. At the time when his brother had gone into battle, Baldulf himself had been on the sea-coast, where he was awaiting the arrival of Duke Cheldric, who was on his way from Germany to bring them support. When he was some ten miles distant from the city of York, Baldulf decided to take the advantage of a night march, so that he could launch an unexpected attack. Arthur heard of this and ordered Cador, duke of Cornwall, to march to meet Baldulf that same night, with six hundred cavalry and three thousand foot. Cador surrounded the road along which the enemy was marching and attacked the Saxons unexpect-edly, so that they were cut to pieces and killed, and those who remained alive were forced to flee. As a result Baldulf became extremely worried at the fact that he could not bring help to his brother. He debated with himself how he could manage to talk with Colgrin; for he was convinced that by consulting together it would be possible for them to hit upon a safe solution — that is, if only he could make his way into his brother's presence.

Once Baldulf had come to the conclusion that no other means of access was open to him, he cut short his hair and his beard and dressed himself up as a minstrel with a harp. He strode up and down in the camp, pretending to be a harpist by playing melodies on his instrument. No one suspected him and he moved nearer and nearer to the city walls, keeping up the same pretence all the time. In the end he was observed by the besieged, dragged up over the top of the walls on ropes and taken to his brother. When Colgrin set eyes on Baldulf he embraced him and kissed him to his heart's desire, as though Baldulf had been restored to him from the dead. Finally, when, after long discussions, they had abandoned all hope of ever escaping, messengers returned from Germany to say that they had brought with them to Albany, which is now known as Scotland, six hundred ships which were commanded by Cheldric and loaded with brave soldiery. When Arthur's advisers learned this, they dissuaded him from continuing the siege any longer, for if so large an enemy force were to come upon them they would all be committed to a most dangerous engagement.

Arthur accepted the advice of his retainers and withdrew into the town of London. There he convened the bishops and the clergy of the entire realm and asked their advice as to what it would be best and safest for him to do, in the face of this invasion by the pagans. Eventually a common policy was agreed on and messengers were despatched to King Hoel in

Brittany to explain to him the disaster which had befallen Britain. This Hoel was the son of Arthur's sister; and his father was Budicius, king of the Bretons. As a result, as soon as he heard of the terrifying way in which his uncle was being treated, Hoel ordered his fleet to be made ready. fifteen thousand armed warriors were assembled, and at the next fair wind Hoel landed at Southampton. Arthur received him with all the honour due to him, and each man embraced the other repeatedly. They let a few days pass and then they marched to the town of Kaerluideoit, which was besieged by the pagans I have already mentioned. This town is situated upon a hill between two rivers, in the province of Lindsey: it is also called by another name, Lincoln. As soon as they had arrived there with their entire force, they were so keen to fight with the Saxons that they inflicted unheard-of slaughter upon them; for on one day six thousand of the Saxons were killed, some being drowned in the rivers and others struck down by weapons. As a result, the remainder were demoralized; they abandoned the siege and took to flight.

Arthur pursued the Saxons relentlessly until they reached Caledon Wood. There they re-formed after their flight and made an effort to resist him. The Saxons joined battle once more and killed a number of the Britons, for the former defended themselves manfully. They used the shelter of the trees to protect themselves from the Britons' weapons. As soon as Arthur saw this, he ordered the trees round that part of the wood to be cut down and their trunks to be placed in a circle, so that every way out was barred to the enemy. Arthur's plan was to hem them in and then besiege them, so that in the end they would die of hunger. When this had been done, he ordered his squadrons to surround the wood, and there he remained for three days. The Saxons had nothing at all to eat. To prevent themselves from dying of sheer hunger, they asked permission to come out, on the understanding that, if they left behind all their gold and silver, they might be permitted to return to Germany with nothing but their boats. What is more, they promised that they would send Arthur tribute from Germany and that hostages should be handed over. Arthur took counsel and then agreed to their petition. He retained all their treasure, and took hostages to ensure that the tribute would be paid. All that he conceded to the Saxons was permission to leave.

THE SAXONS DEPART, ONLY TO RETURN AGAIN

As the Saxons sailed away across the sea on their way home, they repented of the bargain they had made. They reversed their sails, turned back to

Britain and landed on the coast near Totnes. There they took possession of the land, and depopulated the countryside as far as the Severn Sea, killing off a great number of the peasantry. Then they proceeded by a forced march to the neighbourhood of Bath and besieged the town.

When this was announced to King Arthur, he was greatly astonished at their extraordinary duplicity. He ordered summary justice to be inflicted on their hostages, who were all hanged without more ado. He put off the foray with which he had begun to harass the Scots and the Picts, and hastened instead to break up the siege. Arthur was labouring under very considerable difficulties, for he had left behind in the city of Dumbarton his nephew Hoel, who was seriously ill. He finally reached the county of Somerset and approached the siege. 'Although the Saxons, whose very name is an insult to Heaven and detested by all men, have not kept faith with me,' he said, 'I myself will keep faith with God. This very day I will do my utmost to take vengeance on them for the blood of my fellow countrymen. Arm yourselves, men, and attack these traitors with all your strength! With Christ's help we shall conquer them, without any possible doubt!'

As Arthur said this, the saintly Dubricius, archbishop of Caerleon, climbed to the top of a hill and cried out in a loud voice: 'You who have been marked with the cross of the Christian faith, be mindful of the loyalty you owe to your fatherland and to your fellow countrymen! If they are slaughtered as a result of this treacherous behaviour by the pagans, they will be an everlasting reproach to you, unless in the meanwhile you do your utmost to defend them! Fight for your fatherland, and if you are killed, suffer death willingly for your country's sake. That in itself is victory and a cleansing of the soul. Whoever suffers death for the sake of his brothers offers himself as a living sacrifice to God and follows with firm footsteps behind Christ Himself, who did not disdain to lay down His life for His brothers. It follows that if any one of you shall suffer death in this war, that death shall be to him as a penance and an absolution for all his sins, as long as he goes to meet it unflinchingly.'

Without a moment's delay each man present, inspired by the benediction given by this holy man, rushed to put on his armour and to obey Dubricius' orders. Arthur himself put on a leather jerkin worthy of so great a king. On his head he placed a golden helmet, with a crest carved in the shape of a dragon; and across his shoulders a circular shield called Pridwen, on which there was painted a likeness of the Blessed Mary, Mother of God, which forced him to be thinking perpetually of her. He girded on his peerless sword, called Excalibur, which was forged in the Isle of Avalon – long, broad in the blade and thirsty for slaughter. A spear called Rhongomyniad graced his right hand. Arthur drew up his men in companies and then bravely attacked the Saxons, who as usual were deployed in wedges. All that day they resisted the Britons bravely, although the latter launched attack upon attack. Finally, towards sunset, the Saxons occupied a neighbouring hill, on which they proposed to camp. Relying on their vast numbers, they considered that the hill in itself offered sufficient protection. However, when the next day dawned, Arthur climbed to the top of the peak with his army, losing many of his men on the way. Naturally enough, the Saxons, rushing down from their high position, could inflict wounds more easily, for the impetus of their descent gave them more speed than the others, who were toiling up. For all that, the Britons reached the summit by a superlative effort and immediately engaged the enemy in hand-to-hand conflict. The Saxons stood shoulder to shoulder and strove their utmost to resist.

When the greatest part of the day had passed in this way, Arthur went berserk, for he realised that things were still going well for the enemy and that victory for his own side was not yet in sight. He drew his sword Excalibur, called upon the name of the Blessed Virgin, and rushed forward at full speed into the thickest ranks of the enemy. Every man whom he struck, calling upon God as he did so, he killed at a single blow. He did not slacken his onslaught until he had despatched four hundred and seventy men with his sword Excalibur. When the Britons saw this, they poured after him in close formation, dealing death on every side. In this battle fell Colgrin, with his brother Baldulf and many thousands of others with them. Cheldric, on the contrary, when he saw the danger threatening his men, immediately turned and fled with what troops were left to him.

As soon as King Arthur had gained the upper hand, he ordered Cador, duke of Cornwall, to pursue the Saxons, while he himself hurried off in the direction of Scotland. It had reached his ears that the Scots and the Picts had besieged his nephew Hoel in the town of Dumbarton, where Arthur had left him because of his poor health. Arthur therefore hastened to his nephew's assistance, for he was afraid that Hoel might be captured by the barbarians.

Meanwhile the duke of Cornwall, accompanied by ten thousand men, instead of pursuing the fleeing Saxons, headed quickly for their boats, with the intention of preventing them from going on board. Once he had seized their boats, he manned them with the best of his own soldiers and gave those men orders that they were to prevent the pagans from going aboard. Then he hurried off to pursue the enemy and to cut them to pieces without pity once he had found them; this in obedience to Arthur's command.

The Saxons, who only a short time before had attacked like lightning in the most ferocious way imaginable, now ran away with fear in their hearts.

Some of them fled to secret hiding-places in the woods, others sought the mountains, and caves in the hills, in an attempt to add some little breathing-space to their lives. In the end they could find no safe place; and so they came to the Isle of Thanet, with their line of battle cut to pieces. The duke of Cornwall pursued them there and renewed the slaughter. Cador killed Cheldric, took hostages, and forced the remainder of the Saxons to surrender.

ARTHUR CONQUERS SCOTLAND; HIS MARRIAGE TO GUINEVERE

Once peace was restored in this way, Cador set out for Dumbarton. Arthur had already freed the town from the attentions of the barbarians, and he now led his army to Moray, where the Scots and the Picts were under siege. They had fought three times against the king and his nephew, suffering defeat at Arthur's hands and then seeking refuge in this particular district. When they reached Loch Lomond, they took possession of the islands in the lake, hoping to find a safe refuge on them. This lake contains sixty islands and has sixty streams to feed it, yet only one of these streams flows down to the sea. On these islands one can make out sixty crags, which between them support exactly the same number of eagles' nests. The eagles used to flock together each year and foretell any prodigious event which was about to occur in the kingdom: they would all give a high-pitched scream at the same time. It was to these islands that the enemy fled, hoping to be protected by the lake, although they gained little help from it. Arthur collected together a fleet of boats and sailed round by the rivers; he besieged his enemies for fifteen days and reduced them to such a state of famine that they died in their thousands.

While Arthur was killing off the Scots and the Picts in this way, Gilmaurius, king of Ireland, arrived with a fleet and a huge horde of pagans, in an effort to bring help to those who were besieged. Arthur raised the siege and began to turn his armed strength against the Irish. He cut them to pieces mercilessly and forced them to return home. Once he had conquered the Irish, he was at liberty once more to wipe out the Scots and the Picts. He treated them with unparalleled severity, sparing no one who fell into his hands. As a result all the bishops of this pitiful country, with all the clergy under their command, their feet bare and in their hands the relics of their saints and the treasures of their churches, assembled to beg pity of the king for the relief of their people. The moment they came into the king's presence, they fell on their knees and besought him to have mercy on their sorrowing people. He had inflicted sufficient suffering on them, said the bishops, and there was no need for him to wipe out to the last man those few who had so far survived. He should allow them to have some small tract of land of their own, seeing that they were in any case going to bear the yoke of servitude. When they had petitioned the king in this way, their patriotism moved him to tears. Arthur gave in to the prayers of these men of religion and granted a pardon to their people.

When the fighting was over, Hoel looked more carefully at the side of the loch which I have described to you. He was surprised to see so many rivers, islands, rocks and eagles' nests, and, what is more, to find exactly the same number of each. While he was contemplating this remarkable circumstance, Arthur came up to him and told him that in the same neighbourhood there was another pool which was even more extraordinary. It was not very far away from where they were standing. It was twenty feet wide and the same distance long, and its depth was just five feet. Whether it had been shaped into a square by the artistry of man, or by nature, it remained true that, while it produced four different kinds of fish in its four corners, the fish of any one corner were never found in any of the others.

Arthur also told Hoel that there was a third pool in Wales, near the Severn. The local people call it Lin Ligua. When the sea flows into this pool, it is swallowed up as though into a bottomless pit; and, as the pool swallows the waters, it never overflows its banks. When the tide ebbs away, however, the pool belches forth the waters which it has swallowed, as high in the air as a mountain, and floods its banks. Meanwhile, if the people of all that region should approach, with their faces turned towards it, thus letting the spray of the waters fall upon their clothing, it is only with difficulty, if indeed at all, that they have the strength to avoid being swallowed up by the pool. If, however, they turn their backs, they are in no danger, even if they stand on the very brink.

Once he had pardoned the Scottish people, the king moved to York, where he proposed to celebrate the coming feast of the Nativity of Our Lord. As he rode into the city, Arthur grieved to see the desolate state of the holy churches. Samson, the saintly archbishop, had been driven out, and with him all men of the Christian faith. The half-burnt churches no longer celebrated God's holy office. The fury of the pagans had been so great that it had brought everything to an end. Arthur therefore summoned the clergy and the people, and appointed his own chaplain, Piramus, as metropolitan of that see. He rebuilt the churches, which had been razed to the ground, and he graced them with religious communities of men and women. He restored their family honours to the nobles who had been driven out by the Saxon invasions.

There were in York three brothers sprung from the royal line, Lot, Urien and Auguselus, who had been princes in those parts before the Saxon victories. Arthur was determined to do for them what he had done for the others: that is, to restore to them their hereditary rights. He returned the kingship of the Scots to Auguselus; to Urien, the brother of Auguselus, he gave back the honour of ruling over the men of Moray; and Lot, who in the days of Aurelius Ambrosius had married that king's own sister and had had two sons by her, he restored to the dukedom of Lothian and other nearby territories which formed part of it.

Finally, when he had restored the whole country to its earlier dignity, he himself married a woman called Guinevere. She was descended from a noble Roman family and had been brought up in the household of duke Cador. She was the most beautiful woman in the entire island.

ARTHUR EXTENDS HIS EMPIRE FROM IRELAND TO SCANDINAVIA

As soon as the next summer came round, Arthur fitted out a fleet and sailed off to the island of Ireland, which he was determined to subject to his own authority. The moment he landed, King Gilmaurius, about whom I have already told you, came to meet him with a numberless horde of his people, ready to fight against him. However, when Arthur began the battle, Gilmaurius' army, which was naked and unarmed, was miserably cut to pieces where it stood, and his men ran away to any place where they could find refuge. Gilmaurius himself was captured immediately and forced to submit. The remaining princes of the country, thunderstruck by what had happened, followed their king's example and surrendered. The whole of Ireland was thus conquered.

Arthur then steered his fleet to Iceland, defeated the people there and subdued the island. A rumour spread through all the other islands that no country could resist him. Doldavius, king of Gotland, and Gunhpar, king of the Orkneys, came of their own free will to promise tribute and to do homage.

The winter passed and Arthur returned to Britain. He established in the whole of his kingdom a state of lasting peace and then remained there for the next twelve years.

Arthur then began to increase his personal entourage by inviting distin-guished men from far-distant kingdoms to join it. In this way he developed such a code of courtliness in his household that he inspired peoples living far away to imitate him. The result was that even the man of noblest birth, once he was roused to rivalry, thought nothing at all of himself unless he wore his arms and dressed in the same way as Arthur's knights. At last the fame of Arthur's generosity and bravery spread to the very ends of the earth; and the kings of countries far across the sea trembled at the thought that they might be attacked and invaded by him, and so lose control of the lands under their dominion. They were so harassed by these tormenting anxieties that they rebuilt their towns and the towers in them, and then went so far as to construct castles on carefully chosen sites, so that, if invasion should bring Arthur against them, they might have a refuge in their time of need.

All this was reported to Arthur. The fact that he was dreaded by all encouraged him to conceive the idea of conquering the whole of Europe. He fitted out his fleets and sailed first of all to Norway, for he wished to give the kingship of that country to Lot, who was his brother-in-law. Lot was the nephew of Sichelm, king of Norway, who had just died and left him the kingship in his will. However, the Norwegians had refused to accept Lot and had raised a certain Riculf to the royal power, for they considered that they could resist Arthur now that their towns were garrisoned. As soon as Arthur landed on the coast of Norway, King Riculf marched to meet him with the entire population of the country and then joined battle with him. Much blood was shed on either side, but in the end the Britons were victorious. They surged forward and killed Riculf and a number of his men. Once they were sure of victory, they laid siege to the cities of Norway and set fire to them. They scattered the rural population and continued to give full licence to their savagery until they had forced all Norway and all Denmark, too, to accept Arthur's rule.

As soon as he had subdued these countries and raised Lot to the kingship of Norway, Arthur sailed off to Gaul. He drew his troops up in companies and began to lay waste the countryside in all directions. The province of Gaul was at that time under the jurisdiction of the tribune Frollo, who ruled it in the name of the emperor Leo. The moment Frollo heard of the coming of Arthur, he marched out supported by the entire armed force which he had under his command. He was determined to fight against Arthur, but in effect he could offer little resistance. The young men of all the islands which Arthur had subdued were there to fight at his side, and he was reported to have so powerful a force that it could hardly have been conquered by anyone. What is more, the better part of the army of the Gauls was already in Arthur's service, for he had bought the men over by the gifts he had given them. As soon as Frollo saw that he was having the worst of the fight, he quitted the battlefield without more ado and fled to Paris with the few men left to him.

There Frollo reassembled his scattered people, garrisoned the town and made up his mind to meet Arthur in the field a second time. Just as Frollo was considering how to strengthen his army by calling upon neighbouring peoples, Arthur arrived unexpectedly and besieged him inside the city. A whole month passed. Frollo grieved to see his people dying of hunger, and sent a message to Arthur to say that they should meet in single combat and that whichever was victorious should take the kingdom of the other. Being a man of immense stature, courage and strength, Frollo relied upon these advantages when he sent his message, hoping in this way to find a solution to his problem. When the news of Frollo's plan reached Arthur, he was immensely pleased; and he sent word back that he would be willing to hold the meeting that had been suggested. Both sides agreed and the two met on an island outside the city, where the people gathered to see what would happen.

Arthur and Frollo were both fully armed and seated on horses which were wonderfully fleet of foot. It was not easy to foretell who would win. For a moment they stood facing each other with their lances held straight in the air: then they suddenly set spurs to their horses and struck each other two mighty blows. Arthur aimed his lance with more care and hit Frollo high up on his chest. He avoided Frollo's weapon, and hurled his enemy to the ground with all his might. Arthur then drew his sword from the scabbard and was just hurrying forward to strike Frollo when the latter leapt quickly to his feet, ran forward with his lance levelled and with a deadly thrust stabbed Arthur's horse in the chest, thus bringing down both horse and rider. When the Britons saw their king thrown to the ground, they were afraid that he was dead, and it was only with great self-control that they restrained themselves from breaking the truce and hurling themselves as one man upon the Gauls. Just as they were planning to invade the lists, Arthur sprang quickly to his feet, covered himself with his shield, and rushed forward to meet Frollo. They stood up to each other hand to hand, giving blow for blow, and each doing his utmost to kill the other. In the end Frollo found an opening and struck Arthur on the forehead. It was only the fact that he blunted the edge of his sword-blade at the point where it made contact with Arthur's metal helmet that prevented Frollo from dealing a mortal blow. When Arthur saw his leather cuirass and his round shield grow red, he was roused to even fiercer anger. He raised Excalibur in the air with all his strength and brought it down through Frollo's helmet, cutting his head into two halves. At this blow Frollo fell to the ground, drummed the earth with his heels and breathed his soul into the winds. The moment this was made known throughout the army, the townsfolk ran forward, threw open their gates and surrendered their city to Arthur.

As soon as Arthur had won his victory, he divided his army into two and put one half under the command of Hoel, ordering him to go off to attack Guitard, the leader of the Poitevins. With the other half Arthur busied himself in subduing the remaining provinces which were still hostile to him. Hoel soon reached Aquitaine, seized the towns of that region, and, after harassing Guitard in a number of battles, forced him to surrender. He also ravaged Gascony with fire and sword, and forced its leaders to submit.

Nine years passed. Once Arthur had subjected all the regions of Gaul to his power, he returned once more to Paris and held a court there. He called an assembly of the clergy and the people, and settled the government of the realm peacefully and legally. It was then that he gave Neustria, now called Normandy, to his cupbearer Bedivere, and the province of Anjou to his seneschal Kay. He gave a number of other provinces to the noblemen who had served him. Once he had pacified all these cities and peoples he returned to Britain just as spring was coming on.

ARTHUR HOLDS A SOLEMN CROWN-WEARING: THE FESTIVITIES DESCRIBED

When the feast of Whitsuntide began to draw near, Arthur, overjoyed by his great success, decided to hold a plenary court at that season at which he would solemnly wear his crown. He decided, too, to summon to this feast the leaders who owed him homage, so that he could celebrate Whitsun with greater reverence and renew the closest possible pacts of peace with his chieftains. He explained to the members of his court what he was proposing to do and accepted their advice that he should carry out his plan in Caerleon.

This city – situated as it is in Glamorgan, on the river Usk, not far from the Severn Sea, in a most pleasant position, and being richer than other townships – was eminently suitable for such a ceremony. The river flowed by it on one side, and the kings and princes who were to come from across the sea could be carried to the town itself in a fleet of ships. On the other side, which was flanked by meadows and wooded groves, they had adorned the city with royal palaces, and the golden painted gables of its roofs made it a match for Rome. What is more, it was famous for its two churches. One of these, built in honour of the martyr Julius, was graced by a choir of most lovely virgins dedicated to God. The second, founded in the name of the blessed Aaron, the companion of Julius, was served by a monastery of canons, and counted as the third metropolitan see of Britain. The city also contained a college of two hundred learned men, who were skilled in astronomy and the other arts, and who watched the courses of the stars with great attention and so by their careful computations prophesied for King Arthur any prodigies due at that time.

It was this city, therefore, famous for such a wealth of pleasant things, which was made ready for the feast. Messengers were sent to the different kingdoms and invitations were delivered to all those who were due to come to the court from the various parts of Gaul and from the nearby Islands of the Ocean. The following people came: Auguselus, king of Albany, which is now known as Scotland; Urien, king of the men of Moray; Cadwallo Laurh, king of the Venedoti, who are now called the North Welsh; Stater, king of the Demetae, now the South Welsh; and Cador, king of Cornwall. There came, too, the archbishops of the three metropolitan sees: London, York, and Dubricius from Caerleon. The last named, who was the primate of Britain and legate of the Papal See, was so remarkably pious that by merely praying he could cure anyone who was ill. The leading men from the principal cities were there: Morvid, earl of Gloucester; Mauron, earl of Worcester; Anarauth, earl of Salisbury; Artgualchar, earl of Guerensis, which is now called Warwick; Jugein from Leicester; Cursalem from Caistor; Kynniarc, duke of Durobernia; Urbgennius from Bath; Jonathel of Dorchester; and Boso of Rydychen, that is, Oxford.

In addition to these great leaders there came other famous men of equal importance: Donaut map Papo, Cheneus map Coil, Peredur map Peridur, Grifud map Nogord, Regin map Claut, Eddelui map Oledauc, Kynar map Bangan, Kynmaroc, Gorbonian map Coit, Worloit, Run map Neton, Kyrnbelin, Edelnauth map Trunat, Cathleus map Kathel, Kynlit map Tieton and many others whose names it is too tedious to tell. Gilmaurius, king of Ireland, came from the neighbouring islands, with Malvasius, king of Iceland, Doldavius, king of Gotland, Gunhpar, king of the Orkneys, Lot, king of Norway, and Aschil, king of the Danes. From lands across the sea came Holdin, the leader of the Ruteni; Leodegarius, earl of Hoiland; Bedivere the cupbearer, who was duke of Normandy; Borellus of Cenomania; Kay the seneschal, who was duke of Anjou; Guitard of Poitou; the Twelve Peers from the various regions of Gaul, led by Gerin of Chartres; and then Hoel, leader of the Bretons, with the princes who did him homage.

All these marched with a train of accoutrements, mules and horses such as I find it hard to describe. There remained no prince of any distinction this side of Spain who did not come when he received his invitation. Nor was this remarkable: for Arthur's generosity was known throughout the whole world and this made all men love him.

When they had all assembled in the town and the time of the feast had come, the archbishops were led forward to the palace. Since the plenary court was being held in his own diocese, Dubricius made ready to sing Mass in celebration of the moment when the king should place the crown upon his head. As soon as the king was enrobed, he was conducted with due pomp to the church of the metropolitan see. On his right side and on his left there were two archbishops to support him. Four kings, of Scotland, Cornwall, Demetia and Venedotia, preceded him, as was their right, bearing before him four golden swords. A company of clerics of every rank advanced before him, chanting in exquisite harmony.

From another direction the archbishops and bishops led the queen, adorned with her own regalia, to the church of the Dedicated Virgins. Before her walked the four consorts of the kings already mentioned, carrying four white doves according to the custom. All the married women present followed behind her with great rejoicing.

Afterwards, when the procession was over, so much organ music was played in the two churches and the choirs sang so sweetly that, because of the high standard of the music offered, the knights who were there hardly knew which of the churches to enter first. They flocked in crowds, first to this one, then to the other, so that if the whole day had been spent in celebration they would not have been bored. Finally, High Mass was celebrated in both churches.

The king and the queen then took off their crowns and put on lighter regalia. The king went off with the men to feast in his own palace and the queen retired with the married women to feast in hers; for the Britons still observed the ancient custom of Troy, the men celebrating festive occasions with their fellow men and the women eating separately with the other women. When they were all seated as the rank of each decreed, Kay the seneschal, robed in ermine and assisted by a thousand noblemen who were all clad in ermine too, bore in the food. The same number of men, clad this time in miniver, followed Bedivere the cupbearer from another entrance, helping him to pass drinks of all sorts in goblets of every conceivable shape. Meanwhile, in the queen's palace, innumerable servants, dressed in varying liveries, were performing their duties, each according to his office.

If I were to describe everything, I should make this story far too long. Indeed, by this time, Britain had reached such a standard of sophistication that it excelled all other kingdoms in its general affluence, the richness of its decorations, and the courteous behaviour of its inhabitants. Every knight in the country who was in any way famed for his bravery wore livery and arms showing his own distinctive colour; and women of fashion often displayed the same colours. They scorned to give their love to any man who had not proved himself three times in battle. In this way the womenfolk became chaste and more virtuous, and for love of them the knights were ever more daring.

Invigorated by the food and drink which they had consumed, they went out into the meadows outside the city and split up into groups ready to play various games. The knights planned an imitation battle and competed together on horseback, while their womenfolk watched from the top of the city walls and aroused them to passionate excitement by their flirtatious behaviour. The others passed what remained of the day in shooting with bows and arrows, hurling the lance, tossing heavy stones and rocks, playing dice and an immense variety of other games, all this without the slightest show of ill feeling. Whoever won his particular game was then rewarded by Arthur with an immense prize. The next three days were passed in this way. On the fourth day all those whohad done Arthur any service in the office which they held were called together; each was rewarded with a personal grant of cities, castles, archbishoprics, bishoprics and other landed possessions.

Then the saintly Dubricius, who for a long time had wanted to live as a hermit, resigned from his position as archbishop. David, the king's uncle, whose way of life had afforded an example of unblemished virtue to those whom he had instructed in the faith, was consecrated in his place. At the same time Tebaus, the celebrated priest of Llandaff, was appointed in the place of the holy Samson, archbishop of Dol, with the approval of Hoel, king of the Bretons, to whom Tebaus' life and saintly habits had commended him. The bishopric of Silchester was given to Maugannius, that of Winchester to Diwanius and that of Dumbarton to Eledenius.

THE ROMAN ENVOYS CHALLENGE ARTHUR'S RIGHT TO RULE

While Arthur was distributing these benefices among his clergy, twelve men of mature years and respectable appearance came marching in at a slow pace. In their right hands they carried olive branches, to show that they were envoys. They saluted Arthur and handed to him a communication from Lucius Hiberius. This letter read as follows:

Lucius, Procurator of the Republic, wishes that Arthur, king of Britain, may receive such treatment as he has deserved. I am amazed at the insolent way in which you continue your tyrannical behaviour. I am even more amazed at the damage which you have done to Rome. When I think about it, I am outraged that you should have so far forgotten yourself as not to realise this and not to appreciate immediately what it means that by your criminal behaviour you should have insulted the Senate, to which the entire world owes submission, as you very well know. You have had the presumption to disobey this mighty Empire by holding back the tribute of Britain, which tribute the Senate has ordered you to pay, seeing that Gaius Julius Caesar and other men of high place in the Roman State received it for many years. You have torn Gaul away from that Empire, you have seized the province of the Allobroges and you have laid hands on all the Islands of the Ocean, the kings of which paid tribute to my ancestors from the first moment when the might of Rome prevailed in those regions. As a result the Senate has decreed that punishment should be exacted for this long series of wrongs which you have committed. I therefore order you to appear in Rome, so that you may submit yourself to your overlords and suffer the penalty of whatever sentence they may pass; and I appoint the middle of next August as the time for your coming. If you fail to arrive, I shall invade your territory myself and do my best to restore to the Roman State all that you have taken from it by your insane behaviour.

This letter was read aloud in the presence of the kings and the leaders. Arthur then withdrew with them to a gigantic tower near the entrance to the palace, to consider what ought to be done in the face of such a message. As they began to climb the stairs, Cador, duke of Cornwall, who was a cheerful man, burst out laughing.

'Until now,' he said to the king, 'I have been afraid that the life of ease which the Britons have been leading might make cowards of them and soften them up during this long spell of peace. Their reputation for bravery on the battlefield, for which they are more famous than any other people, might well have been completely lost to them. Indeed, when it is obvious that men are no longer using their weapons, but are instead playing at dice, burning up their strength with women and indulging in other gratifications of that sort, then without any doubt their bravery, honour, courage and good name all become tainted with cowardice. For the past five years or thereabouts we have thought of nothing but these follies, and we have had no experience of battle. It is precisely to free us from this sloth that God has stirred up the resentment of the Romans, so that they may restore our courage to what it used to be in the old days.'

As Cador was saying this to them, and much more in the same strain, they reached their seats. When they were all seated, Arthur made the following speech: 'You who have been my companions in good times and in bad, you of whose fortitude both in giving advice and in waging war I have had ample proof in the past, give me now your closest attention, every one of you, and in your wisdom tell me what you consider we should do on receiving such a letter as this. Anything which has been planned with great care by man in his wisdom is realised the more easily when the time for action arrives. It follows that we shall be able to bear this attack of Lucius with great equanimity if we have first of all worked out with one accord how we are best to resist him. For myself, I do not consider that we ought to fear his coming very much, given the trumped up case he uses to demand the tribute he wants to exact from Britain. He says that he ought to be given it because it used to be paid to Julius Caesar and those who succeeded him. When these men landed with their armed band and conquered our fatherland by force and violence at a time when it was weakened by civil dissensions, they had been encouraged to come here by the disunity of our ancestors. Seeing that they seized the country in this way, it was wrong of them to exact tribute from it. Nothing that is acquired by force and violence can ever be held legally by anyone. In so far as the Roman has done us violence, he pleads an unreasonable case when he maintains that we are his tributaries in the eyes of the law. Since he presumes to exact something illegal from us, let us by a similar argument seek from him the tribute of Rome! Let him who comes out on top carry off what he has made up his mind to take! If the Roman decrees that tribute ought to be paid him by Britain simply because Julius Caesar and other Roman leaders conquered this country years ago, then I decree in the same way that Rome ought to give me tribute, in that my ancestors once captured that city. Belinus, that most glorious of the kings of the Britons, with the help of his brother Brennius, duke of the Allobroges hanged twenty of the noblest Romans in the middle of their own forum, captured the city and, when they had occupied it, held it for a long time. Similarly, Constantine, the son of Helen, and Maximianus, too, both of them close relations of mine, wearing the crown of Britain one after the other, each gained the throne of imperial Rome. Do you not agree, then, that it is we who should demand tribute of Rome? As for Gaul and the neighbouring Islands of the Ocean, we need send no answer, for when we snatched those lands from their empire they made no effort to defend them.'

As soon as Arthur had finished his address, Hoel, king of the Bretons, was told to speak first in reply.

'Even if every one of us', said he, 'were to take the trouble to turn all these things over in his mind and to reconsider each point deep within himself, it is my opinion that no one could find better advice to give than that which you have just counselled from your own experience and highly skilled wisdom. Your speech, adorned as it was with Ciceronian eloquence, has anticipated exactly what we all think. We should have nothing but unstinting praise for the opinion expressed by so steadfast a man as you, for the strength of so wise a mind, the benefit of such excellent counsel. If you are prepared to set out for Rome in such a cause as this, then I have no doubt at all about our being victorious. We shall be defending our liberty when in all justice we demand from our enemies what they have sought from us in the first place. Whoever tries to steal from another the things which are that other's, may justly lose to the man he is attacking the things which belong to him personally. Since the Romans propose to remove from us that which is our own, without any doubt at all we, on the contrary, shall take from them what is theirs: that is, if we once have a chance of meeting them in battle. All Britons long for such a confrontation. Do not the Sibylline Prophecies testify in verse that for the third time someone born of British blood shall seize the empire of Rome? As far as the first two are concerned, the prophecies are already fulfilled, for it is well known, as you yourself have said, that those famous princes Belinus and Constantine once won the imperial crown of Rome. Now we have you as the third man to whom the supreme dignity of such an honour is promised. Make haste, then, to take in your hand what God is only too willing to bestow! Hasten to conquer that which in itself is ripe for the conquering! Hasten to exalt us all, for we shall not shrink from being wounded or even losing our lives if it leads to your being exalted! In order that you may accomplish this, I shall stand at your side with ten thousand armed men.'

When Hoel had finished speaking, Auguselus, king of Scotland, began in the following words to declare his thoughts on the matter: 'From the moment I realised that my lord really meant what he said, such joy entered my heart as I cannot describe in his presence. If the Romans and the Germans remain unscathed and we fail to take vengeance on them like true men for the slaughter they have inflicted upon our fellow countrymen in the past, then it will seem as if the campaigns which we have previously waged against so many mighty kings achieved nothing at all. Now that we are promised the opportunity of meeting them in battle, I am overwhelmed with joy and only too eager for the day on which we shall come together. I thirst for their blood, as I would thirst for a spring if I had been prevented from drinking for three whole days. If only I may live to see that day! How sweet will be the wounds which I shall give and receive, once we come together hand to hand! Death itself will be sweet, if only I may suffer it in avenging our ancestors, safeguarding our liberty and exalting our king! Let us attack these emasculated creatures! Let us attack again and again, so that, when we have crushed them, we may seize all their possessions and rejoice in our victory. For my part I will augment our army to the tune of two thousand armed knights, not counting the infantry that go with them.'

It remained only for the others to say what still needed to be said. One after the other they promised Arthur as many men as they owed him as their feudal service. In addition to those whom the Breton leader had promised, sixty thousand armed men were mustered from the island of Britain alone. The kings of the other islands, who had not yet developed the habit of using cavalry, promised as many foot-soldiers as each man

owed, so that from the six islands of Ireland, Iceland, Gotland, the
Orkneys, Norway and Denmark, one hundred and twenty thousand men
were counted. From the various duchies of Gaul, those of the Ruteni, the
Portivenses, the Normans, the Cenomanni, the Angevins and the
Poitevins, came eighty thousand; and from the twelve independent territories of those who accompanied Gerin of Chartres came another twelve
hundred. The total number of the entire army, not including the
foot-soldiers, who were not at all easy to count, was therefore one hundred
and eighty-three thousand, three hundred.

ARTHUR EMBARKS AGAINST THE ROMANS

When King Arthur saw that they were all ready to enter his service, he
accepted their offer and ordered them to return home immediately and
assemble the troops which they had promised. He also instructed them to
rendezvous at the port of Barfleur and then to be ready to march with him
to the lands of the Allobroges, where they would meet the Romans.
finally, he sent word to the emperors by their own messengers to say that
he had no intention whatsoever of paying them tribute and that he was
certainly not coming to Rome in order to receive their legal decision in
this matter. He was coming, on the contrary, to exact from them what they
had decreed in their own judicial sentence that they would demand from
him. The messengers set out. At the same time the kings and princes left
for home, determined to waste no time in carrying out what they had been
ordered to do.

As soon as the contents of this reply were made known, Lucius Hiberius
was ordered by the Senate to send a proclamation to the kings of the Orient
to instruct them to prepare an army and to set out in his company to
conquer Britain. As quickly as possible there duly assembled Epistrofus, the
king of the Greeks; Mustensar, king of the Africans; Ali Fatima, king of
Spain; Hirtacius, king of the Parthians; Boccus of the Medes; Sertorius of
Libya; Serses, king of the Iturei; Pandrasus, king of Egypt; Micipsa, king of
Babylon; Politetes, duke of Bithynia; Teucer, duke of Phrygia; Evander of
Syria; Echion of Boethia; Ypolitus of Crete; and all the leaders and princes
who owed them homage. From among the members of the Senate there
came Marius Lepidus, Gaius Metellus Cocta, Quintus Milvius Catullus,
Quintus Carucius and enough others to bring the total up to four hundred
thousand, one hundred and sixty when they were all counted.

They made all the preparations which they considered necessary and then
set out for Britain towards the beginning of August. When Arthur learned

of their coming, he handed over the task of defending Britain to his nephew Mordred and to his own queen, Guinevere. He himself set off with his army for Southampton, and embarked there with a following wind.

Round about midnight, as he sailed briskly on through the deep sea, surrounded by ships too numerous to count, and following his course closely with joy in his heart, Arthur fell into a very deep slumber. As he lay lulled in sleep he saw a bear flying through the air. At the growling of the bear every shore quaked. Arthur also saw a terrifying dragon flying in from the west and lighting up the countryside with the glare of its eyes. When these two met, they began a remarkable fight. The dragon attacked the bear time and time again, burning it with its fiery breath and finally hurling its scorched body down to the ground. Arthur woke up at this point and described what he had dreamed to those who were standing round. They interpreted it for him, telling him that the dragon was himself and the bear some giant or other with which he was to fight. The battle between the two animals meant the struggle which would take place between him and the giant, and the dragon's victory was that which Arthur himself would win. Arthur, however, was sure that it all signified something different, for he considered that this dream had come about because of himself and the emperor.

Once the night had passed and the dawn began to glow red in the sky, they landed in the port of Barfleur. There they quickly pitched their tents and prepared to await the coming of the kings of the Islands and the leaders of the neighbouring provinces.

ARTHUR AND THE GIANT OF MONT-SAINT-MICHEL

Meanwhile the news was brought to Arthur that a giant of monstrous size appeared from somewhere in Spain. This giant had snatched Helena, the niece of King Hoel, from the hands of her guardians and had fled with her to the top of what is now called the Mont-Saint-Michel. The knights of that district had pursued the giant, but they had been able to do nothing against him. It made no difference whether they attacked him by sea or by land, for he either sank their ships with huge rocks or else killed them with a variety of weapons. Those whom he captured, and they were quite a few, he ate while they were still half alive.

The next night, at two o'clock, Arthur came out from the tents without telling his companions, roused his seneschal Kay and his cupbearer Bedivere and set out for the Mount. Being a man of such outstanding courage, he had no need to lead a whole army against monsters of this sort.

Not only was he himself strong enough to destroy them, but by doing so he wanted to inspire his men.

When they came near to the Mount, they saw a fire gleaming on the top and a second fire ablaze on a smaller peak. Bedivere the cupbearer was ordered by the king to make his way to this second fire by boat. He could not have reached it in any other way, for the hill rose straight up from the sea. As Bedivere began to climb up to the summit, he heard a woman's scream come from above him. This terrified him at first, for he was afraid that the monster was there. His courage soon returned, however, and he drew his sword from its scabbard and climbed up the hillside. On the top he could see nothing at all, except the great fire which he had observed before. Then he made out a newly built tumulus nearby, and at its side an old woman who was weeping and wailing.

The moment she saw him the old woman stopped weeping and began to speak to him instead. 'Unhappy man!' she said, 'What ill fortune has brought you to this place? I pity you, for you are about to suffer death by the most unspeakable tortures. This very night a foul monster will destroy the flower of your youth. The most odious of all giants will come here. Cursed be his name! It is he who carried the king's niece off to this mountain. I have just buried her in this very spot. He brought me, her nurse, with him. Without a moment's hesitation he will destroy you, too, by some unheard-of form of death. How hideous the fate of my fairest nurseling was! When this foul being took her in his arms, fear flooded her tender breast and so ended a life which was worthy of a longer span. Since he was unable to befoul with his filthy lust this child who was my sister soul, my second self, the joy and happiness of my life, in the madness of his bestial desire he raped me, against my will, as I swear by God and my own old age. Flee, sir! flee! If he comes, as he usually does, to have sexual intercourse with me, he will find you here and tear you to pieces and destroy you miserably!'

Bedivere was as much moved as it is possible for a human being to be. He soothed the old woman with kind words, comforted her with the promise of speedy help and returned to Arthur to tell him all that he had discovered. Arthur grieved for the fate of the girl and ordered the other two to leave him to attack the monster alone. Should the need arise, they were to come to his assistance as quickly as they could and attack the giant in their turn. They then made their way to the higher of the two peaks. There they handed their horses over to their squires and began to clamber to the top, Arthur going on ahead.

At that moment the inhuman monster was standing by his fire. His face was smeared with the clotted blood of a number of pigs at which he had been gnawing. He had swallowed bits of them while he was roasting the rest on the spits over the live embers on the spits. The moment he saw the newcomers, whom he did not in the least expect, he rushed to snatch up his club, which two young men would have found difficulty in lifting off the ground. The king drew his sword from its scabbard, held his shield in front of him and rushed forward at full speed to prevent the giant from seizing his club. The giant was quite aware of the advantage Arthur was hoping to gain. He took up his club and dealt the king such a mighty blow on his shield that the shore in both directions was filled with the reverberation of the impact and Arthur was completely deafened. The king grew white-hot with rage. He struck the giant on the forehead with his sword and gave him such a blow that, although it was not mortal, yet blood ran down his face and into his eyes and prevented him from seeing. The giant had warded off the blow with his club and in this way had protected his forehead from a mortal wound. Blinded as he was by the blood which was gushing out, he rushed forward all the more fiercely. Just as a boar hurls itself at the huntsman, despite the latter's boar-spear, so the giant rushed against the king's sword. He seized Arthur round the middle and forced him to the ground on his knees. Arthur gathered his strength and quickly slipped out of the giant's clutches. Moving like lightning, he struck the giant repeatedly with his sword, first in this place and then in that, giving him no respite until he had dealt him a lethal blow by driving the whole length of the blade into his head just where his brain was protected by his skull. At this the evil creature gave one great shriek and toppled to the ground with a mighty crash, like some oak torn from its roots by the fury of the winds. The king laughed with relief. He ordered Bedivere to saw off the giant's head and to hand it over to one of their squires, so that it might be carried to the camp for all to go and stare at.

Arthur said that he had not come into contact with anyone so strong since the time he killed the giant Retho on Mount Arvaius, after the latter had challenged him to single combat. Retho had made himself a fur cloak from the beards of the kings whom he had slain. He sent a message to Arthur, telling him to rip his own beard off his face, and, when it was torn off, to send it to him. Since Arthur was more distinguished than any of the other kings, Retho promised in his honour to sew his beard higher up the cloak than the others. If Arthur would not do this, then Retho challenged him to a duel, saying that whoever proved the stronger should have the fur cloak as a trophy and also the beard of the man he had beaten. Soon after the battle began, Arthur was victorious. He took the giant's beard and the trophy too. From that day on, as he had just said, he had met nobody stronger than Retho.

When they had won their victory, as I have told you, the three returned to their tents with the head, just as dawn was succeeding to night. All their men crowded round them to gape at it and praise the man who had freed the country from such a voracious monster. Hoel, however, grieved over the fate of his niece. He ordered a chapel to be built above her grave on the mountain-top where she had been buried. The peak took its name from the girl's burial place, and to this very day it is called Helena's Tomb.

As soon as all those whom Arthur was awaiting had finally assembled, he marched from there to Autun, where he expected that the emperor would be. However, by the time he reached the river Aube he was informed that the emperor had pitched his camp not far away and was advancing with such an enormous army that it was rumoured that no one could possibly resist him. Arthur was not dismayed, for he had no intention whatsoever of abandoning his plans. Instead, he pitched his own camp on the riverbank, in a spot from which he could easily move his camp forward, or, if the need arose, withdraw under cover.

THE CAMPAIGN AGAINST THE ROMANS

Arthur sent two of his leaders, Boso of Oxford and Gerin of Chartres, together with his own nephew Gawain, to Lucius Hiberius, to tell him either to withdraw from Gallic territory altogether or else to march out the next day to see which of them had more right to Gaul. The young men of Arthur's court were overjoyed at the prospect before them. They began to urge Gawain on to foment some incident in the emperor's camp, to give them an opportunity of fighting with the Romans. They made their way into the presence of Lucius and duly ordered him either to withdraw from Gaul or to come out to fight the very next day. As Lucius was replying that he had not come there in order to withdraw, but rather that he might govern the country, his nephew Gaius Quintillianus who was present was heard to mutter that the Britons were better at boasting and making threats than they were at proving their courage and prowess on the battlefield. Gawain was immediately incensed at this. He drew his sword from the scabbard which was hanging at his belt, rushed at Gaius and cut off his head. He and his fellow envoys then retreated to their horses. The Romans pursued them, some on foot and some on horseback, hoping to avenge the loss of their fellow countryman upon the messengers, who were making off at full speed. Gerin of Chartres suddenly turned round, just as one of the Romans was straining to hit him, couched his lance, pierced the enemy through his protective armour and the middle of his body, and hurled him to the ground with all his might. Boso of Oxford, envious of the mighty deed done by the man from Chartres, wheeled his own horse round and stuck his spear into the throat of the first man he met, mortally wounding him and dashing him from the nag on which he was careering along. In the meantime Marcellus Mutius was making every effort to avenge Quintillianus. He was already threatening Gawain from the rear, and was on the point of laying hold of him, when Gawain swung round and, with the sword which he brandished, clove him through helm and head to his chest, bidding him, when he got to hell, to tell Quintillianus, whom Gawain had just cut down in the camp, that this was why the Britons were so good at boasting and making threats.

Gawain drew his troops up in some order and ordered them to wheel round in formation, each doing his utmost to unhorse one of the enemy. They agreed to his proposals. They all turned back and each of them killed his man. All the same, the Romans continued the pursuit, hitting out at the Britons with their swords and spears, but not succeeding in capturing or unhorsing any of them.

Just as they were riding up to a certain wood, so the story goes, there suddenly emerged from the trees about six thousand Britons, who had heard of the retreat of their leaders and had concealed themselves there in order to bring them help. Out they came, sticking spurs into their horses and filling the air with their shouts. With their rounded shields hung in front of their chests, they attacked the Romans out of the blue and immediately drove them back in flight. The Britons chased after the Romans as one man, hurling some of them from their horses with their spears, capturing others and killing quite a few.

When this was made known to the senator Petreius, he hurried to the assistance of his comrades, accompanied by ten thousand men. He forced the Britons to withdraw to the wood from which they had emerged, but not before he had lost some of his own men in the process. As they fled the Britons turned at bay in the narrow woodland paths and inflicted great slaughter on their pursuers. Meanwhile Hyderus, the son of Nu, was hurrying forward to support them as they retreated. The Britons then made a stand, confronting the same Romans on whom they had previously turned their backs, and doing their level best to deal mighty blows in the most manly way possible.

The Romans, too, stood their ground, in some places managing to kill the Britons, but elsewhere being killed by them. The Britons wanted a fight with all their heart and soul, but once they had begun it they did not care much whether they won or lost. The Romans, on the other hand, who were given careful instructions as to when they should move forward and when retreat by Petreius Cocta, like the good captain he was, behaved with more circumspection, so that he was able to inflict great damage on his opponents.

As soon as Boso noticed this, he called to one side a number of the Britons whom he knew to be among the bravest, and delivered the following speech to them: 'Seeing that we began this skirmish without informing Arthur, we must take great care, now that our men are fully engaged, that we do not have the worst of it. If that does happen, then we shall suffer a great loss of manpower and at the same time have the king cursing us. You must all pluck up your courage and follow me through the ranks of the Romans, so that, if fortune favours us, we can either kill or else capture Petreius.'

They all set spurs to their horses, and, keeping close together, forced their way through the wedge-shaped ranks of the enemy. They reached the spot where Petreius was giving orders to his men. Boso rushed headlong at him, seized him round the neck and fell to the ground with him as he had planned. The Romans came running up to rescue Petreius from his assailants. At the same time the Britons moved forward to give every help to Boso. There followed a tremendous slaughter between the two sides, with much din and confusion, as the Romans tried to free their leader and the Britons strove to hold him captive. Men were wounded on both sides as they dealt and received deadly blows. In this contest it was made quite clear who was the better man with spear, sword and javelin. In the end the Britons advanced with closed ranks, withstood the onslaught of the Romans and made their way, with Petreius in their midst, to the safety of their own lines. Without a moment's respite they then made a counter-attack upon the Romans, who were now for the most part weakened, dispirited, and ready to show their backs, for they had lost their commander. The Britons pressed on against them, striking at them from the rear. They unhorsed them with their blows, plundered them where they lay, and rode on over their looted bodies in pursuit of the others. A few they took prisoner, for they wanted some to hand over to the king.

In the end, when they had done all the damage they could to the Romans, the Britons withdrew to their camp with their spoils and prisoners. They explained what had happened to them and with the joy of victory in their hearts handed Petreius Cocta and the rest of their captives over to Arthur. He congratulated them, and promised them honours and yet more honours in that they had behaved so gallantly even though he was not there to lead them. He decided to throw the captives into prison. He summoned to his presence the men who were to lead them off to Paris the following day and hand them over to the town gaolers for safe keeping, against the time when he should decide what else should be done with them. He ordered Duke Cador, Bedivere the cupbearer, and Borellus and Richerius, two of his leading men, with their personal bodyguards, to lead the party, until they reached a spot beyond which they need not really fear a rescue attempt by the Romans.

It so happened that the Romans got wind of what the Britons had planned. At their emperor's command they chose fifteen thousand of their troops, who, that very same night, were to hurry on ahead of the Britons, along their projected line of march, and were then to attack them and do their utmost to free their fellow countrymen. The Romans put two senators, Vulteius Catellus and Quintus Carucius, in charge of their troops, together with Evander, king of Syria, and Sertorius, king of Libya. That very night they set out with the force I have described, intending to follow the line of march as instructed. They chose a place suitable for an ambush and hid in a place through which they thought their enemies would pass.

After morning came, the Britons duly set out with their captives. They soon came near to the place in question, not realising what a trap their cunning enemies had prepared for them. As the Britons moved forward in their march, the Romans suddenly broke cover. They attacked the Britons, who were expecting nothing of the sort, and smashed their line. Although they were attacked unexpectedly and scattered, the Britons re-formed their lines and resisted bravely. They stationed some of their troops in a circle round the prisoners. The remainder they drew up into companies, which then engaged the enemy. The Britons put Richerius and Bedivere in charge of the force which they set to guard the prisoners. Cador, duke of Cornwall, and Borellus were given command of the others.

The entire Roman detachment had rushed out in a disorderly fashion, without troubling to draw their men up into companies. They attacked with all their might, aiming to slaughter the Britons while the latter were still drawing up their own battle-lines and making plans to defend themselves. The Britons suffered great losses, and would have endured the shame of losing the captives whom they were convoying, if good fortune had not quickly brought the reinforcements of which they were in such need. Guitard, duke of the Poitevins, came to hear of the ambush which I have described, and he marched in with three thousand men. Now that they were able to rely upon this help, the Britons eventually won and so managed to take revenge upon their imprudent ambushers for all the slaughter they had caused. However, they lost many of their troops in the first stage of the battle. Indeed, they lost Borellus, the famous leader of the Cenomanni, who was pierced through the throat by his opponent's spear while he was fighting with Evander king of Syria, and so vomited forth his life with his blood. At the same time they lost four noble princes: Hyrelgas of Periron; Maurice Cador of Cahors; Aliduc of Tintagel; and Her, the son of Hider. It would not have been easy to find braver men than these. However, the Britons did not lose their courage, nor did they despair.

They made every effort to press forward, doing their utmost to guard their prisoners and at the same time to destroy their enemies. In the end the Romans were unable to stand the attack which the Britons launched, and they quickly retreated from the battlefield and began to make for their own camp. The Britons pursued them relentlessly, killing them as they went and taking many captives. They allowed them no respite until they had killed Vulteius Catellus and Evander, king of Syria, and scattered the others completely.

Once they were sure of victory, the Britons sent their prisoners on to Paris. They themselves turned back to their king with those whom they had just captured, promising him hope of a decisive victory because a mere handful of them had triumphed over this immense enemy who had been despatched against them.

Lucius Hiberius bore all these disasters ill. Harassed as he was by a variety of anxieties, he could not make up his mind whether to engage in a full-scale battle with Arthur or to withdraw inside Autun and there await reinforcements from the emperor Leo. In the end he let his misgiving get the upper hand. The next night he marched his troops into Langres, on his way to the city of Autun. This move was reported to Arthur. He made up his mind to outmarch Lucius along this route. That same night he bypassed the city of Autun on his left hand, and entered a valley called Saussy, through which Lucius would have to pass.

THE GREAT BATTLE AGAINST LUCIUS HIBERIUS

Arthur decided to draw up his troops in battle formation. He ordered one legion, the command of which he entrusted to Earl Morvid, to stay constantly in reserve, so that, if need arose, he would know where he could withdraw, rally his companies, and plan new attacks on the enemy. He drew up the rest of his troops in seven divisions, to each of which he allocated five thousand, five hundred and fifty-five fully equipped men. One half of each of the divisions which he drew up consisted of cavalry, and the other half of foot-soldiers. They were given the following standing orders: whenever the infantry showed signs of advancing to the attack, the cavalry of that division, moving forward obliquely with closed ranks, should do its utmost to break the force of the enemy. As was the British custom, the infantry battalions were drawn up in a square, with a right and left wing.

Auguselus, king of Scotland, was put in charge of the right wing, and Cador, duke of Cornwall, the left wing of the first division. Two famous leaders, Gerin of Chartres and Boso of Rydychen (called Oxford in the Saxon language) were put in command of a second division, with Aschil, king of the Danes, and Lot, king of the Norwegians, in charge of a third. Hoel, king of the Bretons, and Gawain, the king's nephew, commanded a fourth. In support of these, four other divisions were placed in the rear. Kay the seneschal was put in charge of one, along with Bedivere the cupbearer; Holdin, the leader of the Ruteni, and Guitard, duke of the Poitevins, commanded the second. Jugein of Leicester, Jonathel of Dorchester, and Cursalem of Caistor took charge of the third, and Urbgennius of Bath of the fourth. Behind all these the king chose a position for himself and for a single legion of six thousand, six hundred and sixty-six men which was under his own command. There he set up the Golden Dragon which he had as his personal standard. To this point the wounded and exhausted could withdraw in case of necessity, as if to a fortified camp.

When all his troops were placed in position, Arthur gave them the following order of the day: 'My countrymen, you who have made Britain mistress of thirty kingdoms, I commend you for your courage, which, far from lessening, seems to me to increase in strength every day, despite the fact that you have waged no war for five long years, during which time you have devoted yourselves to the enjoyment of a life of ease rather than to the practice of war. Nevertheless, you do not seem to have degenerated in the least from your inborn valour. On the contrary, you have retained your courage to the full, for you have just put the Romans to flight, at a moment when, encouraged by the pride which came so naturally to them, they were doing their utmost to deprive you of your freedom. Moving forward with the advantage of numbers on their side, it was they who attacked you, but they were not strong enough to resist your advance and they had to withdraw in shame to that city over there. In a short time they will march out again and come through this valley on their way to Autun. You will be able to attack them when they least expect it and slaughter them like so many sheep. No doubt they imagined, when they planned to make your country pay them tribute and to enslave you yourselves, that they would discover in you the cowardice of eastern peoples. Perhaps they have not heard of the wars you waged against the Danes and Norwegians and the leaders of the Gauls, when you delivered those peoples from their shameful allegiance to the Romans and forced them to submit to my own overlordship. We who had the strength to win a mightier battle will without any doubt at all be successful in this more trifling affair, if only we make up our minds with the same determination to crush these feeble creatures. What rewards you will win, if only you obey my will and my orders, as loyal soldiers ought to do! Once we have beaten the Romans in the field, we can immediately set off for Rome itself. As soon as we march upon Rome, we shall capture it. When we have captured it, you shall occupy it. And yours shall be its gold, silver, palaces, towers, castles, cities and all the other riches of the vanquished!'

As Arthur spoke, they all joined in one great shout of approval, for, as long as he was still alive, they were ready to die rather than leave the battlefield.

Lucius Hiberius found out about the trap that was laid for him. His first inclination was to run away, but he changed his mind. His courage returned to him and he decided to march out through this same valley to meet the Britons. He called his generals together, and spoke as follows: 'My noble leaders,' he said, 'you to whose sovereignty the kingdoms both of the East and of the West owe obedience, remember now the deeds of your ancestors. They did not hesitate to shed their blood in their efforts to conquer the enemies of the Republic. They left an example of bravery and soldierly courage to those who were to come after them, for they fought as if God had decreed that none of them should ever die in battle. They nearly always won, avoiding death in their victory, for they held that no death could come to any man other than that ordained by the will of God. In that way the Republic increased in power as their own prowess became greater. All the integrity, honour and munificence which distinguished men of noble birth flourished in them down the years. This lifted them and their descendants to the overlordship of the whole world. I now want to rouse this same spirit in you. I beg you to remember the bravery of your forefathers. Strong in this courage, you must now march forth to meet your enemies in the valley where they lie in ambush for you. Do your utmost to exact from them what is rightly yours. Do not imagine for a moment that I sought refuge in this city because I feared them, or was afraid of meeting them in battle. On the contrary, I imagined that they would come after us in their senseless bravado and that, as they rushed forward, we might suddenly turn upon them. I thought that we might slaughter them as they tailed after in pursuit. Now, however, since they have behaved in a different way from what we antici-pated, we in our turn must make new plans. We must go out to meet them and attack them as bravely as we possibly can. If they have the first advan-tage. then we must withstand them without letting our lines be broken, and bear the brunt of their initial attack. In this way we shall win without any shadow of doubt. In many a battle the side that stands firm in the first assault achieves victory in the end.'

As soon as Lucius had said these things and added a few other similar remarks, his men agreed with one accord. With heads erect and hands raised they swore an oath, and then armed themselves as quickly as they could. Once they were equipped, they marched out from Langres and made their way to the valley I have described, where Arthur had drawn up his own forces. In their turn they drew up twelve legions, all of them infantry. They were arranged in wedges, in the Roman fashion, each single legion containing six thousand, six hundred and sixty-six men. Separate commanders were appointed to each of the legions, and, according to the orders of these generals, so they were to advance to the assault or stand firm when they themselves were attacked.

The Romans placed Lucius Catellus and Ali Fatima, king of Spain, in command of the first legion; Hirtacius, king of the Parthians, and the senator Marius Lepidus in command of the second; and Boccus, king of the Medes, with the senator Gaius Metellus, in command of the third. They gave the command of the fourth legion to Sertorius, king of Libya, and to the senator Quintus Milvius. These four legions were placed in the first line. Behind them and in their rear were another four. They placed Serses, king of the Iturei, in charge of the first; Pandrasus, king of Egypt, in charge of the second; Politetes, duke of Bithynia, in charge of the third; and Teucer, duke of Phrygia, in charge of the fourth. Behind these again came yet another four legions: to the first of them they appointed the senator Quintus Carucius; to the second Lelius Hostiensis; to the third Sulpicius Subuculus, and to the fourth Mauricius Silvanus.

Lucius himself moved about amongst them, now here, now there, making suggestions and telling them how to proceed. He commanded that a golden eagle, which he had brought with him as a standard, should be set up firmly in the centre. He gave orders that anyone whom the tide of battle had cut off from the others should do his utmost to force his way back to this eagle.

Now at last they stood face to face with javelins raised, the Britons on one side and the Romans on the other. As soon as they heard the sound of the battle trumpet, the legion commanded by the king of Spain and Lucius Catellus charged boldly at the division led by the king of Scotland and the duke of Cornwall, but the latter stood firm, shoulder to shoulder, and the Roman force was not able to breach it. As the Roman legion persisted in its fierce attack, the division commanded by Gerin and Boso moved up at the double. The Roman legion fought bravely, but this fresh division attacked it with a sudden cavalry charge, broke through and came into contact with the legion which the king of the Parthians was directing against the division of Aschil, king of the Danes. Without a moment's delay the two forces met all along the line in a general mêlée, piercing each other's ranks and engaging one another in deadly combat. There ensued the most pitiable slaughter on both sides, with a bedlam of shouting and with men tumbling head foremost or feet first to the ground all over the place and vomiting forth their life with their heart's blood.

At first the Britons had the worst of it, for Bedivere the cupbearer was killed and Kay the seneschal was mortally wounded. When Bedivere met Boccus, king of the Medes, he was run through by the latter's lance and fell dead inside the enemy lines. Kay the seneschal did his utmost to avenge Bedivere, but he was surrounded by battalions of Medes and received a mortal wound. Nevertheless, brave soldier as he was, he cut a way through with the force which he was commanding, scattered the Medes and would have retreated to his own support group with his line of battle unbroken, had he not come up against the legion of the king of Libya, whose counter-attack completely scattered the troops under Kay's command. Even then he fell back with a few men still alive and made his way to the Golden Dragon with the corpse of Bedivere. How the Neustrians grieved when they saw the body of their leader Bedivere slashed with so many wounds! The Angevins, too, mourned as they treated the wounds of their leader Kay in every manner they could think of.

This. however, was no moment for weeping and wailing, with the battle-lines meeting on both sides in a bloodbath and giving them little respite for lamentations of this sort before they were compelled to look to their own defence. Hyrelgas, the Bedivere's nephew, was greatly moved by his uncle's death. He gathered round him three hundred of his own men, made a sudden cavalry charge and rushed through the enemy lines to the spot where he had seen the standard of the king of the Medes, for all the world like a wild boar through a pack of hounds, thinking little of what might happen to himself, if only he could avenge his uncle. When he came to the place where he had seen the king, he killed him, carried off his dead body to his own lines, put it down beside the corpse of the cupbearer and hacked it completely to pieces. With a great bellow, Hyrelgas roused his fellow countrymen's battalions to fury, exhorting them to charge at the enemy and to harass them with wave after wave of assault, for now a new-found rage boiled up within them, and the hearts of their frightened opponents were sinking. They were drawn up, he shouted, in better order in their battalions than their enemies, fighting hand to hand as they were, and they were in a position to attack repeatedly and to inflict more serious losses. The Britons were roused by this encouragement. They attacked their enemy all along the line, and terrible losses were sustained in both armies.

Vast numbers fell among the Romans, including Ali Fatima, king of Spain, Micipsa the Babylonian, and the senators Quintus Milvius and Marius Lepidus. Among the Britons there died Holdin, duke of the Ruteni, Leodegarius of Boulogne, and the three British leaders Cursalem of Caistor, Guallauc of Salisbury, and Urbgennius of Bath. The troops these men had commanded were greatly weakened, and they drew back until they reached the battle-line of the Bretons, which was commanded by Hoel and Gawain. However, this force burst into flame, as it were, rallied those who had been retreating, and compelled the enemy, who, a moment before, had been in pursuit, to withdraw in its turn. The Britons pressed on hard, hurling the fugitives to the ground and killing them. They did not pause in their slaughter until they reached the emperor's own bodyguard. When he saw that disaster had overtaken his men, the emperor hurried forward to give them support.

When the battle began again, the Britons were sadly mauled. Chinmarchocus, duke of Tréguier, fell dead, and with him there died two thousand men. Three other famous leaders were killed: Riddomarcus, Bloctonius, and Iaginvius of Bodloan. Had these men been rulers of kingdoms, succeeding ages would have celebrated their fame, for their courage was immense. In the attack which they launched with Hoel and Gawain, and which I have described to you, no enemy with whom they came to grips escaped alive from their swords and lances. Eventually they reached the bodyguard of Lucius himself. There they were cut off by the Romans and met their end at the same time as their leader Chinmarchocus and his comrades whom I have mentioned.

No better knights than Hoel and Gawain have ever been born. When they learned of the death of their followers, they pressed on even more fiercely. They spurred on this way and that, first in one direction, then in another, in their relentless attack on the emperor's bodyguard. Gawain, fearless in his courage, did his utmost to come up against Lucius himself in the fight. He made every effort to push forward, for he was the bravest of all the knights. He decimated the enemy by his onslaught and as he killed them he moved ever forward. Hoel was in no way less brave. He was raging like a thunderbolt in another sector, encouraging his own men and bringing death to his enemies. He parried their attacks with the utmost courage, giving and receiving blows, but not drawing back for a second. It would be difficult to say which of these two was the braver.

By dint of forcing his way through the enemy troops, as I have said above, Gawain finally found the opening for which he was longing. He rushed straight at the Roman general and fought with him hand to hand. Lucius was in the prime of his youth. He was a man of great courage, strength and prowess, and there was nothing that he wanted more than to join battle with a knight who would force him to prove his worth as a soldier. He accepted Gawain's challenge and fought with him. He was very keen to begin and rejoiced that his opponent was so famous a man. The contest between these two lasted for a long time. They dealt each other mighty blows, holding out their shields to their opponent's onslaught and each planning how he could kill the other.

As Gawain and Lucius fought bitterly in this way, the Romans suddenly recovered. They attacked the Bretons and so brought help to their general. They repulsed Hoel, Gawain and their troops, and began to cut their way into them. It was at this juncture that the Romans suddenly came face to face with Arthur and his division. He had heard a moment before of the slaughter that was being inflicted on his men. He moved up with his own division, drew his wonderful sword Excalibur, and encouraged his fellow soldiers. 'What the devil are you doing, men?' he demanded in a loud voice. 'Are you letting these effeminate creatures slip away unhurt? Not one must escape alive! Think of your own right hands, which have played their part in so many battles and subjected thirty kingdoms to my sovereignty! Remember your ancestors, whom the Romans, then at the height of their power, made tributaries. Remember your liberty, which these halflings, who haven't anything like your strength, plan to take away from you! Not one must escape alive! Not one must escape, I say!'

As he shouted these insults, and many others, too, Arthur dashed straight at the enemy. He flung them to the ground and cut them to pieces. Whoever came his way was either killed himself or had his horse killed under him at a single blow. They ran away from him as sheep run from a fierce lion whom raging hunger compels to devour all that chance throws in his way. Their armour offered them no protection capable of preventing Excalibur, when wielded in the right hand of this mighty king, from forcing them to vomit forth their souls with their lifeblood. Ill luck brought two kings, Sertorius of Libya and Politetes of Bithynia, in Arthur's way. He hacked off their heads and bundled them off to hell.

When the Britons saw their king fighting in this way, they became bolder. They charged as one man at the Romans, attacking them in close formation. While the infantry was assailing them in this way in one sector, the cavalry strove to beat them down and run them through in another. The Romans fought back bitterly. Urged on by Lucius, they strove to take vengeance on the Britons for the slaughter inflicted by their noble king. The fight continued with as much violence on both sides as if they had only just at that moment come to blows with one another. On our side Arthur dealt blow after blow at his enemies, shouting to the Britons to press on with the slaughter. On their side Lucius Hiberius urged his men on, repeatedly leading them himself in daring counter-attacks. He fought on with his own hand, going the rounds of his troops in each sector and killing every enemy who came his way, either with his lance or his sword. The most fearful slaughter was done on both sides. At times the Britons would have the upper hand, then the Romans would gain it.

In the end, as the battle continued between them, Morvid, earl of Gloucester, moved up at the double with his division, which, as I have told you, had been posted higher up in the hills. He attacked the enemy in the rear, when they were expecting nothing of the kind. His assault broke through their lines. As he moved forward he scattered them with tremendous slaughter. Many thousands of Romans were killed. In the end, Lucius himself, their general, was brought to bay in the midst of his troops. He fell dead, pierced through by an unknown hand. The Britons followed up their advantage and finally won the day, but only after a supreme effort.

The Romans were scattered. In their terror some fled to remote places and forest groves, others made their way to cities and towns, and all of them sought refuge in the places which seemed safest to them. The Britons pursued them as fast as they could go, putting them to death miserably, taking them prisoner and plundering them: most of them voluntarily held out their hands to be bound, like so many women, in the hope of prolonging their lives a little. All this was ordained by divine Providence. Just as in times gone by the ancestors of the Romans had harassed the forefathers of the Britons with their unjust oppressions, so now the Britons made every effort to protect their own freedom, which the Romans were trying to take away from them, by refusing the tribute which was wrongly demanded of them.

As soon as victory was assured, Arthur ordered the bodies of his leaders to be separated from the carcasses of the enemy. Once they were gathered together, he had these bodies prepared for burial with royal pomp, and then they were carried to the abbeys of their own native districts and interred there with great honour. Bedivere the cupbearer was borne, with loud lamentations, by the Neustrians to Bayeux, his own city, which his grandfather Bedivere the first had founded. There he was laid to rest with all honour, beside a wall in a certain cemetery in the southern quarter of the city. Kay, who was mortally wounded, was carried away to Chinon, the town which he himself had built. Not long afterwards he died from his wound. As was fitting for a duke of the Angevins, he was buried in a wood belonging to a convent of hermits not far from that town. Holdin, duke of the Ruteni, was carried to flanders and laid to rest in his own city of Thérouanne. At Arthur's command, the rest of the leaders and princes were borne to abbeys in the vicinity. He took pity on his enemies and told the local inhabitants to bury them. He ordered the body of Lucius to be carried to the Senate, with a message that no other tribute could be expected from Britain.

THE TREACHERY OF MORDRED

Arthur spent the following winter in this same region and found time to subdue the cities of the Allobroges. When summer came, he made ready to set out for Rome, and was already beginning to make his way through the mountains when the news was brought to him that his nephew Mordred, in whose care he had left Britain, had placed the crown upon his own head. What is more, this treacherous tyrant was living adulterously and out of wedlock with Queen Guinevere, who had broken the vows of her earlier marriage.

About this particular matter, most noble duke, Geoffrey of Monmouth prefers to say nothing. He will, however, in his own poor style and without wasting words, describe the battle which our most famous king fought against his nephew, once he had returned to Britain after his victory; for that he found in the British treatise already referred to. He heard it, too, from Walter of Oxford, a man most learned in all branches of history.

As soon as the news of this flagrant crime reached his ears, Arthur immediately cancelled the attack which he had planned to make on Leo, emperor of the Romans. He sent Hoel, leader of the Bretons, with an army of Gauls, to restore peace in those parts; and then without more ado he himself set off for Britain, accompanied only by the island kings and their troops. That most infamous traitor Mordred, about whom I have told you, had sent Cheldric, the leader of the Saxons, to Germany, to conscript as many troops as possible there, and to return as quickly as he could with those whom he was to persuade to join him. Mordred had made an agreement with Cheldric that he would give him that part of the island which stretched from the river Humber to Scotland and all that Hengist and Horsa had held in Kent in Vortigern's day. In obedience to Mordred's command, Chelric landed with eight hundred ships filled with armed pagans. A treaty was agreed and Chelric pledged his obedience to the traitor Mordred as if to the king. Mordred had brought the Scots, Picts and Irish into his alliance, with anyone else whom he knew to be filled with hatred for his uncle. In all, the rebels were about eighty thousand in number, some of them pagans and some Christians.

Surrounded by this enormous army, in which he placed his hope, Mordred marched to meet Arthur as soon as the latter landed at Richborough. In the battle which ensued Mordred inflicted great slaughter on those who were trying to land. Auguselus, king of Scotland, and Gawain, the king's nephew, died that day, together with many others too numerous to describe. Ywain, the son of Auguselus' brother Urien, succeeded him in the kingship; and in the wars which followed he became famous because of the many brave deeds that he accomplished. In the end, but only with enormous difficulty, Arthur's men occupied the seashore. They drove Mordred and his army before them in flight and inflicted great slaughter on them in their turn. Profiting from their long experience in warfare, they drew up their troops most skilfully. They mixed their infantry with the cavalry and fought in such a way that when the line of foot-soldiers moved up to the attack, or was merely holding its position, the horsemen charged at an angle and did all that they could to break through the enemy lines and to force them to run away.

However, the perjurer re-formed his army and so marched into Winchester on the following night. When this was announced to Queen Guinevere, she gave way to despair. She fled from York to Caerleon and there, in the church of Julius the Martyr, she took her vows among the nuns, promising to lead a chaste life.

Now that he had lost so many hundreds of his fellow-soldiers, Arthur was more angry than ever. He buried his dead and then marched on the third day to the city of Winchester and laid siege to his nephew, who had taken refuge there. Mordred showed no sign of abandoning his plans. He gave his adherents every encouragement he could think of, and then marched out with his troops and drew them up ready for a pitched battle with his uncle. The fight began and immense slaughter was done on both sides. The losses were greater in Mordred's army and they forced him to fly once more in shame from the battlefield. He made no arrangements whatsoever for the burial of his dead, but fled as fast as ship could carry him, and made his way towards Cornwall.

Arthur was filled with great mental anguish by the fact that Mordred had escaped him so often. Without losing a moment, he followed him as far as the river Camlann, where Mordred was awaiting his arrival. Mordred was indeed the boldest of men and always the first to launch an attack. He immediately drew his troops up in battle order, determined as he was either to win or die, rather than run away again as he had done in the past. From his total force of troops, about which I have told you, there still remained sixty thousand men under his command. From these he mustered six divisions, in each of which he placed six thousand, six hundred and sixty-six armed men. From those who were left over he formed one single division, and, when he had assigned leaders to each of the others, he placed this last division under his own command. As soon as they were all drawn up, he went round to encourage each of them in turn, promising them the possessions of their enemies if only they stood firm and were successful in battle.

On the other side, Arthur, too, was marshalling his army. He divided his men into nine divisions of infantry, each drawn up in a square, with a right and left wing. To each he appointed a commander. Then he exhorted them to kill these perjured villains and robbers who, at the request of one who had committed treason against him, the king, had been brought into the island from foreign parts to steal their lands from them. He told them, too, that this miscellaneous collection of barbarians, come from a variety of countries – raw recruits who were totally inexperienced in war – would be quite incapable of resisting valiant men like themselves, who were the veterans of many battles, provided always that they made up their minds to attack boldly and to fight like men.

While the two commanders were encouraging their men in this way in both the armies, the lines of battle suddenly met, combat was joined, and they all strove with might and main to deal each other as many blows as possible. It is heart-rending to describe what slaughter was inflicted on both sides, how the dying groaned, and how great was the fury of those attacking. Everywhere men were receiving wounds themselves or inflicting them, dying or dealing out death. In the end, when they had passed much of the day in this way, Arthur, with a single division in which he had posted six thousand, six hundred and sixty-six men, charged at the squadron where he knew Mordred was. They hacked a way through with their swords and Arthur continued to advance, inflicting terrible slaughter as he went. It was at this point that the accursed traitor was killed and many thousands of his men with him.

However, the others did not take to flight simply because Mordred was dead. They massed together from all over the battlefield and did their utmost to stand their ground with all the courage at their command. The battle which was now joined between them was fiercer than ever, for almost all the leaders on both sides were present and rushed into the fight at the head of their troops. On Mordred's side there fell Chelric, Elaf, Egbrict and Bruning, all of them Saxons; the Irishmen Gillapatric, Gillasel and Gillarvus; and the Scots and Picts, with nearly everyone in command of them. On Arthur's side there died Odbricht, king of Norway; Aschil, king of Denmark; Cador Limenich; and Cassivelaunus with many thousands of the king's troops, some of them Britons, others from the various peoples he had brought with him.

THE DEATH OF ARTHUR

Accordingly, when the battle between Arthur, king of the Britons, and Mordred – I dare not say his nephew, but rather his betrayer – had ended, and Mordred had been put to death, and here and there numerous warriors had been laid low and many of the enemy had been left for dead, the king – even though he had gained the victory – did not withdraw without some misgiving in his heart. For he had sustained a wound which, although it was not immediately life-threatening, nevertheless boded ill for the near future. He repaid the Creator of all things and His Mother the blessed Virgin Mary with grateful thanks; and the bitterness of his remorse for the loss of his men was balanced by joy at his triumph. After this, exhausted, he leant on his shield, and then sat down on the ground to recover; and as he sat there, he summoned four of the leaders of his people. He ordered them to disarm him gently, lest perhaps by proceeding carelessly they might increase the anguish of his wounds. When the king had been disarmed, a certain handsome youth, tall in stature, whose appearance proclaimed his immense strength, suddenly appeared on horseback, with a shaft of elm in his right hand. This shaft was stiff, not twisted or knotted but straight, and sharpened to a point in the manner of a lance; yet it was sharper for inflicting injury than any lance, since it had been fired to make it hard, and its hardness had been tempered with equal care by plunging it in water. It had been daubed with adder's venom so that, if the person who cast it lacked strength, this would be compensated for by its poison. This bold youth rode straight at the king but halted immediately in front of him, and hurled this missile at him, adding a more serious wound to his already grievous ones. This done, he fled quickly: but he did not escape for long, because the king, moving without hesitation like an active soldier, fixed a quivering spear in the back of the fleeing youth, piercing his innermost heart. The youth immediately breathed his last. But when the author of the king's death had himself been given over to death, a pallor at once came over the king's face, and he explained to those who watched over him that he would not enjoy the breath of life much longer. At this, tears flowed down the faces of those who loved him dearly and all lamented, because they despaired that anyone could safeguard Britain's liberty like him.

At length the king, slightly restored by an improvement in his condition, gave orders to be taken to Gwynedd, since he had decided to stay in the delightful Isle of Avalon because of the beauty of the place, where he could find peace and ease the pain of his wounds). When he arrived there, physicians concerned themselves with the king's injuries with all the diligence of their art, but their efforts were in vain. Because of this the king despaired of any cure in this life, and he commanded the archbishop of London to come to him. The archbishop, in the company of two other bishops — namely Urien of Bangor and Urbegen of Glamorgan — came to the king. (St David, the archbishop of St David's, would also have been present if he had not been prevented by a serious bodily disease.) With these prelates present, the king confessed his deviations from his Christian faith, and rendered himself answerable to his Creator's complaisance. Then he rewarded his followers for their service with the generosity of royal munificence; and he settled the rule of Britain on Constantine, son of Duke Cador. All this done, he received the divine sacraments and bade his last farewell to this wicked world. Stretched out full length on his hair shirt in the manner of those doing real penance, with his hands lifted towards heaven, he commended his spirit into the hands of his Redeemer. O how sad was this day, how worthy of mourning, how charged with lamentation, nor ever to be remembered by inhabitants of Britain without cries of distress! Not undeservedly: for on this day the rigour of justice grew slack, observance of the laws became a rarity, the calmness of peace was shattered, the excellence of liberty was taken captive; because, when glorious Arthur was taken from her midst, Britain was deprived of her unique claim to victory — for she who held dominion is now totally enslaved. But lest I seem to wander too far from the sequence of my narrative, my pen must turn back to the funeral rites of the deceased king.

The three bishops commended the soul returning to Him who bestowed it with deepest prayer through the sweetness of their devotions; the others laid out the royal corpse in a royal manner, embalming it with balsam and myrrh, and prepared it to be committed to burial. On the following day they took the corpse of the dead king to a certain small chapel dedicated to the honour of the Holy Mother of God, the perpetual Virgin Mary, as the king himself had appointed, saying that no other ground should receive his earthly remains. There he wished to be enclosed in the earth; there he wished his flesh to return to its origin; there he commended his dead self to the vigilance of her whom he had venerated with the deepest devotion. But after the cortège arrived at the door of this chapel, the small and narrow opening prevented the entry of a corpse as large as that of the king; and so it had to be left resting outside on its bier, next to the wall. Indeed, the entrance of the chapel was so small and narrow that no one could enter it unless they turned sideways and went in with one shoulder foremost, squeezing with difficulty through the doorway.

The inhabitant of this chapel was a certain hermit, who enjoyed the serenity of this most peaceful dwelling, remote from the squalor of the market-place. The senior bishops entered; the holy services were performed for the soul of the king; and we are told that the dead man's body remained outside. While the bishops performed the last rites, the sky thundered, the earth quaked, storms poured down relentlessly from on high, lightning flashed, and the winds blew from each quarter in turn. After the briefest interval, a mist descended which absorbed the brightness of the lightning, and surrounded the attendants of the royal corpse with such darkness that they saw nothing, even though their eyes were wide open. This mist continued uninterrupted from nine in the morning until three in the afternoon, and the air resounded continually with the crash of thunder. Finally, when the mist dispersed and the air cleared, they could find no trace of the royal corpse. The king had been transported to an abode especially prepared for him; and they looked on a bier deprived of its burden. They were perplexed by the disappearance of the king's body, and could not agree on the truth of what had happened. So an argument arose among them: 'Where did this mighty power come from? Through what violence was he carried off?'

Even today, the shadow of uncertainty remains as to where King Arthur was destined to find his place of rest. Some people say that he is still alive, sound and well, since he was carried off without their knowledge. Others contradict this bold conjecture, affirming without the slightest scruple of doubt that he paid the debt of death, for when the mist had been dispersed and visibility had returned, a sealed tomb appeared to the gaze of those present. It seemed to be both solidly closed and of one piece, so that it appeared to be one single stone, whole and solid, rather than fashioned with the mortar and craft of a builder, piece by piece. They believe that the king is enclosed in its recesses, since it was discovered already sealed and closed. And there is still no small disagreement among them.

Arthur governed the realm of Britain for thirty-nine years in the power of his strength, the wisdom of his mind, the acuteness of his judgement, and through his renown in battle. In the fortieth year of his reign, he was fated to meet the common end of the human lot. Therefore, with Arthur dead, Constantine, the son of Duke Cador, acceded to the British realm.

ARTHUR AND THE ROUND TABLE

THE BIRTH OF ARTHUR

WHEN UTHER PENDRAGON WAS king of all England, there was a mighty duke in Cornwall who waged war against him for a long time. And King Uther sent for this duke, ordering him to bring his wife with him, for she was said to be a wise and beautiful lady, and her name was Igraine. The duke and his wife came to the king, and the great lords of the land made peace between the king and the duke. The king loved this lady well, and he entertained them royally; and he tried to seduce her. But she was a very virtuous woman, and would not yield to the king. She told the duke her husband, saying: 'I suppose we were brought here so that I might lose my honour; husband, let us leave without warning and ride all night to our own castle.' And so they went their way, and neither the king nor his council were aware of their departure. But as soon as King Uther learnt that they had left suddenly, he was furious with rage. He summoned his privy council, and told them that the duke and his wife had gone without his leave.

Then they advised the king to summon the duke and his wife formally: 'If he will not come at your summons, you have good reason to declare war on him.' So that was done, but the duke told the messengers in a few words that neither he nor his wife would come to the king. In a fury, the king told him to prepare himself for war and supply his garrisons well, for within forty days he would drive him out of his biggest castle. When the duke had this warning, he went and garrisoned two of his strong castles; one was called Tintagel, and the other Terrabil. He put his wife Igraine in the castle of Tintagel, and took command of the castle of Terrabil himself. Uther soon arrived with a great army, and laid siege to the castle of Terrabil, pitching his tents there; and there was much fighting, and many people slain. Then, simply because of his anger and his great love of the beautiful Igraine, King Uther fell sick. So a knight named Sir Ulfius came to the king and asked him why he was sick.

'I will tell you,' said the king, 'I am sick with anger and with love of Igraine, and nothing can cure me.'

'Well, my lord,' said Sir Ulfius, 'I will search for Merlin, who will find a remedy that will ease your heart.'

So Ulfius departed, and happened to meet Merlin dressed as a beggar. Merlin asked Ulfius who he was looking for, and Ulfius told him.

'Well,' said Merlin, 'look no further, for I am he; and if King Uther will reward me well, and swear to fulfil my wishes, I will obtain for him what he desires.'

'I promise that if what you ask is reasonable,' said Ulfius, 'you shall have what you want.'

Then Ulfius was glad, and rode quickly back to Uther Pendragon, and told him he had met Merlin.

'Where is he?' said the king.

'Sir,' said Ulfius, 'he will not be long.'

At that Ulfius saw Merlin standing at the entrance of the tent, coming towards the king. When King Uther saw him, he said he was welcome.

'Sir,' said Merlin, 'I know how your heart lies; if you will swear to me as anointed king to fulfil my wish, you shall have your desire.'

So the king swore on the Four Evangelists.

'Sir,' said Merlin, 'this is my wish: the first night that you lie with Igraine you will get a child on her, and when it is born, it shall be delivered to me to bring up as I wish; for it shall be to your honour and to the good of the child.'

'I agree to that,' said the king.

'Get ready then,' said Merlin; 'tonight you shall lie with Igraine in the castle of Tintagel; and you will take on the likeness of the duke her husband; Ulfius shall be like Sir Brastias, and I will be like a knight called Sir Jordanus, both knights of the duke's. Do not let her or her men question you, but say you are not well, and go to bed, and do not get up tomorrow till I come to you, for the castle of Tintagel is only ten miles from here.'

And they did as Merlin instructed. But the duke of Tintagel saw the king riding away from the siege of Terrabil, and that night he sallied out of the castle at a postern gate to harass the king's host. And by making this sally, the duke himself was killed before the king arrived at the castle of Tintagel.

So King Uther lay with Igraine more than three hours after the death of the duke, and begot Arthur on her that night. The next day Merlin came to the king, who kissed the lady Igraine and departed in haste. But when the lady heard what had happened to the duke her husband, and that he was reported to have died before King Uther came to her, then she wondered who might have slept with her in her lord's likeness; so she mourned priffately and said nothing of it. Then all the barons begged the king to make peace with Igraine, and the king entrusted Ulfius to negotiate between them: and in the end the king and she met.

'Our king is a handsome knight and unmarried,' said Ulfius, 'Igraine is a very beautiful lady; it would please us greatly if the the king would make her his queen.'

The barons all agreed, and proposed this to the king, who willingly agreed; and so the two were soon married one morning with great mirth and joy.

And at the same time King Lot of Lothian and Orkney then wedded Morgause, who was Gawain's mother, and King Nentres of the land of Garlot wedded Elaine. All this was done at the request of King Uther. And the third sister, Morgan le Fay, was sent to school in a nunnery, where she learned so much that she became a great expert in witchcraft.

Queen Igraine grew greater day by day, and within six months, as King Uther lay by his queen, he asked her, by the faith she owed to him, whose was the child in her body; and she was too ashamed to answer.

'Do not be dismayed,' said the king, 'but tell me the truth, and I shall love you all the better.'

'Sir,' said she, 'this is the truth. The night that my lord died, at the exact hour of his death according to his knights, a man came into my castle of Tintagel who was like my lord in speech and in appearance, and two knights with him who looked like his two knights Brastias and Jordanus. I went to bed with him as I should have done with my lord, and that night this child was conceived.'

'That is true,' said the king, 'I myself came in the likeness of your husband; do not be dismayed, for I am the father of the child'; and he told her how it had all been brought about by Merlin. And the queen was very joyful when she knew who was the father of her child.

And Merlin came to the king, and said, 'Sir, you must arrange for the upbringing of your child.'

'Tell what you wish to be done,' said the king.

'Well,' said Merlin, 'I know a lord of yours in this land, who is a loyal and honest man and faithful, and he shall bring up your child. His name is Sir Ector, and he has wide estates in England and Wales; ask him to come to speak to you. When the child is born, bring it to me at the private gate of the castle, unchristened.'

And all that Merlin planned was done. When the queen was delivered, the king commanded two knights and two ladies to take the child, bound in a cloth of gold, and told them to deliver him to a poor man at the postern gate of the castle. So the child was given to Merlin; he took it to Sir Ector, and found a holy man to christen him, and named him Arthur.

Then within two years King Uther fell seriously ill. And in the meanwhile his enemies usurped his lands, and attacked his men, and killed many of his people.

'Sir,' said Merlin, 'you must not stay abed, for even if you have to ride in a horse-litter, you must be on the battlefield: if you are there in person, you will win a great victory.'

So they carried the king in a horse-litter at the head of a great army. And at St Albans the king encountered a great host from the North. And that day Sir Ulfius and Sir Brastias did great deeds of arms, and King Uther's men overcame the northerners, killing many and putting the rest to flight. The king returned to London, rejoicing in his victory; but his sickness increased, and he was speechless for three days and three nights. All the barons were full of grief, and asked Merlin what should be done.

'God will have his will,' said Merlin, 'but come to King Uther tomorrow, and God and I shall make him speak.'

So the next day all the barons and Merlin came to the king; and Merlin said aloud to King Uther, 'Sir, shall your son Arthur be king, after your days, of this realm with all that belongs to it?'

Then Uther Pendragon turned and said in the hearing of them all, 'I give him God's blessing and mine, and bid him pray for my soul. He shall claim the crown by right and honour, on pain of losing my blessing.'

At this he yielded up the ghost; and he was buried as befits a king. At this the queen, the lovely Igraine, and all the barons made great sorrow.

ARTHUR IS CHOSEN KING

Then the kingdom was in great danger, for all the great lords gathered their forces, and many thought that they should be king. Then Merlin went to the archbishop of Canterbury, and advised him to send for all the lords of the realm, and all the gentlemen of arms, that they should come to London by Christmas; because Jesus, who was born on that night, would in his great mercy show some miracle, by which men would know who should by right be king of this realm. And so the lords and knights gathered, and in the greatest church in London, men of all ranks were there long before day to say their prayers. And when matins and the first Mass was done, there was seen in the churchyard, near the high altar, a great foursquare stone, like marble; and in the middle of it was an anvil of steel a foot high, and a fine naked sword was embedded in it. Letters were written in gold round the sword which read: *Whoever pulls this sword out of this stone and anvil, is born to be the rightful king of all England.*

Then the people marvelled at it, and told the archbishop.

'I command,' said the archbishop, 'that you all stay within the church and pray; no man shall touch the sword until High Mass is finished.'

So when the Masses were over, all the lords went to look at the stone and the sword. And when they saw the writing, some tried their hand at the task, hoping to be king. But no one could move the sword at all.

'The man who will succeed,' said the archbishop, 'is not here, but God will make him known. But this is my counsel: ten knights, men of good fame, shall be appointed to guard this sword.'

And on New Year's Day the barons announced jousts and a tournament for all comers; and they did this to keep the lords and commons assembled, for the archbishop trusted that God would make known the man who would win the sword.

So upon New Year's Day, when the service was done, the barons rode into the lists, some to joust and some to tourney. Sir Ector, who had lands near London, rode to the jousts; with him rode Sir Kay, his son, and young Arthur who had been brought up as his brother; and Sir Kay had been made a knight some weeks before. As they rode to the jousts, Sir Kay found that he had left his sword at his father's lodging, and asked Arthur to ride back for it. Arthur agreed, and rode quickly back to fetch the sword; but when he came home, everyone had gone to see the jousting, and the door was barred.

Arthur was angry and said to himself, 'I will ride to the churchyard, and take the sword from the stone, for my brother Sir Kay shall not be without a sword this day.'

When he came to the churchyard, Arthur alighted and tied his horse to the stile; he went to the tent and found no knights there, for they were at the jousting. And so he laid hold of the sword by the hilt, and lightly and fiercely pulled it out of the stone. He took his horse and rode back to his brother Sir Kay, and gave him the sword. As soon as Sir Kay saw the weapon, he recognised it as the sword from the stone and rode to his father Sir Ector, and said: 'Sir, here is the sword of the stone, which means that I should be king of this land.'

When Sir Ector saw the sword, he went back to the church, and all three of them dismounted, and went into the church. And he made Sir Kay swear on the Bible to say how he came by that sword.

'Sir,' said Sir Kay, 'from my brother Arthur, for he brought it to me.'

'How did you get this sword?' said Sir Ector to Arthur.

'Sir, I will tell you. When I came home for my brother's sword, I found nobody at home to give it to me; I did not want my brother Sir Kay to be without a sword, so I came here and pulled it out of the stone without any difficulty.'

'Were there any knights guarding this sword?' said Sir Ector.

'No,' said Arthur.

'This means,' said Sir Ector to Arthur, 'that you are to be king of this land.'

'Why should I be king?' said Arthur.

'Sir,' said Ector, ' because God will have it so; for only he who should by right be king of this land can pull out this sword. Now let me see if you can put the sword back where it was, and pull it out again.'

'That needs no skill,' said Arthur, and so he put it in the stone; and Sir Ector tried to pull out the sword and failed,

'Now you try,' said Sir Ector to Sir Kay. And he pulled at the sword with all his might; but it would not move.

'Now you shall try,' said Sir Ector to Arthur.

'I will,' said Arthur, and pulled it out easily. And at that both Sir Ector and Sir Kay knelt before him.

'Alas,' said Arthur, 'my own dear father and brother, why do you kneel before me?'

'No, no, my lord Arthur, it is not so; I was never your father nor of your blood, but now I know that you are of a greater family than I thought.'

And then Sir Ector told him how he had been given him to bring up, and by whose orders, and Merlin's part in it all. Then Arthur was very sad when he learnt that Sir Ector was not his father.

'Sir,' said Ector to Arthur, 'will you be my good and gracious lord when you are king?'

'If I was not, I should be much at fault,' said Arthur, 'for you are the man in the world to whom I owe most, and to my good lady and mother your wife, who has looked after me as if I were her own. And if it is God's will that I am to be king as you say, you shall ask me for anything I can give, and I shall not fail you; God forbid that I should fail you!' 'Sir,' said Sir Ector, 'I will only ask that you make my son, your foster-brother Sir Kay, seneschal of all your lands.'

'That shall be done,' said Arthur, 'and no one save he shall have that office while he and I live.'

Therewithal they went to the archbishop, and told him how the adventure of the sword had been achieved, and by whom; and on the day of epiphany all the barons came there, and all who wished to try their hand were allowed to attempt to take the sword. But no one could pull it out save Arthur; at which many lords were angry, and said it would bring shame on them all if the kingdom were governed by a boy who was not of royal blood. And to settle the dispute, it was agreed that they should meet again in three months; the ten knights were ordered to watch the sword day and night, and they pitched a tent over the stone and the sword, and five always watched. So in three months many more great lords came to try to win the sword, but none could do it. And just as Arthur did at Christmas, he did again then, and pulled out the sword easily, at which the barons were mutinous and angry and asked for another delay till the high feast of Easter. And Arthur was once again the only one who succeeded; so some of the great lords, in their indignation that Arthur should be king, obtained a further delay till the feast of Pentecost.

Then the archbishop of Canterbury, on Merlin's advice, summoned the best knights that he could find, such as Uther Pendragon loved best and trusted most when he was alive, Sir Baudwin of Britain, Sir Kay, Sir Ulfius, and Sir Brastias. All these and many others always guarded Arthur, day and night, till the feast of Pentecost.

And at the feast of Pentecost all ranks of men tried to pull out the sword; but none could do so save Arthur, who pulled it out in the presence of all the lords and common people. All the common people cried at once, 'We will have Arthur as our king without delay, for we all see that it is God's will that he shall be our king. We will kill anyone who denies it!'

And they all kneeled at once, both rich and poor, and begged Arthur for mercy because they had delayed recognising him for so long, and Arthur forgave them, and took the sword between both his hands, and offered it on the altar before the archbishop; and he was knighted by the best man who was there. Soon after, he was crowned, and swore to his lords and the commons to be a true king, to uphold true justice all the days of his life. And many complaints were made to Arthur of great wrongs that were done since the death of King Uther, and of lands that had been wrongfully seized from lords, knights, ladies, and gentlemen. So King Arthur had the lands given back to them that owned them. When this was done, he made Sir Kay seneschal of England; and Sir Baudwin of Britain was made constable; and Sir Ulfius was made chamberlain; and Sir Brastias was made guardian of the north, for it was for the most part in the hands of the king's enemies. But in a few years Arthur won all the north, Scotland, and Wales, through the noble prowess of himself and his knights of the Round Table.

Then the king went into Wales, and announced a great feast at Pentecost after he had worn his crown at a ceremony in the city of Caerleon. To the feast came King Lot of Lothian and of Orkney, with five hundred knights; King Uriens of Gorre with four hundred knights; King Nentres of Garlot, with seven hundred knights; the king of Scotland, who was only a young man, with six hundred knights; a king who was called the king with the Hundred Knights, but he and his men were all splendidly equipped; and King Carados with five hundred knights. And King Arthur was glad that they had come, for he thought that all the kings and knights had come to join his feast in friendship, and he sent them gifts. But the kings refused them, saying they had no pleasure in receiving gifts from a beardless boy of low blood. And they said that they had come to give him gifts with hard swords between the neck and the shoulders: because they were all ashamed to see such a boy as king of so noble a realm as this land. So King Arthur, hearing this, on the advice of his barons withdrew to a strong tower with five hundred good men. And all the kings besieged him, but King Arthur had provisioned the tower well. And within a fortnight Merlin came to the city of Caerleon. All the kings were glad to see Merlin, and asked him, 'Why is that boy Arthur made your king?'

'Sirs,' said Merlin, 'I shall tell you why: he is King Uther Pendragon's son, born in wedlock, gotten on Igraine, wife of the duke of Tintagel.'

'Then he is a bastard,' they all said.

'No,' said Merlin, 'he was conceived more than three hours after the death of the duke, and thirteen days later King Uther wedded Igraine; and so he is no bastard. Let him who wishes say no, he shall be king and over-come all his enemies; and, before he dies, he shall be king of all England for long years, and have under his obedience Wales, Ireland and Scotland, and more kingdoms than I can count.'

Some of the kings were astonished at Merlin's words, and thought it would be as he said; and some, like King Lot, laughed at him in scorn; and many others called him a witch. But they agreed with Merlin that King Arthur should come out and speak with the kings, under a safe conduct. So Merlin went to King Arthur, and told him what he had done, and urged him not to be afraid, but to come out boldly and address them as their king and chieftain; 'for you shall overcome them all, whether they wish it or not'.

Then King Arthur came out of the tower, and had under his gown a hauberk of double mail, and the archbishop of Canterbury, and Sir Baudwin of Britain, and Sir Kay, and Sir Brastias were with him. And when they met there was no meekness, but stout words on both sides; but King Arthur always answered them, and said he would make them obey him if he lived. At this they stormed off angrily; King Arthur told them to be on guard, and they said the same to him. So the king went back to the tower again and armed himself and all his knights.

'What are you trying to do?' said Merlin to the kings; 'you would do better to hold back, for you would not prevail even if there were ten times as many of you.'

'Should we be afraid of a dream-reader?' said King Lot. At that Merlin vanished, and came to King Arthur, and told him to attack them fiercely;

and three hundred good men, the best who were with the kings, went over to King Arthur, and that comforted him greatly.

'Sir,' said Merlin to Arthur, 'do not fight with the sword that you got by the miracle, until you are being driven back, then draw it out and do your best.'

So King Arthur attacked them in their camp. And Sir Baudwin, Sir Kay and Sir Brastias killed men on the right hand and on the left hand; and King Arthur on horseback laid about him with his sword, and did marvellous deeds of arms, so that many of the kings admired his deeds and boldness.

Then King Lot came on Arthur from the rear, with the king with the Hundred Knights, and King Carados. At that Arthur turned with his knights, and struck at those behind and in front, and Arthur was in the front of the battle till his horse was slain underneath him, at which King Lot struck down King Arthur. But his four knights supported him and remounted him. Then he drew his sword Excalibur, which was so bright in his enemies' eyes that it gave light like thirty torches. He drove them back, and then the commons of Caerleon came up with clubs and staves and killed many knights; but the kings rallied their knights who were left alive, and fled from the scene of the battle. And Merlin came to Arthur, and advised him to follow them no further.

Then King Arthur rode into Caerleon where the wife of King Lot of Orkney came to him as a messenger; but she was sent as a spy, to report on the court of King Arthur. She came richly equipped, with her four sons, Gawain, Gaheris, Agravain, and Gareth, and many other knights and ladies. She was very beautiful; and the king was greatly in love with her, and desired to sleep with her; she conceived Mordred, and she was his half-sister through his mother Igraine. So she stayed for a month, and then departed. Then the king dreamed a strange dream which terrified him: he thought that griffins and serpents had come into his land, which burnt and killed all the people. He thought he fought with them, and they did him great harm, and wounded him badly, but in the end he destroyed them. But all this time King Arthur did not know that King Lot's wife was his sister.

THE MARRIAGE OF ARTHUR AND GUINEVERE

Because Merlin had helped Arthur to overcome his enemies, Arthur often took his advice. So one day King Arthur said to Merlin, 'My barons will let me have no rest, but say I must take a wife, and I will only marry according to your advice.'

'You should indeed marry,' said Merlin, 'for a man as noble as you should not be without a wife. Now is there any woman that you love more than the rest?'

'Yes,' said King Arthur,' I love Guinevere, daughter of King Leodegrance of the land of Cameliard, who has in his palace the Round Table which he had from my father Uther. And this girl is the most worthy and beautiful lady that I could ever find.'

'Sir,' said Merlin, 'as to her beauty, she is one of the loveliest women alive, but, if you did not love her so much, I would find you another girl as good and as beautiful; but if a man's heart is set on something, he will be loath to look elsewhere.'

'That is true,' said King Arthur. But Merlin warned the king privately that it was dangerous for him to take Guinevere to wife, for he prophesied that Lancelot should love her, and she him in return.

Then Merlin went to King Leodegrance of Cameliard, and told him that King Arthur wished to marry Guinevere his daughter.

'That is to me,' said King Leodegrance, 'the best news that I ever heard, that so worthy and noble a king wishes to wed my daughter. And as for a dowry, I would give him whatever lands he wished; but he has lands enough and needs no more. So I shall send him a gift which will please him much more, for I shall give him the Round Table, which Uther Pendragon gave me. When it has its full complement, there are a hundred and fifty knights around it. I have a hundred good knights myself, but I lack the other fifty, for so many have been killed in my days.'

So Leodegrance delivered his daughter Guinevere and the Round Table with the hundred knights to Merlin. And Guinevere and Merlin rode freshly, in royal state, by water and by land, until they approached London.

When King Arthur heard of the arrival of Guinevere and the hundred knights with the Round Table, he rejoiced at her coming, and with such a rich present, and said openly, 'This lovely lady is most welcome to me, for I have loved her long, and she is dearer to me than anything on earth. And these knights with the Round Table please me more than great riches.'

And the king quickly gave orders for the marriage and the coronation to be celebrated in the richest manner imaginable.

'Now, Merlin,' said King Arthur, 'go and find me the fifty knights in this country who are most renowned for prowess.'

Within a short time Merlin had found forty-eight knights that were of sufficient repute, but he could find no more. Then the b ishop of Canterbury was fetched, and he blessed the seats with great devotion, and set the forty-eight knights in their places. And when this was done Merlin said, 'Sirs, you must all arise and come to King Arthur to do him homage.'

And so they arose and did their homage, and when they were gone Merlin found in every seat letters of gold that named the knight who had sat there. But two places remained empty.

And the chronicles tell how messengers came to Arthur demanding that he pay tribute to Rome; and the answer that Arthur gave the messengers was fierce and warlike. The king set out for France with a great army, and defeated the men of Rome, and conquered their lands; and he was the greatest emperor and ruler of those days.

ARTHUR TURNS FROM WAR TO ADVENTURES

Soon after King Arthur returned from Rome to England, then all the knights of the Round Table came to the king's court, and held many jousts and tournaments. And some knights did such great feats of arms that they surpassed all their fellows in prowess and noble deeds; but it was especially Sir Lancelot du Lac who excelled all other knights in tournaments and jousts and deeds of arms, both for life and death; and he was never overcome except by treason or enchantment. For this Queen Guinevere favoured him above all other knights, and he loved the queen above all other ladies and girls throughout his life; for her he did many deeds of arms, and saved her from the fire through his noble chivalry.

For ten years King Arthur was a powerful, God-fearing king, at whose court many great adventures took place; and the Round Table was his, at which sat the finest knights in the world; no king on earth was so highly esteemed as he. But a weakness suddenly beset his resolve and he began to lose his former passion for great deeds. He would not hold court at Christmas, nor at Easter, nor at Pentecost. The knights of the Round Table, seeing his prowess decline, began to leave and shun his court. Of three hundred and seventy knights he had had in his household, he now had no more than twenty-five at the most. No longer did adventures befall his court. All the other princes neglected their great deeds because they saw the king's own weakness of spirit, and Queen Guinevere was beside herself with grief.

King Arthur was at Cardueil one Ascension Day. He had risen from the table where he was eating and was pacing up and down the hall. Then looking up he saw the queen sitting at a window, and he went and sat beside her, but when he turned to look at her face he saw tears streaming from her eyes.

'What is the matter, my lady?' said the king.

'Why are you weeping? 'Sir,' she replied, 'I have good reason to weep. And you have no cause to be happy.'

'In truth, my lady, I am not.'

'That is as it should be, sir, for I have seen on just such a day as this, that you had so many knights at your court that they could scarcely be numbered. Now there are so few each day that I feel nothing but shame. Nor does any adventure now befall us, and I fear that God has abandoned you.'

'Truly, my lady,' said the king, 'I have no desire to do great deeds or anything that brings honour; my will has turned to weakness of heart, and I know that because of this I am losing my knights and the love of my friends.'

'Sir,' she said, 'if you were to go to the chapel of Saint Augustine, which stands in the White Forest and can only be found by chance, I think you would regain your will to do great deeds. For God never refused guidance to a forlorn man who prayed with a true heart.'

'My lady,' said the king, 'I will go most willingly. I have heard it described as you say, and three days ago the desire to go there came upon me.'

'Sir,' she said, 'it is a most dangerous place, and the chapel is surrounded by adventures, but the most worthy hermit in the land of Wales has his cell beside the chapel and sustains himself solely by the glory of God.'

'My lady,' said the king, 'I must go there fully armed but without escort.'

'Oh sir,' she said, 'you could surely take a squire with you.'

'I would not dare, my lady, for it is a perilous place and the greater the company, the more harrowing are the adventures encountered.'

'I advise you, my lord,' she said, 'to take a squire with you, and if it please God, it will bring nothing but good.'

'Then I will, if such is your wish, my lady,' said the king, 'but I fear that ill will come of it.'

'No, my lord, may God forbid.'

The king rose from the window and so did the queen, and as he looked before him he saw a squire both tall and strong, and handsome and young. Cahus he was called, and he was the son of Yvain l'Avotre.

'My lady,' said Arthur to the queen, 'I will take this squire with me, if it please you.'

'Sir, it pleases me well, for I have heard much praise of him.'

The king called to the boy, who came and knelt before him; then, bidding him rise, he said: 'Cahus, you will sleep in the hall tonight and see that my horse is saddled at the break of day and my arms are ready, for I want to set out at that very hour. You alone will accompany me.'

'As you wish, sir,' said the boy. It was nearly vespers, and the king and queen went to their bed.

When everyone had dined in the hall the knights went to their lodgings, but the boy stayed there as commanded. He did not trouble to take off his clothes or shoes, for it seemed that the night would be short, and he wanted to be ready to carry out the king's command in the morning. The boy lay down to rest just as I have said, but as soon as he fell asleep he dreamed that the king had gone without him. Stricken with fear he ran to his pony, threw on the saddle and bridle, put on his spurs and girded on his sword; and it seemed in his dream that he galloped out of the castle in pursuit of King Arthur. After riding a long way he plunged into a deep forest, and looking along the path ahead, he saw the hoofmarks of the king's horse, or so it seemed. He followed the trail a long way until he came to a clearing; he thought the king must have dismounted there or nearby, for the trail had come to an end. Then, looking to his right, he saw a chapel in the middle of the clearing, around which he thought he saw a great cemetery with many tombs.

In his dream he decided to go on to the chapel, for he thought the king must have gone inside to pray, so up he rode and dismounted. He tethered his pony and went inside. He could see no one anywhere, except a knight lying on a litter in the middle of the chapel, draped in rich silk, with four candles burning around him in four golden candlesticks. The squire wondered much that the body should have been left there all alone, for statues were its only company. But he was even more perplexed at not finding the king, for now he did not know where to look for him. He removed one of the candles, took its golden candlestick and stuffed it between his hose and his leg, and then left the chapel and remounted his pony. He rode off across the graveyard, through the clearing and into the forest, telling himself that he would not stop until he had found the king.

Just as he was setting off on his way, he saw coming towards him a dark and ugly man, bigger standing up than the squire was on horseback; and it seemed to the boy that the man was clutching a huge, sharp, two-edged knife in his hand. The squire galloped up to him. saying: 'You there! Did you meet King Arthur in the forest?'

'No,' said the man, 'but I have met you, which gladdens my heart, for you left the chapel, you treacherous thief, with the golden candlestick that you wickedly carried off; it was put there in honour of the knight who lies dead in the chapel. I demand that you give it to me so that I may return it there, or else I challenge you.'

'In faith,' said the squire, 'I will not give it to you: I am going to present it to King Arthur.'

'I tell you true,' said the man, 'it will cost you dear if you do not hand it over promptly.'

The boy spurred on in an attempt to gallop past his enemy, but the man came to the attack and struck him in the right side with his knife and thrust it in right up to the haft.

The boy, lying in the hall at Cardueil, awoke from his dream and cried aloud: 'Holy mother! Bring a priest! Help! Help! for death is upon me!'

The king, the queen and the chamberlain heard him shout and jumped up, and they said to the king: 'Sir, you can set off now, for it is dawn. The king put on his shoes and clothes, but the squire was awake, shouting with all the strength he could summon: 'Bring a priest, for I am dying!'

The king ran to him, followed by the queen and the chamberlain bearing great torches. The king asked him what was the matter, and the squire told him of his dream.

'Oh,' said the king, 'then it was but a dream?'

'Yes, sir, but it has come true most horribly.'

And he raised his right arm.

'Sir, look there. See the dagger thrust in me to the haft.'

Then he felt in his hose for the golden candlestick, drew it out and showed it to the king.

'Sir,' he said, 'I was mortally wounded because of this candlestick which I now present to you.'

The king took it and gazed at it in wonder, for never had he seen one so fine. He showed it to the queen.

'Sir,' said the boy, 'do not pull the knife from my body until I have made confession.'

The king summoned his chaplain who heard confession and performed the rites as was fitting. Then the king himself drew out the dagger, and on the instant the boy's soul left his body. The king saw that honour was paid to him and that he was richly shrouded and laid to rest. Yvain l'Avotre, the squire's father, was deeply grieved at the death of his son, and at Yvain's behest King Arthur gave the golden candlestick to the church of Saint Paul's at London, for it had just been built, and he wanted this wondrous adventure to be known to everyone, so that people would pray in the church for the soul of the boy who had been killed because of the candlestick.

In the morning the king armed himself, as I began to relate, for his journey to Saint Augustine's Chapel. The queen said to him: 'Who is to go with you, sir?'

'My lady, my only companion will be God. You can surely see by the adventure which befell the boy that God wishes no one to go with me.'

'May God guard you well,' she said, 'and see you safely back. And may He restore your desire to do great deeds, so that your waning reputation may be exalted once more!' 'May it please God, my lady!' His horse was led to the castle steps and he mounted, fully armed. Sir Yvain l'Avotre gave him his shield and lance, and when the king was thus equipped he looked indeed a knight of great strength and courage. He set himself so firmly in the stirrups that he made the saddle stretch and the horse bow under him, strong and swift though it was; then he thrust in his spurs and the horse leapt forward. The queen was standing at the windows of the hall, and all twenty-five of Arthur's knights had come to the steps. When the king was gone the queen said: 'My lords, what do you think of the king? Does he not look noble indeed?'

'Truly, madam, he does; and it is a great sorrow for the world that he does not carry on the great work that he began, for there is no king or prince so well endowed with all courtly manners and such prowess as he, if he would only do as he used to do.'

At that the knights fell silent, while the king galloped swiftly off and passed into a forest full of adventures.

He rode all day long until he found himself at twilight in the thickest part of the forest, and there he caught sight of a little house beside a chapel, which he felt sure was a hermitage. So the king rode up and dismounted in front of the hut; then he went inside, pulling his horse behind him, though it could hardly get through the door. He laid his lance on the ground and leaned his shield against the wall, and then ungirded his sword and unlaced the top of his mailcoat. Looking ahead he could see barley and meal, and so he led his horse up, took off its bridle and closed the door. And at that moment he thought he could hear people arguing in the chapel: some voices sounded like angels, while others were talking coarsely, like demons, and the king wondered what could be happening.

Just then he found a door in the hut which opened on to a little cloister leading to the chapel. The king went inside the little church and looked around him; he could see nothing but statues and crucifixes, and he could not believe that it was they who had been quarrelling. The noise had stopped as soon as he entered. He wondered much how the hermitage had come to be deserted and what had become of the hermit who lived there. But then, as he went up to the altar, the king saw before him an open coffin, and there lay the hermit, fully clothed. His beard flowed down as far as his belt and his hands were folded on his chest. He was holding a cross to him and the figure of Christ was touching his lips. There was still some life in him, but his end was near. The king stayed by the coffin for a long time, gazing at the hermit with gladness, for he felt that the man had lived a good life.

Night had fallen, but in the chapel there was as much light as if twenty candles had been burning. Arthur wanted to stay by the coffin until the

worthy man had passed away, and he was about to sit down beside it when
a terrible voice shouted to him to be gone, for a judgement was about to be
made in the chapel and it would not be done while he was there. The king
departed, though he would most gladly have stayed, and went back to the
little house and sat down on a seat which had been the hermit's. Then he
heard the din coming from the chapel once more, some talking loudly and
others softly, and he could tell from the voices that on one side were angels
and on the other were demons. He could hear the demons disputing
possession of the hermit's soul and could tell that judgement was near at
hand; and the demons were rejoicing. The king grieved in his heart, for the
voices of the angels had grown silent, and he fell to thinking and had no
desire to eat or drink.

But through his vexed and anguished thoughts he heard in the chapel a
lady's voice, so sweet and high that no man, however distressed, could
have heard the voice and not felt joy. She was saying to the demons: 'Be
gone! You have no right to the soul of this worthy man, whatever he may
have done in the past. My son and I have taken him into our service, and
he was doing penance in this hermitage for his sins.

'True, lady,' cried the demons, 'but he had served us more than your son
or you; for sixty-two years or more he was a murderer and a robber in this
forest. He has been a hermit for only five years, yet now you want to take
him from us.'

'No, in truth,' she said, 'I do not want to take him from you. If he had
truly been in your service as he is in ours, you would have had him freely.'

The demons departed downcast and grieving, while the sweet Mother
of God took the soul of the hermit, which had left his body, and
commended it to the angels, that they should present it to her dear Son in
heaven; and as the angels took it they began to sing in joy.

King Arthur, sitting in the hut and hearing the voice of the sweet
mother of God and the angels, was filled with joy, and deeply happy for
the soul of the worthy man which had been borne to heaven. The king
slept very little that night and stayed fully armed. And when he saw day
break he went to the chapel to pray, expecting to find the hermit's coffin
uncovered. It was not; it was covered by the finest tombstone ever seen,
with a bright red cross upon it; and the chapel seemed to be filled with
incense. When he had finished praying the king left the chapel. He
saddled and harnessed his horse, mounted, took up his lance and shield,
and then left the hut and disappeared into the forest once more. He rode
swiftly on until he came at tierce* to one of the most beautiful glades ever
seen, with a swing gate at the entrance. Just before he rode in, he looked to

---

*   Between 8 and 9 a.m.

his right and saw a girl sitting beneath a tree, holding the reins of her mule. She was very beautiful. The king turned towards her, and said: 'May God give you joy and good fortune.'

'And you, sir, all the days of your life,' she said.

'Is there any house in this glade?' said the king.

'Sir, the only house is the holy chapel of Saint Augustine, and a hermitage which stands beside it.'

'The chapel of Saint Augustine is here, then?'

'Indeed it is, sir. But the glade and the forest around it are so perilous that any knight who enters returns either dead or maimed. But the chapel is a place of such holiness that no wayward soul who goes there can fail to find guidance, so long as he can return alive. May God keep you, sir, for never in a long while have I seen one who seemed a more noble knight. It would be a great pity if you were not, and I will not leave here until I have seen what becomes of you.'

'If it please God, you will see me return.'

'I should then be most happy,' she said, 'and if you do, I shall ask news at leisure of him whom I seek.'

The king rode up to the gate which opened on to the clearing, and passed through. Looking to his right down a defile in the forest, he saw the chapel of Saint Augustine and the hermitage. He rode up and dismounted, and it seemed to him that the hermit was dressed for Mass. He tethered his horse to a tree beside the chapel and then turned to go. But even if all the gold in the world had been at stake he could not have entered the chapel; yet no one was stopping him, for the door was wide open and he could see no one blocking his way. The king felt greatly humbled. Just then he caught sight of a statue of Our Lord and bowed before it; then, looking towards the altar, he saw the holy hermit saying his *Confiteor*, and at the hermit's right hand he could see the most beautiful child that ever a man beheld: he was dressed in an alb, with a golden crown on his head laden with precious stones, which shone with a brilliant light. To the left was a lady so beautiful that no beauty in the world could match hers. And when the holy hermit had said his *Confiteor* he went up to the altar, while the lady took her son and sat on the right-hand side of the altar upon a huge, richly carven chair, setting her son on her knee and kissing him gently.

'Sir,' she said, 'you are my father, and my son, and my lord, and my guardian, and guardian of everyone.'

King Arthur heard these words and saw the beauty of the lady and her child, and was filled with wonder; and he marvelled that she called the child her father and her son. Then he gazed up at a glass window behind the altar, and just as Mass began he saw a great flame, brighter than a shaft of sunlight, pass through and fall upon the altar. The king saw this and wondered, but it grieved him that he could not go inside. And when the hermit began to sing Mass, the king could hear the voices of angels answering; and when the holy Gospel was read, the king looked towards the altar and saw the lady take her child and offer him to the blessed hermit. The king marvelled that he did not wash his hands upon receiving the offering, but he would not have wondered so if he had known the reason, for such a great offering would surely not have been made if his hands had not been clean, and his body clean, too, of all corruption. And when the child was offered to him he placed him on the altar; then began the sacrament, and the king knelt down outside the chapel, praying to God and saying his *Mea Culpa*, and then, looking towards the altar after the preface, it seemed to him that the hermit was holding in his arms a man, bleeding from his side, bleeding from his hands and feet and crowned with thorns: he could see him quite clearly. He looked at him for a long while, and then did not know what had become of him.

The king's heart was filled with pity at what he had seen, and tears started in his eyes. Then he looked back towards the altar and thought he saw the man's body changed into the shape of the child that he had seen before. When Mass had been sung the voice of a holy angel said: '*Ite, missa est.*'

The son took his mother by the hand and vanished from the chapel with the greatest and most beautiful host ever seen, and the flame which had come down through the window disappeared with them.

When the hermit had finished his service and had taken off his robes he came up to the king, who was still outside the chapel, and said: 'Sir, now you may enter, and you might have been joyful indeed in your heart if you had been worthy of admittance at the beginning of the Mass.' The king now entered the chapel quite freely.

'Sir,' said the hermit, 'I know you well, just as I knew King Uther Pendragon your father. Because of your sin you could not enter this chapel today while Mass was being sung. Nor will you do so tomorrow, unless you first atone for your offence to God and to the saint whom we worship here. For you are the richest and most powerful king in the world, and the one to whom the greatest adventures fall, and you should be an example to all the world of valour and great deeds and honour; yet you are the example of baseness to all living men. It will fall out most sorely for you unless you restore your affairs to their former state; for your court was once the greatest of all courts, and the greatest adventures befell it; now it is the least distinguished. Much may he grieve who falls from honour to shame, but he cannot incur any harmful reproach who rises from shame to honour, for the honour in which he is found saves him straightway. But reproach cannot rescue the man if he has left honour for shame, for the shame and the baseness in which he is taken judge him ill.'

'Sir,' said the king, 'I came here to repent, and to find better guidance than I have had. I can see that this is a holy place indeed, and I beg you to pray to God that He may guide me; and I will spare nothing to mend my ways.'

'May God grant that you turn to good,' said the hermit, 'so that you may support and exalt the Law renewed by the death of Christ. But a great misfortune has recently befallen us because of a knight who was lodged at the house of the rich fisher King. The Holy Grail appeared to him, with the lance whose iron head bleeds, but he did not ask what was done with it or who was served from it. And because he failed to ask these questions, all lands are now rent by war; no knight meets another in a forest but he attacks him and kills him if he can, as you yourself will see before you leave this glade.'

'Sir,' said the king, 'may God defend me from a grievous and base death. I came here only to amend my life, and I will do so, if God will lead me back safely.'

'Truly, sir,' said the hermit, 'he who has sinned three years in forty has not been wholly good for all his forty years.'

'Sir,' said the king, 'you speak the truth.'

And the hermit took his leave, commending him to God.

The king returned to his horse as fast as he could and mounted, and hung his shield round his neck and took up his lance, and then rode swiftly away. But he had not ridden the length of a bow-shot before he saw a knight coming towards him at breakneck speed, mounted on a great black horse and carrying a black shield and lance. The head of the lance was huge, and it burned with a great flame, sinister and terrifying, which reached right down to the knight's hand. He levelled his lance to strike the king, but Arthur swerved to one side and the knight galloped past him. The king cried out: 'Sir knight, why do you take me for an enemy?'

'I cannot take you for a friend,' cried the knight.

'And why not?'

'Because you had in your possession the golden candlestick which belonged to my brother, and which was wickedly stolen from him.'

'You know then who I am?' said the king.

'I do. You are King Arthur, who was once a good king but now is bad, and I challenge you as my mortal enemy.'

He drew back and prepared to charge, and the king realised that he could not avoid battle. He lowered his lance as he saw the knight gallop forward with his lance all aflame, and then thrust in his spurs with all his strength and met the knight with his lance, just as the knight met him; and each struck the other so hard that their lances bent, though they did not break, and they were both unseated and lost their stirrups; and both men and both their horses crashed into each other so hard that they saw stars and blood spurted from the king's mouth and nose. They drew back from one another and recovered their breath. The king looked at the Black Knight's burning lance and wondered why it had not been shattered by the great blow it had given him, and thought the knight must be a demon. The Black Knight had no intention of breaking off the fight, and charged at him with all his force; the king saw him coming and hid behind his shield in fear of the flame, but he met the knight with the head of his lance and struck him full in the chest with such fury that he laid him flat over the rump of his horse. But the knight showed great vigour and set himself back in the saddle, and smote the king on the boss of his shield; the burning blade pierced the wood, rent the sleeve of the hauberk and tore into his arm: the king felt the burning of the wound and was filled with rage, while the knight drew out his lance and rejoiced in his heart to see the king wounded.

But the king in his dismay was astonished to see that the knight's lance was no longer burning.

'Sir,' said the Black Knight, 'have mercy on me now. Never could my lance be quenched until it was bathed in your blood.'

'May God desert me,' cried the king, 'if I have mercy on you when I can overcome you.'

And he spurred his horse on with a great leap and struck the knight in the broadest part of his chest, thrusting his lance half a yard into the knight's body, and bringing him and his horse crashing to the ground in a heap. He withdrew his lance and looked down at the knight, stretched out as though dead. He left him there in the middle of the glade and rode off towards the gate. Just as the king was riding away he heard a great noise of knights moving through the forest, and it sounded as though there were twenty or more of them. He saw them emerge from the forest into the glade, armed and well mounted, and ride up to the knight who lay dead.

The king was just about to leave the clearing when the girl he had left beneath the tree came running up to him.

'Oh sir!' she cried.

'Turn back, in God's name, and bring me the head of the dead knight.'

But the king looked back and saw the grave danger and the crowd of knights, all fully armed, and he said: 'Would you have me killed?'

'No sir, truly, but his head would be of great use to me. Never has a knight denied me any gift for which I asked: may God grant that you do not now prove to be the basest.'

'But I am sorely wounded in my shield-arm,' said the king.

'I know that, sir, but you will not be healed unless you bring me the head of that knight.'

'Then I shall venture out,' he said, 'no matter what it may cost me.'

The king looked across the glade and saw that the knights who had ridden up had cut the Black Knight to pieces, and each was carrying off a foot or an arm, a leg or a hand. They were now beginning to ride away into the forest, and when the king saw that the hindmost knight had stuck the head on the end of his lance, he went galloping after him.

'Ho there, sir knight!' he cried.

'Stay and speak with me.'

'What would you, good sir?'

'I beseech you with all my heart,' said the king, 'to give me the head that you are carrying on the end of your lance.'

'I will give it to you,' said the knight, 'on one condition.'

'On what condition?'

'That you tell me who killed the knight whose head I am carrying, which you seem to want so much.'

'I cannot have it otherwise?'

'No,' said the knight.

'Then I shall tell you. Know in truth that King Arthur killed him.'

'And where is he?' asked the knight.

'Look for him until you find him. I have told you the truth; now give me the head.'

'Willingly,' said the knight. And he lowered his lance and the king took the head.

The knight had a horn hanging from his neck and he put it to his lips and blew, and the knights who had ridden off into the forest heard it and came galloping back while the king made for the gate where the girl awaited him. The knights swept up to the one who had given the head to the king, and asked him why he had sounded the horn.

'Because that knight riding away over there,' he said, 'told me that King Arthur killed the Black Knight, and I wanted you to know so that we could hunt him down.'

'We shall not be hunting him down,' cried the knights, 'for that knight who is carrying off the head is King Arthur himself. We cannot do him any harm now, for he has passed the gate. But you will pay for letting him escape when he was so near you.'

They sprang upon the knight and killed him and hacked him to bits, and then each carried off a piece of his body as they had done with the Black Knight.

The king passed through the gate and rode up to the girl who was waiting for him, and presented the head to her.

'Great thanks, sir,' she said.

'It is a gift most gladly given.'

'Sir, you may dismount now. You are safe this side of the gate.'

The king dismounted straightway, and the girl said: 'Sir, have no fear; take off your hauberk and I will bind the wound in your arm, for you can be cured by none but me.'

So the king took off his hauberk, while the girl gathered blood from the knight's head, which still flowed hot, and bound it on the wound. Then she told the king to put on his hauberk once more.

'Sir,' she said, 'you would never have been cured without the blood of this knight, and that is why they cut up his body and were carrying it away, and his head likewise, for they were well aware that you were wounded. And the head will be of great value to me, also; for with this in my possession a castle which was treacherously seized from me may be returned, if I can find the knight whom I seek, who will win it back for me. And now tell me your name.'

'Willingly. Those who know me call me Arthur.'

'Arthur! Is that your name?'

'Yes.'

'Then God help me,' she cried, 'I have less respect for you now: for you have the name of the worst king in the world, and I wish he were here now as you are; but he will never leave Cardueil on his own if he can help it. Instead he guards the queen against abduction, or so I have heard tell. I have never seen either of them. I was on my way to visit his court, but I met twenty knights, one after another, and when I asked them about him they all told me, every one, that the court of King Arthur is the most shameful in the world, and that all the knights of the Round Table have left him because of his baseness.'

'He may grieve much for that,' said the king, 'I heard that he did great good in his early days.'

'What does it matter that he began well, when his end is so shameful? It grieves me much that such a good knight as you should have the name of such a bad king.'

'A man's worth depends not on his name but on his heart.' said the king.

'That is true,' she said, 'but because of the king's name your own displeases me. Where are you headed?' she asked.

'I am going to Cardueil where I shall find King Arthur.'

'Go to!' she cried.

'Both the villains will be together! For so I hold both him and you if you go there!' 'Call us what you will, I commend you to God.'

'May God never guide you again,' she cried, 'if you go to King Arthur's court!'

At that the king remounted and rode off, leaving the girl beneath the tree. He plunged into the deep forest and galloped on as fast as he could towards Cardueil. He had ridden a good ten leagues when he heard a dread voice in the thickest part of the forest; it was shouting: 'Arthur, king of Britain, you may truly rejoice in your heart that God has sent me to you. He commands you to hold court as soon as possible, for the world, which has suffered much harm because of you and your neglect of great deeds, will now profit most greatly from your action.'

With that the voice fell silent, and the king's heart was filled with joy by what he had heard.

He rode on until he came at last to Cardueil, where the queen and the knights were overjoyed to see him. He dismounted at the castle steps and went up to the hall to take off his armour. He showed the queen the wound in his arm, which had been deep and painful but was now healing well. Then he went with the queen to his bedchamber, where he was robed in a gown of silk and ermine, with a coat, a surcoat and a mantle.

'Sir,' said the queen, 'you have suffered much hardship.'

'My lady,' he said, 'worthy men must suffer so if they are to win honour, for honour cannot be won without hardship.'

And he told the queen of all the adventures he had had since his departure, and how he had come to be wounded in the arm, and about the girl who had insulted him because of his name.

'Sir,' said the queen, 'now you can see that a worthy man, rich and powerful, should be deeply ashamed when he falls to base ways.'

'My lady,' said the king, 'the girl showed me that most clearly; but a voice that I heard in the forest gave me much comfort, for it said that God commanded me to hold court as soon as I could, and that I would see the greatest adventure I had ever seen.'

'Sir,' she said, 'you should be joyful indeed when the Saviour remembers you. Now do as He commands.'

'Indeed I shall, my lady, for never have I had so keen a desire for great deeds, honour and largesse as I have now.'

'Sir,' she said, 'may God be praised!'

ARTHUR'S COURT REGAINS ITS FAME

And for many years Arthur's court was renowned throughout the world once more, and many great adventures took place there; and the Round Table was once more filled by the finest knights in the world. He held court at Christmas, at Easter, and at Pentecost; and he renewed his custom at such feasts, that he would not dine until he had seen some marvel which would lead to an adventure. And the last and greatest of these adventures was the quest of the Holy Grail; almost all the knights departed in search of it, and Arthur mourned their going, since he knew that he would not see many of them again. But that tale is not told here, for it is Galahad's story, not Arthur's, even though Arthur's court was the setting for its beginning and its end.

When the Grail quest had finished, Bors arrived at court in the city of Camelot from the faraway lands of Jerusalem, and found much there that brought him great joy, because everyone was very anxious to see him. When he told them about the passing of Galahad and the death of Perceval at the end of the search for the Grail, they were all very saddened at court, but nevertheless they all consoled themselves as best they could. The king commanded that all the adventures that the companions of the quest for the Holy Grail had recounted at his court were to be set down in writing; and when he had done this he said: 'My lords, look among you and count how many of your companions we have lost on this quest.'

They looked and found there were as many as thirty-two missing; and of all these there was not one who had not died in combat.

The king had heard the rumour that Gawain had killed several of them, and he summoned him before him and said: 'Gawain, I order you, by the oath you swore when I knighted you, to answer the question I am going to ask you.'

'My lord,' replied Sir Gawain, 'since you have asked me on my honour as a knight, I shall not fail in any way to tell you, even if it brought me shame as great as ever befell a knight of your court.'

'I want to ask you,' said the king, 'how many knights you think you killed, by your own hand, on this quest.'

Sir Gawain thought for a moment and the king said again: 'By my oath, I want to know, because there are people who are saying that you have killed a very large number.'

'My lord,' said Sir Gawain, 'you obviously wish to be certain of my great misfortune, and I shall tell you, because I see that I must. I can tell you in truth that I killed eighteen by my own hand, not because I was a better knight than any of the others, but since misfortune affected me more than any of my companions. Indeed, it did not come about through my chivalry, but through my sin. You have made me reveal my shame.'

'Certainly, my nephew,' said the king, 'that was truly great misfortune, and I am well aware that it happened through your sin. Nevertheless, tell me whether you believe you killed King Bagdemagus.'

'My lord,' he said, 'I definitely did kill him — and I have never done anything that I regret as much as that.'

'Indeed, my nephew,' said the king, 'if you have regrets about that it is not surprising; because, may God help me, I regret it too. My court has lost more in him than in the four best knights who died on the quest.'

So spoke King Arthur about King Bagdemagus, and as a result Gawain felt worse about the affair than he had done before. And since the king saw that adventures had so declined in the kingdom of Logres that they scarcely took place anywhere, he ordered a tournament to be announced at Winchester, because he did not want his companions to cease wearing arms.

LANCELOT RESUMES HIS AFFAIR WITH GUINEVERE

Lancelot had begun to live chastely as a result of the exhortations of the hermit to whom he had confessed when he had been on the quest for the Holy Grail, and had utterly renounced Queen Guinevere. But when he returned to court it took him less than a month to become just as deeply and ardently in love as he had ever been, and he fell back into sin with the queen just as before. What is more, if he had previously indulged in his sin so carefully and so guardedly that no one had been aware of it, now on the contrary he acted so indiscreetly that Agravain, Sir Gawain's brother, who had never greatly liked Lancelot and took more notice of his erring actions than any of the others, realised what was happening. Agravain watched them so closely that he discovered the whole truth, that Lancelot and the queen loved each other adulterously. The queen was so beautiful that everyone marvelled at her, for at that time she was at least fifty years old but was such a beautiful woman that her equal could not have been found anywhere in the world. Because of this, and since her beauty never failed her, certain knights said that she was the fountain of all beauty.

When Agravain had found out about the queen and Lancelot, he was extremely pleased – more for the harm he thought he would be able to do Lancelot than for an opportunity to avenge the king's dishonour. In that week the day came round for the tournament at Winchester, and a great number of King Arthur's knights attended. However, Lancelot was planning to go in disguise, and told all those around him he felt so unwell that he definitely would not be able to go. Despite this, he wanted Bors and Ector and Lionel and their company of knights to attend. They replied that they would not go, because he was so unwell. So he told them: 'I want and command you to go, and you will leave in the morning, while I remain here. By the time you return I shall have recovered completely, if God is willing.'

'My lord,' they said, 'since it is your wish, we shall go; but we should very much like to have stayed with you and kept you company.'

Lancelot repeated that he did not want them to do that, so thereupon they said no more on the subject.

In the morning Bors left the city of Camelot with his company of knights. When Agravain found out that Bors was going with his knights and that Lancelot was staying behind, he immediately thought that Lancelot's plan was to see the queen after Arthur had left. So he went to his uncle the king and said: 'My lord, there is something I would tell you about in secret, if I did not think it would distress you. I am only mentioning it to avenge your dishonour.'

'My dishonour?' exclaimed the king.

'Is the matter then so important that my dishonour is involved?'

'Yes, my lord,' said Agravain, 'and I shall explain why.'

Then he drew him to one side and told him in confidence: 'My lord, I must tell you that Lancelot and the queen love each other adulterously. Because they cannot meet as they would wish when you are there, Lancelot has stayed behind instead of going to the tournament at Winchester; but he has sent along his knights so that tonight or tomorrow, when you have left, he will be completely free to talk to the queen.'

When King Arthur heard this he could not believe it was true, and in fact was sure that Agravain had invented it.

'Agravain, my nephew,' he said, 'you should never say such a thing, because I could not believe you. I am quite sure that Lancelot could never have had ideas like that, and indeed if he ever did, he was compelled to by the force of love, which neither common sense nor reason can resist.'

'What, my lord!' exclaimed Agravain. 'Are you not going to do anything about it?'

'What do you want me to do about it?' he asked.

'My lord,' said Agravain, 'I should like you to order them to be watched closely until they can be caught together. Then you would know the truth, and next time you would be more ready to believe me.'

'Do what you like about it,' said the king.

'I shall not stop you.'

Agravain said that that was all he was asking for.

That night King Arthur gave considerable thought to what Agravain had said, but he did not let it affect him much, because he did not really believe it was true. In the morning he prepared to leave for the tournament and summoned a great number of his knights to accompany him.

The queen said to him, 'My lord, I should willingly go to the tournament if it pleased you, and in fact I would very much like to go, because I have heard that many very fine knights will be there.'

'My lady,' said the king, 'you are not to go this time.'

And so she said no more on the subject. Arthur was quite intentionally making her stay behind in order to put Agravain's accusation to the test.

When the king was on his way to the tournament with his companions, they talked together quite considerably about Lancelot and said that he was not going to attend. And as soon as Lancelot knew that the king had left with the knights who were going to Winchester, he rose from his bed and dressed. Then he went to the queen and said: 'My lady, if you will permit me, I would like to go to the tournament.'

'Why have you stayed behind after the others?' she asked.

'My lady,' he said, 'it is because I would like to go alone, and arrive at the tournament completely unrecognised by either friends or strangers.'

'Go, then,' she said, 'if you wish. I give you leave.'

He left her straight away and returned to his quarters, where he stayed until nightfall.

When it was dark, and as soon as everyone in the city of Camelot was asleep, Lancelot went to his squire and said: 'You must ride with me, because I want to go to the tournament at Winchester. The two of us must not travel except at night, because I do not want to be recognised on the way at any price.'

The squire carried out his orders; he made himself ready as quickly as he could, and took Lancelot's best horse, because he realised that his lord wished to bear arms at the tournament. When they were outside Camelot and had joined the right path for Winchester, they rode all night through without taking any rest.

The next day, when it was light, they arrived at the castle of Escalot where the king had spent the night. Lancelot went there only because he did not want to travel during the day, in case he was recognised. When he arrived beneath the castle, he rode with his head so low that he could hardly be identified. He did this because some of the king's knights were leaving the castle; and he very much regretted that he had come so early.

King Arthur, who was still looking out of a window, saw Lancelot's horse and recognised it at once because he had given it to him himself, but he did not recognise Lancelot as his head was too low. However, when crossing a street, Lancelot raised his head, and the king noticed him and pointed him out to Girflet: 'Did you see Lancelot just then? Yesterday he was having us believe that he was unwell, and now he is in this castle.'

'My lord,' said Girflet, 'I will tell you why he did that; he wished to be present at the tournament without being recognized and so he did not want to come with us – that is the honest truth.'

Meanwhile, Lancelot, who was quite unaware of all this, entered a house in the town with his squire, and ordered that his identity should not be revealed to anyone there, if they asked. The king stayed at the window waiting for Lancelot to pass once again, until he realised that he had stopped in the town. Then he said to Girflet: 'We have lost Lancelot; he has found somewhere to stay.'

'My lord,' replied Girflet, 'that is quite possible. You see, he only rides at night, in order not to be recognised.'

'Because he wishes to remain unnoticed,' the king replied, 'we shall pretend not to have seen him. Be sure that no living soul is told that you have seen him here – I shall not mention it on my side. Then he will be quite able to remain unnoticed, because we are the only people to have seen him.'

And Girflet swore that he would not tell anyone.

So the king left the window with those who were with him, and Lancelot stayed in the town of Escalot, at the house of a rich baron who had two handsome strong sons, recently knighted by the hand of King Arthur himself. Lancelot began looking at the two knights' shields and saw that they were all as red as fire, without any device on them. That was because it was customary at that time for a newly dubbed knight to bear a shield of only one colour during his first year; if he did not comply it was an infringement of the rule of knighthood. Lancelot said to the lord of the house: 'My lord, I would very much like to ask you as a favour to lend me one of those shields to wear at the tournament at Winchester, as well as the caparison and the other equipment that go with it.'

'My lord,' said the vavasour, 'have you not a shield?'

'No,' he replied, 'not one I wish to wear, because if I wore it I should probably be recognised sooner than I would like; so I shall leave it here with my arms, until I return.'

His host said to him, 'My lord, take whatever you like. One of my sons is unwell and will not be able to bear arms at the tournament, but the other is about to set out.'

Just then the knight who was to go to the tournament came into the room. When he saw Lancelot he was very courteous to him, because Lancelot had the appearance of a fine knight. He asked Lancelot who he was, and the latter replied that he was a foreign knight from the kingdom of Logres, but refused to give him his name or tell him any more about himself. Lancelot would only say that he was going to the tournament at Winchester and that that was why he had come that way.

'My lord,' said the knight, 'I am glad that you have come, because I wanted to go too. Let us set out together, and we can keep each other company on the way.'

'My lord,' replied Lancelot, 'I would rather not ride by day, because the heat is too much for me, but if you could wait till evening, I would accompany you. However, I shall not leave before then under any circumstances.'

'My lord,' said the knight, 'you seem such an excellent knight that I shall do whatever you wish. I shall stay here for the rest of the day out of respect for you, and whenever you decide to go we can leave together.'

Lancelot thanked him for offering to accompany him.

LANCELOT AND THE MAID OF ESCALOT

That day Lancelot remained there and was served and provided with everything that a nobleman could desire. The people in his lodging kept asking him who he was, but they were unable to find out anything. However, his squire spoke to the vavasour's daughter, who was very beautiful and pressed him hard to reveal who his lord was; and when he saw her great beauty, he did not wish to refuse utterly, because that would have seemed an unmannerly thing to do, but said: 'I cannot reveal everything to you, because I should perjure myself and should probably incur my master's anger; but I will certainly tell you all I can without harming myself. In fact he is the finest knight in the world, I can assure you in good faith.'

'May God help me,' said the girl, 'you have said quite enough. You have done me a great favour by saying that.'

Then the girl went straight to Lancelot, knelt before him, and said: 'Noble knight, grant me a gift by the faith you owe to whatever you love most in the world.'

When Lancelot saw such a beautiful and charming girl on her knees before him, he was embarrassed and said: 'Please get up. Be sure there is nothing in the world within my power that I should not do in answer to your request, because you have asked me in such solemn terms.'

She got up and said, 'My lord, I thank you. Do you know what you have granted me? You have promised to wear my right sleeve on your helmet at the tournament instead of a plume, and to bear arms through love for me.'

When Lancelot heard this request he was annoyed; nevertheless he did not dare to refuse it because he had already promised. However, he was very regretful about having granted what she asked, because he realised that if the queen found out about it, she would be so angry with him that, as far as he could see, he would never make his peace with her. Nevertheless, he decided that he would enter the tournament to keep his promise, for otherwise he would be disloyal if he did not do for the girl what he had promised her. She straight away brought him her sleeve attached to a plume, and begged him. to carry out great feats of arms at the tournament for her love, so that she could consider that her sleeve had been put to good use.

'I can tell you faithfully, my lord,' she said, 'that you are the first knight of whom I have ever requested anything, and that I would not have done it even now had it not been for the great goodness there is in you.'

He replied that for her love he would behave in a way that would be beyond reproach.

So Lancelot stayed there all day. In the evening, when it was dark, he left the vavasour's house, and commended him and his daughter to God. He told his squire to carry the shield he had borrowed, and left behind his own. He rode the whole night with his company, until the next morning, a little before sunrise, they came to within one league of Winchester.

'My lord,' said the squire to Lancelot, 'where do you want us to stay?'

'If anyone knew a place near the tournament where we could stay secretly, I should be very pleased, because I do not want to go into Winchester.'

'In faith,' said the knight, 'you are very fortunate; near here, off the main road to the left, is the house of an aunt of mine. She is a very kind woman and will look after us well. She will be delighted to see us when we arrive at her house.'

'In faith,' said Lancelot, 'I would very much like to go there.'

So they left the main road and went secretly straight to where the lady's house was. When they had dismounted and the lady recognised her nephew, you could not have seen greater joy than hers, because she had not seen him since he had been dubbed a knight.

'My nephew,' she said, 'where have you been since I last saw you, and where have you left your brother? Is he not coming to the tournament?'

'No, my lady,' he said, 'he cannot — we left him at home a little unwell.'

'And who is this knight,' she asked, 'who has come with you?'

'My lady,' he replied, 'may God help me, I do not know who he is, except that he seems a good man; and because of the nobility I think there is in him, I am accompanying him to the tournament tomorrow, and we are both bearing the same arms and caparisons of the same kind.'

At the tournament, Lancelot excelled above all other knights; his disguise was both his red shield and the girl's sleeve, for no one believed he would wear a favour in the lists. Only Arthur knew who the knight with the red shield was. But this was to Lancelot's harm, for in the heat of the contest Bors unwittingly gave him a serious wound. Lancelot returned to the house of his companion's aunt to recover, and while he was there the girl from Escalot came to him. As they talked, Lancelot gently told her that his heart was not his own, for it was already given elsewhere; she declared that she would die for love of him, for that was her destiny. A new tournament was proclaimed at Tanebourc, and on the way there, Arthur stayed at Escalot. It so happened that Gawain lodged in the house of the girl who was in love with Lancelot. He offered her his love, but she refused him, and he learnt the story of what had passed between her and Lancelot.

That night Sir Gawain slept very little, because he was thinking of the girl and Lancelot, and in the morning, as soon as it was light, he got up, as did all the others, because the king had already summoned Sir Gawain to come up to court, as he wished to leave the castle. When they were all ready, Sir Gawain went up to his host, commended him to God, and thanked him for the fine welcome he had given him in his house. Then he went up to the girl and said: 'I commend you to God; please know that I am your knight wherever I am, and that there is no place however distant from which I would not come as soon as possible if you called me to help you. And I ask you, for the sake of God, to greet Sir Lancelot for me, because I think you will see him sooner than I shall.'

The girl replied that as soon as she saw him she would greet him for Sir Gawain. Sir Gawain thanked her and then left on horseback. In the middle of the courtyard he found his uncle King Arthur also on horseback, waiting for him with a great company of knights. They greeted each other, and set out, and rode together talking about many things. After a time Sir Gawain said to the king: 'My lord, do you know the name of the knight who won the tournament at Winchester, the one with red arms who wore the sleeve on his helmet?'

'Why do you ask?' said the king.

'Because,' replied Sir Gawain, 'I do not think you know who it was.'

'I do know,' said the king, 'but you do not; and yet you ought to have been able to recognise him from his splendid feats of arms, because no one else could have done as well as that.'

'Indeed, my lord,' said Sir Gawain, 'it is true that I should have recognised him, because many is the time I have seen him acting with as great prowess, but I did not know who it was because he disguised himself as a new knight. However, I have found out and now I know quite certainly who he was.'

'And who was he?' asked the king.

'I shall soon know if you are telling the truth.'

'My lord,' he said, 'it was Sir Lancelot du Lac.'

'That is right,' said the king, 'and he came to the tournament so secretly in order that no knight should refuse to joust with him because he recognised him. He is quite certainly the noblest man in the world and the finest knight alive. If I had believed your brother Agravain, I should have had him put to death, and that would have been such a great crime and dishonour that the whole world would have blamed me for it.'

'Indeed,' replied Sir Gawain, 'what did my brother Agravain say, then? Tell me.'

'I shall tell you,' said the king.

'He came to me the other day and said he was amazed how I could bear to keep Lancelot near me when he was causing me such great shame as to dishonour my wife. He said outright that Lancelot loved her shamefully when my back was turned, and that he had slept with her. According to him, I could be quite sure that he had not remained at Camelot for any other reason than to see the queen freely after I had left for the tournament at Winchester. Your brother Agravain would have had me believe all this, and I would have been dishonoured if I had believed his lies, because I know now that if Lancelot were in love with the queen, he would not have left Camelot while I was away, but would have stayed so as to be able to see her in freedom.'

'Indeed, my lord,' said Sir Gawain, 'Lancelot stayed behind only so that he could attend the tournament more secretly, and you can still see that that is the truth. Be careful that you never believe any man who brings you that kind of news, because I can assure you that Lancelot never thought of loving the queen in that way. In fact I can tell you truthfully that he loves one of the most beautiful girls in the world, and she loves him too and is still a virgin. We also know that he loved King Pelles' daughter with all his heart, and she was the mother of that splendid knight Galahad who brought the adventures of the Holy Grail to their conclusion.'

'If it were true,' replied the king, 'that Lancelot loved the girl deeply, I could not believe that he would have the heart to be so disloyal to me as to dishonour me through my wife; because treason could not take root in a heart that contains such great prowess, unless through the most powerful sorcery in the world.'

So spoke King Arthur about Lancelot. And Sir Gawain told him that he could be quite sure that Lancelot had never aspired to love the queen immorally, as Agravain had accused. 'I shall go further than that, my lord,' he said, 'because I feel that Lancelot is so innocent of the whole affair that there is no knight in the world, however good, whom I would not meet in combat to defend Lancelot if he accused him.'

'What can I say?' said the king. 'If everybody kept telling me every day, or even if I saw more than I have seen, I still should not believe it.'

Sir Gawain begged him not to change his opinion, for it was the truth.

Then they stopped talking. They rode on day by day until they arrived at Camelot, and when they had dismounted there were many people who asked for news about the tournament and about who had won it. However, there was nobody except the king, Sir Gawain and Girflet who could have told them the truth, and they did not yet want to reveal it, as they knew that Lancelot wished to remain unknown. So Sir Gawain said to the queen: 'We do not actually know who it was that won the tournament, as we think it was a foreign knight; but we can tell you that he bore red arms in the jousting, and on his helmet, like a plume, he wore a lady's or a girl's sleeve.'

Then the queen felt sure it was not Lancelot, because she did not think he would bear any token at a tournament that she had not given to him. So she did not inquire any more, except that she asked Sir Gawain: 'Was Lancelot not at the tournament?'

'My lady,' he replied, 'if he was there and I saw him, I did not recognise him; and if he had been there I think he would have won the tournament. However, we have seen his arms so often that if he had been there, unless he had come in disguise, we should have recognised him easily.'

'I can tell you,' said the queen, 'that he went as secretly as he could.'

'Well, my lady,' said Sir Gawain, 'if he was there, he was the knight with red arms who won the tournament.'

'He was not,' said the queen, 'be sure of that, because he is not sufficiently attached to any lady or girl to carry a token for her.'

Then Girflet jumped forward and said to the queen: 'My lady, I can assure you that the knight with red arms who wore the sleeve on his helmet was Lancelot, because when he had won the tournament and had left, I went after him to find out who he was, and I still was not sure as he was so disguised. I went on till I was able to look him clearly in the face. He was riding along, badly wounded, with a knight armed just as he was, for they both had arms of exactly the same kind.'

'Sir Gawain,' asked the queen, 'do you think he is right? By the faith you owe my lord the king, tell me what you know, if you do know anything.'

'My lady,' he said, 'you have begged me in such serious terms that I shall not hide from you anything I know; I can tell you truthfully that it was Lancelot himself who had red arms, who wore the sleeve on his helmet and who won the tournament.'

When the queen heard this, she immediately fell silent, and went into her room crying. She was very upset and said to herself: 'Ah, God, how I have been villainously tricked by the man in whose heart I believed all loyalty to reside, and for whose love I have dishonoured the noblest man alive! Ah, God, who will ever find fidelity again in any man or in any knight, when disloyalty has lodged in the best of all the good ones?'

In that way the queen spoke to herself, because she really imagined that Lancelot had deserted her, and loved the girl whose sleeve he had worn at the tournament. She was so distressed that she did not know what to do next, except that she wanted to take her revenge on Lancelot or the girl, if she could, as soon as she had the opportunity. The queen was deeply hurt

by the news that Sir Gawain had brought, beause she could not bring
herself to believe that Lancelot had the heart to love another woman than
her; she was very miserable all day and turned away from laughter and
enjoyment.

The next day Bors returned to court, and also Lionel and Ector and
their company, from the tournament. When they had dismounted at the
king's lodge, where they ate and slept whenever they came to court, Ector
began asking various people who had remained with the queen, when the
others went to the tournament, where Lancelot had gone, because they
had left him there when they departed.

'My lord,' they said, 'he went from here the day after you left, and he
took only a single squire with him. Since then we have neither seen him
nor heard news of him.'

When the queen knew that Lancelot's brother and his cousins had come,
she summoned Bors before her and said: 'Bors, were you at the tournament?'

'Yes, my lady,' he replied.

'Did you see your cousin Lancelot?'

'No, my lady, he was not there.'

'In faith, he was,' insisted the queen.

'He was not, my lady, save your grace,' he said: 'if he had been there he
would not have failed to come and speak to me and in any case I would
have recognised him.'

'I tell you that he certainly was there,' said the queen.

'I shall describe him: he was wearing red arms, all of one colour, and on
his head he wore a lady's or a girl's sleeve, and it was he who won the tournament.'

'In God's name,' said Bors, 'I certainly hope that it was not my cousin,
because the knight you are speaking of, as I have been told, left the tournament suffering very badly from a wound in his left side I gave him in a joust.'

'Cursed be the hour,' said the queen, 'that you did not kill him, because
he is so disloyal towards me that I should not have thought him capable of
it for anything in the world.'

'How, my lady?' asked Bors.

She told him all her thoughts, and when she had finished all she wanted
to say, Bors replied: 'My lady, do not believe it is as you imagine, until you
know more certainly. May God help me, I cannot believe that he has
deceived you in this manner.'

'I tell you for certain', she said, 'that some lady or girl has caught him
with a magic potion or spell. Never again will I have anything to do with
him, and if by any chance he returned to court, I would prevent him from
entering any part of the king's lodge, and I would forbid him ever to be so
bold as to set foot here.'

'My lady,' said Bors, 'you will do as you wish, but still I can tell you that my lord certainly never had any intention of doing that of which you accuse him.'

'He showed that he did, at the tournament,' said the queen; 'I am sorry that the proof is so evident.'

'My lady,' said Bors, 'if it is as you say, he has never done anything which I regret so much, because he should not transgress against you, of all people, under any circumstances.'

All that week and the next Bors remained in King Arthur's lodge with his company, and they were unusually miserable and pensive because they saw the queen was so angry. During that time no news of Lancelot was brought to court by anyone who had seen him far or near; and King Arthur was most surprised at this.

One day the king and Sir Gawain were together at the windows of the palace, and were talking about various things, when the king said to Sir Gawain: 'Nephew, I keep wondering where Lancelot can be staying so long. It is a long time since I have known him be absent from my court for such a while as on this occasion.'

When Sir Gawain heard this, he smiled and said to the king: 'My lord, you can be sure that he is not bored where he is, because if he were, he would not be long returning; and if he is enjoying himself, no one should be surprised at that, because even the richest man in the world ought to be happy if he had left his heart in the place where I think Lancelot has left his.'

When the king heard this, he was very anxious to know more, and so he begged Sir Gawain, by his faith and the oath he had sworn to him, to tell him the truth.

'Lord,' said Sir Gawain, 'I shall tell you the truth as far as I know it; but it must be kept a secret between the two of us, because if I thought it would be told elsewhere, I should not say anything.'

The king said that he would not repeat any of it.

'My lord,' said Sir Gawain, 'I can tell you that Sir Lancelot is staying at Escalot because of a girl he loves. She is quite certainly one of the most beautiful girls in the kingdom of Logres, and she was still a virgin when we were there. Because of the great beauty I saw in her, I begged her for love not very long ago, but she rejected me, saying that she was loved by a finer and more handsome knight than I was. I was very curious to know who this could be. I pressed her to tell me his name, but she kept refusing. However, she said she would show me his shield, and I replied that that would be good enough for me. So she showed me it, and I recognised it straight away as Lancelot's. I asked her, "Tell me, for love's sake, when this shield was left here." '

She replied that her lover had left it when he went to the tournament at Winchester, that he had borne her brother's arms which were completely red, and that the sleeve he had worn on his helmet was hers.'

The queen was leaning pensively at another window and overheard all that the king and Sir Gawain were saying. She came forward and asked: 'Nephew, who is that girl you find so beautiful?'

'My lady, it is the daughter of the vavasour of Escalot, and if he loves her it is not surprising, because she is endowed with very great beauty.'

'Indeed,' said the king, 'I could not imagine him giving his heart to a lady or a girl unless she were of very high birth. I am sure he is not staying for that reason, but is lying sick or wounded – if I am not mistaken about the injury in his side that his cousin Bors gave him at the tournament at Winchester.'

'In faith,' said Sir Gawain, 'that could well be, and I do not know what to think, except that if he were ill he would have let us know, or at least he would have sent a message to his brother Ector and his cousins who are staying here.'

That day the king, the queen and Sir Gawain talked a great deal together, and the queen left them as distressed as she could possibly be, because she believed that Gawain was telling the truth about Lancelot and the girl. She went straight to her room and summoned Bors to her; and he came at once. As soon as the queen saw him, she said: 'Bors, now I know the truth about your lord, your cousin; he is staying at Escalot with a girl he loves. Now we can say that you and I have lost him, because she has so ensnared him that he could not leave if he wished. That was said just now before the king and me by a knight whose word you would always believe; and I can tell you that he affirmed it was true.'

'Indeed, my lady,' replied Bors, 'I do not know who the knight was who told you that, but even if he were the most truthful in the world, I am certain he was lying when he suggested such a thing, because I know that my lord has such a noble heart that he would not deign to do what he is said to have done. I would beg you to tell me who it was that spoke to you about this, because whoever he may be I shall make him admit before tonight that it is a lie.'

'I am not going to speak any more about it,' she said, 'but you can be sure that I shall never forgive Lancelot.'

'Indeed, my lady,' said Bors, 'that is a pity; since you have taken to hating my lord so much, our men have no reason to stay here. For that reason, my lady, I take my leave of you and commend you to God, because we shall leave in the morning. After we have set out, we shall search for my lord until we find him, if it pleases God; and when we have found him, we shall stay in that part of the country, if he wishes, at some nobleman's house. If he does not wish to stay there, we shall go away to our lands and our men who are longing to see us because we have not been with them for a long time. And I can tell you, my lady,' continued Bors, 'that we should not have stayed in this country as long as we have, if it had not been through love for our lord, and he would not have remained so long after the quest for the Holy Grail except for you. You know for certain that he loved you more loyally than any knight ever loved a lady or a girl.'

When the queen heard this she was as distressed as she could be, and could not stop the tears coming to her eyes. When she spoke she said that the hour should be cursed that ever brought such news to her, 'for I have been badly treated,' she said. Then she spoke again to Bors. 'What, my lord,' she said, 'are you then leaving me in this way?'

'Yes, my lady,' he said, 'because I must.'

Then he left her room and went to his brother and Ector. He told them what the queen had said to him, and they were all distressed. They did not know whom to blame for the situation, but they all cursed the hour that Lancelot first became acquainted with the queen. Bors said to them: 'Let us take leave of the king and depart from here. Then we can search for our lord until we find him. If we are able to take him to the kingdom of Gaunes or the kingdom of Banoic, we shall never have done anything so worthwhile, because then we should be at peace, if he could bear to be away from the queen.'

Ector and Lionel agreed on this, and they went to the king, asking for leave to go to seek Lancelot. He gave it most regretfully, because he cherished their company, especially that of Bors who at that time had a greater reputation, led a better life and practised finer chivalry than any other knight in the kingdom of Logres.

The next day King Ban's descendants left the court, and they rode straight to Escalot. When they arrived, they asked for news of Lancelot wherever they expected to find some information, but they were quite unable to see anyone who could tell them anything. They sought high and low, but the more they asked the less they found out. They rode in that way for eight days without discovering anything. When they took stock of this, they said: 'We are wasting our time, because we shall not find him before the tournament; but he will quite certainly go to that if only he is in this part of the country and able to do as he wishes.'

For that reason they stayed at a castle called Athean, a day's ride away from Tanebourc, and there were only six days to go before the tournament. The king of North Wales was staying near by in a retreat of his, eight leagues from Athean, and as soon as he heard that relatives of King Ban were there, knights who were the most famous in the world and of the greatest prowess and chivalry, he went to see them, because he very much wanted to make their acquaintance. He also hoped, if it were possible, that they would join his side at the tournament against King Arthur and his company. When they saw that the king had come to see them, they considered it an act of great nobility on his part, and they welcomed him courteously, as they knew how. They invited him to stay the night with them there, and the next day he persuaded them to go back with him to his retreat. The king of North Wales kept them at his lodgings with great joy and honour until the day of the tournament, and begged them until they promised to be on his side in the jousting. The king was very happy at this promise and expressed his thanks.

LANCELOT IS FOUND BY HIS COMPANIONS

And the book says that Bors, Lionel, and Ector searched for Lancelot, but could not find him. As they rode, they met with Gawain, who was on the same quest. At last by chance they came to the house where Lancelot was resting because of his injuries. When they arrived, they asked how he was, for he had not been at the tournament at Tanebourc.

The doctor who had been looking after him said to Sir Gawain: 'My lord, I can tell you that he will quite certainly have recovered within a week, so that he will be able to ride and bear arms just as vigorously as he did a little while ago at the tournament at Winchester.'

They replied that they were very pleased at that news.

The next day, as they were sitting at dinner, Sir Gawain laughingly asked Lancelot: 'My lord, did you ever know who the knight was who gave you that wound?'

'Indeed, no,' replied Lancelot, 'but if I could ever find out and by chance I came across him at a tournament, I do not think any favour he ever did me would be so quickly repaid, because before he left I should make him feel whether my sword could cut steel, and if he drew blood from my side, I would draw as much or more from his head.'

Then Sir Gawain began clapping his hands as joyfully as could be, and said to Bors: 'Now we shall see what you are going to do, because you have not been threatened by the most cowardly man in the world, and if he had threatened me like that, I should not be happy until I had made my peace with him.'

When Lancelot heard this, he was quite perplexed, and said: 'Bors, was it you who wounded me?'

Bors was so unhappy that he did not know what to say, because he did not dare to admit it, nor could he deny it. But he replied: 'My lord, if I did it, I am very sorry, and no one should blame me for it; because if you were the knight I wounded, as Sir Gawain is alleging, you were so disguised that I would never have recognised you in those arms – they were like those of a new knight, whereas you have been bearing arms for more than twenty-five years. That was the reason why I did not recognise you. I do not think you should bear me a grudge for what I did.'

He replied that he did not, because Bors had not intended to injure him.

'In God's name, brother,' said Ector, 'I congratulate you for that day, because you made me feel the hard ground at a time when I had no need of it.'

Lancelot replied, laughing, 'Brother, however much you complain about what I did that day, I shall complain even more, because now I know that you and Bors are the two knights who most prevented me from doing as I wished at that tournament, as you were so often in front of me and only intended to injure and dishonour me. I think I would have won the tournament, but the two of you prevented me; and I can tell you that nowhere have I ever found two knights who caused me as much trouble or who made me suffer as much as you two. But you will not hear me speak of it again like this, and I forgive you.'

'My lord,' said Sir Gawain, 'now you know just how well they can strike with lances and swords.'

'Indeed I do,' he said, 'I found that out for myself, and I still have very clear signs to show for it.'

They spoke a great deal about the incident; and Sir Gawain was pleased to speak about it because he saw Bors was as ashamed and abashed as if he had committed the greatest misdeed in the world. So they remained there the whole week in great joy and happiness, glad to see that Lancelot was maintaining his recovery. All the time they were there Bors did not dare to reveal to him what he had heard the queen say, because he feared that Lancelot might be too greatly tormented if he were told the cruel words the queen had spoken about him.

When King Arthur had left Tanebourc with the queen, he rode the first day until he came to a castle of his called Tauroc. That night he stayed there with a great company of knights, and the next morning he commanded the queen to go on to Camelot. The king stayed at Tauroc for three days, and when he left he rode until he came to a certain forest. In this forest Lancelot had once been kept in prison for two winters and a summer, in the castle of Morgan le Fay, who still lived there with a large number of people who kept her company at all seasons. The king entered the forest with his retinue, but they were uncertain of the way and wandered on until they completely lost the right path, and it was dark. Then the king stopped and asked his retinue: 'What are we going to do? We have lost our way.'

'My lord,' they said, 'it would be better for us to stay here than to move on, because we should only put ourselves to more trouble, as there are no houses or castles in this forest so far as we know. We have plenty of food, so let us set up your tent in this meadow and rest now, and tomorrow, if it pleases God, when we set out again we shall find a road that will lead us out of this forest as we wish.'

The king agreed with this; and as soon as they had begun to put up the tent, they heard a horn quite close by which was blown twice.

'In faith,' said the king, 'there are people near here. Go and see who they are.'

Sagramore le Desirous mounted his horse, and went directly to where he had heard the sound of the horn. He had not gone very far when he found a tower, great and strong and closely crenellated, and enclosed all around with a very high wall. He dismounted and went up to the gate, and called. When the porter heard there was someone at the gate, he asked who he was and what he wanted.

'I am Sagramore le Desirous,' he said, 'a knight sent by my lord King Arthur who is close by in this forest; and he informs the people in this castle that he wishes to stay here tonight. So make ready to receive him as you should, because I shall bring him to you straight away with all his retinue.'

'My lord,' said the porter, 'I beg you to wait a moment so that I may speak to my lady, who is up in her room, and I shall return to you at once and give you her reply.'

'What,' said Sagremor, 'Is there no lord here?'

'No,' he replied.

'Then go quickly and return quickly,' said Sagremor, 'because I do not want to wait here long.'

The boy went upstairs to his lady, who was Morgan le Fay, and he repeated the message to her just as Sagramore had told it, that King Arthur wished to stay there for the night. As soon as Morgan heard this news, she was delighted and said to the boy: 'Go back quickly and tell the knight to bring the king here, because we shall receive him as well as we possibly can.'

He went back to Sagramore and told him what his lady had instructed. Then Sagramore left the gate and returned to the king, and said: 'My lord, you are fortunate, because I have found you a lodging where you will be entertained tonight as you wish, so I have been told.'

When the king heard this, he said to those with him: 'Let us mount and ride straight there.'

They all mounted, Sagramore led the way, and when they came to the gate they found it open. So they entered and saw that the place was beautiful, delightful, rich and splendidly kept; they thought they had never seen such a fine and well-arranged castle in their lives. There were such a great number of candles there, producing such intense light, that they were all amazed how this could be, and there was no wall that was not covered in silk cloth.

The king asked Sagremor: 'Did you see any of this decoration just now?'

'Indeed, no, my lord,' he replied.

And the king made a sign of the cross out of astonishment, because he had never seen any church or abbey more richly hung with tapestries than the courtyard there.

'In faith,' said the king, 'if there were great wealth inside, I should not be surprised, because there is an excess of it out here.'

King Arthur dismounted, as also did all the others in his retinue. When they entered the great hall, they met Morgan, and with her at least a hundred people, ladies and knights, who were in her company. They were all dressed so richly that never, at any feast he had ever held in his life, had King Arthur seen people so richly adorned as they all were in the hall. When they saw the king enter, they all cried with one voice: 'My lord, be welcome here, because no greater honour has ever befallen us than that you wish to stay here.'

The king replied, 'May God grant you all joy.'

Then they took him into a room which was so rich that he was sure he had never seen any that was so beautiful and delightful.

As soon as the king had sat down and washed his hands, the tables were set, and all those who had come in the king's retinue were asked to sit down, provided they were knights. The girls began to bring food, as if they had had a month's warning of the arrival of the king and all his companions. Moreover the king had never seen in his life a table as plentifully adorned with rich vessels in gold and silver as this one, and if he had been in the city of Camelot and had done everything possible to ensure a rich meal, he would not have had any more than he had that night at that table, nor would he have been served better or more elegantly. They all wondered where such great plenty could come from.

When they had eaten just as much as they wished, the king, in a room near by, listened to all the different musical instruments he had ever heard of in his life, and they all sounded together so sweetly that he had never heard music that was so gentle and pleasant to the ear. In this room the light was brilliant; before long he saw two very beautiful girls come in carrying two large burning candles in golden candlesticks. They came up to the king and said: 'My lord, if it pleases you, it is now time for you to rest, because the night is well advanced and you have ridden so far that we think you must be exhausted.'

The king replied, 'I would like to be in bed already, because I have great need of sleep.'

'My lord,' they said, 'we have come to accompany you to your bed, since we have been commanded to do so.'

'Certainly,' replied the king.

So he got up at once, and the girls led him to a chamber in which Morgan le Fay had once held Lancelot prisoner. He had spent more than a year there, and to pass the time he had depicted the whole story of his love for Queen Guinevere on the walls of the room. The girls put Arthur to bed there, and when he was asleep they left him and returned to their lady.

Morgan thought a great deal about King Arthur, because she intended him to know the whole truth about Lancelot and the queen, and yet she feared that if she told him everything and Lancelot heard that the king had found out from her, nothing in the world could guarantee that he would not kill her. That night she pondered over the question, whether to tell him or to remain silent; because if she told him she would be in danger of death should Lancelot find out, and if she kept the affair secret, she would never again have such a good opportunity of telling him as now. She kept thinking about this until she fell asleep.

In the morning, as soon as it was light, she arose and went to the king, greeted him very courteously, and said: 'My lord, I beg you for a reward for all the services I have rendered you.'

'I shall grant you it,' said the king, 'if it is something in my power to give.'

'You can certainly give it to me,' she said, 'and do you know what it is? It is that you stay here today and tomorrow. You can be sure that if you were in the finest city you possess, you would not be better served or more at ease than here, because there is no wish you could express that would not be satisfied.'

And he said he would stay, because he had promised her her reward.

'My lord,' she said, 'of all the houses in the world, you are in the one where people were most longing to see you; I can tell you that there is no woman anywhere who loves you more than I do, and so I should, unless human love did not exist.'

'My lady,' said the king, 'who are you that you love me so much, as you say?'

'My lord,' she said, 'I am the person closest to you in blood. My name is Morgan, and I am your sister. You ought to know me better than you do.'

He looked at her and recognised her, and jumped up from the bed as joyful as it was possible to be. He told her that he was very happy about the adventure that God had granted him.

'You see, my sister,' said the king, 'I thought you were dead and had left this world; and since it has pleased God that I should find you alive and well, I shall take you back to Camelot when I leave here, and from now on you will live at court and will be a companion for my wife Queen Guinevere. I know she will be very happy and joyful when she hears the news about you.'

'Brother,' she said, 'do not ask that of me, because I swear to you that I shall never go to court, for when I leave here I shall most certainly go to the Isle of Avalon, which is the dwelling-place of the ladies who know all the magic in the world.'

The king dressed and sat down on his bed. Then he asked his sister to sit beside him, and he began to ask her how she was. She told him a part, and kept a part secret from him. They remained talking there until nine o'clock.

That day the weather was very fine; the sun had risen splendid and brilliant and its light penetrated all parts of the room, so that it was even brighter than before. They were alone, because they took pleasure in talking together, just the two of them. When they had asked each other many questions about their past lives, it happened that the king began looking around him and saw the pictures which Lancelot had painted long before, when he was a prisoner there. King Arthur knew his letters well enough to be able to make out the meaning of a text, and when he had seen the inscriptions with the pictures that explained their meaning, he began to read them. So he found out that the room was illustrated with all Lancelot's deeds of chivalry since he had been made a knight. Everything that Arthur saw he remembered from the news that had constantly been brought to court about Lancelot's chivalry, as soon as he had accomplished each of his acts of prowess.

Thus the king began to read of Lancelot's deeds in the paintings he saw; and when he examined the paintings which related the meeting between him and Guinevere which had been arranged by Galahaut, he was completely astounded and taken aback. He looked again and said under his breath: 'In faith, if these inscriptions tell the truth, then Lancelot has dishonoured me through the queen, because I can see quite clearly that he has had an association with her. If it is as the writing says, it will be the cause of the greatest grief that I have ever suffered, since Lancelot could not possibly degrade me more than by dishonouring my wife.'

Then he said to Morgan: 'My sister, I beg you to tell me the truth about what I am going to ask you.'

She replied that she would be pleased to, if she could.

'Swear that you will,' said the king.

And she swore it.

'Now I am going to ask you,' he said, 'by the faith you owe me and have just pledged me, to tell me who painted these pictures, if you know the truth, and not to refuse for any reason.'

'Ah, my lord,' said Morgan, 'what are you saying and what are you asking me? Certainly, if I told you the truth and the man who did the paintings found out, no one except God could guarantee that he would not kill me.'

'In God's name,' he said, 'you must tell me, and I promise you as a king that I shall never blame you for it.'

'My lord,' she replied, 'will you not spare me from telling you for any reason?'

'Certainly not,' said the king. 'You must tell me.'

'In that case I shall tell you without lying about anything,' replied Morgan.

'It is true, though I do not know whether you know it yet, that Lancelot has loved Queen Guinevere since the first day that he received the order of chivalry, and it was for love of the queen that he performed all his acts of prowess when he was a new knight. You could have known this at the castle of the Dolorous Gard, when you first went there and could not enter because you were stopped at the river; each time you sent a knight, he was unable to go inside. But as soon as Kay went, since he was one of the queen's knights, he was allowed in, and you did not notice this, though some people did.'

'It is true,' said the king, 'that I did not notice it, but all the same it did happen exactly as you say. However, I do not know whether it was for love of the queen or of me.'

'My lord,' she replied, 'there is more to come.'

'Tell me,' said the king.

'My lord,' she said, 'he loved my lady the queen as much as any mortal man can ever love a lady; but he never revealed the fact himself or through anyone else. His love spurred him on to perform all the deeds of chivalry you see depicted here. For a long time he only languished, just like anyone who loves and is not loved in return, because he did not dare to reveal his love. Eventually he met Galahaut, the son of the Giantess, the day he bore black arms and won the tournament organized by the two of you, as you can see related in these pictures here. When he had made peace between you and Galahaut in such a way that all honour fell to you, and when Galahaut saw that Lancelot's strength was declining daily because he could not eat or drink, so deeply did he love the queen, he kept pressing him until in the end he admitted that he loved the queen and was dying for her. Galahaut begged him not to despair, because he would arrange matters so that Lancelot could have what he desired from the queen. And he did just as he promised; he implored the queen until she gave in to Lancelot, and, with a kiss, granted him her love.'

'You have told me enough,' said the king, 'because I can clearly see my shame and Lancelot's treachery; but tell me now who painted these pictures.'

'Indeed, my lord,' she replied, 'Lancelot did them, and I shall tell you when. Do you remember two tournaments held at Camelot, when the companions of the Round Table said they would not go to a joust where Lancelot was on their side, because he always carried off the prize? And when Lancelot knew, he turned against them, making them leave the field and forcing them to retreat into the city of Camelot. Do you remember that?'

'Yes,' replied the king.

'I can still see that tournament in my mind, because never in any place that I have been to have I seen a knight carry out so many feats of arms as he did that day. But why do you speak about that?'

'Because,' she replied, 'when he left court on that occasion he was lost for more than a year and a half, and no one knew where he was.'

'Yes,' said the king, 'that is true.'

'In fact,' she said, 'I held him prisoner for two winters and a summer, and during that time he painted the pictures you can see here. I should still be keeping him in prison, and he would never have escaped, all the days of his life, if it had not been for what he did, the greatest sorcery that a man ever carried out.'

'What was that?' asked the king.

'I swear,' she replied, 'that he broke the bars of that window with his bare hands.'

And she showed him the bars, which she had had repaired since. The king said that it was not the work of a man, but of a devil.

He looked carefully at the paintings in the room, and he thought deeply about them. For a long time he did not say a word. After he had thought for some time, he said: 'Agravain told me about this the other day, but I did not believe him, as I thought he was lying. However, what I have seen here makes me far more certain than I was before. For that reason I can tell you that I shall never be satisfied until I know the whole truth. If it is as these pictures witness, that Lancelot has brought me such great shame as to dishonour me through my wife, I shall never rest until they are caught together. Then, if I do not inflict such justice on them as will be spoken of for evermore, I promise that I shall never again wear a crown.'

'Indeed,' said Morgan, 'if you did not punish them, God and the whole world should certainly hold you in shame, because no true king or true man can tolerate being dishonoured in this way.'

The king and his sister spoke a great deal about the matter that morning and Morgan kept urging him to avenge his shame without delay; and he promised her as a king that he would do so with such vigour that it would always be remembered, if he could manage to catch them together.

'It will not be long,' said Morgan, 'before they are caught together, if you go about it carefully.'

'I shall make sure,' said the king, 'that if one loves the other adulterously as you say, I shall have them caught together before the end of the month, if Lancelot should return to court by then.'

That day the king remained with his sister, and the next day and the whole week; she hated Lancelot more than any other man because she knew the queen loved him. All the time the king was with her she never stopped urging him to avenge his shame when he returned to Camelot, if he had the opportunity.

'My sister,' said the king, 'you do not need to ask me, because not for half my kingdom would I fail to do what I have resolved.'

The king stayed there the whole week, since the place was beautiful and pleasant, and full of game which he spent all his energy hunting. But during that time he did not allow anyone to enter his room while he was there, save only Morgan, because of the paintings which made his shame so evident, and he did not want anyone else apart from himself to know the truth, because he feared the dishonour too much, and feared also that the news would spread.

THE DEATH OF THE MAID OF ESCALOT; THE QUEEN REFUSES TO SEE LANCELOT

Meanwhile Bors and Sir Gawain and the other companions stayed with Lancelot until he had completely recovered and regained all the strength he had had before. As soon as he felt he was better and could bear arms without danger, he said to his doctor: 'Do you not think that I can now do what I like with my body without doing any harm to the wound I have had so long?'

'I can tell you truthfully,' said the good man, 'that you are completely cured and that you do not need to worry any more about any illness you have had.'

'I am pleased at that news,' replied Lancelot, 'because now I can go when I like.'

But Lancelot's joy was the grief of the girl of Escalot, for when Lancelot told her that he was leaving, she declared that she had loved him from the moment she saw him. Lancelot was dismayed, and reminded her that he had told her plainly that his heart was not his own. To this she declared that she could not live without him, and when he departed, she fulfilled her saying, and took to her bed and died. Meanwhile, Lancelot journeyed to Camelot in the company of Bors and the others; and they brought him to Guinevere's chamber.

'My lady,' he said, 'we have brought you Lancelot du Lac, who has been absent from this part of the country for a long time.'

She replied that she could not speak to him then, because she felt too unwell.

Sir Gawain left her room and returned to his companions, saying: 'My lords, I have to tell you that the queen is unwell; we cannot speak to her. But let us rest here until the king comes. If we are bored we can go hunting, as there are plenty of forests near here.'

And they all agreed to this.

That night Bors spoke to the queen and asked her what was wrong with her.

'I am not ill at all,' she said, 'but I have no wish to enter that hall while Lancelot is there, because I have not eyes with which to see him, or a heart that would allow me to speak to him.'

'What, my lady,' said Bors, 'do you then hate him so much?'

'Yes, indeed,' she replied. 'At the moment there is nothing in this world I hate as much as I hate him, nor have I ever in my life loved him as much as I hate him now.'

'My lady,' said Bors, 'that is a great pity for us and all our lineage. It grieves me that things have turned out like this, for many will suffer without deserving it. Moreover destiny arranged the love between you, as I saw it arranged, in such a way that it could only be to our disadvantage. I know that my lord cousin, who is the noblest and most handsome man in the world, has every confidence at present that he can surpass anyone else, if one thing does not prevent him, and that is your anger. Beyond all doubt this would turn him away from all worthy adventures, because if he knew what you have said here, I do not think I should be able to reach him before he killed himself. I think it is a great pity that he, the finest of the best, loves you so deeply, while you hate him.'

'If I hate him mortally,' said the queen, 'he has deserved it.'

'My lady,' said Bors, 'what can I say? I have certainly never seen any nobleman who loved a woman for a long time, who was not finally held to be dishonoured. It is less than five years since the death of Tristan, the nephew of King Mark, who loved fair Iseult so faithfully that he never did anything to harm her in all his life. What more can I say? No man ever became deeply involved in love who did not die as a result. I can tell you that you would be doing something worse than all the other women, because you would be destroying in the body of a single knight all the virtues through which a man can rise in worldly honour and be called noble – I mean beauty and prowess; valour and chivalry, and gentility. My lady, you can maintain all these virtues in my lord so perfectly that none are lost. But just as he is now clothed and covered in all good virtues, in the same way you would strip and deprive him of them. One could say truthfully that you would be removing the sun from among the stars, that is to say the flower of the world's knights from King Arthur's men. You can see quite clearly, my lady, that you would be damaging this kingdom and many others much more than one lady ever did through one knight. That is the great power for good we expect from your love.'

The queen replied to these words and said to Bors: 'If what you say were to happen now, no one would stand to lose as much as I should, because I would lose body and soul. Now leave me in peace, because for the present moment you will not receive any other reply from me.'

'My lady,' said Bors, 'I tell you that you will never hear me mention the matter again, unless you speak of it first.'

Then Bors left the queen and went up to Lancelot; and he said to him secretly, when he had drawn him some way away from the others: 'My lord, I strongly recommend we should leave here, because I do not think we are welcome.'

'Why?' asked Lancelot.

'My lord, my lord,' said Bors, 'my lady the queen has just forbidden you and me and all those who come in your name to enter her lodge.'

'Why?' asked Lancelot.

'Do you know?'

'Yes, I certainly do know,' he replied, 'and I shall tell you when we are away from here.'

'Let us mount, then,' said Lancelot, 'and you will tell me what the reason is, because I am impatient to know.'

Then Lancelot came to Sir Gawain and said: 'My lord, we must depart, my companions and I, as I have to see to some affairs I cannot leave. When you see my lord the king, greet him from me, and tell him I shall come back as soon as I can.'

'In God's name,' said Sir Gawain, 'you cannot leave here in that way – you must wait for my lord the king.'

But Lancelot said that he would not. Then he mounted with his companions, and Sir Gawain accompanied him for some time. Sir Gawain said: 'My lord, in this field at Camelot there will soon be a great and marvellous tournament. Be sure you are there, because there will be few knights from the kingdom of Logres who will not be present.'

Lancelot said he would come, if it was possible for him to do so.

So they parted, and Sir Gawain returned to Camelot, angry because Lancelot had left so soon. Lancelot rode until he arrived at the forest of Camelot, and when they had entered it, he asked Bors to tell him why the queen was angry with him.

'My lord,' he said, 'I shall tell you.'

Then he began to tell him about the sleeve he wore at the tournament at Winchester, 'and it is because of that that the queen is very angry and says she will never forgive you.'

When Bors had told him the whole story, Lancelot stopped and began to cry very bitterly, and no one could get a word out of him. After he had been like this for quite some time, he replied: 'Ah, love! those are the rewards for serving you; because a man who offers himself completely to you cannot escape with less than death, and such is the price you pay to someone who loves you faithfully. Ah! Bors, my cousin, you who know my heart as well as I do, and know for certain that I would not be unfaithful to my lady for anything in the world, why did you not defend me before her?'

'My lord,' said Bors, 'I did everything in my power, but she would not agree with anything I said.'

'Now advise me, then,' said Lancelot, 'and tell me what I can do, because if I cannot find my peace with her, I shall not survive very long. If she had forgiven me for causing her unhappiness and anger, I would have gone joyfully, but in the state in which I am at present, since I have her anger and her ill feelings and have not leave to speak to her, I do not think I can live very long, because my grief and anger will pierce my heart. For that reason I am asking you, my friend, to advise me, because I do not see what I can do for myself after what you have just said.'

'My lord,' said Bors, 'if you can tolerate not being near her or seeing her, I can tell you truthfully that you will not see a month pass, if she does not see you or receive any news about you, without her being even more anxious to have you in her company than you ever were to be with her, and desiring you more; you can be sure that she will send someone to find you, whether you are near or far. That is why my advice is that you should spend your time enjoying yourself in this part of the country, attending all the tournaments that you hear announced. You have with you your fine and noble retinue, and a good many of your kinsmen; you should be pleased about this, because they will accompany you, if you wish, anywhere you want to go.'

He said that he agreed with what Bors advised, but that he did not need any companions. He wished to go alone except only for a squire he would take with him until he decided to dismiss him.

'But you, Bors,' he said, 'you will go away until you see me or a messenger I send to look for you.'

'My lord,' said Bors, 'I am very sorry that you are leaving us like this and going off through this part of the country with such little company, because, if any misfortune should befall you tomorrow, how should we know?'

'Do not worry,' he replied, 'for He who up till now has permitted me to be victorious wherever I have been will not allow by His grace any harm to befall me wherever I am; and if anything did happen to me, you would know sooner than anyone else, be sure of that.'

Then Lancelot went back to his company, who were waiting for him in the middle of the field. He told them he had to go away to see to something and that he could not take many companions with him. He took a squire called Hanguis and told him to follow him; Hanguis said he would willingly go with him, and was delighted.

So in that way he left his close friends, and they said to him: 'My lord, make quite sure you are at the tournament at Camelot, and so armed that we can all recognise you.'

He replied that he would be there, if he were not prevented by some great obstacle. Then he called Bors and said: 'If I am at the tournament, I shall bear white arms with a diagonal band of red on the shield, and in that way you will be able to recognize me.'

Then they separated and commended each other to God.

THE QUEEN IS ACCUSED OF POISONING GAHERIS DE KARAHEU

After King Arthur had stayed with his sister Morgan for as long as he wished, he left with a great company of people. When he was out of the forest, he rode until he came to Camelot. On arriving, and finding out that Lancelot had spent only one day at court, he did not know what to think, because he was sure that if Lancelot loved the queen adulterously as had been alleged, he could not be absent from the court and turn his back on it for as long as he did. This went a long way to set the king's mind at rest, and led him to discount what he had heard his sister Morgan say. However, there was never again a time that he was not more suspicious of the queen than he had been before, because of what he had learnt.

The day after the king arrived at Camelot, it happened that at dinner-time Sir Gawain was eating at the queen's table, and many other knights were there also. In a room beside the hall there was a knight called

Avarlan who mortally hated Sir Gawain, and had a poisoned fruit with which he hoped to kill him. So he decided that if he sent it to the queen, she would sooner give it to Sir Gawain than to anyone else; and if he ate it, he would die straight away.

The queen took the fruit, because she was not on her guard against treachery, and she gave it to a knight who was a companion of the Round Table, called Gaheris de Karaheu. Gaheris, who had a very great affection for the queen, accepted it through love for her and started eating it. As soon as he had swallowed some of it, he immediately fell dead before the eyes of the queen and all those who were at table. They all jumped up straight away and were dumbfounded by what had happened. When the queen saw the knight lying dead before her, she was so distressed by this misadventure that she could not decide what to do, because so many noblemen had seen what had happened that she could not deny it. The news was taken to the king by a knight who had been eating in the queen's room.

'My lord,' he said, 'something extraordinary has just happened in there; my lady the queen has killed a knight through the greatest misdeed in the world. He was a companion of the Round Table and the brother of Mador de la Porte.'

And he related what had happened. The king made a sign of the cross out of surprise, and jumped up from the table to see whether what he had been told was true or not; so did all the others who were in the hall. When the king came to the room and found the dead knight, he said that it was a real misfortune and that the queen had committed a great crime if she had done it intentionally.

'In fact,' said someone there, 'she has deserved death if she really knew that the fruit of which the knight has died was poisoned.'

The queen did not know what to say, so stunned was she by the unfortunate event, except that she replied: 'May God help me, I regret what has happened a hundred times more than I am glad, and had I thought that the fruit I gave him was treacherous, I would not have given it to him for half the world.'

'My lady,' said the king, 'however you gave it to him, the deed is wicked and criminal, and I very much fear that you acted out of greater anger than you admit.'

Then the king said to all those who were round the body: 'My lords, this knight is dead, unfortunately; now see that you treat his body with as great honour as should be paid to such a noble man. For indeed he was a noble man and one of the best knights at my court, and in all my life I have never seen a more loyal knight than him. And I regret his death much more than many people might think.'

Then the king left the room and went back to the main palace and made the sign of the cross over and over again out of surprise at the knight's tragic death. The queen left after the king, and went into a meadow with a great company of ladies and girls, and as soon as she arrived there, she began to grieve bitterly, and said that God had forgotten her when through such ill fortune she killed a man as noble as him.

'And, may God help me,' she said, 'when I gave him the fruit to eat just now I did it with the best of intentions.'

The queen was very sad about what had happened, and her ladies enshrouded the body as well and as richly as they could. They honoured it as it was right to honour the body of a good man, and the next day it was buried at the entrance of St Stephen's Cathedral in Camelot. And when as beautiful and as rich a tomb as could be found in the country had been placed there, the companions of the Round Table put on it, by common consent, an inscription which accused the queen of the knight's death. King Arthur was very sad, and so were all those who were with him; in fact they were so melancholy that they spoke very little of the matter until the tournament.

When Lancelot had left Bors and his brother Ector, he rode up and down in the forest of Camelot, and stayed each night with a hermit who had once confessed him. The hermit treated Lancelot as honourably as he could. Three days before the tournament Lancelot called his squire and said: 'Go to Camelot and bring me a white shield with three diagonal red bands and a white caparison; I have borne those arms so often that if Bors comes to the tournament he will easily be able to recognise me. I am doing it for him rather than for anyone else, because I certainly do not want him to wound me, or to wound him myself.'

The squire left Lancelot to go to the city to fetch the arms he described, and Lancelot went out for a ride in the forest, unarmed except for his sword. That day it was very warm and because of the heat Lancelot dismounted from his horse, took off its saddle and reins, and tied it to an oak tree close by. When he had done this he went to lie beside a spring, and fell asleep straight away, because the place was cool and fresh whereas until then he had been very hot.

As it happened, the king's huntsmen were hunting a large stag and had pursued it in the forest. It came to the fountain to quench its thirst, because it had been chased one way and another for some time. When it had arrived at the fountain, an archer riding a large horse a long way ahead of the others came close to the stag and aimed at it, in order to strike it in the middle of its breast; but it happened that he missed the stag, as it jumped forward a little. However, the shot was not a complete failure, because it struck Lancelot so violently in the left thigh that the blade went right through it, as did also part of the shaft. When Lancelot felt that he was wounded, he jumped up in great pain and distress, and seeing the huntsman coming towards the stag as fast as he could drive his horse, he cried: 'Scoundrel, worthless fool, what harm have I done you that you should injure me while I am asleep? You will regret it, I can tell you, and you will certainly be sorry that you happened to come this way.'

And it was this wound that prevented Lancelot from taking part in the tournament at Camelot, at which all the knights of the Round Table marvelled, and wondered why he had not come.

Sir Gawain said to the king: 'My lord, you can be quite certain Lancelot is ill, because he did not come to the tournament; at the moment there is nothing I would like to know as much as how he is, because I am wondering if he is wounded or whether he has stayed behind because of some other kind of illness.'

'Indeed,' said the king, 'if he is unwell, I am sorry he is not here, because his presence here and that of his companions enhances my court so much that no one can estimate its true value.'

On the third day after the tournament it happened that Mador de la Porte arrived at court. No one there was bold enough to tell him about his brother, because they all realised he was such a valiant knight that, as soon as he heard the truth, he would certainly not let anything prevent him from avenging his brother to the best of his ability. The next day he happened to go to the cathedral in Camelot, and when he saw the tomb which had recently been placed there, he thought it must belong to one of the companions of the Round Table, and he went over to it to see whose it was. When he saw the inscription that read, *Here lies Gaheris of Karaheu, the brother of Mador de la Porte, whom the Queen killed with poison*, he was astounded and aghast, and he could not really believe it was true. Then he looked behind him and saw a Scottish knight who was a companion of the Round Table. He immediately called him and begged him by the fidelity he owed him to answer truthfully what he was going to ask him.

'Mador,' said the knight, 'I know what you are going to ask me. You want me to say whether it is true that the queen killed your brother. It is indeed just as the inscription says.'

'Indeed,' said Mador, 'that is a great tragedy, because my brother was very noble, and I loved him dearly as one brother should another. I shall seek to avenge him as best I can.'

Mador grieved deeply for his brother, and remained there till High Mass had been sung. When he knew that the king was seated at table, he left his brother's tomb in tears and went up to the king in the hall, speaking so loud that all those present could hear him. He began: 'King Arthur, if you uphold what is right as a king should, maintain justice in your court so that if anyone wishes to accuse me I shall act as you please according to it, and if I wish to accuse anyone present, I shall be given justice as the court will ensure.'

The king replied that he could not deny him that, and that whatever Mador might say, he would see that justice was done to the best of his ability.

'My lord,' said Mador, 'I have been your knight for fifteen years and I hold fiefs from you; now I shall return you your homage and your land, because I no longer wish to hold any fief from you.'

Then he went forward and ritually divested himself of all the land he held from the king, and after he had done this, he said: 'My lord, now I request you as a king to grant me justice concerning the queen who killed my brother; if she wishes to deny and disavow that she has acted treacherously and dishonourably, I shall be pleased to prove my case against the finest knight she wishes to represent her.'

When he had said this there was a great noise in the court and many said among themselves: 'The queen is in a sorry plight now, because she will not find anyone to fight against Mador; everyone knows quite certainly that she killed the knight as she has been accused.'

The king was deeply distressed about the accusation, because he could not deny the knight justice, and justice would obviously call for the queen's death. He summoned her to come before him to reply to Mador's charge, and she came full of sadness and anger, because she was well aware that she would not find a knight to fight for her, as they all believed that she had quite definitely killed Gaheris.

THE BARGE BEARING THE MAID OF ESCALOT COMES TO CAMELOT; LANCELOT RESCUES THE QUEEN

And the tale relates how Mador accused the queen of murder, and how Arthur, as the law demanded, gave her forty days in which to find a knight to defend her in single combat against Mador. During this time a strange boat appeared on the river at Camelot, covered in rich silk, floating down on the stream. Gawain and Arthur went to see it, for the men of the river had brought it to shore and moored at the foot of the steps leading down to the water. The boat was covered like a vault, and Sir Gawain lifted up a corner of the cloth and said to the king: 'My lord, let us go aboard, and we shall see what is there.'

So the king jumped aboard straight away, and then Sir Gawain, and when they were inside, they found a beautiful bed in the middle of the boat, adorned with all the riches that can adorn a bed, and in it lay a girl who was not long dead. To judge from how she still looked, she must have been very beautiful.

Then Sir Gawain said to the king: 'Ah! my lord, do you not think death was wicked and horrible, to enter the body of such a beautiful girl as she was not long ago?'

'Yes,' said the king, 'I think this was a girl of great beauty, and it is a pity that she died so young. Because of the great beauty I see in her, I should very much like to know who she was and who her parents were.'

They looked at her for some time, and when Sir Gawain had considered her closely, he recognised her as the beautiful girl whom he had begged for her love, but who had said that she would never love anyone but Lancelot. Then he said to the king: 'My lord, I know who this girl was.'

'And who was she?' asked the king. 'Tell me.'

'Certainly, my lord,' said Sir Gawain.

'Do you remember the beautiful girl about whom I spoke to you the other day, the one I said Lancelot loved?'

'Yes,' said the king, 'I remember it well; you explained that you had sought her love, but that she had completely rejected you.'

'My lord,' said Sir Gawain, 'this girl is the one we were speaking of.'

'That is a tragedy,' said the king.

'I should very much like to know the circumstances of her death, because I think she died of grief.'

The barons had come down from the palace to the foot of the tower to see what there was in the boat. The king ordered that the boat should be uncovered and the girl to be taken out and carried up to the palace; many people came to see her. The king began telling Sir Yvain and Gaheris —Arthur's nephew — the girl's story, and how she died because Lancelot would not grant her his love. They told the others, who were very eager to hear the truth, and the news spread so far one way and another that the queen heard all the details about what had happened.

Sir Gawain said to her: 'My lady, my lady, now I know I was not telling the truth about Sir Lancelot, when I told you he loved the girl from Escalot and that he was staying with her; because without doubt if he had loved her as much as I suggested, she would not now be dead, but Lancelot would have granted her all she sought from him.'

'My lord,' she replied, 'many good men are maligned, and it is a pity because they often suffer more as a result than is supposed.'

Then Sir Gawain left the queen, and she was even more miserable than before, calling herself an unhappy woman, wretched and lacking all sense, and saying to herself: 'You miserable creature, how did you dare to think that Lancelot could have been so inconstant as to love another woman than you? Why have you so betrayed and deceived yourself? Do you not see that all the people in this court have failed you and left you in such great danger that you will not escape alive unless you find someone to defend you against Mador? You have failed everyone here, so that no one will help you, because they are all sure that you are in the wrong and Mador in the right, and for this reason they are all abandoning you and allowing you to be led basely to your death. Nevertheless, despite the blame attached to you, if your lover were here, most faithful of all, who has already rescued you from death in the past, I know he would deliver you from this danger that threatens you. Ah! God,' she exclaimed, 'why does he not know the distress now affecting my heart, for my own sake and for his? Ah! God, he will not know in time, and I shall have to die shamefully. That will make him suffer so much that he will die of grief, as soon as he has heard that I have passed away from this world, because no man has ever loved a woman as much or as loyally as he has loved me.'

The queen lamented in this way and grieved, and blamed and rebuked herself for what she had done, because she ought to have loved and held dear above all others the man she rejected and sent far away from her.

The king had the girl buried in the cathedral of Camelot, and commanded a very rich and beautiful tomb to be placed over her grave, with an inscription reading: *Here lies the girl from Escalot, who died for the love of Lancelot.* This was very richly done in letters of gold and azure.

Lancelot remained with the hermit until he had more or less recovered from the injury caused by the huntsman. One afternoon he mounted his horse, because he wished to go for a ride in the forest. He left the hermitage and started along a narrow path. He had not ridden very far when he found a very beautiful spring beneath two trees, and beside the spring was lying an unarmed knight: he had put down his arms beside him and tied his horse to a tree. When Lancelot saw the knight asleep, he thought he would not wake him but would let him rest, and when he awoke, talk to him and ask him who he was. So he dismounted, tied up his horse fairly close to the other, and lay down on the other side of the spring.

It was not long before the other knight was awakened by the noise of the horses fighting, and when he saw Lancelot before him, he was very curious to know what adventure had brought him there. They sat up and greeted each other, and asked each other who they were. Lancelot did not want to reveal who he was when he saw the other man did not recognise him, but replied that he was a knight from the kingdom of Gaunes.

The book says that the unknown knight told Lancelot of the plight of Queen Guinevere. At once Lancelot prepared to come to her rescue, but he held it best to do so in disguise. Nor did he tell a single mortal man save Bors, and he made Bors swear that he would not reveal to anyone what he was doing or who he was; but he would ride to Camelot alone and in borrowed arms. And at Camelot Guinevere was in despair, because she could not persuade any of the other knights of the Round Table to fight for her.

The night before the battle was due to take place, you could have seen in Camelot all the highest ranking men in the kingdom of Logres, because they had assembled to see what the result of the duel would be for the queen. That night the king spoke angrily to the queen and said: 'My lady, I do not know what to say about you. All the good knights of my court have failed me, and as a result you can be sure that tomorrow will bring you a base and shameful death. I would rather have lost all my land than that this should have happened during my lifetime, because I have never loved anyone in this world as much as I loved, and still do love, you.'

When the queen heard this she burst into tears, and so did the king, and when they had lamented together for some time, the king said to her: 'Did you ask Bors or Ector to undertake the battle for you?'

'No,' replied the queen, 'because I do not think they would have done so much for me, as they do not hold any fiefs from you but come from a foreign country.'

'Still, I suggest that you should ask each of them,' said the king, 'and if both of them should fail you, then I do not know what to say or advise.'

And she said that she would ask them, to find out what would happen.

Then the king left her room as distressed as could be, and the queen straight away commanded Bors and Ector to come and speak to her. They came immediately. When she saw them arrive, she fell at their feet and said, in tears: 'Ah, noble knights, renowned for your valour and high birth, if you ever loved the man called Lancelot, come to my help in my need, not for my sake but his. If you are unwilling to do this, you must know that by tomorrow evening I shall be shamed and basely dishonoured, because all the knights of this court will finally have failed me in my great need.'

When Bors saw the queen so anxious and so unhappy, he took pity on her; he raised her up from the ground, and said, in tears : 'My lady, do not be so dismayed. If by tomorrow evening you do not have a better champion than I should be, I shall enter the battle for you against Mador.'

'A better champion?' asked the queen.

'Where could one come from?'

'My lady,' said Bors, 'I cannot tell you that, but what I have told you I shall keep to.'

When the queen heard this, it made her very happy, because she immediately thought it must be Lancelot about whom he was talking and who was to come to rescue her. Bors then straight away left the queen, with

Ector, and they went to a large room in the palace where they usually slept when they came to court.

The next morning the palace was full of barons and knights who were all awaiting Mador's arrival. Many of them were very anxious about the queen, because they did not think she would find a knight to defend her. Shortly after prime, Mador arrived at court, together with a great company of knights who were all his kinsmen. He dismounted, and then went up to the palace completely armed except for his helmet, his shield and his lance. He was a remarkably big man, and there was scarcely a stronger knight at King Arthur's court.

When he came before the king, he repeated his challenge about the battle which he had given before, and the king replied: 'Mador, the queen's case must be settled according to the principle that if she does not find anyone today who is prepared to defend her, we shall do with her what the court will decide. Now remain here until vespers, and if no one comes forward by then to undertake the battle, your accusation is upheld and the queen is found guilty.'

He replied that he would wait; then he sat down in the middle of the palace, with all his kinsmen around him. The hall was remarkably crowded, but they all kept so quiet that there was not a sound. They stayed like that for a long time.

A little before evening, Lancelot arrived fully armed, lacking nothing that a knight ought to have; however, he came quite alone, without any knight or sergeant. He bore white arms and had a diagonal band of red on his shield. When he arrived at court he dismounted and tied up his horse to an elm tree there, and hung his shield from it. Then he went up to the palace without removing his helmet, and appeared before the king and the barons without a soul there recognising him, except only Ector and Bors.

When he came near the king, he spoke loud enough for all those present to hear him, and said to him: 'My lord, I have come to court because of something unbelievable I have heard related in this country. Some people have led me to understand that a knight is to come here today to accuse my lady the queen of treachery. If this is true, I have never heard of such a mad knight, because we all know, friends and strangers, that in the whole world there is no lady as worthy as she. I have therefore come because of the value I know there is in her, prepared to defend her if there is a knight present who is accusing her of treachery.'

At this, Mador jumped forward and said: 'My lord knight, I am ready to prove that she dishonourably and treacherously killed my brother.'

'And I am ready,' said Lancelot, 'to defend her and prove she never had dishonour or treachery in mind.'

Mador took no notice of this and threw down his gage before the king; Lancelot did the same, and the king received them both.

Then Sir Gawain said to the king: 'I think now that Mador was in the wrong, because, however his brother died, I would swear on the relics of the saints that to my knowledge the queen never had dishonour or treachery in mind. It could soon turn out badly for Mador if this other knight has any prowess in him.'

'I do not know who the knight is,' said the king, 'but I think he is going to win and that is what I should like.'

Then the palace began to empty; everybody, high and low, went down to the jousting-field outside the town, where battles were generally fought in a very beautiful place. Sir Gawain took the knight's lance and said he would carry it on to the field; Bors took his shield. Lancelot mounted at once and entered the field. The king summoned the queen and said: 'My lady, here is a knight who is risking his life for you. You must know that if he is vanquished, you will be sentenced to death, and he will be dishonoured.'

'My lord,' she replied, 'may God be on the side of justice as truly as I never had dishonour or treachery in mind.'

Then the queen took her knight, accompanied him on to the field and said: 'My lord, act in God's name, and may Our Lord help you today.'

Then the knights faced each other, spurred on their horses and came together as fast as they could drive their horses. They struck each other so violently that their shields and coats of mail could not protect them from receiving deep wounds. Mador fell from his horse to the ground, and was quite shaken by the fall as he was big and heavy. However, he soon stood up, although rather lacking in confidence, as he had found his enemy to be strong and fierce at jousting.

When Lancelot saw him standing, he thought it would be unchivalrous to attack him from horseback, so he dismounted and let his horse wander where it wanted. Then he drew his sword, protected his head with his shield, and went to attack Mador where he found him. He gave him such powerful blows on his helmet that he was quite stunned; however, Mador defended himself as best he could and struck Lancelot hard many times in return. But all this did him no good, because before midday had passed Lancelot had wounded him so badly that he was bleeding in more than a dozen places.

Lancelot had harassed and tormented Mador so much on all sides that those present saw clearly that he had lost, and would die if this was what his adversary wanted. They all praised the man fighting Mador, because they thought that they had not seen such a noble knight for a long time.

Lancelot, who knew Mador well and had no wish for him to die, because they had once been companions in arms, saw that he had driven him to the point where he could kill him if he wished, and took pity on him.

'Mador,' he said, 'you are defeated and dishonoured, if that is my will; and you can see that you are a dead man if this battle continues. Therefore I suggest you abandon your accusation, before any harm comes to you, and I shall make sure for you that my lady the queen forgives you for having accused her, and that the king acquits you completely.'

When Mador heard the courtesy and the nobility of his opponent's offer, he recognised straight away that it was Lancelot. He knelt before him, took his sword and handed it to him, saying: 'My lord, take my sword, and I shall put myself entirely at mercy. I can tell you that I do not feel myself dishonoured, because I certainly could not compare myself with such a noble knight as you; you have shown that both here and elsewhere.'

Then he said to the king: 'My lord, you have tricked me by setting Sir Lancelot against me.'

When the king heard it was Lancelot, he did not wait till he had left the field, but instead ran forward to him and embraced him, armed as he was. Sir Gawain came forward and unlaced his helmet. Then you could have seen around him the greatest joy of which you had ever heard tell. The queen was acquitted of Mador's accusation, and she now considered herself silly and foolish for having been angry with Lancelot.

LANCELOT AND THE QUEEN ARE RECONCILED

One day it happened that the queen was alone with Lancelot, and they began to talk of various things. The queen said: 'My lord, I mistrusted you quite wrongly about the girl from Escalot, because I know for sure that if you had loved her as much as various people led me to understand, she would not now be dead.'

'What, my lady?' asked Lancelot. 'Is the girl dead, then?'

'Yes, indeed,' replied the queen, 'and she lies inside St Stephen's Cathedral.'

'That is certainly a great shame,' he said, 'because she was very beautiful. I am very sorry, may God help me.'

They spoke at length about this, and about other things. And if Lancelot had loved the queen before, from now on he loved her more than he had ever done in the past, and so did she him. They acted, however, with such a lack of discretion that many people at court discovered the truth about them, and even Sir Gawain knew it for certain, as did all his four brothers.

It happened one day that all five of them were in the palace, talking in confidence about the matter. Agravain was much more concerned than any of the others. While they were discussing the subject, the king happened to come out from the queen's room, and when Sir Gawain saw him he said to his brothers: 'Be quiet, here comes my lord the king.'

Agravain replied that he would not keep quiet for him, and the king overheard this and said to him: 'Agravain, tell me what you are talking about so loudly.'

'Ah!' said Sir Gawain, 'for God's sake let us say no more on the subject; Agravain is being more unpleasant than usual, and you should not be interested to know, because no good could come of it for you or any noble man.'

'In God's name,' said the king, 'I wish to know.'

'Oh, no, my lord,' said Gaheris, 'that is quite impossible, because there is nothing in what he is saying but fables and the most disloyal lies in the world. For that reason I beg you as my liege lord to stop asking.'

'By my head,' said Arthur, 'I will not. I will go as far now as to request you, on the oath you swore to me, to tell me what you were arguing about just now.'

'It is remarkable how anxious you are to hear about it,' said Sir Gawain.

'Indeed, even if it made you angry with me and you expelled me, poor and exiled, from this country of yours, I still should not tell you, because if you believed it, even if it were the greatest lie in the world, more harm could come of it than has ever come about in your time.'

Then the king was even more distressed than before, and he said that he would know, or he would have them all put to death.

'In faith,' said Sir Gawain, 'you will never know from me, because all I would finally receive would be your hatred, and neither I nor anyone else could fail to regret it.'

Then he left the room, and so did Gaheris. The king kept calling them, but they would not return. They went away as sadly as could be, saying to each other that it was a pity the subject had ever been raised, because if the king discovered the truth and had a conflict with Lancelot, the court would be destroyed and dishonoured, because Lancelot would have on his side all the strength of Gaul and many other countries.

So the two brothers went off, so miserable that they did not know what to do. The king, who had stayed with his other nephews, took them into a room near a garden. Then he closed the door on them, and asked and begged them by the faith they owed him to tell him what he wanted to know. First he turned to Agravain, but he said he would not tell him. Let him ask the others! They too said that they would not speak.

'If you will not tell me,' said the king, 'either I shall kill you or you will kill me.'

Then he ran to a sword lying on a couch, drew it from its scabbard, and went up to Agravain saying that he would not fail to kill him if he did not tell him what he so much desired to know. He raised the sword high to strike his head, and when Agravain saw he was so angry, he shouted: 'Ah, my lord, do not kill me! I will tell you. I was saying to my brother Sir Gawain, and to Gaheris and my other brothers you can see here, that they were disloyal traitors for having so long permitted the scandal and dishonour which Sir Lancelot du Lac is causing you.'

'What,' said the king, 'is Lancelot dishonouring me? What are you talking about? Tell me, because I have never suspected he might be bringing me shame, since I have always honoured and loved him so much that he should never cause me any dishonour.'

'My lord,' said Agravain, 'he is so loyal to you that he is dishonouring you through your wife and has committed adultery with her.'

When the king heard this, his colour changed and he turned pale. He said: 'That is unbelievable.'

Then he began thinking and said nothing for a long time.

'My lord,' said Mordred, 'we have hidden it from you as long as we could, but now it is right that the truth should be known and that we should tell you. So long as we hid it from you, we have also been disloyal and guilty of perjury; now we are freeing ourselves of the blame of that. We are telling you truthfully that it is as we say; now you must see how your dishonour can be avenged.'

As a result of this the king was so pensive and sad and distraught that he did not know what to do. However, when he spoke, he said: 'If you have ever loved me, find a way to catch them together, and if I do not take my revenge on them as one should on traitors, I shall never want to wear a crown again.'

'My lord,' said Gareth, 'advise us, then, because it is a fearsome undertaking to bring so noble a man as Lancelot to his death. He is strong and bold, and his kinsmen are powerful in every way. That means, as you are well aware, that if Lancelot dies, King Ban's kinsmen will wage such a great and vigorous war against you that the most powerful men in your kingdom will find it difficult to withstand it. You yourself, if God does not defend you, could be killed, because they will be more intent on avenging Lancelot than saving themselves.'

'Don't worry about me,' said the king, 'but do as I tell you. Let them be caught together, if you can arrange it; I am commanding you to do this on the oath you swore to me when you were made companions of the Round Table.'

They agreed to do this because he so desired it, and they all three swore it. Then they left the room and went into the palace.

That day the king was more pensive than usual, and it was quite evident that he was angry. At noon Sir Gawain came, together with Gaheris, and when they saw the king, they could tell from his face that the others had told him about Lancelot. For that reason they did not turn towards him, but instead went to the windows of the palace. The hall was quiet; no one present dared to say a word because they saw the king was angry.

At that moment an armed knight arrived who said to the king: 'My lord, I can tell you news from the tournament at Karahés. The knights from the kingdom of Sorelois and from the Waste Land have lost everything.'

'Were there any knights present from here?' asked the king.

'Yes my lord, Lancelot was there and was the winner everywhere.'

The king frowned and lowered his head when he heard this news, and began to think. When he had thought for some time, he got up and said, loud enough for many to hear: 'Ah, God, what grievous shame it is that treason ever took root in such a noble man!'

The king went to his room and lay down sadly on his bed. He knew perfectly well that if Lancelot were caught in adultery and put to death, there would be such a great torment in the country as had never before been caused by the death of a single knight. And yet it was better that Lancelot should die than that a king's dishonour should not be avenged before his death.

LANCELOT AND THE QUEEN ARE TAKEN IN ADULTERY

Then he commanded his three nephews to come to him, and when they were present, he said: 'My lords, Lancelot is returning from that tournament. Now explain to me how he may be caught in the act you revealed to me.

'I certainly do not know,' said Gareth.

'In God's name,' said Agravain, 'I will tell you. Announce to all your sergeants that you are going hunting tomorrow morning, and tell all your knights to accompany you except Lancelot. He will be pleased to stay, and I am quite sure it will happen that as soon as you have left for the hunt, he will go and sleep with the queen. We shall stay behind to establish the truth for you, and we shall be hiding here in a room to catch him and to keep him until you return home.'

The king readily agreed to this. 'But be careful', he said, 'that not a soul knows about it, until it is done as you have described.'

During this conversation Sir Gawain arrived, and when he saw them talking together so confidentially, he said to the king: 'My lord, God grant that nothing but good may come to you out of this discussion, because I fear it may harm you more than anyone else. Agravain, my brother, I beg you not to begin anything you cannot conclude, or to say anything about Lancelot if you do not know it for certain, because he is the finest knight you have ever seen.'

'Gawain,' said the king, 'depart from here, because you are a man I shall never trust again.. You have behaved badly towards me, since you knew my dishonour and permitted it without informing me.'

'My treason certainly never did you any harm,' replied Sir Gawain.

Then he left the room and saw Gaheris, and said: 'Despite everything, Agravain has told the king what we did not dare to tell him. You can be sure that it will cause a great deal of harm.'

'In that case,' said Gaheris, 'I will have nothing to do with it; someone as noble as Lancelot will never be accused of that crime by me. Now let us leave Agravain with what he has started. If good comes of it, may he benefit; but if it turns out badly, he cannot say we had anything to do with it.'

Then they left and went to Gaheris's lodging. As they were going down through the town they met Lancelot and his companions. As soon as they saw one another from a distance, they were very happy.

'Sir Lancelot,' said Gaheris, 'I want to ask you a favour.'

Lancelot agreed readily, provided it was something he could do.

'Thank you,' said Gaheris.

'I want you to come and stay with me tonight together with your company. I can assure you that I am asking this more for your own good than to annoy you.'

When Lancelot heard him say this, he agreed. They turned round and went down to Gaheris's lodge just as they were.

Then squires and sergeants rushed forward to disarm Lancelot and the others who had come from the tournament. At supper-time, they all went to court together, because they truly loved Lancelot. When he arrived, Lancelot was extremely surprised that the king, who usually gave him such a welcome, did not say a word to him this time, but turned his face aside as soon as he saw him coming. He did not realise the king was angry with him, because he did not think he could have heard the news that he had been told. Then he sat with the knights and began to enjoy himself, but not as much as he usually did, because he saw the king was so pensive.

After supper, when the tablecloths had been removed, the king summoned his knights to go hunting the next morning in the forest of

Camelot. Then Lancelot said to the king: 'Lord, I shall accompany you there.'

'My lord,' replied the king, 'you can stay behind this time, because I have so many other knights that I can quite do without your company.'

When Lancelot saw that the king was angry with him, he did not know why; and he was very sorry about it.

In the evening, when it was time to go to bed, Lancelot left with a great company of knights; and when they were at their lodge, Lancelot said to Bors: 'Did you see the look King Arthur gave me? I think he is angry with me for some reason.'

'My lord,' said Bors, 'he has heard about you and the queen. Now be careful what you do, because we risk fighting a war which will never come to an end.'

'Ah,' said Lancelot, 'who was it that dared to talk about it?'

'My lord,' replied Bors, 'if a knight spoke about it, it was Agravain, and if it was a woman, it was Morgan, King Arthur's sister.'

That night the two cousins talked a lot about the subject. The next day, as soon as it was light, Sir Gawain said to Lancelot: 'My lord, I am going hunting with Gaheris. Are you coming?'

'No,' replied Lancelot, 'I am staying behind, because I am not in a position to go as I wish.'

Sir Gawain and Gaheris followed the king to the hunt. And as soon as the king had left, the queen called for a messenger, and sent him to Lancelot, who was still in bed. She commanded him to come to her without fail.

When Lancelot saw the messenger, he was very pleased, and told him to return, because he would follow him. Then he dressed and got ready, and wondered how he could go secretly so that no one would know. He asked Bors' advice, and Bors begged him for God's sake not to go.

'If you go, you will suffer for it; my heart, which has never been apprehensive for you before, tells me so.'

But Lancelot replied that he was determined to go.

'My lord,' said Bors, 'as you wish to go, I shall tell you the best way to take. There is a garden which stretches as far as the queen's room; go through it. You will find the quietest and least frequented path of which I know. But I beg you for God's sake not to fail for any reason to take your sword with you.'

Then Lancelot did as Bors had described, and went along the garden path which led up to King Arthur's house. When he was near the tower, Agravain, who had placed his spies everywhere, knew he was coming, since a boy had told him: 'My lord, Sir Lancelot is coming this way.'

He told him to be quiet.

Then Agravain went to a window looking out over the garden and watched Lancelot hurrying towards the tower. Agravain had a great company of knights with him; he took them to the window and pointed out Lancelot, saying: 'There he is. Now make sure, when he is in the queen's room, that he does not escape.'

They replied that there was no chance of his fleeing, since they would surprise him when he was naked.

Lancelot, who did not suspect that he was being watched, went to the door of the room leading on to the garden, opened it, and went in, passing from room to room until he came to where the queen was expecting him.

When Lancelot was inside, he locked the door after him, as it was not his lot to be killed on that occasion. Then he took off his shoes and undressed and climbed into bed with the queen. However he had not been there long when those who were looking out to capture him came to the door of the room. When they found it locked, they were all confounded, and realised that they had failed in what they had set out to do. They asked Agravain how they could enter, and he instructed them to break down the door, as it was the only way.

They knocked and banged until the queen heard, and said to Lancelot: 'My friend, we have been betrayed.'

'What, my lady?' he said, 'What is it?'

Then he listened and heard all the noise of the men who were trying to force the door, but were unable to.

'Ah, my friend,' said the queen, 'now we are dishonoured and dead; the king will know all about you and me. Agravain has laid a trap for us.'

'Do not worry, my lady,' said Lancelot. 'He has arranged his own death, because he will he the first to die.'

Then they both jumped up from the bed and dressed as best they could.

'My lady,' asked Lancelot, 'have you a coat of mail here or any other armour with which I could protect myself?'

'No,' replied the queen.

'Our misfortune is so great that we must both die, you and I. I am sorrier for your sake, may God help me, than for mine, because your death will be a much greater loss than mine. And yet, if God should grant that you escaped from here alive and well, I know there is no one yet born who would dare to put me to death for this crime while he knew you were alive.'

When Lancelot heard her say this, he went to the door not fearing anything, and shouted to those who were striking it: 'Wait for me, you evil cowards. I am going to open the door to see who will come in first.'

Then he drew his sword, opened the door, and told them to come forward. A knight called Tanaguin who hated Lancelot mortally put himself before the others, and Lancelot, raising his sword, struck him so violently with all his force that neither his helmet nor his iron coif could save him from being split to the shoulders. Lancelot wrenched out his sword, and struck him dead to the ground. When the others saw what had happened to him, they all drew back and left the doorway quite empty. Seeing this, Lancelot said to the queen: 'My lady, the battle is over. When it pleases you I shall go, and shall not be prevented by any man here.'

The queen said she wanted him to be in safety, whatever might happen to her. Then Lancelot looked at the knight he had killed, who had fallen inside the door of the room. He pulled him nearer and closed the door. Then he disarmed him and armed himself as well as he could. Having done that, he said to the queen: 'My lady, since I am armed, I should now be able to go safely, if it pleases God.'

She told him to go if he could.

He went to the door, opened it, and said that they would never hold him. Then he rushed among them, brandishing his sword, and struck the first man he met to the ground so violently that he was unable to get up again. When the others saw this, they drew back and even the boldest of them let him pass.

Seeing that they were leaving him alone, he passed through the garden and went back to his lodging. There he found Bors, who was very worried that he might not be able to return as he wished, because he had realised that King Arthur's kinsmen had been spying on Lancelot in order to be able to catch him in some way. When Bors saw his lord coming fully armed, although he had left unarmed, he knew there had been a fight. He went to meet Lancelot, and asked: 'My lord, what has made you arm yourself?'

Lancelot told him how Agravain and his two brothers had spied on him, because they wished to catch him with the queen, and how they had taken many knights with them.

'And they nearly caught me, too, since I was not prepared for them, but I defended myself vigorously, and with the help of God I managed to escape.'

'Ah, my lord,' said Bors, 'now things are turning out for the worse, because what we have hidden for so long is now in the open. Now you will see the beginning of a war that will never end during our lifetimes; because if until now the king has loved you more than any man, from now on he will hate you even more, since he knows that you have wronged him so much by dishonouring him through his wife. Now you must decide what we are going to do, as I am quite certain that from now on the king will be my mortal enemy. However, may God help me, I am most sorry for our lady the queen, who will be put to death because of you. I should be happier if it were possible for us to decide how she can be rescued from the danger she is in, and brought to safety.'

While they were discussing this, Ector arrived. When he heard what had come about, he was sadder than anyone, and said: 'The best thing I can see is for us to leave and enter the forest out there, but taking great care not to let the king find us, because he is there at present. When it is time for our lady the queen to be judged, she will certainly be taken out there to be put to death. Then we will rescue her, whether those who think they are taking her to her death agree or not. When we have got her with us, we shall be able to leave the country and go to the kingdom of Benwick or the kingdom of Gaunes. If we can manage to lead her to safety, we shall not fear King Arthur or all his power in any way.'

Lancelot and Bors agreed with this plan; they ordered their knights and sergeants to mount, and were thirty-eight in all. They rode until they had left the town and arrived at the edge of the forest, where they knew it was thickest, so that they would be unlikely to be noticed while it was light.

Then Lancelot called one of his squires and said: 'Go straight to Camelot and find out what is happening to my lady the queen and what they plan to do with her. If they have condemned her to death, come and tell us straight away, because despite all the trouble or difficulties we might have in rescuing her, we shall not fail to save her from death as best we can.'

Then the boy left Lancelot, mounted his horse, went by the quickest route to Camelot, and arrived at King Arthur's court.

When Lancelot had left the queen and fled from those who were hoping to catch him, the men at the door of the room, seeing that he had gone, went in and caught the queen. They insulted and taunted her more than they should have done, saying that now they had proof and that she would not escape with her life. They treated her with a total lack of respect, and she heard them, and was as distressed as could be, weeping so bitterly that the wicked knights should have had pity on her.

At noon the king returned from the hunt. When he had dismounted in the courtyard, he was immediately told the news that the queen had been caught with Lancelot; he was much saddened and asked whether Lancelot had been captured.

'No, my lord,' they replied, 'he defended himself very vigorously. No other man could have done what he did.'

'Since he is not here,' said King Arthur, 'we shall find him at his lodge. Take a large number of armed men and go and capture him. When you have caught him, come to me, and I shall deal with him and the queen together.'

Then as many as forty knights went to arm themselves, not because they wanted to but because they had no choice, since the king had commanded them in person. When they arrived at Lancelot's lodge, they did not find him there, and all the knights were pleased about this, because they knew that if they had found him there and had tried to take him by force, they could not have avoided a great and violent battle. So they went back to the king and told him that they had missed Lancelot, because he had left some time previously and had taken all his knights with him. When the king heard this, he said he was very angry, and because he was not able to take his revenge on Lancelot, he would take it on the queen in such a way that it would be spoken about evermore.

THE QUEEN IS CONDEMNED; LANCELOT RESCUES HER FROM THE STAKE, BUT KILLS THREE OF GAWAIN'S BROTHERS

'My lord,' asked king Yon, 'what do you intend to do?'

'I intend,' replied King Arthur, 'that severe justice should be taken on her for this crime she has committed. And I command you first of all, because you are a king, and then the other barons present here, to determine among you how she should be put to death, because she will not escape with her life, and even if you yourself took her side and said she should not die, she would die nevertheless.'

'My lord,' said king Yon, 'it is not the normal custom in this country for a man or a woman to be sentenced to death after noon. But in the morning, if we have no alternative but to make a judgement, we shall do it.'

Then King Arthur fell silent, and was so despondent that he could not eat or drink the whole evening, and did not wish the queen to be brought before him. In the morning, when the barons had assembled in the palace, the king said: 'My lords, what must we do with the queen according to true justice?'

The barons drew aside and discussed the matter. They asked Agravain and the two other brothers what ought to be done, and they said it was their judgement that justice called for her to be put to a shameful death, because she had committed great treachery by sleeping with another knight in place of such a noble man as the king.

'And it is our judgement that she has deserved death by this one thing.'

All the others were obliged to agree with this, because it was obvious that it was what the king wanted. When Sir Gawain saw that the decision of the court meant that the queen's death sentence was confirmed, he said that, if it pleased God, his grief would never allow him to see the death of the lady who had paid him the greatest honour of any in the world. Then

Sir Gawain went up to the king and said: 'My lord, I return to you what-ever fiefs I hold from you, and I shall never serve you again in all my life if you tolerate this treachery.'

The king did not say a word in reply, because his attention was else-where; and Sir Gawain straight away left the court and went to his lodging, lamenting, as much as if he saw everyone dead before him. The king commanded his sergeants to light a great and powerful fire in the joust-ing-field of Camelot, in which the queen would be burnt, because a queen who was guilty of treachery could die in no other way, given that she was sacred. Then a great noise of shouting arose in the city of Camelot, and all the people were as grief-stricken as if she were their mother. Those who had been ordered to prepare the fire made it so great and impressive that everyone in the city could see it.

The king commanded the queen to be brought forward, and she came, crying bitterly. She was wearing a dress of red taffeta, a tunic, and a cloak. She was so beautiful and so elegant that she surpassed any other woman of her age one could have found in the world. When the king saw her, he felt such great pity for her that he was unable to look at her, but commanded her to be taken from him and dealt with as the court had decided in its judgement. Then she was led out of the palace and down through the streets.

When the queen had left the court and the city's inhabitants could see her coming, then you could have heard people on all sides, shouting: 'Ah, my lady, more kindly and courteous than all others, where will the poor people ever find pity now? Ah, King Arthur, you who have treacherously sought her death, you can still repent, and the traitors who have arranged this can die in shame!'

That is what the people of the city were saying as they followed the queen, weeping and shouting as if they were out of their minds.

The king commanded Agravain to take forty knights and to go and guard the field where the fire had been lit, so that if Lancelot came he would be powerless against them.

'My lord, do you then wish me to go?' he asked.

'Yes,' replied the king.

'Then command my brother Gaheris to come with us.'

The king commanded him, but he said he would not go. However, the king threatened him so much that finally he promised to go. So he went back to fetch his arms and all the others did too. When they were armed and had left the city, they saw that they were in fact eighty, all together.

'Listen, Agravain,' said Gaheris, 'do you think I have come to fight with Lancelot if he wants to rescue the queen? I tell you I shall not fight with him; I would rather he kept the queen for the rest of his life than she should die here.'

Agravain and Gaheris went on talking until they were near the fire. Lancelot was in hiding with all his men at the edge of the forest, and as soon as he saw his messenger return, he asked him what news he was bringing back from King Arthur's court.

'Bad news, my lord,' he said.

'My lady the queen has been sentenced to death, and there is the fire they are getting ready to burn her in.'

'My lords,' he said, 'let us mount! There are some people who expect to put her to death but who will die themselves. May God grant, if ever he heard the prayer of a sinner, that I first find Agravain, who caught me in that trap.'

Then they counted themselves to see how many knights they were, and they found they were thirty-two in number. Each one mounted his horse, and took shield and lance. They rode to where they saw the fire.

When the men in the jousting-field saw them coming, they all shouted together: 'There is Lancelot, flee, flee!'

Lancelot, who was riding ahead of all the others, went to where he saw Agravain, and shouted: 'Coward, traitor, you have come to your end!'

Then he struck him so hard that no armour could save him from having a lance thrust through his body. Lancelot, a man of valour and strength, gave him a mighty blow that knocked him to the ground from his horse. As he fell, the lance broke.

Bors, who came riding as fast as he could urge his horse to gallop, shouted to Gareth to defend himself because he was challenging him mortally, and Bors turned his horse towards him and struck him so violently that no armour could prevent him from thrusting the blade of his lance into his chest. Gareth fell from his horse to the ground in such a condition that he had no need of a doctor. The others put their hands to their swords and began to fight. But when Gaheris saw that his two brothers were down, you do not need to ask whether he was angry, because he realised they were dead. Then he turned towards Meliadus the Black, who was actively helping Lancelot and avenging the queen's disgrace. He struck him so hard that he knocked him into the middle of the fire; then he put his hand to his sword, because he was a man of great valour, and struck another knight to the ground at Lancelot's feet.

Ector, who was taking note of all this, saw Gaheris, and said to himself: 'If that man lives much longer, he can do us a lot of harm, as he is so valiant; it is better I should kill him than that he should do us more harm than he has done already.'

Then Ector spurred on his horse, went up to Gaheris, brandishing his sword, and struck him so violently that his helmet flew off his head. When

Gaheris felt his head unprotected, he was stunned, and Lancelot turned to see who it was that Ector was fighting. He did not recognise him, and struck him so hard on his head that he split it to the teeth.

When King Arthur's men saw this blow and saw Gaheris fall, they were quite dispirited; and their opponents pressed them so hard that out of the whole group of eighty there only remained three. One of these was Mordred and the other two were from the Round Table.

When Lancelot saw that there was no one left from King Arthur's household to hold him back from anything, he went up to the queen, and said: 'My lady, what is to be done with you?'

She was delighted by this happy outcome that God had sent her, and said: 'My lord, I should like you to place me in safety somewhere outside King Arthur's control.'

'My lady,' said Lancelot, 'climb on to a palfrey and come with us into the forest. There we shall come to a decision about what it is best to do.'

And she agreed with this.

Then they put her on a palfrey and went into the thickest part of the forest. When they were deep within it, they checked to see if they were all there, and they saw that they had lost three of their companions. Then they asked one another what had happened to them.

'I saw three of our men die at Gaheris's hand,' said Ector.

'What?' said Lancelot, 'was Gaheris present, then?'

'My lord,' said Bors, 'what are you asking? You killed him.'

'In God's name,' said Ector, 'you killed him.'

'Now, we can be sure,' said Lancelot, 'that we shall never be at peace with King Arthur or with Sir Gawain, because of their love for Gaheris. We shall see the beginning of a war that will never come to an end.'

Lancelot was very angry with himself over Gaheris's death, because he was one of the knights he most loved in the world.

Bors said to Lancelot: 'My lord, we ought to decide how my lady the queen is to be led to safety.'

'If we could manage,' replied Lancelot, 'to take her to a castle I once conquered, I do not think she need fear King Arthur. The castle is remarkably strong and so placed that it cannot be besieged. If we were there and had provisioned it well, I would summon to me knights near and far I have often served in the past; there are a great many in the world that would support me, by the oath they have sworn to come to my aid.'

'Where is this castle of which you speak,' asked Bors, 'and what is it called?'

'It is called,' said Lancelot, 'the Castle of the Joyous Gard; but when I conquered it, at the time when I had only recently been dubbed a knight, it was called the Dolorous Gard.'

'Ah, God!' exclaimed the queen. 'When shall we be there?'

They all agreed with Lancelot's idea, and set out along the main path through the forest, saying that however many men might follow them from King Arthur's household, they would all be killed. They rode until they arrived at a castle in the middle of the forest, called Kalec. The lord of it was an earl who was a fine knight of great strength and who loved Lancelot above all men.

When he knew Lancelot had arrived, he was delighted and received him very courteously, treating him with all the honour that he could. He promised to help him against all men, even King Arthur, and said: 'My lord, I would like to give this castle to you and my lady the queen; I think you ought to accept it, because it is very strong and if you wish to stay here you will not have to worry about anyone, or about anything King Arthur can do.'

Lancelot thanked him, but said that he definitely could not stay there.

Then they left the castle and rode day after day until they were four leagues from the Joyous Gard. Lancelot sent messengers ahead to say they were coming, and when the people in the castle knew, they went to meet him as joyfully as if he were God himself, and welcomed him with even more honour than they would have done King Arthur. When they knew he wanted to stay there, and why he had come, they swore to him on the saints that they would lay down their lives to help him. Then Lancelot summoned the knights of the district and they came in great numbers.

When King Arthur saw Mordred returning in flight through the city of Camelot with so few companions, he was amazed how this could be. He asked those who were coming towards him why they were fleeing.

'My lord,' said a boy, 'I have bad news to tell you and all those present here. My lord, I have to tell you that of all the knights that were leading the queen to the fire only three have escaped. One of them is Mordred, and I do not know who the other two are; I think all the others are dead.'

'Ah !' said King Arthur, 'was Lancelot there, then?'

'Yes, my lord,' he replied, 'and that is not all he has done, because he has rescued the queen from death and taken her away with him. He has disappeared with her into the forest of Camelot.'

The king was so shaken by this news that he did not know what to do. At this point Mordred came in and said to the king: 'Lord, things have gone badly for us. Lancelot has got away and taken the queen with him, after defeating us all.'

'They will not be able to go much further, if I can help it,' said the king.

Then he commanded knights and sergeants and all those who were with him to arm, and they mounted as soon as they could. Covered in steel, they left the city and rode up to the forest, and went up and down to see if they could get any news about the people for whom they were searching. But, as it happened, they found no one. The king then suggested they should divide and go different ways in order to find them more easily.

'In God's name,' said King Carados, 'I do not think that is a good idea, because if we separate and Lancelot finds some of us, since he has a great company of strong and bold knights with him, those he meets will undoubtedly pay with their lives, for he will kill them.'

'What shall we do, then?' asked King Arthur.

'Send your messengers to all the seamen in this country's ports, telling them that none should be so bold as to allow Lancelot to pass. In that way he will be forced to stay in this country whether he wishes to or not, and thus we shall easily be able to find out where he is. Then we shall be able to attack him with so many men that he will be captured without difficulty, so that you can take your revenge on him. That is what I advise.'

Then King Arthur called his messengers and sent them to all the ports in the land; and then he returned to the city. As he came to the place where his knights were lying dead, he looked to the right and saw his nephew Agravain, whom Lancelot had killed, lying there. He had been struck in the body by a lance, and the blade had passed right through him. As soon as the king saw him he recognised him, and he was so heartbroken that he could not hold himself in his saddle, but fell to the ground in a swoon on top of the body. When he got his breath back after a time and could speak, he said: 'Ah, my nephew, the man who struck you in that way really hated you; everyone should know that the man who deprived my kinsmen of such a knight as you has brought great grief to my heart.'

He took off Agravain's helmet and looked at him, then he kissed his eyes and his mouth, which by now were cold. After this he had him carried back to the city.

The king was completely grief-stricken and wept as he made his way, still fully armed except for his helmet, through the dead and wounded; he went on looking until he found Gareth, whom Bors had killed. Then you could have seen the king in great distress. He lamented greatly and said that he had lived too long when he saw those he had brought up in great affection die in such a tragic way. When he had had Gareth placed on his shield so that he could be carried back to the city, he went on searching. Then to the left he saw the body of Gaheris whom Lancelot had killed – this was Arthur's favourite nephew except for Gawain.

When the king saw the body of the man he had loved so much, there was no grief that a man can suffer for another that Arthur did not feel. He ran up to him as fast as he could and embraced him very closely. He swooned again and all the barons were frightened that he might die in front of them. He was unconscious for as long as a man could walk a mile;

when he came to he said, loud enough for all to hear: 'Ah, God! Now I have lived too long! Ah, death! If you delay any longer I shall consider you too slow in coming. Ah, Gaheris! If I must die of grief, I shall die for you. My nephew, it is a pity the sword was ever forged that struck you, and cursed be the man who struck you, because he has destroyed both me and my race.'

The king kissed his eyes and his mouth, bloody as they were, and grieved so much that all those watching were astonished. In fact, there was no one there who was not sad, because they all loved Gaheris greatly.

At all this noise and shouting Sir Gawain came out from his lodge, because he believed that the queen was dead and that the lamentation was for her. When he had arrived out in the streets and the people there saw him, they said: 'Sir Gawain, if you want to know great grief and see the destruction of your own flesh and blood, go up into the palace, and there you will find the greatest pain you ever experienced.'

Sir Gawain was quite confounded by this news, and did not say a word in reply, but went along the streets with his head bowed. He did not think the great grief would be over his brothers, because he knew nothing about that yet, but thought it was over the queen. As he was going through the town, he looked to the right and to the left, and saw everyone weeping together, young and old. As he went past, everybody said to him: 'Sir Gawain, go and know your great grief.'

When Sir Gawain heard what they were all saying, he was more dismayed than before, but he did not let it be seen. When he arrived at the palace, he saw everyone there lamenting as much as if they had seen the deaths of all the princes in the world.

Seeing Sir Gawain come in, the king said: 'Gawain, Gawain, know your great grief, and mine too; for here is your brother Gaheris, the most valiant of our race, lying dead.'

He showed him to Sir Gawain, still all bloody as he held him in his arms, lying against his chest. When Sir Gawain heard this he had not the strength to answer a word or to remain standing, but lost consciousness and fell to the ground in a faint. The barons were so grieved and distressed by this that they thought they would never again feel joy. When they saw Sir Gawain fall in that way, they took him in their arms and wept bitterly over him, saying: 'Ah, God! This is a terrible tragedy in every way.'

When Sir Gawain regained consciousness, he got up and ran to where he saw Gaheris lying; then he took him from the king and pressed him hard against his chest, and began to kiss him. As he kissed him he fainted again, and fell to the ground for even longer than before. When he came to, he sat near Gaheris and looked at him. Seeing how hard he had been struck, he said: 'Ah, brother, cursed be the arm that struck you in that way!

Dear brother, the man who struck you certainly hated you. Brother, how did he have the heart to put you to death? Dear brother, how could Fortune allow you to suffer such a base and ugly death when she had endowed you with all good qualities? She used to be so kind and friendly to you, and raised you up. Brother, she has done this to kill me, to make me die of grief for you. It would certainly be quite fitting if I did, and I would not object, because now that I have seen your death, I no longer wish to live, except until I have taken my revenge on the traitor who did this to you.'

Sir Gawain said this, and would have said more, but his heart was so afflicted that he could not say another word. When he had been silent for some time, grieving as much as was humanly possible, he looked to the right and saw Gareth and Agravain lying dead in front of the king on the shields on which they had been brought in. He recognised them straight away, and said, loud enough for everyone to hear: 'Ah, God! I have truly lived too long, when I see my flesh and blood killed so grievously.'

Then he fell on them several times, and was so affected by the great grief he had in his heart that the barons who were present there feared that he might die on the spot. The king asked his barons what he could do for Gawain, saying: 'If he stays here for long, I think he will die of grief.'

'My lord,' they replied, 'we suggest that he should be carried from here, put to bed in another room and watched over until his brothers are buried.'

'Let us do that, then,' said the king.

So they took Sir Gawain, who was still unconscious, and they carried him into another room. He lay there in such a state that no one could get a word, good or bad, out of him.

That night there was such great lamentation in the city of Camelot that there was nobody who was not in tears. The dead knights were disarmed and enshrouded, each according to his lineage. Coffins and tombs were made for them all. For Gareth and Agravain two coffins were made which were as beautiful and rich as those suitable for a king's sons; their bodies were placed in them, one beside the other, in St Stephen's Cathedral, at that time the principal church of Camelot. Between the two tombs the king ordered another to be made, even finer and more splendid than the others, and Gaheris's body was placed in it next to his two brothers. At the moment that he was let down into the earth you could have seen many tears. All the bishops and archbishops of the country came, and all the high-born men, and they paid the dead knights the greatest honour that they could, especially Gaheris, because they had been such good men and fine knights. They had an inscription put on his tomb saying, *Here lies Gaheris, King Arthur's nephew, who was killed by Lancelot du Lac.* They put on the other tombs the names of those who had killed them.

When all the clergy who had come there had conducted the burial service as was fitting, King Arthur returned to his palace and sat among his barons, as sad and pensive as could be. He would not have been so distressed if he had lost half his kingdom. All the other barons were in the same state. The hall was crowded with high-ranking barons, and they were all as quiet as if there had not been a soul there.

Seeing them so still, the king spoke loud enough for everyone to hear, and said: 'Ah, God! For so long you have allowed me to live in great honour, and now in a short time I have been so afflicted by real misfortune that no man has ever lost as much as I have. Because when it happens that someone loses his land through force or treason, that is something which it is quite possible to regain later; but when one loses one's closest friends whom one cannot recover by any means in the world, then the loss is irreversible, then the damage is so great that it cannot possibly be put right. This has befallen me not through God's justice, but through Lancelot's pride. If our grievous loss had come about through Our Lord's vengeance, then we should have found some honour in it and been able to suffer it easily; but instead it has happened through the man we have brought up and enriched in our country over a long period, as if he had been one of our very flesh and blood. It is he who has caused us this loss and this dishonour. You are all my men, and have sworn fidelity to me and hold fiefs from me; therefore I require you on the oath you have sworn to me, to help me, as one should help one's liege lord, so that my dishonour may be avenged.'

Then the king fell silent and waited quietly for the barons to reply. They began to look at one another, urging one another to speak up. When they had been silent for a long time, King Yon stood up and said to the king: 'My lord, I am your bondsman, and I must counsel you with our honour and yours in mind. It is certainly to your honour to avenge your shame. However, anyone who cared about the good of your kingdom would not declare war on King Ban's kinsmen, because we know for a fact that Our Lord has raised King Ban's race above all others. There are no men anywhere in the world who are so noble that, if they declared war on those kinsmen, they would not be the worse for it, provided only that you were not among them. For this reason, my lord, I beg you for God's sake not to begin fighting them if you are not certain of your own superior strength, because I certainly believe they would be very difficult to defeat.'

There was a great deal of shouting in the palace because many barons reproached king Yon for what he had said, and accused him openly of having spoken out of cowardice.

'I certainly did not say that,' he replied, 'because my fear was greater than that of any of you; but I know for a fact that when the war has begun, if they can manage to return to their country safe and well, they will be far less worried about your attacks than you think.'

'Indeed, Sir Yon,' said Mordred, 'I have never heard as noble a man as you give advice as bad as that; I think the king should go to war, and take you whether you want to go or not.'

'Mordred,' replied king Yon, 'I shall go more willingly than you. May the king set out when he wishes.'

'You are arguing quite uselessly,' said Mador de la Porte.

'If you want to declare war, you will not have far to go, because I have been told that Lancelot is between here and the sea in a castle he once conquered when he was beginning to seek adventures, called the Joyous Gard. I know the castle very well, because I was once imprisoned there, and feared I should die, until Lancelot released me and my companions.'

'I know that castle well, too,' said the king.

'Tell me if you think he has taken the queen with him.'

'My lord,' said Mador, 'you can be sure the queen is there, but I do not recommend you to go, because the castle is so strong that it is in no danger of a siege from any side, and those inside are so noble that they would have little fear of your attacks. However, if they saw an opportunity to do you some harm, they would do it without hesitation.'

When the king heard this, he said: 'Mador, you are right about the strength of the castle, and about the self-assurance of those inside. However, you are perfectly aware, as are all those present, that since I first wore a crown I have never waged a war that I did not bring to an end to my honour and to that of my kingdom. For this reason you can be sure that nothing would make me hold back from fighting the men who have caused me such a great loss among my close friends. And now I summon those present here, and I shall call all those who hold lands from me, far and near. When they have assembled we shall leave the city of Camelot, in a fortnight's time. And because I do not want any of you to draw back from this undertaking, I require all of you to swear on the saints that you will continue fighting until our shame has been avenged to the honour of all of us.'

ARTHUR MOUNTS AN EXPEDITON TO BESIEGE LANCELOT AND GUINEVERE IN JOYOUS GARD

Then the saints' relics were brought, and everyone in the palace, poor and rich together, swore that oath. When they had all sworn to keep up the fight, the king summoned through his messengers all those who held fiefs from him, far and near, to be present at Camelot on the stated day, because he then wanted, to set out with all his forces to go to the castle of the Joyous Gard. Thereupon they all agreed and prepared to go to the country north of the Humber. Thus they decided on the war that was later to turn to King Arthur's disadvantage; however superior they were at the beginning, they were beaten in the end.

But rumour, which spreads so quickly through the world, arrived at the Joyous Gard the very next day after the matter had been discussed, since a boy, a sergeant of Ector de Maris, left court immediately and took the news there.

When he arrived, they were anxiously awaiting information from court. He told them that the war had been decided upon, and had been so affirmed that there could be no going back on it, because all the most powerful men at court had taken an oath, and afterwards all others who held fiefs from the king had been summoned.

'Have things then come to this?' asked Bors.

'Yes, my lord,' replied the messenger, 'before long you will see King Arthur and all his forces.'

'In God's name,' said Ector, 'it is a pity they are coming, because they will repent it.'

When Lancelot heard this news, he took a messenger and sent him to the kingdom of Benwick and to the kingdom of Gaunes, ordering his barons to stock their fortresses with provisions, so that, if it happened that he had to leave Great Britain and return to the kingdom of Gaunes, he would find the castles strong and defensible to hold out against King Arthur. Then he summoned all the knights he had served in Sorelois and in foreign lands, to help him against King Arthur. Because he was so highly regarded everywhere, so many men came that if Lancelot had been a king with a territory of his own, most people would not have thought it possible that he could have assembled such a great number of knights as he did on that occasion.

On the day King Arthur had summoned his men to Camelot, they came in such great numbers on foot and on horseback that no man had ever seen such an army. Sir Gawain, who had been ill, was now better, and on the day they assembled there, he said to the king: 'My lord, before you set out, I suggest that out of these barons here you choose as many good knights as were killed the other day when the queen was rescued, and that you promote them to the Round Table in place of those who died, so that we have the same number of knights as before, that is a hundred and fifty. I can tell you that if you do this your company will be more worthy in all ways and will be feared more.'

The king was quite in agreement with what he suggested, and commanded that it should be done, as nothing but good could come of it. Then straight away he called the high-ranking barons and ordered them on the oaths they had sworn him to elect as many of the best knights as were necessary to complete the Round Table, and that they should not refuse anyone for reasons of poverty. They said they would be pleased to do this.

So they drew apart and sat down in the main hall of the palace. They counted how many were missing from the Round Table, and found that the number was seventy-two. Therefore they straight away elected that number and installed them in the seats of those who had died, or had been with Lancelot. But no one was so bold as to sit in the Perilous Seat. The knight who sat at Lancelot's place was called Elianz; he was the finest knight in the whole of Ireland and a king's son. In Bors' seat sat a knight called Balynor, the son of the king of the Strange Isles; he was a very fine knight. Ector's seat was occupied by a Scottish knight, powerful in arms and in the number of his friends; Gaheris's place was taken by a knight who was the nephew of the king of North Wales.

When they had done this on the recommendation of Sir Gawain, the tables were set and they all sat down. That day, seven kings who held fiefs from Arthur and were his liege men served at the Round Table and at the king's table. Then the knights who were to set out for the war prepared their departure, and worked well into the night before they were completely ready.

In the morning, before sunrise, many thousands of men left Camelot, intent on harming Lancelot. As soon as King Arthur had heard Mass in Camelot Cathedral, he mounted with his barons, and they rode until they came to a castle called Lamborc. The next day they travelled as far as they had done the first day; and they rode day after day until they came to within half a league of the Joyous Gard. Because they saw the castle was so strong that it was in no danger from attack, they camped in tents beside the river Humber; but this was a long way from the castle. All that day they saw to settling the camp; they had stationed armed knights in front of them so that, if the people in the castle came out to fight, they would be as well received as one should receive one's enemy. That was how they camped.

However, their adversaries, who had foresight, had sent a great number of men the night before into a nearby forest, to surprise Arthur's army when the occasion arose, and rush out and attack them in front of the castle. Therefore the people in the castle were not at all dismayed when they saw the siege begin, but said to one another that they would leave the enemy in peace for the first night and attack them the next day, if they saw an opportunity. The group of men sent into the forest consisted of forty knights, led by Bors and Ector. The people in the castle had told them that when they saw a red flag raised above the fortress, they were to make a frontal attack on King Arthur's men; those who had remained in the castle would make a sortie at the same moment, so that Arthur's men would be assailed on two sides.

All day the men in the wood kept a look-out on the castle in case they should see the red flag which was their sign to attack, but they did not see it because Lancelot could not allow Arthur's army to be attacked on the first day. Instead he let them rest all day and all night, so that there was no fighting at all. As a result, Arthur's men felt more confident than before, and said among themselves that if Lancelot had had large forces, nothing would have stopped him from coming out to attack them and the whole army, because no true knight would willingly suffer injury from his enemy.

When Lancelot saw how the castle was besieged by King Arthur, the man he had most loved in the world and whom he now knew to be his mortal enemy, he was so saddened that he did not know what to do, not because he feared for himself but because he loved the king. He called a girl, took her into a room, and said to her in secret: 'Go to King Arthur and tell him from me that I cannot understand why he is waging war on me, because I did not imagine I had wronged him so much. If he says it is because of my lady the queen whom he has been led to believe I have dishonoured, tell him I am ready to prove I am not truly guilty of that wrong, by fighting one of the best knights in his court. Moreover, for his love, and to regain his goodwill which I have lost through unfortunate circumstances, I shall put myself under the jurisdiction of his court.'

The book says that the girl made her way to Arthur; but the king refused to countenance any agreement with Lancelot, and insisted on continuing the war. However, the Pope heard of the war, and sent the bishop of Rochester to excommunicate Arthur, because Guinevere's crime had never been proven in a court; the bishop was ordered to make the king take her back and live with her in peace. And Arthur agreed to take her back; but because of Gawain's hatred of Lancelot, he would not agree to end his war with Lancelot. The bishop took this message to Guinevere; and the queen declared in Lancelot's presence that she would return to the king, in the hope that Arthur would forgive Lancelot, or at least allow him to leave Logres unharmed.

'My lady,' said Lancelot, 'if you acted as my heart desired, you would stay; nevertheless, because I want things to work out more to your honour than to my desires, you must return to your lord, King Arthur. Because, if you do not go now, after this offer he has made you, there is no one who would not openly recognise your shame and my great disloyalty. For this reason I want you to send a message to the king saying that you will return tomorrow. I can tell you that when you leave me, you will be so splendidly escorted that never will a high-born lady have been treated so well. I am not saying this, my lady, because I love you more than a knight has ever loved a lady during our lifetimes, but for your honour.'

Then the tears came to his eyes, and the queen also began to cry. When Bors heard that Lancelot was allowing the queen to return to King Arthur, he said: 'My lord, you have agreed this very lightly; may God grant that good may come of it. I certainly think you may never done anything that you will repent so much. You will go to Gaul and my lady the queen will stay in this country, and circumstances will prevent your ever seeing her again at any time. I know your heart so well, and also the great desire you have for her, that I am quite sure that before a month has passed, you would rather have given away the whole world, if it had been yours, instead of granting this. I am afraid you may suffer far more from it than you think.'

When Bors had said this, the other two agreed with him, and began to criticize Lancelot, saying: 'My lord, what fear do you have of the king that you should return my lady to him?'

But he said that he would send her back, whatever was to come of it, even if he was to die through missing her so much. Thus the conversation ended, when they heard Lancelot say that nothing would prevent him from sending the queen back. She returned to the bishop who was waiting for her in the middle of the hall and said: 'My lord, now you may go to my lord the king; greet him from me and tell him that I shall never leave here unless he allows Lancelot to depart without suffering the slightest loss either to his possessions or to his retinue.'

When the bishop heard her say this, he thanked God sincerely, because he could see that the war was over. He commended the queen to God, and everyone in the palace as well, and then he went down from the castle and rode right up to the king's tent. He told him the news he had heard in the castle.

Hearing that they were ready to send the queen back, the king said, in front of all those present: 'By God, if it were true about Lancelot and the queen as I was led to understand, he is not in such a bad position in this war that he would give her up for months, if he loved her adulterously. Because he has carried out my wishes so courteously in what I have asked him, I shall do all that the queen has requested. I shall allow him to leave this country and if he comes across anyone who does him the slightest harm, I shall repay him twofold.'

Then he commanded the bishop to go back to the castle and tell the queen in the name of the king that Lancelot might safely leave the country, and because he had so courteously agreed to his request, the king would even lend him part of his own navy to cross over to Gaul.

The bishop mounted at once, went back to the castle, and told the queen what the king had commanded. Thus the matter was agreed on both sides that the queen would be returned to her lord the next day, and that Lancelot would leave the kingdom of Logres and go with his company to the kingdom of Gaunes, of which they were the lawful lords.

That night the men in the army were happy, and joyful when they saw the war was over, because most of them feared that they would get the worst of it if it lasted much longer. And if they were much happier and more joyful than they had generally been, the men in the castle were tearful and sad, the poor as well as the rich. Do you know why they were so sad? Because they saw that Bors, Lancelot, Ector and Lionel were grieving as much as if they could see the whole world lying dead before them.

GUINEVERE IS RETURNED TO ARTHUR, AND LANCELOT IS BANISHED

That night there was great sadness at the Joyous Gard, and when day broke, Lancelot said to the queen: 'My lady, today is the day you will leave me, and the day I must leave this country. I do not know if I shall ever see you again. Here is a ring you gave me long ago when I first became acquainted with you, and which I have always kept up till now for love of you. Now I beg you always to wear it for love of me as long as you live; I shall take the one you are wearing on your finger.'

She willingly gave it to him. Thereupon they ended their conversation, and went to prepare themselves as splendidly as they could.

That day the four cousins were richly dressed. When they had mounted with all the other men in the castle, they rode to the army under a safe conduct with more than five hundred horses all covered in silk. They went along jousting and showing the greatest joy that you could ever have seen.

The king came to meet them with a large number of knights, and when the moment came that Lancelot saw the king approaching him, he dismounted and took the queen by the reins of her horse, and said to the king: 'My lord, here is the queen, whom I am returning to you. She would have died some time ago through the disloyalty of those in your household, if I had not risked my life to save her. I did not do it because of any kindness I have ever had from her, but only because I know her to be the worthiest lady in the world; and it would have been too great a shame and too grievous a loss if the disloyal men in your household who had sentenced her to death had carried out their intentions. It was better for them to die as a result of their disloyalty than that she should be killed.'

Then the king received her, very miserable and pensive after what Lancelot had said to him.

'My lord,' said Lancelot, 'if I loved the queen adulterously as you have been led to understand, I should not have handed her back to you for months, and you would never have had her through using force.'

'Lancelot,' said the king, 'I am very grateful to you for what you have done; it may stand you in good stead some time in the future.'

Then Sir Gawain came forward and said to Lancelot: 'The king is grateful to you for what you have done. But he requests one more thing of you yet.'

'What, my lord?' asked Lancelot.

'Tell me and I shall do it, if I can.'

'He requests you,' said Sir Gawain, 'to leave his country and never to set foot here again.'

'My lord,' said Lancelot to the king, 'is that what you wish me to do?'

'Because that is what Gawain desires,' said the king, 'it is what I want too. Leave my land on this side of the sea and go across to your very beautiful and rich country.'

'My lord,' said Lancelot, 'when I am in my country, shall I be safe from you? What can I expect from you, peace or war?'

'You can be sure,' said Sir Gawain, 'that you will not be safe from war, because you will have it more violently than you have had it up till now, and it will last until my brother Gaheris, whom you killed wickedly, is avenged by your own death. Moreover I should not take the whole world in exchange for the chance to cut off your head.'

'Sir Gawain,' said Bors, 'stop threatening now, because I can tell you truly that my lord does not fear you. If you go so far as to come after us to the kingdom of Gaunes or to the kingdom of Banoic, you can be sure of being nearer to losing your head than my lord is. You have said that my lord killed your brother treacherously. If you would like to prove this as an honourable knight, I should defend my lord against you, so that if I were defeated, Sir Lancelot would be dishonoured, while if I could get the better of you, you would be in the bad position of being a false accuser. And the war would thus be ended. Indeed, if you agreed, it would be much better for this quarrel to be settled by you and me than by forty thousand men.'

Sir Gawain threw down his gage and said to the king: 'My lord, since he has offered to fight, he will not be able to retract, because I am ready to prove against him that Lancelot killed my brother Gaheris treacherously.'

Bors jumped up and said he was ready to defend himself; and the battle would have been sworn if the king had wanted it, because Sir Gawain desired nothing else, and Bors wished to fight in single combat against him. But the king refused gages from both of them and said he would not allow the battle; however, he said that when they had gone their ways each would have to look after himself, and Lancelot could be sure that as soon as he was back in his country he would find himself in a greater war than he could imagine.

'Indeed, my lord,' said Lancelot, 'you would not be in such a favourable position to continue the war as you are now, if I had done as much to harm you as I did to help you the day that Galahaut, the Lord of the Distant Isles, became your liege man at the very moment when he had the power to strip you of lands and honour, and when you were very close to receiving the humiliation of losing your crown and being deprived of your birth-right. If you remembered that day as you should, you certainly would not be involved in waging this war against me. I am not saying this, my lord, because I fear you, but because of the love you ought to feel for me if you were as grateful for good deeds done for you as a king should be. Indeed, as soon as we are back in our own country with our liegemen, and we have summoned our forces and our friends and provisioned our castles and fortresses, I assure you that if you come and we do all we can to harm you, you will never have done anything that you repent as much as this, because, I can tell you, it will never bring you any honour. You, Sir Gawain, who are so cruelly causing bitterness between us and the king, you certainly should not be doing that, because if you remembered that I once freed you from the Dolorous Tower on the day I killed Caradoc the Great, and released you from his prison where he had left you as if to die, you would not feel any hatred for me.'

'Lancelot,' replied Sir Gawain, 'there is nothing you have done for me that recently you have not made me pay for very dearly; because you have so grievously taken away from me those I loved most, that our lineage has been quite abased, and I am shamed. For this reason there cannot be peace between us, and there never will be for as long as I live.'

Then Lancelot said to the king: 'My lord, I shall leave your territory tomorrow and for all the services I have rendered you since I first became a knight, I shall take away nothing in reward.'

Thereupon the conversation ended, and the king went back to his tents and took the queen with him. Then there was as much joy among them as if God Himself had descended there. But unlike the men in the army, who were joyful and happy, the men in the castle were miserable, because they were distressed at seeing their lord more pensive than he usually was.

When Lancelot had dismounted, he commanded all his retinue to prepare their equipment, because he was planning to leave for the coast the next day, and to cross the sea to Gaunes. The same day, he called a squire named Kanahin and said to him: 'Take my shield from that room and go straight to Camelot; carry it to St Stephen's Cathedral and leave it in a place where it can remain and be seen, so that everyone who sees it in the future will remember my adventures in this country. Do you know why I am paying that place such an honour? It is because I first received the order of chivalry there, and I love that city more than any other; and also because I want my shield to be there to compensate for my absence, as I do not know if it will ever happen that I shall return there, once I have left this country.'

The boy took the shield and together with it Lancelot gave four pack-horses loaded with riches, so that the churchmen could always pray for him, and improve the building. When the people carrying these gifts arrived in Camelot, they were welcomed with great joy. The churchpeople were no less glad at receiving Lancelot's shield than his other gifts; they immediately had it hung up in the middle of the cathedral on a silver chain, and honoured it as if it had been a holy relic.

And the story tells that when Lancelot arrived in Gaunes, Gawain persuaded Arthur to continue the war against him by assembling an army to follow him across the Channel. The king did as his nephew wished, leaving Mordred as regent. The siege lasted for a long time, and Lancelot and Gawain fought in single combat; Gawain was severely wounded, but eventually recovered, and still swore to have his revenge.

THE TREACHERY OF MORDRED

When Sir Mordred had been appointed regent of all England, and King Arthur had been overseas for a long time. Mordred had letters written as though that they came from overseas, and the letters specified that King Arthur had been killed in battle with Sir Lancelot. So Sir Mordred held a parliament, and called the lords together, and made them choose him as king; and he was crowned at Canterbury, and held a feast there for fifteen days. Afterwards he went to Winchester, and captured Queen Guinevere, and said plainly that he would wed her even though she was his uncle's wife and his father's wife. And so he named a day when they were to be wedded; at which Queen Guinevere was greatly grieved. But she did not dare to say what she thought, but pretended to agree to Sir Mordred's wishes. She asked Sir Mordred to let her go to London, to buy all kinds of things for the wedding. And Mordred trusted her well enough, and gave her leave to go. And when she came to London she took the Tower of London, and in all haste possible she filled it with every kind of provisions, and garrisoned it with men she could trust, and held it in defiance of him.

When Sir Mordred realised how he had been deceived, he was extremely angry. In short, he went and laid a mighty siege about the Tower of London, and made many great assaults on it; he bombarded it with many great engines, and shot great guns. But none of this helped Sir Mordred, for Queen Guinevere would never, neither for fair speech nor foul, trust herself in his hands again.

Then the bishop of Canterbury said to Sir Mordred : 'Sir, what are you doing? This displeases God and puts shame on you and all knighthood. Is not King Arthur your uncle, your mother's brother, and your father as well; how can you wed your father's wife? Leave this idea alone or I shall curse you with book and bell and candle.'

'Do your worst,' said Sir Mordred, 'I shall defy you.'

'Sir,' said the bishop, 'I am not afraid of doing my duty. And you have also spread the word that my lord Arthur has been killed, which is not true, and you are a traitor.'

'Peace, you false priest,' said Sir Mordred, 'for if you anger me any more I shall strike off your head.' So the bishop departed and did the cursing with the greatest pomp and solemnity. Sir Mordred sought the bishop of Canterbury in order to kill him and the bishop fled, and took part of his goods with him, and went to a place near Glastonbury. There he lived as a priest hermit in a chapel, in poverty and in holy prayers; for he foresaw that a fearful war was at hand.

Sir Mordred sent letters to Queen Guinevere to get her by fair means or foul to come out of the Tower of London; but she replied that she had rather kill herself than be married to him. News came to Sir Mordred that King Arthur had raised the siege of Sir Lancelot's castle, and he was coming home with a great army, to take his revenge on Sir Mordred; so Sir Mordred sent writs to all the barons of this land, and many people supported him. For the general opinion among them was that with Arthur there was always war and strife, but with Sir Mordred there would be peace and joy. Thus was King Arthur defamed, and evil things were said of him. And many of these men had been raised by King Arthur from nothing, and given lands; but they could not say a good word for him. Look, all you Englishmen, do you not see what mischief was done here! Arthur was the greatest king and knight in the world, and most loved the fellowship of noble knights, and supported such men; but these Englishmen could not be content with him. And this was always how things went in this country; and men say that we have not yet lost nor forgotten that custom. It is a great fault of us Englishmen; nothing pleases us for long.

Sir Mordred went with a great host to Dover, for he had heard that Arthur would land there, with the intention of driving his own father from his lands; and the greater part of England supported Sir Mordred, because the people were so eager for novelty.

And when Sir Mordred was at Dover with his host, King Arthur came with a great navy of ships, and galleys, and carracks. Sir Mordred was ready and waiting to prevent his own father from landing in the country of which he was king. They launched boats, both large and small, full of noble men of arms; and there was much slaughter of gentle knights on both sides. But King Arthur was so courageous, and his knights followed him so fiercely, that they landed despite Sir Mordred and all his men, and put him and his army to flight.

When the battle was over, King Arthur had those who had died on his side buried. And Sir Gawain was found in a great boat, lying more than half dead. When Arthur learned that Sir Gawain was laid so low, he went to him; and there the king grieved beyond measure, and took Sir Gawain in his arms, and he fainted there three times. And when he recovered he said: 'Alas, Sir Gawain, my sister's son, you are the man in the world that I loved most; you and Lancelot were the two men who gave me joy, and now all the joy I had in this world is gone.'

'My uncle, King Arthur,' said Sir Gawain, 'I am certain my death-day has come, and it is all through my own haste and wilfulness; for I have been struck on the old wound which Sir Lancelot gave me, and that will be fatal. If Sir Lancelot and you had not quarrelled, this unhappy war would never have begun; and of all this I am the cause, for I would not make peace with him. I beg you that I may have paper, pen, and ink, so that I may write to Sir Lancelot in my own hand.'

When paper and ink was brought, Gawain sat up, weak as he was, supported by King Arthur, for he had been confessed a little while before; and this is what he wrote: 'To Sir Lancelot, flower of all noble knights that I ever heard of or saw in all my days, I, Sir Gawain, King Lot's son of Orkney, sister's son to the noble King Arthur, send you greeting, and let you know that on the tenth day of May I was struck on the old wound that you gave me outside the city of Benwick; and through the same wound that you gave me I have come to my death-day. And I want all the world to know that I, Sir Gawain, knight of the Table Round, sought my death, and that it was not your fault; so I beseech you, Sir Lancelot, to return to this kingdom, and see my tomb, and pray some prayer for my soul. And the very day that I wrote this letter, I was hurt to the death in the same wound that I had of your hand, Sir Lancelot; and I could not have been killed by a nobler man. And, Sir Lancelot, for all the love that was ever between us, do not delay, but cross the sea in all haste, so that you and your knights can rescue Arthur, the noble king who made you knight; for he is hard pressed by a false traitor, my half-brother, Sir Mordred. He has had himself crowned king, and would have wedded my lady Queen Guinevere, and would have done so if she had not shut herself in the Tower of London. And so the tenth day of May last, my lord Arthur and all of us landed and fought them at Dover; and we put that false traitor, Sir Mordred, to flight, but it was my misfortune to be struck upon the wound you gave me. And this letter was written only two and a half hours before my death, written with my own hand, and signed in my heart's blood. And I request and require you, most famous knight of the world, to see my tomb.'

And then Sir Gawain wept, and King Arthur wept; and then they both fainted. And when they both awoke, the king had Sir Gawain given the last rites. And then Sir Gawain begged the king to send for Sir Lancelot, and to cherish him above all other knights. And so at the hour of noon Sir Gawain yielded up the spirit; and then the king had him buried in a chapel in Dover Castle; and there all men may see his skull with the wound that Sir Lancelot gave him in battle.

Then the king was told that Sir Mordred had encamped at Barham Down. And the next day the king rode against him, and there was a great battle between them, and many were slain on both sides; but in the end Arthur's men held the field, and Sir Mordred and his forces fled to Canterbury.

THE LAST BATTLE IN THE WEST

And then the king had all the towns searched for those of his knights who had been killed, and he buried them; and he had the wounded tended to with the best remedies available. And many people joined King Arthur, saying that Sir Mordred had wrongfully made war on him. And then King Arthur marched with his host along the coast, westward towards Salisbury; and there was a day agreed between King Arthur and Sir Mordred, when they should meet on the downs near Salisbury, not far from the seaside; and the date agreed was the Monday after Trinity Sunday. Sir Mordred raised many troops around London, for those of Kent, Sussex, Surrey, Essex, Suffolk, and Norfolk mostly supported Sir Mordred, as did those who loved Sir Lancelot.

So on the night before Trinity Sunday, King Arthur dreamed a wonderful dream, and this was his dream: he seemed to be sitting in a chair made fast to a wheel, in the richest cloth of gold; and the king thought there was, far below him, hideous deep black water in which were all kinds of serpents, and worms, and wild beasts, foul and horrible. Suddenly the wheel turned upside-down, and he fell among the serpents, and every beast took him by a limb; and then the king cried as he slept: 'Help!' And then his squires awoke the king; he was so stunned that he did not know where he was and then dozed off, neither sleeping nor properly awake. It seemed to the king that Sir Gawain came to him with a number of beautiful ladies. And when King Arthur saw him, he said: 'Welcome, my sister's son; I thought you were dead, and now I see you alive.'

'Sir,' said Sir Gawain, 'God has given me leave to warn you of your death; for if you fight tomorrow with Sir Mordred as you have agreed, you and most of the men on both sides will be killed. And God has sent me to you of His special grace, to give you warning that in no way are you to fight tomorrow; you shall make a truce for a month and a day; and offer him generous terms. For within a month Sir Lancelot with all his noble knights will come, and rescue you honourably, and kill Sir Mordred, and all his followers.' Then Sir Gawain vanished.

And the king called his knights, squires, and yeomen, and ordered to fetch his noble lords and wise bishops unto him. And when they were come, the king told them his vision and what Sir Gawain had told him; and how he had warned him that if he fought on the next day he would be killed. Then the king ordered Sir Lucan the Butler, and his brother Sir Bedivere, with two bishops with them, to make a truce for a month and a day with Sir Mordred, and to offer him whatever lands and goods they thought necessary. So they went to Sir Mordred, and found him with his grim host of a hundred thousand men. They talked with Sir Mordred for a long time; in the end it was agreed that Sir Mordred should have Cornwall and Kent, during Arthur's life, and after that the whole of England, when he was dead.

And it was agreed that King Arthur and Sir Mordred should meet between both the armies, and each of them should bring fourteen men; and they came to report this to Arthur. And when Arthur was about to go to meet Mordred, he warned all his army that if they saw a sword drawn, they were to attack fiercely, and kill that traitor, Sir Mordred, 'for I do not trust him in the least'. In the same way Sir Mordred warned his that if they saw a sword drawn, 'attack fiercely, for I do not trust this treaty, and am sure my father will be revenged on me.'

And so they met as they had arranged, and everything was agreed; and wine was fetched, and they drank. But an adder came out of a little bush on the heath, and it stung a knight on the foot. And when the knight felt that he had been stung, he looked down and saw the adder, and drew his sword to kill the adder, meaning no harm. And when the two armies saw that sword drawn, they blew their trumpets and horns, and shouted fearsomely. And so the two armies met. And King Arthur mounted his horse, and said: 'Alas, this unhappy day!' and rode to join his troops; and Sir Mordred did likewise. And a grimmer battle was never seen in Christian lands; but King Arthur rode through Sir Mordred's men many times, and did everything a noble king should; and Sir Mordred pressed him hard and put him in great danger. And thus they fought all day long, until it was nearly night; and by then a hundred thousand were laid dead upon the down. Then Arthur was mad with rage when he saw all his men killed.

Then the king looked round and saw that of all his army and of all his good knights, no more than two knights were left alive, Sir Lucan the Butler, and his brother Sir Bedivere; and they were badly wounded.

'Where are all my noble knights?' said the king. 'Alas that I should ever see this saddest of days, for I too have come to my end. But would to God I knew where that traitor Sir Mordred was, who has caused all this mischief.'

Then King Arthur saw Sir Mordred leaning on his sword among a great heap of dead men.

'Now give me my spear,' said Arthur to Sir Lucan, 'for over there is the traitor who has caused all this anguish.'

'Sir, let him be, said Sir Lucan, 'for he is unhappy; and if you survive this unhappy day you will be well revenged on him. Remember your night's dream, and what the spirit of Sir Gawain told you last night; yet God of his great goodness has preserved you until now. Therefore, for God's sake, my lord, leave this, for you have won the field; for there are three of us alive, and no one save Sir Mordred of the enemy. If you leave off now this wicked day of destiny is past.'

'Give me death, give me life,' said the king, 'now I see him alone over there, he shall never escape me, for I shall never have a better chance.'

Then the king took his spear in both his hands, and ran toward Sir Mordred, crying: 'Traitor, now is your death-day come.'

And when Sir Mordred heard Arthur, he ran to him with his sword drawn. And King Arthur struck Sir Mordred under the shield with his spear, so that more than six feet went through his body. And when Sir Mordred felt that he had his death wound he thrust himself with his remaining strength up to the guard of King Arthur's spear. And he struck his father Arthur, with his sword held in both his hands, on the side of the head, piercing the helmet and the brainpan; at which Sir Mordred fell stone dead to the ground. Arthur fell unconscious to the ground, and Sir Lucan the Butler and Sir Bedivere led him, weak as they were, between the two of them, to a little chapel not far from the seaside. And when the king was there he felt more comfortable.

ARTHUR IS BORNE TO AVALON

Then they heard men shouting on the battlefield. 'Sir Lucan,' said the king, 'go and tell what that noise on the battlefield means.'

So Sir Lucan went as best he could, for he was grievously wounded in many places. And he saw by moonlight that robbers had come to strip the knights of many a good ring and of many a rich jewel; and those who were not dead, they killed for their armour and their riches. When Sir Lucan realised what was happening, he came to the king, and told him what he had heard and seen. 'So it would be best,' said Sir Lucan, 'if we could bring you to some town.'

'I wish it could be done,' said the king. 'But I cannot stand, my head works so.'

'Ah, Sir Lancelot,' said King Arthur, 'I have missed you sorely today: alas, that I ever fought against you, for now I go to my death, as Sir Gawain warned me in my dream.'

Then Sir Lucan picked up the king on one side, and Sir Bedivere on the other, and as they lifted him the king fainted; and Sir Lucan fainted with the effort, and part of his guts fell out of his body, and his heart failed him. And when the king awoke, he saw Sir Lucan, lying foaming at the mouth, with part of his guts at his feet. 'Alas,' said the king, 'he died for my sake, trying to help me when he had more need of help than I. He would not complain, his heart was so set on helping me: now Jesus have mercy upon his soul!'

Then Sir Bedivere wept for the death of his brother. 'Now is not the time for mourning and weeping,' said the king, 'if I might live, the death of Sir Lucan would grieve me for evermore; but my time is short, so take Excalibur, my good sword, and go with it to the water's edge, and throw my sword into the water, and come again and tell me what you have seen.'

'My lord,' said Bedivere, 'I will do as you say, and tell you what happens.'

So Sir Bedivere left the king, and as he went he looked at that noble sword, whose pommel and haft was all of precious stones; and he said to himself: 'If I throw this rich sword in the water, no good will ever come of it, but only harm and loss.'

And then Sir Bedivere hid Excalibur under a tree, and came quickly back to the king, and said he had been to the water's edge and had thrown the sword in the water.

'What did you see there?' said the king.

'Sir,' he said, 'I saw nothing but waves and winds.'

'That is not the truth,' said the king, 'go back and do as I have ordered; by our friendship, do not hesitate but throw it in.'

Then Sir Bedivere went once more, and took the sword in his hand; and he thought it was a sin and shame to throw away that noble sword. So he hid the sword, and returned, and told the king that he had been to the water's edge, and done as he ordered.

'What did you see there?' said the king.

'Sir,' he said, 'I saw nothing but the wind on the waters and the white waves.'

'Ah, disloyal traitor,' said King Arthur, 'you have betrayed me twice. Who would have thought that you who are so dear to me would betray me for the richness of the sword. But now go again in haste, for your long delay puts me in danger of my life, for I have caught cold. And unless you do as I say, I shall kill you with my own hands if I see you again; for you would have me dead for the sake of my sword.'

Then Sir Bedivere left him, and found the sword, and went to the water side; and he bound the girdle round the hilt, and threw the sword as far into the water as he could; and an arm and a hand came up out of the water and caught it, and brandished it three times; and then hand and sword vanished into the water. So Sir Bedivere came back to the king, and told him what he saw.

'Help me from here,' said the king, 'for I am afraid I have delayed too long.'

Then Sir Bedivere took the king on his back, and carried him to the water's edge. And when they reached the bank, a little barge with many fair ladies in it came into sight, and among them was a queen; they all had black hoods, and wept and shrieked when they saw King Arthur.

'Now put me into the barge,' said the king. And so he did softly; and three queens received him with great mourning; they sat down, and King Arthur laid his head in one of their laps. And then the queen said: 'Ah, dear brother, why have you stayed so long? Alas, this wound on your head has grown cold.'

And so then they rowed from the land, and Sir Bedivere watched all those ladies as they left him alone on the bank. Then Sir Bedivere cried: 'Ah my lord Arthur, what shall become of me, now that you leave me here alone among my enemies?'

'Comfort yourself,' said the king, 'and do the best you can, for I can be no help to you; for I will go into the vale of Avalon to be healed of my grievous wound: and if you never hear of me again, pray for my soul.'

And the queens and ladies wept and shrieked pitifully. As soon as Sir Bedivere had lost the sight of the barge, he wept, and went his way into the forest where he walked all that night. In the morning he was aware of a chapel and an hermitage in a clearing between two ancient woods.

Sir Bedivere went into the chapel, and saw a hermit stretched out on the ground in prayer, next to a newly cut tombstone. When the hermit saw Sir Bedivere he recognised him, for he had been bishop of Canterbury, until Sir Mordred forced him to flee.

'Sir,' said Bedivere, 'what man is buried there for whom you pray so fervently?'

'My son,' said the hermit, 'I cannot say for sure, but I think that I know. Only last night, at midnight, there came a number of ladies, and brought a dead man, and prayed that I would bury him; and they made an offering of an hundred tapers, and gave me a hundred gold coins.'

'Alas,' said Sir Bedivere, 'that is my lord King Arthur, who lies buried here in this chapel.'

Then Sir Bedivere fainted; and when he recovered he asked the hermit if he might stay with him, to live in fasting and prayers. 'For I never wish to leave here,' said Sir Bedivere, 'but will spend all the days of my life here praying for my lord Arthur.'

'You are welcome,' said the hermit, 'for I know you better than you think: you are the bold Bedivere, and Sir Lucan the Butler was your brother.'

Then Sir Bedivere told the hermit all that had happened, and he lived there with the hermit, putting on poor clothes, and humbly serving him in fasting and in prayers.

And of Arthur I find nothing more written in the true accounts of his life, nor did I ever read of the certainty of his death. All that the books say is that he was taken away in a ship in which were three queens; one was King Arthur's sister, Queen Morgan le Fay; the second was the Queen of North Wales; the third was the Queen of the Waste Lands. And Nimue, the Lady of the Lake, who had done much for King Arthur, was also there. More of the death of King Arthur I could never find, except that ladies brought him to be buried; and the hermit who was once bishop of Canterbury bore witness that a man brought by ladies was buried there. Nonetheless the hermit did not know for certain that it was indeed the body of King Arthur.

Yet men say in many parts of England that King Arthur is not dead, but conveyed by the will of Our Lord Jesus into another place; and men say that he will come again, and he will win back the Holy Cross from the heathen. I will not say it shall be so, but rather this: here in this world he changed his life. But many men say that there is written upon his tomb this verse in Latin: *Here lies the once and future king.*

EPILOGUE: LANCELOT AND GUINEVERE

So I leave Sir Bedivere with the hermit, living in a chapel beside Glastonbury, in their prayers, and fastings, and great abstinence. And when Queen Guinevere learned that King Arthur was dead, and all the noble knights, Sir Mordred and all the others, she went in secret with five ladies to Amesbury; and there she became a nun, and wore white clothes and black; and she did as great penance as any sinful lady in this land. No-one could make her cheerful; she lived in fasting, prayers, and giving alms, so that everyone marvelled at her change from worldly affairs to the ways of virtue. And there she was abbess and ruler, as was fitting.

And when Lancelot heard that Sir Mordred was crowned king in England, and made war against King Arthur, his own father, he was mad with rage and said to his kinsmen: 'I am deeply sorry that that double traitor Mordred ever escaped my hands, for he has done much harm to my lord Arthur; for from the doleful letter that my lord Sir Gawain sent me, I am sure that King Arthur is hard pressed. And Gawain's words in his letter will never go from my heart, for he was as noble a knight as ever was born; and I was born in an unlucky hour, to kill Sir Gawain, Sir Gaheris, and my own friend Sir Gareth.'

'Leave your complaints,' said Sir Bors, 'and first revenge yourself for the death of Sir Gawain; pray at Sir Gawain's tomb, and then revenge my lord Arthur, and my lady Queen Guinevere.'

And they prepared ships and galleys as quickly as they could for Sir Lancelot and his army to cross into England. And he came to Dover, where he landed with seven kings, and the number of his army was hideous to behold. There Sir Lancelot asked the men of Dover what had become of King Arthur: and the people told him how he was killed, and that Sir Mordred and a hundred thousand men died in one day.

'Alas,' said Sir Lancelot, 'this is the most grievous news that I ever heard. Now show me the tomb of Sir Gawain.'

And at the tomb Sir Lancelot knelt down and wept, and prayed heartily for his soul. And that night he held a wake and made offerings for his soul; all those who came had as much flesh, fish, wine and ale as they desired, and every man and woman had twelve pence. Sir Lancelot himself gave out this money, in a mourning-gown, weeping and asking them to pray for the soul of Sir Gawain. And the next day all the priests and clergy who could be found sang a Mass of requiem; after which Sir Lancelot lay two nights on his tomb in prayers and weeping.

Then on the third day Sir Lancelot summoned the kings, dukes, earls, barons, and knights.

'My fair lords,' he said, 'I thank you all for coming into this country with me, but we came too late, and that will grieve me as long as I live, but no man can gainsay death. I myself will ride in search of my lady, Queen Guinevere, for I am told she has had great pain and discomfort and has fled into the west. Wait for me here; but if I do not come again within fifteen days, take your ships and your men, and sail to your own lands.'

And then Sir Bors said: 'My lord Sir Lancelot, you will find few friends if you ride alone through this kingdom.'

'Be that as it may,' said Sir Lancelot, 'stay here, for I will set out on my journey, and neither man nor child shall go with me.'

So he departed and rode into the west, and searched there for seven or eight days; and at last he came to a nunnery, and Queen Guinevere saw Sir Lancelot as he walked in the cloister. And when she saw him, she fainted three times, and her ladies could scarcely support here. When she could speak, she called her ladies to her, and said; 'You marvel that I should faint like this, but in truth, it is the sight of that knight who stands over there; so I ask you to call him to me.'

When Sir Lancelot was brought to her, she said to all the ladies: 'Through this man and me has all this war arisen, and the death of the noblest knights in the world; for through our love is my most noble lord slain. Therefore, Sir Lancelot, I can scarcely hope to win the salvation of my soul; and yet I trust through God's grace after my death to have a sight of the blessed face of Christ, and at the day of doom to sit on His right side, for there are saints in heaven who were once as sinful as I. Therefore, Sir Lancelot, I require and beseech you, for all the love that ever was between us, that you never see me again face to face; in God's name, leave my company, and return to your kingdom. Guard your realm from war and ruin; for much as I have loved you, I cannot bear to see you, for through you and me is the flower of kings and knights destroyed. Sir Lancelot, Sir Lancelot, go to your realm, and marry, and live with your wife in joy and bliss. As for me, pray for me to our Lord that I may amend my misspent life.'

'Now, sweet lady,' said Sir Lancelot, 'you ask me to return to my own country, and to wed some other lady? That I shall never do, for I have made promises to you which I shall never break; but your fate shall be my fate: I too will follow that path to please our Lord, and will always pray especially for you.'

'If you will do this,' said the queen, 'keep your promise, for I believe you will turn back to worldly things.'

'Lady, say as you please, but I have never been false to my promise, and God save me from doing other than to forsake the world as you have done. For in the quest of the Holy Grail I would have forsaken the vanities of the world if you had not ruled my heart. And if I had done so I would have surpassed all the knights in that quest save Sir Galahad, my son. And therefore, lady, since you seek perfection, it is only right that I should seek perfection too. For as God is my witness, in you I have had my joy on earth; and if you had now so wished, I would have taken you back to my own kingdom. But you wish otherwise; and I promise you faithfully, I will do penance and pray while my life lasts. So, my own lady, I ask you to kiss me once and never again.'

'No,' said the queen, 'that I will never do; it is time to abstain from such things.'

And so they parted. But there was no man so hard-hearted that he would not have wept to see their grief, as sharp as if they had been stung with spears. And the ladies led the queen to her chamber.

And Sir Lancelot mounted his horse, and rode all that day and all night in a forest, weeping, until he saw a hermitage and a chapel between two cliffs; and then he heard a little bell ringing for Mass, and he alighted, and tied his horse to the gate, and heard Mass. And he that sang Mass was the bishop of Canterbury. Both the bishop and Sir Bedivere knew Sir Lancelot, and they talked after Mass. But when Sir Bedivere had told the whole history, Sir Lancelot's heart almost burst for sorrow. And he knelt, and prayed the bishop to confess him and absolve him. And when this was done, he asked the bishop that he might be his brother. Then the bishop put a habit on Sir Lancelot, and there he served God day and night with prayers and fastings.

And Sir Bors de Ganis made the great army that waited at Dover go home again; and Sir Bors, Sir Ector de Maris, Sir Blamore, Sir Bleoberis, with others of Sir Lancelot's kin, rode the length and breadth of England in search of Sir Lancelot. At last Sir Bors came to the chapel where Lancelot was, and begged the bishop that he too might take the habit. And he lived there in prayers and fasting. And within half a year, Sir Galihud, Sir Galihodin, Sir Blamore, Sir Bleoberis, Sir Villiars, Sir Clarras and Sir Gahalantine all found the hermitage; and when they saw Sir Lancelot's holy way of life, they had no desire to depart, but took the same habit.

And so they lived in great penance for six years; and at the end of this time Sir Lancelot was consecrated priest by the bishop, and for a twelve-month he sang Mass. And all the other knights read the offices, and helped to sing Mass, and rang bells, and did all kinds of manual work. For they saw Sir Lancelot endure such penance, in prayers, and fastings, that he grew thin and pale. But one night, there came a vision to Sir Lancelot, and commanded him to go to Amesbury: 'For when you come there, you will find Queen Guinevere dead. Take your companions with you, fetch you her corpse, and bury her by her husband, the noble King

Arthur.' And this vision appeared to Sir Lancelot three times in one night.

Sir Lancelot rose before daybreak, and told the hermit of his vision. 'Get yourselves ready,' said the hermit, 'and obey the vision.'

Then Sir Lancelot took his eight fellows with him, and they walked from Glastonbury to Amesbury, a little more than thirty miles. And it took them two days to make the journey, for they were weak and feeble from fasting. When Sir Lancelot came into the nunnery at Amesbury, Queen Guinevere had died only half an hour before. And the ladies told Sir Lancelot that Queen Guinevere told them all before she died that Sir Lancelot had been a priest for almost a year, 'And he is coming here as fast as he can to fetch my corpse; and he will bury me beside my lord, King Arthur.'

And in their hearing the queen prayed aloud: 'I beseech Almighty God that I may never see Sir Lancelot again in this world'; and she prayed thus for two days before her death.

Then Sir Lancelot looked on her face; he did not weep greatly, but sighed. And so he fulfilled all the rites and services for the queen himself. And her body was placed on a bier drawn by horses; with a hundred torches always burning around the corpse of the queen, Sir Lancelot with his eight fellows followed the bier, singing and reading many a holy prayer, and frankincense burned in a censer by the corpse.

And when they had come to the chapel the hermit who was once bishop of Canterbury sang the Mass of requiem with great devotion. And then the queen was wrapped in a rich waxed shroud, from the top to the toe, thirty times; and then she was put in a lead coffin, and then in a coffin of marble. And when she was laid in the earth Sir Lancelot fainted, and lay still for a long while until the hermit came and roused him, and said: 'You will displease God with such a display of sorrow.'

'Truly,' said Sir Lancelot, 'I hope I do not displease God, for my sorrow was not, nor is not, for any sinful joy. For when I remember her beauty, and her grace, and the nobility and honour of the king, when I saw his corpse and her corpse so lie together, my heart failed me when I thought how by my sin and my pride they were both laid low, who had no equal among Christian people. At the thought of their kindness and my unkindness, I could bear it no longer.'

And after that Sir Lancelot took little meat or drink, and sickened more and more, and dwindled away. For neither the bishop nor his companions could make him eat, and no one else would have recognised him. Day and night he prayed, and sometimes he slept a broken sleep; he always lay full length on the tomb of King Arthur and Queen Guinevere. Within six weeks Sir Lancelot fell sick, and lay in his bed; and he sent for the bishop

and his faithful companions. Then Sir Lancelot said with a hollow voice :
'Lord bishop, I pray you to give me the rites that every Christian man
should have.'

'You are not yet in need of them,' said the hermit, 'it is care and grief
that ail you, and by the grace of God you will be better in the morning.'

'My lords,' said Sir Lancelot, 'my weary body longs for its grave, and I
know better than I can say that the time is come; so give me my rites.' So
when he had received the sacrament, and all that a Christian man ought to
have, he asked the bishop that his companions would take his body to
Joyous Gard. (Some men say it was Alnwick, and some men say it was
Bamborough.) 'I would rather it were otherwise, but long ago I vowed to
be buried at Joyous Gard, so take me there.'

Then his companions wept bitterly; and in due time they all went to
their beds, for they all slept in one chamber. And so after midnight,
towards daybreak, the bishop began to laugh heartily in his sleep. And all
of them awoke, and came to the bishop, and asked him what was wrong.

'Ah, Jesus have mercy on me,' said the bishop, 'why did you wake me? I
was never in all my life so cheerful and so well at ease.'

'Why so?' said Sir Bors.

'Truly,' said the bishop, 'Sir Lancelot was with me and more angels than
I ever saw men in one day. And I saw the angels lift up Sir Lancelot into
heaven, and the gates of heaven opened before him.'

'It is nothing but an empty dream,' said Sir Bors, 'for I am sure there is
nothing amiss with Sir Lancelot.'

'If you are so sure,' said the bishop, 'go to his bed, and you will see the
truth.'

When Sir Bors and his companions came to Lancelot's bed they found
him stone dead, and he lay as if he were smiling, and the sweetest scent about
him. Then there was grief beyond telling. And the next day the bishop said
his Mass of requiem; and after that, the bishop and all the nine knights put
Sir Lancelot in the same horse-bier that Queen Guinevere was laid in before
she was buried. And they all went together with the body of Sir Lancelot,
day by day, till they came to Joyous Gard; and they always had a hundred
torches burning around him. And there they laid his corpse in the body of
the quire, and sang and read many psalms and prayers over him.

And as they were holding the service, Sir Ector, Lancelot's brother, who
had sought him for seven years, came to Joyous Gard. When he saw the
lights in the quire of Joyous Gard, he dismounted, and came into the
quire. Sir Bors went to Sir Ector, and told him that it was his brother, Sir
Lancelot, who lay there dead; and Sir Ector threw his shield, sword, and
helm from him. And when he saw Sir Lancelot's face, he fell down in a
faint. And when he recovered, he lamented for his brother.

'Ah, Lancelot,' he said, 'you were head of all Christian knights, and I declare that you, Sir Lancelot, who lie there, were never matched by any earthly knight. And you were the most courteous knight who ever bore a shield. And you were the truest friend to your lover who ever bestrode a horse. And you were the truest lover of a sinful man who ever loved woman. And you were the kindest man that ever struck with sword. And you were the finest man who ever came among knights in combat. And you were the meekest man and the gentlest who ever ate in hall among ladies. And you were the sternest knight to your mortal foe who ever put spear in the rest.'

And they wept and grieved without restraint.

So they kept Sir Lancelot's corpse for fifteen days, and then buried it with great devotion. After that they all went with the bishop of Canterbury to his hermitage, where they remained for more than a month. Then Sir Constantine, son of Cador of Cornwall, was chosen king of England. And Constantine sent for the bishop of Canterbury, and he was restored to his bishopric, and left the hermitage: but Sir Bedivere was a hermit there to his life's end. And Sir Bors, Sir Ector, Sir Blamore and Sir Bleoberis went into the Holy Land where Jesus Christ lived and died, as Sir Lancelot commanded them to do, before he left this world. And these four knights fought many battles against the miscreants or Turks. And there they died on a Good Friday for God's sake.

GAWAIN

INTRODUCTION

'Then [in the time of William the Conqueror] in the country of the Welsh which is called Ros [Pembrokeshire] the tomb of Walwen was found, who was nephew to Arthur, his sister's son, and by no means unworthy of him. He ruled in the part of Britain now called Walweitha [Galloway]; he was a soldier of outstanding bravery, but he was driven out of his kingdom by the brother and nephew of Hengest [the Saxon leader], though he killed many of them before he went into exile....' This is Gawain's first appearance in literature, in the *Deeds of the Kings of Britain* by William of Malmesbury, written in 1125. He does not appear in earlier Welsh stories, though it has been argued that he is the same as Gwalchmei, one of the heroes in the Welsh romance of *Culhwch and Olwen*, who is named as Arthur's nephew.

Gawain plays a prominent part in Geoffrey of Monmouth's *History of the Kings of Britain*, because a sister's son had a special relationship with his uncle in Celtic society, and he is therefore shown as Arthur's right-hand man. He retained this prominent place in the historical and supposedly historical versions of Arthur's story down to the fifteenth century; in Malory's *Morte Darthur*, Arthur's support of his quarrel with Lancelot is one of the chief causes of the downfall of the Round Table, and his deathbed letter to Lancelot is one of the most moving passages in the story.

In the French romances, however, he had a much less certain reputation. There are romances in which he is portrayed as a paragon of knightly virtues, but he always has a reputation as a ladykiller, which degenerates into that of a seducer and ultimately rapist in less sympathetic accounts of his exploits. At the other extreme, he achieves the Grail adventure instead of Perceval in the German romance *Diu Krone*. He is an ambivalent figure, and not only in terms of his behaviour and exploits: even in Malory, there are remains of magical powers once ascribed to him, for when he fights Lancelot in single combat, his strength grows greater until the sun is at its zenith, and then gradually fades away.

Unlike Arthur, Tristan, Perceval or Galahad, all of whom have a generally accepted story attached to their names, Gawain's exploits are diffuse, and very much typical of the subject matter of chivalric romance. In the unfinished *Story of the Grail* by Chrétien de Troyes, his adventures alternate with those of Perceval, and he has a parallel quest: Perceval seeks the Grail, Gawain the lance which appears in the same procession as the Grail. Where Perceval is unsophisticated and clumsy in worldly matters, Gawain is courtly and polished, and his great reputation precedes him wherever he goes. This remains the case in the romances which immediately follow Chrétien, but in the second or third decade of the thirteenth century, with the appearance of the religious versions of the Grail story and the single-minded passion of the story of Tristan and Iseult, Gawain is seen as a sinner and inconstant lover: he fails miserably in the quest for the Grail in the great French version of the story, and never has one specific lady attached to his name in the stories about him.

The two stories about Gawain which follow look on the bright side of his reputation. The first, *The Romance of Gawain* (or Walewein, as the Dutch author calls him). This is an adventure story in the best traditions of chivalric tales, beginning with one of the most extraordinary openings in all Arthurian romance: the appearance of a flying chess-set at Arthur's court in the middle of a feast. Gawain sets out in pursuit of it, and it turns out to belong to the appropriately named king Wonder. For we are in the midst of marvels: in quick succession we meet a magic healing bed, a sword which attacks unworthy knights who try to handle it, and a talking fox. With the latter, we are almost in the realm of folklore, and the whole story has a directness about it which is at odds with the supposed sophistication of its subject. It is excellent entertainment, with no great moral purpose: beside the adventures there are the detailed descriptions of impossibly heroic duels beloved of knightly audiences. (The author makes Gawain an expert in the tending of wounds, particularly his own - a very necessary skill.) The story moves rapidly forward, with none of the breathing-spaces for expression of the characters' emotions beloved of Chrétien de Troyes. Many of the adventures are found in other romances in which Gawain figures, but elsewhere he always belongs to the supporting cast. It is only here, among all the French and German romances, that he really comes into his own as a hero; the result is a kind of anthology of his typical deeds, vivid, imaginative, and all thoroughly enjoyable.

With *Sir Gawain and the Green Knight* we are on very different territory. There is one central marvel, the awesome figure of the Green Knight who allows Gawain to behead him at the opening of the poem on condition that Gawain accepts the return blow a year and a day later. He is an interloper into an entirely realistic world, and Gawain's adventures require no other suspension of disbelief. This poem, by an unknown hand, is the supreme achievement of medieval English Arthurian poetry, on a par with Malory's prose version of the stories. Only one copy survives, which contains three other poems of the same period and probably by the same writer. All are in the West Midland dialect, with a strong Scandinavian influence, which is at its most marked in *Sir Gawain and the Green Knight.* This seems to have been the first of the poems to be written, about 1370 to 1390. It has been suggested that it was commissioned by John of Gaunt, and there is strong evidence for some connection between him and the poet, if not for the actual commission. The identity of the unknown genius now generally known as 'the Gawain-poet' has long been a matter for debate. No suggestion yet put forward has gained more than a handful of supporters; attempts to marshal internal evidence, whether in the form of puns or numerology, all fail to point to a convincing case for the author's identity. All that can be said with certainty about him is that he was well acquainted with courtly life, could read Latin and French, and was probably a scholar of some merit. He might well have been, or become, a clerk in minor orders, since his later poems are distinctly religious in tone.

The story hinges on two distinct themes which the author has skilfully welded into one. The Green Knight's challenge to Gawain is an example of a mythical story or folktale that we may call the Beheading Game. The approaches of his hostess at castle form the other part, the Temptation. In the case of the Beheading Game, this may be one of a small number of tales taken over intact into the Arthurian romances from a Celtic original. The earliest form of the story is found in the Irish exploits of Cuchulainn, in which it is part of the contest for the championship of Ulster. From Ireland it passed to France, where three romances made use of this theme: in two cases Gawain is the hero. The common feature of all versions is a supernatural being who is beheaded without apparent harm and who returns his half of the bargain with a harmless blow.

The Temptation story is less specific; it is very probably the imaginative contribution of the poet, to provide proof of Gawain's virtue, and hence to motivate the outcome of the return blow; the theme of the acceptance of the one token that will help him in his coming trial, and its discovery, is brilliantly handled. The exchange of spoils, which is an integral part of the temptation theme, shows that the poet is a masterly constructor of stories. As a kind of light-hearted wager, Gawain and his host agree to exchange spoils: the host goes hunting each day, while Gawain stays in the castle with his wife. This apparently unequal bargain becomes the crux of the plot. The Temptation arises out of the Challenge, and the issue of the Challenge depends on the outcome of the Temptation.

If the plot is brilliantly handled, the poetry is a mirror of mood and imagination, whether it be the details of Gawain's arming before his departure or the loving portrayal of the Green Knight's magical axe. The greatest passages are those in which the poet depicts Nature and her ways, a theme which underlies the poem in several aspects. Two stanzas at the opening of the second part describe the changing seasons between Christmas and Michaelmas, and surpass all conventional poetry of this kind. They are followed by the harsh weather which Gawain encounters on his journey northwards, where in the sound of the words and in the rugged rhythms the very spirit of winter re-echoes. The northern countryside in which the poet lived rises up before us in its severe and impressive beauty. The three days' hunting sweeps across this background, days in which the essence of the chase is exactly caught: exhilaration, danger, triumph and noble ritual, at the end of each a homecoming to a warm welcome and a blazing fire when the last horn has been blown. On the day of the tryst at the Green Chapel, the countryside grows grim once more; the hills are mist-mantled, there is a hoar-frost in the oakwoods, snow in the valleys outside. The people of this harsh, real world are equally alive; their feasts and merry-making, gaiety and good cheer are far from the delicate but artificial world of the French romances, and their conversations are unforced and natural.

But just as Nature dominates the real world, so natural magic dominates the spiritual plane of the poem. The Green Knight is a superhuman being with strange powers, who moves in an aura of mystery, the shadow of his ancient role as the incarnation of spring who must be slain in winter in order to renew life for the next year. In the Temptation, he becomes a gay, friendly lord, owner of a fair castle; but this is only a disguise, even if the poet, uneasy at the pagan implications of his subject-matter, blames the whole mystery on Morgan le Fay. The strange legendary world of Norse and Saxon literature is never far from the poet's mind; Gawain encounters dragons, trolls and giants on his journey northward. The contrast between the Green Knight's two shapes is cunningly exploited, to heighten the climax of the poem.

The poet handles what could have been a mere adventure with such high intent that it becomes in his treatment a moral and didactic example. Gawain, the model of knighthood, only escapes the fatal return blow because he holds out against the lady's adulterous temptations. This is a far cry from the French writers' attitude; Gawain is often portrayed by them as overwhelmingly attractive to women, who succumb without any of the courtly conditions. Yet they would have agreed with his punishment, for by breaking his word in concealing the girdle, he had dishonoured the order of knighthood. The English poet takes even these worldly ideals onto a higher plain: Gawain's device, the pentangle, borne on his shield, is a religious rather than armorial symbol, and he is frequently called 'Mary's knight'. There is an idealism throughout that raises the poem far above the level of the other English romances. Some writers have seen *Sir Gamain and the Green Knight* as a poem with a didactic moral; but it is rather a moral reflection on human weakness when set against the highest ideals.

SIR GAWAIN AND THE GREEN KNIGHT

I

After the battle and the attack were over at Troy,
The town beaten down to smoking brands and ashes,
That man enmeshed in the nets of treachery — the truest
Of men — was tried for treason; I mean
Aeneas, the high-born, who, with his noble kinsmen,
Conquered many countries and made themselves masters
Of almost all the wealth of the Western isles.
Romulus goes off in haste towards Rome, raises
At first that fine city with pride, bestowing
On her his famous name, which she still has now.
Ticius builds new towns in Tuscany
And Langaberde lays out homes in Lombardy
And, joyfully, far over the French sea,
Felix Brutus founds Britain by ample down
                    and bay;
        Where war, and joy, and terror
        Have all at times held sway;
        Where both delight and horror
        Have had their fitful day.

And after Britain was founded by this brave fighter
Rough fellows were fathered here who relished a fray
And made much mischief in troubled times.
More marvels have occurred in this country
Than any other since then, so far as I know.
But of all the kings who've commanded this land
Men say king Arthur was the greatest in courtesy.

Let me tell you, then, a tale of adventure,
A most striking one among the marvels of Arthur
Which some will consider a wonder to hear.
If you listen closely to my words a little while
I'll tell it to you now as I heard it told
in town:
A bold story, well-proven,
And everywhere well-known,
The letters all interwoven
As custom sets it down.

Christmas time. The king is home at Camelot
Among his many lords, all splendid men –
All the trusted brothers of the Round Table
Ready for court revels and carefree pleasures.
Knights in great numbers at the tournament sports
Jousted with much joy, as gentle knights
Will do, then rode to the court for the carol-dances.
The festival lasted fifteen long days
Of great mirth with all the meat that they could manage.
Such clamour and merriment were amazing to hear:
By day a joyful noise, dancing at night –
A happiness that rang through rooms and halls
With lords and ladies pleasing themselves as they pleased.
So in delight they lived and danced there together:
The knights of highest renown under Christ Himself,
The loveliest ladies that ever on earth drew breath,
The handsomest king that ever kept court,
All in that hail were beautiful, young and, of
their kind,
The happiest under heaven
A king of powerful mind;
A company so proven
Would now be hard to find.

With the New Year so young it had hardly begun,
Those seated at the dais were given double servings.
Then, when the sound of the chanting in the chapel subsided,
The king came with all his knights to the hail
And loud cries leapt out from clerics and laymen:
'Noel!' they shouted, again and again 'Noel!'
Then noble knights ran forward with New Year gifts,

Handed out what they had, shouting, with loud
Guessing-games about each others' gifts.
Even when they guessed wrong the ladies laughed —
And, believe me, those who won weren't angry at all.
This merrymaking took place before the meal.
When they had washed they took their tables
In their right ranks, highest first, as was fitting.
Queen Guinevere, the gayest of all the gathering,
Sat at the high dais which was hung with adornments,
A canopy over her, silken curtains all round:
Damasks of Toulouse and rich drapes from Turkestan
Sewn and set off by the most detailed designs
In rich metals and jewels, beautifully beaten
                    and wrought —
          No woman lovelier,
          Her grey eyes glancing about;
          In beauty she had no peer,
          Of that there was no doubt.

But Arthur refused to eat till the rest were served.
He was in merry mood, like a mischievous boy.
He liked a life of action and couldn't abide
Long stretches of lying about or sitting idle;
His blood burned, his restless mind roused him.
But that day he was driven by a different resolve;
He had nobly decided never to eat at feasts
Such as these, until someone had told him
A strange story or a splendid adventure —
Something marvellous and beautiful that he might believe,
With the clamour of battle, attacks, the clash of arms —
Or till someone entreated him to spare a knight
To join with in jousting, jeopardising their limbs
And even their lives on the field, yielding advantage
As the favours of fortune touched the luckier one.
Such was Arthur's new custom with his court,
At feasts and festivals, with the fine company
                    in his hall.
          So now, in his kingly way,
          He stands fearless and tall,
          Alert on that New Year's day,
          And jests among them all.

In this regal manner he remains for quite a while
Talking of courtly trifles before the High Table
Where the knight, Gawain, is next to Guinevere,
With Agravain a la Dure Main at her other side –
Both sons of the king's sister, trusted brother knights.
Bishop Baldwin is head of the High Table
With Iwain, Urien's son, to keep him company.
A canopy over her, silken curtains all round:
Damasks of Toulouse and rich drapes from Turkestan
Sewn and set off by the most detailed designs
In rich metals and jewels, beautifully beaten and wrought –
No woman lovelier,
Her grey eyes glancing about;
In beauty she had no peer,
Of that there was no doubt.
All these are seated and served with honour
And likewise those on the long side-tables.
The firstcourse comes with a burst of trumpets
Whose banners hung from them in brilliant colours.
And now a clatter of kettledrums, a chifflng of fifes:
Wild music that ricochets off walls and rafters;
And the listeners' hearts leap with the lively notes.
Costly and most delicious foods are carried in:
Great mounds of steaming meat – so many dishes
There's little space in front of the lords and ladies
To set all the heaped silver platters that rapidly
                    appear.
           Each man eats as he wishes,
           Lustily takes his share;
           Each pair has twelve full dishes,
           Bright wine, and foaming beer.

Well, I won't tell you more about the meal;
You can be sure, of course, there was little lacking.
But now another sound was stirring – one
Which would allow the king to come and dine.
The first course had barely been served
To all the court, the music hardly hushed,
When there hove into the hail a hideous figure,
Square-built and bulky, full-fleshed from neck to thigh:
The heaviest horseman in the world, the tallest as well,
His loins and limbs so large and so long

I think he may have been half giant;
Anyway, I can say he was the mightiest of men
And, astride his horse, a handsome knight as well.
But if he was broad of back and chest
His build, mid-body, was elegantly slender,
His face befitting his form, his bold lineaments
                    cut clean.
            But the hue of his every feature
            Stunned them: as could be seen,
            Not only was this creature
            Colossal, he was bright green —

Green all over, the man and his garments as well!
A surcoat snugged him tight at the waist
And, over that, a tunic, closely trimmed inside
With fine fur, the cloth resplendent and furnished
With borders of bright ermine; the hood, turned back,
Looped from his coat-collar and was also lipped with fur.
Neat stockings, tightly drawn up, clung to his calves,
All green, and green also the spurs that hung below,
And they glinted gold against the striped silk hose
Of his stockinged feet fixed in the stirrups.
And all his garments this unearthly green
Down to the bars of his belt, and the shining stones
That richly studded the magnificent array
Around the saddle, and around himself: a silken ground
The details of whose embroidery would be difficult
To describe, with its delicate birds and butterflies
In bright green, and a hem of hammered gold;
The cords of the breast-harness, the beautiful crupper-cloth,
The burnished bridle-stud of baked enamel,
Even the steel of the stirrups on which he stood,
The saddle-bows and the broad saddle-skirts —
All glinted with the greenish glow of jewels;
And the steed he rode of the same bright
                    green strain:
            A horse of massive limbs,
            Most difficult to restrain;
            A useful mount! — with gems
            Studding his bridle and rein.

And he was fresh-looking, this fellow decked out green.
The hair of his head matched his horse's coat:
Bright hair, curling and cascading down his back;
And, bunched on his chest, a bushy beard
Which, with the locks that hung from his head,
Was well-trimmed just above the elbow-joints
So half his arms were hidden beneath hair
Which cleaved to his neck like a king's cape.
The horse's mane was like that mantle of hair,
Groomed and combed, and neatly knotted,
Plaited and filigreed in gold and green –
One hank of hair to each strand of gold.
The tail and the forelock were alike in detail;
The bright green bands around them both
Were strung all along with studded stones
And knit together with a knotted thong
Along which a row of bells rang brilliantly.
No one watching had ever before beheld
A horse like that – and such a horse man had never crossed
                    their tracks:
        To them he looked as bright
        As summer lightning that cracks
        The sky, and no man might
        Withstand his dreadful axe.

And yet he wore no hauberk, bore no helm,
No mail or metal plate – no arms or armour at all:
No spear to thrust, no shield against the shock of battle,
But in one hand a solitary branch of holly
That shows greenest when all the groves are leafless;
In the other hand he grasped his axe – a huge thing,
A dreadful weapon, difficult to describe:
The head of the big blade over a yard in length,
The spike of green steel and wrought gold,
The blade brightly polished, with a broad edge
Beautifully cast to bite keen as a razor;
The shaft he grimly gripped it by, a straight staff
Wound with iron bands right to the end,
Engraved all about with elegant green designs,
Circled with lace-work lashed to the end
And looped round and round the long handle
With plenty of priceless tassels, attached

With bright green buttons, richly braided.
And now he shoves past them all, heaves into the hall
And rides right up to the High Table, afraid
Of nothing. He greeted no one, just glared over their heads.
The first words he spoke were these: 'Where is', he said,
'The leader of this lot? I'd be pleased indeed
If he came forward and traded a few words
                      with me.'
          He looked at every knight,
          Strutted, and rolled his eye;
          Stopped, fixed them in his sight
          To find whose fame stood high.

And they gazed at him a long moment, amazed.
Everyone wondered what it might mean
That a man and his mount could both be coloured
The green of sprouting grass, and even greener —
Like emerald enamel that glowed on a ground of gold.
They studied him, waited, stalked up warily, stood
Wondering what in the world the man might do.
They'd seen strange things, but never a sight like this;
They thought it must be a sort of magic, or a dream.
Most of the men were too terrified to reply;
Struck dumb by his words, they waited, stock-still.
A pall of torpor settled over the hall
As if all dozed. Their talk dropped and their tongues
                      went dry,
          Not only, I think, from fear,
          But also from courtesy,
          To give the king they revere
          Chance of a first reply.

The king, from the high board beholds these curious things,
Then, quite free of fear, greets him graciously.
He says: 'Well, sir, you're surely welcome here.
I am the master of this hall and my name is Arthur.
Do dismount and bide with us a while —
Whatever your wish, we'll learn about it later.'
'No, so help me, He that reigns in heaven!
To pass time in this place was not my plan at all.
But because your name, my lord, is so renowned —
Your castle and your court — and your knights known

As the hardiest on horseback, in armour the most
Formidable, the fiercest at melées and tournaments,
The bravest and best in the wide world,
And because they say the bright crown of courtesy
Itself sits here — these things have brought me by,
Nothing but these for, as sure as I bear this branch,
I travel in peace and seek no trouble.
Had I come belligerently, were I bent on war,
I have a hauberk at home, and a helm also,
A shield and a sharp spear, both shining bright;
And I have other weapons to wield, that's for certain.
But, since I want no war, my dress is innocent.
So, if you're as bold as everybody says,
You'll grant me graciously the sport that I seek
                    by right.'
          'Well, if you're hungering,
          Sir knight, sir courteous knight,
          To try your strength,' said the king,
          'You'll certainly have your fight.'

'No, no, I'm not brewing for trouble, I tell you — besides,
It's clear there's no one here but beardless boys.
If I bore armour, if I sat on a battle-steed,
No man could match me among these milksops.
I need only some diversion for the new season.
It's Yuletide and New Year. Here are many young men.
If any now hold himself bold enough,
If any so hot-blooded or so hare-brained,
Has the stomach to strike one stroke for another,
I'll give him the gift of this beautiful battle-axe
Which weighs heavy enough for his every wish.
And I shall bear the first blow, as I am, bare-necked.
Now, if any man has the mettle to meet my challenge
Let him step down and seize this weapon.
There, I throw it down, let him take it as his own.
I'll receive the first blow right here, without blenching,
If he but allow me to return that blow however
                    I may;
          And yet I'll give him respite:
          A whole year, plus a day —
          So, if your liver's not white,
          Quick now, who's ready to say?'

If they were astounded at first, the crowd in the court
Went even quieter now, both high and low.
The horseman swivelled himself about in the saddle
And rolled his red eyes around, most horribly,
Bunched together his brows of bristling green,
Wagged his beard this way and that, and watched.
When no word came he gave a great hacking cough,
Carked his throat clear, most eloquently, and spoke:
'And this is supposed to be Arthur's house,' he cried,
'Whose fame flies through the remotest regions!
Where are your boasts of valour now, your bold victories,
Your pride, your prizes, your wrath and rousing words?
Am I right? All the pageantry and power of the Round Table
Made nothing by the words of one man?
You're all white with fear, and not a whack fallen!'
And he laughed so loud the king blanched with anger,
Then his brow darkened in shame, his face flushed
                    blood-dim —
          He grew as wild as the wind;
          The whole hall turned grim.
          Then, being of noble kind,
          The king strode up to him

And replied: 'By heaven, sir, your request's very silly,
But as you ask for a silly thing I'll see you have it.
No man here is scared by what you've said.
Give me your great battle-axe, in the name of God.
I'll easily provide what you've pleaded for!'
He leaps down lightly, seizes the man's hand
Who also dismounts in high disdain.
Arthur takes the axe. He grips the huge handle,
And swings it, practising to hack him down.
The fellow pulls himself up to his full height,
Taller than any man in the hall by a head and more.
He stands there, looking serious, smoothing his beard —
Remote, expressionless. He draws his coat down,
Unafraid, no more dismayed by the thought of an axe-blow
Than if a knight nearby had fetched him a flagon
                    of wine.

Beside the queen, Gawain
Bows to the king, gives sign:
'Please, my good liege, it's plain
This little fight is mine.

'I would ask you', continued Gawain, to his master and king,
'To bid me rise from my bench and stand beside you,
So that I can quit the table courteously
Without causing displeasure to my lady queen.
I wish to give counsel before this wise court
For, truth to tell, it does not appear proper to me
That a demand like this, delivered with such disdain,
Should be dealt with – whether you wish or no – directly,
By you alone, while all around you sit many men
Than whom few under heaven are firmer in will
Or stronger in body when a battle begins.
I am the weakest and the least in wit;
Loss of my life is therefore of little account.
I am, by birth, your nephew; besides that, nothing.
My one virtue, your blood that runs in my veins.
Since this affair's so foolish and unfit for you
And since I asked soonest, please leave it to me.
If I have blundered, let the whole hall, without blame,
                              decree.'
        The nobles thereupon
        Confer, and all agree:
        Gawain should take him on,
        And let the king stay free.

Then the king commanded the knight to stand
And he rose up promptly, prepared himself correctly
Knelt down before the king and felt the cold weapon;
And the king graciously gave it him, held up his hand
And granted him God's blessing, commended him, praying
That his heart and his hand remain resolute:
'Take care, cousin,' said the king, 'how you swing at him,
For, if you strike him right, I'm really sure
You'll withstand any blow he plans to give you back.'
Gawain, axe in hand, goes towards the man
Who bravely waits for him, afraid not a whit.
Then the green knight speaks to sir Gawain:
'Let's repeat our agreement before we go further,

But first I entreat you, sir, teach me
Your true name, that I may trust you.'
'In good faith', said the good knight, 'I am called Gawain,
And I am to make this cut at you, come what may,
And a twelvemonth from now I'll take another one
From you, with whatever weapon you choose, to pay
                it back.'
      The knight gives him reply:
      'Ah, sir Gawain – what luck!
      I am pleased exceedingly
      That you will make the stroke.

'Yes, by heaven, sir Gawain,' the knight says,
'I'm delighted I'll get this gift from your hand.
You have repeated precisely and truthfully
All the conditions of the covenant I asked of the king,
Save that you will assure me by your troth,
You will seek me yourself, wherever your search
Takes you in the world – and you'll win the same wages
As you give me before this fine company.
'Where shall I find you, sir, where are you from?
By Him that made me, I know nothing of your home;
Neither do *I* know you, your court, or what you're called –
Nothing. So please tell me now your name
And I'll use all my wits to find my way to you:
I swear by that, and there's *my* troth on it.
'Enough for New Year's day, no more needs saying,'
Continued the man in green to the courteous Gawain.
'You'll not discover that until you've dealt your blow.
When you have struck properly then I'll provide you with
All you need know about my castle and name.
Only then need you learn where I live, to keep the contract.
And if I keep quiet the bargain's even better:
You can remain here, all year, in your own country!
          Enough said!
     Now grip this axe until
     We see of what stuff you're made.'
     'Gladly, sir, that I will!'
     Says Gawain. He strokes the blade.

On the ground the green knight girds himself;
He lets his head fall forward, revealing the flesh.

His long locks tumble down over his crown
Baring the nape of his neck for the blow.
Gawain sets his left foot slightly forward;
He grips the axe and lifts it over his head
Then brings it down, neat and quick, on the bare nape
So that the sharp blade shattered the neck-bone,
Bit through the flesh and sliced the knight in two.
The flashing blade bit a deep groove in the ground,
The head sprang from the body and hurtled to earth
And some fumbled it with their feet as it rolled around.
Blood spurted from the great body and splattered the green,
But still he didn't fall, didn't falter at all,
But strode forward steadily on firm thighs,
Reached out fiercely among the ranks of knights,
Gripped his handsome head and quickly picked it up;
Then hurried to his horse, caught hold of the halter
Stepped into the stirrups and swung up,
Holding his head, by its own hair, in his hand
Then sat there in the saddle, stubbornly,
As if nothing had happened – though now he was wearing
                              no head.
            He twisted around. Amazed
            At that gross trunk that bled,
            In pure terror they gazed,
            And marvelled at what he said,

For now he holds the head in his hand up high
And turns it to face the noblest at the table.
It lifts its eyelids, gives them a long stare, then
Slowly opens its mouth, and these words come out:
'Be prepared to do as you promised, Gawain;
Seek me faithfully until you find me, sir.
As you have pledged in the presence of these noble knights,
You will go to the Green Chapel, to receive
Such a blow as you have dealt – you now deserve it! –
That blow to be borne on New Year's morning.
Men know me as the knight of the Green Chapel,
And, if you ask, you cannot fail to find me.
Come, therefore – or be known as a craven coward!'
With a quick twist he tugs at the reins
And, still holding his head, rides through the hall doorway.
His horse's hooves kick fire from the flintstone.

Which way he was headed no one could readily say,
Nor could they name the country whence he came.
             And so?
      Well, the king and his chosen knight
      Laughed as they watched him go —
      Yet they had to admit
      They'd seen a marvel too.

Though Arthur's heart stood still in wonder,
He showed no sign of it, but said aloud
To his queen, in his most courteous manner,
'Dear lady, please don't be dismayed.
Such deeds are welcome at the Christmas season,
Like the interludes, the laughing and singing
And the carol-rounds with royal lords and ladies.
Nevertheless, now I may proceed with my meal
For I have seen a marvel, I mustn't deny it.'
He caught Gawain's eye, and lightly said to his knight:
'Now sir, hang up your axe; it's hacked enough for today.'
And they hung it high on a drape over the dais,
That men might gaze upon it as a marvel
And point to it, and tell the tale of its power.
Then they went together to the table,
The king and his knight, who were now served in splendour,
With double helpings of the daintiest things:
All kinds of fine fare, and more music.
So they passed their time in delight, until at last
             night fell.
      Now, Gawain, think of your quest,
      And let no terror quell
      Your courage in the test
      You have taken on. Think well!

II

This novel event was Arthur's New Year present
At the dawn of the year; he yearned for such adventures.
Yet they all wanted for words as they went to their tables,
For now the business in hand is heavy, burdensome.
Gawain was glad to begin the sport in the hall
But, if the game grew serious, think it no surprise,
For if men are feather-wits when the wine's flowing,
Time races on, nothing remains unchanged;
Our endings rarely square with our beginnings.
Yuletide once past, the year followed fast behind,
Each new season turning in its time:
After Christmas, the crabbed fasting-time of Lent
When people eat fish for meat, and simple fare.
Then the world's fresh weather fights with winter:
Cold shrinks into the ground, clouds rise;
Warm rain shuttles down in flashing showers
Over the flatlands; flowers poke up,
fields and groves put on their freshest green;
Birds start building – they call out loudly
For the calm of summer that spreads its balm on valleys
and slopes.
Rich hawthorn-blossoms swell
And burst in rows; in the copse
New bird-sounds run, pell-mell,
Through the glorious full tree-tops.

And then broad summer, when balmy winds
Out of the west breathe on bush and seed,
And plants under a wide sky dance in joy;
When dew gathers and slips in drops from wet leaves
As they bask in the sumptuous beams of the bright sun.
Then autumn, with sombre shadows striding towards
Winter, warning the grain to grow to fullness.
On dry days he drives the rising dust
Up from the folding fields, where it spirals high.
In the huge heavens, winds wrestle with the sun;
Tawny leaves are ripped from the linden-tree
And lush grass in the field leans over, and greys.
Whatever rose up earlier now ripens and rots;
The year dwindles, all days seem yesterdays.

Winter winds on as it will, as it has done
of old.
And when the Michaelmas moon
Burns on the icy wold
Gawain fears he must soon
Make his quest through the cold.

Till All Hallows' day he stays with Arthur
Who, on that holiday, held a feast in his homage
With much revelry and rejoicing of the Round Table.
The lords, out of courtesy, with their comely ladies,
Came in sorrow for love of the young knight,
And yet, though sad, they *still* made jests,
Not showing their feelings but suppressing their sorrow.
After the meal, in gloomy mood, Gawain came to the king
Concerning his journey, and said straight out:
'It is time, my lord, to take my leave of you.
You know what it's about, and I'll not bother you
With all my difficulties, and the small details.
I'm duty bound to depart tomorrow, without delay,
To get my blow from the man in green, as God decrees.'
Then the best men of the court gathered together:
Iwain and Erik, and many more besides;
Sir Doddinvale de Savage, the duke of Clarence,
Lancelot, Lionel, that good man, Lucan;
Sir Bors, sir Bedivere, big men both,
Mador de la Port, and also many more
Of great renown. They gathered around the king.
Now, heavy with care, they counselled the knight
And many suffered their sorrow secretly,
Regretting that the good Gawain should make the quest
And bear such a horrible blow, and not hit back,
but wait.
Gawain put on good cheer.
'Why should I hesitate?'
He said. 'Kind or severe,
We must engage our fate.'

He stays on all that day. Next dawn he dresses,
Calls early for his arms; they are duly carried in.
first, a red silk carpet is spread on the floor
And the lustrous gilt armour laid on it, glistening.

Dressed in a doublet of worked silk from Turkestan
And a king's cape, cleverly made, closed at the neck,
Its inside hems fringed with shining fur,
He strolls among the armour and strokes the steel.
They fix steel sabatons onto his feet,
Lap his legs in gleaming metal greaves,
Their brilliant knee-joints newly burnished,
And fasten them, with knotted filigree, to his knees.
fine thigh-pieces, lashed with leather thongs,
Cover his thick thighs, and close over them.
A coat of link-mail, its rings glinting,
Clasps him round, over a tunic of finest cloth;
Polished armpieces, with gay-coloured elbow-guards,
Are fastened to his arms and, last, gauntlets of steel.
In all, the finest-fitting gear to guard him on
                              his ride:
          His coat-armour, trimmed by hand,
          His gold spurs proudly tied;
          Girt with a silken band,
          His broadsword swung at his side.

Buckled up, the knight glowed in his bright armour;
The smallest lace or loop gleamed gold.
Clothed in this manner, he goes to hear Mass
Solemnly celebrated at the great altar.
Then he comes to the king, and his court-companions,
Takes his leave courteously of the lords and ladies;
Escorting him out, they kissed him, commending him to Christ.
By then Gringolet stood ready, girt with a saddle
That, studded with new nails cut specially
And bordered with gold, gleamed brightly.
The bridle was richly barred and wrapped with gold.
The furnishings of the breast-harness, of the fine skirts,
Crupper and caparison, matched those of the saddle-bows,
And all was gilded with new gold nails
That flickered and flashed like tiny sun-flares.
He takes hold of the helm, which is strongly stapled
And thickly padded inside, and quickly kisses it.
It sat high on his head, held with a hasp
Behind, and a bright strap clasping the visor
Embroidered and set with the best gems
On a broad silk hem, with birds on the seams:

Parrots preening their wings, depicted among
Turtle-doves, and true-love knots, so numerous
It must have taken the ladies seven seasons
                        to sew.
            The circlet round his crown
            Was even more precious, though;
            Its device of diamond-stone,
            Burned with a dusky glow.

Then they show him the shield, its gules shimmering,
And its pentangle picked out in pure gold.
He grips the girdle of the shield, flicks it quickly
Round his neck. It fits him neatly.
Now, though it delay me, I propose to say
Why the pentangle bedecks the noble knight:
It is a design that Solomon devised, a sign
And token of truth — quite rightly too,
For its figure comprises five points
And its lines overlap and link with each other
With no ending anywhere; and men in England
Call it, accordingly, the Knot without End.
Therefore it suits the knight in his bright armour
Ever faithful, five times, five ways in each.
Gawain was known as a good knight, like gold
Purified of fault, his virtues clearly and openly
                        revealed.
            The pentangle he was wearing
            On surcoat and on shield
            Bespoke his gentle bearing
            And trust that would not yield.

First, he was found without fault in his five senses;
Again, his five fingers never failed him,
And all his faith in the world was in the five wounds
That Christ received on the Cross, as the Creed tells;
And whenever this warrior was embroiled in battle
His sole and steadfast thought was simply that
His courage came, finally, from the five joys
The courteous Queen of Heaven had from her child;
Therefore, painted in comely colours, he carried
Her gracious image; it glowed inside his shield
And when he gazed thereon his courage never wavered.

Of the fifth group of five he honoured constantly
The first four were generosity, good fellowship,
Cleanness, and courtesy, uncurbed and unimpaired;
Lastly, compassion, surpassing all: these final five,
More firmly fixed on that knight than on any other,
These five, compounded by faith, conjoined in him,
Each one woven with the other, each one unending,
Fastened on five points that never faltered,
Nor strayed from each other, but stayed together
Always without end, as I have found, no matter where
A man might begin the design, or strive to close it.
Therefore the knot on this new shield was fashioned
Royally, in red gold on red gules:
Such is the pure pentangle which people of old
                    were taught.
        He is ready now in his gay
        Armour; his lance is brought.
        He took it, gave them good-day –
        For evermore, he thought.

He jabbed the steed with his spurs and sped away
So fast that sparks flew from the flintstone.
At the sight of the knight riding off, they sighed.
Grieving for Gawain, all the lords and ladies
Said truthfully to each other: 'By heaven, it's a pity
That he is gone, with his huge gift for life!
To find his equal will be far from easy.
It would have been wiser to proceed discreetly,
To have endowed the noble knight with a dukedom.
He would have been a lord of men, a magnificent leader;
A much better destiny than being destroyed, his head
Struck off by an elfish man out of selfish pride.
Whoever heard of king heeding the counsel
Of capricious knights in the nonsense of Christmas games?'
Much warm water flowed from their eyes
When the good man went from their dwelling
                    that day.
        He bade them well, then took
        Himself, without delay –
        As I heard tell from the book –
        Along his tortuous way.

Now the knight rides through the realm of Logres:
Sir Gawain, in God's service, finding it no game.
At times, companionless, he takes his rest at night
Where he finds little of the food to his liking.
No good friend but his horse in those woods and hills,
And no one save God to speak to on his way,
While he is nearing the wastes of northern Wales.
He keeps to the right of the isles of Anglesey,
Fords the foreshore by the promontory, first
Wading over at Holyhead, then heaving ashore once more
Into the forest of Wirral, the wilderness. Few there
Were loved by God or men of goodwill.
And wherever he went, asking those whom he met
If they knew anything of a knight in green
Or, by chance, of the Green Chapel in the region around,
They said, no, no, they'd never seen him,
Nor even heard of a man in that land, dressed all
                    in green.
      He turns down dreary ways
      Where dark hillsides lean,
      His mood changing as the day's,
      But the chapel could not be seen.

He clambers over rough slopes in curious regions;
Estranged from his friends, he rides on, ranging far.
At each water-ford, or river-reach that he crossed
He found, more often than not, a foe before him –
One so foul and violent he had to fight him.
Among those hills he met so many marvels
It's hard to tell a tenth part of them all.
Sometimes he wars with dragons, or with wolves,
With wodwos, who watched him from woodland crags;
With bulls and bears; sometimes with savage boars,
And giants from the high fells, who followed him.
Had he not been brave and sturdy, not served God,
He would have died, been destroyed many times.
But if those fights were fierce, winter was worse,
When chilling water spilled out of the clouds
Freezing as it fell, pelting the pale ground.
Almost killed by sleet, he sleeps in all his armour
More nights than enough among the rough rocks,
Where plummeting cascades from the summits ran cold

Or hung over his head in hard ice-blades.
This way, in danger, in pain and hardship,
Over the land the knight rides till Christmas Eve,
                    alone;
            Then, in despair on his ride,
            He cries in a plangent tone
            That Mary be his guide
            To a house, a warm hearthstone.

Through the morning he rides on merrily, beside a hill,
Into a dark wood, wonderfully wild.
High hills all around; below, a grove of oaks,
Huge and hoary, more than a hundred of them.
Hazel and hawthorn were tangled together there,
And everywhere rough mounds of hairy moss.
Hunched on bare branches, doleful birds
Piped out pitiful calls in the bitter cold.
The knight glides under them on Gringolet
Through bogs and quagmires, quite alone,
Fearing the whims of fate, worried that he would
Never see the Lord's service, who, on that same night,
Was born of a maid to assuage our sorrow.
And he implored Him, saying, 'I beseech thee, Lord,
And Mary, mild Mother, so dear to us,
That I might soon hear Mass in a Holy Place
And Matins in the morning – I ask it meekly,
And therefore promptly say my Paternoster, Ave
                    and Creed.'
            And, riding as he prayed,
            He repented each misdeed,
            And signed himself, and said:
            'May Christ's Cross lend me speed!'

Hardly had he made the sign three times
When, in the midst of the wood, he saw a moated castle
On open ground, rising from a mound; boughs
Of massive trees by the moats enclosed it.
Built on meadow-ground, with a beautiful park all round,
It was the finest castle ever kept by a knight.
A spiked palisade, its palings tight together,
Surrounded many trees, and ran two miles around.
The knight studied the stronghold from the side

As it glimmered and glowed among the tall oak trees.
He removed his helm in reverence, humbly thanked
Both Jesus and Saint Julian for their bounteous deed
And their great courtesy in granting him his plea.
'Now, grant me a good night's lodging,' he beseeched.
Then, with his gold spurs, he urged Gringolet on.
By good chance he had chosen the main road
And it brought him to the drawbridge quick
                    and straight.
      The bridge was drawn upright
      And shut tight every gate;
      Against the wind's worst might
      Those walls were inviolate.

The horseman waited at the bank, hesitated at the brink
Of the double ditch that ran around the castle.
The walls sank down far into the dark water,
And rose to a huge height over it;
The fine stone soared up to the cornices.
Its battlements were formed in a style most fitting,
With graceful turrets spaced out at intervals
And a row of lovely loopholes with locking shutters.
A better barbican the knight had never seen.
Further in, he descried the wall of the high hall
With its bold, regular towers and tough battlements
And clusters of painted pinnacles, cleverly joined,
Their high carved tops far up in the sky.
He also caught sight of the chalk-white chimneys
That shimmered immaculately on the tower-tops:
From any vantage-point so many turrets and towers
Amid the parapets, and scattered so thickly,
It seemed a pure fancy, or a model made from paper.
From his horse, the knight thought it so inviting
He wondered: 'If I can work my way inside,
A respite here in the Holy Season would be a time
                    of grace.
      He called out. After a time,
      A porter, high up, whose face
      Smiled down, acknowledged him
      And welcomed him to that place.

'Good sir,' said Gawain 'would you take a message for me
To the lord of the castle, and ask for lodging?'
'Yes, by Saint Peter, though I'd guess', replied the porter,
'You're welcome to lodge here as long as you like.'
He hurried off, and straightway came back
With many more people, to receive the knight properly.
They let fall the drawbridge, walked out towards him
And knelt down in courtesy on the cold ground
To greet the man in a manner they gauged befitting.
They let him ride through the great gates, now wide
Apart. He bade them stand, passed over the bridge
Where several of the men steadied his saddle.
He dismounted, and more men stabled his steed.
And then the knights and their squires descended
To greet him, and lead him off to the lord's hail.
As he unhasped his helmet, everyone hurried
To seize it in their hands, and serve this noble man.
They relieved him of sword and shield and bore them off.
Then, courteously, he greeted each man among them.
They all pressed forward proudly to honour the prince
And brought him to the hail, still in his bright armour
Where a fire burned fiercely in the big grate.
Then the lord of the castle came forth from his chamber
To greet with high honour the man in his hail.
He said: 'You may stay as long as you like.
All here in this hall is yours, to do whatever you have
                    in mind.'
          'My warmest thanks!' They embrace
          Gladly, their arms entwined.
          'May Christ reward your grace;
          You are indeed most kind.'

Gawain gazed at the man that greeted him,
And a powerful prince he looked, the castle's lord:
A towering fellow, trim, and in his prime.
His wide beard glistened like a beaver's hide.
Stern-looking, on stalwart legs he strode forward,
fiery-faced, his eye fierce, and his speech
Noble, an excellent thing, the knight thought,
For him to be master of the men of that castle.
The lord turned towards a side-room, straightway ordered
That a servant be given to Gawain, to tend him.

In a trice, at his call, many came and took him
To a bright room with regal bedding:
Curtains of silk cloth with gilded hems,
Delicate coverlets of lovely smooth sable,
With parti-coloured panels and stitch-worked seams,
And the curtains ran along cords on red-gold rings.
Silks of Toulouse and Turkestan spread down the walls
And fine carpets, matching them, covered the floor.
And there, with merry quips, they quickly removed,
To his great relief, his mail and gleaming raiments,
And promptly fetched him fine fresh robes
To choose from and change into, as he wished.
No sooner had he chosen one with flowing skirts
That suited him, and put it on, than it seemed to everyone
By his appearance that spring was clearly beginning
For its glorious colours, as it lightly covered his limbs,
Caught fire and glowed and, surely, they thought,
Christ had never created a creature like
                   this knight.
      They saw, no matter where
      He came from, this man might
      Be a prince without any peer
      Wherever bold men fight.

A seat with sumptuous furnishings, its cover-cloths
And quilted cushions crafted masterfully,
Was fetched and set before the fire where
The coals glowed. A glorious cloak of brilliant silk,
Opulently appointed, was placed over his shoulders.
It was fringed inside with the finest animal-fur,
Earth's best ermine, the broad hood also of fur.
He sat there, looking most handsome in that seat.
Warmth ran through his limbs and his liveliness
Returned. Soon they set up a trestle-table
Laid with a new cloth and napkins, spotless white,
A salt-cellar, and cutlery, all silver.
He washed in his good time, and went to his food.
Serving-men, with becoming grace, brought bowls
Of several excellent soups, exquisitely seasoned,
Steaming and brimming over, then dishes of various fish:
Some baked in bread, some broiled on the embers,
Some boiled, or stewed with spices, in their juice,

All served with delicate sauces that he relished.
And he politely proclaimed it a feast, again
And again, whereon they bade him again and again,
                    'Please eat!
          This fast is for your good;
          Tomorrow's fare will be meat.'
          Gawain was in jovial mood,
          Flushed with the wine and heat.

Then they asked, and ascertained in a tactful way,
By detailed questions put to the knight discreetly,
That he was of Arthur's court; and he courteously revealed
That he was a knight and kinsman of king Arthur,
That royal and renowned lord of the Round Table;
That it was, in fact, Gawain who sat before them,
And he'd arrived, as chance decided, at Christmastide.
When the lord learned that Gawain was staying with him
He laughed loudly, delighted with his luck.
And all the folk in the hall were full of joy
And presented themselves without ado because all virtue,
Excellence, strength and good breeding belonged
To this reputable person, praised everywhere,
Whose honour was held highest before all men.
And each man said quietly to his companion:
'Now we shall see a marvellous show of manners,
And learn from the intricate turns of his conversation;
Without even seeking we'll see just what
Good talk can be, for the prince of courtesy walks
Among us. Surely God has showered his grace
On us in granting us a guest such as Gawain
At the season when all on earth sing the birth of God
                    above!
          Surely we shall receive
          From him a knowledge of
          Fine ways and, I believe,
          The subtle speech of love.'

By that time dinner was done. The fine company
Rose. Night was now closing in.
Chaplains made their way to the chapel
And bells rang out richly, as befitting
The blessed evensong, of the festive season.

The lord attends; his lady is there also.
She goes in gracefully, to her private pew
And straightway Gawain enters the chapel as well.
The lord takes hold of a fold of his gown and leads him
To a seat, acknowledges him, speaks his name,
Adding, moreover, that his presence gladdens him more
Than anything. Gawain thanks him again. They embrace,
Then sit together silently through the service.
Later, the lady wished to look on the knight:
She came from her pew, accompanied by peerless women,
But she, in looks and complexion, the loveliest of all:
Well-groomed, graceful, perfectly poised –
Even lovelier than Guinevere, thought Gawain.
He goes forth into the chancel, to greet her formally.
Another lady led her by the left hand,
An elderly lady, one clearly much older than her,
Who was held in high honour by everyone there.
These two were quite unlike in every way:
One was winsome and young, the other withered.
A glow of roseate colour shone on the first,
While rough and wrinkled cheeks hung from the other.
Kerchiefs and clusters of pearls adorned the younger;
Her breast and bright throat, showing bare,
Glowed more freshly than the first snow on the hills.
The other, swathed in a gorget that hid her neck,
Her swart chin wrapped in chalk-white veils,
Her forehead muffled up in folds of silk,
Was trellised round with trefoils and jingling rings,
And nothing of her uncovered but her black brows,
Her two eyes, her nose and naked lips –
All sour to the sight, all strangely bleared:
A beautiful lady, by God, let it not be
                    denied!
          Squat body, and thick waist,
          Her buttocks full and wide;
          Much daintier, to his taste,
          The young one at her side.

Gawain, gazing on the one who looked so gracious,
Received the lord's consent to go forward in greeting.
He faces the old one first, bows very low;
The fairer one, very lightly, he embraces

In comely fashion, kisses her, speaks to her courteously.
They beg his acquaintance; he eagerly requests,
In all solicitude, to be their true servant.
They take him between them and, talking, lead him
To a side-room where first of all, they call
For spices, which men speed to bring them unstintingly,
With beakers of warming wine at each return.
The jubilant lord leapt about in joy
Telling them, time and again, to amuse themselves.
He snatched his hood off, gaily snared it on a spear
Declaring 'He wins the honour of wearing this
Who makes up the most amusing Christmas game —
And, by my faith, with the help of my friends, I'll fight
The best of you before I give this garment up.'
With whirling words and laughter the lord enjoys himself
That night, with many games for sir Gawain, to make
                    him glad,
          Until, the hour being late,
          'Bring lights!' the fine host said.
          Gawain gave all goodnight
          And went off to his bed.

So the morning when men are mindful of the time
When the Lord for our destiny, was born to die,
For whose sake joy wakens in every house in the world,
Fell to them there as well that day: delicious foods,
Both at the formal dinner and the more casual meals,
Were plentifully served, by strong men at the long dais.
The ancient lady sat in the loftiest place
With the lord, I believe out of courtesy, beside her.
Gawain and the lovelier lady sat together
At the central board where the food was served first.
Then all in the hail were subsequently served
According to their state — the appropriate form.
There was meat, great mirth and much delight,
Difficult indeed to describe to you now
If I tried to tell it in all its finer details.
But I do know that Gawain and the lovely lady
Delighted in each other's bright company,
And in the deft dalliance of courtly conversation.
No innuendo darkened their delicate speech;

Their witty word-play surpassed the sports of the other lords.
　　　　With blares
　　　　　Of trumpets, drums' loud measures
　　　　　And pipes with their pleasing airs,
　　　　　All tended to their pleasures
　　　　　As these two looked to theirs.

Great mirth and merriment that day and the next,
And the third, as pleasure-filled, followed hard.
They celebrated St John's day with joy and jubilation.
This was the final festive day, for in the grey
Of morning they knew many guests were going.
So they whiled away the night in high style,
Drinking wine and dancing the finest carols.
At last, very late, all who were not of that place,
All those who were going, slowly took their leave.
Gawain gave them farewell. The lord leads him aside,
Brings him to his own bedroom, beside the fire;
There he detains him, shows his delight, thanks him
For the high honour he has heaped on them all
In staying at his house for that solemn season,
And in gracing his court with his gay company:
'Indeed, as long as I live, I'll be the better for it,
That Gawain has been my guest at God's feast.'
'My thanks are to you,' says Gawain, 'for in good faith,
I claim the honour as mine, may the High King reward you.
I am most eager to please you, to perform your every wish,
Both small and great, as I am bound by my knight's
　　　　　　　　decree.'
　　　　　The lord tries hard to hold
　　　　　Gawain in his company
　　　　　Much longer, but he is told
　　　　　By the knight it cannot be.

Then he put many questions to his guest, courteously
Asked him what grim business forced him at that time
To ride so resolutely from the king's court alone,
Even before the end of the festive season.
'Indeed, sir,' said Gawain, 'your question comes home.
A difficult and urgent duty spurred me on:
I am summoned to seek a particular place
Of whose location I have no notion at all.

And I must not miss it on New Year's morning
For all the rich land in the realm of Logres.
My lord, please let me put you a question:
Tell me truthfully if you've heard any man mention
The Green Chapel, or the ground that church stands on,
Or the knight who keeps it, clothed in bright green.
A meeting with that man at such a landmark,
If I'm still alive, was set by solemn agreement,
And there's but little time till the New Year.
If God permit, I would set my gaze on him
More willingly, by God's Son, than I would on anything
In the world. So, by your leave, I'm bound to proceed;
There are barely three days more. I must make ready
For I'd rather meet quick death than defeat in my quest.'
The lord laughed. 'In that case you can stay,
Because I will show you well before where to go.
Let the whereabouts of the Green Chapel worry you no longer.
You can rest at ease, lie in as long as you please
Until late morning on the first day of the year,
Then ride to the meeting place at midday, to do what you
                              must do.
          Stay until New Year's day,
          Then you can rise, and go.
          We'll set you on your way.
          It's only a mile or so.'

At this, Gawain, most gratified, laughed gladly:
'My heartfelt thanks – indeed, you have helped exceedingly!
My quest is at an end. I shall spend, at your behest,
Therefore, a longer time, and do as you would wish.'
Then the knight took hold of him, sat beside him,
And bade the ladies enter to please them better,
And they passed a delightful time before the fire.
The lord, in his levity, let forth shrieks of glee
Like someone losing his wits, or unaware of his acts,
Calling out to the knight in a loud cry:
'So, you have chosen to do what I asked of you!
Will you promise, here and now, to hold to that vow?'
'Most certainly I will, sir,' said the noble knight,
'While I bide in your house I'm bound by your command.'
'Well, because you've come so far and travelled hard,
Then kept late nights with me, you're not quite rested.

You need nourishment and sleep, that's easily seen.
So remain in your room and rest at your leisure
In the morning, till Mass, then go to your meal
With my wife, as soon as you wish. She will sit
With you for company till I come back to court.
                    Understood?
            Quite early I shall rise
            For hunting in the wood.'
            With this, Gawain complies,
            And bows, as polite men should.

'Furthermore,' said the lord, 'let's settle on a bargain.
Whatever I win at hunting will henceforth be yours;
And you, in turn, will yield whatever you earn.
There, my fine fellow, swear on it truly,
Whether we win or lose,' demanded the lord.
'By God,' replied Gawain, 'I'm ready for that.
I must say I'm glad you wish to play this game.'
'Bring us all drinks, the bargain's driven!'
Said the lord of the castle. And they laughed delightedly,
And drank wine, chatted, dallied, and delayed,
The lords and ladies, as long as it pleased them to.
Then, with French phrases, and lingering, light douceurs,
They stayed on even longer, speaking softly,
And kissed each other, and kindly took their leave.
Then their serving-men slowly led them away,
Lighting each to his room with the glow of a bright
                    torch-flame.
            But, before bed, their accord
            Again and again they proclaim.
            He knew very well, that lord,
            How to draw out his game.

III

Even before daybreak everyone was up.
The guests who were going called their grooms,
And they hurried out to saddle their stout horses,
Get all their gear in order, pack their saddle-pockets.
Guests of the highest rank, dressed ready for riding,
Leapt up lightly, took hold of their bridles,
Each person going where it most pleased him.
The beloved lord of the castle was not the last:
Rigged out for riding, he appeared with his many men.
Straight after Mass he ate a light meal, hastily,
And hurried to the field, flourishing his bugle.
By the time daylight was gathering over the ground
He and his men were waiting on their huge horses.
His clever huntsmen coupled the hounds in their leashes,
Opened the kennel door and called them forth.
They blew their bugles loudly: three bare notes.
At that the hounds bayed, making a great furore,
And those that broke away were whipped and turned back.
There were, I'm told, a hundred men of the boldest
                    hunting blood.
          The keepers of the hounds
          Took up their posts and stood
          Waiting, while bugle-sounds
          Echoed around the wood.

Creatures in the wild, hearing the hounds, awoke
Trembling; terrified deer raced through the dale.
They sped away to safer ground, but straightway
Were blocked by the beaters, with bellows and cries.
They let the high-antlered harts go by
And the big bucks with their huge horn-branches
For the lord had forbidden, in the closed season,
That any man interfere with the male deer.
The hinds were held back with shouts of 'Hey!' and 'Hold!'
While the does charged down to the deep dale,
And there you might see men loosing their long
Arrows: at each forest-break the big shafts flew,
Their broad heads biting the tawny hides,
And they cried out, bleeding and dying on the banks,
The hounds racing headlong after the rest.

Hunters, their horns blaring, hurried after:
A mighty cracking sound, as if a cliff were splitting.
Any wild beast beaten back from the high ground,
Who slipped between the bowmen, was driven down
To the stations by the water, and slaughtered there.
The huntsmen who kept those posts were so adept
With their sleek hounds, they quickly stopped them
And, fast as the eye could follow, dragged
                    them down.
          The lord galloped, and dismounted,
          In ecstasy galloped on,
          Riding daylong, undaunted,
          Until the light was gone.

And so the lord enjoys his sport at the forest-border,
And the good man, Gawain, remains in bed,
Lying snug, while the light streams down his walls.
Under luxurious coverlets, all canopied about,
And drowsing in soft slumber, he dimly hears
A small sound at the threshold. He listens. Now the door
Opens. He pokes his head out of the bedclothes,
Lifts back the corner of the curtain, just a little,
Looks warily out to see what it could be.
He sees the lady there, and she is lovely to look upon.
She draws the door close-to behind her, silently,
And moves towards the bed; the man, embarrassed,
Sinks back again soundlessly, feigning sleep.
She steps up lightly, steals towards the bedside,
Brushes back the curtain and cautiously creeps in,
And sits, very softly, on the bed's edge,
Lingering there at leisure to watch him waking.
The lord kept low for a long time also,
Turning over in his mind what this might mean
And what it implied, for it seemed to him a marvel.
But he murmured to himself: 'It would be more seemly
To find out, in the course of a conversation, what she wants.'
Soon he woke, and stretched, and turned towards her,
Unlocked his eyelids, and looked surprised,
Then made the sign of the Cross, as if by prayer to escape
                    his plight.
          There glowed on her lovely face
          A hue both red and white.

She seemed the image of grace,
Her small lips laughing and bright.

'Good morning, sir Gawain,' said the lady merrily.
'What a careless sleeper, to let someone slip in here.
I have trapped you beautifully; unless we strike a bargain
I shall bind you in your bed – of that you can be sure.'
And the lady laughed, made jests and jibes.
'And a very good morning to you,' said Gawain gaily.
'You may do with me as you wish and I'll be pleased:
In a moment I surrender – and I seek your mercy.
Truly I have no choice, trapped here as I am.'
He jests with her, to joyful peals of merriment.
'But, lovely lady, would you grant me leave
And release your prisoner, prompt him now to rise
That he might slip from his bed to find more fitting clothes?
Then I'd be more at my ease to talk with you.'
'No, no, my fine sir,' said the sweet lady,
'You shall not budge from your bed.
I have another notion. I shall tuck you up tightly on either side
And then talk with my knight whom I have neatly trapped,
For, yes, I am certain now that you are sir Gawain
Revered by the wide world everywhere you ride.
Your knightly character and courtesy are highly renowned
By all lords and ladies – indeed, by all who live.
And now, you are next to me, and we are alone.
My lord and his loyal men are far away in the forest;
Those in the hail lie sleeping, their ladies also.
The door is shut firm and fastened with a hasp.
And since I have in my house the person whom all prefer
I intend to savour each second: each passing word
                    I'll treasure.
        Both my mind and body
        Are only for your pleasure.
        I'm here perforce, and ready
        To serve you at your leisure.'

'In good faith,' says Gawain, 'that's certainly flattering.
However, I'm not the man whom you have in mind.
I'm not nearly worthy enough, as I well know,
To inspire such reverence as you have described.
I should be happy, by heaven, if I could please you

And be deemed fit, in word and deed, to devote myself
To serving you – a service of purest joy!'
'In good faith, sir Gawain,' said the lady gaily,
'Your excellence exceeds, your powers surpass all others.
To consider them lightly would show little courtesy;
There are many ladies who would love beyond the world
To hold you in their power, as I have you now,
To while away the time with tender words,
To find solace in love, free at last from sorrow:
They would prefer that pleasure to the richest possession.
But praise Him who reigns in heaven on high,
By whose grace I have wholly in my hand the man desired
                    by all.'
          She brought him excellent cheer,
          Being so beautiful,
          And the knight, with tact and care,
          Answered her words in full.

'Mary reward you, madam,' he said merrily,
'For, truly, I find your kindness most noble.
Most men receive recognition for generous deeds;
The respect I receive is through no merit of mine.
You yourself gain in honouring me this way.'
'Not so,' said the noble lady, 'I know otherwise,
For were I worth all the women who live on earth,
If I held the world's wealth in my very hand,
How could I make a better bargain in a husband?
With the qualities of heart and mind I have come to find
In you – your youth, your grace and gaiety,
Of which I have heard tell, and now know to be true,
There is no man in the world I would choose before you.'
'Beautiful lady, I know you could have chosen better;
Yet I am proud of the price you have placed on me.
I shall hold you as my sovereign, serve you steadfastly,
And I shall be your knight, may Christ reward you!'
Thus they discussed many things till mid-morning
And the lady made as if she loved him dearly.
Gawain, more restrained, showed marvellous courtesy.
Were she the brightest beauty, the knight had little love
To spare from his sorrowful quest, which he might not
                    forestall.
          The cut that lays him low

Assuredly will fall.
She told him she would go,
And he agreed withal.

She said goodbye, laughed, gave a sidelong look;
Then, while she stood there, astonished him with these words:
'May He who rewards fine speeches praise your performance.
However, it's hard to be sure you're really sir Gawain.'
'Why?' he replied, and quickly questioned her,
Afraid that he may have behaved boorishly.
But the lady blessed him and spoke to him, explaining:
'Gawain is rightly held to be a gracious knight
And courtesy contained in him so completely
He could never dally so long with a lady
Without being moved – if only by some touch or trifle
At a speech's end – out of kindness, to beseech a kiss.'
Gawain said: 'Well, best let it be as you wish:
I shall kiss at your command, as becomes a knight,
And more: I'll not displease you, no need to plead further.'
She comes nearer at that, catches him in her arms,
Leans down lovingly and kisses the lord.
They commend each other becomingly to Christ
And she goes out gracefully without more ado.
With that, rather hurriedly, he prepares to rise,
Calls to his chamberlain, chooses his clothes.
Once ready, he leaves his room and repairs to Mass,
Then to his meal, which the men had made for him.
All that day he made merry, until the rise
                    of the moon.
          Never so graciously,
          By the young one and the crone,
          Was knight received. All three
          Enjoyed themselves as one.

And all the while the lord is at his sport
Hunting the barren hinds in wood and heath.
By sundown, he has slain so many beasts –
Does and other deer – it is a marvel to recall.
Then at last all the menfolk flocked together
And deftly built a small hill of the deer they'd killed.
Those of noblest rank went up with their retinue
And chose all those they liked with the choicest fat

And ordered them neatly cut up, as custom demands.
They strolled around studying them, and found
Two finger-widths of fat on even the worst of them.
They slit open their slots, seized the first stomach,
Cut it out with a keen knife and knit it up.
Next they lopped off the legs, peeled back the pelt,
Tore the belly open, took out the bowels,
But deftly, not to destroy the first knot.
They gripped the gullet hard, swiftly severed
The weasand from the wind-pipe, and shucked out the guts.
They sheared off the shoulders with their sharp knives
And poked the bones through slits, preserving the sides.
They rent the breast, pulled the bones wide apart,
Then got to work on the gullet. One
Ripped it swiftly, right up to the leg-forks,
Nimbly cleaned out the innards; then they commenced
To free all the fillets that ran along the ribs.
They cleaned the backbones quite correctly
In a straight sweep, down to the hanging haunch,
Lifted the haunch up whole, and lopped it off.
The loose parts, properly speaking, men call the *mumbles.*
        Right down
    The leg-forks they released
    The flesh on every one,
    And quickly split each beast
    Along the long backbone.

And then they hewed off both the head and neck,
And, with a chop, severed the sides from the chine.
They kept a tidbit for the crows, tossed it into the trees,
Then rent a hole in the full flanks near the ribs,
And hung the beast from branches by the hocks.
Each huntsman was handed his proper portion
While their dogs feasted hungrily on a fine doeskin,
On the lights and liver, the lining of the paunches,
And on bread sopped in the blood that spilled around.
The kill was boldly blown, the hounds bayed loudly,
And all headed for home, their meat packed up neatly,
Proudly sounding all their hunting horns.
By then the day was done, and the company came
Into the lovely hall where the knight was quietly waiting,
        beside

A dancing fire at the hearth.
The lord enters with pride,
And when they meet there's mirth
And joy on every side.

The lord commanded all the men to come to the hall
And bade both the ladies down, with their maids-in-waiting.
Before all the folk in the hall he orders his hunters
To fetch his venison and set it before him on the floor.
With gracious ceremony he summons Gawain
And tells the tale of all the animals he's slain;
He shows him the fine flesh hewn from the ribs:
'What do you say to that for sport? Is it worth your praise?
Do I deserve your thanks for my skill at the hunt?'
'Before God,' said Gawain, 'these are the finest beasts
I've seen for seven years in a winter season.'
'I give them all to you, Gawain,' was the lord's answer,
'Our contract agrees you can claim them as your own.'
'That's right,' he replied, 'and I say the same to you.
What I have won with all honour, here in your hall,
Is yours indeed, as we agreed. I give it with goodwill.'
Now he clasps him with both arms around the neck
And kisses him as courteously as he can.
'There, take my trophies for I got no more than that,
Had they been greater I'd gladly give them to you.'
'That's very fine,' replied the lord, 'many thanks, but maybe
They were greater – so I wish you would tell me where,
With your subtlety, you won such a wonderful prize.'
'That's not part of the pact,' he said, 'ask me no more.
You've received what's yours. That's all, you may rest
                              assured.'
            They laughed, and ribbed each other
            With many a jaunty word,
            Then went to dine together
            Where fine food steamed on the board.

After that they both sat together before the fire
Where the women brought them beakers of wine;
And, in their raillery, they decided to repeat
Next day the same bargain they had made before:
Whatever happened, they would hand their winnings over
Exchanging at night the new things they had gained.

Both of them gave their oath before the gathering.
More beverages were brought, and their mirth rekindled.
Then, at last, the lords and the ladies left,
Bidding goodnight, and quickly repaired to their bedrooms.
The rooster had not roused, cackled and crowed three times
Before the lord leapt from his bed, and his men too.
Once more, both Mass and meal were quickly over
And, before daybreak, off to the forest in their hunting array
     they hurry.
   Sounds of their hunting-horns
   Over the wide plains carry
   To the hounds, loosed among thorns,
   Who hurtle towards their quarry.

Soon they mount a search at the edge of a marsh,
The huntsmen goading the hounds that had the scent,
Rousing them fiercely, raising a frightful din.
The hounds, hearing the shouts, hurried forward
And sprang along the trail, a throng of forty or so,
And such a riot of yelps and yaps arose
That all the rocks around rang with the sound.
The hunters, with shouts and horn-blasts, urged them on.
At that, the pack strung together and sprinted
Down a track between a pool and a beetling crag.
By the edge of a rock outcrop, near the marsh's rim,
Where rough rocks had fallen hugger-mugger,
They rushed in to flush their quarry, the hunters following.
They spread around the crag and the jagged mound
Till they were certain they'd trapped inside their circle
The beast that the bloodhounds had discovered.
Then they beat the bushes furiously, forcing him out.
Maddened, he charged at the men that checked his way,
Barrelling out, the most marvellous boar.
A long-time loner, cut off from his kind,
But still a redoubtable beast, the stoutest of boars,
Grunting at them grimly, and they were all dismayed
For, with his first thrust, he destroyed three dogs
Then, in no way hurt himself, spurted away.
The men shouted 'Ho!' very loudly, again and again;
Set horns to their mouths, sounded the hunting-call,
And joyful cries rose from the milling hounds

And men, as they ran at the boar in a swelling roar
                    of sound.
          He stops often, and growls,
          Then jabs at the pack around;
          There are horrible yelps and yowls
          Each time he maims a hound.

Then the men push forward to fire arrows at him;
They loosed the long shafts, struck him in showers,
But the tips were knocked aside by his tough hide
And no point could pierce his bristling brow;
Though the smooth-shaven shafts were shattered to pieces,
As soon as they hit him, the heads slewed off.
Then, under the welter of their pelting arrow-blows,
Crazed by their baiting, he hurled himself at the hunters,
Goring them savagely as he bored forward.
Many among them were fearful, and they fell back.
But the lord, on a light horse, gallops at him hard;
Like a bold knight on a battlefield, he blows his bugle,
Sounding the rally as he rides through bush and briar
Chasing the doughty boar till, once more, darkness came.
In this way they pass the whole day at the hunt,
While our gracious knight reclines at his leisure,
In luxurious pleasure, under bedcovers rich and
                    bright-hued.
          Nor was the lady neglecting
          To greet him in this mood,
          For she came again – expecting
          To change his attitude.

She creeps to the curtain, peeps in at the knight.
Gawain gave her first a cordial greeting,
And she, polite and eager, replied in kind.
She sat down lightly beside him, laughing;
Then, with a loving look, she started speaking:
'If you are Gawain, sir, it seems to me most strange
That, being inclined to breeding and fine manners,
You've no patience with the ways of polite society,
Or, being taught them, banish them from your thoughts.
For you have surely forgotten what I showed you yesterday
In the finest lesson that my lips could form.'
'And what was that?' said the man, 'for I am unaware

Of it. But if it be true, I am much to blame.'
'But I taught you to kiss,' the kind lady said,
'To make your claim quickly when the lady is willing;
Such behaviour becomes every knight who earns the name.
'Dear lady, don't say such things,' the man said.
'I dare not do that for fear of being refused –
For, if refused, my offer would wear a fool's face.'
'In honesty, none could refuse you,' she nobly replied,
'And, of course, you have the sinew to subdue by force,
Those churlish enough to wish to rebuff you.'
Gawain agreed. 'Indeed, what you say is true
But such force is unworthy in one of Arthur's court,
As is a gift not made with goodwill in mind.
But see, I'm at your command, to kiss as you please:
You may take one when you like and leave off at
                    your whim.
         She graciously leans his way
         And neatly kisses him –
         And of love's turnings they say
         Much in the interim.

'Now, if you won't be angry with me,' she went on,
'I would like to learn from you, sir. How does it happen
That one so young and lively as you, so active,
So courteous and chivalrous, so esteemed in every house,
And of all chivalrous deeds, if one need choose, the chief—
 Don't you agree? – are the deeds of love and war,
For the text and the very title of those volumes
Which deal with knightly deeds describe in detail how men
Have hazarded their lives in the cause of love,
Suffered for love's sake long ordeals, then
Avenged themselves with valour, vanquished sorrow
And brought great joy to a lady's bedroom,
And you, known as the noblest knight in all the land,
Your fame and honour following you everywhere –
How does it happen that I have sat beside you twice
Right here, and never heard the smallest word from you
About love-lore – not the least little thing.
Now, one so courteous and correct in his vows,
Would, I think, be yearning to show a young woman
At least a tiny token of the crafts of love.
Does it mean, despite your fame, you're in the dark?

Or do you think — shame on you! — I'm too slow to follow?
                              Not so!
                    I've come alone to sit
                    And learn new ways. Please show
                    The treasures of your wit.
                    My lord, being gone, won't know.'

'In good faith,' murmured Gawain, 'may God reward you!
It gives one great pleasure — great gladness —
That one so worthy as you should come to this room
And take pains with so poor a person, and sport
With your knight — I'm flattered by your fine favours.
But to take on the task of explaining true love,
To discourse, moreover, on the themes of love and war
To you, who, without doubt, are as deft
In that fine art as an army of fellows like me
Will ever be, even if we live long lives —
That would be stupid, esteemed lady, in the extreme.
I'll grant your other requests to the best of my skill
For I am deeply beholden, and will always be
Your loyal servant, may the Lord save me.
This way, whatever other motive she had in mind,
The lady lured him on, enticing him to sin.
But he held himself back so well no blemish appeared.
There was no sin on either side, nothing but innocent
                              pleasure.
                    They laughed. She lingered on;
                    And then, taking her measure,
                    Kissed him — and thereupon
                    Gracefully left, at her leisure.

Now the knight gets up and goes to Mass;
The morning meal was cooked and served with ceremony.
Then, all day long, Gawain amused himself with the ladies
While the lord galloped and cantered over his lands,
Chasing the wild boar that raced over the banks
And bit the best of his hounds, cracking their backs.
When he stood at bay the bowmen broke his will;
Gathering in groups, they shot shock-volleys of arrows,
Forced him to flee, to go for the open ground.
He could still make the hardiest start aside.
But in the end he was spent and could spurt no more,

So, quick as he could, he gained higher ground
And found a hole near a rock, where the river ran by.
He got the bank at his back, began to scrape,
A foul cud foaming at the corners of his mouth
As he honed his tusks. The hunters hovered, held back,
Weary of wounding him from afar, but still afraid.
He'd hurt so many hunters. Close in now? No one would try
          that task.
     No sense at all in waging
     More lives on such a risk
     With his mad brain raging
     Behind that murderous tusk.

Then the lord surged up, spurring his steed fiercely,
And saw him standing at bay, surrounded by hunters.
He leaps down lightly, leaves his mount,
Unsheathes a bright sword, strides forward,
Quickly wades the stream to where the beast waits
Watching the man warily as he lifts the weapon.
His big bristles stood up, and he snorted so loud
They were much afraid the lord might be worsted.
Then the boar made a rush, right at the man,
And with a crash they tumbled together, splashing
In white water. But the beast was defeated.
Right from the start the man had sighted him well
And he drove the big blade deep into his chest,
Shoved it in to the hilt, shattering the heart.
He crashed over. The water washed him away, with his
          last growls.
     Quickly, before he sank,
     In a splash of yelps and howls,
     He was dragged onto the bank
     And rent by a hundred jowls.

They blew the death of the boar with a blare of horns;
Every man shouted and hallooed, loud as he could.
The huntsmen placed in charge of that hard chase
Had their hounds bay at the beast.
Then one of them, wise in the crafts of the wood
Began with elegant care, to cut up the boar.
First he hacks off the head, sets it up high,
Then splits him roughly right along the spine,

Uncoils the bowels, roasts them on red-hot coals,
Dunks bread-sops in them, divides them among his dogs;
Then slices the boarflesh into broad gleaming slabs,
Pulls out the guts, and cuts them away, as is proper.
Then sews the two halves in a single whole.
Then they truss him up on a stout stick.
Now, with their swine hanging, they swing off homeward.
The boar's head was borne before the lord himself,
Who had dealt the death-blow in the stream after that swift
                    mêlée.
          It seemed to him, till he saw
          Gawain, a long delay.
          Then he called him and once more
          The knight came for his pay.

The lord laughed loudly and merrily then;
He greeted sir Gawain, and joked with him joyfully.
The good ladies were called, the whole house gathered.
He points to the pieces of boarflesh, tells them the tale
Of his great mass and vast length, how malicious he was,
And how wildly he'd fought as he fled into the woods.
Gawain hastened to praise his hunting prowess;
He commended the skills he'd so clearly displayed,
For a beast of such bulk and muscle, he maintained,
Or with such broad flanks, he'd not seen before.
They patted the huge head, praised it again,
Recoiled, feigning fear, so that the lord might hear.
'Now, Gawain,' said the good man, 'as you know, this game,
By our fixed and final contract, is yours completely.
 'True,' he replied, 'and by our terms it's also right
That I must give you back the gains that are mine.
He clasped the knight round the neck, and kissed him.
Then straightway served him again in the same way.
'This evening', said Gawain, 'we're still even, you see,
In all the covenants that, since my coming, we
                    have made.'
          'By Saint Giles!' the lord said,
          'What a fine game you've played!
          You'll heap wealth on your head
          If you conduct such trade.'

The serving-men then set up trestle-tables,
And spread white cloths over them. Clear light
Gleamed on walls as the servants set waxen torches,
And then brought food for all the folk in the hall.
A happy murmuring arose, then merry music
And mirth around the hearth. All sorts of singing
During the dinner, and after, rang through the room:
Old Christmas tunes and the newest carols and dances,
The most delightful pleasures a man could describe.
And our handsome knight stayed close beside the lady
Who dallied with him, offering subtle sallies,
Giving furtive and fetching glances, and he
Was caught in confusion, vexed in himself, perplexed;
But, out of good breeding, decided not to rebuff her,
But to deal with her delicately, though his plan might
                    go awry;
          They stayed on in that way
          Till the end of their revelry
          Then the lord called him away
          For some fireside causerie.

And there they drank and debated, deciding anew
The selfsame terms for tomorrow, New Year's Eve;
The knight begged permission to depart next morning
As it was now approaching the hour when he must go;
But to little avail, for the lord prevailed upon him:
'Stay,' he replied, 'I assure you, hand on heart,
You'll get to the Green Chapel and achieve your errand
On time, on the morn of New Year's Day, well before prime,
So rest in peace in your room, be at your ease
While I hunt in the holt and keep the covenant
To exchange my gains with you when I get home.
I have tested you twice and I have found you true
But *"third time, winner takes all"* — recall my words
Tomorrow. Meanwhile, let's have more merriment,
For a man can find misery whenever he wants.
Gawain agreed to that, and agreed to remain there.
Drinks were brought, then torches when the day
                    was done.

As if rocked on a raft,
Gawain sleeps on and on.
The lord, intent on his craft,
Rises at earliest dawn.

After Mass, he and his men took a quick mouthful.
A magnificent morning! He calls for his mount.
All the hunters who would follow him on horse
Were girt up and in saddle at the castle gates.
Fresh light over the fields: frost on the ground,
Sun climbing through a wrack of ruddy clouds
Dissolving them in wide light, driving them off.
The huntsmen loosed their hounds by a leafy wood
And the rocks rang with the sound of hunting horns.
Some sniffed the trail down which the fox lay lurking,
And cunningly crossed it, weaving about, in their way.
A small whelp smells him, and yelps; the hunters call.
Up come his companions, panting madly
And, packed together, they take off on his tracks.
The fox flicks ahead of them; they soon sight him
And they're after him again as fast as they can go,
Deriding him fiercely, with a furious din.
He twists quickly through a tangled thicket,
Then edges back, and bides his time in a hedge;
He hops over a hawthorn hedge by a small stream
And slinks out stealthily through the valley,
Hoping to outwit the hounds and escape in the woods;
Suddenly, before him stood a band of hunters
By a gap in the trees, and three growling hounds,
                              all grey.
          He twisted back, with a start,
          And boldly sprang away
          To the woods, fear at his heart,
          The smell of death in the day.

When the pack gathered, and put him up,
What a din! A delicious pleasure to hear those dogs!
When he veered into view they abused him bitterly,
A sound as if the cliffs were crashing down.
And the huntsmen hallooed mightily when they met him.
He was greeted with snarling snouts, and growls;
He was threatened, called 'cur' and 'thief',

And the dogs closed on his tail so he couldn't delay.
When he sped, going for open ground, he was headed off;
So he wound back, rapidly – Reynard was so wily.
In this way, he led them all astray, the lord and
His men, till the height of morning, among the mountains.
In his room at home the knight sleeps soundly
In the cold morning, ringed by rich awnings.
But, for love's sake, the lady was awake,
Nursing her heart's wish, lest her will weaken.
She suddenly got up, and went on her way
In a bright gown that brushed the ground lightly;
It was hemmed and lined with the finest fur.
She wore no headpiece, but in her hairnet were
Studded gemstones, in clusters of twenty or so.
Her fair face and her throat were both
Quite bare, and her breast and her white shoulders.
She deftly enters the bedroom.
The door behind her
Closes; she throws wide the window, calls the knight
To rouse him with her rich voice and joyful words:
                    'I say,
          How can you sleep, good sir,
          On such a splendid day?'
          He heard, through a drowsy blur,
          Her words wafting his way.

Drugged with heavy dreams, the man muttered
As one who, on waking, is shaken by the thought
That today his fate would gaze into his face
At the Green Chapel, where he must meet that man
And withstand his foul axe, and not fight back.
But soon as he had summoned his reason
He broke from his reverie and replied to her brightly.
The lady approaches the bed, laughs pertly,
Leans over, and lightly kisses his lips,
And he greets her warmly, in a most grateful manner.
He saw she looked lovely in her rich robes,
Her features flawless, and her colour so fine
It warmed his blood, and a great blessedness welled up
In him. They smiled shyly, prattled on merrily,
And all was bliss between them, all joy
                    and light.

Their speech was calm and clear
And everything stood right.
Yet danger was waiting near
Should Mary neglect her knight

For that lovely lady pressed him hard, persisted
Urgently, spurring him to the brink, and he thinks:
'I must accept her affection, or refuse, and offend her,'
Concerned with courtesy, lest he be thought a boor,
But more concerned about a misdeed should he err
And betray the man to whom the hall belonged.
'God help me,' he thought, 'that's not going to happen!'
With a short laugh he lightly laid aside
All the fine phrases that tripped from her tongue.
'You merit much blame', exclaimed the lady,
'If you lack love for the person you lie beside
Who is hurt now beyond anyone in the world.
Perhaps you already love a lady and, preferring her,
You've pledged your word, promised her so firmly
You cannot break it – that's what I've come to believe.
Is it true? Be honest with me, I beg of you.
Don't disguise truth with guile, for all the love
                    on earth.'
        'I have no love, by St John,
        I swear for all I'm worth!
        No one at all – and need no one
        Right now,' he replied in mirth.

'That's the worst word of all,' the woman said.
'But you have given a true answer, and it grieves me.
Come, kiss me quickly, then I must hasten away.
I must go on in sorrow, as a woman will who has loved.'
Sighing, she leans across and lightly kisses him;
Then goes her way, saying as she gets up,
'Now, my dear, as I depart allow me this:
Please give me a small present – a glove perhaps –
To remember you by, and rid myself of my grief'
'By heaven,' he said, 'I wish I had something worthy
Of your loving friendship – the finest gift in the land!
Truth to tell, you deserve much more,
By rights, than any gift that I might give.
But a love token would be of little avail,

A dubious honour indeed, to hold in your house –
A glove of Gawain as a keepsake in your care!
I have come here on a quest through rough country
And have no bearers with saddlebags full of fine things.
Because of your love, that distresses me, dear lady.
But each man as he can. Please, it's no impoliteness that
            I offer.'
       'No, no – but since, sweet knight,
       You've no gift for my coffer,'
       Said the lady, 'it is right
       You take whatever I proffer.'

She gave him a ring wrought in red-gold.
On it, a glittering stone stood out
That gleamed with light-beams, bright as the sun.
Be assured it was worth a fine fortune.
Nevertheless, the knight refused it, replying nimbly:
'I cannot take gifts at this time, good lady,
For I really may not tend you anything in return.'
She importuned him eagerly; again he refused
And swore, as before, he could and would not accept it.
Regretting his refusal, she then replied:
'If you refuse my ring because it appears costly
And because you'll feel yourself deeply beholden,
I shall give you my girdle, a gift of lesser worth.'
She loosed a belt she wore about her waist
Looped round her gown under her lovely mantle.
It was of green silk, sewn with a trim of gold,
Its margins highly embroidered by a fine hand.
She pleaded with him once more, with pleasant smiles,
That he might take it, unworthy as it was for a knight.
And he told her he would never even touch
Keepsake or gold, till God had sent him grace
Or before he had finished the task he had taken on.
'And now, I pray you, do not be displeased,
And do stop pressing me. My mind is firm. To that, pray be
            resigned.
       Yet I am deeply beholden
       For you have been so kind;
       Through times dark or golden
       I'll serve you with heart and mind.'

'Do you refuse my girdle', the lady replied,
'Because it is so simple? It may well seem so.
A poor rag, really — a most improper gift.
Yet the person who knows the power of its knots
Would perhaps gauge it at a greater price,
For with this green lace girt about his waist,
While he keeps it closely wound around him
He cannot be cut down by any man nor slain
By any cleverness or cunning under the whole heavens.'
The knight, pondering her words, now began to wonder
If it might be a talisman in his terrible plight
When he came to the Green Chapel to get his gains:
Maybe death could be foiled with this marvellous device!
Patient now as she pressed him, he allowed her to speak.
She gave him the girdle once more, most eagerly.
He accepted, and she granted the gift with goodwill
And besought him, for her sake, never to uncover it
But loyally to conceal it from her lord. He conceded:
No one will know except themselves, no matter what
                        the price.
            He thanked her, time and again,
            For her gift and her advice.
            By then she had kissed Gawain
            The hardy, not once, but thrice.

The lady makes ready to go and leave him be
For she knows she'll get no greater satisfaction.
When she has gone Gawain gets up from the bed
And dresses in the best and richest raiment.
He hides the love-lace that the lady gave him,
Conceals it carefully where he can find it later,
Then rapidly makes his way towards the chapel,
Goes to a priest in private and beseeches him
To instruct him how to conduct his life and learn
How his soul might be saved when he leaves the earth.
Then he fully confessed, admitting his misdeeds,
Both large and lesser, and begged for mercy,
And he also called on the priest for absolution.
He absolved him completely, so wholly cleansed him
That it might have been the dawning of Judgement Day.
Then he was free to please himself and the ladies
At carols and dancing and delightful pleasures

Much more than ever before, till the fall
               of night.
          Each man he honoured there
          And all exclaimed outright:
          'I think, since his coming here,
          He has never shone so bright.'

Let him stay in that haven, may love come his way!
The lord is still at his sport in the far fields.
He has finished off the fox he'd followed so long:
As he leapt over the hedgerow to look at the rascal
At a place where the hounds were giving hot chase,
Reynard ran quickly through a thicket
With the yapping rabble hard at his heels.
The lord, catching sight of the wild creature, slyly
Waited, withdrew a bright sword, and struck.
He shied away from the sharp blade, tried to evade him,
But the hounds rushed at him before he could run back
And fell on him in front of the horse's feet
And harried their clever quarry, snapping and snarling.
The lord leaps down and lifts him up by the pelt,
Snatches him out briskly from their busy snouts,
Holds him above his head, and bellows 'Halloo',
And the fretting hounds mill round, barking furiously.
The hunters, with their many horns, hurry along
Rightly sounding the rally, till they recognise their lord.
By then the noble men of the company were coming up
And those who carried bugles blew them and cried out
And those who had no horns bellowed and hallooed:
The most cheering cry that a man might hear.
They roared for the soul of Reynard – a resounding
               full note.
          The dogs are fondly praised
          With strokes on head and throat,
          And then Reynard is raised
          And stripped of his tawny coat.

Then, with nightfall nearing, they headed home,
Proudly blowing on their stout bugles.
At last the lord dismounts by his beloved castle,
Where he finds a fire in the hearth, the knight beside it,
The good man, sir Gawain whose heart was glad

As he'd treasured the love of the ladies in full measure.
His robe of rich blue reached to the ground,
And he looked fine in a surcoat, softly furred.
A mantling hood, that matched it, hung from his shoulders,
Both trimmed with fur from the finest ermine.
He rose, met his host in the middle of the room,
Greeted him with great pleasure, exclaiming:
'This time, my lord, I'm first to keep our agreement
Which we made final that time when the wine was flowing.'
Then he embraces the knight and kisses him thrice
With as much energy and glee as he could muster.
'By heaven,' said the lord, 'you've had enormous luck
In gaining that booty, if you drove a good bargain.'
'Don't bother your head about bargains,' he said.
'I've openly returned whatever, by rights, I owe you.'
'By Mary, mine are much less impressive,'
Said the lord. 'I worked a long day and won nothing.
A miserable fox-fur, may the devil take it!
A paltry reward to pay for such riches!
And you have given me three kisses that no man can
                    excel.'
          'By the Cross, our bargain's good,'
          Said Gawain. 'I thank you well.'
          The lord, right where they stood,
          Told how the bold fox fell.

With mirth, music and the finest fare,
They made as merry as any man might
And they laughed with the ladies, joked and jested.
Gawain and his host were most happy indeed
Like men who are light-headed, or a little tipsy.
The lord and his retinue played plenty of ruses
Till the time fell for the last farewell
And for all to go from the hall and be off to bed.
Gawain turns, and graciously takes his leave of the lord,
Greeting that noble knight with gratitude:
'May I give you thanks for this marvellous time,
And God bless you for your great honours at this feast.
Were you willing, I'd yield myself up as your man,
But, as you know, I must go on in the morning.
Please grant me, as you promised, a guide to lead me
To the gate of the Green Chapel, where God

Would have me face my fate on New Year's Day.'
'Indeed,' he said, 'I did agree to that, and you'll see
My promise fulfilled perfectly, and with pleasure.'
He promptly singles out a servant to point the way
And direct him over the dales with the least delay
By a quick path that goes through thickets and groves
of trees.
> The lord, for his uncommon
> And countless courtesies,
> He thanked, and the noble women,
> And gave them his goodbyes.

He spoke to them softly, his heart heavy,
And kissed them, expressing great gratitude for their kindness,
And they, in turn, gave him their compliments,
Commending him to Christ, with grave sighs.
Now he courteously takes his leave of that noble company;
He spoke a warming word to each man he stood before
For his fine service, and the trouble he had taken,
And for tending him so faithfully all that time.
And each man there was as sorry to see him go
As if they had lived their whole lives with him.
Servants, bearing lights, led him to his bedroom
And, as he needed sleep, brought him to bed.
Whether, once there, he slept, I dare not say,
For the morning was much on his mind as he thought
and thought.
> Let him lie there and wait,
> He almost has what he sought.
> If you're patient, I'll relate
> All that the morning brought.

IV

Night passes and New Year's Day draws near,
Dawn drives out the dark as the Lord decrees.
A time of wild weather; the wind increases,
Clouds rain down over the cold ground;
A nagging northerly pinches the skin,
Blown snow whips about, nipping the animals;
Wind whistles in gusts and howls off the heights,
Packing the dales with deep drifting snow.
Lying wide awake, the knight listens:
At each cock-crow he told the time exactly.
Though he closed his eyelids he dozed but little.
Before first light he leapt briskly out of bed,
For a lamp still burned on in the bedroom.
He roused his chamberlain, who replied straightway.
He bade him bring his suit of mail, and his saddle.
The man gets up, goes to fetch his clothes for him,
Then soon arrays sir Gawain in splendid style,
Beginning with warm clothes against the biting cold,
Then his mail-armour, which the men had safely stored:
Chest-pieces, plate-armour perfectly polished,
And his coat of mail, its metal rings rubbed clean of rust.
All seemed brand new and he was thankful
              indeed.
      As he buckled on each piece
      It shone like a burnished bead,
      The finest from here to Greece.
      Then he asked for his steed.

Gawain arranged the best of the gear himself:
His coat-armour, its crest a bright blazon
Worked in velvet, with vivid gems pointing the virtues,
Beaten and beautifully set, with embroidered seams
And a marvellous lining of finest fur.
Nor did he leave off the lace-girdle, the lady's gift;
For his own good, Gawain could not forget that.
When he'd buckled his blade about his firm haunches
He wound his love-token twice around him,
Tucked it quickly about his waist, content
That the green silk-girdle suited him well;
Against its ground of royal red it glowed richly.

But he wore the green belt not for its beauty
Nor for its pendants, all neatly polished,
Nor for the gold that glinted on its end-knots,
But to save himself when it behoved him to suffer
And stand defenceless against death when he met that man
     again.
    Now that he is ready
    He strides outside, and then
    He turns and, in a body,
    Thanks all the servingmen.

His great horse Gringolet was waiting for him.
He had been proudly stabled; he stood there, towering,
Fretting at the reins, fit — and itching to be off.
The knight strode up to him, studied his coat
And muttered softly, swearing on his oath,
'Here are men who care, and mind about honour.
Much happiness to the man who maintains these men.
And may the fine lady find happiness and long life.
Whenever they cherish a guest out of their charity
Heaping honour on their heads, may the Lord
In high heaven reward them, and all in this hall!
If I am still to dwell on this earth a while
I will certainly, God willing, return with a great gift.
He steps up into the stirrup, bestrides the big horse.
His man hands him his shield; he slings it over his shoulder.
With the spikes of his gilt heels he spurs Gringolet
Who springs off at once — no more need to prance on the stones
     and rear.
    Now man and horse ride tall
    And the man bears lance and spear.
    'May Christ protect this hall;
    May all things prosper here.'

The bridge was drawn down, the wide gates
Unbarred. Both halves slowly opened.
As he crossed the bridge-boards the knight blessed himself.
He praised the porter, who knelt before the knight
To give him good-day and pray God to keep him;
Then went off on his way with his one attendant
To point out the route to that perilous place
Where soon he must suffer that mighty blow.

They rode by banksides under bare branches,
They climbed by cliffs where the cold hung.
Clouds, high overhead; down below, danger.
Mist drizzled on the moors, dissolved the summits.
Each peak wore a hat, a huge mist-mantle.
Brook-waters boiled, sluiced over the slopes;
White water raged against the riverbanks.
The way they took through the woods was wild,
But soon it was time for the morning sun to
                    come up.
          In a field of fresh snow
          That lay on a high hilltop
          The servant reined in, and now
          Bade his master stop.

'See I have come this distance with you, sir,
And you are not far now from the notable place
That you have sought so long and so zealously.
But I shall tell you the truth as I know you well
And as you are a much-loved lord and man;
If you observe my words to the letter you'll be better served.
The place you're headed for is held to be perilous
For in those wastes lives the worst man in the world.
He is fearless and brutal and delights in fighting;
He is mightier than any man you might imagine.
His body is bulkier than four of the best
In Arthur's house, or Hector's, or any man's.
He chooses to challenge whoever might appear
At the Green Chapel; however skilled at arms
He will put him down, destroy him with one blow.
For he is vicious; his violence knows no mercy:
Whether churl or chaplain rides by his church,
Whether monk, or priest, or any other man,
He thrives on killing them all, as he loves his life.
So I tell you as truly as you sit upon that saddle
Go if you will — but, if he has his way, you'll be slain.
Believe me, though you have twenty lives to trade for
                    your own:
          He's lived here since long ago;
          In fights he cuts all down;
          Against his deadly blow
          No sure defence is known.

'So it's wise, sir Gawain, to leave him be.
When you go, for God's sake take a different track.
Ride home through another region, where Christ can help you.
I'll hurry home meanwhile, and I promise
And swear, by God and all his good saints –
So help me! – and by the holy relics and all else,
To keep your secret loyally, and tell no one you ran
From any knight or man that's known to me.
'Many thanks,' he murmured, then replied somewhat drily,
'I'm touched by your care for my welfare. I wish you well.
I'm sure you'd keep my secret quite securely,
But however firmly you held it, should I fail here
And scuttle off, fleeing in fright, as you suggest,
I'd be a fraud and coward, and could not be forgiven.
No – I shall go to the chapel, whatever happens,
And say to the man you speak of whatever I wish,
Come foul fortune or good, wherever my fate
                    might dwell.
          Tough he may be, his arm
          Might wield a club that can kill,
          But the Lord will save from harm
          All those who serve Him well.'

'Mother of God!' cried the man, 'if your mind's made up
To take your troubles entirely on your head –
If you wish to lose your life, I won't argue.
Put on your helmet, hold your spear at your side
And ride down the track that takes you close to that cliff;
Descend to the very depths of that wild valley
Then glance a little around the glade; on your left hand,
Chance is, you will see that selfsame chapel
And its massive master, grimly guarding it.
Farewell, noble Gawain, for I would not
Keep you company for all the gold in the ground
Nor walk with you one foot further through this wood.'
Brusquely, the man wrenches his bridle around,
Kicks his horse with his heels, quick and hard,
And gallops off and away, leaving Gawain
                    still there.

'I'll neither groan nor weep,'
Muttered the knight, 'I swear.
It's God's will: I must keep
My word, and not despair.'

He goads Gringolet further on, follows the path,
Rides along a bank beside a forest-fringe,
Negotiates a steep slope down into a dale.
He surveys the scene; it seems to him dreary, wild –
No place to hide, no haven to protect him,
But on both sides, sheer beetling banks:
Rough crags and piles of jagged rocks
Like snapped spears that appeared to scratch the sky.
He halted, reined in his horse, rested a moment,
Gazing around for a glimpse of the Green Chapel.
He thought it strange that nothing caught his notice,
Save something a short way off, where a kind of mound
Rose up, a barrow on a slope by a flowing stream
Where a rushing waterfall ran down. There,
The stream bubbled; it seemed to be boiling.
The man forced his horse towards the mound,
And leapt off lightly by a linden-tree.
He hitched his horse's bridle to a rough branch,
Stalked over to the mound and walked around it,
Wondering what on earth such a barrow could be.
Both at the end and sides it had big vents,
The bump completely grown over with clumps of grass;
And nothing inside, save the deep dark of a cave,
Or the crevice of an old crag – he couldn't tell which
                    from there.
            The Green Chapel! Lord, what a sight!
            A place, more likely, where
            In the dark of midnight
            The devil says morning prayer.

'An utter desert,' muttered Gawain. 'What a desolation,
With its sinister shrine, and tufts of weed everywhere!
A fitting spot for that fellow in his green gown
To do his devil's rites and unholy duties!
All my five senses say it is the fiend
Who's brought me down here to destroy me!
What an unhappy place! An evil chapel – devil

Take this accursed church, the worst I've ever chanced on.'
His helmet firm on his head, lance in hand,
He strode up to the roof of that rough abode.
At that height, from behind a boulder, he heard
Way off, beyond the brook, a weird sound.
Listen to that! It clattered against cliffs, as if to shatter them:
A sound like a scythe being ground against a stone.
Listen! It sang, and whirred, like wild mill-water
In a race. It clanged and rang out, rushing
Towards him. 'By God, this instrument is meant
To honour me alone; it is for me he hones
                        his blade!
          God's will be done.
          To cry 'Alas' is of little aid.
          Yet, even if I'm to die,
          No noise will make me afraid.'

With that, the knight called out with all his might:
'Who's master here, who keeps his covenant with me?'
Without halting, Gawain stalks up to the place:
'If anyone wants anything let him walk out now,
And finish this business off – now or never.
'Be patient,' came a call from the bank above him.
'You'll very soon get what I promised you.'
The sound went on again as he ground for a while.
The grindstone whined, then stopped; and the man
Stepped down, wound his way by a crag, and whirled
Out of a gap in the rock-wall with a grisly weapon:
Danish-made, its bright blade whetted for the blow,
Colossal and sharp, its shaft cunningly shaped.
Gauged by the gleaming lace he gripped it by
It was all of four feet broad, or more.
And the man in green was dressed as he'd seen him first:
The same bushy beard, thick thighs, and hair
Hanging down – save now he saunters firmly on foot
Wielding his weapon like a walking stick.
When he reached the water he refused to wade across
But vaulted over on the huge handle, not halting,
But striding, fiercely angry, over a wide field
                        of snow.

And Gawain bowed his head,
In greeting — but not too low.
'Well, sir,' the other said,
'I see you can keep your vow.

'Gawain,' said the green knight, 'may God protect you.
I wish you a pleasant welcome to my place!
You've judged your journey well, as a true man should,
And you're perfectly correct on the pact we agreed upon:
A twelvemonth ago, you took what fell to you then;
Now, on this New Year's Day I shall pay you back.
We're on our own down here in this lonely dale,
No man stands between us, we can strike as bitterly as
We please. Take your helm from your head. Prepare yourself!
And do not resist for I didn't restrain you
When you hacked my head off with your first smack.'
'By the God who gave me soul and spirit,
I shan't begrudge you your blow nor any harm that happens.
But take one stroke only; I'll stand still meanwhile.
Do whatever you wish — I'll neither resist
                    nor care.'
        He dropped his head, waiting.
        His neck showed white and bare,
        He made as if this thing
        Would never cause him fear.

Now the man in green gets ready, steadies himself,
Sweeps back the grim weapon to hack at Gawain.
He flourishes it with all the force in his big body
And brings down a dreadful blow, as if to destroy him.
Had it descended as hard as he seemed to intend
He would have been bisected by that blow,
But Gawain, glancing sideways as the axe swung,
Flinched his shoulders to evade the sharp blade
As it flashed towards the flint to topple him.
Suddenly the man in green stopped his motion
Then scolded him with a spate of fine phrases:
'You're not Gawain,' he said, 'so noble and so good.
He's not afraid of a whole army by hill or dale.
And now you tremble in terror even before I touch you.
I never knew he was such a lily-livered knight!
Did I flinch, or flee from you when your blow felled me?

Did I cavil, or create a fuss at king Arthur's house?
My head flew to my feet but I never flicked an eyebrow;
And you – I haven't even touched you and you're trembling.
It's clear I'm the better man here, the case is white
                    and black.'
            Gawain replied: 'Enough!
            I won't flinch when you hack –
            Though once my head is off
            I cannot put it back.

'But swing promptly, man, and bring me to your point.
Deliver me to my destiny – but don't delay!
I'll stand up to your stroke and start away no more
Till your steel strike me squarely.
There's my oath on it.'
'Here is your bargain, then!' He heaved the blade up high
And gazed at him savagely as if somewhat crazed.
He gathered himself for a great blow, then held
His hand, letting him stand there, still unharmed.
Gawain readied himself, steady in every limb,
Still as a stone, or the stump of a tree
That grips the rocky ground with a hundred roots
The man in green chatted on cheerily, mocking him:
'Now you've recovered your nerve I have to hit you.
May the great knighthood of king Arthur guard you
And keep your neckbone from this blow – if it can.'
Gawain, afire with fierce rage, replied,
'Get on, man. No more threatening. Strike!
It seems to me you've made yourself afraid.'
'All right,' the knight said, 'after such a speech
I'll no longer delay your quest, nor let you break
                    your vow.'
            He stands ready to swing,
            Face puckered. Imagine how
            Gawain is suffering
            For there is no hope now.

He lifts the weighty weapon, lets it fall
Straight: the blade brushes the bare neck;
But though the arm swung fiercely he felt no harm
For his neck was only nicked, a surface scratch;
Yet when the blade broke the fatty flesh

And bright blood shot over his shoulder to earth
Seeing his own blood-spots mottle the snow,
He leapt forward, feet together, a spear-length,
Seized his helmet, and slammed it on his head;
With a heave of his shoulders he hastily swung his shield
In front of him, drew his sword and spoke out fiercely.
Not any morning since the one when his mother bore him
Can he have been half so happy a man:
'Stop striking – now! Not one blow more!
I have received your stroke without strife or resistance.
If you give me more you'll get repaid:
It will be quick and fierce – you can count on what
                              you've heard.
          Only one stroke will fall.
          That was our accord
          Last year in Arthur's hall.
          So stop. That was your word.'

The man drew back. Upending his big weapon,
He shoved the shaft into the ground, leaned over the blade
And studied the knight who stood there before him
In his fine armour, his fear of being harmed
Quite vanished. That sight warms the blood in his veins.
He pokes fun at him, cracks merry jokes
In a loud tone that rebounds off the stones:
'My good fellow, no need now to be so fierce!
In our fight no one has slighted you nor
Broken the conditions of our contract made at court.
I promised one stroke only. You have handsomely paid
Your debt – you're freed from all other dues.
Perhaps I'd have struck you with much more power
Had I been nimbler, and hurt you horribly.
That first stroke was only a joke, a threat in jest;
I didn't hack you open, I hit you but lightly – rightly so
Because of our agreement fixed on that first evening
When you behaved well in my hail and gave me all
Your winnings as a wise and good man must.
And the second stroke I dealt you for that day
When you kissed my wife and returned my rights to me.
My arm missed both times: mere feints, no harm
                              to show.

Who pay their debts can rest
Quite unafraid. And so,
Because you failed the test
Third time, you took that blow.

'For that woven garment you wear is my own girdle.
My wife wove it, so I know it well.
I have missed no facts concerning your acts and kisses,
Nor my wife's wooing of you; I brought it all about.
I sent her to test you out. You withstood her stoutly.
You're the most faultless warrior who walks on foot!
As a pearl is more precious than a snow-pea
So is Gawain, upon my oath, among other knights.
Yet here you lacked a little: your loyalty
Was wanting – not out of greed, not out of wantonness,
But because you loved your life – and I blame you much less
For that.' Gawain stood still, his mind in pain,
So shaken with guilt, so grief-struck that he quaked within.
The blood rushed from his heart, flushing his face.
He shrivelled in shame at what the bold man told him,
And the first words that he spoke were these:
'A curse upon my cowardice – and my covetousness!
There's villainy in both, and virtue-killing vice!'
He grasped the love-knot and loosened its clasp,
And hurled it hard in anger towards the man.
'There, take that tawdry love-token! Bad luck to it!
Craven fear of your blow, and cowardice, brought me
To give in to my greed and go against myself
And the noble and generous code of knightly men.
I am proved false, faulty – those failings will haunt me.
From falsehood and faithlessness come a hollow heart and
                    ill-fame,
        And I confess to you
        That I am much to blame.
        What would you have me do
        That I may cleanse my name?'

The lord laughed, and replied reasonably
And warmly: 'Any harm you've done is now undone.
You've clearly confessed and freed yourself of fault.
You've paid your penance at the point of my blade;
I hold you absolved of all offence, and as fresh-made

As if, since birth, you had never sinned on earth.
And I give you back the girdle with the golden border.
It's green like my gown – so take it, Gawain,
To recall this contest when you ride away
Among proud princes, as an emblem to remember
Your quest and challenge at the Green Chapel. But the feast
Continues at my castle. Let us hurry home
And resume our festival and our New Year revels
                    once more.
          With my wife,' insisted the lord,
          'Who was your foe before,
          You'll find a new accord;
          Of that I'm very sure.'

But Gawain declines, catches hold of his helm
And politely puts it on, thanking the man most warmly:
'I have lingered long enough. Good luck to you,
And may He who bestows all honour show you His bounty.
And commend me to your lovely lady, your courteous wife –
Both her and the other, my two honoured ladies,
Who so neatly tricked their knight with their nice ploy.
Yet it's no wonder if a fool's made mad
By the wiles of a woman, and suffers woe.
Adam in paradise was thus deceived by one,
Solomon by more than one; Samson also –
Delilah sealed his fate – and, after that, David
Was betrayed and brought to sorrow by Bathsheba.
Since these were gulled by their guiles, how fine it would be
To love women warmly, yet believe no word that
They say. They were the noblest men we've known;
Fortune favoured them, they were the finest, the most blessed
                    by heaven.
          But by women they'd used
          Their wits were teased and riven.
          Now I, likewise abused,
          Perhaps will be forgiven.

'As for your girdle,' said Gawain, 'God reward you,
I shall bear it with the best will – not for its gleaming gold,
Not for its fine-knotted cloth, nor its many pendants,
Not because of its cost or its handsome handiwork –
But I shall see it always, as a sign of my fault

Wherever I ride, remembering with remorse, in times of pride,
How feeble is the flesh, how petty and perverse,
What a pestilent hutch *and* house of plagues it is,
Inviting filth! And, if my vanity flare up,
When I see this love-lace it will humble me.
Now I would ask one thing, if you won't be offended:
Since you are lord of these lands where I have spent
Many days in your friendship – may the One who reigns
High in heaven reward you royally! –
By what name are you known? It's the last thing I'll ask.'
'Very well, I shall tell you,' the knight replied,
'By name I am known as Bertilak de Hautdesert.
Through the power of Morgan le Fay, part of my menage –
By her wiles in witchcraft and her cleverness
She has mastered magic skills once kept by Merlin,
For it is well known that long ago she fell in love
With that wise wizard, as your knights have heard at your own
                    hearthside.
          'Morgan the Goddess': so
          Titled, since none can ride
          So tall, but with a blow
          She will cut down his pride –

'She had me to go in this guise to your hail
To test your mettle, gather whether there's truth
In the rumours of the Round Table's renown;
She worked this marvel on me to befuddle your brains
And cause Guinevere grief, kill her with fear
Of a ghastly apparition that spoke like a ghoul
And twisted his head in his own hand at the High Table.
It is she who lives in my home, the hoary lady;
Arthur's half-sister, and your own aunt as well:
The duchess of Tintagel's daughter, who bore,
Through union with Uther, the noble Arthur, now king.
So I beseech you, come back and greet your aunt
And celebrate in my hall. The whole house loves you.
And, as much as any man, I wish you well, for
The truth that you bear, and there's my oath on it.'
Gawain again said, 'No – not by any means.'
They embraced and kissed, commending each other to Christ,
The Prince of Paradise, and parted right where
                    they stood.

Gawain tugged at the rein,
Turned homeward fast as he could.
And the knight in bright green
Turned to wherever he would.

And now Gawain rides along wild ways
On his good steed Gringolet, his life spared by grace.
Sometimes he stayed in a dwelling, often out in the open;
He battled, and fought off vicious attacks in the valleys;
Too many adventures to mention in this tale.
His neck-wound ceased to hurt him, slowly healed,
And he bore the green belt wound around him
Crosswise as a baldric, bound fast to his side,
Its laces tied under his left arm in a tassel,
Sign of the sorry fault that had found him out.
And thus, quite sound, the knight comes to the court.
When the king found Gawain come home, cries
Of gratitude and great joy broke out, mounting as the king
And queen kissed him and all the court greeted him,
And all his trusted brother knights of the hall
Questioned him, marvelling as he told tales of the quest
And all the galling trials he had undergone:
The challenge at the Green Chapel, the antics of the man
In green, the loving friendship with the lady – and the girdle.
He bade them scan his bare neck for the scar,
That shameful hurt at the lord's hand, with himself
                    to blame.
        Grieving as he retold
        The whole tale, his blood came
        Rushing, now hot, now cold,
        And his face flushed in shame.

'Look, my lord,' he said, touching the love-token.
'This band belongs with the wound I bear on my neck:
Sign of the harm I've done, and the hurt I've duly received
For covetousness and cowardice, for succumbing to deceit.
It is a token of untruth and I am trapped in it
And must wear it everywhere while my life lasts.
No one can hide, without disaster, a harmful deed.
What's done is done and cannot be undone.'
The king and the whole court comfort the knight,
Laughing loudly, and they cordially decree

Right then, that lords and ladies of the Round Table
And all in their Brotherhood should wear a baldric
Bound crosswise round them, a band of green
The same as sir Gawain's, to keep him company.
All agreed it was good for the Round Table's renown;
He who wore it would be honoured evermore,
As it is recounted in the best books of old Romance.
These marvellous things took place in the age of Arthur
As the books of Britain, Brutus' isle, all tell.
Since Brutus, that bold man, first landed here
After the battle and the attack were over
> at Troy,
> This land has often known
> Adventures like these. I pray
> That He of the thornèd crown
> Bring us all to His joy. *AMEN*

HONI SOYT QUI MAL PENSE

THE ROMANCE OF GAWAIN

THE FLYING CHESS-SET APPEARS AT KING ARTHUR'S COURT

There are many adventures about King Arthur which have never yet been written down. I am beginning a marvellous tale of this sort; if I could find it in French, I would translate it for you into Dutch: it is a fine tale indeed! All the angels in heaven must lend me courage and sense and wisdom for the task, and reinforce my creative powers so that all those who hear the tale may find noble virtues in it. May the Lord grant me as much wisdom as this book demands so that I may carry out my task from start to finish without coming to grief! For this I pray to God that through his grace he may forgive me for the errors, whether at the start or the finish, that I commit in the telling. This was the prayer of Penninc, writer of this book. He spent many sleepless nights on it before he considered that he had finished his task. Now he asks you all to be silent, if you are courteous: even if it is too much for him, he will now relate the marvellous tale of King Arthur.

King Arthur was holding court in his hall at Caerleon, as was his royal custom, with a number of his knights, who I will name as best I can: Yvain and Perceval, Lancelot and Duvengael, and the courtly Gawain (whose equal was not to be found there). Kay the seneschal was there too. When the barons had gathered and had finished their meal and washed their hands, they witnessed a great marvel: they saw a chess-set fly in through the window and settle itself on the floor, all ready for anyone to play. It stood there, yet not one of those high-placed lords dared approach it. Now I should like to describe the chess-set for you: its legs were made of red gold, and the rims of silver. The board itself was of ivory and inlaid with precious stones. Indeed, the pieces belonging to the chess-set were more valuable than all of Arthur's kingdom. Everyone there saw it; suddenly it rose up and flew off to wherever it had come from.

This disappointed King Arthur and he said, 'By my royal crown, that chess-set seemed a splendid one, and there must be a reason why it appeared here. Whoever shall set out in pursuit of that chess-set and deliver it into my hands, shall have all my land, and shall hold my crown as his own after my death.'

But of all the knights who were present, not a single one dared set out. They all sat there in silence. The king said, 'Whoever wishes to be judged a noble knight in my court, must obtain this chess-set for me. If we let it slip away, no one will ever honour us again.'

Still all who sat there were silent. None of them spoke a single word in answer. When the king heard this, he spoke, 'By my royal crown and by the heavenly host, and by all the power that I have wielded by God's grace, if no one will get the chess-set for me, I shall ride after it myself. I don't intend to delay any longer or it will have flown far beyond my reach. I am the one who desires it, so I shall either retrieve it before I return to Caerleon, if disaster or mishap do not prevent me, or I shall perish with this wish unfulfiled.'

Sir Gawain, foremost in knightly deeds of virtue, was ashamed when he heard that there was no one who dared to accept that promise from his lord the king. He stepped forward and spoke, 'King Arthur, my lord, I have listened carefully to what you said: will you honour the promise you have made to the man who accepts your quest?'

The king answered at once, 'Indeed I shall, and may it bring me good fortune! If there is any knight at my court who can deliver it into my hands, I will give him all my land and it would be my wish that my crown be his own after I depart this life! I shall not go back on my word.'

When Sir Gawain heard this he had his armour prepared, and armed himself without delay. Then he spoke, 'Wherever I find the chess-set I shall hand it over to you, or may I perish in the attempt!'

Once Gawain was armed Gringolet was brought before him – whom he loved and had chosen in his heart before all other horses – and he sprang into the saddle and made the sign of the cross with his right hand. Then the warrior took his leave of the king and queen and all those who were in that hall with the king. They answered together, 'Farewell! May God protect you from shame and harm and may your quest turn out well!'

He rode off at these words; the knights who remained were very excited and said, 'If it turns out ill for him, he will have little reason for complaint, for he dared to accept the quest which no other man dared undertake, and of which no one had heard that it had ever happened to another man. We think that he acts unwisely.'

'Sir Gawain, take care in what you do,' said the king to his nephew as he rode off, 'and heed the advice I give you: always take care of yourself and your horse so that you do not pursue the chess-set in such a way that you come to grief.'

Sir Gawain set his spurs to Gringolet with all his might. And when Sir Kay saw this, he ran to the window of the hall and cried – these are his very words – 'Sir Gawain, listen: if you had taken a cord and had tied it to the chessboard, you might now be able to reel it in so that it would not have escaped you.'

Sir Gawain said, 'Sir Kay, stop your spiteful taunts, and let me have my adventure! Whether it is sweet or sour, whether it turns out well or poorly, Sir Kay, I will not call on you for advice.'

And so he rode off in haste, bold as a lion. Sir Kay spoke, 'Spur on, Sir Gawain, the chess-set lies ahead; it must not escape you.'

The king and those who were with him said, 'Sir Kay, enough of your words. Why don't you let the knight go, and God protect him? You yourself did not dare to accept the quest that he has taken upon himself.'

Gawain rode off while they stayed behind, talking freely about Gawain.

The king and the queen went up to the battlements and gazed out after Gawain. There was no one there, neither great nor small, who did not rush to the windows to see which way Gawain would go. He rode at full gallop as if he would not spare himself, after the chess-set: and the chess-set flew before him, now high, now low, now forwards, now backwards, now far off, now close by, or so I have been told. Sir Gawain saw it float ahead of him and he could have caught it in his hand, but he let it go because of what they might say up in the hall: if they were to see him capture it and if it then escaped him, they would mock him. He did not let it go for any other reason. And so Sir Gawain rode at a trot through open country until he came to a valley. At that the king stood up and said, 'Sir Gawain, may God guide you! I can no longer watch you.'

At that he turned about, and the nobles with him, away from the windows in the hall; and they all said the same thing: 'Sir Gawain, may God in heaven above keep you from disgrace and harm and from dishonourable behaviour; and may He allow you to return safely, to your honour, with the chess-set.' After that they spoke of other matters.

GAWAIN'S PURSUIT OF THE CHESS-SET

So the warrior rode off in pursuit of the chess-set, the object of his quest. Soon Gawain realised that a mountain was blocking his way: it seemed to him to reach to heaven! When he reached it he exclaimed, 'Help me, Lord, Child of Mary; how can I ride around this obstacle? I see no way, neither straight nor crooked, by which I may follow the chess-set. It would be a dismal day if the chess-set escaped me.'

At that moment Gawain became aware that the mountain had suddenly gaped open: the chess-set flew in, and he followed. But the mountain at once returned to normal when Gawain was inside: the opening was now suddenly closed. Gawain was compelled to remain inside, and bewail his fate alone in the darkness within the mountain! He could not hear a single living creature; there was nothing but stones to whom he could speak! It seemed to him that his heart would break because he had lost the chess-set. It was more than he could bear – that he should pursue the prize so far only to land in such straits. He said to himself, 'Even if the mountain were open and I could leave, if I were to return to court without the chess-set I would forfeit all my honour, and I would be ridiculed by Sir Kay: such treatment at his hands would be very hard to bear. I would rather die and rot in this mountain, as I now expect I shall unless God and a favourable fate help me!'

That night he suffered great anguish, from the moment when the sun ceased to shine, until it rose again. The youthful knight fell to his knees in prayer and said, 'Oh Lord, you who died for us and for our sake tasted that bitter death, help me now out of this predicament! If I were out on the open plain, though there were foes surrounding me and they all sought to slay me, I would defend myself against them with shield and spear! But here I am doomed to die without having struck a single blow! This fact alone grieves me sorely.'

Then he crossed himself and rose to his feet, and quickly went to Gringolet, taking the reins in his hands, and bewailing the loss of the chess-set. He took up the reins at once and wandered about in that mountain alone until he saw in the distance a point of daylight, as if it were a star.

He was making his way towards that light when he stumbled on a dragon's nest in which four small dragons were sleeping. The older dragon, though Gawain did not know it, had ventured forth from the mountain to search for food for its young ones. They had remained behind, so when Gawain saw the four dragons, he didn't know what best to do. But he acted quickly, and, drawing his sword, he rushed up to them and struck a blow in their midst. The eldest bore the brunt of that attack, for Gawain cleaved it neatly in twain. The second he hurt so grievously that it died as a result of its wounds. He cut off the foot of the third, but the fourth defended itself, and burned with anger towards Gawain. It had dodged him despite its drowsiness, and it was fierce, even if it was small. It charged Sir Gawain with both claws and fangs bared. Sir Gawain defended himself with hands and with sword and shield; he defended himself bravely and desperately, and tried to kill the dragon, but he could not. It lay in a hollow where neither man nor woman had been before. Then the dragon raised its tail and struck Gawain such a blow, that he fell to the ground, though he smarted sorely for it. But Gawain jumped up and seized the dragon with both hands, by both its lower and upper jaws, and he rent its maw so wide open that its head split and hung down in two parts. He at once took up his sword, but the other dragon, that had lost its foot, had singled out Gringolet, Sir Gawain's horse, and charged wildly towards him. Straight away Gringolet perceived that the dragon was headed for him, so he raised his foot and dealt the serpent such a mighty blow, so precisely aimed against its healthy leg, that it was smashed to pieces — the dragon fell to the earth. Whereupon Gawain rushed up with his sword and quickly deprived it of its life. He strode quickly to Gringolet, readied himself and mounted, and rode off without delay to where he saw daylight gleaming. Now may the Virgin Mary preserve him!

And so he rode through the mountain until he came to a place where the mountain was split open. The older dragon used to come and go through that gap with the prey off which it and its young lived. When Gawain saw it coming he was not the least bit pleased, so he jumped to one side so that the dragon might not see him. He readied himself and took up immediately both shield and spear, and he prepared to make a stand: he gripped his spear in both hands and stood before the opening, spear-point poised for the thrust. And the dragon came rushing at him and expected to enter without resistance, when Gawain struck it with his spear so well that he pierced it quite through; the dragon fell down in the opening and began to writhe in pain. Gawain tried to remove the shaft of his spear, but it broke in two! The stump hurt the dragon so severely, that the flames burst forth from its throat; then Gawain thought that he would certainly succumb to the heat. Fearing for his life, he moved quickly to one side to avoid the flames which issued from the dragon's throat. If its tail had not remained outside it would have cost Gawain his life, so great was the pain he caused it. The dragon struck such mighty blows with its tail against the rocks that they fell away on either side of the opening. Three knights could have ridden through the hole that the dragon made. If Gawain had been hit, I believe it would have been the death of him, even if he had had the strength of twenty men. Sir Gawain stood there and laughed, saying, 'Now the dragon has opened the door for me! I can go out of the mountain and ride wherever I wish.'

But the dragon did not lie still for long: the broken spear-head hurt it so much that it raised itself as soon as it could and rushed towards Sir Gawain. On it came, burning like fire; no one ever saw such a gruesome beast! When Gawain saw it, he grew fearful and let his sword slip out of his hand. The dragon chose to harm Gawain as best it might: it dealt him twenty or more heavy blows in quick succession! Then suddenly it took up Sir Gawain in its tail, intending to carry him to its young for their food: for this reason it let him live. But Gawain, fortunately for him, had killed them all before. The knight was in dire straits: If he had stood in front of the dragon, instead of behind him as he now did, he would have been burnt at once, without a doubt. Gringolet could not endure the heat within those walls: he ran out through the opening and stood to one side. This dismayed Gawain, who said, 'The Devil holds me so firmly captive that I cannot escape, bound fast in his tail as I am. If only I could confess my sins, then I would be content before my death. May the same God who granted me life, help me and protect me and give aid to my soul, for my life has come to an end.'

The dragon flew off quickly, carrying Gawain in its tail, and went on down a narrow path. Gawain was exhausted by the injuries that the dragon had inflicted on him. But suddenly it got caught in an opening; it could not pass through: the walls on either side were too narrow. It had passed through often enough before, but now the spear-stump which was still sticking in its side prevented it.

When Gawain saw that, he was glad. He said, 'Lord God, through Your grace, may You now protect me, against this fierce dragon, that has caused me such anguish.'

Gawain was forced to remain where he was. The two of them were caught so firmly that they could not move either forward or backward. Gawain could barely speak a word, so tightly did the dragon's tail grip him. The dragon dealt him a great many blows with its tail against the rocks, and thrust him into a pit so that he could hardly speak, let alone move a muscle. At that moment the dragon rent Gawain's armour with its claws. He was still coiled in its tail and so firmly gripped that he was going to be hard pressed to escape the plight he found himself in. Nevertheless he freed one hand and felt for his sword at his side: it had gone! Neither before nor since did Gawain find himself in such dire need, and he truly expected to die. Then he found at his side a dagger: this made him glad, and he thanked God, as he had ample reason to do. Gawain drew that knife and stabbed the dragon again and again. He caused it very little harm and he did not succeed in hindering it in the least. If it had had free movement of its head Gawain would have had reason to regret his attempts at wounding the dragon, but the spear-stump prevented it from attacking him with fire. Gawain, who was barely alive, took up that dagger and stabbed the dragon precisely in its navel so that its heart burst. The dragon bellowed loudly: its death was near. And yet Gawain's situation was desperate: he lay under the dragon's foot. Blood came pouring out of its wound onto him – it was hotter than fire. Gawain said to himself, 'This is no earthly creature; it is the Devil from hell who has come to torment me and who has wrought such tortures upon me! And still I cannot escape from it although it has been robbed of life. Even though I was stronger than all five dragons, I am not now able to prevent my being cooked and broiled – the Devil holds me so firmly captive – in the blood that flows from these wounds. It seems hotter to me than any fire!'

Gawain lay under that creature in the pit, drenched in the dragon's blood that streamed about his shoulders, and in great pain upon him. He quickly drew the dagger out of the dragon and slashed at its tail until he had quite cut it apart and thus freed himself. Praise be to God, he has escaped! So he cheerfully gives thanks to God in His kingdom on high. Then he rejoiced when he saw that the dragon that had caused him so much harm lay dead; but he said, 'I do not want you to cause anyone else distress, either now or in the future. I do not expect you will; but to make sure I shall cut off your feet.'

He did this, and then said, 'I trust that you will never again oppress anyone as you once did. My good coat of mail was no match for you: you have shredded it and through the tears in my mail coat I have sustained many deep wounds.'

Gawain was both happy and sad: he was very pleased that he had killed the dragon, but on the other hand it grieved him that he had lost his sword. He also had to make do without his shield, though it might cost him his life: it lay in pieces beneath the dragon. But for that he had had his revenge. His lance was also broken in two, and Gringolet had fled, leaving him there alone in mortal danger. He had fifteen wounds which the dragon had dealt him, and his life was full of woe. Yet Gawain would have paid no heed to the wounds and suffering that the dragon had caused him if he had known where to go to get news of the chess-set, wherever it might be.

And so he wandered about throughout the mountain, not knowing what to do next. And by chance he found his good sword, which he dearly loved and valued. Pleased, he picked it up and promptly hung it at his side in its sheath (which he still had). Gawain sighed and shuddered: his wounds hurt him very much. Meanwhile his wanderings had brought him to the spot where the mountain opened out, where he stood and looked out at a beautiful landscape. When Gringolet saw him there, he trotted up to his master as best he could, for he had been badly injured by the blows that the dragon had dealt him with its claws. Gawain sat down and examined his wounds; men said of him that he would never be found wanting for bandages and salves. No man alive had more need of his skills; but there was no water to be had. So he had to bathe all his wounds with his own blood, and bind them up as best he could. When he had finished this task, he got up and walked over to his horse. As he stood there and looked down at the valley below, it seemed to him that he was at such a height that it would be impossible for a man below to fire an arrow so high that it would reach him there, and he could not see how he and his horse could make their way down to the valley. For the mountain was so steep that, although a man might reach the top, he could not slide down again without falling into the water on all sides. For around that mountain there flowed a mighty, broad and rapid river, out of which the mountain seemed to have been raised like a church tower, straight out of the river. And in the mountain there was the opening, through which the dragon had often passed and behind which it had built its nest, out of reach of men: it was a difficult stronghold to take.

Gawain was very sorry that he had entered the mountain. It was a marvel that he had not sustained greater injury, for the dragon had been so fierce. Now he said, 'I have survived the terror inflicted upon me by the dragon. But I am still in great danger, for if I stay here any longer, I will have nothing to eat or drink. All I can do is to jump from this mountain into the river. If I die, I will drift to where people will recognise me. Up here there is little honour to be won. If I were to die here,' the knight said, 'Men would never come to know what had become of me.'

GAWAIN COMES TO THE COURT OF KING WONDER

And so he stood fearfully by his horse Gringolet, tightened his saddle-belt and mounted in a bound. He crossed himself profusely; Gringolet made for the river and jumped into the abyss below. If he had been lord and master of Paris, he would gladly have given it up to have been back in Caerleon! He clung firmly to his horse as he had good reason to do, and they leapt into the river. Gringolet began to swim; Gawain could now wash his painful and bloody wounds. Gringolet was so exhausted from swimming that he could hardly go on, but he swam until he felt land beneath his feet; it was an island in the river, and he stood still in order to catch his breath. It was lucky that he found it: he had little more than his head above water. Gawain was lucky to have his good steed which had saved him. When Gringolet had rested, he swam on to the other side.

Gawain dismounted at once in a beautiful meadow and sat down in the green grass. He was in bad shape physically, for he had emerged from a very dangerous place. Gringolet lay there as if he were dead. This greatly disturbed Gawain; he pulled up some grass, strode over to his horse and began to curry and rub him, to see if he could keep him alive. Then he jumped to his feet, which made Gawain very happy. As the knight stood by his horse's side, he had nothing with which to defend himself: he had neither shield nor spear if the need arose. Even though he was unarmed, he was brave. His coat of mail had many a rip and tear, and through these his handsome body was exposed: this was the dragon's doing. All he had to save him was his horse, Gringolet. Again he tightened the girth and mounted in a bound. Yet he saw no road along which he might follow the chess-set. So he rode in haste straight across the lovely meadow until he found that he had come to a road, which he then followed as best he could. Then he saw what seemed to him a castle made of gold, and Gawain thought to himself that he would lodge there if he could; he was determined to try. He rode off towards the castle in great haste. It seemed to him to stand in a lake, and to be built upon a pillar. In it there lived the King of Wonder. Do you know why he was called Wonder? It was because he could alter his shape to that of any animal that lived either on land or in rivers, and he could assume the shape of every feathered bird. I believe that no one has ever seen a more beautiful castle than his: it was adorned in gold with inscriptions both inside and outside. That castle cannot be taken, for the water that flows around it is half a mile wide.

Gawain had chosen the road that took him to the gates, and he dismounted as soon as he reached the stronghold, where he saw all manner of wonderful things that the king had created. Leaving his horse behind him, he went in, and he found King Wonder and his son Alidrisonder: between them was the chess-set that had caused him so much suffering; they were playing a game of chess. Then Gawain was in a better mood than he had been for a long time, for he had found the chess-set which he had sought for so long. Then he bowed and greeted the king and his youthful son. They returned his greeting in true fashion, arose from their game and welcomed Sir Gawain; and they then led him inside, taking him by the sleeve for he was in need of rest: since the previous morning he had suffered a great deal. His armour was badly damaged: he felt ashamed that one could see his bare flesh in so many places. King Wonder noticed this and called for two pages to take Sir Gawain and lead him to a chamber. Yet another page took it upon himself to go to Gringolet; Gawain had left him at the bridge below when he had come up. The page took Gringolet, who had emerged quite battered from the river, and led him up to a clean stable, where he groomed him and provided him with everything he needed. He curried and rubbed him vigorously, removed his saddle and bridle and covered him without delay. Then he fetched some grain and fed him well, before returning to the court above. The other two pages were with Gawain in his chamber; one fetched water without delay, neither too cold nor too warm, and poured it quickly into a tub; the other page had remained with him and quickly helped him out of his armour. Then they washed him and tended the many deep wounds which they found on him. When they had finished they led him quickly to a bed that was sumptuous and costly, and perfect in every way: the bedposts were of fine gold and the headboards of ivory, which were splendidly carved and sculpted. And there was a marvellous device there: four golden angels who sang beautifully and clearly. Sir Gawain realised that the song emanating from them came through a conduit that King Wonder had had installed beneath the castle. Each of them had in his hand a sapphire and a ruby, in the other hand a carbuncle: this dispelled the darkness with its light so that at midnight it was as bright as if it were morning within the keep of that stronghold. And the bed possessed this power: if a man were laid upon the bed, even though he were severely wounded or bruised or had any wounds on his body, he had only to lie on it for an hour until sleep overcame him, and when he woke up again he would be as whole and healthy as he had ever been before. This was why King Wonder had him laid upon it and tucked under its covers. He slept deeply, and the clear-voiced angels left off their singing.

When the king saw that Gawain was asleep, he summoned a page and commanded him to fetch Gawain's armour. They set about polishing and cleaning it: wherever they noticed that a ring was missing, they put in a new one. Gawain was not aware of this, for he was still asleep. When they had finished with his armour they replaced the equipment which he lacked, shield and spear with which he might defend himself if the need arose; and they found for him a green mantle of silk, exceedingly well made. King Wonder asked his pages, 'Tell us, has the meal been prepared?'

'No, sire, Lord knows.'

'Then make haste with it, for it is time for us to eat. I fear that our guest has not eaten anything all day!'

At that boards were laid upon trestles; a cloth was spread upon them. Gawain awoke out of his sleep as whole and healthy as he had ever been before; that is why the king had let him sleep, so that he would be healed of all his hurts before the evening fell.

'God help me!' exclaimed Gawain, 'Where am I? Am I lying here stark naked? I have neither stockings nor shoes, nor any clothes to wear!'

The king heard this, and had clothes of white silk brought to him. They were brought, and he was pleased when he took them from the pages; they were the most costly clothes that had ever been seen. So many marvels had been embroidered on them that one could not have bought their like for a fortune. Gawain was delighted, and dressed himself. The king had at the same time ordered a surcoat to be made, scarlet and trimmed with ermine. This was brought to Gawain, as well as new stockings and new shoes for the knight to wear. Then they fetched a washbasin of red gold with which they might serve him, and a ewer of the same material – the man who had had it made was rich indeed. They gave him water and he washed his hands; a towel was brought with which he might dry his hands; he had everything he could wish for.

Meanwhile King Wonder and his son Alidrisonder, together with six chosen knights, each of them handsome, wealthy and of noble birth, came to see Sir Gawain; the king said, 'You have arisen, Sir, and how do you feel?'

'I feel no pain at all; I have healed very quickly.'

'For that may God and His Son be praised,' said the king. Then they took the youth with great joy there were many eminent people present – and they led him to where all those tables stood; some were made of ivory and some of stone and yet others were made of ebony. The king's table, at which Gawain was to eat, was made of gold. He was placed all by himself in a chair adorned with jewels and costly gems. Neither lightning nor thunder could harm the man who sat in that seat. Sir Gawain began to eat as did all of those nobles, both at the upper and the lower ends of the hall. At the ebony table sat the counts and dukes of great wealth; at the ivory table sat eminent men, the knights, but their retinue sat below at tables of marble. Cool wine was served at the tables both above and below. Even if Gawain had sought for better lodgings during the space of a year, I believe he could have found no better. He sat at the king's side, who was very pleased at his coming. Before them stood the jugs of gold, from which the wine would be served, and there were a great many cups, as well as costly dishes. The king was pleased and said to Sir Gawain, 'Sir, take your pleasure, I implore you, of all such things as are here.'

Sir Gawain, to be sure, was well mannered; he laughed and said, 'Sire, here is enough. I want for nothing. I am very much satisfied.'

So they sat and talked. Gawain saw in that hall torches fitted in candle stands made entirely of gold, and they were so bright that it was as if it were midday in that great hall. As Gawain looked about him, he saw many knights but not a single woman or girl, which seemed strange to him.

The nobles sat enjoying themselves and they ate and made merry. Then the king said, 'Knight, if it please you, I should very much like to know your name.'

Gawain answered at once: 'Gawain is my name. If it be your wish and pleasure – for I am your guest and you are my host – tell me yours if you please, and where it is that I find myself.'

The king answered him, 'Sir Gawain, you are in the land of Wonder, where all the senses are charmed. Wonder is my own name.'

Sir Gawain said, 'Your name is truly Wonder, for your castle is full of wonders, and I have never seen the like in all my travels. But there is one thing which amazes me: there are many knights here, but no women and girls. Do you not have a queen here?'

At this the king opened a window through which Gawain could see, sitting in a hall on the other side of the wall, very many beautiful women. At that moment the queen sat down in a dignified manner; having washed her hands, she sat at a sumptuous table, and she was about to eat with a great number of her ladies in waiting who were all at her service. Sir Gawain said, 'Sire, according to what custom and for what reason – please tell me this – why do you live thus separated?'

The king replied, 'Sir Gawain, you see many marvels here which are of my making. But the queen has never been inclined to come and see how such things were made; she has always preferred to live in her own quarters.'

With this, the tablecloths were cleared, water was brought and they washed their hands. After the meal wine was served, as is the custom among men of standing. It was poured and passed around, the nobles drank. Then they put the jugs and cups aside. Then Alidrisonder said, 'Sir Gawain, I am curious to know what quest it is you have undertaken that brings you to the land of Wonder. Are you simply traveling, or looking for a joust, or are you seeking adventure? Do you come in peace, or with evil intent? You will surely find someone to oppose you before you turn away from here. Or is it your wish to remain with these knights? My lord is very much pleased with you, and he would be glad if you were to join his household.'

Gawain answered, 'May the Almighty God reward you for this splendid offer, but that is not my intention! You must know that I have come here in quest of the chess-set that I saw before you today.'

And he told Alidrisonder how the quest had begun at Arthur's court, when, as the king and his knights were sitting at table, the chess-set flew in through the window and settled itself on the floor. None of the knights had dared to touch it, and it had flown off again. At this Arthur swore that he would leave his crown and kingdom to anyone who set out in pursuit of the chess-set and brought it back to him. And so he, Gawain, had set out to seek the chess-set, since no one else dared to undertake the quest. 'I swore that I would hand it over to him if I ever succeeded in capturing it. So you see, sire, I caught sight of it and followed the chess-set to the Land of Wonder, expecting to capture it here. But now it seems that it has escaped me and is entirely out of my reach.'

Then the king said, 'God knows, Sir Gawain, if you had captured it, you could have spared yourself the greater trials that you must now endure. But my chess-set will remain beyond your grasp unless you dare to accept the conditions that I will put to you. If your desire for the chess-set is so great, then you must win it from me with spear and shield.'

Gawain's reply was courteous: 'I should be foolish indeed if I were to repay your goodness and the honour you have done me with evil. No, sire, without a doubt, if we were to injure each other in battle, I could never again gain honour: I would be denied any claim to fame. Wherever I came, men would say: 'That is the man who abused his host after he had treated him well!' I would rather I were imprisoned in a dungeon for forty days, where I could see neither sun nor moon than that such a disgrace should befall me here.'

All the lords said: 'You have spoken like a true man.'

The king said, 'In that case, Sir Gawain, will you grant my request and win the chess-set in a chivalric manner? Then it will be at your disposal.'

Sir Gawain said, 'I shall do as you desire.'

'Sir Gawain, then you must go in search of the Sword with the Two Rings. If you get it and bring it to me then I will give you the chess-set without fail. It is in the possession of a rich and mighty king named Amoraen. His castle is such that it may never be taken, and the good sword lies within its walls. The powers of the sword are these: it is said that no man may approach it unless he has been chosen by fate to do so. If anyone else should draw the sword, it will cut him in two at the middle. Only the most excellent of all men who were ever born may wear that sword. Sir Gawain, if you should fulfil this request and obtain the sword for me then I shall give you my chess-set at once to do with as you please.'

Gawain replied: 'If I were to possess it, then no man could buy the chess-set from me for gold or silver; I would deliver it into your power to do with as you please. But, my lord, there is one thing I lack and it troubles me greatly.'

The king said, 'Tell me what it is, and I will help you to the best of my power.'

He replied, 'I have neither shield nor lance; my hauberk is badly torn: if anyone were to strike me, he would pierce me through. It is for this reason that I am very concerned.'

The king said, 'Wait until tomorrow. Your armour has been repaired and readied for you.'

At this they ended their conversation. Then they prepared for sleep; Sir Gawain found himself in a good and costly bed, upon which he slept through the night until it was almost morning. Then Gawain dressed himself and asked whether anyone knew where his armour was. Two pages brought it to him at once and armed him properly and quickly. The knight was very pleased when he saw his hauberk shining brightly. He asked where the king was; but the latter had in the meanwhile risen and made his way to Gawain, and he greeted him in a very courtly fashion. Gawain said, 'May God give you joy and great honour, and keep you till I return! I will get the Sword with the Two Rings for you, provided that God spares me, before I return to the land of Wonder.'

GAWAIN BEGINS THE QUEST FOR THE SWORD WITH THE TWO RINGS

So Gawain left that mighty castle; on the drawbridge a page held Gringolet for him, along with his lance and shield. He climbed into his saddle and rode off without delay.

Presently Gawain was aware of a forest in front of him, where many birds sang, for it was only just dawn. Soon after he entered he heard someone moaning and complaining so woefully that Our Lord would have taken pity on him: he repeated, 'Alas! Alas! I do not know what to do! My old trouble only grows worse and worse!'

Gawain spurred on his horse and rode to see if he could help him. He saw riding towardshim a handsome youth on a miserable horse: it was skinny and lame; its mane was lank and long; its ears drooped downward; it limped on both fore and hindleg. It had been left to wander here and there, in all weathers, in that wood for many years. Indeed, it was no more than skin and bones. Its rider was thoroughly disheartened, and he beat the horse repeatedly with a stick, but it was no use: the horse could not go another step; it needed to stand still and rest or it would have fallen to earth.

Gawain saw this, and was sorry for the lad; he was well-built and handsome and yet rode such a wrteched horse. His nose was handsome and straight; his forehead broad and smooth; his eyes were a beautiful grey; his hair was curled and fair. He looked honourable enough to be count of that land. But he wrung his hands so that red blood streamed out from under his nails. Gawain greeted the youth as soon as he came up to it, and wished him good day. The youth said, 'May God reward you, Sir! It will never again be good day for me: I have come to the end of my good days!'

Gawain said, 'Tell me the reason for your sorrow.'

The youth said, 'It will be of no use to you to hinder me; let me pass, Sir, and may God keep you! Even if I were to tell you all my woes it would not help you. It is years ago that I lost my only brother. He was handsome, wise and virtuous, and no one living in the kingdom could match him. Yet the man who took him from me walks daily before my eyes, nor did he offer me any compensation for it, Sir, as true Christian love demands. Instead, wherever he sees me or comes near, he mocks and taunts me, even in church. I avoid him, but that does not prevent him from mocking me as if I were a fool. For he is convinced that I deserve nothing better than this abuse. Now I have challenged him before the king to a fight. But something else troubles me more: it is our custom in this land that no squire may challenge a knight to combat, for it would be considered an insult. So I must first be dubbed a knight: I have left both my goods and my estate in the hands of my lord the king, and hoped that I could journey to King Arthur to beg him to dub me knight; for he whom Arthur knights is certain of victory. That is why I set out, but misfortune has befallen me! Today I tried to cross the ford at the edge of the forest, but the evil custom that prevails there meant that my good sword was taken from me as well as my hauberk and my horse, as toll for the crossing. This sorry horse was given me in return. I cannot get another, for I have left my entire estate in the hands of the king and must return on the appointed day to do battle. Men will say that I have fled abroad out of fear; my beautiful wife will be disinherited and my children will miss me, for I will have to travel in foreign lands.'

At this he wept and wrung his hands.

Gawain understood his predicament and said, 'If someone were to give you a horse, would you then return from King Arthur's court in time for your combat as you swore?'

The squire answered, 'God knows I would, but that is beyond my grasp.'

Gawain said, 'Here, take mine. You will not find a better one anywhere.'

The squire said, 'You mock me, Sir; you would not go willingly on foot and give me your horse.'

Gawain dismounted immediately and said, 'Here, take my horse.'

The squire accepted it and was joyful. 'But I give it to you on the condition that you do your utmost to return quickly from Arthur's court to your challenge, and so retain your estate. Now go and return as soon as you are able and always be mindful of knightly virtue.'

Then the squire mounted Sir Gawain's horse and rode off in haste, having thanked him profusely for the favour and the honour that Gawain had done him: the youth was very happy indeed. Gawain strode up to the horse that the lad left there and mounted it, to see if it could carry him: it could neither amble nor trot. He dismounted and left it there; he had to leave that place on foot, and make his way on foot through the forest.

Though he was not accustomed to walking, he came in a little while to a castle and a river. This castle was the one from which the toll was levied and from which evil deeds were perpetrated with overweening pride. As soon as the castellan saw him he quickly rode out to Gawain on his high-spirited horse: when he came up to him, he said, 'Knight, clearly the customs of this land are unknown to you: you are under arrest. Pay us what you owe us and spare us a long struggle!'

Gawain answered him immediately and said, 'Why am I under arrest?'

'Because you are trying to make off without paying your toll.'

Then Sir Gawain enquired further: 'What toll is it that I owe?'

'The hauberk you are wearing and your shield and your sword, and if you had brought a horse with you, that, too, you would have to give me!'

Sir Gawain said, 'I gave my own horse to the youth whom today you have robbed of his hauberk and horse with your toll and evil custom. He is riding it now to Cardueil.'

'He did well to find such a fool and to persuade you to do that! Hurry up and give me your shield and your hauberk and your sword; I want them this minute!'

Sir Gawain countered, 'Who gets the toll?'

The man said, 'I do.'

Sir Gawain answered, 'You can have your toll, but only if you dismount and stand on your feet. I'd sooner see you in hell than give it to you on your horse.'

The man dismounted immediately and said, 'You play for high stakes! The Devil brought you here!'

In a single motion he drew his sword, but Gawain immediately drew his. He said, 'I will give you a toll before you go, since that is what you want!'

Gawain defended himself against his opponent to see whether he could put an end to the evil custom which had caused such harm. But the fellow's pride was so great that he thought that his equal was not to be found living in any land. He raised his sword at once and struck at Gawain with such great ferocity that he was disappointed to find him holding out so long. Gawain covered himself and used his shield cleverly; he received many a blow, but they did not go unreturned. Suddenly he raised his sword and struck his enemy so hard that he cleaved through both helmet and noseguard straight down to his teeth. Then he pulled out his sword with both hands and he said, 'There, take your money!'

The man was dead before he touched the earth.

Gawain took the fine horse that stood at his side, which he badly needed. He said to the horse, 'Easy, calm down; your master has received his desserts. He lies here in silence and has what he longed for. He says he will take my hauberk and sword as surety until I return.'

Then Sir Gawain mounted and rode up to the castle that had been the source of such an evil custom for many a day. And when the gatekeeper saw him he began to shut the gate and said, 'By my faith, you'll remain outside, I won't let you in!'

When Gawain saw this he spurred his horse – it was both mettlesome and swift – so that it galloped through the gates before the gatekeeper could close them. Gawain said, 'You failed to shut me out; and you'll live to regret it, mark my words!'

He dismounted at once, drew his sword in a flash and struck off the gatekeeper's head. Then he threw it before him into the court and quickly seized the keys. He locked the gates so that no one could come into the castle from outside before he wanted them to; nor could anyone get out before he had done as he wished. Then he went on, carrying his sword drawn and naked in his hand. Whoever he encountered there within the castle and in the great hall died; he spared no one . Wherever they fled, he dragged them out and struck them dead, until no one remained; he deprived them all of their lives. He did this to stamp out the evil custom that had caused such harm.

When he had finished, he returned to his horse, unlocked the gate and led it outside. Then he went back and locked all the doors in the castle, mounted and threw the keys into the river. He rode quickly away and left the castle locked firmly behind him. I believe no one will ever enter it unless he breaks down the walls. And so he set out in search of adventure, while the squire to whom he had given his horse rode swiftly to Cardueil. The king and those who were with him stood at the windows and saw a youth riding up on Gringolet. They were astonished by this and said to each other, 'What has become of our lord Gawain? It can only be that the man who now approaches has taken his life.'

Sir Kay was there; he spoke last, saying ironically, 'What you say is not true. The youth you see approaching is a messenger with news of the chess-set. All is well with Sir Gawain, and he has acquired the chess-set. He has simply sent his squire before him to the court. Gawain has now realised where his audacious boasts will lead him. And I told him clearly before he started that it would bring him shame if he dared undertake the quest that no one else would embark upon.'

The king said, 'Desist from such talk, Kay; we have heard quite enough of it.'

Kay was pleased; he laughed and said, 'By God, your Majesty, Sir Gawain will certainly bring you honour! Prepare to welcome him without delay!'

The king retorted, 'Sir Kay, if you please, we have had enough of such talk, and we can do without your spiteful taunts. If I have lost Gawain, you will regret it!'

As the youth came nearer, the knights said, 'Shall we seize him and strike off his head at once? Sire, you must decide which manner of death is best by which we may avenge Gawain.'

But Sir Lancelot said, 'King Arthur, for the sake of God and your own honour wait until the youth has arrived and you have learned the truth about what he seeks and desires before you pronounce his death. Men have so often spoken of Sir Gawain's goodness: he is courteous, merciful and brave. I think it likely that he gave him his horse.'

So the king and his knights waited until the youth came riding into the courtyard and alighted from his horse. The king went out to meet him and the youth made haste to greet Arthur, but his welcome was not a very warm one. The king said, 'Tell me where you came by this horse.'

The squire answered immediately, 'Sire, by your leave, it is three days ago today that a daring knight gave it to me, because he was so moved to pity by my sorry state. I met him in the forest one morning, when I was riding a horse that could hardly move, it was so feeble. My own had been taken from me at a castle where their evil custom was to demand as toll any knight's horse, weapons and armour. When that knight saw that I was in such need, out of the goodness of his heart, he dismounted immediately and gave me his good horse, For, as matters stood, I was in great danger of losing my estate, my honour, and my life.'

The king spoke, 'Now I am sure of it: that was my knight, Sir Gawain! Where is he?'

'Sire, when I saw him last he had set out on foot through the wood in the direction of the castle of the evil toll. After that I do not know where he went.'

Then the king said, swearing, 'By God, now I know that Gawain has lost his life, for that toll is of such a nature that no man may escape it. Squire, tell me what it is you desire.'

The squire answered: 'Your Majesty, my sorrow is great: my brother, sire, was slain some years ago, and the man who did it mocks me as if I were a fool. My lord, I have challenged him to combat for this matter. Now I ask of you, lord king, that I may be your servant, by your grace, and that you dub me knight if it please you, and let me depart from your court for my combat, to keep my word. If I remain here any longer I will have cause to regret it, and it will cost me my life!'

The king promptly dubbed him knight and girded a good sword on him; and he said to the youth, 'Do not delay! Go, and think of winning honour from this day on; strive always to be virtuous wherever you are. Aid widows and orphans and protect all whom you find in fear, even at the risk of your own life.'

The youth rode out as quickly as he could, through the gates and along the road he saw before him. He dared not wait if he was to arrive in time for the combat that he had taken upon himself, and if he was to be in the lists at the appointed hour. He rode on without pausing. And where he had been mistreated, there was now no trace of that evil custom, for Gawain had paid in full all that had been demanded of him.

GAWAIN RESCUES THE KNIGHT WHO HAS ACCUSED HIS BROTHER'S MURDERER

Meanwhile Gawain came to a mountain; he reached the top of it and there he saw the land below, from the foot of the mountain into the valley, covered with knights, riding on large and richly armed horses. He saw them coming in large numbers towards a castle that stood before him. A squire rode up behind him on a handsome horse, carrying a sword and two shields. When they had greeted each other, Sir Gawain asked him: 'Lad, where are all these great barons riding?'

'They are not travelling far, but are going to a certain king's court, by the name of Amadis.'

'Dear friend, what will they do there?'

'I will tell you all about it, Sir: that knight who rides over there, with his sword girded at his side, has been challenged on a charge of murder to trial by combat because he wilfully took a young lad's life. The challenger who has called him to combat has failed to appear because he does not dare come to the lists. He is a very worthy squire, and he said that he would travel to Arthur's court to ask the king to knight him. For this he was granted leave with honour. But he has not dared return since, and his friends bear the shame for it.'

Then Sir Gawain enquired, 'Will none of his kinfolk stand by him in his need?'

The lad answered, 'By God, not one! Of all the men whom you see here, none of them stands on his side. But twenty times more would have come here if they could have been certain that he would appear today in the lists. I beg your leave, but I must go ...' said the lad. 'Go! May God reward you! It is time for you to follow your lord before he gets too far ahead of you.'

The lad spurred his horse and rode away as fast as he could.

Sir Gawain came to where he saw a fair lime-tree standing in the field; he made for it and halted beneath it, to observe how the combat would proceed. He dismounted and left his horse tied to a stake because he wished to see whether the opponents would meet, and how the combat would turn out. He saw many knights riding in company with the man that had accepted the challenge. When they had all assembled, it seemed to Gawain that there were two thousand or more of them. But on the other side there was not even the champion, let alone anyone else. All the same, they began to prepare the lists outside the castle so that the ladies and girls in the castle would be able to watch the contest on the plain below. Thus they hastily set about their preparations, pounding stakes into the ground. They stretched ropes between these so that no one should enter except the combatants. When all was in readiness, the king addressed the man who had been challenged, 'Knight, if the time seems right to you, go and await your opponent in the lists. I expect he will come soon.'

He took his horse at once and rode haughtily into the lists, and waited because he was obliged to do so, until shortly after midday. Still the youth did not appear.

Then the knight spoke, 'Sire, when you deem the time has come, let me depart.'

All the men who were with him said, 'The time has long passed. The youth is not coming to the lists today; his time is up.'

The king answered at once, 'The more haste, the less speed; he who waits is wise. Wait in patience, friend. Something may have happened to delay him; give him just a little more time.'

They waited until evening, and still the youth did not come. Then the knight spoke angrily to the king, 'By the Lord in heaven! The time has long passed, now let me be on my way!'

All the men who were with him said, 'He has kept his word, your Majesty, in your court; you may now in all honour allow him to leave the lists.'

The king thought to himself, 'You are all wasting your time; if I have my way, the matter will be otherwise.'

'Wait just a bit,' he then said. Shortly thereafter they saw the youth riding towards them on Gringolet; he rode in haste and at great speed towards the lists. His horse flew under him like an arrow from the bow. Thus he rode into the lists shortly after vespers. His horse was exhausted from the ride: he had moistened the road with both foam and blood. The knight himself was tired and worn out. He dismounted, and went up to the king. He said, 'My Lord King Amadis, you see now that I have come to the lists. I can see ranged against me many famous knights, each armed, who have come here with the man who accepted my challenge, and who will fight for him in his defence against me. But I have no one here of my kinfolk to support me, even though they would protect me with might and main.'

The king answered at once, 'I shall come to your aid far better than if all your kin were by your side and I were only looking on; of this you may rest assured.'

They set about arming themselves on both sides. All the knights who accompanied the accused were required to swear before the king that they would grant the youth a lasting safe-conduct. And so the combatants entered the lists. The king stood at the window in order to watch the outcome of the fight. All the members of his court flocked to the windows as well to see whether those high nobles who waited on the other side would in any way mistreat the youth. Then the two knights crossed lances with such force that both their spears were splintered. Casting these aside, they drew their swords and exchanged strokes fiercely and unceasingly. The youth was rightly angry on account of his brother's death: his grief so increased his courage that he was prepared to do anything when he saw the man who had so falsely taken his brother from him. The chips flew from their shields, and each was eager to slay the other. The evil knight raised his sword and slashed at the youth with such arrogance and hatred that he deprived him entirely of his shield, and hacked many rings of mail out of his hauberk of good steel. But the young knight determined that he would avenge himself on him as soon as he might, and he dealt him such a blow with his sword, that he split his foe's helmet to the noseguard, and struck his head in half below the ears. The sword passed through at an angle, emerging to strike the joint of the shoulder upon which he slung his shield, and struck off the arm, which fell steaming to the ground. His enemy fell to the ground, dead before he hit the earth.

At this his friends were furious! As soon as they saw him fall there was not a single man among them who did not ride at once against the youth in the lists. This one wielded a lance, another his sword, a third said, 'Shall we take him prisoner?'

They stabbed him so that he fell to earth. Then they rode over him with their horses, back and forth; one stabbed him from above, another from below; they dealt him many blows, and injured him seriously. But the young knight was alone, and there was nothing he could do. However, Gawain saw all this and quickly untied his horse from the lime tree. He rode to the aid of the youth in the field, coming into the lists as if he were a wild lion. Never have you seen a flock of sparrows scatter as those knights scattered when Gawain came among them. He wielded his lance to the best advantage; whoever he struck was doomed to defeat. He forced knights to quit the saddle: one broke a leg, one his arm, and one after the other, in quick succession, they fell sweating to the ground. Gawain cried, 'Traitors! you swore to grant the youth safe-conduct, and this is your reward.'

He rode at once into the host, and no one dared resist him. If anyone did come to meet him, Gawain wounded him so badly with his lance that he did not recover in less than forty days. He knocked head-over-heels those who had taken a lofty tone before he rode into the field; they had cause to regret his appearance. He forced his way to where both the champions were lying still on the field; but one was alive and the other dead. Gawain singled out the man who was attacking the youth hardest and cried out, 'Defend yourself!'

With those words he ran him through the body with the point of his spear and tossed him, dead, out of his saddle. Gawain dismounted from his own horse and took up the young knight as soon as he could; he helped him up quickly and placed him on his horse Lyaert, that he had won at the castle of the evil custom.

And so Gawain made his stand on foot, while the young knight sat comfortably in his saddle. Gawain took the shield and spear of the dead man and gave them to his companion. Suddenly a knight rode up on Gringolet to one side of Gawain, intending to run him through before he noticed. As soon as the youth saw this, he raised his lance and struck the knight so that the lance broke in three pieces before the grip. The knight fell to the sand, and Gringolet came running up to his master as soon as he saw him. Gawain made haste to mount, and with good reason. Many men approached who were eager to harm the two of them. But Gawain held the field against them all, and did not budge an inch from his companion's side. Never has anyone, I believe, read of such marvels as those that Gawain performed there. This was all too clear to those who paid the price! He spared neither horse nor man, dealing many a hard blow on those polished helmets of steel. The other knight also acquitted himself well; fifty knights and squires, all of whom had been slain by Gawain and his companion, lay dead on the field.

The king was standing at the window and saw all the deeds performed by Gawain. Only now did he remember the promise of safe-conduct which he had made to the young knight. He said, 'It is high time that I went to help him with that crowd of armed men slashing and hewing at him. But I believe that the knight at his side, who is fighting for him so heroically, is an angel from heaven sent by God to help the young knight; never has a knight done such deeds.'

And so the king himself led five hundred chosen knights, in order to fulfil his oath, all splendidly armed, who rode out through the gates. They galloped to where Sir Gawain and the young knight both fought side by side; they were now greatly in need of rest. Sir Gawain noticed the king's arrival and said, 'Sire, why do you make such haste? You might as well turn around: it is over! I expect that we shall hold out against those left here, if we are lucky. My only worry is that nightfall will rob us of all our sport.'

The king answered him and said, 'Knight, I have done wrong, and for that I am sorry. But it is because of you that I left the young knight in danger: I watched you and became so engrossed that I completely forgot the safe-conduct which the lad had requested, for I saw you do such marvellous deeds.'

But the friends of the dead knight still stood firm, and swore that his death would be avenged. So they drew up in battle order and came up to where the king was talking to Gawain. Suddenly they saw that the enemy was approaching and left off talking to defend themselves against this renewed attack. Night fell: it was high time to stop fighting, but the dead knight's friends had sworn that they would capture the knight who had inflicted their loss, and take their revenge upon him. Both sides fought vehemently and fiercely. The king himself was a hardy knight; it was he who struck the first blow as the armies engaged once more, against a knight who rode out ahead of the enemy host. He was called Sir Alangremant, the bravest knight there was, and his brother followed him, Sir Bancram the Valiant. The king took up his shield and his spear to defend himself against the knight who bore down fearlessly upon him; he commended his soul to God in heaven. At the king's side rode the youth, who rejoiced at the aid which the king had brought him. But Sir Gawain dismounted and wisely let his horse cool off: Gringolet was tired. Then he unlaced his helmet and watched the progress of the battle between the king and Alangremant. They took up their lances in their hands and the reins by the knots; they spurred their horses, which were brave and swift. Alangremant struck the king a little to one side of his shield, and would have sent him tumbling from his horse had his lance not slipped from his grasp and broken into splinters just above the grip. The king faltered in the saddle; yet he did not miss, but hit Alangremant on the mark, piercing his shield quite through; so too he pierced his hauberk and leather jerkin through to his skin with the spear, and lifted him out of the saddle on the point of his spear; he flung him backwards out of the saddle fourteen feet out onto the field, and let him fall dead to the ground. His horse galloped quickly back whence it had come with empty saddle: it had lost its master.

All this was observed by Sir Bancram who grieved for his brother, but he was somewhat wiser than Sir Alangremant. He said, 'If I were to fall into the king's hands it would go as badly with me as it has for my brother. It seems better for me to turn back now, and make an honourable retreat.'

However, the knights who had remained behind were angry, and said, 'How stupid we were to let the two best knights in the host ride out alone into the hands of the king! Now the king's men are doomed to die!'

There were at least eighteen hundred of them, and a fearsome charge ensued! That host descended upon the king and he and his men began to fight fearlessly against the knights who attacked them. The young knight fought aggressively at his lord the king's side; the struggle was very fierce and violent. The battle lasted well into the night, for the moon shone brightly, and they could all see. The king's men began to lose heart: when the enemy approached in such a great mass, they turned tail and left their king behind in great peril. Now the young knight was hard pressed to defend the king. The king defended himself as well, but they both knew that to stay there was to die, and to flee was to incur great shame. Both of them hoped that someone might come to their aid.

Gawain saw this and thought to himself, 'It is time to fight again!'

He quickly fixed his helmet upon his head, mounted his horse Gringolet, and rode into that host as if he were a falcon among a flock of wild geese. He exacted his dues from every man he found before him. The young knight saw this, and rejoiced exceedingly. The three of them joined battle and began to hew with their swords at the men who before had instilled such fear in their hearts; for Gawain brought courage to one and all. The others wielded their swords with furious arm as birds do their feathers. And as the hauberks became hot, the rings of mail flew about the field like chaff. The enemy knights fell to earth two, three at a time, by fours and fives at once. Now this man is killed, now this taken captive, so that within a short time – though Gawain was sorry for it – not one of them escaped without having been slain or captured or maimed by deep wounds!

The enemy quickly retreated, and the king returned triumphantly and conducted Gawain into the castle: everyone rejoiced on account of the king's guest. The prisoners were quickly led away to a place from which they could not escape. Servants hastened to relieve the knights of their horses and led them to their stalls. The pages came running at once to Gawain and his young companion and helped them out of their armour. The queen sent two rich and costly cloaks and had them draped about the knights so that they would not catch cold: they had had a warm day's work. In the meantime the queen herself and all her attendants were ready. She entered the hall, and taking Gawain by the hand she said, 'Sir, welcome to such hospitality as we can offer! I wish that you would remain with us for ever, since you have done us such a great honour!'

Thereupon they approached a couch that stood before the hearth and sat down upon it. At this his host the king came forward and sat down by their side. It was almost midnight before they could sit down to eat. The king obliged Gawain to sit in the place of honour opposite the queen, with the young knight on one side, and the king on the other. They sat down and talked in friendly and noble fashion. When they had finished their meal they talked of going to sleep. Four servants entered carrying each a large and bright torch and held them carefully over the spot where Gawain's bed had been prepared. It was brighter there than a mirror with all that light. Gawain took his leave of his lady the queen. She commended him graciously to God and bade the servants see to it that he would sleep well. They still did not know his name, nor where he had been born.

The torch-bearers led the way and showed him to his chamber, that was painted entirely in gold. They sat the noble knight down on an ivory chair and dutifully removed his shoes and washed his feet with warm water. They had laid a carpet on the floor so that his feet would not be soiled.

Then he lay down to sleep under the covers of that costly and splendid bed: he was given a pillow and a splendid, soft kerchief. They served him as best they could. He said, 'I'm quite comfortable; I desire nothing else than that you should care as best you can for the knight who came here with me this evening.'

They at once took their leave and led the knight by his sleeve to the chamber where he was to sleep and laid him upon a magnificent bed. They commended him to God and left, each to his own master. Both knights and squires went as quickly as they could to their beds, to rest: they needed it.

In the early morning Gawain awoke as the larks began to sing, and said, 'I have slept too long; if I had been wiser, I would have ridden a mile by now.'

He arose, dressed himself and donned his socks and shoes. Not a single knight or servant was yet up in that hall. Gawain found a basin and towel and washed his hands and face. He said, 'Lord of the heavenly throne, show me today where I might find the true way to the sword that has caused me so much trouble.'

At that moment, the king emerged from his own chamber and entered the hall. Gawain wished him good morning. The king said, 'Why have you risen so early? It seems to me quite the wrong thing to do. Here in this court there is no one awake, neither count nor duke, nor knight nor squire either. Why did you not remain in bed and rest a little longer?'

Gawain said, 'I have many miles yet to ride on my journey; and this combat has delayed me. I could not pass by because I saw that they shamefully intended to harm the young knight; otherwise I would have continued on my way.'

All the members of the court had meanwhile awoken, and the queen entered the hall with her ladies-in-waiting. Gawain greeted them all, but first and foremost the queen. She answered thus cordially, 'Sir, I understand that the hospitality here is not to your liking.'

Gawain responded: 'Lady, it is very much to my liking. But I cannot hide from you the fact that I have other things to do now.' At that the young knight entered and Gawain turned to the king and his wife, 'I beseech you by your honour that you find it in your grace to give help and counsel to this knight. Protect him against his enemies and help him to resume his estate and dwell in honour.'

The king said, 'By Our Lord, I shall do as you desire.'

Then Gawain called for his horse. But the queen, a most courtly woman, then replied: 'Sir, do not think of getting your horse; I beg you not to ride from this court today. Rest yourself a day or two more; then journey wherever you will.'

Gawain replied that it was no good asking him to stay: he must be on his way. Then his horse was fetched and his armour, quite cleaned and repaired. The king said, 'I should very much like to know your name before you go.'

Sir Gawain mounted his horse. He said, 'It would not be proper for me to refuse, but there has never been a mortal man who wished to know my name, who was not obliged to ask for it first. My name is Gawain.'

When the king heard this he was delighted and said, 'Are you Arthur's sister's son, of whom nothing but good is spoken, and who has put an end to many an evil practice? Praise be to God that I have lived to see you at my court: there is no limit to your fame! Now dismount and let your horse be led to stable at once and stay here with me, sir, and stand by my side. All my possessions and all my land I give to you to hold and dispose of as you see fit; moreover, so help me God, I will be at your service if you will accept it and remain with me for the rest of my life!'

'Even if you were to give me the world,' said Gawain, 'I would not stay. But if I saw that you suffered pain and sorrow, sire, it would grieve me and by my faith I would readily risk my life for you.'

Then he took his leave of the lady, the king's wife, the queen, and of all those who accompanied her in that hall. They answered: 'Farewell! May the Lord our God protect you from shame and harm and may He grant you success!'

And so he took his leave and rode away. The young knight lamented very grievously indeed that his master, who had saved his life, should thus ride away. He said, 'May God reward you for the good that you have done on my behalf!'

GAWAIN COMES TO THE COURT OF KING AMORAEN AND IS GIVEN THE SWORD WITH THE TWO RINGS

Gawain rode day and night, through forests and woods and meadows; this adventure brought him many trials. One day he came riding to the seashore, and watched the ships as they sailed to and fro in the sunshine. But he lamented because he could not find what he sought. He said, 'What good is it continuing? For I have not been able to obtain a single clue concerning the goal of my quest.'

Suddenly he saw in the distance a high, narrow, towering rock which men called Ravenstene. Though it seemed narrow, with the waves swirling at its base, it was certainly half a mile wide at the top. Gawain wondered at this when he saw it; there was a castle perched on top of it: it had a great many towers, all made of bright marble, some large and others small. He rode on for a mile or so, thinking that he would dearly love to get to that castle in the hope of hearing news of the sword, about which he still knew nothing. But it was quite impossible. There was nothing but water to be seen; he saw before him no path, nor even a tunnel, which would take him to the castle.

But then he noticed at his feet a great number of hoof-prints in the sand that led in the direction of the castle. He realised that the way to reach it was to wait untill the tide had ebbed, and then it was a mile across the sands, even though the water was wide when the tide came in. So he followed the track of hoof marks in the sand, and his horse carried him to that island. But the tide came in quickly as Gawain was crossing: the waves swirled about him, and it was impossible for him to turn back, for the water behind him was too deep. He reined his horse in at the base of the cliff and looked upward along the rock-face towards the castle: but he could not see it. He said, 'Now I have paid dearly indeed for seeking the Sword with the Two Rings! It is certain to cause me more grief and now it is a complete mystery to me where I may be.'

But at that instant he saw a path before him, which led through an open gate. So he thought to himself, 'I must enter this gate and try my luck inside. I believe this is the road to the castle, and may God Himself protect me.'

The road led upward through a tunnel to the top of the mountain, where Sir Gawain saw the castle, so magnificently situated.

He saw many knights there taking their ease; they were playing chess or backgammon, or hitting a ball; everywhere on the yard before the castle games of dice were being played. When he saw that, Sir Gawain dismounted and left his horse behind, wishing simply to ask what castle that might be. Two pages came up to him and greeted him courteously. They said, 'Please give us your horse and let us bring it to stable, while you go to meet our master.'

He gave one of the pages his horse while the other kneeled before him and removed his spurs, unbuckled his sword and quickly took off his armour. He had on underneath handsome clothes of fine linen and on his feet he wore splendid shoes, studded with red gold. Gawain said, 'Now tell me what might be the name of this castle to which I have journeyed alone?'

'Ravenstene, my lord' said the page. 'And tell me next who might be lord of this castle?'

'The mighty King Amoraen; he it was who had it built.'

When Gawain heard that he was very pleased indeed. He said, 'Tell me which one of those men might be your master, King Amoraen?'

The page replied at once, 'That is him sitting over there under the lime tree between the two girls. Round him are many young knights who are playing all kinds of games. I will take you there.'

And so Sir Gawain approached the king; and as soon as the king saw him he rose from his seat and the knights left off their games. The king welcomed him, saying 'Sir Gawain, I am greatly honoured that you have come to my court! I have often thought of setting out in search of you or offering a reward to anyone who brought you here.'

The king and Sir Gawain took each other by the hand and all the lords of that land escorted Gawain with due honours to the hall inside the castle. The ladies were eager to see Sir Gawain, for no one else was as handsome as he was. They entered the hall which was as splendid as any paradise. The floor over which the king led him was covered with splendid carpets. Sir Gawain and his host sat down near the hearth on a couch that was covered by a fine cloth; at their feet lay another splendid carpet. The nobles took their seats in the hall, and both knights and ladies admired Sir Gawain to their hearts' content. Sir Gawain said to the king, 'Sire, it puzzles me greatly how it is you know me; for I have never seen you, to the best of my knowledge, nor any of your knights!'

The king said, 'I will tell you as soon as we have eaten.'

Water was brought; everyone washed their hands and sat down at table in that hall. The dishes were served in such quick succession that no one could make a list of them, they were so numerous. Wine of fine quality, fresh and clear, was poured for everyone who wished it. When they had eaten their fill, spiced wine was served. And when they had finished their meal the tablecloths were removed but the tables themselves were left standing.

Then King Amoraen spoke, 'Sir Gawain, now I will tell you the answer to the question you asked earlier. More than ten years ago that I married a young girl: I should be more grateful to God if she were still alive, than I am now He has taken her away. She was the daughter of the king of Ireland and the most beautiful girl one might find! Through my marriage I received wealthy towns, high castles and many an estate, and she brought me more dignity than I can relate. May she enjoy God's mercy! When I went to fetch her I travelled to King Arthur's court, and your uncle did me great honour. It was there that I heard of you, for all the knights honoured you greatly and called you the Father of Adventure. When we left the court you happened to come into the castle at the same time; you reined in at once and greeted us courteously; you would not move until we had passed. When I had gone on my way, I was angry that I did not know who you were, nor the names of the three knights who were with you, and who had also greeted us. So I asked a page whom we met on the road a little while later. He told me that one of them was Yder, another Lancelot, and the third Ywain. He named you as Sir Gawain, and said that your virtue and honour were greater than those of any man at the king's court. 'He protects everyone who requires help in their need. His virtue is so great, he defends widows and orphans and everyone whom he finds living in fear, risking his own life in the process.' I never saw you again after that before this very day, but the moment I saw you I recognised you. I believe the Lord Himself has sent you here to me, for no one but you can help me in my present dilemma.'

Gawain replied, 'Tell me, if you would, of your problem. If it is anything that lies within my power, then by my honour I will help you gladly, Your Majesty.'

The king said, 'Sir Gawain, you can indeed, and far better than any other man now living. If you succeed on the quest then I shall give you the Sword with the Two Rings. If I dared produce it I would show it to you, but I cannot: for whoever sets eye on it will lose his life. Only the flower of knighthood can claim it. The mighty King Wonder has asked me for it many times; and his son Alidrisonder has all his life tried to win it from me by means of stratagems. Sir, it is still in my possession. But it is at your disposal, on one condition, with one stipulation: that you will grant me a request.'

Gawain rejoiced at hearing the king name the sword which he was seeking.

'Sire, would I dare wear the sword, if you were to give it to me?'

'Yes indeed, Sir Gawain, you might wear the good sword all your life, if I were to give it to you sheathed: no man against whom you drew the sword could stand before you. If I were to give you the sword and you drew it against me, I would not be able to defend myself, even though I have had it in my power all my life. The man who wrought it was skilled indeed. When he had finished it, he inscribed on it: *Whichever mortal man who acquires or possesses this sword I advise to keep it well: it is a very dangerous sword. If he wishes to pass it on to another man, and remain alive, let him do so sword in sheath, and may he never show it fully drawn; in this way he may preserve his friend, and the man to whom he willingly gives the sword may wield it freely.* There is not a man alive today who knows its nature. It is dangerous and evil, but it spares the man who wears it. Sir, I will give you this sword if you will grant my request.'

Sir Gawain said, 'Your Majesty, show me that sword! I will do anything you desire, provided it is within my power.'

Then the king went to where it lay wrapped in a linen cloth, and brought it to Gawain. When he unwrapped it from the cloth and Gawain saw it, he thought to himself that he had never seen such a good sword: both pommel and hilt, as well as sheath, were of red gold; the belt attached to the sheath was made of shining gold lace; the metalwork on the belt and lining the belt-holes was also entirely of gold. Never has such a magnificent weapon been seen! Sir Gawain said, 'Your Majesty, would you draw the sword from its sheath?'

'You would pay dearly, Sir Gawain, if I were to draw the sword: it is so dangerous. Though you were wearing all the armour you have ever worn, believe me, it would cleave it all clean through; you would never be able to escape.'

Gawain answered: 'Then show me both pommel and hilt, and the sheath as well: but let me see its edge!'

The king drew it at once, and before he had pulled it halfway out of the sheath, it sprang, pommel over hilt, to the earth before Gawain, as if it were a man who had sinned and wished to do penance. The king stepped forward at once and grasping the sword between pommel and hilt he returned it to its sheath, saying, 'By Our Lord! The sword has shown you great honour; never before has any man remained standing before it.'

Gawain answered at once, saying, 'Your Majesty, tell me what it is you desire of me; I do not want you to spare me. In whatever way I can help you, I will do so if you will give me the sword.'

The king was glad and said cheerfully, 'If you will then promise me, in the name of knighthood and the Virgin Mary, that you will not fail to journey wherever I send you, then I will give you the Sword with the Two Rings.'

'I will make that promise,' said Gawain, 'but still I do not know what it is you desire.'

Then the king gave him the sword that was without fault; he said, 'Sir Gawain, no better knight could wear this sword and there is none to whom I would rather give it! Therefore I make you its guardian. Keep the promise you have made to me and it will remain with you for evermore.'

And so Gawain received the sword, and there was no happier man alive. He said again, 'Tell me, sire, where I must travel. I would not delay any longer the fulfilment of my pledge!'

'Then you must fetch a girl, Sir Gawain, whom you do not know. I have loved her for a long while, and it grieves me that I cannot win her myself. Her name is Ysabele; she is more beautiful than Venus, the Goddess who reigns over love; she is fairer than Olympias who was Empress of Rome; she is much fairer in my opinion than Iseult of Ireland or Iseult of the White Hands. This is the woman that I love! I will go mad for love, Sir Gawain, if you do not fetch her for me.'

'Her father is the mighty King Assentin; and he has shut up my love for safe keeping in a castle in far away Endi. The castle is surrounded by twelve walls; each in turn has eighty towers, strong and splendid, built upon it. Between every two walls there runs a moat. The gates, through which one enters, are of copper and bronze, bound with iron and steel. At each gate are stationed eighty heavily armed men, ready to go to battle at a moment's notice. All this is to protect the girl so that no man could win her nor come into the castle without it first being known what his intentions were. Within those walls she possesses every luxury, for she never comes out at any season of the year. In the morning she walks among the orchards, in the pleasure gardens that are to be found there, luxuriant and splendid. There is an arbour there more than half a mile wide. It houses a marvellous array of plants: pepper, anise and ginger, figs and nutmeg grow there, and pomegranates, almonds and chestnuts and many other things that I am not well able to name. Lilies, roses and other flowers grow there and many a sweet herb. There is the sweet sound of song-birds. She walks there in the morning among the roses.'

'She has another arbour, in which there stands a tree, very broad at the base and made entirely of fine red gold. It has countless branches of gold; each branch is hollow on the inside, and on every branch is perched a little bird of gold, beautiful and finely crafted. On each splendid little leaf there hangs a little golden bell which rings sweet and clear. In the centre there is a hollow chamber in which sixteen men work eight bellows, with which they force a current of air through the tree from its roots to its very top. And when the little birds are moved by the wind they twitch as if they were alive; then each bird sings its song six and seven in chorus; and the little bells sound, some with high notes, some with low. When they burst out in song anyone who hears that sweet music, even if he is mortally wounded, will be healed of all his pain in a short space of time, so sweet is the song one may hear there. There is also a clear, sparkling fountain beneath a most costly and splendid olive tree. The stream which feeds it flows from the earthly paradise itself. A golden eagle has been fashioned there which covers the well with its wings so that nothing evil may come near that magnificent fountain. Around the well there are bay trees and rose bushes and many sweet herbs in bloom.'

'That is where the young girl whom I love and who will drive me mad with love-longing takes her pleasure in strolling chastely with her companions among the lilies and the roses. If she wishes to wash her hands at the well or drink from it a drop of water, she need only turn the eagle's beak and out pours clear water from the fountain. One drop from the fountain would restore a man, however old, to the strength and appearance of a thirty year old. This is how Ysabele spends her days; if God grants you the grace to fetch this girl for me, then you will have deserved the sword and fulfiled your oath; for by no other means may you acquit yourself of your debt to me.'

Gawain answered the king courteously, saying, 'May Almighty God allow me to bring her here to you and thus redeem the sword that you have given me!'

It was far into the night before they put an end to their conversation. They went to sleep in the hall and conveyed Gawain to his bed with much honour. The king and all the other nobles went each to his own bed to sleep, as did the squires, girls and pages. Gawain rested till daybreak, and as soon as he saw the first light of day he arose as quickly as he could in order to fulfil his pledge.

Everyone in the castle gathered to see Gawain depart. Gawain said to the king, 'May God be with you, your Majesty. I shall fetch the girl for you and redeem the sword and fulfil my pledge, by Jesus Christ of Nazareth, before I return to Ravenstene, provided God spares my life.' Gawain was armed at once and Gringolet, the horse whom he loved before all others, was led before him. He mounted and crossed himself with his right hand.

Gawain sets out in search of Ysabele, daughter of King Assentin

And so the hero took his leave of all the nobles and commended himself to the care of both God and His Mother as he rode out of the hall and the castle, wearing the Sword with the Two Rings. He rode down the path, to the tunnel through which he had passed before. The tide was out: his horse was brave and swift and Gawain kept him under tight rein till they reached the shore. He was much concerned as to which direction he should take in order to find the girl; this was his greatest difficulty. So he took a road to his right which led away from the shore and the sea, and rode twelve miles or more that day, through inhospitable thickets and coppices, until he came upon a river that was very deep and wide, and on the other side he saw a knight riding on a very large horse, and he seemed fierce indeed. His weapons and shield and banner were red, and he wore red armour. Judging by his countenance and bearing he was a fierce and heartless man. Then he saw riding at the knight's side a girl, finely dressed in green silken garments. Upon her head he saw two braids of golden hair which hung over her shoulders as far as the saddle-bow, but they were tattered and tangled: the Red Knight, who was very angry with her, had pulled at them, torn her clothes and laid bare her beautiful body and limbs! In his hand he carried a whip, made from eight strong thongs, with which he inflicted much pain on the girl and with which he lashed the girl savagely in the face; her neck and throat were covered in blood. She said, 'Knight, deliver me from the misdeeds that this man has inflicted upon me without cause.'

Sir Gawain cried, 'If I could meet you face to face, evil knight, I would repay you for your treatment of this girl! But it seems to me it will be difficult.'

Wherever Gawain turned his gaze, up-river and down, he saw no bridge nor any other means by which he could cross the river. But the girl's laments grieved Gawain so, that he could no longer bear to watch as she was dealt so many blows. He suddenly turned his horse and headed for the river, as fast as he could ride. Gringolet found his footing on the bank and gave a mighty leap, landing over halfway across the river, and he swam on to the other bank. Then Sir Gawain dismounted, and dried his horse with his cloak. When he had adjusted his horse's bridle Sir Gawain became aware of three shields flashing in the distance; the sun shone so brightly that they sparkled like stars of bright silver and gold; and he saw a column of dust rising. Then it occurred to him that they were knights who pursued the Red Knight and wished to rescue the girl, and therefore rode after him. But he could not be sure whether they wished to help him or to harm him, and they were still a good mile distant. So, unsure of their intentions, he mounted his good horse Gringolet and set out in pursuit at once to deliver the girl. He rode until he saw the knight, and when he was within earshot Sir Gawain called out, 'Wait, speak with me a moment before you travel on!'

The other spurred his horse, and acted as if he had not heard, giving not a single word in answer. He neither spoke nor laughed, but he raised the whip and dealt the girl hard and repeated blows to the face; now and again he jabbed her with his shield. When Gawain saw this he became even more enraged than before. Then he spurred his horse forward and intended to requite him for it. The evil knight turned around and said, 'You are not at all wise to follow me. Do you think that because of you I would leave off striking the girl? Not I!'

Sir Gawain answered, 'Friend, what has the girl done to you? It is wrong to strike a woman: if you do not leave off, you will regret it, I warn you beforehand.'

The evil one answered him, saying, 'You talk like an idiot! If you were wise you would turn away from me now. I will not on your account leave off whipping and striking her. If you wish to prevent me I shall teach you the same game – you would come away from it in shame and it would cost you your life!'

At that he raised the whip and struck the girl, who suffered such sorrow, so hard in the face that a stone would have taken pity on her! She cried, 'Oh woe is me! Deliver me from this torment if you can. If I survive the harsh wounds that I have received at his hand I will be at your service. Do it for the honour of womankind!'

Sir Gawain said, 'If he strikes you just once more he will seal his own doom! That is my warning.'

Then that evil knight turned to face Gawain and told him to defend himself with his shield. They both raised their shields, and charged each other as quickly as arrows from a bow. When they had crossed lances and both their spears were splintered, their hauberks had lost every ring of chain mail. They offered each other no quarter. Their horses were both swift: they reeled and fell. People would talk of that joust for many a day afterwards. When the Red Knight saw Gawain on foot, he rejoiced in his heart and thought already to have emerged victorious from a difficult situation; he did not hesitate, but drew his sword. Gawain saw this and said, 'Our duel will be a short one.'

Then he drew the Sword with the Two Rings, and struck the Red Knight so that he cleaved his helmet clean through down to his teeth. Then brains and red blood came streaming from that wound and spilled out onto the earth. The girl said, 'Thank you for that blow; I have been delivered and will gladly become your servant: you have avenged me against the evil Red Knight. You have also avenged one of my brothers, a brave knight who died at his hand: great sorrow and many blows were all the compensation he gave me.'

Then Gawain went to where that knight lay wounded, mortally ill and weak, and did his best to ease his pain. He took his own helmet and went with it to the river to fetch water and he revived the Red Knight; and when he came to from his swoon, Gawain took the wound and closed it with his hands. The knight spoke through clenched teeth, 'Noble knight, I beg mercy, I have done most heavy penance for my misdeeds. I have for many years now deserved death and now it has come. You have taken my life; it is my own fault,' said the evil Red Knight, 'My sins are not slight or few; I deserve to die and worse, if only on account of my wrongs against this girl.'

'Then repent, friend, and pray to the Virgin Mary for mercy. Your soul may yet receive salvation, if you repent now of all that you have done to harm the girl.'

Thereupon the Red Knight answered, 'If I thought I could thus obtain forgiveness, I would eagerly confess my sins to you. But I have sinned so greatly that my soul can never be saved.'

'The sins of the entire world,' said Gawain, 'are insignificant compared to God's mercy. God received bitter wounds on our account: He can absolve you of your sins, if you make your confession now fully and clearly.'

'I shall reveal to you all my sins; but I regret most of all what I did today, when this fair young girl came riding with her brother, a brave young knight, riding at her side. They were singing and riding to and fro through the woods for their amusement. Three knights were riding with me; each has a girl who had been stolen from their husbands and family; we took them before their very eyes. We have been kidnappers and murderers for fully twenty years. We never once let anyone escape, whom we had captured, without torturing him first. When I saw this fair girl I rode nearer and killed her brother then and there. The girl herself I tormented often and dealt her many heavy blows. Ask her if she will forgive it me. My three companions have remained behind and would come to my assistance if they saw anyone coming to rescue the girl. They are evil and fierce, so be on your guard. You mustn't stay here a moment longer! If they should find you here with me you would surely lose your life.'

At this Gawain said, 'May almighty God in His mercy forgive you all your sins. Fair girl, in your mercy forgive this knight for all the sins that he has committed against you. Your only revenge can be that the Devil should take him into the torment of hell; he will not be the better for this fate. If you do as I ask, you will release both your brother's soul and that of this knight from the torment of hell-fire.'

Then the girl answered, 'He has caused me great distress and he has killed my dear brother whom I loved more than any other man alive; but I will forgive his sins so that my brother's soul may find grace with Our Lord.'

Lying there near death as he was, the knight took a straw and said, 'Girl, at this hour I beg your mercy, and that you forgive me my sins.'

The girl took the straw, the token of all his sins against her, and at that answered him, 'May God who tasted a bitter death for us, forgive you your sins, even though you have caused me great distress, and pain that will last for many days to come.'

Now the dying knight's strength began to fail him, for he could hardly speak. Gawain asked if there was anything else he desired. 'I beg you to have masses said for me, and see that I am buried in holy ground.'

Sir Gawain said, 'I will do as you ask; in return, promise me that, if you are able, you will come to me wherever I may be, when I call on you.'

Gawain took up a handful of earth from under his right foot, and said, 'Open your mouth; in God's name I bless you, that it be pleasing both to God and His Mother.' And so the knight died.

In the meanwhile the other three knights had come so close that Gawain could by no means escape. He quickly readied himself and mounted his horse Gringolet. He had already drawn the naked sword with which he would defend himself; he was without a lance, for he had shattered it when he avenged the girl against the evil Red Knight. One of the three knights who rode towards Gawain saw his comrade lying there dead. This grieved him greatly and he determined to avenge him. Without uttering a word he drew closer, he spurred his horse against Gawain, with his lance at the ready, intending to pierce him through. Gawain took cover behind his shield, and holding his good sword naked in his hand he struck the lance in two with a single blow. Meanwhile the second knight arrived and was eager to take his life, but Gawain did the same to him. Then the last of the three arrived; he thought he had come too late. This knight struck Gawain such a blow with his lance that the chain-links of his hauberk flew off in all directions, and he himself was well-nigh lifted out of the saddle. The other two did not hesitate to draw their swords without a word and they rode closer, intent upon avenging their comrade. The girl was distressed and prayed earnestly to God on behalf of Sir Gawain that he might retain his honour against those three foes that day.

And when the girl saw Gawain in such difficulty, she wept bitterly, saying, 'I am worse off than when I saw my brother struck dead before my eyes! How can my heart bear to see this knight die? For his sake I shall go mad with grief.'

'Noble girl,' said Gawain, 'do not lament, there is nothing here to harm me.'

At that he swung his sword and dealt one of his foes such a blow that neither his kin nor any other man could ever help him; he fell out of his saddle and tumbled without delay to the earth. Gawain had made peace with one of his foes, but the others still attacked him fiercely. One of them thrust at Sir Gawain and struck him squarely, piercing his shield quite through and stopping only at his hauberk. At that Gawain raised his sword, quickly cut the lance in three places, and dealt that fierce and evil knight such a blow that without uttering a word he fell to earth. As Gawain fought the last knight, the knight who lay there came to out of his swoon and saw Gawain's sword; he recognised it by its rings. He cried out to his comrade, 'That sword is dangerous; you cannot escape!'

The other knight answered, 'Don't be a a coward, but mount and grit your teeth against the pain; help me to avenge our comrades!'

The knight silently mounted, and they both attacked my lord Gawain, one from behind, one from the fore. Sir Gawain decided to avenge himself upon the knight who had scorned the Sword with the Rings, and said, 'If I have my way you will not remain standing before me for long.'

The other knight quickly replied, 'I care nothing for your threats. My sword will soon end your life!'

But Gawain raised his sword and struck off his head!

At this, the knight who had suffered that first blow, seeing his comrade lying dead, said, 'You could have escaped the sword if you had listened to me. It seems to me that all I can do is to beg for mercy!'

So he dismounted at once, and fell to his knees on the ground in front of Gawain and said, 'Have mercy upon me, knight, and I will renounce my evil practices; I promise you by my faith that never again will a lady or a girl suffer distress because of me. Let me live, for God's sake!'

Sir Gawain said, 'The crimes you have committed are serious, but if you would do penance for them then there may be help for you yet.'

The knight quickly took his sword and laid it on the ground before Gawain. 'Sir, I am prepared to pledge an oath to do everything you require.'

'Then raise your hand and swear by the hilt of this sword. I shall dictate the oath: that you shall honour the Holy Church and further God's creation and help widows and orphans; and that you shall protect all those whom you find living in fear, and take pains to avenge their suffering; promise me on your word of honour that you will help these three girls return whence they have been abducted, and that you will renounce all the evil practices which you have formerly pursued.'

The other knight swore to him on his word that he would keep that promise. 'For that oath, I shall let you go and forgive you your misdeeds. See that you keep your word!'

And thus it was that they put an end to the fighting.

Now it was time to seek lodgings for the night, for the sun was setting. The knights were in urgent need of rest, and had no time to lose if they were to reach any shelter where they might find help and hospitality. The girl whom Gawain had rescued said joyfully, 'Knight, my uncle lives within a mile or so, though I don't know exactly where. I beg you to ride there with me.'

'By God, if that is the case,' spoke Gawain, 'I will gladly do so.'

Then he invited the other knight and the three girls to ride with them. 'Thank you, but I shall seek shelter tonight beyond the river, and will take these three girls with me.'

'May God guide you,' spoke Gawain, 'and may you always do what you have promised and sworn to do.'

The knight rode off, and the girls after him. Gawain remained behind with the dead, whom he was very anxious to bury. But he could not leave the girl without taking her first to her uncle. Sir Gawain took the two horses that were standing there riderless and tied their reins together; he sat the girl on the better of the two, and mounted his own horse. They rode off at a fast gallop through the darkness over the wild fields, and left the dead where they lay. After a mile in the pitch darkness, Gawain heard the noise of a great host gathering in a castle and he saw a well-built squire come riding through the gates on horseback, armed from head to foot. Gawain greeted him courteously and said, 'May all the angels in heaven give you a good night!'

The squire was well mannered , but it was evident that he was deeply concerned. He said, 'May God reward you, sir! I could well use a good night.'

Gawain asked, 'Has anyone harmed you? Is this castle perhaps under siege, judging by the noise I hear inside?'

'There is much more sorrow here than words can say! The brother of the lord of the castle has met with great misfortune. One of his sons has been killed by an unknown knight, who has abducted one of his daughters as well, and they do not know where she has been taken. I must ride all this night to summon a great host of my lord's men; tomorrow at daybreak we shall ride in search of that girl.'

Sir Gawain said, 'Let us ride back and bring joy to all those noble barons: I have brought the girl for whom you were going to search tomorrow: here she is!'

So they rode into the castle and pages and servants came forward with torches and candles, and they all forgot their sorrow: they went to see the girl. When they recognised her, they were full of joy and sorrow: joy at her return, sorrow at her dreadful injuries. The girl's uncle wept when he saw his niece thus scarred. He said, 'Niece, you have suffered great torment; I can see your wounds. I hope that you will be avenged.'

That girl answered at once, 'Uncle, I have been well avenged upon the evil Red Knight who had caused me this great suffering, and on his companions as well, thanks to this knight here. He has endured many heavy blows today at the hands of those four knights, but he slew three of them and the fourth begged for mercy. Gawain let him live because he sued for mercy. Look at the horses; they are still entirely stained red with the blood of those who lie there dead!'

The girl's uncle said to Gawain, 'May the Lord God reward you for having saved my niece's life: your reward will be greater still if you remain with us a while.'

'Sir, would that she had never received those blows before my eyes! But the knight who did this to her has repented and asked the girl humbly for forgiveness. I did not wish to leave behind his horse and those of his comrades, and I give them gladly to the girl for her pain. If I had taken better spoils I would gladly give them to her, in God's name.'

The girl said, 'I accept them gladly! May the Lord God reward you for all the good you have done me this day.'

Three pages took the horses in hand and led them to the stables.

They all escorted Gawain into the hall with the girl at his side, where they attended to Gawain's every need. Two squires knelt down on the ground in front of Sir Gawain and removed his leggings and spurs; they unbuckled his sword and quickly removed his armour: a set of garments, newly cut, were brought at once, straight from the tailor, and Gawain dressed himself in these. Then water was brought and they washed their hands before sitting down to table; the table was well set with dishes and rare delicacies. Gawain was given the seat of honour beside the girl, and the girl's uncle came and sat down at their side. The pages entered, bringing the meal, and they served Gawain and the other knights; nor did they wait long before they replaced the first dishes with new ones. There was an abundance of wine, red and white, cool and clear, enough for all who wished to drink of it. When they had had their fill and eaten enough of that food, the tablecloths were removed. They did not delay for Gawain's sake, so that he could rest and sleep after a day that had exhausted him.

But he was not thinking of sleep, but of the quest on which he had embarked. So when the tables had been removed and the beds were prepared, he said to the girl, 'Noble girl, we must part.'

The girl replied, 'Why, knight, do you wish to leave us? That would be a great disgrace for me. You shall ride nowhere, by Our Lord, this night – wait until dawn. Rest yourself now, after the heavy blows you suffered today.'

But Sir Gawain answered, 'I would not remain here for all the treasure in the world, nor will I wait until dawn; I must return to the slain knight whom I left behind. Listen, noble barons: I must fulfil my promise – your niece, this girl, was witness to it – that I would bury him. I mean no disrespect: if it were not for this, then I would remain here with you.'

They were all grieved that Gawain was to take leave of them so soon; but the girl's uncle ordered his horse to be saddled: he wished to ride with him and accompany my lord Gawain with all those present at his court. But Gawain refused: 'You shall not ride with me! I shall return alone to the dead knight whom I left behind. Be content with the company of these barons and console this girl who suffers such great grief: that is the best thing for you to do. I ask of you, sir, by your knightly virtue, have my armour made ready. It is time I went.'

Two squires fetched his armour and helped him don it. Another squire, as I understand, brought Gringolet forward. And his host had a sumpter horse loaded with silver and with gold and said, 'You must take this with you; as well as two squires and two steeds who will ride at your side, and I give them to you, sir, because you have done my niece such honour today.'

Sir Gawain said, 'Please, I have no desire for your gifts. But if you gave them to the girl, I would be grateful. I have delayed here long enough. Do you know what I would be glad to accept? A shield; mine has been pierced through and through. In the battle to free the girl I lost both shield and lance, so give me these – I will accept no more from you – and I will be grateful.'

At once he was given a lance, long and strong, and a shield painted in gold and blue, which he accepted. Then the girl rose to her feet and went straight to Gawain and kissed him on the mouth in front of her uncle and her kin: she did not let that stop her. She said, 'Knight, I must suffer great sorrow at this parting. May almighty God protect you since you no longer wish to stay here!'

Gawain answered, saying, 'Do not be sad! Though I must go now, I hope that I shall return. I shall always be your knight.'

With that Sir Gawain mounted Gringolet and took leave of his host and of all the knights in the hall: they were sorry to see him go. Gawain spurred his horse and rode off at a gallop. Through the gate and over the field he rode at great speed; before midnight he had drawn so close to the dead man that he saw a great number of torches and candles burning brightly near the body, and he heard clear voices singing the Kyrie Eleison. Gawain rode bravely and without fear towards this sound when he heard it, because he wished to see what was happening. But this was not to be: the bright lights and the singers vanished, nor could he tell where they had gone. No living man may be present when God Himself performs miracles, and look upon His holiness. And so Gawain arrived at the place where he found the dead knight lying before him in the sand. He saw not one of God's creatures, save for the dead man lying as he had left him there before. Then he dismounted and came closer to the dead man, and tethering his horse to his lance he drew his sword and traced a circle in the sand around him so that none of God's enemies might come near to him.. In his lap he laid his sword, the naked steel drawn from its sheath. The Pater noster and his creed he said many times for the dead man's soul and commended it to the protection of St Michael.

It was shortly before or after midnight that he heard great cries and weeping, as well as screams, the gnashing of teeth, and the loud clapping of hands. The dead man cried out, 'I am lost! Cursed be the hour that I was born! Mother, wherever you may be, you did not teach me to realise the importance of virtue, otherwise I would have escaped the torment that I must now suffer for evermore. You, too, father, may your bones suffer in the torments of hell! It is because of you that I am in such straits: you encouraged me, and rejoiced at my misdeeds. If you had chastised me, I would have avoided the evils that I have wrought against God. Teach your children well, you wise folk!'

When Gawain had heard this lament from the dead man, he saw at the same time that a flame shot forth from his throat. Many demons approached, armed with forks and with meat hooks, with which they pulled at him and at his comrade who lay there as well, both of whom Gawain had deprived of their lives that day. The demons said, 'You have served us for many a year, you shall have your reward!'

They began to stab and beat them and inflicted many harsh torments upon them, playing with them as if they were balls. Gawain feared for himself when he saw them coming closer to him. He at once drew his sword, gripping it firmly between pommel and hilt, commended himself to God and to the Virgin Mary and signed himself with the sword: the Devils flew off on their way to the northeast making a terrible noise. They tossed the two for whom they had come between them like a ball.

As the day dawned, Gawain said, 'Thanks be to the Lord that I have escaped with my life!'

He put the dead man on his horse and rode away at top speed to a nearby chapel. There he dismounted at once and carried his companion inside. Then Gawain rang a bell which was hanging there. A priest came and asked him what he desired. 'Let us bury this dead man – it would be the right thing to do – and let us sing a Mass for him.'

'Who will assist me?'

'I shall,' said Gawain, 'I can read well, for I attended school for years in my childhood.'

So the priest donned his robes and sang a mass for the dead man's soul and commended him to St Michael. Then Gawain took his sword and dug a pit in the earth; he fulfiled his promise when he laid the dead knight in it. Then he mounted without delay and rode off to search for the girl who he had promised on his word to deliver to King Amoraen in return for the Sword with the Two Rings, saying to himself, 'Though I may wander about for years, I shall at last come to where the king said she is to be found: in the castle of Endi.'

GAWAIN COMES TO KING ASSENTIN'S CASTLE, AND MEETS ROGES, THE TALKING FOX

And Sir Gawain rode on, through forest and narrow passes and through wastelands where he suffered more heavy hardships than I am able to describe. Then one day he came to a river and saw on the other side a splendidly built castle. He thought to himself, 'I shall ride along this river till I can cross to the castle.'

But if he had known the true nature of the river, he would have done better to ride off: it was by nature a most perilous river, though on the surface the water was clear. When Gawain had ridden about a mile, he saw before him a bridge spanning the width of the river. Never was there an iron or steel razor so sharp as the edge of that bridge which Sir Gawain found before him; this disturbed him greatly. He said to himself, 'Blessed Mary, is this the bridge over which one must cross? My horse would rather swim over than cross here: it would carry no one over that.'

At that he dismounted and, tightening his saddle girth, prepared to ford the river. But he thought, 'This river is unfamiliar to me. I shall test the depth to see if I can ride across.'

So he took his lance in hand and walked to the edge of the river. He tested the depth with his lance, which at once burst into flames: wherever anything touched the water it was burned and reduced entirely to cold ashes. Then Sir Gawain was amazed and said, 'Lord, how can this be? I have never heard of such wonders as I see here before me – water that burns like fire and a bridge sharper than a razor. By God, I must turn back in dishonour without having accomplished my quest, and I can see no way for me to avoid this. Lord God, what will become of me? Is this all an enchantment of elves or magic to lead me astray?'

And when the flames had died down in the river Gawain moved to another spot, where the water was clear, and taking his lance in hand he said, 'I will test my luck again; though the water is treacherous, here it seems fordable to me.'

He raised his lance and where the water seemed to him so clear, there he plunged it downwards. Before it could even touch the water he saw the point of the lance turn to ash and the rest burst into flames down half its length. This dismayed him greatly and he said, 'My God, dear Lord, how can this be? I pray to almighty God for mercy; I see that my sins are great. My disgrace will be too great for me to appear before my liege lord Arthur, if he should come to learn of my failure; and if Sir Kay should hear of it, then my disgrace will be all the greater! Mercy, my dear Lord God, why have you thus undone me?'

Then he saw a lime tree, not far off. Gawain sadly mounted his horse and rode towards it. At that moment the water in the river there shone bright, as if it were gold. Gawain, said, 'By God, I must have been dreaming! The water is pure and good, and flows brightly here before me..'

Again he rode to the edge of the river and, testing the water with his feet, he burned himself sorely: the flames shot up as they had done earlier upon his lance! But Gringolet pulled back: if they had remained standing there they would both have lost their lives! Gawain was despondent, and rode off without delay, until he reached the lime tree. Its branches grew wide and spreading, and covered a beautiful lawn. It stood in a garden with a wall running all around it. Gawain began to hope that he would soon learn how it was that the river burned and behaved so strangely. He found a little gate opening into the garden, and there within the walls he saw many rich herbs and plants. The garden was fragrant with wild roses and there were columbines, violets, and lilies that stain one's hands. Gawain entered the beautiful arbour, and dismounted at once for he needed to spend the night there. He had seen no other shelter within seven miles, other than the castle beyond the river of fire. He took the lance head, and, thrusting it into the ground before him, he tethered Gringolet to it. Gawain said to his horse, 'Gringolet, you must stay here for a while, then you shall enter the garden; I will remove your bridle.'

Gawain was so sleepy that he very nearly fell to the earth; he took his shield, which was painted with gold, walked under the lime tree and threw it down on the green grass where many a flower blossomed; he laid his head upon it and was soon overcome by sweet sleep. But if he had known what was going to happen he would not have done so. He had slept there for a short while when the master and lord of the garden, a fox called Roges, arrived, and saw Gawain in his garden. He silently approached the spot where the knight lay and stole from him the Sword with the Two Rings that he wore at his side. The fox hid the sword and then took Gawain's horse and quickly led it out through the gate to a hiding-place by the wall, where he left it. He went back to Gawain and sat down at his side; he began to tear at his hauberk, pulling out rings of mail so that his bare skin could be seen through it. And still Gawain did not awake. Then the fox noticed the golden shield under Gawain's head; he seized it and began to hack it into a great many little splinters. Thus the fox robbed Gawain of both shield and sword; and his armour was torn all over. The fox had also robbed him of his horse.

Suddenly Sir Gawain awoke. He saw the fox sitting at his side and said, 'Did the Devil bring you here?'

When he saw the fox, he raised his fist and struck him on the neck so that he was sent sprawling. Gripped by fear, he reached for his sword, thinking it hung at his side, and was dismayed when he found it had gone. He seized the fox, held him fast and said, 'It seems to me that Satan himself must be master of this enemy; my armour is useless, I have lost my hauberk and my shield and cannot defend myself in the least. I have lost my good sword; and Gringolet has vanished.'

Gawain was still afraid that the fox might be the Devil. At this the fox spoke, 'Noble knight, let me live! I will give you your good sword, and your horse is quite safe.'

'Tell me how it is that you can speak.'

'Indeed I will, knight. Have mercy for your honour's sake! It was very foolish of me to have sought to harm you. When I saw the sword I knew that I had met my match, for on the pommel I saw inscribed that the knight who would wear it must all the days of his life be the best under the sun.'

'Will you then this day tell me all that I ask of you if I grant you your life?'

The fox answered, 'For the love of God, indeed I shall.'

Then Sir Gawain granted him his life then and there: though a man had killed his father, if he begged for mercy Gawain would forgive him his misdeeds.

Then Sir Gawain asked him, 'How is it that you talk and know so many sly tricks? Do you live beneath this lime tree? You have brought ruin upon me, and you are dressed in the hide of a fox, yet you have a human voice! It is as if you were a man!'

Thereupon the fox answered and he said, 'My dear lord, I have lived beneath this lime tree for many years and brought ruin upon anyone who tried to rest in my garden. And I shall tell you why: my father is a noble man with many virtuous qualities, and I am myself a wretch and must live all my life in foreign lands and in misfortune. And so I dwell beneath this lime tree, alone in this wild wasteland: no one can capture me as long as I am in the enclosed garden.'

Sir Gawain said, 'Tell me then, have you ever been baptised or are you still a heathen? And where were you born? Tell me your name and who your father is.'

The fox said, 'Roges, my lord, is my name, if it please you. My father has the same name – King Roges of Ysike.'

'Friend, you must tell me: did he himself disfigure you thus and banish you from the land or were you born this way?'

The fox answered, 'There was a time, my lord, when I was a handsome child and much loved by my father before my lady, my mother, died; with her death my happiness ended. She taught me all the skills of a knight; but also she taught me how to fly about, just like a falcon or a sparrow-hawk, and to swim in the water like a fish with its fins. All this I do well and I speak six different languages. For this reason I stood in awe of no man, small or great. Then she died; and so I must remain in this miserable state eternally, unless God Our Lord help me.'

'So your present condition is not your own fault?'

'No, sir; my father, who is a worldly sovereign and king, sent me as a squire to a neighbouring king's court after my mother's death. While I was there, his barons advised him to marry again, and he took a girl to wife who brought this misery upon me; but she herself suffers as much. It had been more than a year since I had seen my father when he called me back to court. I was welcomed there with a great show of honour: my father and all the other lords were pleased at my arrival and my step-mother welcomed me and had me seated by her side. which pleased my father greatly. And a great feast was held.'

'After the feast my lady retired to her chamber and my father followed her. When they were thus together there my lady spoke to my lord, 'Now I will never believe that you love me. You have had such a fair child for such a long time, yet I had never laid eyes upon him! From now on, do not ever separate him from me. I want to keep him with me to serve me, my lord. You will be praised and honoured for it. He is chivalrous and handsome; it would be disgraceful and scandalous if you were to send him abroad again for his education; he might become jealous of me and think that it was by my advice. By your grace, my lord, grant me this request.' My father said, 'I will give him to you to teach, and may you bring one another mutual honour."

'So when they returned to the hall, that lady spoke to me, 'Roges, my son, where are you? Come here, I wish to speak with you.' I had no thoughts of false tricks and I said, 'Gladly, my lady! I will always come to you when it is your pleasure.' We went into a little chamber. My lady took me by the hand; she made me sit at her side on the bed. She said, 'I am delighted that you have come; I was never allowed to see you before, but now I hope that I shall have my way with you. Your father has given you to me to serve me, and if you will do so, I will bring you honour; I will give you a horse and saddle so you may ride at your father's side.' I answered, 'This is a pleasant command.' She said, 'I favour you more than I can say: kiss me now on the mouth before we leave this bed.'

I said, 'My lady, that would be a sin! And if my father knew then I would be lost."

'She said, 'Harm will come of it if you refuse. And even if you wished, you could not leave before you have done what I desire. If you do not do it, harm will come to you of it, I warn you.' 'I would be cursed if I dishonoured my father in this way!' 'It will cost you your life and honour unless you do it immediately. I have you so firmly in my power that you must do it, however much it may displease you.' I said, 'Lord God, may I escape this with honour!"

'At this I tried to get up off the bed. My lady — she was not slow —grabbed me and pulled me back and said, 'You shall sit down, wretch; it will cost you your life or mine, by God!' She raised a terrible outcry. With her hands she tore at her hair and scratched her face. Red blood began to flow from the wounds in many places, covering her hands in gore; and she struck herself in the mouth. When I saw this I feared that it was the Devil's doing. She tore at her hair and ripped her clothes completely from head to toe until she was stark naked. She cried out, 'Woe is me, wretch! Will no one come to my aid before this Devil who stands here has deprived me of my life? You have treated me disgracefully and indecently! I expected only honour from you. Why have you treated me like a woman of easy virtue?"

'The entire court was in tumult when they heard my lady's outcry and rushed to the chamber. My father was the first to enter and said, 'My sweet love, who has brought this misery upon you?' 'This devil, my lord, whom you see here, whom you call your son! In all my days I have never been in such fear for my life as when he tried to assault me on that bed against my will. I was very nearly no match for him! He was beating me and hitting me:, but I managed to escape his grasp; I thought to escape with my honour intact. Then he attempted the most shameful of deeds and he said that he would have his will with me, come what might, forcing himself upon me against my will. I screamed, for he hurt me sorely!' My father answered, 'By Our Lord, my lady, if you recover from this you shall be fully avenged. I shall have him broken on the wheel, and when death has taken him I shall immediately have his body burned in a fire outside my gates here, and the ashes thrown to the winds. No father has ever done this to his child, but this is how I will avenge you!' At this my friends were very distressed. I said, 'My lord, have mercy on your son! Do not visit such woe, such misery upon me without knowing why. If I am to blame then do with me as you wish, but I swear by God that it never occurred to me to do what my lady accuses me of.' 'Her appearance is witness enough,' said my father, 'No plea will help you now; you must die this very day.'

'He ordered his knights to seize me and keep me under close guard. But though there were many brave knights present, not one of them would lay a hand upon me. Two of my mother's brothers were there and they had brought a hundred knights to the court with them. Indeed, if anyone there had attempted to seize me, he would have lost his life for it. It was for this reason that they all held back. My father said, 'This is a great disgrace that I can move none out of all my retinue to take this murderer captive!' He looked around him, yet no one there stepped forward. 'It seems to me that my authority counts for nothing!' said my father, 'If there is anyone here who would serve me truly, let him seize this murderer — by Our Lord in heaven, I would give him half my kingdom! I cannot bring myself to kill him or do him harm. And yet I see before my own eyes my wife so sorely abused! For the love of Our Lord, who shall avenge my injury?"

'My uncle arose without a word and went up to his elder brother, my other uncle, and said, 'I would take my nephew from this court, if it could be done with honour.' His brother said, 'Let us go before the king and pledge that we shall put him to death, if you agree. In this way the king's honour is preserved, and we shall come away unscathed.' They agreed on this, and went to my father. My uncle greeted him courteously and said, 'My lord, after what has transpired you are eager to be avenged for the base deed that your son has perpetrated. My lord, this shall be done: my brother and I will avenge you, if you would not object. For he has brought us great shame."

"I would by no means refuse,' said my father, 'Just remove him from my sight: I can no longer bear to see him standing before me, so great is the grief he has done me. Burn him outside in a fire, and bring his ashes back to me: then I shall discharge you from your obligation.' My uncle said, 'We will carry out your command: it is not for us to refuse it."

'And so my uncles left off talking, strode over to me, and seized me; and their men rallied around them.. My stepmother was very happy that she would thus get even with me; but then she asked who the two barons were. 'Who are the men who are taking away your son? It seems to me that they pay him such respect that I can never believe, my lord, that they would kill him. It seems to me that they will not carry out their task willingly. No one has abandoned him; an entire retinue follows him. Who are they, my lord?' Then my father spoke, 'They are two of his mother's brothers.' 'By God, now I shall never be avenged upon him!' said my lady, 'I shall seek my revenge upon him myself! He shall assume the shape of a fox, while both his uncles look on, and he shall remain in that form until one condition, which I shall set, is fulfilled: if God should grant him that he should see in one place the mighty King of Wonder and his son Alidrisonder together in his court along with Sir Gawain and the daughter of a certain king named Assentin, only then will he be freed from this spell. But this will never befall him; I expect that he shall die before it does.' '

'Then my kinsmen and my friends lamented loudly: they knew well that I did not deserve to suffer such a cruel fate. However, Duchess Alene, one of my mother's sisters was at court; she immediately answered the queen of Ysike: 'You have brought upon us great grief because of our nephew; May God visit upon you such rewards, my lady, as you deserve! If I could think of an equally severe curse, then you would not escape it. I know — this shall be your fate! Until our nephew is freed from this spell you shall become a toad and sit still within the castle gate, at the threshold, and all those who pass you by will beat you and hit you and spit upon your hide! This is as evil a fate, I should think, as that which you have decreed upon Roges.' '

'And so I departed, and they remained behind, grieving for me. My father's wife went in great sorrow to take her place at her threshold and I departed against my will. Since then I have not returned. I was utterly at a loss as to where I should go in order to find Sir Gawain, though whoever speaks of him praises his virtue. Perhaps you know him: if I were to find him, I am sure he would not neglect to help me make amends and shorten my woe. For this reason I remained here, my lord, and built this park and this garden with him in mind. I thought that he might enter it while searching for the girl whose father has had her put under guard in the castle that you see standing on the far side of this river. There is no one so brave that he dare fetch her, except Gawain, that daring knight whom men call the Father of Adventure. Now I have told you all. Tell me about Gawain in return, if you know of him.'

'I have often heard tidings of Gawain. If we mean the same one, those who praised him did not do well: Gawain is base and evil! Why do you praise him so much?'

The fox said, 'If I had not promised not to harm you, you would never escape without my first having sought out Sir Gawain, to tell him how you have slandered him! In my opinion he is neither base nor evil.'

'I will tell you where he may be found, but first, Roges, tell me why this water thus bursts into flame.'

' Have you never heard of this river? It is the true purgatory. All souls, having departed from the body, must come here to bathe if they are to attain God's grace.'

'I would not believe it,' said Gawain, 'unless I saw it myself.'

And the fox answered: 'My lord, I shall show you; you shall see with your own eyes that you've no cause to call me a liar. Do you see those black birds flying yonder, that now dive head first into the water? They are under water now: how do they appear as they emerge?'

Sir Gawain replied, 'Much whiter than snow.'

'Look carefully, my lord; those are living souls, the one of a child, the other of a father. Those black birds are bound and tainted with foul sins until they are permitted to cross the bridge that you see here. Then they bathe themselves and are purified and fly off to the heavenly kingdom to live in eternal bliss. I have answered your question; tell me now where Gawain is to be found.'

'Sir Gawain is here, nearby: you could easily speak with him.'

'So you are he, my lord! I shall never leave your side until you have helped me in my need. Please bring an end to my misery!'

'I do not intend to refuse you: if it lies within my power, I will help you gladly.'

'Then sit down here on the grass,' said the fox, and he ran off to fetch Gawain's sword and gave it into his hand; he said, 'Take this as proof that I shall serve you, my lord. I am very sorry indeed that I have mistreated you! Tell me, on your word of honour, whether you are my lord Gawain.'

'I would have told you long ago, Roges, if you had asked. I was born in the land of Arthur; I am Gawain, King Arthur's nephew. I might well regret that I still live, now that you have torn my armour!'

The fox said, 'I have erred, but I wish to make up for it, be sure of that.'

'Many men err and repent of it afterwards; but anyone who trusts a fox is a fool, for they never do as they promise.'

'My lord, do not fear this of me. Wait here. I shall fetch your horse; and good weapons are waiting for you, though they have not been used for some years; my mother gave them to me so that I might wear them with honour. Remove yours, if you would. I'll fetch the others without delay.'

So Gawain removed his armour as best he could, and the fox returned with the new armour. Sir Gawain donned it and it fitted him well; he cut quite a dashing figure in it. Then Roges led his horse in and left him standing in the garden, and ran off quickly to fetch his shield from where it hung. He brought a lance as well and gave it all to Gawain at once and said, 'My lord, do not spare these weapons when you are in need. And I will carry your hauberk, my lord, more than a hundred miles to a wild dwarf; he will fix these mail rings so that they will never come loose; and I will bring it back within three days. Now tell me if there is anything else you desire.'

Then spoke Sir Gawain, 'What I desire is difficult: to be on the other side of this river. But that lies beyond my grasp.'

The fox replied, 'God knows, wherever it is you wished to travel, you would not come to the end of the river even if you were to ride for many miles. Even if you reached the river's mouth, my lord, you still could not cross it. Its source is in the depths of hell where wretched souls are tormented, and it flows to the ends of the earth.'

'Then we shall never cross it,' spoke Gawain, 'We are both doomed to remain in sorrow. I had hoped to help you, and that you would accompany me to be freed from your present misery. But I cannot help you. If only we could win the girl upon whom I set my hopes! Your salvation depends on her, if you are to recover.'

The fox said, 'Even if you could cross this river, how would it be possible for you to breach that strong castle? No-one has entered unless he was invited first. Even if all the men in the world were to lend you their aid you still could not win the first gate — and there are twelve of them! They are made of copper and bronze and bound with iron and with steel; beneath each gate there runs a moat; and there are as many strong and splendid walls wrought of grey marble. Looking at it, I ask myself: who can ever take this castle? At each gate are stationed eighty men-at-arms. My lord, how do you expect to win this castle tomorrow? 'If I find the first gate open and I am able to enter it, then, I believe, I shall win the rest!'

The fox spoke, 'Then I will show you how to cross that river.'

Gawain answered, 'Roges, friend, even if I have to ride through hell, I will do so in order to cross it.'

'You will be on the other side this very evening , I assure you. Your horse, however, must stay here; if you took him with you, he would certainly be killed, so let him graze here in the garden. I shall guard him well for you, my lord.'

'If what you say is true, my despair has changed to hope!'

Then the fox said, 'Come, let us be on our way. If you dare to follow me I shall lead you up to the castle, before we part. Once there, do your best. If I had the power, I would do more to help you.'

ROGES THE FOX BRINGS GAWAIN INTO KING ASSENTIN'S CASTLE

Sir Gawain followed the fox out of the garden; the fox locked the garden gate and they went a little way, to a spot at the edge of the river. There the fox opened a trap-door in the ground. And he commanded Gawain, if he desired to have the girl, 'Down you go!'

'This looks to me like a snare!'

'I swear that it is not – my salvation depends upon you! We must enter through this trap-door if we are to cross this river that you saw in flames this day. I believe that no one else knows the way along which I shall lead you. The only entrance to the castle is by this underground path.'

Gawain was very anxious to see the girl; he came closer and crossed himself, for he was afraid that the fox intended to betray him. He stepped through the trap-door, and the fox took him by the sleeve and said, 'Let us go; I shall lead the way.'

The trap-door fell shut immediately once they were inside. Even if a man were to stand on top of it and search for it with all the skill he possessed, he would not find the place where it opened, so cleverly was it made. Under the ground it was as dark as hell itself, but the fox knew the way: he went straight ahead until they reached the other end. Gawain saw that the door was open; they stepped out, and the door swung shut. He looked at the ground to see where he had just emerged; but he could not find the spot.

But when he saw the castle his heart leapt for joy. They approached the fortress along the river bank, and it seemed to Gawain to be the finest castle that he had ever seen. They cautiously approached the gate; it was almost sunset, and the gate seemed to be bolted fast. 'It seems that guests are not welcome here,' said Gawain. The fox said, 'Tables have been set, my lord; they are about to eat.'

Sir Gawain said, 'How do you know that?'

'My lord, I see pages there inside carrying tablecloths and dishes, for this wicket-gate is standing wide open.'

'I wouldn't give three figs,' said Gawain, 'for the lot of them if things go in my favour!'

Then he drew the Sword with the Two Rings and wiped it clean on his sleeve. The fox said, 'My dear lord, God go with you! I must leave. God knows I have done everything I could for you, but I dare not go in there.'

Sir Gawain said, 'Friend, you have guided me well. Turn back now; I will see if I can get in.'

He pushed the wicket-gate open and went inside holding his naked sword in his hand. The men who were seated at table jumped up immediately, and leaving their food behind they spoke with great haste: 'A plague on the man who left the wicket-gate open! Tell us, knight, who it was advised you to enter? What do you seek in this stronghold? You'll be thrown out at any event.'

Gawain answered at once, 'It seems to me you are being rash, for surely you see that night approaches; where else should I look for lodging?'

'What concern of that is ours?' they said. Sir Gawain replied, 'If I turn back, you will be sorry. I would rather die here inside than go out again.'

'Then you shall stay inside – dead!'

They drew their swords and their knives and set upon him at once. But Gawain drew his sword and lashed out stoutly on all sides: whatever he struck, the good Sword with the Two Rings cut clean through. The chain mail rings flew forth from hauberks like chaff in the wind. The knights who guarded the first gate began to fear for themselves so they left Sir Gawain standing there alone and fled towards the next gate. They cried out, 'Open up, let us in! We shall lose our lives if you leave us here any longer!'

The guards raised the gate at once, and demanded what the matter was. 'The strongest and the best knight who has ever lived and borne arms has entered the fortress! He has put us all to flight! Look, here he comes, he draws near!'

The others exclaimed, 'Are you cowards, to be defeated by one knight? Our lord will be angry with you for abandoning your post!'

'But he is the strongest and the best; no one has any right to blame us! He will soon take your bulwark as well.'

At that moment Sir Gawain came up, without the least hesitation. The guards at the second gate addressed him, 'If you take one more step forward we will kill you at once! It would be best for you to throw down your sword, for you have no business in this stronghold.'

Sir Gawain answered calmly 'Do you not see that night has fallen? I thought to myself that I might ask for shelter here. I found the wicket-gate open, and so I entered. The guards refused to let me in, so I drew my sword, and they fled, calling to you to open the gate; I came in with them.

Now I ask you in the name of knightly virtue that you allow me to remain here inside.'

But they retorted, 'Knight, there is no help for you now: give yourself up, you are under arrest! Even though you made it through the one gate, you will not be able to boast that you won the rest.'

Sir Gawain said, 'I seek no quarrel. If I owe you anything I will gladly pay you.'

At that they became still angrier and pressed forward upon Gawain. As he felled the guards at the second gate, those who had fled from the first gate said to their comrades: 'Now we have been avenged for your haughty words.'

They answered, 'You have brought this misery upon us: why did you leave the wicket-gate unlocked and wide open? If you had closed it, this never would have happened. Now we must flee for our lives!'

Then they left Gawain behind and retreated in haste. Sir Gawain was more pleased with his sword than he had ever been before. He rested a bit and then followed them, strolling at his leisure. The others cried, 'In the name of mercy open the gate and let us in! Our lives are in danger!'

Those who were inside answered, 'What is the matter?'

and opened the gate. The men from the first and second gates said, 'We have all been betrayed!'

'Why did you allow your gate to be taken? Why did you not defend yourselves? Does a mighty army follow at your heels?'

'No.'

'Do you need our help to defeat one man?'

'Let us in, secure the stronghold, and lock him out, that is best. Blow the horn for more reinforcements, for he will win the castle from us if we are not careful.'

'Are you mad to say such things? Or are you convinced that we are cowards?'

At that moment Gawain entered as boldly as a lion. The men inside drew their swords and said with great vehemence, 'Knight, you will die here! Remove your helmet and your shield and we will let you live until dawn.'

'I would be a fool if I were to give you my weapons, nor do I care for your threats', Gawain replied. They began to hew with their swords at Gawain's helmet of steel, cutting off the precious and costly gems with which it was adorned. Gawain hacked so furiously that the sparks lit up everything in sight. Those who were most eager to have at him he struck in such wise that they might show off their scars afterwards! And it cost many knights their lives: soon they had to leave off further fighting and flee. Gawain followed after them as quickly as he was able, gripping his naked sword in his hand, for he was eager to enter through the fourth gate if he could.

At the fourth gate, the rabble of fleeing knights cried out, 'Open up, open up! Make haste!'

The men inside became anxious when they heard the clamour; they undid the gate and saw Gawain driving that bevy of knights before him at the point of his sword, like a flock of sheep, so that they all strove to be the first to reach the gate. They told the men they found inside to ready their weapons. And when these saw their great wounds and the blood flowing forth from them, they armed themselves in haste. They said, 'Who has done this to you?'

'A knight has got inside, and he will win the castle from us! Close the gate; that is the best thing to do.'

At that moment Gawain strode into the stronghold driving them all before him. The defenders began to attack Gawain, and three hundred men pressed forward into the fray. Gawain stood thinking how best to defend himself against those blows. He left the gate-opening and stood with his back to a wall so that he could not be attacked from any other direction than the front. Great misery was in store for the first man who attempted it. Then a cry was raised on all sides, 'Forward, take him quickly! He will be easy to take, for he is exhausted from fighting.'

But Gawain felled whoever he struck. He cut off at the knee the legs of the knight who attacked him first. He fought like a lion! If anyone was so bold as to attack him, Gawain inflicted scars that he might well show off wherever he touched him with his sword. He did such damage that before long there lay in front of him so many severed limbs, hands and feet and other extremities, that he was almost covered by them, and he stood up to his ankles in blood. Once more, the guards fled.

This suited Gawain well: he was so tired that he thought that he would never be able to fight again. If they had stood their ground they would surely have taken his life. Once Gawain was safe he removed his helmet and rested a bit, and calmly wiped the sweat off his brow. The others cried out, 'We are lost! He is near! What are we to do?', when they saw him, and they trampled one another underfoot. When Gawain saw this, he put his helmet back on and came nearer. At that they all were gripped by a terrible fear and expected to lose their lives. Luckily for them they found the gate unlocked and they all entered; but Gawain also entered as soon as he had the chance. This was his great mistake: an army may still overcome one man, even if he has terrified them! The sword in which he trusted had made him so haughty that he might easily be overcome, so worn out was he from fighting. But when the knights who held the fifth gate wanted to settle the matter, it was late and the moon waned and finally set. The night became as dark as pitch: this suited Gawain well. He went over to the attack and fiercely slashed at whoever came near him. His enemies cried out, 'Where is he, where? He would be wise to give himself up! He must die soon!'

Gawain began to believe that this was the truth, as he could scarcely fight for weariness. So he escaped from the mêlée.

But the others were furious, and were so thoroughly confused that they did not know what they were doing, and started to fight among themselves as they made their way towards the sixth gate. Sir Gawain gripped his naked sword in his hand and followed them. They cried out anxiously, 'Open up, for the love of God, or we are all doomed!'

The men who were inside answered them, saying, 'Stay outside. Why did you allow your gate to be taken? We are in bed, it is late. If we were to open up for you, we would be lost. We shall guard our gate until dawn.'

Sir Gawain stood below at the base of the drawbridge: this rendered their return by that route a dangerous endeavour! They had to escape by jumping off the bridge into the moat, so terrified were they of Gawain's sword.

Yet he had still not achieved his goal, even though all those whom he had met at the fifth gate had lost their lives, so that neither squire nor serjeant remained. This grieved Gawain greatly and he prayed to Our Lord and to good St. Michael for all of those souls who had died there and who had lost their lives at his hands. Then he prayed to God that He would forgive him the sin that he had committed in this way. Afterwards he was very quick to thank Our Lord joyously for the extraordinary honour that he had done him that day. It was on account of their overweening pride and their lack of charity in refusing him shelter for the night that they had died.

As for Gawain, he quickly turned back to the fifth gate. Here he saw a bright light in a hall, and tables standing by the hearth. The guard had just sat down to table when Gawain arrived at the gate. Gawain walked boldly into that hall, and shut the door at once and locked it fast in case anyone wanted to attack him. Then he quickly removed his armour. It seemed a foolish thing to do, but he was so tired that he thought he would not live much longer if he kept his armour on. The first thing he removed was his hauberk; he inspected the mail rings to see whether any were lacking. He found them all sound and intact.

Sir Gawain found clean wash-basins and white towels laid out there. So he went up to them and washed his hands and his eyes at once. He laid his armour and weapons at his side. His sword, in which he placed such great trust, he laid drawn and naked by his right hand, and he looked at the blade of steel: it pleased him extraordinarily well, for it had delivered him from danger. He took up a cup of good wine and drank a draught. At that Gawain was in better spirits than he had been before. He tested his appetite on the thigh of a roast chicken. But exhaustion very quickly compelled him to fall asleep there as he sat. He sat there in that hall, sleeping until bright morning came, oblivious to everything until dawn.

But at the sixth gate, when it grew light, the defenders cried, 'Men, it is time to ready ourselves for battle!'

Then they all armed themselves with care. Before they opened either a window or a door they conferred amongst themselves about how they might best ride out without risk. Then they sent a messenger to the seventh gate, and to the eighth and ninth as well, telling them that the castle was under siege, and that three or four men should come at once from each of those gates. When the reinforcements arrived, they said, 'Tell us what is happening and why you need us.'

'The castle is under siege by a great host. Our comrades from the outer defences came up to our gate last night in great difficulty. They called to us in the name of mercy that we should come to their aid outside; but we dared not open the gate: we feared the host. They were defenceless, and lost their lives or jumped quickly from the bridge into the moat.'

'Should the king be told that his castle is under siege?'

'Indeed not! The king has already suffered great losses, though he does not know it. We are in great trouble: if he should learn of it, he would want to know who has besieged it; but we could not tell him who had slain his men and wreaked this havoc. But let us prepare a force of three hundred men and ride out; and let us leave the gates open, in case we have to retreat. Let us see who has besieged our castle and find out who they are and where they are from. Once we have discovered the truth we will tell the king.'

The others agreed, and so the defenders prepared themselves for battle without further delay. Three hundred well-armed knights rode out through the gate. Before long they arrived outside the gate and saw the bodies of the slain and the streets stained red with blood; otherwise they saw not a single one of God's living creatures. They said to each other, 'The enemy have retreated to safety. Let us pursue them without delay! Let us ride until we find them!'

So they rode out through the gate: they made such a great commotion that Gawain awoke from his sleep at the sound of it. It was some time before he remembered how it was he came to be there. When he noticed the tables laden with food before him, he thought to himself, 'I must eat before I leave here, because I do not know where else I shall find food.' He drank some wine to raise his spirits and ate his fill; then he armed himself and prepared himself to go, once he was ready, out of the hall.

The knights who had ridden out in search of the enemy found no one, for the simple reason that no one was there. They cried out, 'Woe is us! We cannot even say to the king who did this, for they have escaped! What else can we do except tell him the truth?'

They turned back, dispirited. Meanwhile, Gawain took up his good and sturdy sword and held it drawn before him; he crossed himself and stepped out of the door, to find the sixth gate standing open. Once inside the gate he saw no one who might deny him entry. But those who had ridden out now returned and saw Gawain walking swiftly ahead of them, alone and on foot. Gawain heard them coming, as quickly as he could, he shut the gate and locked it fast, leaving the three hundred men outside. And because the men from the seventh, eighth and ninth gate had gone with them, he was able to make his way as far as the tenth gate.

Gawain was given a hostile reception here. As soon as he entered he found a crowd of men who attacked him without delay, believing that he was just one of the host who had slaughtered their comrades. He jumped to one side and threw his back against a wall, with a pillar to either side, and quickly defended himself. He said, 'Come closer, if you want to attack: I am waiting for you!'

Then the others halted, and said, 'Your defence will avail you nothing; even if the knights who have remained outside were here, we would kill them all! Not one of them would ever escape!'

'I left no one outside, for no one else attacked the castle,' answered Gawain. They drew their swords and stormed Gawain from all sides. It was thus that they welcomed their guest. But Gawain's weapons were so good that he made room as best he could: whoever he struck with it he sent tumbling ignominiously to the ground. Then the others said, 'Will we allow ourselves to be frightened by this one knight? And will we allow him to take the castle from us by force?'

They took up spear and lance and advanced towards him. Gawain kept his wits about him and sought cover behind his shield: he sliced the spears in two as if they were mere reeds. At that they exclaimed, 'He is a fiend! We are no match for him! Let us send a messenger inside to our lord the king to ask him to come to our aid, or we are lost.'

Gawain, Father of Adventure, thought to himself when he heard this, 'May God grant me strength and good fortune so that you may not escape me!'

At that same moment, the young girl whom Gawain sought came before her father and his lords, and said, 'Greetings, my lord! I dreamt last night that great woe and deep sorrow are in store for you, but I dare not tell you about it unless you command me to do so.'

The king replied, 'Dearest daughter, tell me your dream, and I will grant anything you wish.'

'Father, a very strange dream came to me last night. It seemed to me that a knight, a youth well-versed in all virtues, came riding here from a distant land – so distant, that no one would believe it! Upon his shoulders stood a head that seemed to be that of a girl. What might this mean?'

'Fair girl, if you would like to know, I shall gladly tell you. That knight travels through the worldseeking adventure, and whoever he finds in any danger, he seeks to help, even if it means his own death: this is what the girl's head which you saw on the knight signifies. Is there anything else in your dream?'

'I saw something else: his surcoat was, I believe, made from the hide of a lion.'

'The lion's hide that you saw is the courage that he carries within his heart. He is courteous, and seeks to do away with injustice and evil. When anyone tries to harm him he defends himself bravely with his sword. And he has never forsaken anyone who sought his help. This is the significance, no more, no less, of that lion's skin that he wears.'

'Father, there is a third thing that I dreamt. He brought with him a great serpent, and out of its throat fire spewed forth: this did you great harm. It had absolutely no mercy on you nor on your retainers: they were overwhelmed; before they departed he had slain nearly two-thirds of them, so help me God!'

'The fiery serpent was a sword that will cause me still greater harm and trouble if he should enter my fortress. But if Fortune smiles upon me he will not take it so easily.'

Tables were set up in the hall, and the king and his barons sat down to eat. But before they had finished washing their hands a messenger came striding into the hall and halted before the king: 'Get up,' he said with great vehemence, 'from your table, your Majesty! Let your meal be! Your stronghold is under siege: a knight has forced his way in. He will capture the castle from us. He has already achieved some success: he has entered the first gate and he may easily win two more. What's more he has slain two-thirds or more of your men!'

The king said, 'Although it hurts me, it is a good thing that such a knight lives. The misery and distress that now confronts me appeared to my daughter in a dream. My knights are ready. Rise, all of you, and make haste! Where are my weapons? Fetch them for me! Go! Let each man hasten to fetch his arms!'

The king was quickly helped into his armour and a strong charger was brought before him, which he mounted in a bound. He took the shield and the lance which were brought to him; it was a large, sturdy lance, painted cinnabar red. A metal band was wound about it from the point to the grip. This he took in hand without delay and rode off to find Gawain, who had caused his men pain and great woe that day.

Even now Gawain was not idle: he fought like a lion! The king was strong and brave and bore down upon him at full gallop. He held his lance at the attack and thought to pierce him through at the first blow. He struck Gawain a hard blow on the right elbow so that his sword flew out of his hand and landed several feet away from him. At that Sir Gawain was overcome by fear and great despair: because of the crowd that pressed upon him he could not win it back! The king rejoiced, as did the men who were with him; they said, 'You shall not escape! We shall kill you now!'

'No,' said the king, 'I want him captured alive.'

Suddenly Gawain saw a knight in front of him with a drawn sword; just as the king rushed towards him, he lunged at the knight and wrenched the sword out of his hand, and wielding it with two hands he said, 'If I must die, then you too will regret it!'

He struck the king so squarely on his steel helmet that the sword cut through it; but he did not wound him: this blow left him unharmed! The king turned his horse about and charged towards Sir Gawain without delay. Gawain defended himself against the blow and jumped to one side; in return he dealt the king such a blow that he was rendered both deaf and blind: that blow was a mighty one indeed! But Gawain's sword broke in two at the hilt, above the grip. The king fell to the ground, knocked unconscious by the blow.

But Sir Gawain feared for his life, for he did not know what to defend himself with. His attackers advanced on him. When the king came to, he was in a rage and mounted his horse in a bound. But Gawain caught hold of the lance and wrenched it from the king's grasp, saying, 'Though I have no sword I shall defend myself with this.'

GAWAIN IS CAPTURED BY ASSENTIN, AND MEETS YSABELE

As a reaper fells stalks of grain, Gawain felled his opponents boldly with the lance. Finally the king drew his sword, and seeing that they immediately fell upon Gawain with all their might. They cut asunder the strong steel bands upon the lance in seven places or more, and overwhelmed Sir Gawain. And so he was led by his attackers towards the castle. Then one of them saw Sir Gawain's sword and tried to pick it up. The sword dealt him such a blow that he went away a sadder man, leaving the good sword where it lay: and it did the same to more than a few of them. They left it there against their will.

When they entered the castle, the girl knew as yet nothing of her father's anger and woe until, standing with her attendants at the window, she saw him approaching. Then she made haste to go down and meet him. Gawain, whom he had brought with him as a prisoner, stood at his side. The king said, 'Now be of good cheer, daughter! See if you recognise this man: it is he who came wielding that serpent in his hand! It seems to me that I have experienced your dream to my own misfortune.'

The girl said, 'Father, I am saddened by your injuries; but I ask you to grant me the request that you promised me today.'

The king answered, 'I have no intention, daughter, of refusing you your request. But if you were to ask me to spare this man's life, that I could not grant you. Beyond that, ask of me what you will.'

The moment Gawain was brought before her the girl became so inflamed with inward love for him that she did not know what to do. But many and various are the thoughts of women once they have set their minds on a thing. She was overwhelmed by love for the knight, even though she had never seen him before. She answered the king at once, 'My lord, I do not ask for his life. He has caused us both great woe, my lord, and serious injury. Now I ask of you, father, by your grace, that you give him to me until tomorrow; you needn't worry about it, for I shall return him to you. Let me cool my anger on him this night, do you the same tomorrow.'

The king said, 'So be it, daughter. Will you return him to me tomorrow?'

'Indeed I will, if he lives that long. But if he is dead I shall give you his body, in God's name.'

Four strong and sturdy knights took hold of Gawain at once and led him to her side. Her ladies in waiting vied with one another to catch a glimpse of Gawain as he was led by. Because they thought him so handsome they all prayed earnestly to God and the blessed Virgin Mary that he would escape with his honour! Thus Gawain was led a prisoner to where the girl wanted him to be; he was thrown into a dungeon and the door locked fast behind him. 'Take good care of your guest,' said the knights to the girl.

'I shall, by my faith, take such good care of him, this I say to you in all frankness, that he were better off dead so terrible will be his torment,' answered the girl. 'I would be sorry if news were to reach the court – for I am a woman – that I had taken the life of a man. I do not want to kill him, but his torment and his misery will be great enough.'

At that all four of the knights took leave of the girl. The girl said, 'Tell my father that tomorrow I will return this prisoner, if he should live so long, for he will have been hard pressed by torments. And I thank my father for granting me the first request that I ever dared ask of him.'

The knights soon came before the king, who was overwhelmed by grief, and said, 'My lord, my lady the young princess sends you her cordial greetings and thanks you for the great honour that you have done her today. She will return the knight she holds prisoner tomorrow if he should live that long. But it is more likely that he shall die: so great is his torment that no one is able to describe it.'

The king replied that this did not trouble him; but if he should live to see the dawn, then he would have him put to death with the greatest pain. 'Speak to me no more of the matter. I am very grieved by the losses that I have incurred today! We must bury the dead, and see that the wounded are cared for.'

The king rode down to the tenth gate and his physicians came as soon as they were able. When the king reached the spot where he saw Gawain's sword lying on the ground, he rode forward and commanded his men to bring it to him. 'My lord, it would slay us,' said all of his men, 'we have tried it: no one here is capable of taking up that sword!'

The king himself got down off his horse and said, 'It is your cowardice that prevents you from doing so.'

He took cover behind his shield and tried to pick it up where it lay. The sword dealt him such a blow that it cut cleanly through his shield and helmet and only stopped when it struck the iron cap he wore under it. The king jumped back at once. 'It is the Devil, not a sword!' said the king, 'No one can approach it. If it had remained in the hands of the knight who brought it here, he would have done even more damage than he did! But thank God, he has been captured. I do not expect he will ever see it again.'

The king and his companions rode down to the sixth gate, where the men guarding it said: 'There is a huge army outside, which has come on account of the knight who was taken prisoner here.'

'Then let us make ready for battle, even though nightfall approaches,' said the king. The gates were quickly opened and the men who waited outside tried to force their way in before they were fully opened. The guards at the sixth gate attacked them before getting a good look at them and they set out after them in pursuit. Thereupon the defenders cried out desperately, 'Stop, stop, Your Majesty! If you kill us, it is your loss: we are your own men!'

When the king realised this he ordered all his other men to sheath their swords at once. He demanded to know how the fighting had begun. But there was no one present who could tell him: they did not know. 'My lord, we can tell you only what we know. Just before midnight your mighty walls were besieged by an immense host, and all those who guarded the first five gates, both great and small, were killed to a man! They called to us and wanted us to open the gates. Yet we dared not do it, for we feared the great host.'

'And does not a single man remain?'

'My lord, we have suffered a heavy blow! As soon as it was dawn, we ordered the gates to be opened and rode out to discover who had laid siege to the castle. But when we arrived outside not a soul was to be seen. As soon as we decided to go back inside we saw a single knight of quite average stature: he had slipped in through the gate with his bloodied sword drawn. But just as we were about to seize him he managed to close the gates. My lord, that is why we are outside and he remains inside. This is all that we are able to report.'

'It seems to me,' said the king, 'that I have suffered a great loss. The man who has wrought this destruction has been captured. My men were fools to have let him enter. I had at least a thousand men to guard my sturdy castle; but now it seems to me that there are hardly four hundred left. I shall man my gates again as best I can, but in future we will have twice as many men on guard.'

The king's men began to gather together the dead, dispersed over the ground, wherever they lay. The king ordered them to be loaded onto waggons so that they might be taken immediately into the castle. So the dead were buried and the living were stationed where they were needed. The bodies were all laid upon a burial ground so that they could be buried in the morning, while the king, full of grief, went to his hall to remove his armour, and all his nobles with him.

Gawain now lay in a place where he saw neither sun nor moon, and because of this his spirits were low indeed. The young princess, who knew all the secret entrances of the dungeon, secretly opened a door, because she wished to hear if he would reveal his thoughts. As she listened, Gawain said, 'Dear Lord, I would think nothing of death here, if only I could catch a glimpse of the beautiful girl whom I am seeking; then I would be content to die. Her beauty is so great that I could not care less about the pain I endure here if only she herself will take my life. But if her father cools his anger upon me, then I shall be sorry. In my heart it seems I see her: she stands with arms spread wide and the love for her that I have cherished for so long embraces me in those arms. Love for her has utterly overpowered me! If it be her wish, she may slay me; still I shall bear her love firmly in my heart even if she never knows it. She is the rose that surpasses all other flowers!'

All this the girl heard from where she stood and though she spoke not a word, she thought, 'It would be a great sin for me to take this knight's life:

How could my heart approve of that! He loves me even more than I do him.'

The king and his lords sat down at table and began to eat. But they had little appetite: their hearts were filled with sorrow. When the meal was over, the king, exhausted by the day's events, wished to go to sleep. When he and his men had retired to bed, the girl quickly went and had the door of the dungeon unlocked, and Gawain was brought out. When he saw the girl his heart blossomed like the dawn: he very nearly went up to her, surrounded by her men as she was, to kiss her on her mouth; but he thought better of it, hoping that she might yet take pity upon him. Two knights seized him by his arms and brought him before the princess. He had still not taken off his armour. Then the girl ordered that his armour be removed at once, and his hands and feet be harshly bound together, and that he be led before her and thrown at her feet. 'Now the hour of my torment,' said Gawain, 'and of my misery draws near. In God's name, do with me as you please, fair girl. Kill me; whatever torments you inflict on me will be a pleasure.'

The girl thought to herself, 'It would never, it seems to me, – given my father's explanation of my dream – be to my advantage to kill this knight. I wish that I could spend a year with him outside the castle; I would much rather enjoy his sweet face, his sweet body, the delights he could bestow upon me, if he wished, than stroll in the garden that my father values so highly and in which stands the wonderful golden tree with its magic birds and the eagle that shelters the fountain. I would rather give up all of this and lose the love of my father, than forsake this knight who lies here bound before me.'

She said to the knights who had brought Gawain from the dungeon to the hall, 'My lords, God knows that I would eagerly be avenged upon this knight who has injured my father so severely, but it would grieve me if it were to become known publicly that I, a girl, should have caused a knight such suffering. Go now, my lords, for it is not seemly that you see it; for I shall inflict great torment upon him.'

The knights left the chamber, and as soon as they were outside Ysabele immediately shut the door and locked it firmly. Now she forgot all her woe because she had her beloved there with her in her private domain. Never in all the world was there a girl who loved a knight so deeply and so intensely as she did Sir Gawain. She knew that she was safe there and that she had no cause to fear. If her sense of shame had not prevented her, she would have embraced the knight immediately and covered him with kisses. But she resisted the urge with great difficulty, and hurried to release the noble man from his bonds. At this Gawain asked, 'Ah, fair girl, shall I die or shall I live? If I am to die, then I entrust my soul to you. If you are to take my life, I would die in your lap, full of joy and sorrow.'

The girl spoke, 'You will not meet death here at my hands. If I could, I would quickly deliver you entirely out of my father's power, and I know a way to do so.'

The girl took him by the hand, drew him quickly to his feet and led him into the next chamber. Never in all the world was there ever such a beautiful chamber: it sparkled and shone brilliantly with the splendour of red gold. Many a heroic story, was painted there in cinnabar and azure, in silver and pure gold. The paintings and the wonders that were wrought there — the History of Troy as well as the wondrous deeds of Alexander — would take too long to describe to you. In the floor a passageway had been built in such a way that no one could tell where the entrance was. It brought only great calamity and woe to the craftsman who had made it: as soon as he had finished the passageway and completed his task he was immediately given his wages. Ysabele ordered him to be thrown immediately into the river, where he drowned; so no one knew about the passageway except the girl. Ysabele sat down next to Sir Gawain on a couch covered with sheets of white silk. There she told him everything about herself, and showed him the passageway. The beautiful girl and the noble knight enjoyed one another's company: the passionate love and the delight that they experienced I shall not describe for you, for I am not capable of expressing it. And whether the two of them also played the game of love, I am unable to tell you. They gave free rein to their desires; Ysabele had forgotten her father and his great sorrow: she would rather that he were dead than that she should forget Gawain, the brave and daring knight.

Her father, King Assentin, thought that Gawain was bound in harsh captivity. Little did he suspect that he was amusing himself so well in sweet play with his daughter. Assentin occupied himself constantly in imagining by which of numerous torments he would have him killed, while Gawain and Ysabele enjoyed each other's love. But Ysabele had dug her own grave, for there was a knight at court who spared no effort to sully the girl's reputation. By subtle means he espied all the pleasure that she blithely enjoyed with the knight of high renown. Gawain, who loved the girl with all his heart, thought that they were out of all danger, and they enjoyed repeatedly their games of love and their sweet joy. This made the knight extremely jealous, for had cunningly made a hole in the wall through which he saw the pleasure which Gawain was having with the gentle girl. So the cruel knight went at once to the king whom he found in a chamber alone. He fell to his knees at once and said, 'Your Majesty, my heart weeps for great grief! You have been betrayed deplorably by your daughter, the fair Ysabele, by means of a cunning trick. A great disaster hangs over your head!'

The king answered, 'Tell me about this; it would be an unnatural thing for my daughter to disgrace me when others treat me well and show me honour. But how am I to believe this?'

The knight spoke, 'My lord, have me tortured on the rack if it is not true! Come and see for yourself.'

At these words the king and the cruel knight set out together. He led his lord immediately to the chamber in which the lovers sat, to the spot where he could look through the wall. The king saw at a glance the handsome knight Gawain sitting free with his daughter; the two of them were alone at a splendid table. They had all manner of good foods in abundance and three or four kinds of wine. And before the meal was finished, they had, at the urgings of love, kissed one another a hundred times.

The king said quietly, 'Woe is me! Who is one to trust or believe now that even my own child wishes to deprive me of my worldly honour! For this she shall die under great torment!'

He rushed off as if he was out of his mind, and the knight followed at his heels. When he reached the hall, he threw everyone into commotion by ordering them to arm themselves. Assentinled them all to where Gawain and Ysabele sat in the chamber, unaware of the danger which threatened them. Once all of his men had arrived, the king told them about the scandalous deed that Ysabele his daughter had done, and about how she had fallen in love with the knight who had slain so many of their companions. His men were furious the moment they heard this. So the king ordered the door to be broken down at once, and they began to pound it with battering-rams. Ysabele thought for sure that her heart would break, she was so terrified. She said to her beloved, 'Sweet love, our love is to come to a grievous end: my father has found out! We have been spied upon and found out! Quick, flee through the passageway or you are certain to perish! I shall stay out here: even if you were to offer resistance, you would not be able to help me at all before my father would slay me.'

'Dearest,' said my lord Gawain, 'I would be a coward if I fled while you lost your life. I would rather perish with you! Help me to arm myself, Ysabele; God will be our shield this day. At least I shall not die without having defended myself.'

The girl helped the knight as best she could. But Sir Gawain lamented the fact that he did not have the Sword with the Two Rings. Suddenly he took her in his arms and kissed her passionately on her red mouth. He said, 'Dearest, put your faith in Our Lord; all may yet be well.'

At that moment the king's men started to splinter and smash the door, calling out to those inside, 'Where are you, scoundrel, vagabond? You are done for, it is here you'll stay!'

And they battered the door even harder than before. But Gawain remained calm: he took up position before the door with sword drawn, ready to receive any guests who wished to pass through it. At that very moment they smashed the door to bits. Gawain did not know how he would escape with his life. With the most gruesome of blows he received the first man who tried to get in, and two more who followed. Many spears were splintered on the noble knight. Assentin, urged on his men: 'Are you going to let yourselves be beaten by a single knight? You'll have to go about it differently if you wish to capture him, craven wretches!'

The king himself now entered the room and made straight for Sir Gawain. He slashed adroitly at Gawain, wielding his sword with both hands, trying to split his head to the teeth, but he missed. Sir Gawain, who feared neither loss nor risk, returned the blow at once. All manner of costly and precious stones flew off his helmet; and because of the force of the blow the king fell to the ground at once, unconscious. He heard nothing, nor could he speak, nor did he know what had happened to him. A great number of men rushed forward and carried the king back out of the press. Fearing for his life they quickly removed his helmet and threw water on his face.

The king soon revived and said, 'My lords, have no fear: I am not wounded. Fetch my sword! He cannot hold out for long and he will either die or collapse from exhaustion in the mêlée!'

At this the king was pulled to his feet and handed his sword; he advanced against Gawain with fifty famous knights. They began to hack and hew at Gawain from all sides. Never has a man fought so well! In the small area in which he could move, he shattered sturdy shields and strong helmets; he pierced them all through. Blood ran from freshly made wounds and gushed forth like water in a stream. His enemies cried, 'This man who does us such harm has been sent here by the Devil; otherwise he would not be able to cause such carnage here today!'

King Assentin was infuriated by such talk and said, 'You are cowards! If you had acquitted yourselves bravely we would have killed or captured the knight by now. He is a man just like you.'

At these reproaches, the entire host began to slash and thrust in earnest at Sir Gawain. They kept this up until by sheer force they brought him to the ground, deprived him of his sword, bound him and maltreated him seriously. And they led him to their lord who received him cruelly and immediately had his daughter seized. If the girl had wished to, she could easily have escaped through the passageway, but since she saw that the man upon whom all her happiness depended had been taken captive by his enemies, she, too, wished to die and live no longer.

They put her in a dungeon that was filthy and cold. And Gawain the brave knight was put in an adjoining one, where he was harshly bound and clapped in such heavy irons that a horse could not have borne them. He lamented the plight of his beloved, saying, 'Alas, dear, sweet friend, sweet love, never in all the earthly kingdom was a love so sorely betrayed as ours!! I would rather that I might die three deaths for your sake, and that you would be released from prison and pardoned completely! Who was that scoundrel who had us locked up separately? If you were here with me in this place, we would both better be able to bear our misfortune!'

Though Gawain's anguish was great, the girl's was much greater: she wrung her hands and tore her hair. Unceasingly she bewailed the fate of her lord Gawain in that filthy and squalid place. Assentin, the fierce and cruel king, had promised to kill them both under great torments: and each of them lamented sorely the fact that they had been separated so that they could not console one another in their sorrow. The girl thought that they would be buried alive or burned in a fire; the knight thought, 'Now I shall be hanged here or laid on the rack.'

YSABELE AND GAWAIN ESCAPE WITH THE HELP OF THE RED KNIGHT'S GHOST, AND SET OUT IN SEARCH OF KING AMORAEN

Suddenly, after midnight, a ghost appeared to Gawain in the filthy dungeon. The apparition spoke to him, saying: 'Knight, fear no more at this time. I shall free you: I am the spirit of the evil Red Knight whom you slew because of the harm that I inflicted upon the girl. Because you buried me and administered the sacraments as I desired, I shall release you from this prison.'

Gawain was astonished and terrified at this; he said, 'God has watched over me! May you be forgiven your sins for remembering me in my hour of need!'

Suddenly his chains burst asunder and the dead man took Gawain by the hand and led him out of the dungeon to the cell of Ysabele, where they found her crying and weeping. The dead man freed her: her chains soon burst asunder. Then Gawain said, 'Fair love, have no fear. Our fortunes have already taken a turn for the better. We are free, we can go!'

The dead man led the girl and Gawain outside. No lock in the castle was so strong that it did not open when the dead man approached. Then he took Gawain to where he found his own armour. Then he hurriedly led Gawain into the stables and gave him the best horse he could find there. Next he conducted Gawain to where he had left the Sword with the Two Rings; Gawain picked it up with no difficulty, and they went on until they stood before the outermost gate. Gawain mounted that horse and placed the girl in the saddle before him. Thus rode the two of them: setting spur to the horse they galloped off, the dead man still in the lead. And when they arrived at the secret passageway that passed under the river they had to dismount, for no horse could pass through that tunnel. The dead man descended first into the underground passageway. Gawain followed close behind and led his beloved by the hand.

At last they arrived on the other side of the river. At this the girl rejoiced: it seemed to her that she had forgotten all her sorrow now that she had her lover safely with her. The dead knight led Gawain all the way up to the stronghold in which the fox lived, who was very eager to learn how Sir Gawain had fared. When the dead knight had brought Gawain into the fox's domain he took his leave, and vanished. Gawain and Ysabele remained in the garden; the fox ran up to him and greeted him with great joy. Ysabele was much perplexed at how a fox could speak! The fox asked the knight how he had fared on his expedition. Gawain told him of his adventures and told him that this was King Assentin's daughter, whom he loved dearly. At this the fox rejoiced even more, and said, 'By the Holy Ghost, Now I must find the mighty King Wonder and Alidrisonder his son! If I were able to see both of them together along with you two, I would at once become human again!'

Gawain answered: 'I will on no account abandon you until you have seen the four of us.'

The fox thanked him earnestly for these words. Then Sir Gawain asked him, 'Have you taken good care of my brave horse Gringolet and my helmet as well?'

The fox answered, saying, 'Yes, indeed, my lord.'

'Then tomorrow we must set out in search of King Wonder.'

Within the garden there stood a most beautiful palace; and the fox led Gawain and the fair girl Ysabele together up into it and saw to it that they were happy. They had all they could wish for there that evening. Afterwards they went to sleep. In the morning the fox inquired as to what horse the girl should ride. Gawain answered, 'Don't let that delay you: I shall put her on the horse in front of me!'

The fox brought him his horse; Gawain mounted at once and with joy in his heart placed the fair girl Ysabele before him. Then they rode away from there, the fox leading the way. The weather was fair and clear; the sun shone in all its early morning glory. They met neither man nor woman, nor any living creature. But as night began to fall, a young well-armed knight came riding on a strong horse. He came face to face with Sir Gawain, and when my lord Gawain saw him, he greeted him first in a courtly manner. The other knight looked at him with disdain and rode past without a word.

Gawain was silent and rode on. He was so mild mannered that he did not wish to show his annoyance. But when the villain who had not deigned to greet him had passed by, he turned his horse and peered after Gawain, saying to himself, 'Bah! How can I allow this lout to pass now when he has with him such a beautiful harlot! He will leave her here even if it costs me my life!'

He called to Gawain, 'Knight, you there riding on the plain with the comely girl, turn back and leave a hostage behind. It is the girl I want, no other hostage will do!'

'Do you wish to provoke me with this?' said Sir Gawain, 'I've done you no wrong!'

The other knight replied: 'Are you jesting? Do you take me for a fool? You had better desist while you can, or much sorrow will come your way!'

'If it is the girl you want, then it will certainly cost one of us dearly!'

The other knight said, 'I shall win the girl here on this meadow with my sword.'

They both turned their sturdy chargers and stood at the edge of the meadow a great distance apart, in order to deliver the greatest possible thrust. The other knight laughed for joy that he was to have a joust. He spurred the horse on which he sat with spurs of red gold. Nor was Sir Gawain slow to action: he fiercely gave his brave horse Gringolet the spur. They bore down upon one another with shield and lance like dragons: each aimed a mighty thrust at the other. And the strange knight struck brave Gawain so mightily against his helmet that his head was stunned by the blow, and his lance was utterly shattered by the force of the impact. But my lord Gawain struck him in return so mightily that both horse and rider went crashing down violently to earth. The knight lay there for some time afterward speechless; but when he came to and he saw Gawain sitting upon his horse and himself lying there like that, he said, 'Knight, whatever has happened, I'm not vanquished yet. Allow me to mount and I shall slay you as I have slain many others before!'

Gawain said, 'I could easily avenge myself upon you if I had a mind to do so, but arise at your leisure and mount your horse, since you are so proud!'

'These are chivalrous words; if you surrender your sword and shield and beg for mercy I would consider it, and treat you mercifully.'

Sir Gawain answered him, saying, 'Knight, what prompts you to say this? Do you not realise that you lie here at my feet in the sand? If I wished I could kill you at once. Get up, mount your horse and do whatever you wish!'

That degenerate knight got up at once, mounted his horse and drew his sword. He began to hew fiercely at Sir Gawain as if he wanted to cut him to pieces. And when my lord Gawain saw that he would have to fight, he began to return the other knight's blows, and he very nearly struck him down with the very first blow; he said, 'By God's grace, knight, you know full well that I have done you no harm yet you seek to slay me.'

Then my lord Gawain attacked him, but the strange knight still defended himself well; he had a horse that was mettlesome and he launched many fierce attacks and counter-attacks against Gawain. It was as if the grass had been sprinkled with crimson drops. And yet the stranger was hard pressed, for he could by no means escape the Sword with the Two Rings. Sir Gawain pressed him so hard that he was at his wits' end, but because of his great pride he would not ask for mercy. His heart became weak and cold because of the blood that he had lost, and his fear of death became acute. My lord Gawain drove him back and forth over the field of battle, until with his good sword, sharp of edge, he caused his head to fly off and land two paces further on: the body fell dead to earth; the soul went whither God commanded.

When Ysabele saw the knight die in combat, she rejoiced; she did not mourn him in the least. My lord Gawain let the fool lie where he was and took the knight's horse and placed Ysabele on it. They set out on their way and rode off at full gallop. The fox ran ahead of them over the field. He was happy that Sir Gawain had defeated the scoundrel. Then the sun began to set and evening was upon them. But they saw neither castle nor house nor any other dwelling towards which they might ride. Night fell swiftly, and they had to ride on in the dark until the moon and stars gave them light. Far off in the distance they saw a light shining bright as a torch. They made straight for this until they could make out the form of a pavilion; when they arrived at its door they peered through and saw tables set up. The tent was brightly lit and inside a duke was seated with many knights; squires served them in courtly fashion. Sir Gawain said, 'Fair love, I hope we may dine here tonight in peace, if it please those who are sitting here now.'

The girl said, 'I assure you, I have never been so hungry before.'

So Gawain dismounted and helped the girl down off her horse; he tied both the horses to a tree standing nearby. Taking the girl by the hand, he entered the pavilion fully armed, though he doffed his helmet out of courtesy. He greeted the duke before all others, because he seemed to him to be a nobleman. The duke aked him, 'Who are you and what do you mean by riding here through this wilderness at this time of night?'

Gawain answered, 'My lord, we had no other choice in order to escape danger.'

The duke spoke, 'And this girl, is she your sister or your lover?'

Gawain answered, 'My lord, she is my lover.'

'You may rest here, and I shall gladly entertain you today in honour of all knighthood and all womankind.'

'May God reward your courtesy, my lord,' said Gawain. The duke immediately said to him, 'Knight, wash your hands, both you and your lover.'

Ysabele and the brave knight washed their hands and took their seats at the best part of the table. They were then served with both food and drink to their heart's content. And as they were sitting comfortably the duke said, 'Where is my son? It is not his custom to stay away like this: where can he be?'

GAWAIN AND YSABELE ARE CAPTURED BY THE DEAD KNIGHT'S FATHER, BUT ESCAPE

As he said this, at that very moment they heard a shrieking and crying out, 'What will become of us? Our young lord is dead!'

Men approached the pavilion leading a sumpter horse loaded with game; upon another sumpter was draped a dead body without a head. They carried the head with them, by the hair. They dismounted in front of the pavilion and left the game behind.

They led into the pavilion the sumpter upon which the dead man lay; many deep and fresh wounds could be seen upon him. By then the body was cold through and through, and the bleeding had stopped. But as soon as they entered the pavilion, it began immediately to bleed afresh. All the wounds opened wide: the blood flowed forth on all sides. Sir Gawain saw this and said to himself, 'May God in heaven help me! This is surely the knight whom I slew in the field. His wounds are bleeding anew because I am the one who slew him. This will bring me great misfortune.'

As soon as the duke saw his dead son, he cried out, 'Who has robbed me of my son? I can never again be happy!'

And overwhelmed by great sorrow he took up the head and pressed it to his breast. He kissed the eyes and the mouth, which were pale and grue-some, for all the blood had drained from them. Seven times he fainted and revived, and if he had not been taken away from it by force, he would have died on the body.

And because the dead body had begun to bleed again, and more and more profusely, the knights there said to their lord, 'My lord, the man who has caused you such anguish is here inside this tent; we believe we can say for sure that it was your guest who did it. Who else could have done it?'

The duke answered, 'If I knew the truth of the matter I would feel the better for it; for I would avenge myself so well, that men would speak of it from now until doomsday.'

It had never been Sir Gawain's habit to tell a lie, and when the duke began to accuse Gawain of the deed, he confessed, a thing that many men would hesitate to do. 'You are a bold murderer to dare to confess publicly to the murder of my son!'

Sir Gawain rejoined, 'My lord, you speak in haste. I have never deserved the name of murderer. It was your son who sought to fight with me and wrest my lover from me. He called me a numbskull and a fool, and rushed to the attack and said that I would receive my just desserts. He charged at me with his lance and I threw him from the saddle with a single blow. But when he got to his feet again – which I allowed him to do – he refused to acknowledge defeat, but instead began to swear that he would slay me then and there God granted me the good fortune that I was able to send him reeling, stunned, to earth. I dismounted and cut off his head. I have told you the absolute truth, just as it all happened.'

The duke replied, 'Alas, if a nobleman had slain him then I would not be so upset. But that a peasant has killed him is a fact that weighs heavily on my heart! I shall avenge myself on you as I wish.'

He commanded his knights to seize the knight and his lover, too, that evil harlot, that vile vixen, and to cause her such disgrace as she had never suffered before. The duke's retainers were not slow to rush as one man at the brave Gawain. Before he had sat down to table he had removed his weapons, for it would have been discourteous to eat while armed. Now he regretted the fact that he did not have the good Sword with the Two Rings with him here. All of those knights pressed upon him and dealt him heavy blows: some threw benches and trestles while others drew their swords, or grabbed pikes and battle-axes, and lances and staves. Gawain seized a sturdy shield from one of the knights; he took courage from this and began to defend himself by lashing out in all directions. He killed four men with four blows: they measured their length on the ground. The fox caused great turmoil: he did great damage by tearing at the knights' legs and faces with both claws and teeth. With great effort and many blows a group of men had captured Ysabele and they intended to carry her off at once and rape her, but a nobleman prevented them, saying that he would not allow anyone to dishonour her in that way, regardless of whatever else she might suffer.

Gawain and Ysabele are hard pressed indeed. For all his exertions, and although he killed many knights, Gawain had to concede defeat, for the duke's forces were growing by the minute; many knights had in the meanwhile armed themselves and joined in the fight. In the end, they overwhelmed him by sheer force and bound him hand and foot. As soon as this battle was over the duke said, 'He shall be held until dawn, at which time I shall ride to my castle without delay. There my barons will deliberate to decide how best to dispose of him. And his lover, the vile slut, I shall have put to death, to avenge myself on him who has caused me all this suffering.'

And his men immediately did as the duke had commanded. In the morning, at dawn, he set out with his retinue, and Ysabele was carried away with malevolent glee. As for the fox, when he saw that he could not help his lord, he let himself be captured. The pavilion had been packed away, and Gawain's death was postponed until the duke had decided how he might soon have him put to death in the most merciless and degrading manner.

The duke arrived in great sorrow at his castle, and he calls his friends and kinsmen to come to his aid, and, above all else, to come and look upon the young duke, their lord. The duke's son was laid out and buried, according to the custom of the land. Then the duke came and desired that the murderer who had caused him so much grief should be tried and punished at once. But a knight answered, 'My lord, send for his brother to witness the vengeance. He would be very angry if he was not here; and he will soon return from the tournament to which he has gone. He will help you torture the knight who has brought this misery upon you. Leave the knight in the dungeon until he arrives: then he may be slain before both him and all of us.'

The duke agreed to this, for Gawain had been firmly clapped in irons, while Ysabele wore shackles about her legs; and that hideous dungeon was so deep that they nearly perished there for cold. The prison was at the edge of the sea, and the waves streamed in upon them through so many holes that the two of them stood in water up to their knees. Both of them would have lost their lives if it had not been for the comfort that they gave one another in their misery. Sir Gawain said, 'Sweet love, it is unjust that you suffer such ill luck: it is my fault that this misfortune has befallen you. If I had not found you, you would not be in such distress.'

Ysabele answered, 'Alas, that you should say this, sweet love! I would not wish to be in paradise if I knew you to be in such misery.'

The next day they were given bread and water, but only a little: they had eaten it in a trice. The jailer was a very cruel man: he heard them complain often of their hunger and the severe cold; he paid no heed to their lamentations but told them that Gawain would be broken on the wheel, and that his lover would be given without more ado to the stableboys and filthy servants to do with as they pleased. He also took up a staff with which from a distance he struck Gawain; Gawain rushed towards him, but he did not get far on account of the irons with which his legs were shackled. Ysabele embraced Gawain to comfort him, and wet his face with her tears. Gawain did the same, weeping for the girl whom he saw suffering such misery. She said, 'My love, let us receive death embracing thus, for there is no escaping it here.'

The jailer returned the next day to the girl and to Sir Gawain and he brought food for them: it was a loaf of bread so small that one man alone could have eaten four of them; and a quarter-portion of water was given to the two of them to share. Yet again the jailer struck the knight. He said, 'Why are you so hostile towards me? You should not treat any prisoner in this way.'

The man was cruel and heartless and he hit Sir Gawain with the staff all the harder, at which he began to get angry. 'Why do you hit me from a distance? Why don't you come closer to me?'

The jailer replied, 'Sir murderer, I would much rather you suffered shame than that I should fall into your hands.'

At that he hit him a third time and struck the girl squarely on her hand so that it began to bleed. Gawain was beside himself, and he flew into a frenzy: 'Scoundrel, you've struck the girl! You'll regret it!'

Then he gripped the chains in his hands with all his might and pulled them apart, an impossible feat: it was the might of God that did it. He ran after the jailer, seeking revenge for his blows, and caught him by the sleeve just as he set one foot outside the door. He pulled him violently back in, and grabbing him by the throat he threw him down at his feet and struck him so that he gave up the ghost then and there.

Gawain picked up the staff with which he had been struck. He went over to where the girl stood; he said, 'Gentle love, I have avenged you for the blows that you have suffered.'

Then he searched the dungeon until he found a stone with which to strike off her chains. 'If only I had the Sword with the Two Rings, the duke would not be able to stop me: I would slay him in his hall with all his men! But I must take things as I find them.'

At that he walked over to where the jailer lay; he took his sword and his keys, and went over to the dungeon door and locked it. In high spirits he went over to Ysabele and said, 'Brave beloved, I know for certain that God in His power has provided for us. Tonight we shall set out from here in the hope that He hears our prayers. Whoever tries to stop us will meet with great sorrow and shame.'

But the girl replied, 'You must not lay a hand on anyone, for you might well stir up all the knights in the hall and start another battle; we would be lucky to escape again.'

'Do not worry; I think we will get our way.'

They remained there in silence until it was nearly midnight. Then Gawain said, 'We won't be seen, let us go now at once!'

He took the girl by the hand and led her silently and stealthily out of the dungeon, holding his naked sword at the ready. Thus the two of them set out: as they wound their way through the catacombs they had no idea of where they were, nor did they know where they were going. They came to a door and they found that it was locked; but they saw light in the room behind it. Gawain examined the keys that the jailer had used to carry with him, found one that fitted the door and quickly opened it. There were four knights sleeping on four costly beds; on the wall nearby hung their good swords and their armour. Gawain did not want to harm them or take their armour, and by great good luck, in the very same place he also found all of his own good and sturdy armour. He armed himself at once, and the girl helped him as best she could. No one there awoke.

Gawain found a candle and lit it, and they left the room. By the light of the candle they found a stairway which led to the hall above; but the door they found there was locked. Again Gawain opened it with the keys; they crossed the length of the hall and descended the stairs at the other end, where Gawain again opened the door; neither knight nor squire said or did anything to stop them. When they had gone a little way they came to a stable and found its door ajar. Inside, the stableboys had drunk so much that night that they all of them lay snoring in a stupor and did not hear Sir Gawain. As they went in, the fox suddenly sprang up with his paws against Sir Gawain. He said, 'Lord, is that you? I have been very worried about you. Gringolet your good horse is here in the stable.'

Suddenly the horse saw his master and pulled his tether from the wall and ran over to him, neighing and prancing for joy. 'Look at this friendly beast; he is the best horse in the world!' said Gawain. But the girl replied, 'Let us go quickly, I beg of you!'

Gawain took a palfrey, saddled and bridled it, and did the same to his own horse. He led them towards the outer gate, which he unlocked then and there, for he had the key with him. They opened the gate wide and walked out in high spirits.

Gawain lifted Ysabele onto the palfrey and gave her the horse's reins. He himself leapt up onto Gringolet, and they set out at a leisurely pace. The fox fell into a trot at their side. Sir Gawain said, 'I do not know how to find King Amoraen's court, but I must go there, for I promised him that

I would take you there. That is why he gave me the Sword with the Two Rings, which I have lost in a miserable way.'

The girl was very upset; she said, 'If you take me and present me to some strange king to love then I will be a miserable wretch indeed! I would sooner take my own life. How could you justify such a deed, my sweet love? For I have never played false with you! I have left great wealth and immense power behind!'

Gawain spoke, 'Ysabele, I know this well. Do not be sad! I promise you that I shall not desert you!'

She said, 'My lord, I thank you for these words.'

They rode on and before long they happened to come to the meadow where the duke had set up camp, and where Sir Gawain had been captured so ignominiously. There, lying on the ground he found the Sword with the Two Rings, which no one had been able to take away; Gawain dismounted and picked it up off the grass. He girded it about his waist, delighted that he had found it! He said, 'Look, Ysabele, with this as security I can ransom you from King Amoraen. This sword is of such great value that the king would not exchange it for anything, except for you alone. But we must ride on fast, for I am sure that we will be pursued from all directions once it is discovered what we have done.'

At dawn they encountered a page; Gawain called to him and asked him if he knew the shortest route to Ravenstene. The page replied, 'My lord, it is scarcely twenty miles if you travel by sea; and if you are not averse to travelling by water, you can soon be at the quay. But if you travel overland, you have sixty miles to go from here. The choice is yours, my lord.'

Gawain asked the girl for her advice. She said, 'The less delay the better! Let us go on board ship, if you agree!'

They rode in haste towards the quay until they saw the masts of ships on the sea. There were twenty ships or more ready to sail, so they chartered one and set sail at once; a favourable wind filled all their sails. The ship was well trimmed and swift; they had cast off without delay so that they arrived before vespers at Ravenstene.

When the jailer was missed, the news spread like wildfire. No one knew what had become of Gawain and the girl Ysabele. The news pained the duke greatly and he ordered his men to search for Gawain and the fair girl. And when they could not be found, the duke ordered them to be pursued at once. Thirty men took to the sea and thirty more set out to search by land. But Gawain and the girl had escaped their clutches. When the duke's men reached the quay, they found that the wind was against them. At this they were disappointed and furious. Neither did those who followed Gawain by land, intent upon harming him, have the least bit of success.

They turned back whence they had come. They had accomplished little of any use; they were angry and exasperated.

GAWAIN COMES TO KING AMORAEN'S CASTLE TO GIVE HIM YSABELE, BUT FINDS THAT THE KING IS DEAD

As for Gawain, he was overjoyed when he arrived at Ravenstene and saw the castle standing there before him. He met a young nobleman, and asked, 'Squire, may God keep you from harm's way! Tell me, how fares my lord Amoraen, the gentle king?'

The squire answered, 'My lord, would that I had not been reminded of him' At that his eyes filled with tears and he began to weep. He spoke to Sir Gawain, 'My lord, King Amoraen is, I hope, in paradise: he has departed this world.'

'May God preserve his soul!' said Gawain in reply. At that he took leave of the young nobleman, and turned to Ysabele, 'See here, sweet love, the mighty King Amoraen is now dead. He would have become your lover if things had gone according to his will.'

'God has watched over me,' she said, 'for even if he had possessed me, it would not have come to that!'

Gawain and Ysabele went up to the castle and were welcomed thére with honour: Gawain showed the nobles there that his mission had been accomplished. Gawain, the Father of Adventure, was greatly honoured and feted there that day! They stayed there for three days, and when they left, most of the knights accompanied them a half mile's ride from Ravenstene.

Now the fox was eager to regain his human shape, and Gawain had promised him that he would ride over hill and dale and that he would not rest until such time as he found King Wonder and his son Alidrisonder. 'There is no one I'd rather hear news of than those two, I assure you. There is a chess-set there that I must have, which I shall take back to court, if luck is with me. But there I must leave the good Sword with the Two Rings: that is the only way I can acquire it. I swore a solemn oath that I would acquire the chess-set for the king. Now the time has come when, God willing, I hope to obtain it.'

Thus they rode a considerable distance, speaking of these things, as I understand. The fox followed them all the while. The sun burned brightly overhead so that they were drenched in sweat, for it was a wasteland where there was not a single tree to be found anywhere. But at last they arrived at a pleasant spot that was fair and green, where water bubbled forth from a well, clear and bright and cold as ice. They thought they were in the earthly paradise. When they arrived there they saw an olive tree spreading its branches over the well.

Sir Gawain dismounted on that green meadow and helped the girl down off her horse. He let the palfrey and his own Gringolet graze on the pasture. The fox, too, lay down in the grass beside them. Gawain had sat down next to his love, at the edge of the well, which the olive tree shaded pleasantly with its branches. He had removed his helmet and with his hand he dipped into the well and drank from the water that was pure, sweet and cool. Ysabele did the same. And so they sat there for quite some time enjoying each other's company. Both of them would have liked to have shown the other more frank proofs of their love than they did, but they did not want the fox to witness their pleasure. When they had sat at the edge of the well for some time Gawain became exceedingly drowsy. He did not wish to sleep in her lap for fear of discomforting her, so he laid his head down upon his shield and immediately fell into a very deep sleep. And the girl, who was true to him and loved him dearly, could not keep herself from kissing the knight, even though the fox could see it all then and there.

But when she looked up she saw a huge knight come riding in the distance on a massive charger, black as a raven. He was neither ambling nor trotting, but rather he came storming on like one being chased by a Devil, spurring his horse furiously on. The moment the girl saw this she was so utterly terrified that she could not utter a word. The Black Knight had no other intention than to carry off the girl, who was not able to stir a limb. He bore straight down upon the girl, who sat utterly paralysed with terror, stooped down and swung her up onto his horse in front of him. Then he spurred off again. When the fox saw this he immediately began to whimper and weep. He began frantically to buffet Gawain's head with his paws so that he awoke at once, and said, 'Are you possessed by the Devil, that you are behaving this way? Are you mad?'

The fox said: 'It is you who are mad: it is your fault that my lady Ysabele has been lost. A knight as black as ink has carried her off by force on a horse as black as pitch. He was none other than the Devil himself! Alas! What are we to do?'

Sir Gawain almost took leave of his senses. He put his helmet upon his head, took up his lance — be assured of this — and leapt fearlessly into the saddle. The fox ran swiftly ahead like a hare being chased in the hunt; Gawain followed him. Though it had been Beelzebub himself he would not have given up; he would have followed him to hell if need be.

All the while the fox ran ahead and Gawain followed riding as hard as he could until they caught sight of the knight, who seemed to pay little attention when he heard Gawain approaching. He simply continued on his way, neither slowing down nor speeding up: he wasn't concerned in the least about Gawain. Sir Gawain rode now so close behind him that he could have stabbed him with his lance if he had wished; but because the Black Knight held the girl and Gawain feared that he might harm her, he stayed his hand and addressed the Black Knight angrily: 'Enough, enough, you've gone far enough! Give me that girl at once! One of us is sure to die here!'

The Black Knight helped Ysabele down off his horse and said to her, 'Fair girl, I long to become your knight. Please do not think my actions false or base; when I saw you sitting there, so beautiful under the olive tree, I became inflamed with such intense love that I thought my heart would break. If I have done you ill, I shall make it all up to you myself. I shall run a course here on your behalf.'

Sir Gawain did not hold his tongue; he said, 'It is no good declaring your love! I shall this day ordain you priest and tonsure your pate with my sword!'

GAWAIN FIGHTS THE BLACK KNIGHT, WHO PROVES TO BE ESTOR, BROTHER OF LANCELOT

Both of them retreated to the edge of the meadow on their chargers. Each had his own battle lance with a sharp, slender lance head at its tip. They both turned about and spurred their horses dauntlessly towards each other, holding their fearsome lances poised in knightly fashion. Like a Devil from hell the Black Knight charged, his crest flying in the wind. Gawain charged straight at him; that joust was fierce, the impact of their collision mighty. Their chargers collided with such a shock that their shields shattered with the violence of the impact. They bled profusely from nose and mouth. They were so utterly stunned by the great violence with which they had collided into one another, both with body and shield, that they both fell ignominiously to earth. They lay there, speechless, for quite some time.

But the fox began to cool his anger on the Black Knight with his teeth. He attacked him fiercely and tore loose many a ring of mail from his armour. Then the Black Knight's horse stepped forward and dealt the fox a blow. If he had hit him squarely he would have been seriously wounded; nevertheless he sent him flying into the grass three paces away, so that he lay there unconscious and stunned, bleeding profusely from the head and not able to stir. The two knights lay for quite some time on the ground, not moving a limb. Ysabele suspected that her sweet lover was more dead than alive,so she ran over to where he lay and quickly unfastened his helmet and removed it from his head, for she wished to let the wind blow in his face. But that was to cause Gawain more harm than good. The Black Knight, had he been in his right mind, would never, I feel certain, have attacked Gawain when he was without his helm; but because of the blow that Sir Gawain had dealt him, he was so stunned that he had taken leave of his senses; he rushed forward like a crazed she-lion whose cubs are in danger. He drew his sword and made straight for Gawain. If he had been in control of his wits, neither torment nor torture would have compelled him to commit such a base act. The knight raised his sword and was about to slay the noble knight as he lay bareheaded in the girl's lap.

But God would not allow it. As soon as Gawain came to his senses and saw the grim knight bearing down upon him, he threw up his shield to defend himself and took the mighty blow on his shield. His day of doom would certainly have arrived if he had not done so! That steel sword was so good that it cleaved entirely through the sturdy shield, believe me, and it dealt Gawain a great wound to the head. 'It wouldn't be wise for me to sleep through such blows,' said Gawain. 'Barbarian, evil, infamous scoundrel! By God, for this disgraceful deed you shall soon die!'

During this tirade he donned his helmet with such painful effort that it was a marvel he managed it at all. Gawain had sworn that he would on no account draw the Sword with the Two Rings against a Christian. Now he regretted his oath, for he was in dire need of the sword. So he drew another sword and attacked the Black Knight so furiously that it seemed as if he would pound him into the ground. But the Black Knight replied in kind to his attack; he made him feel the weight of his blows. He struck Gawain on the helmet so that the precious gems fell upon the grass. But Gawain pressed hard against the Black Knight, attacking him with his sword, and he nearly bore him down to the ground.

Then the Black Knight rushed at Sir Gawain in a counter-attack: he flung his shield onto his back and gripped his sword in both hands. He attacked Gawain with all his strength, sending the rings of mail flying! Though Sir Gawain was swift and strong he could not find the right defence. The Black Knight pressed his attack more and more, stabbing and slashing unremittingly like an all-consuming dragon. He wounded Gawain in four places, so that the blood ran so profusely over his limbs that he became very anxious. Gawain thought to himself, 'He will soon strike me senseless if this tempestuous attack lasts much longer. But it seems to me that he has taken leave of his senses: if I take care and do not launch a counter attack before he is overcome by exhaustion and out of breath, then I can bring him down.'

Meanwhile the Black Knight still rained blow upon blow in a frenzy so that it was a wonder that Gawain endured it! When at last he saw the Black Knight show signs of exhaustion he grasped his shield firmly by the straps and rushed forward to attack the Black Knight, and he said, 'Though your attack be ever so fierce, may you now pay the price!'

Gawain dealt him such a mighty blow that he fell on his head immediately, and so violently that his brains nearly dropped into his throat. He lay there unconscious for a long time, utterly stunned.

Ysabele danced for joy and said, 'My lord, there is nothing to stop you now: remove the tyrant's helmet and cut off his head at once! And God knows, it would be no crime, for you pledged an oath and swore that you would slay him if you vanquished him.'

'That shall not happen,' said Gawain to the girl. 'It would be a dishonourable deed if I were to slay such a brave knight in that way. I won't be frightened into doing it. I shall help him come to and I shall do battle with him then.'

He immediately went over to the knight and removed both his helmet and his iron cap and in doing so bared his face. But when he looked into that face, Gawain began to weep, for he saw that it was Lancelot's brother Estor, whom he held in great esteem. He said, 'Alas, Lancelot, now you will bear great hatred against me!'

Gawain carried with him for such emergencies both flax and salve; there was no one in those days who knew more about wounds than he: he had often had cause to use it himself. He removed the brave knight Estor's armour and proceeded to bind those wounds which he found to be the deepest and most serious He bound them gently and with skill. But Estor, the all too daring knight, had still not moved a muscle. Gawain took a ring from his finger and with its stone he blessed all the wounds, great and small, until the knight began to stir. Gawain hoped earnestly that he would live.

As soon as he saw him stir, he put his own helmet on his head. He would not have wanted Estor to recognise him even for a thousand pounds in gold; that is why he covered his face. And that knight, who could hardly have been in worse shape, addressed Sir Gawain, 'I see that I am in the company of a nobleman: I have never encountered such a courtly foe, who treated the man who wished to slay you by force so well.'

Gawain made no reply, for he did not want Sir Estor to recognise his voice.

Then Sir Gawain noticed a knight coming towards them unarmed. He wore a surcoat of scarlet and a mantle, and he rode across the meadow singing as he came. Two handsome squires followed in his wake. He saw Gawain sitting there next to the knight on the grass. He rode casually towards him as if he suspected that Gawain was uncomfortable with the situation. This man was courtly and well mannered. He rode up to the two knights; and when he reached them he was amazed: he could see that both their shields had been shattered, their sturdy mail-coats torn, their helmets dented, and their leggings covered in blood. And he noticed that bright red blood oozed continually from between the rings of Gawain's mail-coat. From his shoulders to his hands he was covered in blood. He greeted Gawain and said, 'God knows your plight grieves me sorely. The knight who lies there before you hasn't long to live now, it seems to me, for I see so many deep gashes and tears in his armour. He will have to be very stout-hearted and remarkably strong if he is to recover.'

Still Gawain said nothing, lest Estor should recognise him; but he took the knight in scarlet aside and said, out of earshot, 'My lord, if I may, I would earnestly ask of you a favour. This knight and I have fought for a long time here, and badly wounded each other. I fear that he may die, and this would be a disaster, for if we had recognised one another beforehand, we would never have fought. So please help this wounded knight: he needn't fear death in the least, so long as someone cares for him; I have tended and bandaged his wounds. My lord, do not be offended that I do not remove my helmet: it is simply that this knight would at once recognise my face.'

The knight replied, 'It is lucky for you that I have come here. My castle stands in the valley below, and I shall take the knight there. Have no fear for him: I shall not let him want for anything, though he remain with me for twenty weeks.'

But when Estor recovered, he complained that he did not know his opponent's name; for he wanted to be able to praise him for his great courtesy.

Gawain thanked the knight sincerely and took his leave. He mounted his horse in great sorrow, and placing the girl before him in the saddle he rode back towards the green olive tree to fetch the girl's palfrey. The fox followed behind, both sad and happy: happy because Gawain had come away from there, but on the other hand tears ran down over his whiskers because he was so afraid that Gawain would not recover. And Ysabele wept out of anxiety at seeing Gawain so severely wounded. 'Dearest, you should not be afraid,' said Gawain, 'I shall soon be whole again.' Before long they arrived at the tree where they found the girl's horse. She dismounted, and Gawain, who was very well versed in the care of wounds, removed his armour at once. Gawain showed Ysabele how to bind his wounds, and when this was done, he got up and helped her up onto her palfrey and mounted his horse at once.

They set out again, for Gawain would have been very sorry to have been recognised. As always, the fox followed close behind. They rode on till shortly before nightfall. As evening began to fall they approached a large and splendid castle. Gawain spoke, 'It would be to our advantage if we were to receive lodgings here today.'

The girl said, 'Let us go, then, my lord.'

They rode towards the castle and found a very warm welcome there, for the lord there was the same squire, the same young knight whom he had encountered long ago riding towards him in the wild forest, on that scrawny horse that could hardly put one foot before the other. Now the squire had overcome his difficulties and had reclaimed his estate. He had become a knight of great renown, and he welcomed the brave knight Gawain as his guest. He knelt before him and said, 'My dear lord, I bid you welcome to my castle! My life, my goods, they are all at your disposal: because of you I am lord of my estate, which would never have come about if it had not been for you, and you alone.'

Gawain bade his host rise and said, 'God knows, I am pleased that you have overcome your troubles.'

They spoke of many things together that evening in the hall, until it was time to dine. They had their fill of everything that was to be had in the castle. Ysabele sat between them and in a courteous fashion the choicest morsels were carved before her there. Neither Gawain nor the girl had ever been to a place where they were entertained so well, for everyone took great pains to please them then for the sake of their lord. I am not able to recount it all for you. When the tables were removed, the cup-bearer entered, bringing various spices as well as many sorts of wine: white and red, heady and sweet, malmsey, spiced wine, every imaginable kind.

Afterwards they all retired to bed. In a chamber with walls of marble there stood two sumptuous beds, made up with dazzlingly white linen. My lord Gawain and the girl went there to sleep. Whether or not they came together in love that night the story does not tell. They had for quite some time been weary from riding so long across country and deserved to enjoy the rest and peace provided them in that palace. And so they slept soundly until the nightingale and the lark, as well as many other kinds of birds, began to sing so loudly in the courtyard that they were all awakened by it.

GAWAIN AND HIS HOST ARE BESIEGED BY THE DEAD KNIGHT'S FATHER

The first one to rise there, so the story tells us, was Sir Gawain's host. But when he looked out he saw pavilions had been pitched round the castle on all sides: green ones, blue, yellow and red ones. And on many of them great eagles of gold could be seen. The knight's heart sank when he saw such a huge army. 'Lord God, have mercy!' he cried.' 'Who has brought us to such straits? Why has this great army come upon me so unexpectedly? Now I shall lose both my possessions and my life, unless God helps me.'

He quickly left the window and went to find Gawain in his chamber. Gawain rose and saw that so many pavilions had been pitched that the entire countryside was covered with them! Gawain marvelled greatly at this and he told his host to send a messenger out to them without delay and inquire after their intentions. A young knight was chosen at once who would carry the message.

When he reached the pavilions he saw one that was very costly; it was chequered with different coloured panels of muslin and silk. Knights began to press around the messenger: they repeatedly said that if he were not a messenger they would seize him and hang him to the disgrace of those inside the castle. They led him quickly to the rich pavilion, and made him dismount. They went into the tent with him, where he saw a lord sitting at a game of chess with many knights about him, all of high rank. When the messenger entered the pavilion he kneeled and greeted the lord, saying, 'My lord, those inside the castle send you their sincerest greetings, and ask you whether you have come here to harm the castle or to honour it. If they knew that they had done you any wrong, they would eagerly wish to set it right. My lord is not aware of having done anyone wrong.'

The duke replied fiercely, 'Tell your lord this: he will not escape with his life unless he immediately sends me the knight whom he foolishly granted lodgings late last night, and the girl who is with him. Unless he sends me in chains that manifest murderer whom he harbours there in his domain he will never again know peace: I would sooner hang him in front of his castle.'

As soon as the messenger heard this, he took his leave and returned to the castle and informed his lord that it was the duke who lay in siege on the plain, and that he had sworn to kill him unless he sent him with the utmost expediency the knight who had sought lodgings there last night. 'He will be furious if you refuse, for he intends publicly to prove him a murderer. It is for you to decide how to deal with this.'

Then Gawain said, 'I know who this duke is: he has repeatedly caused me grief.'

So Gawain soon told him how he had slain the young knight, the duke's son, and how the duke had captured him and the girl, and how they had escaped from their perilous situation. When the lord of the castle heard this he said to my lord Gawain, 'Do not be in the least bit afraid. I shall send out messengers at once to my friends and to my kinsmen. They will come here and risk their lives on my behalf.'

Messengers were despatched in all directions to seek aid and help in lifting the siege, and it was not long before help arrived. After three weeks had gone by so many reinforcements had arrived at the castle in that short time that its occupants felt a little less fearful than they had before.

But they were greatly outnumbered, and their force seemed insignificant compared to the duke's host. Encouraged by Gawain's exhortations, messengers were despatched to the duke, to tell him that if he wanted the brave knight he would have to undertake to win him by the sword, and that they were now at open war. The defenders were quick to elect my lord Gawain as their common leader, to issue commands and draw up their order of battle. What fine swords, helmets, spears there were, and pennons in yellow, grey, red and green! There were five thousand strong horses in their host! Before they would allow these to be destroyed they would slay many a man. Dressed as if for a bridal procession, the army of the besieged sallied forth and saw the opposite host well-armed and drawn up in ranks, with their standards unfurled, silken pennons on their lances and peacock feathers on their helmets. Both sides were eager to slay one another on that field of battle.

The armies met with a tremendous crash of lance on shield. The fighting was extremely fierce; many men perished there. Gawain thrust his pennoned lance through the body of a knight and tossed him out of the saddle: at that a loud cry was raised by the duke and his men! All of them were intent upon avenging the knight, for he was the duke's kinsman. Many a battle-proven sword was drawn there on both sides. They began to hack and slash at one another, and many brave men perished there. The duke was greatly to be feared; he brought knights down in great ignominy, their heads cleaved through to the teeth. He killed four men before Gawain's eyes: but he was powerless to help, for he had enough to do himself. They banished all thought of peace or reconciliation. The duke had in his host many knights of great physical prowess; if it had not been for Gawain's strength the besiegers would have been utterly defeated for they lost many brave knights. The duke fought dauntlessly; he encouraged those of his men who were afraid: he lent courage to his entire host by his own example; with his sword he cut many men in half at the waist; with a thrust he laid low both man and horse. Never was such a press of battle seen, nor battle-cry and din of arms heard! Bitter fighting was going on everywhere.

Sir Gawain made his way, slashing savagely, through the enemy ranks: he cleaved through helmets and shields; he turned the green grass red with blood as he went, and just as the scythe mows the hay, so he felled the enemy and cast them underfoot. Gawain was highly praised and many fingers were pointed his way. Many a man cried out, 'Look at him there! there's no braver man to be found for miles!'

The duke was angered greatly by the carnage that Sir Gawain wrought there. He bore down upon the lord of the castle with a stout and sturdy lance, driving his spurs of shining gold into both flanks of his horse, that ran as swiftly as does a bird being chased in the wood. His opponent was not in the least afraid; he rode to meet him at full tilt. It was a fierce joust when they bore down upon one another. So great was the velocity of the duke's horse that he brought both the lord of the castle and his mount crashing down.

Sir Gawain was seized with dread when he saw his host fall: he feared greatly for his life. He did not care in the least for his own life so long as he could help him in his time of need. Gawain seized a lance, sturdy and long, and bore down upon the doughty duke, who turned to meet him. The knights charged one another fiercely. They shattered their sturdy shields with their lances in that collision. The pennons of red velvet went straight through them. Each dealt the other a gaping wound. Their lances were shattered asunder, but they did not stop to rest at all: they drew their brightly polished swords and charged at one another on their horses and proceeded to show each other what their intentions were. There they dealt out great and mighty blows, so that bright sparks shot forth and their helmets rang. Each rendered the other dizzy with his blows. Gawain was angry that the duke was pressing him so hard, so he dealt him five blows in succession such that it was a wonder that any man could withstand the least of them! If the duke's men had not soon come to his aid, he would have been killed, but his men saw his dire position and came up in force. He had already been compelled to flee before Gawain into the open field, and he bellowed at him for all to hear, 'You brutal murderer, though you have shattered my helmet, I shall avenge my son!'

Then the duke begged his friends and his kinsmen to stand by him.

There was not much time for talking, for the fighting had become very fierce. The clash of good swords of steel resounded in the mountains and valleys. Many a sturdy lance was thrust clean through a man's body, so that his entrails spilled out; and those who met a bitter death screamed terribly before they died. There one saw hauberks lose their rings, helmets cleaved, shields quartered. No matter how sturdy those hats of steel were, they were hewn apart, so that blood gushed out all the same. Bright, shining suits of armour were hewn clean through with swords of steel. Silken surcoats were torn to shreds, pennons were stained crimson by red blood. Sir Gawain cut a path through the enemy with his sword: he had already felled sixty who never again got up. The field was well-nigh covered with dead knights and horses; there the clash of swords was loud, the din of battle and shouting intense.

The duke had a huge host of foot-soldiers and they were all well versed in warfare with lances and pikes. They had forced many to give way and many to retreat. But Gawain had cut a great breach in their line: he killed fully a hundred with the might of his hand and put that host so utterly to flight that they were pursued and killed without resistance. But the noblemen came to their aid. Life and limb were taken there without quarter. The press of battle was intense. Gawain sent many a knight tumbling from his horse while Ysabele stood watching high up on the ramparts and saw Gawain perform marvels with his sword. If he had not fought so well, the defenders would never have been able to boast that they had vanquished the duke in battle.

But Sir Gawain realised that his men were hard pressed and in dire need; he saw how they received thrusts and blows. Squires were always at his side to hand the noble knight lances with which he avenged his men. Nevertheless the duke's numbers were so great that the defenders were compelled by necessity to quit the field and flee; for the duke was so formidable that no one dared face him there. His household knights stood by him and assisted him at every attack, for they were famous men, praiseworthy knights renowned for great deeds: they repeatedly bathed their swords in gore and stained the grass red with blood that gushed from gaping wounds, so that they put the defenders to flight and followed close on their heels, hacking and cutting them down with all their might.

Gawain realised the seriousness of this assault. In a loud voice he called out, 'Where would you flee, noble lords? Defend yourselves! You are being slain without offering resistance!' At this, they turned round and raised a great war-cry. Gawain ripped open the stomach of one of his foes with a long and sturdy lance: it came out the other side fully the length of an ell. Then he tossed the dead man to the ground and rode on to meet another. Five strong knights he pierced through before that lance broke. Then he quickly drew his sword with which he attacked both man and beast so fiercely that no one could face him there. I believe his sword was drunk on the blood. The lord of the castle, Gawain's host, was gravely wounded and in a sorry state; he had almost reached the end of his strength. Nevertheless, despite his pain he got to his feet and fought on with his sword. He had little hope of getting a horse and yet he got hold of more than five horses during that battle. But each time he had captured one and was about to climb into the saddle, an enemy came forward to pull him back down again. Gawain saw this and bore down on one of the enemy knights unhorsing him in that mêlée. He seized the horse before it could escape and brought it immediately to his host and said, 'Make haste and mount! This entire army is weary: they won't be able to hold out much longer.'

He mounted, and side by side they rode again into the press. The host praised Gawain profusely and thanked him sincerely for the gift. Now the counter-attack raged in earnest: Gawain wrought great slaughter among the duke's men and put many of them to flight. They defended themselves well; but all the same, much against their will, the besiegers were pursued and chased, scattered and stricken by terror: they were cut down and slain in droves. Hardly a one was able to escape; the tables had turned against them. Gawain caught up with the duke, and hurled him from his horse so that he fell at his feet: he captured him and had him taken to the castle.

The duke's men then began to cry out in loud voices, 'All is lost! He who was our shield before has now been captured! If we can, the best thing for us to do now is flee!'

Then every man left remaining on the field fled. The men who were slain in that pursuit were too many to count, and if nightfall had not intervened, not one would have escaped. The defenders pulled back hastily to their castle, as we heard tell. They had lost three hundred men from among the knights and foot-soldiers, all of them brave and able-bodied men. Disgrace was the attackers' only reward. They had to leave more than five thousand of their comrades lying outside their tents. That evening there was great sorrow on both sides for the losses incurred in the heavy fighting; but more than anyone else it was the attackers who suffered most, lamenting the loss of their lord. Never again would they undertake or strive by any means to wage war against the inhabitants of that castle.

That evening Gawain was entertained with all manner of comforts. But he was despondent, the story says, because his host had lost so many men in the battle on his account. Everyone went to sleep, knights, squires and pages, until the breaking of dawn next morning. Gawain slept soundly, for he was very tired indeed. Ysabele, his sweet love, was in very good spirits because he had won the battle. That morning, at first sunlight, Gawain went to see the duke in his prison cell. The duke implored him earnestly to have mercy on him despite his misdeeds, and he said that if he let him live he would forgive Gawain for the death of his son. Gawain took pity on him and made his peace with him, but he made him solemnly swear that he would make reparation for the damage his host had incurred by his actions. The duke was set free then and there, and he was allowed to ride back to his men, who rejoiced greatly at his return. And he hastened to leave the place where he had won so little honour.

GAWAIN, YSABELE AND ROGES COME TO THE COURT OF KING WONDER; ROGES REGAINS HIS HUMAN FORM

Gawain returned to his host and asked to take his leave, but his host would not hear of it. He kept the noble knight with him and entertained him lavishly for fourteen nights. Then the day came for Sir Gawain to ride on his way: he thanked his host for the great honour that he had shown him; but he also lamented the damage that the host had incurred on his account. His host escorted him on his way with many men, until they had to take leave of one another. Then Gawain rode on his way, through forest and field, and with him his fair love. At their side in that meadow scampered the fox, who was very happy that my lord Gawain had emerged from the battle unharmed and had escaped the power of the duke, who had nearly tortured him to death. Each day they rode a great distance until they arrived at the foot of a castle, where they observed a group of splendidly dressed knights who had set up a tilt and were riding courses against it with gusto. My lord Gawain approached them and asked one of the knights where they came from. The knight answered him frankly, saying, 'My lord, they are members of King Wonder's household. The king himself is sitting under that tree yonder, watching these exercises, along with Alidrisonder, his son.'

When Sir Gawain had heard this he immediately said to the fox, 'Now be of good cheer, for you shall be delivered from your torment before too long.'

So they rode quickly over to the tree where the king and his son sat. And my lord Gawain, the noble man, dismounted, and Ysabele followed suit: if a king of such rank was seated, he did not wish to approach on horseback. When he came to where he could make out the mighty king he bowed, and greeted him in courtly wise. Ysabele was his match in courtesy: she too greeted the king and his son as well, who both jumped to their feet and vied with one another to embrace Sir Gawain in their arms. Their happiness was complete: the king and his son, Gawain and the fair Ysabele stood together, all four of them, side by side. And the fox peered up at them and as soon as he had looked all four of them in the eye, he shook his sleek red fur from his shoulders in full view of everyone, and he began to change his shape. Those who saw it felt their hearts race in amazement! And he became the handsomest youth they had ever seen.

Gawain gave thanks to Our Lord for Roges' release, and told all their adventures to King Wonder and his son Alidrisonder. They were amazed and astounded by them; and they asked the brave knight about the good Sword with the Two Rings. But at the same time as the fox was released from his enchantment, his stepmother's trials came to an end. For a long time she had sat at the threshold, as toads are wont to do, but now her shape and manners quickly changed. Her hair and skin became that of a fair and beautiful woman, and she walked back up into the hall. There was great rejoicing at the sight: for by that sign they were certain that the fox had become a man. The king was beside himself with joy, and the court rejoiced with him.

Gawain gave the noble King Wonder the good Sword with the Two Rings, which he gladly accepted, for he valued it more than anything else. In return, he promised to give the knight the chessboard and its costly pieces as soon as they arrived at the palace. He had Gawain escorted with a great show of honour and joy in his company to his splendid castle. There all the folk of both low rank and high turned out to greet him festively. And when they had all returned the horses were led to the stables; their every need was well attended to. Many noble rulers were present there, who all to a man honoured my lord Gawain. They led him up into the hall; they proceeded to remove his armour. Garments were quickly brought for him, and a cloak of oriental workmanship, which shone with a lustrous sheen. Rich garments of red silken velvet were quickly produced for Ysabele. And the youth who had been a fox was clothed in royal fashion.

That evening they were entertained honourably in every imaginable way: they had their fill of the finest beverages, the best foods that were to be found; after the meal an abundance of spiced wines, rare candied fruits and herbs were theirs to enjoy. Thereafter everyone retired at their leisure, to sleep. In a chamber glittering with gold, Gawain, the girl Ysabele and the trustworthy youth, son of the King of Ysike, were given three beds, resplendently covered with costly coverlets. They slept soundly until they heard the sweet song of birds. As they became aware of the breaking of dawn they awoke; they got up and made their way to the hall. There they found their host King Wonder and his son, who were very annoyed that they had risen so early. Gawain said, 'There is no time to lose: we must leave without delay.'

But no matter what Gawain said, he was compelled to remain there the entire week. When Gawain was given leave to go, the king escorted him out together with his son, though they were displeased that he wished to depart so soon. Nevertheless they did not wish to let Gawain go without an escort of knights and squires and sumpter horses, all in his honour; they accompanied him for a distance of three miles. My lord Gawain was sorry that the king had ridden with him so far. As soon as he could, he asked the king to turn back. Then Gawain and his fair love and Roges rode hard each day for a month before they finally arrived at the main gate of Cardueil and made their way to the palace. Gawain arrived with the magic chess-set, in the company of his fair beloved, and a great tumult and din arose: the news spread like wildfire that Sir Gawain had returned. King Arthur left the hall with many men and came forth to greet him. Ladies and girls vied with one another on all sides to greet him. Gawain and Ysabele were brought up into the hall and a great celebration ensued. The mighty King Assentin had come to King Arthur's court to look for his daughter, and he was pleased when he learned that the brave knight Gawain had won his daughter's love and he agreed to their marriage. And king Roges of Ysike had come to see his son. The celebration lasted thirty days. Gawain, the noble and excellent knight, presented his uncle with the flying chess-set in front of both lords and ladies so that all might see it; it lit up the entire hall, such was its brilliance and excellence. Then Gawain recounted to King Arthur all his good fortunes, and on the other hand his misfortunes, of many a bitter and fierce battle. He also told him of the wonderful way in which the fox had turned into a man. The king marvelled exceedingly at this. And Gawain, the brave knight, then married the fair girl Ysabele; and it was he who wore the crown after King Arthur's death.

Roges, king of Ysike, rode back to his realm in high spirits with his son, when the celebrations had ended, though it was a long time before they arrived in their realm. The entire population turned out in joy when they heard the news of their arrival. Roges' stepmother approached him as soon as he appeared, and begged on her knees to be granted mercy. And Roges, at his father's request, forgave her for what she had done, for she had been fearfully punished for it. After his father's death, as I understand, his son inherited that kingdom.

Penninc, who composed this book was unwise not to have brought it to an end. Pieter Vostaert continued it as best he could according to the text that he found which Penninc left behind: it seemed to him a pity for it to be left unfinished, because without an ending all Penninc's labours would have been in vain. Now he bids you all earnestly that you should pray on his behalf to Our Lord God that at the end of his life he should have done such a noble deed with penance and good works, so that he might turn his gaze towards the kingdom of heaven with joy, and for all of you he wishes the same. May the Almighty God grant it us! Amen.

TRISTAN AND ISEULT

TRISTAN

THE STORY OF TRISTAN AND ISEULT seems to have been told
for the first time in a single poem which no longer survives, written around
the middle of the twelfth century. We know a little about it from the
surviving fragments of other poems about Tristan, all of which relate the
main episodes of the story in the same way, although individual details
vary. In effect, modern scholars argue that there was once something like
The History of the Kings of Britain for the Tristan legend, one key text from
which all other reworkings were largely derived. What has come down to
us are fragments of a version by Thomas, who wrote at the Plantagenet
court in England some time after 1150; parts of a poem by Eilhart von
Oberge, writing in Germany in about 1170, and a similar fragment by
another Norman poet, Béroul, of about 1180. It was a theme which
caught the imagination of the writers of that period, and it is possible that
Chrétien de Troyes also wrote a version of it.

The central theme of these romances, the love of Tristan for Iseult, wife
of his uncle, Mark, is found in Welsh literature, and scholars generally
accept that the original Tristan was Drust, son of the Pictish king, Talorc,
who ruled in Scotland about 780, and that the legends were later given a
new setting in Cornwall. The so-called Tristan stone at Castledore refers
to another character of similar name, and its only connection with the
legend is that it may have suggested the new site of the stories; in Welsh
legend, Essyllt's lover is always Tristan 'son of Tallwch' and the Cornish
Drustanus' father is named in the inscription as Cunomorus. The shape of
the legend was drawn by Welsh writers from Irish sources: the central
triangle of lord, wife and lover comes from the story of Diarmaid and
Grainne, which has been added to an episode about Drust telling how, by
defeating a hero in single combat, he rescued a foreign king from having to
surrender his daughter as tribute. This theme, similar to the story of
Theseus in Greek myth, may have suggested the addition of other details
from the Theseus legends: the half-bestial nature of his adversary (as with
the Minotaur) and the use of the black and white sails as a signal of failure
or success. Other incidents were drawn into the story from sources as far
afield as India and Arabia, brought perhaps by travelling merchants; and

merchants figure in the poem as the cause of Tristan's arrival in Cornwall from Brittany. The power of the central love-story has attracted all kinds of lesser folklore in which the same triangle of characters is repeated.

The original romance seems to have been a relatively sophisticated story, with a complex sequence of episodes. It is not connected with Arthur and his court, nor is it essentially a courtly romance. The version by Béroul, on which the first of the two accounts that follow is largely based, does not adopt a 'courtly' attitude towards the lovers: some episodes are of a primitive cruelty, as when Iseult is about to be burnt for adultery and a company of lepers suggest that a more fitting fate would be for her to be given to them as their whore. It is a tale of passion and fate, rather than courtly love, and there is a wide range of reactions to the central problem of the romance, that of reconciling the lovers' treachery towards Mark with their close relationship to him. A theologian might see the various versions as a study in free will and predestination: Eilhart sees the love-potion as the sole cause of the lovers' destiny – once they have tasted 'the most unlucky drink', they are doomed. Béroul, on the other hand, is less inclined to use the love-drink as the sole reason for their conduct, but he ends in a mire of equivocal oaths and legal niceties: Mark is in the wrong for refusing Tristan the customary trial by battle, and Iseult escapes the judgement of God by swearing an ambiguous oath. The heart of the tale is one of star-crossed lovers, and its beauty lies in the simplicity and freshness of the telling.

But subtler minds saw more in the story than this. Chrétien's version might well have been a study of feeling, much in the manner of another of his romances, *Cligès*, and later writers seized on the opportunities for analysing the lovers' emotions. The surviving parts of Thomas's version are concerned with the truth of Tristan and Iseult's love: the effect of the love-potion is not an external force but a symbol of an internal emotion – free will rather than predestination, if you like – and Tristan's marriage to the second Iseult becomes another of the tests of the lovers' fidelity. The romance also moves towards the ideas of courtly love: Thomas introduces the *Salle aux Images* (hall of statues) to which Tristan retreats secretly to worship an image of Iseult of Cornwall, a concept which comes near to the veneration of the troubadours for their ladies. But there is none of the restraining *mezura* ('measure in all things') of the troubadours elsewhere in the story; physical desire and spiritual union are as one.

Gottfried von Strassburg, working in the early thirteenth century, realised the full possibility of the story as a study in the mystic power of love. Tristan and Iseult are seen as two perfect beings, and they alone are fit for the transcending experience. Gottfried tells us that he speaks only to those 'noble hearts' who can understand his message, and he uses his materials skilfully and subtly, as in the crux of the story, the famous scene where Tristan and Iseult drink the love-potion, thinking it is common wine. Gottfried leaves us uncertain whether the drink merely confirms a love already begun, or is in itself the *coup de foudre*. For his own purposes he is well enough content to let it be regarded as a supernatural force; with this excuse he can tell his story of open adultery, treachery and broken oaths as a special case, and invoke the magic philtre as justifying each transgression. On the other hand, the 'noble hearts' who understood his true meaning could see the potion merely as the surrogate of love's power, a symbol of its workings.

For in Gottfried's universe, Tristan and Iseult's love puts their relationship above the everyday ways of the world. They are no longer subject to the ordinary laws of men, but can only be judged in terms of their fidelity to each other and to love's ideals. The tension that arises between the two worlds, their unresolved discontent, shows that this is not an intensified version of courtly love, but a more disturbing force. Passion is the word we have now come to use for this force, and it is a commonplace of our view of love. But to Gottfried's contemporaries this was novelty indeed.

Tristan and Iseult are equal in love. There is no question of knight serving lady; instead, they are both servants of *Frau Minne*, Lady Love. Caution becomes impossible, compromise unthinkable once her mystic joys have been tasted; love becomes the fountain of all goodness, and even provides them with physical sustenance. The climax of Gottfried's poem is the depiction of a magic retreat, the Cave of Lovers.

But if love is a higher ideal than those of the courtly world in which the lovers move, it affords them no protection. Its joys are balanced by its sorrows; and its sorrows stem from the lovers' concern for their reputation. When Mark discovers them lying with a naked sword between them and is persuaded of their innocence, they return to court 'for the sake of God and their place in society'. Mark represents the opposite side of love: lust and appetite aroused by Iseult's beauty. As such he cannot find peace either; sometimes a pitiful figure, he wavers between the unpalatable truth and the comfort of illusion. Despite its outward gaiety, the court of Cornwall which he rules is similarly tainted; suspicion is everywhere, misunderstanding and distrust abound. Only Brangane and Kurvenal remain loyal; and even their steadfastness is tested. Iseult, fearing lest Brangane should reveal their secrets, tries to have her killed, but repents as soon as she fears the deed is really done. For loyalty only exists between the lovers themselves; all external claims are brushed aside and there is left

> A man, a woman; a woman, a man:
> Tristan, Iseult; Iseult, Tristan.

Their true world is an enclosed, charmed garden; in the everyday world, no matter how splendid and gay, they move guiltily, forced to deny their desires, and the air grows thick with sorrow and evil.

The story of Tristan and Iseult is remarkably consistent in these early versions, and the version of *Tristan and Iseult* which follows draws on all of them in turn; since the outline of the story remains the same, the various different approaches can be interwoven almost seamlessly, and given that none of the surviving texts is complete, what follows is a tapestry of different colourings. But the fire and force of the tale, the lovers' adversity and passion, are, I hope, undimmed.

The Tristan story was only brought into the Arthurian world in the decades after Gottfried von Strassburg wrote his masterpiece. In the original, there is a hint that Mark is Arthur's neighbour, with Iseult's demand that Arthur and his court should witness her oath. It is not until later in the thirteenth century that versions of the Arthurian stories which included Tristan as a member of Arthur's court began to appear. Indeed, it is possibly fairer to say that the Tristan story came to include most of the Arthurian tales, in the vast compilation called *The Romance of Tristan*. This was so large that when Malory came to work on it, it provided him with slightly over a third of his material for the *Morte Darthur*; and even that was only drawn from the first two volumes of the three-volume copy he had in front of him. We feel a sense of his weariness when he tells us at the end of 'The Book of Sir Tristram' that 'here is no rehearsal of the third book'. And modern readers find even Malory's excerpted version hard going; it is the most idiomatic section of his work, in terms of its depiction of the idea of the knight errant and his adventures and tournaments. Given that, today, reading a description of a tournament is rather like an American trying to wade through a report of a cricket match for, or an Englishman trying to get to grips with an American football match, it is not surprising that many readers skip this section. Yet there is an enthusiasm about Malory's writing on tournaments, and they are such an essential part of the medieval vision of Arthur, that I have deliberately included one here, if only to emphasise that we are in a very different world from that of the early Tristan stories.

For Tristan and Iseult are a kind of parallel version of Lancelot and Guinevere, renowned as lovers without any great question as to the why and wherefore; their reputation as lovers is everything, and the morality or otherwise of their affair is hardly discussed. Mark is evil and treacherous, and it is he who eventually kills Tristan; Malory only mentions Tristan's death in passing, and the version here, from the end of *The Romance of Tristan*, is, I believe, given in English for the first time. And chivalry itself is no longer an unquestioned and unassailable ideal; we have the figure of

Palamides, the unsuccessful lover, who is driven by love into jealousy, unchivalrous behaviour and then into treachery. It is a striking portrait, as is that of Dinadan, the knight who questions the ideal of knight-errantry and the enthusiasm for tournaments. Tristan calls him the best 'japer' that he knows, but Dinadan's mockery of chivalry has a cutting edge, for all the entertainment he provides. He is one of my favourite Arthurian oddities, and his appearance is always welcome. The love of Tristan and Iseult is no longer a passionate flame; it is somehow more domestic, as they settle in at Joyous Gard, lent to them by Lancelot. But it is how a large number of medieval readers would have come across the story, and it is a tale worth the telling.

TRISTAN AND ISEULT

THE CHILDHOOD OF TRISTAN

MY LORDS, IF YOU WOULD HEAR a high tale of love and of death, here is that of Tristan and Queen Iseult; how to their full joy, but to their sorrow also, they loved each other, and how at last they died of that love together in the space of one day, she by him and he by her.

Long ago, when Mark was king over Cornwall, Rivalen, king of Lyonesse, heard that Mark's enemies waged war on him; so he crossed the sea to bring him aid; and so faithfully did he serve him with counsel and sword that Mark gave him his sister Blanchefleur, whom King Rivalen loved most tenderly.

He wedded her in Tintagel Minster, but hardly was she wed when the news came to him that his old enemy Duke Morgan had fallen on Lyonesse and was laying waste town and field. Then Rivalen manned his ships in haste, and took Blanchefleur with him to his far-off land; but she was with child. He landed below his castle of Kanoël and gave the queen into the keeping of his marshal Rohalt, and after that set off to wage his war.

Blanchefleur waited for him continually, but he did not come home, till she learnt one day that Duke Morgan had killed him in a vile ambush. She did not weep: she did not cry or lament, but her limbs failed her and grew weak, and her soul was filled with a strong desire to be rid of the flesh, and though Rohalt tried to soothe her, she would not hear. For three days she awaited reunion with her lord, and on the fourth she brought forth a son; and taking him in her arms she said: 'Little son, I have longed a while to see you, and now I see you, the fairest thing ever a woman bore. In sadness came I hither, in sadness did I bring forth, and in sadness has your first feast day gone. And as by sadness you came into the world, your name shall be called Tristan; that is, the child of sadness.'

After she had said these words she kissed him, and as soon as she had kissed him she died.

Rohalt, faithful to his lord, took the child, but already Duke Morgan's men had surrounded the castle of Kanoël and were besieging it. There is a wise saying: 'Foolhardy was never hardy,' and he was compelled to yield to Duke Morgan at his mercy: but for fear that Morgan might slay Rivalen's heir, the marshal hid him among his own sons.

When seven years were passed and the time had come to take the child from the women, Rohalt put Tristan under a good master, the squire Gorvenal, and Gorvenal taught him in a few years the arts that go with being a knight. He taught him the use of lance and sword and shield and bow, and how to cast stone quoits and to leap wide dykes as well: and he taught him to hate all lies and felony and to keep his given word; and he taught him the various kinds of song and harp-playing, and the hunter's craft; and when the child rode among the young squires you would have said that he and his horse and his armour were all of a piece. Seeing him so noble and so proud, broad in the shoulders, loyal, strong and right, all men praised Rohalt for such a son. Rohalt, remembering Rivalen and Blanchefleur, of whose youth and grace all this was a resurrection, loved him indeed as a son; but in his heart he revered him as his lord.

Now all his joy was snatched from him on a day when certain merchants of Norway, having lured Tristan to their ship, bore him off as a rich prize, though Tristan fought hard, as a young wolf struggles, caught in a trap. But it is a tried and tested truth, and every sailor knows it, that the sea will not bear a felon ship, and gives no aid to rapine. The sea rose and cast a dark storm round the ship and drove it eight days and eight nights at random, till through the mist the mariners caught sight of a coast of awful cliffs and seaweed rocks on which the sea would have ground their hull to pieces. Then they did penance, knowing that the anger of the sea came because of the lad whom they had stolen in an evil hour. They vowed to set him free and got ready a boat to put him ashore if they could. At this the wind and sea fell and the sky shone, and as the Norwegian ship grew small in the offing, a quiet tide cast Tristan and the boat upon a beach of sand.

Painfully he climbed the cliff and saw, beyond, a lonely rolling heath and a forest stretching out as far as the eye could see. And he wept, remembering Gorvenal, his father, and the land of Lyonesse. Then the distant cry of a hunt, with horse and hound, came suddenly and lifted his heart, and a tall stag broke cover at the forest edge. The pack and the hunt streamed after it with a tumult of cries and winding horns, but just as the hounds were racing clustered at the haunch, the quarry turned to bay at a stone's throw from Tristan; a huntsman gave him the thrust, while all around the hunt had gathered and was winding the kill. But Tristan, seeing by the gesture of the huntsman that he made to cut the neck of the stag, cried out:

'My lord, what would you do? Is it fitting to cut up so noble a beast like any farmyard pig? Is that the custom of this country?'

And the huntsman answered: 'Fair friend, what startles you? Why yes, first I take off the head of a stag, and then I cut it into four quarters and we carry it on our saddle-bows to King Mark, our lord. So do we, and so since the days of the first huntsmen have the Cornishmen done. If, however, you know of some nobler custom, teach it us: take this knife and we will learn it willingly.'

Then Tristan kneeled and skinned the stag before he cut it up, and quartered it all in order, leaving the crow-bone all whole, as is correct, and putting aside at the end of the head, the haunch, the tongue and the great heart's vein; and the huntsmen and the kennelmen stood over him with delight, and the master huntsman said: 'Friend, these are good ways. In what land did you learn them? Tell us your country and your name.'

'Good lord, my name is Tristan, and I learnt these ways in my country of Lyonesse.'

'Tristan,' said the master huntsman, 'God reward the father that brought you up so nobly; doubtless he is a baron, rich and strong.'

Now Tristan was skilled in both speech and silence, and he answered: 'No, lord; my father is a townsman. I left his home without his knowledge on a ship that traded to a far place, for I wished to learn how men lived in foreign lands. But if you will accept me as one of the hunt I will follow you gladly and teach you other crafts of venery.'

'Tristan, I marvel there should be a land where a townsman's son can know what a knight's son does not know not elsewhere, but come with us since you wish to, and welcome: we will bring you to King Mark, our lord.'

Tristan completed his task; to the dogs he gave the heart, the head, offal and ears; and he taught the hunt how the skinning and the ordering should be done. Then he thrust the pieces upon pikes and gave them to this huntsman and to that to carry, to one the snout, to another the haunch, to another the flank, to another the chine; and he taught them how to ride by twos in rank, according to the dignity of the pieces each might bear.

So they took the road and spoke together, till they came to a great castle and round it fields and orchards, and living waters and fish-ponds and ploughlands, and many ships were in its harbour, for that castle stood above the sea. It was well fenced against all assault or engines of war, and its keep, which the giants had built long ago, was made of great stones, like a chessboard of green and blue.

And when Tristan asked its name: 'Sir,' they said, 'we call it Tintagel.'

And Tristan cried: 'Tintagel! God's blessing on you and on all those who inhabit you.'

(It was there, my lords, there that Rivalen had taken Blanchefleur to wife, though their son did not know it.)

When they came before the keep the horns brought the barons to the gates, and King Mark himself. And when the master huntsman had told him the whole story, and King Mark had marvelled at the good order of the cavalcade, and the cutting of the stag, and the high art of venery in all that had been done, yet he wondered most of all at the stranger boy, and could not take his eyes off him, troubled and wondering why he felt such tenderness towards him, and his heart would not yield the answer; but, my lords, it was blood that spoke, and the love he had long since borne his sister Blanchefleur.

That evening, when the boards were cleared, a singer out of Wales, a master, came forward among the barons in hall and sang a harper's song, and as this harper touched the strings of his harp, Tristan who sat at the king's feet, spoke thus to him: 'Oh master, that is the first of songs! The Bretons of old wove it once to celebrate the loves of Graëlent. And the melody is rare, and rare are the words: master, your voice is subtle: play it well.'

But when the Welshman had sung, he answered: 'Boy, what do you know of the craft of music? If the townsmen of Lyonesse teach their sons to play harps, and viols too, rise, and take this harp and show your skill.'

Then Tristan took the harp and sang so well that the barons softened as they heard, and King Mark marvelled at the harper from Lyonesse, the place to which Rivalen had taken Blanchefleur away so long ago.

When the song ended, the king was silent a long space, but he said at last: 'Son, blessed be the master who taught you, and may God bless you: for God loves good singers. Their voices and the voice of the harp enter the souls of men and wake dear memories and cause them to forget many griefs and many sins. It was for our joy that you came to this house; stay near us a long time, friend.'

And Tristan answered: 'I will serve you willingly, sire, as your harper, your huntsman and your liege.'

And so he did; and for three years a mutual love grew up in their hearts. By day Tristan followed King Mark in the law-courts and in the saddle; by night he slept in the royal room with the councillors and the peers, and if the king was sad he would harp to him to soothe his care. The barons also cherished him, and above all, the king loved him. But Tristan could not forget either Rohalt his father, or his master Gorvenal, or the land of Lyonesse.

My lords, a storyteller who wants to please must not stretch out his tale too long, and this tale is so varied and so great that it needs no straining after effect. Then let me shortly tell how Rohalt himself, after long wandering by sea and land, came to Cornwall, and found Tristan, and showing the king the ruby that once was Blanchefleur's, said: 'King Mark, here is your nephew Tristan, son of your sister Blanchefleur and of King Rivalen. Duke Morgan holds his land wrongfully; it is time such land came back to its lord.'

And Tristan (to be brief), when his uncle had armed him knight, crossed the sea, and was hailed by his father's vassals, and killed Rivalen's slayer and took possession of his land again.

Then remembering how King Mark could no longer live in joy without him, he summoned his council and his barons and said this: 'Lords of Lyonesse, I have retaken this place and I have avenged King Rivalen by the help of God and of you. But two men, Rohalt and King Mark of Cornwall, nourished me, an orphan and a wandering boy. So I should call them fathers also. Now a free man has two things thoroughly his own, his body and his land. To Rohalt then, here, I will release my land. Hold it, father, and your son shall hold it after you. But my body I give up to King Mark. I will leave this country, dear though it be, and in Cornwall I will serve King Mark as my lord. Such is my judgement, but you, my lords of Lyonesse, are my lieges, and owe me counsel; if then, some one of you will counsel me otherwise, let him rise and speak.'

But all the barons praised him, though they wept; and taking with him Gorvenal only, Tristan set sail for King Mark's land.

THE MORHOLT OUT OF IRELAND

When Tristan came back to that land, King Mark and all his barons were in mourning; for the king of Ireland had manned a fleet to ravage Cornwall if King Mark refused, as he had refused these fifteen years, to pay a tribute his fathers had paid. Now that year the king of Ireland had sent to Tintagel, to carry his summons, a giant knight named the Morholt, whose sister he had wed, and whom no man had yet been able to overcome: so King Mark had summoned all the barons of his land to council, by sealed letters.

On the day assigned, when the barons were gathered in hall, and when the king had taken his throne, the Morholt said: 'King Mark, hear for the last time the summons of the king of Ireland, my lord. He summons you to pay at last that which you have owed so long, and because you have refused it too long already he orders you to surrender to me this day three hundred youths and three hundred girls drawn by lot from among the Cornish people. But if anyone would prove by trial of combat that the king of Ireland receives this tribute without right, I will take up his wager. Which among you, my Cornish lords, will fight to redeem this land?'

The barons glanced at each other but all were silent.

Then Tristan knelt at the feet of King Mark and said: 'Lord king, by your leave I will do battle.'

And in vain King Mark tried to turn him from his purpose, thinking, how could even valour save so young a knight? But he threw down his gage to the Morholt, and the Morholt took up the gage.

On the appointed day he had himself clad for a great feat of arms in a hauberk and in a steel helm, and he entered a boat and sailed to the isle of St Samson's, where the knights were to fight each to each alone. Now the Morholt had hoisted to his mast a sail of rich purple, and coming fast to land, he moored his boat on the shore. But Tristan pushed off his own boat with his foot, and said: 'One of us only will go from here alive. One boat will be enough.'

And each rousing the other to the fray, they went ashore on the island.

No man saw the sharp combat; but three times the salt sea-breeze had wafted or seemed to waft a cry of fury to the land, when at last towards the hour of noon the purple sail showed far off; the Irish boat appeared from the island shore, and there rose a clamour of 'The Morholt!' But suddenly, as the boat grew larger on the sight and topped a wave, they saw that Tristan stood on the prow holding a sword in his hand. He leapt ashore, and as the mothers kissed the steel upon his feet he cried to the Morholt's men: 'My lords of Ireland, the Morholt fought well! See here, my sword is broken and a splinter of it stands fast in his head. Take that steel, my lords; it is the tribute of Cornwall.'

Then he went up to Tintagel and as he went the people he had freed waved green boughs, and rich cloths were hung at the windows. But when Tristan reached the castle with joy, songs and bells sounding about him, he fainted in the arms of King Mark, for the blood ran from his wounds.

The Morholt's men landed in Ireland quite downcast. For whenever he came back into Whitehaven the Morholt used to rejoice in the sight of his clan upon the shore, of the queen his sister, and of his niece Iseult the Fair. They had cherished him of old, and if he had been wounded, they healed him, for they were skilled in balms and potions. But now their magic was vain, for he lay dead and the splinter of the foreign sword still lay in his skull, till Iseult plucked it out and shut it in a chest.

From that day Iseult the Fair knew and hated the name of Tristan of Lyonesse.

But over in Tintagel Tristan languished, for there trickled a poisonous blood from his wound. The doctors found that the Morholt had thrust into him a poisoned barb, and as their potions could never heal him they left him in God's hands. So hateful a stench came from his wound that all his dearest friends fled from him, all save King Mark, Gorvenal and Dinas of Lidan. They could only stay near his couch because their love overcame their abhorrence. At last Tristan had himself carried into a boat on the shore, away from men; and lying facing the sea he awaited death, for he thought: 'I must die; but it is good to see the sun and my heart is still high. I would like to try the sea that brings all chances. . . . I would have the sea bear me far off alone, no matter to what land, as long as it heals me of my wound.'

He begged so long that King Mark accepted his desire. He bore him into a boat with neither sail nor oar, and Tristan wished that his harp only should be placed beside him: for he could neither lift the sails, nor ply the oars, nor wield a sword; and as a seaman on some long voyage casts to the sea a beloved dead companion, so Gorvenal pushed out to sea that boat where his dear friend lay; and the sea drew him away.

For seven days and seven nights the sea drew him on; at times, to charm his grief, he harped; and when at last the sea brought him near a shore where fishermen had left their port that night to fish far out, they heard as they rowed a sweet and strong and living tune that ran above the sea, and feathering their oars they listened, immovable.

In the first whiteness of the dawn they saw the boat at large: she went at random and nothing seemed to live in her except the voice of the harp. But as they approached, the air grew weaker and died; and when they hailed her, Tristan's hands had fallen lifeless on the strings, though they still trembled. The fishermen took him in and bore him back to port, to their lady who was merciful and perhaps would heal him.

It was that same port of Whitehaven where the Morholt lay buried, and their lady was Iseult the Fair.

She alone, being skilled in philtres, could save Tristan, but she alone wished him dead. When Tristan knew himself again (for her art restored him) he knew himself to be in the land of peril. But he was yet strong to hold his own and found good crafty words. He told a tale of how he was a seer who had taken passage on a merchant ship and sailed to Spain to learn the art of reading all the stars; of how pirates had boarded the ship; and of how, though wounded, he had fled into that boat. He was believed, nor did any of the Morholt's men know his face again, so hardly had the poison used it. But when, after forty days, Iseult of the Golden Hair had all but healed him, when already his limbs had recovered and the grace of youth returned, he knew that he must escape, and he fled and after many dangers he came again before Mark the king.

THE QUEST OF THE LADY WITH THE HAIR OF GOLD

My lords, there were in the court of King Mark four barons, the basest of men, who hated Tristan with a hard hate, for his greatness and for the tender love the king bore him. And I know their names well: Andred, Guenelon, Gondoïne and Denoalen. They knew that the king meant to grow old childless and to leave his land to Tristan; and their envy swelled and by lies they roused the anger of the chief men of Cornwall against Tristan. They said: 'There have been too many marvels in this man's life. It was marvel enough that he beat the Morholt, but by what sorcery did he try the sea alone at the point of death, or which of us, my lords, could voyage without mast or sail? They say that warlocks can. It was surely a wizard's trick, and that magic harp of his pours poison daily into the king's heart. See how he has bent that heart by power and chain of sorcery! He will be king yet, my lords, and you will hold your lands of a wizard.'

They won over the greater part of the barons and these pressed King Mark to take to wife some king's daughter who should give him an heir, or else they threatened to return home, each man into his keep, and wage war on him. But the king turned against them and swore in his heart that so long as his dear nephew lived no king's daughter should come to his bed. Then in turn Tristan, ashamed to be thought to serve for hire, threatened that if the king did not yield to his barons, he would himself go overseas to serve some great king. At this, King Mark made a pact with his barons and gave them forty days to hear his decision.

On the appointed day he waited alone in his chamber and sadly mused: 'Where shall I find a king's daughter so fair and yet so distant that I may feign to wish her my wife?'

Just then by his window that looked upon the sea two swallows intent on building their nest came in quarrelling together. Startled, they flew out, but they let fall from their beaks a woman's hair, long and fine, and shining like a beam of light. King Mark took it, and called his barons and Tristan and said: 'To please you, lords, I will take a wife; but you must seek her whom I have chosen.'

'Fair lord, we all wish it,' they said, 'and who may she be?'

'Why,' said he, 'she whose hair this is; nor will I take another.'

'And whence, lord king, comes this hair of gold; who brought it and from what land?'

'It comes, my lords, from the lady with the hair of gold, the swallows brought it to me. They know from what country it came.'

Then the barons saw themselves mocked and cheated, and they turned with sneers to Tristan, for they thought him to have counselled the trick.

But Tristan, when he had looked on the hair of gold, remembered Iseult the Fair and smiled and said this: 'King Mark, can you not see that the doubts of these lords shame me? You have devised this trick in vain. I will go and seek the lady with the hair of gold. The search is perilous: nevertheless, my uncle, I wish once more to put my body and my life into peril for you; and that your barons may know I love you loyally, I take this oath, to die on the adventure or to bring back to this castle of Tintagel the queen with that fair hair.'

He fitted out a great ship and loaded it with corn and wine, with honey and all manner of good things; he manned it with Gorvenal and a hundred young knights of high birth, chosen among the bravest, and he clothed them in coats of homespun cloth so that they seemed merchants only: but under the deck he hid rich cloth of gold and scarlet as for a great king's messengers.

When the ship had taken the sea the helmsman asked him: 'Lord, to what land shall I steer?'

'Sir,' said he, 'steer for Ireland, straight for Whitehaven harbour.'

At first Tristan made believe to the men of Whitehaven that his friends were merchants of England come peacefully to barter; but as these strange merchants passed the day in the useless games of draughts and chess, and seemed to know dice better than the market price of corn, Tristan feared discovery and did not know how to pursue his quest.

Now it chanced once at the break of day that he heard a cry so terrible that one would have called it a demon's cry; nor had he ever heard a brute bellow in such wise, so awful and strange it seemed. He called a woman who passed by the harbour, and said: 'Tell me, lady, where does that voice come from? Hide nothing from me.'

'My lord,' said she, 'I will tell you the truth. It is the roar of a dragon, the most terrible and dauntless on earth. Each day it leaves its den and stands at one of the gates of the city: nor can any come out or go in till a girl has been given up to it; and when it has her in its claws it devours her.'

'Lady,' said Tristan, 'do not mock me, but tell me: can a man born of woman kill this thing?'

'Gentle sir,' she said, 'I cannot say; but this is for certain: twenty tried and tested knights have ventured against it, because the king of Ireland has proclaimed that he will give his daughter, Iseult the Fair, to whoever shall kill the beast; but it has devoured them all.'

Tristan left the woman, and returning to his ship, armed himself in secret; and it was a fine sight to see so noble a charger and so good a knight come out from such a merchant ship. But the harbour was empty of people, for the dawn had barely broken and none saw him as he rode to the gate. And he had hardly passed it, when he met suddenly five men at full gallop flying towards the town. Tristan seized one by his hair as he passed, and dragged him off his horse and held him fast: 'God save you, my lord,' said Tristan, 'and where does the dragon come from?'

And when the other had shown him the road, he let him go.

As the monster neared, he showed the head of a bear and red eyes like coals of fire and hairy tufted ears, lion's claws, a serpent's tail, and a griffin's body. Tristan charged his horse at him so strongly that, though the beast's mane stood on end with fright, yet he drove at the dragon: his lance struck its scales and shivered. Then Tristan drew his sword and struck at the dragon's head, but he did not so much as cut the hide. The beast felt the blow: with its claws he dragged at the shield and broke it from the arm; then, his breast unshielded, Tristan used the sword again and struck so strongly that the air rang all round about: but in vain, for he could not wound it. Meanwhile the dragon vomited from its nostrils two streams of loathsome flames, and Tristan's helm blackened like a cinder and his horse stumbled and fell down and died. But Tristan, standing on his feet, thrust his sword right into the beast's jaws, and split its heart in two.

Then he cut out the tongue and put it into his belt, but as the poison came in contact with his flesh the hero fainted and fell in the high grass that bordered the marsh.

Now the man he had stopped in flight was the seneschal of Ireland and he desired Iseult the Fair: and though he was a coward, he was daring enough to return with his companions secretly, and he found the dragon dead; so he cut off its head and bore it to the king, and claimed the great reward. The king could scarcely credit his prowess, yet wished justice to be done and summoned his vassals to court, so that there, before the barons assembled, the seneschal should furnish proof of the victory he had won.

When Iseult the Fair heard that she was to be given to this coward, at first she laughed long, and then she bewailed her fate. But the next day, fearing some trick, she took with her Perinis her squire and Brangane her maid, and all three rode secretly towards the dragon's lair: and Iseult saw such a trail on the road as made her wonder – for the hoofs that made it had never been shod in her land. Then she came on the dragon, headless, and a dead horse beside him: nor was the horse harnessed in the fashion of Ireland. Some foreign man had slain the beast, but they did not know whether he was still alive.

They searched for him for a long while, Iseult and Perinis and Brangane together, till at last Brangane saw the helmet glittering in the marshy grass: and Tristan still breathed. Perinis put him on his horse and bore him secretly to the women's rooms. There Iseult told her mother, Queen Iseult, the tale and left the hero with her, and as the queen unharnessed him, the dragon's tongue fell from his belt. Then the queen of Ireland revived him by the virtue of a herb and said: 'Stranger, I know you for the true slayer of the dragon: but our seneschal, a felon, cut off its head and claims my daughter Iseult for his wage; will you be ready two days hence to give him the lie in battle?'

'Queen,' said he, 'the time is short, but you, I think, can cure me in two days. By killing the dragon I conquered Iseult, and by overcoming the seneschal perhaps I shall reconquer her.'

Then Queen Iseult brewed him strong brews, and on the next day her daughter Iseult the Fair prepared a bath and anointed him with a balm her mother had conjured, and as he looked at her he thought, 'So I have found the Queen of the Hair of Gold,' and he smiled as he thought it.

But Iseult, noting it, thought, 'Why does he smile, or what have I neglected of the things due to a guest? He smiles to think I have forgotten to burnish his armour.'

And now fate decreed that Iseult should discover her heart's torment! Her heart was turned, her eye impelled to where his equipment lay. I have no idea how she could do such a thing, but she took up the sword in her hands. She drew it, looked at it, and studied it closely in one place and another. Then she saw where the piece was missing and examined the gap, long and minutely, and thought: 'Heaven help me! I think I have the missing piece, and what is more, I shall try it!'

Iseult fetched the piece and inserted it — and the gap and the cursed splinter fitted each other and made as perfect a whole as if they were one thing, as indeed they had been, not two years past. But now her heart froze within her on account of the old wrong that she had suffered. Her colour came and went from red to deathly pale and fiery red again, for grief and anger.

'Oh,' she said, 'luckless Iseult! Alas, who brought this vile weapon here from Cornwall? With it my uncle was slain, and his slayer was called Tristan! Who gave it to this minstrel? After all, his name is Tantris.'

At once she began to turn the two names over in her mind and consider their sound.

'These names trouble me. I cannot think what there is about them. They sound so very similar. Tantris and Tristan — they surely somehow go together?'

Trying the names over on her tongue she seized on the letters of which each is formed and soon found that they were the same. She then divided their syllables and, reversing them, found the key to the name. She found what she had been looking for. Forwards she read 'Tristan', backwards she read 'Tantris'. With this she was certain of the name.

'I knew it!' said the lovely girl.

'If this is how things stand, my heart informed me truly of this decep-
tion. How well I have known all the time, since I began to take note of him
and study him in every detail of his appearance and behaviour and all that
has to do with him, that he was a nobleman born. And who would have
done this but he? Sailing from Cornwall to his deadly enemies, we have
twice saved his life. Saved? Nothing will save him now! This sword shall
make an end of him! Now, quick, avenge your wrongs, Iseult! If the sword
with which he slew your uncle lays him low in turn, ample vengeance will
have been done!' She seized the sword and stood over Tristan where he
was sitting in a bath.

'So you are Tristan?' she said.

'No, my lady, I am Tantris.'

'I know you are Tantris *and* Tristan, and the two are a dead man!
Tantris will have to answer for the wrong that Tristan has done me! You
will have to pay for my uncle!'

'No, lady, no! In God's name, what are you doing? Consider your sex
and spare me! You are a woman, well born and of tender years. If you earn
the name of murderess, enchanting Iseult will be dead to honour for ever.
The sun that rises from Ireland and has gladdened many hearts, alas, will
be extinguished. Shame on those dazzling white hands – how ill a sword
becomes them!'

At this point her mother the queen entered at the door.

'Daughter, what do you mean by this? Is this ladylike behaviour? Are
you out of your senses? Is this some joke, or are you really angry? What is
that sword doing in your hands?'

'Oh, my lady mother, remember the great wrong that has been done to
us. This is the murderer Tristan, the man who killed your brother! Now is
our opportunity to revenge ourselves by plunging this sword through him
– we shall never have a better chance!'

'Is this Tristan? How do you know it?'

'I am certain it is Tristan! This is his sword: look at it and note the fragment beside it, and then judge if he is the man! Only a moment ago I
inserted the piece into this cursed gap, and, oh, misery, I saw it made a
perfect whole!'

'Ah, Iseult, what memories have you revived in me?'
was her mother's swift reply.

'That I was ever born! If this is Tristan, how deceived I am!'

But now Iseult went and stood over him with poised sword.

'Stop, Iseult!' said her mother, turning towards her.

'Stop! Do you not know what I have pledged?'

'I do not care. I swear he is going to die!'

'Mercy, lovely Iseult!' cried Tristan.

'Villain!' answered Iseult.

'Are you asking for mercy? Mercy is not for you. I shall have the life out of you!'

'No, daughter,' interposed her mother, 'we are not in a position to take vengeance, except by breaking our oath and dishonouring ourselves. Do not be so hasty. His life and goods are under my protection. However it came about, I have granted him full immunity.'

'Thank you, my lady,' said Tristan.

'For I relied on your honour; I entrusted my goods and my life to you, and you received me on those terms.'

'You liar,' said the girl.

'I know very well what was said. She did not promise Tristan her protection, either for life or property!' And with these words she ran at him for the second time, and Tristan again cried 'Lovely Iseult, mercy, mercy!'

But her mother, the most trusty queen, was there and he had no need to be anxious. And even if he had been tied to the bath at this time, and Iseult had been there alone with him, he would not have died at her hands. How could the good, sweet girl, who had never known bitterness or rancour in her womanly heart, ever kill a man? Only, because of her grief and anger, she outwardly behaved as if she wished to do so, and indeed might easily have done so, had she had the heart – but it failed her utterly for so bitter a deed! Yet her heart was not so good that she knew no hate or animosity, since she saw and heard the cause of her grief. She heard her foe and saw him, and yet was unable to slay him. Her tender womanliness was not to be denied, and it snatched her from her purpose.

Those two conflicting qualities, those warring contradictions, womanhood and anger, which accord so ill together, fought a hard battle in her breast. When anger in Iseult's breast was about to slay her enemy, sweet womanhood intervened.

'No, don't!' it softly whispered. Thus her heart was divided in purpose – a single heart was at one and the same time both good and evil. The lovely girl threw down the sword and immediately picked it up again. Faced with good and evil she did not know which to choose. She wanted and yet did not want, she wished both to do and refrain. Thus uncertainty raged within her, till at last sweet womanhood triumphed over anger, with the result that her enemy lived, and the Morholt was not avenged.

Iseult then flung the sword away, burst into tears, and cried: 'Alas, that I ever lived to see this day!'

'My dearest daughter,' that wise woman her mother replied, 'the sorrows that weigh on your heart are the ones I share, only mine are worse and much more cruel, I say it to my grief. Mercifully this grief does not touch you so deeply as me. My brother, alas, is dead. This was my greatest affliction. But now I fear further grief through you, which, I tell you, daughter, affects me far more deeply than the other, for I have loved nothing so much as you. Rather than that anything should happen to you, I would renounce this feud. I can abide one sorrow more easily than two. Because of that vile man who threatens us with judgement by combat, I find myself so placed that unless we see to it urgently, your father the king, and you and I, will suffer lasting disgrace and never be happy again.'

'Ladies,' said Tristan, 'it is true that I have made you suffer, though under great duress. Yet you know that my hand was forced by nothing less than death, to which no man willingly submits so long as he can save himself. But however events turned out then, and however matters stand now in respect of the steward, set it all aside. I shall bring it to a happy conclusion – that is, if you let me live and death does not prevent me. Queen Iseult, and you too, Iseult, I know that you are always thoughtful, good, sincere, and understanding. If I may broach a certain matter to you in confidence, and if you will refrain from unfriendly behaviour towards me, and from the animosity, too, which you have long borne towards Tristan, I have some good news to tell you.'

Iseult's mother, Queen Iseult, looked at him for some time, and her face grew redder and redder.

'Oh,' she said, her bright eyes filling with tears, 'now I hear it clearly and know for a fact that you are he! I was in doubt until this moment. Now you have told me the truth, unasked. Alas, alas, Lord Tristan, that I should ever have you in my power as well as I have now, yet not so as to be able to use it or so that it could serve me! But power is so very varied: I think I may use this power on my enemy and pervert justice thus far against a wicked man. God, shall I, then? I think most assuredly – yes!'

At this point noble, discerning Brangane, Iseult's companion, came softly gliding in, smiling, and beautifully attired. She saw the naked sword lying there and the two ladies looking very woebegone.

'What is the matter?' asked Brangane quietly.

'What is the reason for all this? What are you three up to? Why are these ladies' eyes so dimmed with tears? This sword lying here – what does it mean?'

'Look,' said the queen, 'Brangane, dearest cousin, see how deceived we are! In our blindness we have reared a viper for a nightingale, and ground corn for the raven that was meant for the dove. Almighty God, how we have saved our foe, thinking him a friend, and twice with our own hands shielded Tristan, our enemy, from grim death! Look at him sitting there – that man is Tristan! Now I am in two minds as to whether to avenge myself! Cousin, what do you advise?'

'Do not do it, my lady, put it from your mind. Your happy nature is too good for you ever to think of such a crime or abandon yourself so far as to contemplate murder, and against a man, at that, to whom you have given your protection! You never meant to do so, I trust to God. Should you barter your honour for the life of an enemy?'

'What would you have me do, then?'

'Think it over for yourself, my lady. Withdraw, and let him leave his bath. You can discuss what will suit you best in the mean time.'

And so all three retired to their private chamber to talk the matter over.

'Listen, you two,' said the elder Iseult, discerning woman that she was.

'Tell me, what can this man mean? He informed us that if we would renounce the enmity which we have long borne him, he would have some good news to tell us. I cannot imagine what it could be.'

'Then my advice is that nobody should show him any hostility till we have discovered his intentions,' said Brangane.

'They may well be good and tend to the honour of you both. Who knows if he has not come to Ireland to enhance your reputation? Take care of him now and never cease to praise the Lord for one thing – that through him this monstrous, scandalous fraud of the steward's is going to be exposed. God was looking after us while we were searching; for if Tristan had not been quickly found, he would soon have died. In that event, young Iseult, things would be worse than they are. Do not show him any unfriendliness, for if he were to grow suspicious and succeed in escaping, nobody could blame him. So think this over, both of you. Treat him kindly as he deserves. Tristan is as well born as you are, and he is well bred and intelligent, and lacking in no fine quality. Whatever your feelings towards him, entertain him courteously. You can rely on it that, whatever his motives were, some serious purpose has brought him.'

The ladies rose and left their chamber, and went to the secret place where Tristan was now sitting on his couch. Tristan did not forget himself – he leapt up to meet them, threw himself before them, and lay in supplication at the feet of those gracious and charming women, saying as he prostrated himself: 'Mercy! Ladies, have mercy on me! Let me profit from having come to your country for the sake of your honour and advantage!' The dazzling trio looked away, and exchanged glances. And so they stood, and so he lay.

'My lady,' said Brangane, 'the knight has lain there too long.'

'What do you wish me to do with him?' the queen asked swiftly.

'My feelings do not allow me to be his friend. I cannot think of anything that I could suitably do.'

'Now, dear lady,' replied Brangane, 'do as I say, you and mistress Iseult. I am utterly certain you can scarcely love him in your thoughts because of

your old grief; but at least promise him his life, the two of you, then
perhaps he will say something to his advantage.'

'Very well,' said the ladies. And with that they told him to get up.
When the promise had been duly given, all four talked together.

Tristan returned to the matter in hand.

'Now, your majesty,' he said, 'if you will be my good friend, I will
arrange within these two days for your dear daughter to wed a noble king,
well suited to be her lord – handsome and magnanimous, a rare, illustrious
knight in the use of lance and shield, born of a lineage of kings and, to
crown all, far wealthier than her father!'

'On my word,' said the queen, 'if I could be sure of this I should willingly do whatever I was asked.'

'I will soon provide you with guarantees, ma'am,' answered Tristan.

'If I do not confirm it at once, following our reconciliation, then withdraw your protection and leave me to my ruin.'

'Speak, Brangane,' said the prudent woman, 'what do you advise?'

'I approve of what he has said, and I advise you to act accordingly. Put
your doubts aside, stand up, both of you, and kiss him! Though I am no
queen, I mean to share in this peacemaking – I too was related to the
Morholt, however humble my station.'

And so she and the queen kissed him: but the younger Iseult could not
bring herself to do so.

When the queen and Brangane had made their peace with him, Tristan
spoke once again: 'Now the good Lord knows that I have never felt so
happy as now! I have anticipated and weighed all the dangers that could
befall me, in the hope that I might win your favour – only now I do not
hope, I am sure of it! Lay your cares aside.'

'Tell me,' asked the queen, 'would it be remiss of me if I were to inform
his majesty and effect a reconciliation?'

'By no means, ma'am,' answered Tristan.

'He has every right to know it. But take good care that I come to no
harm from it.'

'Have no fear, my lord. That danger is past.'

This concluded, the older ladies withdrew to their cabinet and considered his good fortune and success in every detail of this enterprise. They
spoke of his cleverness, the mother from one angle, Brangane from
another. Iseult was left with Tristan, who said to her: 'King's daughter, my
life is not only in your power but is yours of right. My life is yours because
you have twice returned it me. Once, long ago: for I was the wounded
harper whom you healed of the poison of the Morholt's shaft. Nor should
you repent the healing: were not these wounds had in fair fight? Did I kill
the Morholt by treason? Had he not defied me and was I not held to the

defence of my body? And now this second time also you have saved me. It was for you I fought the beast . . . But let us leave these things. I would only show you how my life is your own. Then if you kill me, as you have the right to do, for the glory of it, you may ponder for long years, praising yourself that you killed a wounded guest who had wagered his life to win you.'

Iseult replied: 'These are strange words. Why should he that killed the Morholt seek me also, his niece? Doubtless because the Morholt came for a tribute of girls from Cornwall, so you came to boast in return that you had brought back the girl who was nearest to him to Cornwall, a slave.'

'King's daughter,' said Tristan, 'no. . . . One day two swallows flew to Tintagel and bore one hair out of all your hairs of gold, and I thought they brought me goodwill and peace, so I came to find you overseas. See here, amid the threads of gold upon my coat your hair is sewn: the threads are tarnished, but your bright hair still shines.'

Iseult put down the sword and taking up the coat of arms she saw upon it the hair of gold and was silent for a long space, till she kissed him on the lips to prove peace, and she put rich garments on him.

On the day of the barons' assembly, Tristan sent Perinis secretly to his ship to summon his companions to come to court adorned as befitted the envoys of a great king. One by one the hundred knights passed into the hall where all the barons of Ireland stood. They entered in silence and sat all in rank together: on their scarlet and purple the gems gleamed.

And then Queen Iseult, the glad dawn, entered, leading by the hand her sun, the wonder of Ireland, the resplendent maiden Iseult. The girl glided gently forward, keeping even pace with her dawn, on the same path, with the same step, exquisitely formed in every part, tall, well moulded, and slender, and shaped in her attire as if love had formed her to be her own falcon, an ultimate unsurpassable perfection! She wore a robe and mantle of purple samite cut in the French fashion and accordingly, where the sides sloped down to their curves, the robe was fringed and gathered into her body with a girdle of woven silk, which hung where girdles hang. Her robe fitted her intimately, it clung close to her body, it neither bulged nor sagged but sat smoothly everywhere all the way down, clinging between her knees as much as each of you pleases. Her mantle was set off by a lining of white ermine with the spots arranged in a diamond pattern. For length it was just right, neither dragging nor lifting at the hem. At the front it was trimmed with fine sable cut to perfect measure, neither too broad nor too narrow, and mottled black and grey, so blended as to be indistinguishable. The sable beside the ermine curved all along its seam, where sable and ermine match so well! Where the clasps go, a tiny string of white pearls had been let in, into which the lovely girl had inserted her left thumb. She had brought her right hand further down, you know, to where one closes the mantle, and held it decorously. From here it fell unhampered in a last fold revealing this and that – I mean the fur and its covering that love had shaped so rarely in body and in spirit! Rapacious feathered glances flew thick as falling snow, ranging from side to side in search of prey. I know that Iseult robbed many a man of his very self! On her head she wore a circlet of gold, perfectly slender and ingeniously wrought. It was encrusted with gems, fabulous stones, emerald and jacinth, sapphire and chalcedony, which, despite their small size, were very dazzling and the best in all the land. These were so finely inlaid in their various places that no goldsmith's cunning ever set stones with greater artistry. Gold and gold, the circlet and Iseult, vied to outshine each other. There was no man so discerning who, had he not seen the stones already, would have said that there was a circlet there, so much did her hair resemble gold, and so utterly did it merge with it.

Meanwhile, noble Brangane, the lovely full moon, came gliding in, leading Tristan, her companion, by the hand. The stately, well-bred girl went modestly at his side, in person and carriage beyond all measure charming, in spirit proud and free. Her companion, too, escorted her with dignity. He was marvellously blessed with every grace that goes to make a knight: everything that makes for knightly distinction was excellent in him. His figure and attire went in delightful harmony to make a picture of chivalrous manhood. He wore rare, fine clothes of scarlet and gold of quite unusual splendour. They were not the sort of thing that is given away at court, the gold was not worked into the cloth in the amount that is usual there! You could scarce trace the silken ribbing – it was so swamped with gold and sunk so deep in gold, here, there and everywhere, that you could barely see the fabric! Over its outer surface lay a net of tiny pearls, its meshes a hand's breadth apart, through which the scarlet burned like glowing embers. It was copiously lined with silk, more purple than a violet and quite as purple as the iris. This cloth of gold took fold and grain as smoothly as cloth of gold ought. It became the fine man most rarely and was altogether to his taste. On his head he wore an aureole of cunning workmanship – an excellent chaplet that burned like candlelight and from which topaz and sardonyx, chrysolite and ruby, shone out like stars! It was bright and full of lustre and made a lambent ring about his head and his hair. And so he entered, magnificent and gay. His bearing was fine and princely, his whole array was splendid, his person most distinguished in every particular. The throng began to make way for him as he came into the palace.

When the king had taken his throne, the seneschal arose to prove by witness and by arms that he had slain the dragon and thus had won

Iseult. Then Iseult bowed to her father and said: 'King, I have here a man who challenges the lies and felony of your seneschal. Promise that you will pardon this man all his past deeds, who stands to prove that he and none other slew the dragon, and grant him forgiveness and your peace.'

The king said, 'I grant it.'

But Iseult said, 'Father, first give me the kiss of peace and forgiveness, as a sign that you will give him the same.'

Then she found Tristan and led him before the barons. And as he came the hundred knights rose all together, and crossed their arms upon their breasts and bowed, so the Irish knew that he was their lord.

But among the Irish many knew him again and cried, 'Tristan of Lyonesse, that slew the Morholt!' They drew their swords and clamoured for his death.

But Iseult cried: 'King, kiss this man upon the lips according to your oath!' And the king kissed him, and the clamour died away.

Then Tristan showed the dragon's tongue and offered the seneschal battle, but the seneschal looked at his face and dared not.

Then Tristan said: 'My lords, you have said it, and it is truth: I killed the Morholt. But I crossed the sea to offer you a just blood-fine, to ransom that deed and get me quit of it. I put my body in peril of death to rid you of the beast; thus I have conquered Iseult the Fair, and having conquered her I will bear her away on my ship. But that these lands of Cornwall and Ireland may know no more hatred, but love only, learn that King Mark, my lord, will marry her. Here stand a hundred knights of high name, who all will swear with an oath upon the relics of the holy saints, that King Mark sends you by their embassy the offer of peace and of brotherhood and goodwill; and that he would by your courtesy hold Iseult as his honoured wife, and that he would have all the men of Cornwall serve her as their queen.'

When the lords of Ireland heard this they acclaimed it, and the king also was content.

Then, since that treaty and alliance was to be made, the king her father took Iseult by the hand and asked of Tristan that he should take an oath; to wit that he would lead her loyally to his lord, and Tristan took that oath and swore it before the assembled knights and barons of Ireland. Then the king put Iseult's right hand into Tristan's right hand, and Tristan held it for a space in token of seizin for the king of Cornwall.

So, for the love of King Mark, did Tristan conquer the queen of the hair of gold.

Tristan ordered a ship to be made ready as well his own, to be reserved for Iseult and himself and his chosen companions. While Tristan and his compatriots were preparing for the voyage, Iseult, the prudent queen, was brewing a love-drink so subtly devised and prepared, and endowed with such powers, that if any man and woman drank it together, they would at once and always love each other. They would share one death and one life, one sorrow and one joy.

The wise lady took this philtre and said softly to Brangane: 'Brangane, dear niece, do not be sad, but you must go with my daughter. Resign your-self to your fate, and listen to what I say. Take this flask and guard it above all your possessions. See to it that no one at all gets to hear of it and above all take care that nobody drinks any! When Iseult and Mark have been united in love, make it your task to pour out this liquor as wine for them, and see that they drink it all – just those two – and do not let anyone share with them, not even yourself! For this is a love-philtre! I most dearly and urgently commend Iseult to your care. The better part of my life is bound up with her. Remember that she and I are in your hands, by all your hopes of Paradise! Need I say more?'

'Dearest lady,' answered Brangane, 'if you and she both wish it, I shall gladly accompany her and watch over her honour and all her affairs, as best I can.'

Tristan and all his men took their leave and left Whitehaven rejoicing. Out of love for Iseult, the king and queen and the whole court followed him down to the harbour. The girl he never dreamt would be his love, his abiding anguish of heart, radiant, exquisite Iseult, rode weeping beside him. Her mother and father passed the brief hour with much lamenting. Many eyes began to redden and fill with tears. Iseult brought distress to many hearts, for to many she was a source of secret pain. They wept unceasingly for their eyes' delight, Iseult. Many hearts and many eyes wept there together, both openly and in secret.

And now that the two Iseults, the sun and her dawn, and the fair full moon, Brangane, had to take their leave, sorrow and grief were much in evidence. That faithful alliance was severed with many a pang. Iseult kissed the pair of them many, many times.

When the Cornishmen and the ladies' Irish attendants had embarked and said goodbye, Tristan was last to go on board. The dazzling young queen, the flower of Ireland, walked hand in hand with him, sad and dejected. They bowed towards the shore and invoked God's blessing on the land and on its people. And then they put to sea; and, as the sails filled, they began to sing the anthem 'We sail in God's name' with high, clear voices, and they sang it again as the ships gath-ered speed.

Now Tristan had arranged for a separate cabin to be given to the ladies for their comfort during the voyage. The queen occupied it with her ladies-in-waiting; no one else might enter, apart from Tristan, who was sometimes admitted, to console the queen as she sat weeping. She wept and she lamented through her tears that she was leaving her home, her familiar people and her friends, and had set sail with strangers to a place unknown to her. And so Tristan would console her as tenderly as he could: when he came and found her sorrowing he took her in his arms gently and quietly, but in no other way than a liege might care for his lady. The loyal man hoped to comfort the girl in her distress. But whenever he put his arm round her, Iseult the Fair recalled her uncle's death.

'Enough, lord,' she said.

'Keep your distance, take your arm away! Why do you keep on touching me?'

'But am I offending you?'

'You are — because I hate you!'

'But why?' he asked.

'You killed my uncle!'

'But that has been put by.'

'I hate you all the same, since but for you I should not have a care in the world. You are the cause of all my troubles, winning me by trickery and deceit from those who brought me up, and taking me God knows where, as if I had been sold, with no idea of what is to become of me!'

'Fair Iseult, take heart! Better to be a great queen in a strange land, than humble and forgotten at home.'

'Take my word for it, Lord Tristan,' answered the girl, 'whatever you say, I would prefer obscurity and peace of mind, to the cares that come with great wealth!'

'You are right there,' replied Tristan, 'yet if you can have wealth and ease together, the two are better as a team than separately. But suppose I had not come forward and you had had no alternative but to marry the seneschal, how would you have felt then? Are these your thanks for my coming to your aid and saving you from him?'

'Even if you saved me from him, you have since so overwhelmed me with care that I would rather have married the steward than set out on this voyage with you. However worthless he is, he would have mended his ways, if he had been my companion for any time and truly loved me.'

'I don't believe it,' answered Tristan.

'No one believes that the leopard can change his spots. Lady, do not be downcast. I shall soon give you a king for your lord in whom you will find a good and happy life, wealth, noble excellence and honour for the rest of your days!'

Meanwhile the two ships sped on their course. They both had a favourable wind and were making good headway. But the fair company aboard,

Iseult and her train, were unused to such hard going in wind and water. Quite soon they were in great distress. Their captain, Tristan, gave orders to put to shore and lie at anchor in a harbour for a while. When they had made land, most of those on board went ashore for exercise. But Tristan went to see his radiant lady and to pass the time of day with her.

He sat down beside her, and the sun was hot above them; as they talked, they were athirst and he called for something to drink.

Now, apart from the queen, there was nobody in the cabin but the youngest of the ladies-in-waiting.

'Look,' said one of them, 'here is some wine in this little bottle.'

It held no wine, much as it resembled it. It held their lasting sorrow, their never-ending anguish, even their very death. But the child was not to know that. She rose and took the draught, hidden in its vial. She handed it to Tristan and he handed it to Iseult. She drank after long reluctance, then returned it to Tristan, and he drank, and they both of them thought it was wine. At that moment Brangane entered, recognised the flask, and saw only too clearly what had happened. She turned as pale as death, and almost fainted with shock. Her heart beat fast within her as she went and seized that cursed, fatal flask, bore it off and flung it into the wide wastes of the sea!

'Alas for me,' cried Brangane, 'alas that I was ever born! Wretch that I am, I have ruined my honour and trust! May God show everlasting pity that I ever came on this journey! Why did death not snatch me when I was sent on this ill-starred voyage with Iseult! Ah, Tristan and Iseult, this draught will be your death!'

Now when the woman and the man, Iseult and Tristan, had drunk the draught, in an instant that arch-disturber of tranquillity was there: Love, waylayer of all hearts, had stolen in! Before they were aware of it she had planted her victorious standard in their two hearts. They who were two and divided now became one and united. No longer were they at variance: Iseult's hatred was gone. Love, the reconciler, had purged their hearts of enmity, and so joined them in affection that each was mirror to the other. They shared a single heart. Her anguish was his pain: his pain, her anguish. The two were one both in joy and in sorrow. Yet, from fear and shame, they hid their feelings from each other. She was ashamed, as he was. She went in fear of him, as he of her. However blindly the craving in their hearts was centred on one desire, they did not know where to start, and hid their desire from each other.

When Tristan felt the stirrings of love he at once remembered loyalty and honour.

'Felons, that charged me with coveting King Mark's land, I have stooped far lower, for it is not his land I covet. Fair uncle, who loved me as an orphan even before you knew I was of the blood of your sister Blanchefleur, you that wept as you bore me to that boat alone, why did you not drive out the boy who was to betray you? Ah! What thought was that! Iseult is yours and I am but your vassal; Iseult is yours and I am your son; Iseult is yours and may not love me.'

'Leave this, Tristan,' he was continually thinking to himself, 'pull yourself together, take no notice of it.'

But his heart was driven towards her. He fought against his own desire, turning this way and that to escape the trap in which he found himself. He was afflicted by a double pain: when he looked at her face and sweet love began to wound his heart and soul, he thought of honour, and it drew him back. But this in turn was the sign for love, his liege lady, whom his father had served before him, to attack him again, and once more he had to submit. Honour and loyalty harassed him powerfully, but love tormented him in the extreme, making him suffer more than honour and loyalty together. His heart smiled upon Iseult, but he averted his eyes: yet his greatest grief was when he failed to see her. Like every prisoner, he fixed his mind on escape and how he might elude her, and returned again and again to that thought. He took his heart and soul and searched them for some change: but there was nothing there but love – and Iseult.

And so it was with her. Finding this life unbearable, she too made ceaseless efforts. When she recognised the mire of bewitching love had spread and saw that she was deep in it, she endeavoured to reach dry ground. The lovely woman fought back with might and main, but stuck fast at every step. She was succumbing against her will. Desperately she twisted and turned with hands and feet only to plunge ever deeper in the blind sweetness of love for this man. Her senses failed to discover any path, bridge, or track that would advance them half a step, half a foot, without love being there too. Whatever Iseult thought, whatever came uppermost in her mind, there was nothing there, of one sort or another, but love – and Tristan.

This was all below the surface, for her heart and her eyes were at variance – modesty turned her eyes away, love drew her heart towards him. That warring company, a woman and a man, love and modesty, confused her utterly; for the woman desired the man, and yet she turned away. But what was the good of that? A woman and her modesty are by common consent so fleeting a thing, so short-lived a blossoming, they do not long resist. Thus Iseult gave up her struggle and accepted her situation. Without further delay the vanquished girl resigned herself body and soul to love and to the man.

Iseult gave him a hidden glance now and again; her bright eyes and her heart were now in full accord. Secretly and lovingly her heart and eyes darted at the man, while the man gave back her looks with tender passion. Since love would not release him, he too began to give ground. Whenever there was a suitable occasion the man and the woman came together to feast each other's eyes. These lovers seemed to each other fairer than before – such is love's law, such is the way with affection. It is so this year, it was so last year and it will remain so among all lovers as long as love endures.

The ships put out to sea again and, except that love had led astray two hearts on board, sailed gaily on their course. The two lovers were lost in their thoughts. They were burdened by the pleasing malady that works such miracles as changing honey to gall, turning sweetness sour, setting fire to moisture, converting balm to pain; that robs hearts of their natures and stands the world on its head. This tormented Tristan and Iseult. The self-same woe afflicted them, and in the strangest way. Neither could find rest or comfort except when they saw one another: yet when they saw each other they were deeply troubled. When from time to time they tried to observe each other through eyes which love had misted, their flesh assumed the hue of their hearts and souls. Love the dyer did not deem it enough that she was hidden in the recesses of two noble hearts: she meant to show her power in their faces. Indeed, they bore many marks of it, since their colour did not long stay the same. They blushed and blanched, blanched and blushed in swift succession as love painted their cheeks for them.

With this they both grew aware that their thoughts for each other ran somewhat in the direction of love. Love's huntsmen as they were, they laid their nets and their snares for one another, they set up their coverts and lurking-places, with question and answer. They had much to say to each other. The words with which Iseult began were innocent enough: she approached her friend and lover in a roundabout way. She reminded him of all that had happened: how he had come floating in a skiff to Whitehaven, wounded and alone; how her mother had taken charge of him and how she had duly healed him; how, in every detail, she had learned the whole art of writing, under his tuition, and Latin and stringed instruments. She recalled – scarcely daring to talk of it directly – his valiant exploit, and the dragon, too, and how she had twice recognised him, first in the marsh where he lay wounded and then in the bath.

'Alas,' said Iseult, 'when I had such an opportunity to kill you in your bath, God in heaven, why did I do as I did? Had I known then what I know now, I swear you would have died!'

'Why, lovely Iseult?' he asked, 'why are you so distressed, what is it that you know?'

'All that I know distresses me, all that I see afflicts me. The sky and sea oppress me, my life has become a burden to me!'

She pressed her arm against him – such was the beginning of their daring! The bright mirrors of her eyes filled with hidden tears. Her heart began to swell within her; her head drooped on her breast. As for her friend, he took her in his arms, neither too closely nor yet too distantly.

'Come now, sweet lady,' he whispered tenderly, 'tell me, what is vexing you, why do you complain so?'

'*Lameir* is what distresses me,' answered love's falcon, Iseult, 'it is *lameir* that so oppresses me, *lameir* it is that pains me so.'

Tristan pondered the word: did she mean *l'ameir*, which is love, *l'ameir*, which is bitterness, or *la meir*, the restless sea? He disregarded the first, and asked about the others. Not a word did he say of love, mistress of them both, their common hope and desire. All that he spoke of was 'sea' and 'bitter'.

'Fair Iseult, is the tang of the sea too strong for you? Is it this you find so bitter?'

'No, my lord, no! Neither of them troubles me, neither the sea nor its tang is too strong for me. It is *lameir* alone that pains me.'

When he knew the meaning of the word, 'I swear, lovely woman,' he whispered, 'it is the same with me; *lameir* and you are what distress me. My dearest lady, sweet Iseult, you and you alone and the passion you inspire have turned my wits and robbed me of my reason! Nothing in the wide world is dear to my heart but you.'

Iseult answered, 'And so are you to me.'

When the two lovers perceived that they had one mind, one heart, and one will between them, this knowledge began to assuage their pain: each looked at the other and spoke with ever greater daring. Then all reserve was gone. He kissed her and she kissed him, lovingly and tenderly, a blissful beginning for love's remedy. Whenever they could find an occasion, this traffic passed between them, it stole to and fro so secretly that none discovered their mind save far-seeing Brangane, who could not help but know of it. Quietly she kept glancing in their direction and, seeing how intimate they were, she thought to herself: 'Alas, it is plain to me that these two are falling in love!' It did not take her long to see that they were in earnest, or to detect in their demeanour the pain within their hearts. She was harrowed by their suffering, for she saw them pining and languishing, sighing and sorrowing, musing and dreaming and changing colour. They were so lost in thought that they neglected all nourishment, till Brangane was greatly alarmed and feared this hardship might prove the end of them.

'Now pluck up your courage,' she thought, 'and find out what is happening!'

One day the three of them sat talking alone.

'There is nobody here but we three,' she said.

'Tell me, both of you, what is the matter with you? I see you fettered by your thoughts and sighing all the time.'

'Noble lady, if I dared tell you, I would,' answered Tristan.

'Tell me anything you like.'

'I dare not say any more, unless you first assure us on your holy word of honour that you will be kind and gracious to us – or else we are past all saving.'

Brangane gave them her word. She promised and assured them on her honour, calling Heaven to witness, that she would do exactly as they wished.

'First think of God and then of your hopes of paradise,' said Tristan 'consider our sufferings and the fearful plight we are in. I do not know what has come over us: but we have both of us gone mad in the briefest space of time and are in unimaginable torment – we are dying of love and can find neither time nor occasion for a meeting, because you are always in our way. And I tell you, if we die, it will be nobody's fault but yours. It is in your hands, whether we live or die!'

Turning to Iseult, Brangane asked: 'Is your distress as great as he paints it?'

'Yes, dear cousin,' said Iseult.

'May God have pity on us, for the Devil laughs at us!' said Brangane. 'I can see that I have no choice but to act to my own sorrow and your shame. Rather than let you die, I will allow you good opportunity for whatever you wish to embark on. But oh! that path has no returning. For already love and his strength drag you on and from this moment on you shall never know joy without pain again. The wine possesses you, the draught your mother gave me, the draught the king alone should have drunk with you: but the old enemy has tricked us, all three; friend Tristan, Iseult my friend, take here my body and my life, for guarding you so carelessly. Through me and in that cup you have drunk not love alone, but love and death together.'

That night, as the lovely Iseult lay brooding and pining for her beloved, there came stealing into her cabin her lover and her physician – Tristan and love. Love the physician led Tristan, her patient, by the hand: and there, too, she found her other patient, Iseult. She quickly took both sufferers and gave him to her, her to him, to be each other's remedy. Love the ensnarer united them and knit their two hearts together by the toils of her sweetness with such consummate skill that the bond was never loosed to the end of their days. The lovers held each other; life and desire trembled through their youth, and Tristan said, 'Now let death come!'

And as dawn broke, on the ship that heeled and ran to King Mark's land, they gave themselves up utterly to love.

THE TALL PINE TREE

Let us not make a long story of it. Young though she was, Iseult devised the best ruse that she could at this juncture, namely that they should simply ask Brangane to lie at Mark's side during the first night in perfect silence and keep him company. He could be denied his due in no better way, since Brangane was beautiful and a virgin. Thus love instructs honest minds to practise perfidy, though they ought not to know what goes to make a fraud of this sort.

This is what the lovers did. They begged and implored Brangane till they brought her to the point where she promised to do the deed. But she promised it most reluctantly. It was not just once that she turned red and then pale at this request under the stress of great emotion: after all, it was a strange one.

'Dearest mistress,' said Brangane, 'your mother, my lady the good queen, entrusted you to me, and I ought to have shielded you from such calamity during this God-forsaken voyage. But instead, owing to my carelessness, sorrow and shame have come upon you, so that I have little cause for complaint if I have to endure the disgrace with you, and it would even be right and proper that I alone should suffer it, provided that you could escape it. Merciful Lord, how couldst Thou so forget me!'

'Tell me, my noble cousin,' Iseult asked Brangane, 'what do you mean, why are you so distressed? I must know what is troubling you.'

'Madam, the other day I threw a flask overboard.'

'So you did: but what of that?'

'Alas,' replied Brangane, 'that flask and the draught it contained will be the death of you both!'

'But why, cousin?' asked Iseult. 'How can that be?'

'It is like this.'

And Brangane told them the whole story from beginning to end.

'It is in God's hands!' said Tristan.

'Whether it be life or death, it has poisoned me most sweetly! I have no idea what the other will be like, but this death suits me well! If my adored Iseult were the death of me in such fashion, I would woo death everlasting!'

Whatever our contentment of love, we must never lose sight of honour. When we are unwilling to seek anything but the body's delight it means the ruin of honour. However much the life that Tristan led was to his liking, his sense of honour restrained him. His loyalty laid regular siege to him so that he kept it well in mind and brought Mark his wife. Honour and loyalty pressed him hard: these two, who had lost the battle to love when Tristan had decided in her favour, this vanquished pair now vanquished love in turn.

Tristan at once despatched messengers to land in two ship's boats and sent news to Mark of how things had gone with regard to the Fair Maid of Ireland. Mark promptly summoned whomever he could. Within that same hour a thousand messengers were hastening to assemble the knights of Cornwall. Natives and strangers alike were made welcome in great number. Mark received in this pair with whom he passed his life both the worst and the best; yet he welcomed them as warmly as a man should welcome that which he most esteems.

As King Mark came down to greet Iseult upon the shore, Tristan took her hand and led her to the king and the king took her hand. He led her in great pomp to his castle of Tintagel, and as she came in hall amid the vassals her beauty shone so that the walls were lit as they are lit at dawn. Then King Mark blessed those swallows which, by happy chance, had brought the hair of gold; and he blessed Tristan as well, and the hundred knights who, on that ship of adventure, had gone to find him joy of heart and joy of eyes; yet to him also that ship was to bring sharp torment and mourning.

Mark at once summoned his barons, to come to court within eighteen days in a style appropriate for his wedding. This was duly done. They came in magnificent array. Many a dazzling cavalcade of knights and ladies arrived there to see their eyes' delight – radiant Iseult! They gazed at her with indescribable fervour, and accorded her this unvarying tribute: '*Isot, Isot la blunde, marveil de tu le munde!*

'Iseult is indeed a marvel throughout the world! What they say of this heavenly girl is true: like the sun she brings joy to the world! No land on earth ever gained so enchanting a maiden!'

After the wedding, and when the marriage contract had been signed, (namely that Cornwall and England were made subject to her provided that, if she bore no issue, Tristan should inherit) and when homage had been done to her, that night, when she was to go to bed with Mark, she, Brangane, and Tristan had gone to great trouble in advance to lay their plans and ensure that all went smoothly. There were none but these four in Mark's chamber: the king himself and the three. Mark was the first to disrobe and get into bed. Brangane had donned the queen's robes – they had exchanged clothes between them – and Tristan now led her towards Mark to suffer her ordeal. Her mistress Iseult put out the lights and Mark clasped Brangane to him.

I do not know how Brangane took to this business at first. She endured it so quietly that it all passed off in silence. Whatever her companion did with her, whatever demands he made on her, she met them to his satisfaction with brass and with gold. I am convinced that it can rarely have happened before that such fine brass was passed as bed-money for a payment due in gold. Indeed I would wager my life on it that false coin of such nobility had never been struck since Adam's day, nor had so acceptable a counterfeit ever been laid beside a man.

While these two lay in bed disporting themselves, Iseult was in great fear and anguish.

'Lord God help and preserve me lest my cousin prove unfaithful to me!' Such was her constant thought.

'If she plays this bed-game overlong and too intently I fear she will take such a liking to it that she will lie there till daylight, and all will be revealed!' But no, Brangane's thoughts and feelings were true and unsullied. When she had done duty for Iseult and her debt had been discharged, she quitted the bed.

Iseult was ready waiting there, and went and sat by the bed as if she were the same person.

The king, for his part, at once asked for wine in obedience to tradition, since in those days it was invariably the custom that if a man had lain with a virgin and taken her maidenhead, someone would come with wine and give it them to drink together, the one like the other. This custom was observed. Mark's nephew, Tristan, at once brought lights and wine. The king drank, and so did the queen. (Many assert that it was the same draught through which Tristan and Iseult were plunged into their love-passion: but none of that philtre remained. Brangane had thrown it into the sea.) When they had honoured the tradition and drunk as custom required, the young Queen Iseult, in great distress and with secret pain in her heart, laid herself down beside her lord the king who, clasping her close to him, then resumed his pleasures. To him one woman was as another: he soon found Iseult, too, to be of good deportment. There was nothing to choose between them – he found gold and brass in either. Moreover, they both paid him their dues, one way and another, so that he noticed nothing amiss.

Then Iseult lived as a queen, but lived in sadness. She had King Mark's tenderness and the barons' honour; the people also loved her; she passed her days amid the frescoed walls and floors strewn with flowers; she had fine jewels and purple cloth and tapestry from Hungary and Thessaly too, and songs of harpers, and curtains upon which were worked leopards and eagles and popinjays and all the beasts of sea and field. And her love too she had, love high and splendid, for as is the custom, among great lords, Tristan could always be near her, even in his leisure and his dalliance, night and day: for he slept in the king's chamber as great lords do, among the lieges and the councillors. Yet still she feared; for though her love were secret and Tristan unsuspected (for who suspects a son?), Brangane knew.

And Brangane seemed in the queen's mind like a witness spying; for Brangane alone knew what manner of life she led, and so had her at her mercy. And the queen thought: 'Ah, if some day she should weary of being a servant in the chamber where once she passed for queen . . . If Tristan should die from her betrayal!' So fear maddened the queen, but not in truth the fear of Brangane, who was loyal; her own heart bred the fear.

These lovers should not have feared Brangane, Brangane who was faithful, but themselves, for hearts so stricken will lose their vigilance. Love pressed them hard, as thirst presses the dying stag to the stream; love dropped upon them from high heaven, as a hawk slipped after long hunger falls right upon the bird. And love will not be hidden. Brangane indeed by her prudence served them well, nor were the queen and her lover ever careless. But in every hour and place every man could see that terrible love that rode them, and could see in these lovers their every sense overflowing, like new wine working in the vat.

Brangane was assiduous in the service of Iseult: she served her in all her wishes with regard to her lover Tristan. They conducted this affair so discreetly that nobody grew suspicious. None paid attention to what they said, to how they comported themselves or to any concern of theirs. No one had any doubts about them. They were at their ease and as contented as a pair of lovers should be who can choose their meetings at their own time and convenience. The lover and his beloved were at all times hot in pursuit of love. Many times in the day did they ensnare each other's eyes with tender glances, in the crowd and in the presence of others, where glances are full of significance and mean whole conversations, and through which it is possible to communicate on all matters of mutual affection. They continued so night and day without danger of observation. Walking, sitting, and standing, they were open and unconstrained both in speech and in demeanour. At times they embroidered their public conversation, in which they were marvellously adept, with words that were meant to stick — one might often observe love's handiwork in golden words caught up in their talk. But nobody had any idea that their words or acts were inspired by any affection other than what came from the close kinship which all knew existed between Mark and Tristan, with which they trafficked dishonestly and won their sport by cheating. With this, love beguiled the wits of very many people, none of whom could conceive of the true nature of their friendship, which was indeed perfect between them. Their thoughts and wishes were in concord: it was 'yes' and 'yes' and 'no' and 'no' with them. As to 'yes' and 'no', 'no' and 'yes', believe me, there was none of it, there were no differences between them. Yes or no, they were both of one mind. And so they passed their time delightfully together, now thus, now so. At times they were happy, at others out of humour, as is love's custom with lovers; for in their hearts she brews pain besides pleasure, sorrow and distress as well as joy. And distress for Tristan and his lady Iseult was when they could not contrive a love-meeting.

Thus in one way and another these two were both mournful and happy. Nor did it fail to happen now and again that there was anger between them – anger without malice, I mean. And if anyone were to say that anger is out of place between such perfect lovers, I am absolutely certain that he was never really in love, for such is love's way. With it she kindles lovers and sets fire to their emotions. For as anger pains them deeply, so affection reconciles them, with the result that love is renewed and friendship greater than ever. But how their anger is roused, and how they are appeased without the help of others, you need no telling. Lovers who are very often able to have each other's company are apt to imagine that some other is more loved than they, and they will make a great quarrel out of a caprice, and for a tiff will make peace right royally. And there is good reason why they should do so. We must uphold them in this, since affection will grow rich, young, and fresh from it, and take fire in its attachment. On the other hand, it grows poor, old, cold, and frigid when it lacks its fire; when anger is spent, affection does not quickly grow green again. But when lovers fall out over a trifle it is loyalty, fresh and ever new, that will always be the peacemaker.

This renews their loyalty, this refines their affection like gold. Thus Tristan and Iseult passed their time in joy and sorrow. There was joy and sorrow between them in tireless succession. I mean joy without mortal sorrow, for as yet they were free of mortal pain and of such calamity as stares into one's heart. They said not a word of their affairs, they kept their secret very close, and long continued so. They were both in excellent spirits and free and gay at heart. Queen Iseult was on the best of terms with everyone, and everyone spoke about Tristan. His name was on every lip, and he was marvellously feared in the land.

But there were four barons at court who had borne Tristan especial hatred of old for his prowess. These four watched the queen; they had guessed that great love, and they burnt with envy and hatred, and now a kind of evil joy. They planned to give news of their watching to the king, to see his tenderness turned to fury, Tristan thrust out or slain, and the queen in torment; for though they feared Tristan, their hatred mastered their fear. One day, the four barons called King Mark to speak with them, and their leader, Andred, said: 'Lord king, your heart will be troubled and we four also mourn; yet are we bound to tell you what we know. You have placed your trust in Tristan, and Tristan would shame you. In vain we warned you. For the love of one man you have mocked ties of blood and all your barons. Learn then that Tristan loves the queen; it is a proven truth and many a word is spoken of it.'

The king shrank and answered: 'Coward! What thought was that? Indeed I have placed my trust in Tristan. And rightly, for on the day when the Morholt offered combat to you all, you hung your heads and were dumb, and you trembled before him; but Tristan dared to fight him for the honour of this land, and suffered mortal wounds. Therefore do you hate him, and therefore do I cherish him above you, Andred, and beyond any other; but what then have you seen or heard or known?'

'Nothing, lord, save what your eyes could see or your ears hear. Look and listen, sire, if there is yet time.'

And they left him to taste the poison.

Then King Mark watched the queen and Tristan; but Brangane noted it and warned them both. The king watched in vain, so that, soon wearying of an ignoble task, but knowing, alas, that he could not kill his uneasy thought, he sent for Tristan and said: 'Tristan, leave this castle; and having left it, remain apart and do not think of returning to it, and do not cross again its moat or boundaries. Felons have charged you with an awful treason, but ask me nothing; I could not speak their words without shame to us both. For your part say nothing to try to appease me. I have not believed them . . . had I done so . . . But their evil words have troubled all my soul and only by your absence can my disquiet be soothed. Go, doubtless I will soon recall you. Go, my son, you are still dear to me.'

When the felons heard the news they said among themselves, 'He is gone, the wizard; he is driven out. Surely he will cross the sea on far adventures to carry his treacherous service to some distant king.'

But Tristan had not the strength to depart altogether; and when he had crossed the moats and boundaries of the castle he knew he could go no further. He stayed in Tintagel town and lodged with Gorvenal in a townsman's house, and languished, more wounded than when once the shaft of the Morholt had tainted his body.

In the closed towers Iseult the Fair drooped also, more wretched still. For it was her task all day long to feign laughter, and all night long to conquer fever and despair. And all night as she lay by King Mark's side, fever still kept her waking, and she stared into the darkness. She longed to fly to Tristan and she dreamt dreams of running to the gates and of finding there sharp scythes, traps laid by the felons, that cut her tender knees; and she dreamt of weakness and falling, and that her wounds had left her blood upon the ground. Now these lovers would have died, but Brangane came to their rescue. In peril of her life, she found the house where Tristan lay. There Gorvenal admitted her gladly, knowing what salvation she could bring. So she found Tristan, and to save the lovers she taught him a device, the most subtle ruse of love ever devised.

Behind the castle of Tintagel was an orchard fenced around with stout and pointed stakes; in it were numberless trees and fruit on them, birds and clusters of sweet grapes. And furthest from the castle, by the stakes of the palisade, was a tall pine tree, straight and with heavy branches spreading from its trunk. At its root a living spring welled quietly into a marble basin, then ran between two winding borders the length of the orchard and onwards till it flowed at last within the castle and through the women's rooms.

And every evening, by Brangane's counsel, Tristan cut twigs and bark, leapt the sharp stakes and, when he came beneath the pine, threw them into the clear spring; they floated light as foam down the stream to the women's rooms; and Iseult watched for their coming, and on those evenings she would wander out into the orchard and find her friend. Lithe and in fear would she come, watching at every step for what might lurk in the trees observing, foes or the felons whom she knew, till she spied Tristan; and the night and the branches of the pine protected them.

And so she said one night: 'Oh, Tristan, I have heard that the castle is fairy and that twice a year it vanishes away. So is it vanished now and this is that enchanted orchard of which the harpers sing.'

And as she said it, the sentinels bugled dawn.

Iseult had refound her joy. Mark's thought of ill-ease grew faint; but the felons felt or knew which way lay truth, and they guessed that Tristan had met the queen. Till at last Duke Andred (whom God shame) said to his peers: 'My lords, let us take counsel of Frocin the Dwarf; for he knows the seven arts, and magic and every kind of charm. He will teach us if he will the wiles of Iseult the Fair.'

The little evil man drew signs for them and characters of sorcery; he cast the fortunes of the hour and then at last he said: 'Sirs, high good lords, this night shall you seize them both.'

Then they led the little wizard to the king, and he said: 'Sire, bid your huntsmen leash the hounds and saddle the horses, proclaim a seven days' hunt in the forest and seven nights abroad therein, and hang me high if you do not hear this night what kind of conversation there is between Tristan and Iseult.'

Unwillingly, the king did so; and at nightfall he left the hunt, taking the dwarf as pillion, and entered the orchard, and the dwarf took him to the tall pine tree, saying: 'Fair king, climb into these branches and take with you your arrows and your bow, for you may need them; and keep still.'

That night the moon shone clear. Hidden in the branches, the king saw his nephew leap the palisades and throw his bark and twigs into the stream. But Tristan had bent over the round well to throw them and in so doing had seen the image of the king. He could not stop the branches as they floated away, and there, yonder, in the women's rooms, Iseult was watching and would come.

She came, and Tristan watched her motionless. Above him in the tree he heard the click of the arrow when it fits the string.

She came, but with more prudence than her wont, thinking, 'What has happened, that Tristan does not come to meet me? He has seen some foe.'

Suddenly, in the clear moonlight, she too saw the king's shadow in the pool. She showed the wit of women well, she did not lift her eyes.

'Lord God,' she said, low down, 'grant I may be the first to speak.'

'Tristan,' she said, 'what have you dared to do, calling me hither at such an hour? Often have you called me to beseech, you said. And queen though I am, I know you won me that title and I have come. What do you want of me?'

' Queen, I would have you pray the king for me.'

She was in tears and trembling, but Tristan praised God the Lord who had shown his friend her peril.

'Queen,' he went on, 'often and in vain have I summoned you; never would you come. Take pity; the king hates me and I know not why. Perhaps you know the cause and can charm his anger. For whom can he trust if not you, chaste queen and courteous, Iseult?'

'Truly, Lord Tristan, you do not know he doubts us both. And I, to add to my shame, must acquaint you of it. I swear that my love never went out to any man but he that first received me. And would you have me, at such a time, implore your pardon of the king? Why, if he knew of my passage here tonight he would cast my ashes to the wind. My body trembles and I am afraid. I go, for I have waited too long.'

In the branches the king smiled and had pity.

And as Iseult fled, ' Queen,' said Tristan, 'in the Lord's name help me, for charity.'

'Friend,' she replied, 'God aid you! The king wrongs you but the Lord God will be by you in whatever land you go.'

So she went back to the women's rooms and told Brangane, who cried: 'Iseult, God has worked a miracle for you, for He is compassionate and will not hurt the innocent in heart.'

And when he had left the orchard, the king said smiling: 'Fair nephew, that ride you planned is over now.'

But in an open glade elsewhere, Frocin the Dwarf read in the clear stars that the king now meant his death; he blackened with shame and fear and fled into Wales.

THE DISCOVERY

King Mark made peace with Tristan. Tristan returned to the castle as of old. Tristan slept in the king's chamber with his peers. He could come or go, the king thought no more of it.

Mark had pardoned the felons, and as the seneschal Dinas of Lidan found the dwarf wandering in a forest abandoned, he brought him home, and the king had pity and pardoned even him.

But his goodness did not quench the ire of the barons, who swore this oath: if the king kept Tristan in the land they would withdraw to their strongholds as for war; and they called the king to parley.

'Lord,' said they, 'drive Tristan away. He loves the queen as all who choose to do so can see. As for us, we will bear it no longer.'

And the king sighed, looking down in silence.

'King,' they went on, 'we will not bear it, for we know now that this is known to you and that you still will not move. Let us talk, and take counsel. As for us, if you will not exile this man, your nephew, and drive him out of your land for ever, we will withdraw within our bailiwicks and take our neighbours with us from your court: for we cannot endure his presence longer in this place. Make your choice!'

'My lords,' he said, 'once I listened to the evil words you spoke of Tristan, but I was wrong in the end. But you are my lieges and I would not lose the service of my men. Give me advice then, I order you, for you owe me counsel. You know me for a man who is neither proud nor over-bearing.'

'Lord,' they said, 'call Frocin here. You mistrust him for that night in the orchard. Still, was it not he that read in the stars of the queen's coming there and to the very pine tree too? He is very wise, take advice from him.'

And he came, that hunchback of hell: the felons greeted him and he planned this evil.

'Sire,' he said, 'let your nephew ride hard to-morrow at dawn with a brief drawn up on parchment and well sealed with a seal: bid him ride to King Arthur at Cardueil. Sire, he sleeps with the peers in your chamber; you must go out when the first sleep falls on men, and if he loves Iseult so madly, why, then I swear by God and by the laws of Rome, he will try to speak with her before he rides. But if he do so unknown to you, or to me, then kill me. As for the trap, let me lay it, but say nothing of his ride to him until the time for sleep.'

And when King Mark had agreed, this dwarf did a vile thing. He bought from a baker a pennyworth of flour, and hid it in the turn of his coat. That night, when the king had supped and the men-at-arms lay down to sleep in the hall, Tristan came to the king, as the custom was, and the king said: 'Fair nephew, do my will: ride tomorrow night to King Arthur at Cardueil, and give him this brief, with my greeting, that he may open it: and stay with him for only one day.'

And when Tristan said: 'I will take it on the morrow;' the king added: 'Yes, and before day dawns.'

But, as the peers slept all round the king their lord, that night, a mad thought took Tristan that, before he rode, he knew not for how long, he would say a last word to the queen before dawn. And there was a spear's length in the darkness between them. Now the dwarf slept with the rest in the king's chamber, and when he thought that all slept he rose and scattered the flour silently in the spear's length that lay between Tristan and the queen; but Tristan watched and saw him, and said to himself: 'It is to mark my footsteps, but there shall be no marks to show.'

At midnight, when all was dark in the room, no candle nor any lamp glimmering, the king went out silently by the door and with him the dwarf. Then Tristan rose in the darkness and judged the spear's length and leapt the space between, for his farewell. But that day in the hunt a boar had wounded him in the leg, and in this effort the wound bled. He did not feel it or see it in the darkness, but the blood dripped upon the couches and the flour strewn between; and outside in the moonlight the dwarf read the heavens and knew what had been done and he cried: 'Enter, my king, and if you do not hold them, hang me high.'

Then the king and the dwarf and the four felons ran in with lights and noise, and though Tristan had regained his place there was the blood for witness, and though Iseult feigned sleep, and Perinis too, who lay at Tristan's feet, yet there was the blood for witness. And the king looked in silence at the blood where it lay upon the bed and the boards and marking the flour.

And the four barons held Tristan down upon his bed and mocked the queen also, promising her full justice; and they bared and showed the wound whence the blood flowed.

Then the king said: 'Tristan, now nothing longer holds. To-morrow you shall die.'

And Tristan answered: 'Have mercy, Lord, in the name of God that suffered on the Cross!'

But the felons called on the king to take vengeance, saying: 'Do justice, King: take vengeance.'

And Tristan went on, 'Have mercy, not on me – for why should I fear to die? Truly, but for you, I would have sold my honour high to cowards who, under your peace, have put hands on my body – but in homage to you I have yielded and you may do with me what you will. But, lord, remember the queen!'

And as he knelt at the king's feet he still complained: 'Remember the queen; for if any man of your household make so bold as to maintain the lie that I loved her unlawfully, I will stand up armed to him in a ring. Sire, in the name of God the Lord, have mercy on her.'

Then the barons bound him with ropes, and the queen also. But if Tristan had known that trial by combat was to be denied him, he would have resisted them. For he trusted in God and knew no man dared draw sword against him in the lists. And truly he did well to trust in God; for though the felons mocked him when he said he had loved loyally, yet I call you to witness, my lords who read this, you who know of the philtre drunk upon the high seas, and who understand whether his love were disloyalty indeed. For men see this and that outward thing, but God alone sees the heart; in the heart alone is crime and the sole final judge is God. Therefore did He lay down the law that a man accused might uphold his cause by battle, and God Himself fights for the innocent in such a combat.

For this reason Tristan claimed justice and the right of battle and was careful to fail in nothing of the homage he owed King Mark, his lord.

But had he known what was coming, he would have killed the felons.

THE CHANTRY LEAP

Dark was the night, and darker still when the news ran that Tristan and the queen were held and that the king would kill them; and wealthy townsmen and common men alike wept, and ran to the palace.

And the murmurs and the cries ran through the city, but such was the king's anger in his castle above that neither the strongest nor the proudest baron dared to move him.

Night ended and the day drew near. Mark, before dawn, rode out to the place where he held pleas and judgement. He ordered a ditch to be dug in the earth and knotty vine-shoots and thorns to be laid therein.

In the morning he had a ban cried through his land to gather the men of Cornwall; they came with a great noise and the king spoke to them: 'My lords, I have made here a faggot of thorns for Tristan and the queen; for they have fallen.'

But they all cried, with tears: 'A sentence, lord, a sentence; an indictment and pleas; for killing without trial is a shame and a crime.'

But Mark answered in his anger: 'Neither respite, nor delay, nor pleas, nor sentence. By God that made the world, if any dare petition me, he shall burn first!'

He ordered the fire to be lit, and Tristan to be called.

The flames rose, and all were silent before the flames, and the king waited.

The servants ran to the room where watch was kept on the two lovers; and they dragged Tristan out by his hands though he wept for his honour; but as they dragged him off in such shame, the queen still called to him: 'Friend, if I die that you may live, that will be great joy.'

Now, hear how full of pity is God and how He heard the lament and the prayers of the common folk, that day.

For as Tristan and his guards went down from the town to where the faggot burned, near the road upon a rock was a chantry; it stood at a cliff's edge, steep and sheer, and it turned to the sea-breeze. In the apse were glazed windows. Then Tristan said to those with him: 'My lords, let me enter this chantry, to pray for a moment the mercy of God whom I have offended; my death is near. There is but one door to the place, my lords, and each of you has his sword drawn. So you can be sure that, when my prayer to God is done, I must come past you again when I have prayed to God, my lords, for the last time.'

And one of the guards said: 'Why, let him go in.'

So they let him enter to pray. But he, once in, dashed through and leapt the altar-rail and the altar too and forced a window of the apse, and leapt again over the cliff's edge, thinking to die, but not of that shameful death before the people.

Now learn, my lords, how generous was God to him that day. The wind took Tristan's cloak and he fell upon a smooth rock at the cliff's foot, which to this day the men of Cornwall call 'Tristan's Leap'.

His guards still waited for him at the chantry door, but vainly, for God was now his guard. And he ran, and the fine sand crunched under his feet, and far off he saw the faggot burning, and the smoke and the crackling flames; and fled.

Gorvenal had fled the city, sword girt and bridle loose, lest the king burn him in his lord's place: and he found Tristan on the shore.

'Master,' said Tristan, 'God has saved me, but oh! master, to what end? For without Iseult, I may not and will not live, and I had rather died of my fall. They will burn her for me, then I too will die for her.'

'Lord,' said Gorvenal, 'do not act in anger. See here this thicket with a ditch dug round about it. Let us hide therein where the track passes near, and we will hear what travellers say; and, if they burn Iseult, I swear by God, the Son of Mary, never to sleep under a roof again until she is avenged.'

There was a poor man of the common folk that had seen Tristan's fall, and had seen him stumble and rise after, and he crept to Tintagel and to

Iseult where she was bound, and said: ' Queen, weep no more. Your friend has fled safely.'

'Then I thank God,' said she, 'and whether they bind or loose me, and whether they kill or spare me, I care but little now.'

And though blood came at the cordknots, so tightly had the traitors bound her, yet still she said, smiling: 'If I wept for my own death when God has loosed my friend, I would be worth little.'

When the news came to the king that Tristan had leapt that leap and was lost to him, he paled with anger, and ordered his men to bring forth Iseult.

They dragged her from the room, and she came before the crowd, held by her delicate hands, from which blood dropped, and the crowd called: 'Have pity on her – the loyal queen and honoured! Those who betrayed her brought mourning on us all – our curses on them!'

But the king's men dragged her to the thorn faggot as it blazed. She stood up before the flame, and the crowd cried out in anger, and cursed the traitors and the king. None could see her without pity, unless he had a felon's heart: she was so tightly bound. The tears ran down her face and fell upon her grey gown where ran a little thread of gold, and a thread of gold was twined into her hair.

Just then there approached a hundred lepers of the king's, deformed and broken and horribly white, and limping on their crutches. And they drew near the flame, and being evil, loved the sight. And their chief Ivan, the ugliest of them all, cried to the king in a quavering voice: 'O king, you would burn this woman in that flame, and it is sound justice, but too swift, for very soon the fire will fall and her ashes will very soon be scattered by the high wind and her agony be done. Throw her rather to your lepers where she may drag out a life forever asking death.'

And the king answered: 'Yes; let her live that life, for it is better justice and more terrible. I can love those that gave me such a thought.'

And the lepers answered: 'Throw her among us, and make her one of us. Never shall lady have known a worse end. And look', they said, 'at our rags and our abominations. She has had pleasure in rich stuffs and furs, jewels and walls of marble, honour, good wines and joy, but when she sees your lepers always, King, and only them for ever, their couches and their huts, then indeed she will know the wrong she has done, and bitterly desire even that great flame of thorns.'

And as the king heard them, he stood a long time without moving; then he ran to the queen and seized her by the hand, and she cried: 'Burn me! rather burn me!'

But the king gave her up, and Ivan took her, and the hundred lepers pressed around, and to hear her cries all the crowd rose in pity. But Ivan had an evil gladness, and as he went he dragged her beyond the borough bounds, with his hideous company.

Now they took that road where Tristan lay in hiding, and Gorvenal said to him: 'Lord, here is your friend. Will you do nothing?'

Then Tristan mounted the horse and spurred it out of the bush, and cried: 'Ivan, you have been at the queen's side a moment, and that is too long. Now leave her if you would live.'

But Ivan threw his cloak away and shouted: 'Your clubs, comrades, and your staves! Crutches in the air – for a fight is on!'

Then it was a sight to see the lepers throwing their capes aside, and stirring their sick legs, and brandishing their crutches, some threatening, all groaning. Tristan was too noble to strike them. There are singers who sing that Tristan killed Ivan, but it is a lie. He was too much a knight to kill such things. Gorvenal, indeed, snatching up an oak sapling, crashed it on Ivan's head till his blood ran down to his misshapen feet. Then Tristan took the queen.

Once near him, she felt no further evil. He cut the cords that bound her arms so tightly; and he left the open country and plunged into the. wood of Morois. There, in the thick wood, Tristan was as safe as in a castle keep. And as the sun fell they halted all three at the foot of a little hill. Fear had wearied the queen, and she leant her head upon his body and slept.

But in the morning, Gorvenal stole from a woodman his bow and two good arrows plumed and barbed, and gave them to Tristan, the great archer, and he shot a fawn and killed it. Then Gorvenal gathered dry twigs, struck flint, and lit a great fire to cook the venison. And Tristan cut branches and made a hut and garnished it with leaves. And Iseult slept upon the thick leaves there.

So, in the depths of the wild wood a savage life began for the lovers; but soon they loved it well.

THE WOOD OF MOROIS

They wandered in the depths of the wild wood, restless and in haste like beasts that are hunted; and often they did not dare to return at night to the place where they had found shelter yesterday. They ate only the flesh of wild animals. Their faces sank and grew white, their clothes ragged, for the briars tore them. They loved each other and they did not know that they suffered.

One day, as they were wandering in these high woods that had never yet been felled or ordered, they came upon the hermitage of Ogrin. The old man limped in the sunlight under a light growth of maples near his chapel: he leant upon his crutch, and cried: 'Lord Tristan, hear the great oath which the Cornishmen have sworn. The king has published a ban in every parish. Whoever seizes you shall receive a hundred marks of gold for his reward, and all the barons have sworn to give you up alive or dead. Do penance, Tristan! God pardons the sinner who turns to repentance.'

'And of what should I repent, Ogrin, my lord? Or of what crime? You that sit in judgement upon us here, do you know what cup it was we drank upon the high seas? What we drank then was great and good, and we are still both drunk with it. I would rather beg my whole life long and live on roots and herbs with Iseult than be king of a wide kingdom without her at my side.'

'God aid you, Lord Tristan; for you have lost both this world and the next. A man who is traitor to his lord is worthy to be torn by horses and burnt upon the faggot, and wherever his ashes fall no grass shall grow and all planting shall be waste, and the trees and the green things shall die. Lord Tristan, give back the queen to the man who espoused her lawfully according to the laws of Rome.'

'He gave her to his lepers. From these lepers I myself conquered her with my own hand; and henceforth she is altogether mine. She cannot pass from me nor I from her.'

Ogrin sat down; but at his feet Iseult, her head upon the knees of that man of God, wept silently. The hermit told her and retold her the words of his holy book, but still while she wept she shook her head, and refused the faith he offered.

'Ah me,' said Ogrin then, 'what comfort can one give the dead? Do penance, Tristan, for a man who lives in sin without repenting is a man quite dead.'

'Oh no,' said Tristan, 'I live and I do no penance. We will go back into the high wood which comforts and guards us all around. Come with me, Iseult, my friend.'

Iseult rose up; they held each other's hands. They passed into the high grass and the underwood: the trees hid them with their branches and they disappeared beyond the curtain of the leaves.

The three of them together made steadily for the wilds, journeying over forest and heath for well on two days. Tristan had long known of a cavern in a savage mountainside, on which he had chanced when his way had led him there out hunting. The cavern had been hewn into the wild mountain in heathen times, in the days when giants ruled in the isle of Albion. They used to hide inside it when, desiring to make love, they needed privacy. Wherever such a cavern was found it was barred by a door of bronze, and bore an inscription to love – *la fossiure à la gent amant*, which is to say 'the cave of lovers'.

The name was well suited to the thing. The story tells us that this grotto was round, broad, high, and perpendicular, snow white, smooth, and even, throughout its whole circumference. Above, its vault was finely keyed, and on the keystone there was a crown most beautifully adorned with gold-smiths' work and encrusted with precious stones. Below, the pavement was of smooth, rich, shining marble, as green as grass. At the centre there was a bed most perfectly cut from a slab of crystal, broad, high, raised well from the ground, and engraved along its sides with letters, announcing that the bed was dedicated to the goddess of love. In the upper part of the grotto some small windows had been hewn out to let in the light, and these shone in several places.

Where one went in and out there was a door of bronze. Outside, above the door, there stood three limes of many branches, but beyond them not a single one. Yet everywhere downhill there were innumerable trees which cast the shade of their leafy boughs upon the mountainside. Somewhat apart, there was a level glade through which there flowed a spring – a cool, fresh brook, clear as the sun.

Above that, too, there stood three limes, fair and very stately, sheltering the brook from sun and rain. The bright flowers and the green grass vied with each other most delightfully, each striving to outshine the other. At dawn and dusk you could hear the sweet singing of the birds. Their music was even lovelier here than elsewhere. Both eye and ear found their pasture and delight there: the eye its pasture, the ear its delight. There were shade and sunshine, air and breezes, both soft and gentle. Away from the mountain and its cave for fully a day's journey there were rocks unrelieved by open heath, and wilderness and waste land. No paths or tracks had been laid towards it of which one might avail oneself. But the country was not so rough and fraught with hardship as to deter Tristan and his beloved from halting there and making their abode within that mountain cave.

When they had taken up their quarters, they sent Gorvenal back to put it out at court and wherever else was necessary that, after many griefs and hardships, Tristan and fair Iseult had arrived back in Ireland in order to proclaim their innocence before the land and people. Further, he was to take up residence at court as Brangane should instruct him and earnestly assure the truehearted girl, their common friend, of their love and friendship. He was also to find out what was rumoured of Mark's intentions – whether he might be plotting some villainy against their lives, and in that case inform them at once. And they begged him to keep Tristan and Iseult in his thoughts and to return once every twenty days with such intelligence as would enable them to counter such moves. He did as he was asked. Meanwhile Tristan and Iseult had taken up their abode together in this wild retreat.

Some people are smitten with curiosity and astonishment, and plague themselves with the question how these two companions, Tristan and Iseult, nourished themselves in this waste land? I will tell them and assuage their curiosity. They looked at one another and nourished themselves with that! Their sustenance was the eye's increase. They fed in their grotto on nothing but love and desire. The two lovers who formed its court had small concern for their provisioning. Hidden away in their hearts they carried the best nutriment to be had anywhere in the world, which offered itself unasked ever fresh and new – I mean pure devotion, love made sweet as balm that consoles body and sense so tenderly, and sustains the heart and spirit – this was their best nourishment. Truly, they never considered any food but that from which the heart drew desire, the eyes delight, and which the body, too, found agreeable. With this they had enough. Love drove her ancient plough for them, keeping pace all the time, and gave them an abundant store of all those things that go to make heaven on earth. Nor were they greatly troubled that they should be alone in the wilds without company. Tell me, whom did they need in there with them, and why should anyone join them? They made an even number: there were simply one and one. Had they included a third in the even pair which they made, there would have been an uneven number, and they would have been much encumbered and embarrassed by the odd one. Their company of two was so ample a crowd for this pair that good King Arthur never held a feast in any of his palaces that gave keener pleasure or delight. In no land could you have found enjoyment for which these two would have given a brass farthing to have with them in their grotto. Whatever one could imagine or conceive elsewhere in other countries to make a paradise, they had with them there. They would not have given a button for a better life, save only in respect of their honour. What more should they need? They had their court, they were amply supplied with all that goes to make for happiness. Their loyal servitors were the green lime, the sunshine and the shade, the brook and its banks, flowers, grass, blossoms, and leaves, so soothing to the eye. The service they received was the song of the birds, of the lovely, slender nightingale, the thrush and blackbird, and other birds of the forest. Siskin and calander-lark vied in eager rivalry to see who could give the best service. These followers served their ears and sense unendingly.

Their high feast was love, who gilded all their joys; she brought them King Arthur's Round Table as homage and all its company a thousand times a day! What better food could they have for body or soul? Man was there with Woman, Woman there with Man. What else should they he needing? They had what they were meant to have, they had reached the goal of their desire.

Now some people are so tactless as to declare (though I do not accept it myself) that other food is needed for this pastime. I am not so sure that it is. There is enough here in my opinion. But if anyone has discovered better nourishment in this world, let him speak in the light of his experience. There was a time when I, too, led such a life, and I thought it quite sufficient.

The grotto was secluded in the midst of this wild solitude, for love and her concerns are not assigned to the streets nor yet to the open country. She is hidden away in the wilds, the country that leads to her refuge makes hard and arduous going – mountains are strewn about the way in many a massive curve. The tracks up and down are so obstructed with rocks for us poor sufferers that, unless we keep well to the path, if we make one false step we shall never get back alive. But whoever is so blessed as to reach and enter that solitude will have used his efforts to most excellent purpose, for he will find his heart's delight there. Whatever the ear yearns to hear, whatever gratifies the eye, this wilderness is full of it. He would hate to be elsewhere.

I know this well, for I have been there. I, too, have tracked and followed after wildfowl and game, after hart and hind in the wilderness over many a woodland stream and yet passed my time and not seen the end of the chase. My toils were not crowned with success. I have found the secret catch that gives access to the cave and have, on occasion, even pressed on to the bed of crystal. But I have never had my repose on it. However hard the floor of marble beside it, I have so battered the floor with my steps that, had it not been saved by its greenness, in which lies its chiefest virtue, and from which it constantly renews itself, you would have traced love's authentic tracks on it. I have also fed my eyes abundantly on the gleaming wall and have fixed my gaze on the medallion, on the vault and on the keystone, and worn out my eyes looking up at its ornament! The sun-giving windows have often sent their rays into my heart. I have known that cave since I was eleven, yet I never set foot in Cornwall.

Those truehearted inhabitants of love's lands, Tristan and his mistress, had arranged their leisure and exertions very pleasantly in the woods and glades of their wilderness. They were always at each other's side. In the mornings they would stroll to the meadow through the dew, where it had cooled the grass and the flowers. The cool field was their recreation. They talked as they walked to and fro, and they listened as they went to the sweet singing of the birds. Then they would turn aside to where the cool spring murmured, and would hearken to its music. Where it entered the glade they used to sit and rest and listen to its purling and watch the water flow, a joy of which they never tired.

But when the bright sun began to climb and the heat to descend, they withdrew to their lime tree in quest of its gentle breezes. This afforded them pleasure within and without their breasts – the tree rejoiced both their hearts and their eyes. With its leaves the fragrant lime refreshed both air and shade for them; from its shade the breezes were gentle, fragrant, cool. The bench beneath the lime was flowers and grass, the best painted lawn that ever lime tree had. Our constant lovers sat there together and told love-tales of those whom love had ruined in days gone by. They debated and discussed, they mourned for Phyllis of Thrace and poor Canacea who had suffered such misfortune in love's name; they talked of how Biblis had died brokenhearted for her brother's love; how lovelorn Dido, queen of Tyre and Sidon, had met so tragic a fate because of unhappy love.

When they tired of stories they slipped into their refuge and resumed their well-tried pleasure of sounding their harp, and singing sadly and sweetly. They busied their hands and their tongues in turn. They performed amorous lays and their accompaniments, varying their delight as it suited them: for if one took the harp it was for the other to sing the tune with wistful tenderness. And indeed the strains of both harp and tongue, merging their sound in each other, echoed in that cave so sweetly that it was dedicated to sweet love for her retreat most fittingly as '*la fossiure à la gent amant*'.

All that had been rumoured in tales of old on the subject of the grotto was borne out in this pair. Only now had the cave's true mistress given herself to her sport in earnest. Whatever frolics or pastimes had been pursued in this grotto before, they did not equal this; they were neither so pure nor so unsullied in spirit as when Tristan and Iseult disported themselves. These two beguiled love's hour in a way no lovers surpassed – they did just as their hearts prompted them.

There were amusements enough for them to follow by day. They rode out into their wilderness, hunting wildfowl and game with their crossbow now and then, when fancy took them, and sometimes they chased the red deer with Houdenc their hound, who as yet could not run without giving tongue. But it was not long before Tristan had trained him to run most perfectly through field and forest on the scent of hart and hind and of all varieties of game without giving cry. And so they spent many a day, not for what such sport brings the hunting-bag, but solely for the amusement it affords. They exercised hound and bow, I am convinced, more for their pleasure and recreation than for their table. What they did was entirely as they pleased, and as they felt inclined.

The summer passed and the winter came: the two lovers lived hidden in the hollow of a rock, and on the frozen earth the cold crisped their couch with dead leaves. In the strength of their love neither one nor the other felt these mortal things. But when the open skies had come back with the springtime, they built a hut of green branches under the great trees. Tristan had known, ever since his childhood, that art by which a man may sing the song of birds in the woods, and at his fancy, he would mimic the call of the thrush, the blackbird and the nightingale, and of all winged things; and sometimes in reply a throng of birds would come on to the branches of his hut and sing their song full-throated in the new light.

The lovers had not ceased to wander through the forest, for none of the barons ran the risk of their pursuit, knowing well that Tristan would have hanged them from the branches of a tree. One day, however, one of the four traitors, Guenelon, whom God blast, drawn by the heat of the hunt, dared to enter the Morois. And that morning, on the forest's edge in a ravine, Gorvenal, having unsaddled his horse, had let him graze on the new grass, while far off in their hut Tristan held the queen and they slept. Then suddenly Gorvenal heard the cry of the pack; the hounds pursued a deer, which fell into the ravine. And far on the heath the, hunter showed and Gorvenal knew him for the man whom his master hated above all. Alone, with bloody spurs, and striking his horse's mane, Guenelon galloped on; but Gorvenal watched him from ambush: he came fast, he would return more slowly. He passed and Gorvenal leapt from his ambush and seized the rein and, suddenly, remembering all the wrong that man had done, hewed him to death and carried off his head in his hands. And when the hunters found the body as they followed, they thought Tristan would come in pursuit and they fled in fear of death, and after that no man hunted in that wood. And far off, in the hut upon their couch of leaves, Tristan and the queen lay sleeping.

There came Gorvenal, noiseless, the dead man's head in his hands that he might lift his master's heart at his awakening. He hung it by its hair outside the hut, and the leaves made a garland for it. Tristan woke and saw it, half hidden in the leaves, and staring at him as he gazed, and he grew afraid. But Gorvenal said: 'Have no fear, he is dead. I killed him with this sword.'

Then Tristan was glad, and from that day on no one dared enter the wild wood, for terror guarded it and the lovers were lords of it all: and then it was that Tristan fashioned his bow called Failnaught which struck home always, man or beast, whatever it aimed at.

My lords, on a summer day in the month when men mow the hay, a little after Whitsuntide, as the birds sang dawn, Tristan left his hut and girded his sword on him, and took his bow and went off to hunt in the wood; but before evening, great evil was to fall on him, for no lovers ever loved so much or paid their love so dear.

When Tristan came back, broken by the heat, the queen said: 'Friend, where have you been?'

'Hunting a hart,' he said, 'that wearied me. I would lie down and sleep.'

So she lay down, and he, and between them Tristan put his naked sword, and on the queen's finger was that ring of gold with emeralds set in it, which Mark had given her on her bridal day; but her hand was so wasted that the ring hardly held. And no wind blew, and no leaves stirred, but through a crevice in the branches a sunbeam fell upon the face of Iseult, and it shone white like ice. Now a woodman found in the wood a place where the leaves were crushed, where the lovers had halted and slept, and he followed their track and found the hut, and saw them sleeping and fled at once, fearing the terrible awakening of that lord. He fled to Tintagel, and going up the stairs of the palace, found the king as he held his pleas in hall amid the vassals assembled.

'Friend,' said the king, 'what have you come to seek, in haste and breathless, like a huntsman that has followed the dogs on foot? Have you some wrong to right, or has any man driven you?'

But the woodman took him aside and said in a low voice: 'I have seen the queen and Tristan; I was afraid and fled.'

'Where did you see them?'

'In a hut in Morois; they slept side by side. Come swiftly and take your vengeance.'

'Go,' said the king, 'and wait for me at the forest's edge where the red cross stands, and tell no one what you have seen. You shall have gold and silver as you wish.'

The king had his horse saddled and girded on his sword and left the city alone, and as he rode alone he remembered the night when he had seen Tristan under the great pine tree, and Iseult with her clear face, and he thought: 'If I find them I will avenge this awful wrong.'

At the foot of the red cross he came to the woodman and said: 'Go first, and lead me straight and quickly.'

The dark shade of the great trees engulfed them, and as the king followed the spy he felt his sword, and trusted it for the great blows it had struck of old; and surely had Tristan wakened, one of the two would have been left for dead. Then the woodman said: 'King, we are near the place.'

He held the stirrup, and tied the reins to a green apple-tree, and saw in a sunlit glade the hut with its flowers and leaves. Then the king threw back his cloak with its fine buckle of gold and drew his sword from its sheath and said again in his heart that they or he should die. And he signed to the woodman to be gone.

He came alone into the hut, sword bare, and watched them as they lay: but he saw that they were apart, and he marvelled because between them was the naked blade.

Then he said to himself: 'My God, I may not kill them. For all the time they have lived together in this wood, these two lovers, yet is the sword here between them, and throughout Christendom men know that sign. Therefore I will not kill, for that would be treason and wrong. But I will leave a sign so that when they wake, they will know that I found them here, asleep, and spared them and that God had pity on them both.'

And still the sunbeam fell upon the white face of Iseult, and the king took his ermine gloves and put them up against the crevice whence it shone. And he laid his sword between them, and exchanged his ring for that of the queen, and took Tristan's sword away with him.

Then in her sleep a vision came to Iseult. She seemed to be in a great wood and two lions near her fought for her, and she gave a cry and woke, and the gloves fell upon her breast; and at the cry Tristan woke, and made to seize his sword, and saw by the golden hilt that it was the king's. And the queen saw on her finger the king's ring. and she cried: 'O, my lord, the king has found us here!'

And Tristan said: 'He has taken my sword; he was alone, but he will return, and will burn us before the people. Let us fly.'

So by great marches, with Gorvenal alone, they fled towards Wales.

OGRIN THE HERMIT

After three days it happened that Tristan, in following a wounded deer far out into the wood, was caught by nightfall, and took to thinking thus under the dark wood alone: 'It was not fear that moved the king . . . he had my sword and I slept . . . and had he wished to kill, why did he leave me his own sword? . . . Oh, my father, my father, I know you now. There was pardon in your heart, and tenderness and pity . . . yet how was that, for who could forgive in this matter without shame? . . . It was not pardon, it was understanding; the fire of thorns and the chantry leap and the leper ambush have shown him God upon our side. Also I think he remembered the boy who long ago harped at his feet, and my land of Lyonesse which I left for him; and the Morholt's spear and blood shed in his honour. He remembered how I made no avowal, but claimed a trial at arms, and the high nature of his heart has made him understand what men around him cannot; he can never know of the spell, yet he doubts and hopes and knows I have told no lie; and he would have me prove my cause. Oh, to win at arms by God's aid for him, and to enter his peace and to put on mail for him again . . . but then he must take her back, and I must yield her . . . it would have been much better had he killed me in my sleep. For till now I was hunted and I could hate and forget; he had thrown Iseult to the lepers, she was no more his, but mine; and now by his compassion he has wakened my heart and regained the queen. For queen she was at his side, but in this wood she lives a slave, and I waste her youth; and for rooms all hung with silk she has this savage place, and a hut for her splendid walls, and I am the cause that she treads this ugly road. So now I cry to God the Lord, who is king of the world, and beg Him to give me strength to yield back Iseult to King Mark; for she is indeed his wife, wed according to the laws of Rome before all the barons of his land.'

And as he thought thus, he leant upon his bow, and all through the night considered his sorrow.

Within the hollow of thorns that was their resting-place Iseult the Fair awaited Tristan's return. The golden ring that King Mark had slipped there glistened on her finger in the moonlight, and she thought: 'He that put on this ring is not the man who threw me to his lepers in his wrath; he is rather that compassionate lord who, from the day I touched his shore, received me and protected me. And he loved Tristan once, but I came, and see what I have done! He should have lived in the king's palace; he should have ridden through king's and baron's fees, finding adventure; but through me he has forgotten his knighthood, and is hunted and exiled from the court, leading a random life . . .'

Just then she heard the feet of Tristan coming over the dead leaves and twigs. She came to meet him, as was her wont, to relieve him of his arms, and she took from him his bow and his arrows, and she unbuckled his swordstraps. And, 'Friend,' said he, 'it is the king's sword. It should have slain, but it spared us.'

Iseult took the sword, and kissed the hilt of gold, and Tristan saw her weeping.

'Friend,' said he, 'if I could make my peace with the king; if he would allow me to sustain in arms that neither by act nor word have I loved you with a wrongful love, any knight from the marshes of Ely right away to Dureaume who would contradict me would find me armed in the ring. Then if the king would keep you and drive me out I would cross to the Lowlands or to Brittany with Gorvenal alone. But wherever I went and always, queen, I should be yours; nor would I have spoken thus, Iseult, but for the wretchedness you bear so long for my sake in this desert land.'

'Tristan,' she said, 'the hermit Ogrin is near by. Let us return to him, and cry mercy to the King of Heaven.'

They wakened Gorvenal; Iseult mounted the steed, and Tristan led it by the bridle, and all night long they went for the last time through the woods of their love, and they did not speak a word. By morning they came to the hermitage, where Ogrin read at the threshold, and seeing them, called them tenderly: 'Friends,' he cried, 'see how love drives you still to further wretchedness. Will you not do penance at last for your madness?'

'Lord Ogrin,' said Tristan, 'hear us. Help us to offer peace to the king, and I will yield him the queen, and will myself go far away into Brittany or the Lowlands, and if some day the king suffer me, I will return and serve as I should.'

And at the hermit's feet Iseult said in her turn: 'Nor will I live longer so, for though I will not say one word of penance for my love, which is there and remains for ever, yet from now on I will be separate from him.'

Then the hermit wept and praised God and cried: 'High King, I praise Thy Name, for that Thou hast let me live so long as to give aid to these!'

And he gave them wise counsel, and took ink, and wrote a little letter offering the king what Tristan said.

That night Tristan took the road. Once more he saw the marble well and the tall pine tree, and he came beneath the window where the king slept, and called him gently, and Mark awoke and whispered: 'Who are you, calling me in the night at such an hour?'

'Lord, I am Tristan: I bring you a letter, and lay it here.'

Then the king cried: 'Nephew! nephew! for God's sake wait awhile,' but Tristan had fled and joined his squire, and mounted rapidly. Gorvenal said to him:

'Ah, Tristan, you are mad to have come. Let us escape quickly by the nearest road.'

So they came back to the hermitage, and there they found Ogrin at prayer – but Iseult weeping silently.

THE FORD

Mark had awakened his chaplain and had given him the letter to read; the chaplain broke the seal, saw that the greetings were in Tristan's name, and then, when he had made out the written words, told him what Tristan offered; and Mark listened without saying a word, but his heart was glad, for he still loved the queen.

He summoned by name the choicest of his barons, and when they were all assembled they were silent and the king spoke: 'My lords, here is a writ, just sent me. I am your king, and you my lieges. Hear what is offered me, and then counsel me, for you owe me counsel.'

The chaplain rose, unfolded the writ, and said, upstanding: 'My lords, it is Tristan that first sends love and homage to the king and all his barons, and he adds,

Oh king, when I slew the dragon and conquered the king of Ireland's daughter it was to me they gave her. I was to guard her at will and I yielded her to you. Yet scarcely had you wed her when felons made you accept their lies, and in your anger, fair uncle, my lord, you would have had us burnt without trial. But God took compassion on us; we prayed to him and he saved the queen, as justice demanded: and me also, for though I leapt from a high rock, I was saved by the power of God. And since then what have I done that is blameworthy? The queen was thrown to the lepers; I came to her succour and bore her away. Could I have done less for a woman, who all but died innocent through me? I fled through the woods. Nor could I have come down in the vale and yielded her, for there was an order to take us dead or alive. But now, as then, I am ready, my lord, to sustain in arms against all comers that the queen never had for me, nor I for her, a love dishonourable to you. Publish the lists, and if I cannot prove my right in arms, burn me before your men. But if I conquer and you take back Iseult, no baron of yours will serve you as will I; and if you will not have me, I will offer myself to the king of Galloway, or to him of the Lowlands, and you will never hear of me again. Take counsel, King, for if you will make no terms I will take back Iseult to Ireland, and she shall be queen in her own land.

When the barons of Cornwall heard how Tristan offered battle, they said to the king: 'Sire, take back the queen. They were madmen that defamed her to you. But as for Tristan, let him go, and war it in Galloway, or in the Lowlands. Bid him bring back Iseult on such a day and that soon.'

Then the king called thrice clearly: 'Will any man rise in accusation against Tristan?'

And as none replied, he said to his chaplain: 'Write me a letter in haste. You have heard what you shall write. Iseult has suffered enough in her youth. And let the letter be hung upon the arm of the red cross before evening. Write speedily.'

Towards midnight Tristan crossed the sandy heath, and found the letter, and bore it sealed to Ogrin; and the hermit read the letter, learning how Mark consented by the counsel of his barons to take back Iseult, but not to keep Tristan for his liege.

Rather let him cross the sea, when, on the third day hence, at the Ford of Chances, he has given back the queen into King Mark's hands.

Then Tristan said to the queen: 'Oh, my God! I must lose you, friend! But it must be, since I can thus spare you what you suffer for my sake. But when we part for ever I will give you a pledge of mine to keep, and from whatever unknown land I reach I will send some messenger, and he will bring back word of you, and at your call I will come from far away.'

Iseult said, sighing: 'Tristan, leave me your dog Houdenc, and every time I see him I will remember you, and will be less sad. And, friend, I have here a ring of green jasper. Take it for the love of me, and put it on your finger; then if anyone should come saying he is from you, I will not trust him at all till he show me this ring, but once I have seen it, there is no power or royal ban that can prevent me from doing what you bid, whether it is wisdom or folly.'

'Friend,' he said, 'here I give you Houdenc.'

'Friend, ' she replied, 'take this ring in reward.'

And they kissed each other on the lips.

Now Ogrin, having left the lovers in the hermitage, hobbled upon his crutch to the place called The Mount, and he bought ermine there and fur and cloth of silk and purple and scarlet, and a palfrey harnessed in gold that went softly, and the folk laughed to see him spending upon these the small moneys he had amassed so long; but the old man put the rich stuffs upon the palfrey and came back to Iseult.

'Queen,' said he, 'take these gifts of mine that you may seem the finer on the day when you come to the Ford.'

Meanwhile the king had had cried through Cornwall the news that on the third day he would make his peace with the queen at the Ford, and knights and ladies came in a crowd to the gathering, for all loved the queen and would see her, save the three felons who still survived.

On the day chosen for the meeting, the field shone far and wide with the rich tents of the barons, and suddenly Tristan and Iseult came out at the forest's edge, and caught sight of King Mark in the distance among his barons. 'Friend,' said Tristan, 'there is the king, your lord, his knights and his men; they are coming towards us, and very soon we may not speak to each other again. By the God of Power I conjure you, if ever I send you a word, do my bidding.'

'Friend,' said Iseult, 'on the day that I see the ring, neither tower, nor wall, nor stronghold will hinder me from doing the will of my friend.'

'Why then,' he said, 'Iseult, may God reward you.'

Their horses went abreast and he drew her towards him with his arm.

'Friend,' said Iseult, 'hear my last prayer: you will leave this land, but wait some days; hide till you know how the king may treat me, whether in anger or kindness, for I am afraid. Friend, Orri the woodman will look after you in hiding. Go by night to the abandoned cellar that you know and I will send Perinis there to say if anyone misuses me.'

'Friend, none would dare. I will stay hidden with Orri, and if anyone mistreats you, let him fear me as the enemy himself.'

Now the two troops were near and they saluted, and the king rode a bowshot before his men, and with him Dinas of Lidan; and when the barons had come up, Tristan, holding Iseult's palfrey by the bridle, bowed to the king and said: 'Oh king, I yield you here Iseult the Fair, and I summon you, before the men of your land, that I may defend myself in your court, for I have had no judgement. Let me have trial at arms, and if I am conquered, burn me, but if I conquer, keep me by you, or, if you will not, I will be off to some far country.'

But no one took up Tristan's wager, and the king, taking Iseult's palfrey by the bridle, gave it to Dinas, and went apart to take counsel.

Dinas in his joy gave all honour and courtesy to the queen, but when the felons saw her so fair and honoured as of old, they were stirred and rode to the king, and said: 'King, hear our counsel. That the queen was slandered we admit, but if she and Tristan re-enter your court together, rumour will revive again. Rather let Tristan go apart awhile. Doubtless some day you may recall him.'

And so Mark did, and through his barons ordered Tristan to leave without delay.

Then Tristan came near the queen for his farewell, and as they looked at one another the queen, ashamed by the crowd, blushed, but the king pitied her, and spoke to his nephew thus for the first time: 'You cannot leave in these rags; take from my treasury gold and silver and white fur and grey, as much as you will.'

'King,' said Tristan, 'I will take neither a penny nor a link of mail. I will go as I can, and serve with high heart the mighty king in the Lowlands.'

And he turned rein and went down towards the sea, but Iseult followed him with her eyes, and so long as he could yet be seen a long way off, she did not turn.

Now at the news of the peace, men, women, and children, great and small, ran out of the town in a crowd to meet Iseult, and while they mourned Tristan's exile they rejoiced at the queen's return.

And to the noise of bells, and over pavements strewn with branches, the king and his counts and princes were her escort, and the gates of the palace were thrown open that rich and poor might enter and eat and drink at will.

And Mark freed a hundred of his slaves, and armed a score of squires that day with hauberk and with sword.

But Tristan that night hid with Orri, as the queen had counselled him.

THE ORDEAL BY IRON

The three felons, Denoalen, Andred and Gondoïne, believed themselves safe; Tristan was far over the sea, far away in the service of a distant king, and they were beyond his power. Therefore, during a hunt one day, as the king rode on his own in a glade where the pack would pass, and listened to the hounds, they all three rode towards him, and said:

'Oh king, we have something to say. Once you condemned the queen without judgement, and that was wrong; now you acquit her without judgement, and that is wrong. She is not quit by trial, and the barons of your land blame you both. Counsel her, then, to claim the ordeal in God's judgement, for since she is innocent, she may swear on the relics of the saints and hot iron will not hurt her. For so custom runs, and in this easy way are doubts dissolved.'

But Mark answered: 'God strike you, my Cornish lords, how you hunt my shame! For you have I exiled my nephew, and now what do you want? Would you have me drive the queen to Ireland too? What new complaints have you to plead? Did not Tristan offer you battle in this matter? He offered battle to clear the queen for ever: he offered and you heard him all. Where then were your lances and your shields?'

'Sire,' they said, 'we have counselled you loyal counsel as lieges and to your honour; henceforward we hold our peace. Put aside your anger and give us your safe-guard.'

But Mark stood up in the stirrup and cried: 'Out of my land, and out of my peace, all of you! Tristan I exiled for you, and now go you in turn, out of my land!'

But they answered: 'Sire, it is well. Our keeps are strong and fenced, and stand on rocks not easy for men to climb.'

And they rode off without a salutation.

But the king spurred his horse to Tintagel straight away, without waiting for huntsman or for hound; and as he sprang up the stairs the queen heard the jangle of his spurs on the stones.

She rose to meet him and took his sword as she was wont, and bowed before him, as it was also her wont to do; but Mark raised her, holding her hands; and when Iseult looked up she saw his noble face in the same anger she had seen before he condemned her to the fire of thorns.

She thought that Tristan had been found, and her heart grew cold, and without a word she fell at the king's feet.

He took her in his arms and kissed her gently till she could speak again, and then he said: 'Friend, friend, what evil tries you?'

'Sire, I am afraid, for I have seen your anger.'

'Yes, I was angered at the hunt.'

'My lord, should one take so deeply the accidents of a sport?'

Mark smiled and said: 'No, friend; nothing in the hunting vexed me, but those three felons whom you know; and I have exiled them from my land.'

'Sire, what did they say, or dare to say of me?'

'What does it matter? I have exiled them.'

'Sire, I wish to ask a question, but from whom shall I learn the answer unless from you? I am alone in a foreign land, and have no one else to defend me.'

'They would have it that you should quit yourself by solemn oath and by the ordeal of iron, saying that God was a true judge, and that as the queen was innocent, she herself should seek such judgement as would clear her for ever. This was their incessant clamour and demand. But let us leave it. I tell you, I have exiled them.'

Iseult trembled, but looking straight at the king, she said: 'Sire, call them back; I will clear myself by oath. But this is my part of the bargain: that on the appointed day you call King Arthur and Lord Gawain, Girflet, Kay the seneschal, and a hundred of his knights to ride to the Sandy Heath where your land borders on his, and a river flows between; for I will not swear before your barons alone, lest they should demand some new thing, and lest there should be no end to my trials. But if my warrantors, King Arthur and his knights, be there, the barons will not dare dispute the judgement.'

But as the heralds rode to Cardueil, Iseult sent her squire Perinis to Tristan secretly: and he ran through the underwood, avoiding paths, till he found the hut of Orri, the woodman, where Tristan for many days had awaited news. Perinis told him all: the ordeal, the place, and the time, and added: 'My lord, the queen would have you on that day and place come dressed as a pilgrim, so that none may know you, unarmed, so that none may challenge you, to the Sandy Heath. She must cross the river to the place appointed. Beyond it, where Arthur and his hundred knights will stand, be there as well; for my lady fears the judgement, but she trusts in God.'

Then Tristan answered: 'Go back, friend Perinis, return to the queen, and say that I will do her bidding.'

And you must know that as Perinis went back to Tintagel he caught sight of that same woodman who had betrayed the lovers before, and the woodman, as he found him, had just dug a pitfall for wolves and for wild boars, and covered it with leafy branches to hide it, and as Perinis came near the woodman fled, but Perinis drove him, and caught him, and broke his staff and his head together, and pushed his body into the pit with his feet.

On the appointed day King Mark and Iseult, and the barons of Cornwall, stood by the river; and the knights of Arthur and all their host were arrayed beyond.

And just before them, sitting on the shore, was a poor pilgrim, wrapped in cloak and hood, who held his wooden plátter and begged for alms.

Now as the Cornish boats came to the shoal of the further bank, Iseult said to the knights: 'My lords, how shall I land without dirtying my clothes in the river-mud? Fetch me a ferryman.'

And one of the knights hailed the pilgrim, and said: 'Friend, tuck up your coat, and try the water; carry the queen to shore, unless you fear such a burden.'

But as he took the queen in his arms she whispered to him: 'Friend.'

And then she whispered to him, lower still: 'Stumble on the sand.'

And as he touched shore, he stumbled, holding the queen in his arms; and the squires and boatmen with their oars and boat-hooks drove the poor pilgrim away.

But the queen said: 'Let him be; great hardship on his journey has weakened him.'

And she threw to the pilgrim a little clasp of gold.

Before the tent of King Arthur was spread a rich Nicaean cloth upon the grass, and the holy relics were set on it, taken out of their covers and their shrines.

And round the holy relics on the sward stood a guard more than a king's guard, for Lord Gawain, Girflet, and Kay the seneschal kept ward over them.

The queen, having prayed to God, took off the jewels from her neck and hands, and gave them to the beggars around; she took off her purple mantle, and her overdress, and her shoes with their precious stones, and gave them also to the poor that loved her.

She kept upon her only the sleeveless tunic, and then with arms and feet quite bare she came between the two kings, and all around the barons watched her in silence, and some wept, for near the holy relics a brazier was burning.

And, trembling a little, she stretched her right hand towards the relics and said: 'Kings of Logres and of Cornwall; my lords Gawain, and Kay, and Girflet, and all of you that are my warrantors, by these holy things and all the holy things of earth, I swear that no man has held me in his arms saving King Mark, my lord, and that poor pilgrim. King Mark, will that oath stand?'

'Yes, queen,' he said, 'and God see to it.'

'Amen,' said Iseult, and then she went near the brazier, pale and stumbling, and all were silent. The iron was red, but she thrust her bare arms among the coals and seized it, and bearing it took nine steps.

Then as she cast it from her, she stretched her arms out in a cross, with the palms of her hands wide open, and all men saw them fresh and clean and cold. Seeing that great sight the kings and the barons and the people stood for a moment silent; then they stirred and praised God.

THE LITTLE FAIRY BELL

When Tristan had come back to Orri's hut, and had loosened his heavy pilgrim's cape, he saw clearly in his heart that it was time to keep his oath to King Mark and to flee from the land.

But he still delayed for three days, because he could not drag himself away from that earth, but on the fourth day he thanked the woodman, and said to Gorvenal: 'Master, the hour is come.'

And he went into Wales, into the land of the great Duke Gilain, who was young, powerful, and frank in spirit, and welcomed him nobly as a God-sent guest.

And he did everything to give him honour and joy; but he found that neither adventure nor feast could soothe what Tristan suffered.

One day, as he sat by the young duke's side, Tristan's spirit weighed upon him, so that without knowing it he groaned, and the duke, to soothe him, summoned into his private room a fairy thing, which pleased his eyes when he was sad and relieved his heart; it was a dog, and the servants brought it in to him, and they put it upon a table there. Now this dog was a fairy dog, and came from the duke of Avalon; for a fairy had given it him as a love-gift, and no one can well describe its kind or beauty. And it bore at its neck, hung on a little chain of gold, a little bell; and that tinkled so gaily, and so clear and so soft, that as Tristan heard it, he was soothed, and his anguish melted away, and he forgot all that he had suffered for the queen; for such was the virtue of the bell and such its property that whoever heard it was oblivious to pain. And as Tristan stroked the little fairy thing, the dog that took away his sorrow, he saw how delicate it was and fine, and how it had soft hair like samite, and he thought how good a gift it would make for the queen. But he dared not ask for it outright since he knew that the duke loved this dog beyond everything in the world, and would yield it to no prayers, nor to wealth, nor to wile; so one day Tristan having made a plan in his mind said this: 'Lord, what would you give to the man who could rid your land of the hairy giant Urgan, that levies such a toll?'

'Truly, the victor might choose what he would, but none will dare.'

Then Tristan said: 'Those are strange words, for good comes to no land save by risk and daring, and not for all the gold of Milan would I renounce my desire to find him in his wood and bring him down.'

Then Tristan went out to find Urgan in his lair, and they fought hard and long, till courage conquered strength, and Tristan, having cut off the giant's hand, bore it back to the duke.

And 'Sire,' said he, 'since I may choose a reward according to your word, give me the little fairy dog. It was for that I conquered Urgan, and your promise stands.'

'Friend,' said the duke, 'take it, then, but in taking it you take away also all my joy.'

Then Tristan took the little fairy dog and gave it in ward to a Welsh harper, who was cunning and who bore it to Cornwall till he came to Tintagel, and having come there put it secretly into Brangane's hands, and the queen was so pleased that she gave ten marks of gold to the harper, but she put it about that the queen of Ireland, her mother, had sent the beast. And she had a goldsmith work a little kennel for him, all jewelled, and encrusted with gold and enamel inlaid; and wherever she went she carried the dog with her in memory of her friend, and as she watched it sadness and anguish and regrets melted out of her heart.

At first she did not guess the marvel, but thought her consolation was because the gift was Tristan's, till one day she found that it was a fairy thing, and that it was the little bell that charmed her soul. Then she thought: 'What have I to do with comfort since he is sorrowing? He could have kept it too and have forgotten his sorrow; but with high courtesy he sent it to me to give me his joy and to take up his pain again. Friend, while you suffer, so long will I suffer also.'

And she took the magic bell and shook it just a little, and then by the open window she threw it into the sea.

ISEULT OF THE WHITE HANDS

Apart, the lovers could neither live nor die, for it was life and death together; and Tristan fled his sorrow through seas and islands and many lands.

He fled his sorrow still until at last he came back to his land of Lyonesse, and there, Rohalt, loyal as always, welcomed him with happy tears and called him son. But he could not live in the peace of his own land, and he turned again and rode through kingdoms and through counties, seeking adventure, from Lyonesse to the Lowlands, from the Lowlands on to the Germanies; through the Germanies and into Spain. And many lords he served, and many deeds did, but for two years no news came to him out of Cornwall, neither friend nor messenger. Then he thought that Iseult had forgotten.

Now it happened one day that, riding with Gorvenal alone, he came into the land of Brittany. They rode through a wasted plain of ruined walls and empty hamlets and burnt fields everywhere, and the earth deserted of men; and Tristan thought: 'I am weary, and my deeds profit me nothing; my lady is far off and I shall never see her again. Or why for two years has she made no sign, or why has sent no messenger to find me as I wandered? But in Tintagel Mark honours her and she gives him joy, and that little fairy bell has done its work all too well; for little she remembers or cares for the joys and the mourning of old, little for me, as I wander in this desert place. I, too, will forget.'

On the third day, at the hour of noon, Tristan and Gorvenal came near a hill where an old chantry stood, and close by it a hermitage; and Tristan asked what wasted land that was, and the hermit answered: 'Lord, it is Breton land which Duke Hoel holds, and once it was rich in pasture and ploughland, but Duke Riol of Nantes has wasted it. For you must know that this Duke Riol was the duke's vassal. And the duke has a daughter, fair among all kings' daughters, and Duke Riol would have taken her to wife; but her father refused to let one of his vassals wed her, and Duke Riol tried to carry her away by force. Many men have died in that quarrel.'

And Tristan asked: 'Can the duke hold his own in war?'

And the hermit answered: 'Hardly, my lord; yet his last keep of Carhaix holds out still against Riol, for the walls are stout, as stout as the heart of the duke's son Kaherdin, a very good knight and bold; but the enemy surrounds them on every side and starves them. They are scarcely able to hold their castle.'

Then Tristan asked: 'How far is this keep of Carhaix?'

'Sir,' said the hermit, 'it is but two miles further on this way.'

Then Tristan and Gorvenal lay down, for it was evening.

In the morning, when they had slept, and when the hermit had chanted, and had shared his black bread with them, Tristan thanked him and rode hard to Carhaix. And as he halted beneath the high walls, he saw a little company of men behind the battlements, and he asked if the duke were there with his son Kaherdin. Now Hoel was among then; and when he cried 'Yes,' Tristan called up to him and said: 'I am Tristan, king of Lyonesse, and Mark of Cornwall is my uncle. I have heard that your vassals do you a wrong, and I have come to offer you my arms.'

'Alas, Lord Tristan, go on your way alone and God reward you, for in here we have no more food; no wheat, or meat, or any stores but only lentils and a little oats remaining.'

But Tristan said: 'For two years I dwelt in a forest, eating nothing save roots and herbs; yet I found it a good life, so open the gate.'

They welcomed him with honour, and Kaherdin showed him the wall and the dungeon keep with all their devices, and from the battlements he showed the plain where far away gleamed the tents of Duke Riol. And when they were down in the castle again he said to Tristan: 'Friend, let us go to the hall where my mother and sister sit.'

So, holding each other's hands, they came into the women's room, where the mother and the daughter sat together weaving gold upon English cloth and singing a weaving song. They sang of Doette the Fair who sits alone beneath the whitethorn, and round her blows the wind. She waits for Doon, her friend, but he tarries long and does not come. This was the song they sang. And Tristan bowed to them, and they to him.

Then Kaherdin, showing the work his mother did, said: 'See, friend Tristan, what a workwoman is here, and how marvellously she adorns stoles and chasubles for the poor minsters, and how my sister's hands run thread of gold upon this cloth. Sister, you are rightly called "Iseult of the White Hands".'

But Tristan, hearing her name, smiled and looked at her more kindly.

And on the morrow, Tristan, Kaherdin, and twelve young knights left the castle and rode to a pinewood near the enemy's tents, where they laid an ambush and captured a waggon of Duke Riol's food; and from that day, by escapade and ruse they attacked tents and convoys and killed men, and they always came back with some booty; so that Tristan and Kaherdin began to be brothers in arms, and kept faith and tenderness, as history tells. And as they came back from these rides, talking chivalry together, Kaherdin praised his sister, Iseult of the White Hands, for her simplicity and beauty.

One day, as the dawn broke, a sentinel ran from the tower through the halls crying: 'Lords, you have slept too long; rise, for an assault is on.'

And knights and townsmen armed, and ran to the walls, and saw helmets shining on the plain, and pennons streaming crimson, like flames, and all the host of Riol arrayed for battle. Then the duke and Kaherdin deployed their horsemen before the gates, and from a bow-length off they stooped, and spurred and charged, and they put their lances down together and the arrows fell on them like April rain.

Now Tristan had armed himself among the last of those the sentinel had roused, and he laced his shoes of steel, and put on his mail, and his spurs of gold, his hauberk, and his helm over the gorget, and he mounted and spurred forward with his shield before him, crying: 'Carhaix!'

And as he came, he saw Duke Riol charging, his reins free, at Kaherdin, but Tristan came in between. So Tristan and Duke Riol met. And at the shock, Tristan's lance shivered, but Riol's lance struck Tristan's horse on its breastbone, and brought it to the ground. But Tristan, standing, drew his sword, his burnished sword, and said: 'Coward! Here is death ready for the man that strikes the horse before the rider.'

But Riol answered: 'I think you have lied, my lord!'

And he charged him.

And as he passed, Tristan let fall his sword so heavily upon his helm that he carried away the crest and the nasal, but the sword slipped on the mailed shoulder, and glanced on the horse, and killed it, so that of force Duke Riol must slip the stirrup and leap and feel the ground. Then Riol too was on his feet, and they both fought hard in their broken mail, their escutcheons torn and their helmets loosened and lashing with their dented swords, till Tristan struck Riol just where the helmet buckles, and it yielded and the blow struck so hard that the baron fell on hands and knees; but when he had risen again, Tristan struck him down once more with a blow that split the helm, and it split the headpiece too, and touched the skull; then Riol cried mercy and begged his life, and Tristan took his sword.

So he promised to enter Duke Hoel's keep and to swear homage again, and to restore what he had wasted; and by his order the battle ceased, and his host went off discomfited.

Now when the victors were returned Kaherdin said to his father: 'Sire, keep Tristan with you. There is no better knight, and your land has need of such courage.'

So when the duke had taken counsel with his barons, he said to Tristan: 'Friend, I owe you my land, but I shall be quit with you if you will take my daughter, Iseult of the White Hands, who comes of kings and of queens, and of dukes before them in blood.'

And Tristan answered: 'I will take her, sire.'

So the day was fixed, and the duke came with his friends and Tristan with his, and before all, at the gate of the minster, Tristan wed Iseult of the White Hands according to the Church's law.

But that same night, as Tristan's attendants undressed him, it happened that in drawing his arm from the sleeve they drew off and let fall from his finger the ring of green jasper, the ring of Iseult the Fair. It rang on the stones, and Tristan looked and saw it. Then his heart awoke and he knew that he had done wrong. For he remembered the day when Iseult the Fair had given him the ring. It was in that forest where, for his sake, she had led the hard life with him, and that night he saw again the hut in the wood of Morois, and he was bitter with himself that ever he had accused her of treason; for now it was he who had betrayed her, and he was bitter with himself also, pitying his new wife and her simplicity and beauty. See how these two Iseults had met him in an evil hour, and he had broken faith with both!

Now Iseult of the White Hands said to him, hearing him sigh: 'Dear lord, have I hurt you in anything? Will you not speak a single word to me?'

But Tristan answered: 'Friend, do not be angry with me; for once in another land I fought a foul dragon and was near to death, and I thought of the Mother of God, and I made a vow to Her that, should I ever wed, I would spend the first holy nights of my wedding in prayer and in silence.'

'Why,' said Iseult, 'that was a good vow.'

And Tristan watched through the night.

THE MADNESS OF TRISTAN

In her room at Tintagel, Iseult the Fair sighed for the sake of Tristan, and named him, her desire, of whom for two years she had had no word, whether he lived or not.

Within her room at Tintagel she sat singing a song she had made. She sang of Guron taken and killed for his love, and how by guile the count gave Guron's heart to her to eat, and of her woe. The queen sang softly, catching the harp's tone; her hands were cunning and her song good; she sang low down and softly.

Then Kariado, a rich count from a far-off island, entered; he had travelled to Tintagel to offer the queen his service, and had spoken of love to her, though she disdained his folly. He found Iseult as she sang, and laughed to her: 'Lady, how sad a song! As sad as the osprey's; they say he sings for death, and your song means that to me: I die for you.'

And Iseult said: 'So let it be and may it mean so; for you never come here but to stir in me anger or mourning. You were always the screech owl or the osprey that boded ill when you spoke of Tristan; what news do you bear now?'

And Kariado answered:

'You are angry, I do not know not why, but who listens to you? Let the osprey be harbinger of my death; here is the evil news the screech owl brings. Lady Iseult, Tristan, your friend, is lost to you. He has wed in a far land. Look elsewhere, for he mocks your love. He has wed in great pomp Iseult of the White Hands, the king of Brittany's daughter.'

And Kariado went off in anger, but Iseult bowed her head and broke into tears.

Now far from Iseult, Tristan languished, till one day he had to see her again. Far from her, he would surely die; and he had rather die at once than day by day. And he desired some death, but if the queen might know that he had died seeking her, then death would come easily.

So he left Carhaix secretly, telling no man, neither his kindred nor even Kaherdin, his brother in arms. He went in rags and on foot (for no one notices the beggar on the high road) till he came to the sea shore.

In the harbour, he found a great ship ready; the sail was up and the anchor-chain short at the bow.

'God save you, my lords,' he said, 'and send you a good journey. To what land sail you now?'

'To Tintagel!' they said.

Then he cried out: 'Oh, my lords! take me with you!'

And he went aboard, and a fair wind filled the sail, and she ran five days and nights for Cornwall, till, on the sixth day, they dropped anchor in Tintagel Haven. The castle stood above, well defended. There was but the one armed gate, and two knights watched it night and day. So Tristan went ashore and sat upon the beach, and a man told him that Mark was there and had just held his court.

'But where,' said he, 'is Iseult, the queen, and her fair maid, Brangane?'

'In Tintagel too,' said the other, 'and I saw them lately; the queen sad, as she always is.'

At the hearing of the name, Tristan suffered, and he thought that neither by guile nor courage could he see his friend, for Mark would kill him.

And he thought, 'Let him kill me and let me die for her, since every day I die a little. But you, Iseult, even if you knew that I was here, would you not drive me out?'

And he thought, 'I will try guile. I will seem mad, but with a madness that shall be great wisdom. And many shall think me a fool that have less wit than I!'

Just then a fisherman passed in a rough cloak and cape, and Tristan, seeing him, took him aside and said: 'Friend, will you not change clothes?'

And as the fisherman found it a very good bargain, he answered: 'Yes, friend, gladly.'

And he changed and ran off at once for fear of losing his gain. Then Tristan shaved his wonderful hair; he shaved it close to his head and left a cross all bald, and he rubbed his face with magic herbs distilled in his own country, and it changed in colour and skin so that none could know him, and he made him a club from a young tree torn from a hedgerow and hung it round his neck, and went barefoot towards the castle.

The porter was sure that he had to do with a fool and said: 'Good morrow. fool, where have you been this long while?'

And he answered: 'At the Abbot of Saint Michael's wedding, and he wed an abbess, large and veiled. And from the Alps to Mount Saint Michael they came, the priests and abbots, monks and canons, all dancing on the green with croziers and with staves under the high trees' shade. But I left them all to come hither, for I serve at the king's board today.'

Then the porter said: 'Come in, Lord Fool; you are the Hairy Urgan's son, I know, and like your father.'

And when he was within the courts the serving men ran after him and cried: 'The fool! the fool!'

But he made play with them, though they cast stones and struck him as they laughed, and in the midst of laughter and their cries, as the rout followed him, he came to the hall where, at the queen's side, King Mark sat under his canopy.

And as he neared the door with his club at his neck, the king said: 'Here is a merry fellow, let him in.'

And they brought him in, his club at his neck. And the king said: 'Friend, welcome; what seek you here?'

'Iseult,' said he, 'whom I love so well; I bring my sister with me, Brunehild, the beautiful. Come, take her, you are weary of the queen. Take my sister and give Iseult to me, and I will hold her and serve you for her love.'

The king said laughing:

'Fool, if I gave you the queen, where would you take her, pray?'

'Oh! very high,' he said, 'between the clouds and heaven, into a fair chamber all of glass. The beams of the sun shine through it, yet the winds do not trouble it at all. There would I bear the queen into that crystal chamber of mine, created of roses and the morning.'

The king and his barons laughed and said: 'Here is a good fool at no loss for words.'

But the fool as he sat at their feet gazed fixedly at Iseult.

'Friend,' said King Mark, 'what reason have you to think that the queen would heed so foul a fool as you?'

'Oh! sire,' he answered gravely, 'many deeds have I done for her, and my madness is from her alone.'

'What is your name?' they said, and laughed.

'Tristan,' said he, 'that loved the queen so well, and still till death will love her.'

But at the name the queen grew angry and faint at once, and said: 'Get out of here, you evil fool!'

But the fool, marking her anger, went on: 'Queen Iseult, do you remember the day, when, poisoned by the Morholt's spear, I took my harp to sea and landed by chance on your shore? Your mother healed me with strange drugs. Have you no memory, queen?'

But Iseult answered: 'Out, fool, out! Your folly and you have passed the bounds of a fool's licence!'

But the fool, still playing, pushed the barons out, crying: 'Out! madmen, out! Leave me to talk with Iseult, since I come here for the love of her!'

And as the king laughed, Iseult blushed and said: 'King, drive this fool away from me!'

But the fool still laughed and cried: ' Queen, do you mind you of the dragon I slew in your land? I hid its tongue in my hose, and, burnt by its venom, I fell by the roadside. Ah! what a knight was I then, and it was you that succoured me.'

Iseult replied: 'Silence! You wrong all knighthood by your words, for you are a fool from birth. Cursed be the seamen that brought you here; they should have cast you into the sea!'

'Queen Iseult,' he went on, 'do you mind you of your haste when you would have slain me with my own sword? And of the hair of gold? And of how I stood up to the seneschal?'

'Silence!' she said, 'you drunkard! You were drunk last night, and so you dreamt these dreams.'

'Drunk indeed, and so I am still,' said he, 'but of such a drink that its effect will never fade. Queen Iseult, do you remember that hot and open day on the high seas? We thirsted and we drank together from the same cup, and since that day I have been drunk with a fearful wine.'

When the queen heard these words which she alone could understand, she rose and wished to go.

But the king held her by her ermine cloak, and she sat down again.

And as the king had his fill of the fool he called for his falcons and went to hunt; and Iseult said to him: 'Sire, I am weak and sad; let me go rest in my room; I am tired of these follies.'

And she went to her room in thought and sat upon her bed and mourned, calling herself a slave and saying: 'Why was I born? Brangane, dear sister, life is so hard to me that death were better! There is a fool outside, shaved criss-cross; he has come in an evil hour, and he is a wizard, for he knows every part of me and my whole life; he knows what you and I and Tristan only know.'

Then Brangane said: 'It may be Tristan.'

But 'No,' said the queen, 'for he was the first of knights, but this fool is foul and crooked. A curse on the day and the ship that brought him here!'

'My lady!' said Brangane, 'calm yourself. You curse too much these days. Perhaps he comes from Tristan?'

'I cannot tell. I do not know him. But go and find him, friend, and see if you know him.'

So Brangane went to the hall where the fool still sat alone. Tristan recognised her and dropped his club and said: 'Brangane, dear Brangane, before God! have pity on me!'

'Foul fool,' she answered, 'what devil taught you my name?'

'Lady,' he said, 'I have known it long. By my head, that once was fair, if I am mad the blame is yours, for it was your task to watch over the wine we drank on the high seas. The cup was of silver and I held it to Iseult and she drank. Do you remember, lady?'

'No,' she said, and as she trembled and left, he called out: 'Pity me!'

He followed and saw Iseult. He stretched out his arms, but in her shame and sweating agony she drew back, and Tristan was angry and said: 'I have lived too long, for I have seen the day that Iseult wants nothing to do with me. Iseult, how hard love dies! Iseult, a river in full spate is a mighty thing; on the day that it dries up it is nothing; love that changes is like that river.'

But she said: 'Brother, I look at you and doubt and tremble; I do not recognise Tristan.'

' Queen Iseult, I am Tristan indeed who loves you; remember for the last time the dwarf, and the flour, and the blood I shed in my leap. Remember last of all that ring I took in kisses and in tears on the day we parted. I have kept that jasper ring and it has comforted me.'

Then Iseult knew Tristan for what he was, and she said: 'Heart, you should have broken of sorrow not to have known the man who has suffered so much for you. Pardon, my master and my friend.'

And her eyes darkened and she fell; but when the light returned she was held by him who kissed her eyes and her face.

So three full days passed. But, on the third, two maids that watched them told the traitor Andred, and he put spies well-armed before the women's rooms. And when Tristan would enter they cried: 'Back, fool!'

But he brandished his club laughing, and said: 'What! May I not kiss the queen who loves me and awaits me now?' And they feared him for a mad fool, and he passed in through the door.

Then, being with the queen for the last time, he held her in his arms and said: 'Friend, I must flee, for they are wondering. I must flee, and perhaps shall never see you again. My death is near, and far from you my death will come of desire.'

'Oh friend,' she said, 'fold your arms round me close and embrace me so hard that our hearts may break and our souls go free at last. Take me to that happy place of which you told me long ago, the fields from which none return, but where great singers sing their songs for ever. Take me now.'

'I will take you to the happy palace of the living, queen! The time is near. We have drunk all joy and sorrow. The time is near. When it is finished, if I call you, will you come, my friend?'

'Friend,' said she, 'call me and you know that I shall come.'

'Friend,' said he, 'God send you His reward.'

As he went out the spies would have held him; but he laughed aloud, and flourished his club, and cried: 'Peace, gentlemen, I go and will not stay. My lady sends me to prepare that shining house I promised her, of crystal and of rose, shot through with morning.'

And as they cursed and drove him off, the fool went leaping on his way.

THE DEATH OF TRISTAN

When he came back to Brittany, to Carhaix, it so happened that Tristan, riding to the aid of Kaherdin his brother in arms, fell into an ambush and was wounded by a poisoned spear; and many doctors came, but none could cure him of the ill. And Tristan weakened and paled, and his bones showed.

Then he knew that his life was ebbing, and that he must die, and he had a desire to see once more Iseult the Fair, but he could not seek her, for the sea would have killed him in his weakness, and how could Iseult come to him? In sorrow and suffering, he awaited death.

He called Kaherdin secretly to tell him his pain, for they loved each other loyally; and as he would have no one in the room save Kaherdin, nor even in the neighbouring rooms, Iseult of the White Hands began to wonder. She was afraid and wished to hear, and she came back and listened at the wall by Tristan's bed; and as she listened one of her maids kept watch for her.

In his room, Tristan had gathered up his strength, and had half risen, leaning against the wall, and Kaherdin wept beside him. They wept for their good comradeship, broken so soon, and their friendship: then Tristan told Kaherdin of his love for that other Iseult, and of the sorrow of his life.

'Fair friend,' said Tristan, 'I am in a foreign land where I have neither friend nor cousin, save you; and you alone in this place have given me comfort. My life is ebbing, and I wish to see once more Iseult the Fair. Ah, if only I knew of a messenger who would go to her! For now I know that she will come to me. Kaherdin, my brother in arms, I beg it of your friendship; try this thing for me, and if you carry my word, I will become your liege, and I will cherish you beyond all other men.'

And as Kaherdin saw Tristan broken down, his heart reproached him and he said: 'Fair comrade, do not weep; I will do what you desire, even at the risk of death I would do it for you. Neither distress nor anguish will prevent me from doing it as best I can. Give me your message, and I will get ready.'

And Tristan answered: 'Thank you, friend; this is my request: take this ring, which is a sign between her and me; and when you come to her land disguise yourself at court as a merchant, and show her silk and stuffs, but make sure that she sees the ring, for then she will find some ruse by which to speak to you in secret. Then tell her that my heart salutes her; tell her that she alone can bring me comfort; tell her that if she does not come I shall die. Tell her to remember our past time, and our great sorrows, and all the joy there was in our loyal and tender love. And tell her to remember that draught we drank together on the high seas. For we drank our death together. Tell her to remember the oath I swore to serve a single love, for I have kept that oath.'

But behind the wall, Iseult of the White Hands heard all these things; and Tristan continued: 'Hasten, my friend, and come back quickly, or you will not see me again. I will expect you in forty days, but come back with Iseult the Fair. And tell your sister nothing, or tell her that you seek another doctor. Take my fine ship, and two sails with you, one white, one black. And as you return, if you bring Iseult, hoist the white sail; but if she is not with you, the black. Now I have nothing more to say, but God guide you and bring you back safe.'

With the first fair wind Kaherdin headed for the open sea, weighed anchor and hoisted sail; the ship ran before a gentle breeze, the seas curling from its bow. They took rich merchandise with them, dyed silks of rare colours, enamel of Touraine and wines of Poitou, for by this ruse Kaherdin planned to reach Iseult. Eight days and nights they ran full sail to Cornwall.

Now a woman's wrath is a fearful thing, and all men fear it, for according to her love, so will her vengeance be; and their love and their hate come quickly, but their hate lives longer than their love; and they will make play with love, but not with hate. So Iseult of the White Hands, who had heard every word, and who had so loved Tristan, waited for her vengeance on the man she loved most in the world. But she hid it all; and when the doors were open again she came to Tristan's bed and served him with food as a lover should, and spoke to him gently and kissed him on the lips, and asked him if Kaherdin would soon return with one to cure him . . but all day long she thought upon her vengeance.

And Kaherdin sailed and sailed till he dropped anchor in the harbour of Tintagel. He landed and took with him a cloth of rare dye and a cup well chiselled and worked and made a present of them to King Mark, and courteously begged of him his peace and safeguard that he might trade in his land; and the king gave him his peace before all the men of his palace.

Then Kaherdin offered the queen a buckle of fine gold; and 'Queen,' said he, 'the gold is good.'

Then taking from his finger Tristan's ring, he put it side by side with the jewel and said: 'See, O queen, the gold of the buckle is the finer gold; yet that ring also has its worth.'

When Iseult saw what ring that was, her heart trembled and her colour changed, and, fearing what might next be said, she drew Kaherdin apart near a window, as if to see and bargain the better; and Kaherdin said to her under his voice: 'Lady, Tristan has been wounded by a poisoned spear and is about to die. He sends you word that you alone can bring him comfort, and reminds you of the great sorrows that you bore together. Keep the ring – it is yours.'

But Iseult answered, weakening:

'Friend, I will follow you; get ready your ship tomorrow at dawn.'

And on the morrow at dawn they raised anchor, stepped mast, and hoisted sail, and the ship left land joyfully.

But at Carhaix Tristan lay and longed for Iseult's coming. Nothing now held him any more, and if he lived it was only because he awaited her coming; and day by day he sent watchers to the shore to see if some ship came, and to learn the colour of her sail. There was nothing left in his heart save this one desire.

He had himself carried to the cliff of the Penmarks, where it overlooks the sea, and all the daylight long he gazed far off over the water.

But, all you who love, hear the sorrow of this story! Iseult was already near; already the cliff of the Penmarks showed far away, and the ship ran swiftly, when a storm arose suddenly and struck the sail, and forced the ship round, and the sailors bore away and greatly against their will they ran before the wind. The wind raged and huge seas ran; the air grew thick with darkness until the ocean itself turned dark, and the rain drove in gusts. The yard snapped, and the sheet; they struck their sail, and ran with wind and water. In an evil hour they had forgotten to haul their pinnace aboard; it leapt in their wake, and a great sea broke it away.

Then Iseult cried out: 'God does not will that I should live to see him, my love, not even one time more. God wills that I shall drown in this sea. Oh Tristan, had I spoken to you but once again, it is little I should have cared for death coming afterwards. But now, my love, I cannot come to you; for God so wills it, and that is the core of my grief.'

And thus the queen mourned while the storm endured; but after five days it died down. Kaherdin joyfully hoisted the sail, the white sail, right up to the top of the mast; the white sail, that Tristan might know its colour from afar: and already Kaherdin saw Brittany far off like a cloud. But scarcely had he done so when a calm came, and the sea lay even and untroubled. The sail hung slack, and the sailors steered the ship now up, now down, the tide, beating backwards and forwards in vain. They saw the shore afar off, but the storm had carried their boat away and they could not land. On the third night Iseult dreamt this dream: that she held in her lap a boar's head which streaked her skirts with blood; then she knew that she would never see her lover again alive.

Tristan was now too weak to keep his watch from the cliff of the Penmarks, and for many long days, confined within walls, far from the shore, he had mourned for Iseult because she did not come. Sorrowing and alone, he mourned and sighed restlessly: he was near death from desire.

At last the wind freshened and the white sail showed. Then it was that Iseult of the White Hands took her vengeance.

She came to where Tristan lay, and she said: 'Friend, Kaherdin is here. I have seen his ship upon the sea. She is scarcely in sight – yet I recognise her; may he bring whatever will heal you, friend.'

And Tristan trembled and said: 'Beautiful friend, you are sure that the ship is his indeed? Then tell me what is the manner of the sail?'

'I saw it plain and well. They have shaken it out and hoisted it very high, for they have little wind. As to its colour, why, it is black.'

And Tristan turned his face to the wall, and said: 'I cannot keep this life of mine any longer.' He said three times: 'Iseult, my friend.'

And in saying it the fourth time, he died.

Then throughout the house the knights and the comrades of Tristan wept aloud, and they took him from his bed and laid him on a rich cloth, and they covered his body with a shroud. But at sea the wind had risen; it filled the sail fair and full and drove the ship to shore, and Iseult the Fair set foot upon the land. She heard loud mourning in the streets, and the tolling of bells in the minsters and the chapel towers; she asked the people the meaning of the knell and of their tears. An old man said to her: 'Lady, we suffer a great grief. Tristan, who was so loyal and so true, is dead. He was open to the poor; he ministered to the suffering. It is the greatest evil that has ever fallen on this land.'

But Iseult, hearing them, could not answer them a word. She went up to the palace, following the way, and her cloak was random and wild. The Bretons marvelled as she went; nor had they ever seen a woman of such beauty, and they said: 'Who is she, and where is she from?'

Near Tristan, Iseult of the White Hands crouched, maddened at the evil she had done, and calling and lamenting over the dead man. The other Iseult came in and said to her: 'Lady, rise and let me come by him; I have more right to mourn him than you have, believe me. I loved him more.'

And when she had turned to the east and prayed to God, she moved the body a little and lay down by the dead man, beside her friend. She kissed his mouth and his face, and clasped him closely to her, and so gave up her soul, and died beside him of grief for her lover.

When King Mark heard of the death of these lovers, he crossed the sea and came to Brittany; and he had two coffins hewn, for Tristan and Iseult, one of chalcedony for Iseult, and one of beryl for Tristan. And he took their beloved bodies away with him upon his ship to Tintagel, and near a chantry, to the left and right of the apse, he had their tombs built round. But in one night there sprang from the tomb of Tristan a green and leafy briar, strong in its branches and in the scent of its flowers. It climbed the chantry and fell to root again by Iseult's tomb. Three times the peasants cut it down, but three times it grew again, as full of flowers and as strong. They told the marvel to King Mark, and he forbade them to cut down the briar again.

TRISTAN THE COURTIER

LORDS, YOU HAVE HEARD the tale of Tristan as they tell it in Brittany, where men say that was a knight of Cornwall and Brittany only, and never journeyed to Arthur's court. But other men, the men of Logres, have tales of the great exploits of Tristan in their country and of his encounters and friendships with the foremost knight of the Round Table, of which he was a member; and they say that the tale of the men of Brittany is not proven and certain. They say that Tristan was indeed born in sorrow, as the Breton tale says; and that it was at the court of his uncle, King Mark, that he was brought up. And they agree that he killed the Morholt, and so freed Cornwall from its fearful tributes of young men and girls. Of the poison on the Morholt's sword they also tell, and how Tristan became Tantris and sailed, without oar or rudder into Ireland, to seek healing at the hands of those who hated him. And they say that these were his adventures after he came to Ireland.

HOW SIR TRISTAN AND ISEULT THE FAIR FELL GREATLY IN LOVE

And so it happened that Tristan landed in Ireland near the castle where Anguish, king of Ireland, was, with his queen; and he took his harp, despite his sickness, and played such a song as they had never heard in Ireland before. And the king sent for him, and asked his name; and he said that it was Tantris, and that he had been wounded fighting for the sake of his lady. And because of his marvellous playing on the harp, the king as a great favour had Tantris put in his daughter's care, because she was expert in surgery. And when she had examined him, she found that there was poison in the bottom of his wound, and so she healed him in a little while. And for this Tantris fell greatly in love with Iseult the Fair, for she was at that time the most beautiful woman in the world. And Tantris taught her to play the harp, and she began to have a great liking for him. And at that time Sir Palamides, the Saracen, was in that country, and much favoured by the king and the queen. And every day Sir Palamides came to Iseult the Fair and offered her many gifts, for he loved her exceedingly well. Tantris observed all this, and knew that Sir Palamides was a noble knight and a mighty man. And Sir Tantris was very jealous of Sir Palamides, for Iseult the Fair told Tantris that Palamides was minded to be christened for her sake. So there was great envy between Tantris and Sir Palamides.

Soon after this, King Anguish proclaimed a great joust and a great tournament for a lady that was called the Lady of the Launds, his cousin. And whoever won the tournament was to wed her three days later, and have all her lands. This proclamation was made in England, Wales, Scotland, and also in France and in Brittany. One day Iseult the Fair came to Sir Tantris and told him of this tournament. He answered: 'Fair lady, I am but a feeble knight, and only lately I would have died without your care. Now, fair lady, what do you want me to do in this matter? You know well, my lady, that I should not joust.'

'Ah, Tantris,' said Iseult the Fair, 'why will you not take part in that tournament? I know for certain that Sir Palamides will be there, and will do what he may; and therefore Tantris, I beg you to be there, for otherwise Sir Palamides is likely to win the honours.'

'Madam,' said Tantris, 'that may well be the case, for he is a proved knight, and I am only a young knight and newly made; and in my first battle I had the misfortune to be badly wounded, as you see. But if you would look more kindly on me as my lady, I will be at that tournament. But you will keep my secret and let no one know that I shall joust except for those whom you trust to keep your secrets; and I will hazard my poor person there for your sake, that perhaps Sir Palamides will know when I come into the lists.'

'Then,' said Iseult the Fair, 'do your best, and I will provide horse and armour for you.'

'Let it be as you wish,' said Sir Tantris, 'I will be at your command.'

So at the day of jousts there came Sir Palamides with a black shield, and he overthrew many knights, and all the people marvelled at him. For he put to the worse Sir Gawain, Gaheris, Agravain, Bagdemagus, Kay, Dodinas le Savage, Sagramore le Desirous, Guivret le Petit, and Girflet le Fise de Dieu; all these Sir Palamides struck down to the ground on the first day. And then all kinds of knights were in fear of Sir Palamides, and many called him the Knight with the Black Shield. So that day Sir Palamides won great honour.

Then King Anguish came to Tantris, and asked him why he would not joust.

'Sir,' he said, 'I was hurt only lately, and as yet I dare not risk myself.'

Then a squire from France came up and recognised Sir Tristan: when he caught sight of Sir Tristan he bowed deeply to him. Iseult the Fair saw the courtesy with which the squire addressed Sir Tristan; but Sir Tristan ran quickly to him and begged him heartily on no account to tell his name.

'Sir,' said the squire, ' I will not reveal your name unless you command me.'

Then Sir Tristan asked him what he was doing in that country.

'Sir,' he said, 'I came here with Sir Gawain to be made a knight, and if it please you, I wish to be knighted by you.'

'Come to me tomorrow secretly, and I shall make you a knight on the tournament field.'

Then Iseult the Fair suspected greatly that Tantris was some famous knight proven in battle, which reassured her; and she was more in love with him than ever before. And so in the morning Sir Palamides made ready to come into the field as he did the first day. And there he struck down the king with the Hundred Knights, and the king of Scots. Meanwhile Iseult the Fair ordained and arrayed Sir Tristan in white harness and mounted him on a white horse. And she had him put him out at a secret side gate, and so he came into the field like a bright angel. Shortly Sir Palamides caught sight of him, and aimed his spear at Sir Tantris, who did likewise. And Sir Tristan struck down Sir Palamides to the ground. And then there was a great noise from the crowd: some said Sir Palamides had a fall, some said the Knight with the Black Shield had a fall. And Iseult the Fair was very glad. And then Sir Gawain and his nine companions wondered what knight it might be that had struck down Sir Palamides. So no one would joust with Tantris, but they all avoided him, both great and small.

And when Sir Palamides had received this fall, he was very much ashamed, and as secretly as he could he withdrew from the field. Sir Tristan caught sight of him as he went, and rode after Sir Palamides and overtook him; he ordered him to turn, for he wanted to try his strength against him before he departed. Then Sir Palamides turned against him, and they lashed at each other with their swords. But at the first stroke Sir Tristan struck Palamides, and gave him such a blow upon the head that he fell to the ground. So then Tristan told him to yield, and do as he commanded, or else he would slay him. When Sir Palamides saw his face, he was in such dread of his blows that he granted all that he asked.

'Well said,' said Sir Tristan, 'this is what you are to do. First, on pain of your life leave my lady Iseult the Fair alone, and in no way approach her. Secondly, for a year and a day you will not wear armour or harness of war. Now promise me this, or here shall you die.'

'Alas,' said Palamides, 'I am shamed for ever.'

Then he swore as Sir Tristan had commanded him; in despair and anger Sir Palamides cut off his armour and threw it away.

So Sir Tristan returned to the castle where Iseult the Fair was; and by the way he met a lady who sought Sir Lancelot, and she asked Sir Tristan who he was. For she had been told that it was he who had struck down Sir Palamides, by whom ten knights of King Arthur's were struck down. Then the lady begged Sir Tristan to tell her who he was, and whether or not he was Sir Lancelot du Lac, for she thought that there was no other knight in the world who could do such deeds of arms except for Lancelot.

'Fair lady,' said Sir Tristan, 'I assure you that I am not Sir Lancelot, for my prowess was never as great as his; may God make me as good a knight as the good knight Sir Lancelot!'

'Now, gentle knight,' said she, 'put up your visor'; and when she saw his face she thought she had never seen better, nor a knight who bore himself as well as him. When the lady knew for certain that he was not Sir Lancelot, she took her leave, and departed from him. And then Sir Tristan rode in secret to the side gate where Iseult the Fair was waiting to welcome him, and she thanked God that he had done so well. And soon the king and the queen learnt that it was Tantris who had struck down Sir Palamides; and he was made much of, more than ever before.

And the book says that the queen of Ireland knew Tantris by his sword, for it was broken, and the piece that was lacking was the piece that the queen had taken from the Morholt's wound. So she was certain he was Tristan, and told Iseult, not knowing that her daughter loved him. When Iseult learnt of this, she was in utter despair, for she knew that her mother was cruel and harsh, and would not forgive him; and she loved him deeply. The queen told her husband King Anguish that she knew who the stranger was, and that he was the knight who had killed her brother the Morholt; and the king challenged Tristan, saying that he was astonished that he should show his face in Ireland. But Tristan answered the king boldly and owned to his name, saying that he had done no more than his duty to his lord as a knight of Cornwall. And the king gave him justice in what he said but banished him from Ireland for his own safety, for others might take vengeance on him. And Tristan went to take his leave of Iseult.

'O gentle knight,' said Iseult the Fair, 'I am full of woe at your departing, for I never saw a man whom I held in such goodwill.'

And at this she wept with all her heart.

'Lady,' said Sir Tristan, 'I must tell you that my name is Sir Tristan of Lyonesse. And I promise you faithfully that I shall be your knight all the days of my life.'

'I thank you for that,' said Iseult the Fair, 'and I promise you in return that I shall not be married within seven years except with your assent; and whoever you wish me to marry I will take as my husband.'

And then Sir Tristan gave her a ring, and she gave him another; and he left her making great sorrow and lamentation; and he went to the court among all the barons, and took his leave from both great and small, saying openly: 'Fair lords, I have to depart now: if there is any man here that I have offended, or if any man has a grievance against me, let him make his complaint before I go, and I shall amend it as best I can. And if there are any who will accuse me of wrongdoing, say it now or never, and here is my body to make it good, body against body.'

And they all stood still; there was not one that would say one word, even though there were some knights of the queen's blood, and of the Morholt's blood; but they would not meddle with him.

HOW SIR TRISTAN QUARRELLED WITH KING MARK OVER SIR SEGWARIDES' WIFE

So Sir Tristan departed, and went to sea, and with a fair wind he arrived at Tintagel in Cornwall; and when King Mark heard the news that Sir Tristan had arrived, and was healed of his wounds, he was very glad, and so were all the barons.

So Tristan returned to the court of King Mark, and lived in great joy for a long time, until in the end King Mark and Sir Tristan grew jealous of each other and quarrelled, for they both loved one lady, the wife of Sir Segwarides. And this lady loved Sir Tristan exceedingly; he loved her likewise, for she was a very fair lady. Then King Mark understood this and was jealous, for King Mark also loved her exceedingly.

It so happened one day this lady sent a dwarf to Sir Tristan, and ordered him, if he loved her, to be with her the next night.

'Also she orders you not to come unless you are well armed, for her lover is said to be a good knight.'

Sir Tristan answered the dwarf: 'Send my lady greetings, and tell her I will not fail to come within the appointed time.'

And the dwarf departed with this answer. And King Mark saw the dwarf with Sir Tristan with a message from Segwarides' wife; so he sent for the dwarf, and forced him to tell him why he came with a message from Sir Tristan.

'Now,' said King Mark, 'go where you like, but upon pain of death tell no one that you spoke to me.'

And the night when the assignation between Segwarides' wife and Sir Tristan was to take place, King Mark armed himself, and took two knights whom he trusted with him; and he rode before Sir Tristan to lie in wait for him. And as Sir Tristan came riding upon his way with his spear in his hand, King Mark suddenly came hurtling upon him with his two knights, and all three struck him with their spears, and King Mark hurt Sir Tristan severely on the breast. And then Sir Tristan levelled his spear, and struck his uncle, King Mark so hard that he threw him to the ground, and bruised him so badly that he fainted, and it was a long time before he could bestir himself. And then he attacked one knight, and the other, and struck them to the cold ground, so that they lay still. And Sir Tristan rode on, badly wounded, to the lady, and found her waiting for him at a side gate.

And there she welcomed him, and they embraced each other; she had his horse stabled in the best fashion, and then she unarmed him. And so they supped lightly, and went to bed with great joy and pleasure; and in the heat of his passion he forgot the new wound that King Mark had given him. And so Sir Tristan bled on both the upper and lower sheets, and on the pillows. And in a little while a servant warned her that her lord was no more than a bowshot away. So she made Sir Tristan get up, and arm himself, and take his horse, and so depart. By then Segwarides, her lord, had arrived; and when he found her bed disturbed, he looked at it closely by candlelight, and saw that a wounded knight had lain there.

'Ah, false traitress,' he said, 'why have you betrayed me?'

And as he said this, he drew his sword, and said: 'Unless you tell me who has been here, here you shall die.'

'Ah, my lord, mercy,' said the lady, and held up her hands, saying, 'Do not kill me, and I shall tell you who has been here.'

'Tell me the truth, and quickly,' said Segwarides. Terrified, she said: 'Sir Tristan was with me, and on the way, as he came to me, he was badly wounded.'

'Ah, false traitress,' said Segwarides, 'where is he now?'

'Sir,' she said, 'he has armed, and departed on horseback, and is not yet half a mile away.'

Then he armed himself, and got his horse, and rode after Sir Tristan; in a little while he overtook him, and called, 'Turn back, false traitor!' And Sir Tristan turned to face him. Segwarides struck Sir Tristan with a spear which shattered; and then he drew his sword and struck hard at Sir Tristan.

'Knight,' said Sir Tristan, 'do not strike me again, even though I shall not retaliate, because I have wronged you.'

'No,' said Segwarides, 'that shall not be, for either you shall die or I.'

Then Sir Tristan drew his sword, and charged him fiercely, and he struck Sir Segwarides in the waist so that he fell to the ground in a swoon.

Sir Tristan left him there, and rode to Tintagel; he went secretly to his lodging, for he did not want it to be known that he was hurt. Sir Segwarides' men rode after their master, whom they found lying in the field badly wounded, and brought him home on his shield; it was a long time before he recovered. Nor did King Mark want it known that Sir Tristan and he had met that night; but Tristan did not know that King Mark had met him. But as long as King Mark lived he never loved Sir Tristan after that; though there was fair speech, there was no love there. And many weeks and days passed, and all was forgiven and forgotten; for Sir Segwarides did not dare to challenge Sir Tristan, because of his prowess, and also because he was nephew to King Mark; so he let matters be.

One day Bleoberis de Ganis, a good knight and cousin to Sir Lancelot du Lac, came to the court of King Mark, and there he asked of King Mark a boon, to give him whatever gift that he might ask before his court. When the king heard his demand, he was amazed, but because he was a knight of the Round Table, and of great renown, King Mark granted him his request.

'Then,' said Sir Bleoberis, 'I will have the fairest lady in your court that I wish to choose.'

'I cannot refuse,' said King Mark; 'choose as you wish.'

And so Sir Bleoberis chose Sir Segwarides' wife, and took her by the hand, and went on his way with her.

When Sir Segwarides heard that his lady had gone with a knight of King Arthur's court, then he armed himself and rode after the knight to rescue his lady. King Mark and all the court were angry that she had been taken; there were certain ladies who knew that she and Tristan loved each other. One of these ladies rebuked Sir Tristan horribly, and called him coward knight, because he had stood by and watched a lady being taken away from his uncle's court so shamefully be taken away. But she implied that they had been deeply in love with each other. But Sir Tristan answered: 'Fair lady, it is not for me to interfere in such matters while her lord and husband is present here; and if he had been absent, then for the honour of this court I might have been her champion. If Sir Segwarides is unsuccessful, I may speak with Sir Bleoberis before he leaves this country.'

Then one of Sir Segwarides' squires came to the court and said that when Sir Segwarides tried to rescue his lady, Sir Bleoberis overthrew him and badly wounded him. When Sir Tristan heard of this he was ashamed; he was soon armed and on horseback, and Gorvenal, his servant, bore his shield and spear. He overtook Sir Bleoberis, and called on him to surrender the lady. But Sir Bleoberis said that he feared no knight from Cornwall, and stood his ground. He and Sir Tristan unseated each other at the first charge, and fought fiercely with swords, until Sir Bleoberis called for a truce while they talked to each other. When he learnt Tristan's name, he said that he and Tristan were both sister's children to Sir Lancelot du Lac, one of the best knights of the world.

'That is truth,' said Sir Tristan, 'and I will not with my goodwill fight any longer with you, for the great love I have to Sir Lancelot du Lac.'

'In good faith,' said Bleoberis, 'as for me, I will be loath to fight with you; but since you follow me here to have this lady, I shall proffer you kindness, courtesy, and gentleness. This lady shall choose between us; whoever she chooses, let him have her in peace.'

'I agree,' said Tristan, 'for I think she will leave you and come to me.'

So when she had to choose between them, she said to Sir Tristan: 'Sir Tristan of Lyonesse, only a little while ago you were the man in the world whom I most loved and trusted, and I thought you loved me above all ladies; but when you saw this knight lead me away you made no effort to rescue me, but let my lord Segwarides ride after me; until then I thought you loved me, but now I will leave you, and I shall never love you again.'

And so she chose to go with Sir Bleoberis.

When Sir Tristan saw her do so he was furious with the lady, and ashamed to go to the court.

'Sir Tristan,' said Sir Bleoberis, 'you are at fault, but rather than earn your displeasure, I would like you to take her, if she will go with you.'

'No,' said the lady, 'so God help me, I will never go with him; for I loved him best of all and thought that he loved me. Sir Tristan, ride back as you came, for even if you had overcome this knight, as you might well have done, I would never have gone with you. And I shall beg this knight for the sake of his knighthood, that before he leaves this country, he will lead me to the abbey where my lord Sir Segwarides lies.'

'As God is my help,' said Bleoberis, 'I have fulfilled my quest; she shall be sent to her husband again, especially for your sake, Sir Tristan; but if she would go with you I would like you to have her.'

'I thank you,' said Sir Tristan, 'but because of her love I shall beware what kind of lady I shall love or trust; for if her lord, Sir Segwarides, had been away from the court, I should have been the first that should have followed you.'

And so they took their leave and departed.

And so Sir Tristan rode to Tintagel, and Sir Bleoberis rode to the abbey where Sir Segwarides lay badly wounded, and there he delivered his lady, and departed; and when Sir Segwarides saw his lady, he was greatly comforted; and then she told him that Sir Tristan had done great battle with Sir Bleoberis, and caused him to bring her again.

HOW SIR TRISTAN WON ISEULT THE FAIR FOR KING MARK

After this, King Mark was always scheming as to how he might destroy Sir Tristan. And so he thought of sending Sir Tristan into Ireland to win Iseult the Fair for him. For Sir Tristan had so praised her beauty and her goodness that King Mark said that he would wed her; and he begged Sir Tristan to make his way to Ireland for him as his messenger. But his intention was that the Irish should slay Sir Tristan. Notwithstanding, Sir Tristan would not refuse the mission despite the danger and peril he might be in, but prepared to set out with a retinue of the finest knights at court. So Sir Tristan departed and took the sea with all his fellowship. And when he was at sea a storm blew up, and drove them back into the coast of England; and there they arrived hard by Camelot, and were very glad to have reached dry land.

And when they had landed, Sir Tristan set up his pavilion upon the land of Camelot, and hung his shield upon the pavilion. The same day there came two knights of King Arthur's, Sir Ector de Maris and Sir Morganor; they touched the shield, and told him to come out of the pavilion to joust, if he wished to joust.

'You will be answered,' said Sir Tristan, 'if you will wait a little while.'

So he made himself ready, and first he struck down Sir Ector de Maris, and then he struck down Sir Morganor, all with one spear, and badly bruised them. And when they lay upon the ground they asked Sir Tristan who he was, and of what country he was knight.

'Fair lords,' said Sir Tristan, 'you must know that I am from Cornwall.'

'Alas,' said Sir Ector, 'I am ashamed that any Cornish knight should ever overcome me.'

And Sir Ector in a fury took off his armour, and went on foot, and would not ride. And a little time after this Sir Tristan fought in single combat for King Anguish, to prove that the king had not encompassed the death of a knight; and he defeated Sir Blamore who had accused the king, for which King Anguish promised Sir Tristan that he should have whatever he asked, without fail.

One day King Anguish asked Sir Tristan why he had not claimed his reward.

'Sir,' said Sir Tristan, 'now is it time; this is all that I will desire, that you will give me Iseult the Fair, your daughter, not to myself, but to my uncle, King Mark; he shall have her to wife, for so have I promised him.'

'Alas,' said the king, 'I would give away all the land if you would wed her yourself.'

'Sir, if I did, then I would be shamed for ever in this world, and false to my promise. Therefore,' said Sir Tristan, 'I pray you hold to your promise: for this is my desire, that you will give me Iseult the Fair to go with me into Cornwall to be wedded to King Mark, my uncle.'

'You shall have her to do what you please with her,' said King Anguish; 'if you want to wed her yourself, that would be my choice, and if you will give her to King Mark, your uncle, that is your choice.'

So Iseult the Fair was made ready to go with Sir Tristan, and Brangane went with her as her gentlewoman.

Then the queen, Iseult's mother, gave to her and Brangane, and to Gorvenal, Tristan's squire, a drink, and commanded them that on the day King Mark should wed, they should give him that drink, so that King Mark should drink to Iseult the Fair; 'And then,' said the queen, 'they will love each other all the days of their life.'

So this drink was given to Brangane, and to Gorvenal. And soon after Sir Tristan set sail with Iseult the Fair; and when they were in their cabin, it happened that they were thirsty. They saw a little flask of gold standing nearby, and it seemed by the colour and the taste that it was noble wine. Then Sir Tristan took the flask in his hand, and said, 'My lady Iseult, here is the best drink that ever you drank, that Brangane, your maiden, and Gorvenal, my servant, have kept for themselves.'

Then they laughed and made good cheer, and either drank to other freely, and they thought no drink they had ever pledged to each other was so sweet or so good. But once that drink was in their bodies, they loved each other so well that their love never departed for weal nor woe.

And soon after Mark and Iseult were richly wedded in the noblest manner. But, as the French book says, Sir Tristan and Iseult the Fair were always in love. Then there were great jousts and great tourneying, and many lords and ladies were at that feast, and Sir Tristan was the most praised of all. A little while after the feast had ended, two ladies who were with Queen Iseult tried out of hate and envy to destroy Brangane, hand-maiden to Iseult the Fair. She was sent into the forest to fetch herbs, and there she was met, and bound hand and foot to a tree, and was there for three days. And by good fortune, Sir Palamides found Brangane, and saved her from death, and brought her to a nearby nunnery to recover. When Iseult the queen missed her maiden, she was as grieved as any queen ever was, for of all earthly women she loved her best, because she had come with her from her homeland. And so one day Queen Iseult walked into the forest to calm her thoughts, and there she sat by a well and wept. And suddenly Palamides came to her, and had heard her weeping, and said: 'My lady Iseult, if you will grant me what I ask, I shall bring Brangane safe and sound to you.'

And the queen was so glad of his offer that she granted him whatever he might ask.

'Well, my lady,' said Palamides, 'I trust in your promise; if you will wait here half an hour I shall bring her to you.'

'I will await you,' said Iseult the Fair. And Sir Palamides rode to the nunnery, and he came back with Brangane; but she would rather not have come again, because for love of the queen she stood in danger of her life. Notwithstanding, half against her will, she went with Sir Palamides to the queen. And when the queen saw her she was very glad.

'Now, my lady,' said Palamides, 'remember your promise, for I have fulfilled my promise.'

'Sir Palamides,' said the queen, 'I do not know what you desire, but I tell you that though I promised you anything, I thought no evil, nor, I warn you, will I do evil.'

'My lady,' said Sir Palamides, 'you shall not know what I desire as yet, but in the presence of my lord your husband, I will have my desire that you have promised me.'

And at this the queen departed, and rode home to the king, and Sir Palamides rode after her. And when Sir Palamides came before the king, he said: 'Sir king , I require you, as you are a righteous king, that you will judge and give me my rights.'

'Tell me your cause,' said the king, 'and you shall have your rights.'

'Sir,' said Palamides, 'I promised your queen, Iseult, to bring back Brangane, whom she had lost, on the understanding that she should grant me a boon that I would ask; she did not begrudge it or hesitate, but granted my request.'

'What do you say to this, my lady?' said the king.

'It is as he says, so God help me,' said the queen; 'to tell the truth, I promised him what he asked because I longed to see her.'

'Well, my lady,' said the king, 'you may have been hasty to grant him whatever he asked, but I decree that you should perform your promise.'

'Then,' said Palamides, 'I will have your queen, to lead her and govern her wherever I choose.'

At this the king stood still, and thought of Sir Tristan, and believed that he would rescue her. And he quickly answered: 'Take her, whatever may come of it, for I do not think she will be with you for long.'

'As for that,' said Palamides, 'I will take my chance.'

And Sir Palamides took her by the hand and said: 'My lady, do not refuse to go with me, for I ask nothing but your own promise.'

'I am not afraid to go with you,' said the queen, 'even if you have me at a disadvantage because of my promise, for I am sure that I shall be worshipfully rescued from you.'

'Be that as it may,' said Sir Palamides. So Queen Iseult mounted behind Palamides, and he rode on his way.

The king at once sent for Sir Tristan, but he was nowhere to be found, for he was in the forest hunting: for that was always his custom, if he was not bearing arms, to chase and to hunt in the forests.

'Alas,' said the king, 'now I am shamed for ever, because my lady and my queen shall be ill-used by my consent.'

Then one of Sir Tristan's knights came to the king; his name was Lambegus.

'My lord,' said this knight, 'since you trust my lord, Sir Tristan, for his sake I will ride after your queen and rescue her, or else I shall be beaten.'

'I thank you for that,' said the king, 'as I live, Sir Lambegus, I will reward you.'

And then Sir Lambegus armed, and rode after them as fast as he might; and in a little while he overtook Sir Palamides, who left the queen.

'Who are you?' said Palamides, 'are you Tristan?'

'No,' he said, 'I am his servant, and my name is Sir Lambegus.'

'I am sorry for that,' said Palamides, 'for I had rather you were Sir Tristan.'

'I believe you,' said Lambegus, 'but when you fight with Sir Tristan you shall have your hands full.'

And then they charged each other and shattered their spears; and then they drew their swords, and hacked at each other's helm and hauberk. In the end Sir Palamides gave Sir Lambegus such a wound that he fell down like a dead knight to the ground.

Then he looked round for Iseult the Fair, and did not know where she had gone. Sir Palamides was beside himself with grief. The queen ran into the forest, where she found a well, and thought she would drown herself in it. But as good fortune would have it, a knight that had a castle nearby, named Sir Adtherp found the queen in her distress and rescued her and brought her to his castle. And when he learnt who she was he armed himself, and took his horse, and said he would be avenged on Palamides; and he rode on till he met him. But Sir Palamides wounded him sorely, and forced him to tell him why he did battle with him, and how he had led the queen to his castle.

'Now bring me there,' said Palamides, 'or you shall die at my hands.'

'Sir,' said Sir Adtherp, 'I am so wounded I may not go on, but ride this way and it shall bring you into my castle, and the queen is there.'

Then Sir Palamides rode until he came to the castle. And from a window Iseult the Fair saw Sir Palamides; she had the gates shut and fastened strongly. And when he saw he could not come into the castle, he put off his bridle and his saddle, and put his horse to graze, and sat himself down at the gate like a man who was out of his wits.

When Tristan came home and learned that Iseult the Fair had gone with Sir Palamides, he was mad with rage.

'Alas,' said Sir Tristan, 'I am shamed today!' Then he cried to Gorvenal his squire: 'Hasten to arm me and bring my horse, for I know Lambegus has no might nor strength to withstand Sir Palamides: if only I were in his place!' So Sir Tristan was quickly armed and horsed, and Gorvenal rode after him into the forest, where he found his knight Lambegus almost wounded to death; and Sir Tristan took him to a forester, and commanded him to look after him well. He rode on and found Sir Adtherp badly wounded, who told him how the queen would have drowned herself if he had not been there, and how for her sake he had done battle with Sir Palamides.

'Where is my lady?' said Sir Tristan.

'Sir,' said the knight, 'she is secure enough within my castle, if she can stay within it.'

'I thank you for that,' said Sir Tristan, 'and for your good deeds.'

And he rode till he came near to the castle; and he saw Sir Palamides sitting asleep at the gate, and his horse grazing in front of him.

'Gorvenal,' said Sir Tristan, 'go and wake him, and tell him to make ready.'

So Gorvenal rode to him and said: 'Sir Palamides, arise, and put on your armour.'

But he was in such a daze that he did not hear what Gorvenal said. So Gorvenal came back and told Sir Tristan that Palamides was either asleep or mad.

'Go back,' said Sir Tristan, 'and tell him to get up, because his mortal enemy is here.'

So Gorvenal rode back and prodded him with the butt of his spear, and said: 'Sir Palamides, get ready, for Sir Tristan is over there, and sends word to you that he is your mortal foe.'

And at this Sir Palamides got up quietly, without a word, got his horse, saddled him and bridled him, and leapt lightly into the saddle, and took his spear in his hand; and they both levelled their spears and charged fast at each other; and Tristan struck down Sir Palamides over his horse's tail. Then Sir Palamides put his shield before him and drew his sword. And there began strong battle on both parts, for they both fought for the love of one lady, and the whole time she lay on the wall of the castle and watched as they fought furiously. Both were badly wounded, but Palamides was much more severely wounded. So they fought, tracing and traversing for more than two hours, until for grief and sorrow Iseult the Fair almost fainted.

'Alas,' she said, 'I loved one of them and still do, and the other I do not love; yet it would be a great pity if I should see Sir Palamides slain; for by the time the battle ends, Sir Palamides will be a dead knight: because he is not christened, I would be sorry that he should die a Saracen.'

And with that she came down and beseeched Sir Tristan to fight no more.

'Ah, my lady,' said he, 'what do you mean, will you bring shame on me? You know I will do as you say.'

'I do not want to dishonour you ,' said Iseult the Fair, 'but for my sake spare this unhappy Saracen, Palamides.'

'My lady,' said Sir Tristan, 'I will stop fighting at this time for your sake.'

Then she said to Sir Palamides, 'These are your orders: you are to go out of this country while I am here.'

'I will obey your command,' said Sir Palamides, 'but it is much against my will.'

'Then go on your way,' said Iseult the Fair, 'to the court of King Arthur, and there commend me to Queen Guinevere, and tell her that I send her word that there are in this land only four lovers, that is, Sir Lancelot du Lac and Queen Guinevere, and Sir Tristan of Lyonesse and Queen Iseult.'

And so Sir Palamides departed with great grief. And Sir Tristan took the queen and brought her back to King Mark, and great joy was made at her homecoming. Who was cherished but Sir Tristan! Then Sir Tristan had Sir Lambegus, his knight, fetched from the forester's house, and it was long before he was whole, but in the end he recovered well. And they lived in joy and play a long while. But Sir Andred, cousin to Sir Tristan, always lay in watch for Sir Tristan and Iseult the Fair, to catch them and slander them. So one day Sir Tristan talked with Iseult the Fair in a window, and Sir Andred caught sight of them, and told the king. Then King Mark took a sword in his hand and came to Sir Tristan, and called him false traitor, and would have struck him. But Sir Tristan was close to him, and ran under his sword, and took it out of his hand. And then the king cried: 'Where are my knights and my men? I order you to slay this traitor.'

But not one of them would move for his words. When Sir Tristan saw that there was no one who would be against him, he shook the sword at the king, and made as though he would have struck him. And then King Mark fled, and Sir Tristan followed him, and struck upon him five or six strokes flat on the neck, and made him fall on his nose. And then Sir Tristan went his way and armed himself, and took his horse and his man, and so he rode into the forest.

And there one day Sir Tristan met two brothers who were King Mark's knights, and there he struck off the head of one, and wounded the other to the death; and he made him bear his brother's head in his helm to the king, and he wounded thirty more there. And when that knight came before the king to give his message, he died before the king and the queen. Then King Mark called his council and asked advice of his barons as to what was best done with Sir Tristan.

'Sir,' said the barons,' 'we counsel you to send for Sir Tristan, for many men will side with Sir Tristan if he is in difficulty.'

'And sir,' said Sir Dinas the seneschal, 'Sir Tristan is called without equal and unmatched by any Christian knight; we know no other knight of his might and hardiness, unless it is Sir Lancelot du Lac. And if he departs from your court and goes to King Arthur's court, he will win such friends there that he will not care for your ill will. And therefore, sir, I counsel you to take him into your grace.'

'I agree,' said the king, 'that he is sent for, that we may be friends.'

Then the barons sent for Sir Tristan under a safe conduct. And when Sir Tristan came to the king he was welcomed, and no mention was made of what had happened, and there was game and play. And then the king and the queen went hunting, and Sir Tristan with them.

The king and the queen pitched their tents in the forest beside a river, and there was daily hunting and jousting, for there were always thirty knights ready to joust with all comers. And there by chance came Sir Lamorak de Galis and Sir Driant; Sir Driant jousted well, but in the end he had a fall. Then Sir Lamorak offered to joust. And when he began he dealt with the thirty knights so that there was not one of them whom he did not unseat, and some of them were badly hurt.

'I wonder,' said King Mark, 'what knight does such deeds of arms?'

'Sir,' said Sir Tristan, 'I know him to be as noble a knight as few who are now alive, and his name is Sir Lamorak de Galis.'

'It would be a great shame,' said the king, 'if he went away now, unless some of you can give him a better joust.'

'Sir,' said Sir Tristan, 'he has done as much as any knight alive today, and it would be great shame and villainy to tempt him any more at this time, for he and his horse are both weary; for the deeds of arms that he has done this day would be good enough for Sir Lancelot du Lac.'

'As to that,' said King Mark, 'I command you, as you love me and my lady the queen, Iseult the Fair, to take your arms and joust with Sir Lamorak de Galis.'

'Sir,' said Sir Tristan, 'you are telling me to do a thing that is against knighthood; it will be easy to give him a fall, for my horse and I are both fresh, but neither he nor his horse are; and he will take it as a great unkindness, for one good knight is always loath to take another at a disadvantage. But because I will not displease you, I will obey your commandment.'

And so Sir Tristan armed and took his horse, and Sir Lamorak met him mightily, and what with the force of his own spear, and of Sir Tristan's spear, Sir Lamorak's horse fell to the ground, with him in the saddle. As quickly as he could, he got clear of the saddle and his horse, and put his shield before him and drew his sword, saying, 'Alight, knight, if you dare!' 'No,' said Sir Tristan, 'I will not contiue the fight, for what I have done to you is to my dishonour and to your renown.'

'I cannot thank you for that,' said Sir Lamorak, 'since you have outmatched me on horseback, I beg you, if you are Sir Tristan, fight with me on foot.'

'I will not,' said Sir Tristan 'for I am indeed Sir Tristan de Lyonesse, and I know that you are Sir Lamorak de Galis. What I have done to you was against my will, but I was ordered to do it; but even if you ask me, it would be to my shame to do more.'

'As to shame,' said Sir Lamorak, 'on your side or on mine, be ashamed if you must, for though. a mare's son has failed me, now a queen's son shall not fail you. If you are such a knight as men say you are, I ask you to dismount and fight with me.'

'Sir Lamorak,' said Sir Tristan, 'I know your courage is great, but no knight who is fresh should strike down a weary knight, for no knight or horse can endure a fight for ever. So I will not fight you, for I regret what I have done.'

'I will be quits with you for that,' said Sir Lamorak, 'if I ever have my chance.'

So he departed with Sir Driant, and on the way they met a knight that was sent from Morgan le Fay to King Arthur; and this knight had a fine horn harnessed with gold, and the horn had this virtue: that no lady or gentlewoman could drink from that horn unless she were true to her husband; if she were false she would spill all the drink, and if she were true to her lord she might drink in peace. And because of Queen Guinevere, and to shame Sir Lancelot, this horn was sent to King Arthur; and Sir Lamorak forced that knight to tell him why he carried that horn.

'You will take this horn,' said Lamorak, 'to King Mark, or die for it; for I tell you plainly, to shame and reprove Sir Tristan, you will bear that horn to King Mark, his uncle, and say to him that I sent it to test his lady.'

So the knight went on his way to King Mark, and brought him that rich horn, and said that Sir Lamorak sent it to him; and he told him the virtue of the horn. Then the king made Queen Iseult drink from it, and a hundred other ladies, and there were only four ladies of all those who drank without spilling. 'Alas,' said King Mark, 'this is a great misfortune', and swore a great oath that she and the other ladies should be burnt.

Then the barons gathered and said plainly they would not have those ladies burnt because of a horn made by sorcery, which came from as false a sorceress and witch as any then living. So many knights vowed that if they ever met Morgan le Fay, they would show her scant courtesy. Sir Tristan was very angry that Sir Lamorak sent that horn to King Mark, for he knew that it was done to spite him, and vowed to avenge himself.

Then Sir Tristan used to go to Queen Iseult whenever he might, by day or night, and Sir Andred his cousin always watched him in order to take him with Iseult the Fair. And so one night Sir Andred learnt the hour and the time when Sir Tristan was going to his lady. Then Sir Andred summoned twelve knights, and at midnight he set upon Sir Tristan secretly and suddenly, so that Sir Tristan was taken naked abed with Iseult the Fair; he was bound hand and foot, and kept until day. And then by the command of King Mark, and of Sir Andred, and of some of the barons, Sir Tristan was led to a chapel that stood on the rocks at the edge of the sea to be judged: and he was led there bound, with forty knights.

And when Sir Tristan saw that there was no escape and that he must die, he said: 'Fair lords, remember what I have done for the country of Cornwall, and in what danger I have been for the good of you all; for when I fought for the tribute of Cornwall with the Morholt, the good knight, I was promised a great reward when you all refused to take up the challenge; so do not let me die shamefully, for it is shame to all knighthood if I die like this; for I never met a knight as good as or better than myself.'

'You are a false traitor, and vain as well,' said Sir Andred, 'for all your boasting you shall die this day.'

'O Andred, Andred,' said Sir Tristan, 'you are my kinsman, and now you are my deadly enemy; if it was only between you and me, you would not put me to death.'

'I would indeed!' said Sir Andred, and with that he drew his sword, and wanted to kill him.

When Sir Tristan saw him ready to attack he pulled the two knights to whom he was bound towards himself, and wrenched his hands free; and he leapt at his cousin, Sir Andred, and wrested his sword out of his hand, and then he struck Sir Andred so that he fell to the ground. And so Sir Tristan fought till that he killed ten knights, and had seized the chapel. There was a great outcry, and more than a hundred men came to aid Sir Andred. When Sir Tristan saw the people coming, he remembered he was naked, and shut the chapel door; he broke the bars of a window, leapt out and fell on the rocks by the sea where neither Sir Andred nor his fellows could get at him.

Meanwhile Sir Tristan's men sought their master. When they heard he had escaped they were very glad; and they found him on the rocks, and they pulled him up with towels. And then Sir Tristan asked them where Iseult the Fair was, for he thought that she had been seized by Andred's people.

'Sir,' said Gorvenal, 'she has been put in a house of lepers.'

'Alas,' said Sir Tristan, 'that is an evil place for such a fair lady, and if I have anything to do with it, she shall not be there for long.'

So he took his men and went to the place where Iseult the Fair was, and fetched her out, and brought her into a forest to a fine manor-house, and Sir Tristan lived there with her.

And Tristan told his men to leave him because he could not support them. So they all departed except for Gorvenal. One day Sir Tristan went into the forest to hunt, and it so happened that he fell asleep there; and a man came whose brother Sir Tristan had slain. When this man found him he shot him in the shoulder with an arrow, and Sir Tristan leapt up and killed him. And in the meantime King Mark was told that Sir Tristan and Iseult the Fair were in that manor-house, and as soon as he could do so, he came with many knights to slay Sir Tristan. And when he came there he found him gone; and he took Iseult the Fair home with him, and kept her closely guarded so that she could not get a message to Tristan, nor he to her. And when Sir Tristan came back to the old manor he found the track of many horses, and learned his lady was gone. Sir Tristan was in great sorrow and in great pain for a long time, for the arrow with which he was hurt was poisoned.

HOW SIR TRISTAN WENT INTO BRITTANY

Then Iseult the Fair managed to get a message to a lady who was cousin to Brangane to go to Sir Tristan, and tell him that he could not be healed by her.

'For your lady, Iseult the Fair, cannot help you; she orders you to hurry to Brittany, to King Hoel, and there you will find his daughter, Iseult of the White Hands, and she will help you.'

Then Sir Tristan and Gorvenal found a ship and sailed into Brittany. And when King Hoel learned that it was Sir Tristan he was glad to see him.

'Sir,' he said, 'I have come to this country to get help from your daughter, for I am told that there is no one else that may heal me but her.'

And within a while she healed him.

There was an earl called Grip who made great war upon the king, and got the better of the king, and besieged him. And Sir Kaherdin, King Hoel's son, made a sally; but he was badly wounded, and almost died. Then Gorvenal went to the king and said: 'Sir, I advise you to ask my lord, Sir Tristan, to help you in your need.'

'I will take your advice,' said the king. And so he went to Sir Tristan, and begged him to help him in his wars because his son, Sir Kaherdin, could not go into the field.

'Sir,' said Sir Tristan, 'I will go to the field and do what I may.'

Then Sir Tristan made a sally from the town with such men as he could raise, and did such deeds that all Brittany spoke of him. At last, by great might and force, he slew Earl Grip with his own hands, as well as more than a hundred knights. And when he returned, Sir Tristan was received in great honour, with processions. Then King Hoel embraced him and said: 'Sir Tristan, I will resign all my kingdom to you.'

'God forbid,' said Sir Tristan, 'for I am in your debt because of what your daughter has done for me.'

Then by the persuasion of King Hoel and Kaherdin his son, there arose great love between Iseult and Sir Tristan, for that lady was both good and fair, and a woman of noble blood and fame. And because Sir Tristan had such cheer and riches and lived so pleasantly he almost forsook Iseult the Fair, and agreed to wed Iseult of the White Hands. And in the end they were wedded; but when they were abed, Sir Tristan remembered his former love, Iseult the Fair. And the memory of Iseult the Fair was so vivid that he was dismayed, and he could do no more than embrace and kiss Iseult of the Whie Hands; as for other desires of the flesh, Sir Tristan never thought of these with her. So the French book tells us; and it adds that the lady thought that there were no pleasures in love beyond kissing and embracing.

And a knight from Brittany came over the sea to the court of King Arthur, where he met Sir Lancelot du Lac, and told him of the marriage of Sir Tristan.

Sir Lancelot exclaimed: 'Shame on him, as a knight untrue to his lady; I cannot believe that so noble a knight as Sir Tristan should be false to his first lady, Iseult the Fair, queen of Cornwall; but tell him that of all knights in the world I loved him most, but now the love between him and me is done for ever, and I give him warning from this day forth that I am his mortal enemy.'

But the book says that Iseult the Fair learnt of Tristan's marriage; and she guessed that he still loved her, and not his new bride, and begged him to bring Iseult of the White Hands and Kaherdin to Cornwall. Tristan persuaded them both to take ship and set sail with him. The ship was driven by fierce winds far past Cornwall, and at last they landed in North Wales, where, in strange country, Tristan and Kaherdin were parted from Iseult of the White Hands as they searched for the right road, and could not find her again. So they rode into Cornwall without her, and only came there after many adventures.

When they landed in Cornwall, they rode to Sir Dinas the seneschal, a trusty friend of Sir Tristan's, who rode to the court of King Mark, and told the queen, Iseult the Fair, that Sir Tristan was near by. Then Iseult the Fair swooned for pure joy; and when she recovered she said: 'Gentle seneschal, help me to speak to him, or my heart will break.'

Then Sir Dinas and Brangane brought Sir Tristan and Kaherdin in secret to the court, to a chamber where Iseult the Fair had agreed to meet him; and as to the joy that was between Iseult the Fair and Sir Tristan, no tongue can tell it, nor heart think it, nor pen write it. And as the French book mentions, the first time that Sir Kaherdin saw Iseult the Fair he was so enamoured of her that he could never withdraw his love. And in the end, Sir Kaherdin died for the love of Iseult the Fair. He wrote to her in secret letters and ballads as good as any that were written in those days. And when Iseult the Fair read his letters she had pity on him, and without telling anyone she wrote another letter to comfort him.

And Sir Tristan was all this time hidden in a turret at the command of Iseult the Fair, and when she could she came to him. One day King Mark was playing chess under a chamber window; and Sir Tristan and Sir Kaherdin were in the chamber above King Mark. By mischance Sir Tristan found the letter that Kaherdin sent to Iseult the Fair, as well as the letter that she wrote to Kaherdin; and Iseult the Fair was in the room at the same time. Then Sir Tristan went to Iseult the Fair and said: 'Madam, here is a letter that was sent to you, and here is your reply to it. Alas for my faithful love for you and for the many lands and riches I have forsaken for your love! You have betrayed me, and that gives me great pain. But as for you, Sir Kaherdin, I brought you out of Brittany into this country, and I won back the lands of your father, King Hoel, and I wedded your sister Iseult of the White Hands for the goodness she did to me. And yet, as I am a true knight, she is still a virgin; but as for you, Sir Kaherdin, I will have my revenge for the falsehood and treason you have done me.'

And with that Sir Tristan drew out his sword and said: 'Sir Kaherdin, defend yourself,' and then Iseult the Fair fell fainting to the ground. And when Sir Kaherdin saw Sir Tristan about to attack him he saw no other way out, but leapt out at a bay-window, over the head of King Mark who sat playing chess. And when the king saw someone come hurtling over his head, he said: 'Fellow, who are you, and why did you leap out of the window?'

'My lord the king,' said Kaherdin, 'I happened to fall asleep in the window above your head, and as I slept I fell out of it.'

And this was Kaherdin's excuse.

Then Sir Tristan was in great fear that the king would discover that he was there; so he retreated into the tower and armed himself in such armour as he had to fight anyone who came for him. But when Sir Tristan saw that no one came, he sent Gorvenal for his horse and his spear, and he rode out of Tintagel openly into the forest, where he met a knight of his called Sir Fergus. And he made great sorrow, so much that he fell down off his horse in a swoon, and this lasted three days and three nights. Then Sir Tristan sent Sir Fergus to discover what news there was at the court. And on the way Sir Fergus met a lady who came from Sir Palamides, to find out how Sir Tristan was. Sir Fergus told her how he was almost out of his mind.

'Alas,' said the lady, 'where shall I find him?'

And Sir Fergus told her where Tristan was. Then Sir Fergus found Queen Iseult sick in her bed, as full of grief as any earthly woman. And when the lady found Sir Tristan, she was in despair, because she could not cure him, for the more she cared for him the greater was his pain. In the end Sir Tristan took his horse and rode away from her. And then it was three days before she could find him, and she brought him meat and drink, but he would not take it; and once again Sir Tristan escaped from the lady.

It so happened that he rode by the castle where he had fought Sir Palamides and Iseult the Fair had parted them. And there the lady met Sir Tristan again, weeping and moaning; and she went to the lady of that castle and told her of Sir Tristan's misadventure.

'Alas,' said the lady of that castle, 'where is my lord, Sir Tristan?'

'Right here by your castle,' said the lady.

'It is good that he is so near; he shall have the best meat and drink I can give him; and I have a harp of his on which he taught me, for he is the best harper in the world.'

So the two ladies brought him meat and drink, but he ate little of it. That night he let his horse go, and unlaced his armour. After that Sir Tristan went into the wilderness, and broke down the trees and boughs; and when he found the harp that the lady sent him, then he would play on it, weeping as he did so. And sometimes when Sir Tristan was in the wood and the lady did not know where he was, she would sit down and play on that harp: then Sir Tristan would come and listen to it, and sometimes he would play himself. He lived in this way for a quarter of a year, but at last he ran away, and she could not find out where he had gone. He went naked and grew lean and poor of flesh; he fell in the fellowship of herdsmen and shepherds, and they would give him some of their meat and drink each day. If he did anything stupid they would beat him with rods, and they clipped his hair with shears and made him like a fool.

And one day Dagonet, King Arthur's fool, came into Cornwall with two squires with him; and as they rode through that forest they came past a well where Sir Tristan often went; the weather was hot, and they alighted to drink of that well, and in the meanwhile their horses broke loose. Sir

Tristan found them, and first he soused Sir Dagonet in the well, and after him his squires, and the shepherds laughed at that. Next he ran after their horses and brought them again one by one; and, wet as the men were, he made them mount and ride on their way. In revenge for being laughed at, Dagonet and the squires returned later to the shepherds and beat them. Sir Tristan saw them beating the men who gave him meat and drink, and ran up and seized Sir Dagonet by the head, and gave him such a fall to the ground that he bruised him badly and he lay still. Sir Tristan pulled Dagonet's sword out of his hand, and ran to one of his squires and struck off his head, and the other fled. And so Sir Tristan went on his way with that sword in his hand, running as if he were completely mad. Then Sir Dagonet rode to King Mark and told him what had happened in that forest.

'And therefore,' said Sir Dagonet, 'beware, King Mark, of coming to that well in the forest, for there is a fool naked, and that fool and I met together, and he almost killed me.'

'Ah,' said King Mark, 'that is Sir Matto le Breune, that went out of his mind because he lost his lady; for when Sir Gaheris struck down Sir Matto and won his lady of him, he was never in his right mind, and that was a pity, for he was a good knight.'

Then Sir Andred, cousin to Sir Tristan, made a lady that was his paramour spread a rumour that she had been with Sir Tristan when he died. And she told King Mark's court that she buried him by a well, and that before he died he begged King Mark to make his cousin, Sir Andred, king of the country of Lyonesse. Sir Andred did this because he wanted to have Sir Tristan's lands. And when King Mark heard tell that Sir Tristan was dead he wept and mourned greatly. But when Queen Iseult heard of these tidings she was so grieved that she was almost out of her mind; and one day she got a sword in secret and took it to her garden, and there she forced the sword through a plum tree up to the hilt, so that it stuck fast, and it stood breast high. And as she was about to run upon the sword and to kill herself, King Mark saw all this and how she kneeled down and said: 'Sweet Lord Jesu, have mercy upon me, for I may not live after the death of Sir Tristan of Lyonesse, for he was my first love and he shall be the last.'

At these words King Mark came and took her in his arms, and then he took up the sword, and carried her away with him into a tower. He had her kept there, and watched her carefully; after that she lay at death's door for a long time.

In the meanwhile Sir Tristan ran naked in the forest with the sword in his hand, until he came to a hermitage, where he lay down and slept; and as he slept the hermit stole away his sword, and laid meat down by him. The hermit kept him there for ten days; after which he departed and came to the herdsmen again. And there was a giant in that country called Tauleas, who for fear of Sir Tristan had never dared to leave his castle for more than seven years. When he heard that Sir Tristan was dead, according to the rumour from the court of King Mark, Tauleas went wherever he wished. And one day he came to the herdsmen as they wandered and pastured their beasts, and sat down to rest among them. There came a knight of Cornwall with a lady; and when the giant saw him he left the herdsmen and hid under a tree; so the knight came to the well, and there he alighted to rest. And as soon as he had dismounted this giant Tauleas came between the knight and his horse, and took the horse and leapt on it. He rode to the knight and took him by the collar, and pulled him up in front of him on his horse, and tried to cut off his head. Then the herdsmen said to Sir Tristan: 'Help that knight.'

'You help him,' said Sir Tristan.

'We dare not,' said the herdsmen. Then Sir Tristan saw the knight's sword lying there; he ran and took up the sword and struck off Tauleas' head, and went back to the herdsmen.

Then the knight took up the giant's head and took it with him to King Mark, and told him of his adventures in the forest, and how a naked man rescued him from the giant.

'Where did this adventure happen?' said King Mark.

'At the well in your forest where many adventurous knights meet; that is where the madman is.'

'Well,' said King Mark, 'I will go and see that wild man.'

So within a day or two King Mark commanded his knights and his hunters to be ready to go hunting the next day, and in the morning he went to that forest. And when the king came to that well he found a fair naked man lying there with a sword by him. Then King Mark blew his horn and his knights came to him; and the king commanded them to take the naked man gently, and bring him to his castle. They did so, softly and gently, and put a mantle on Sir Tristan, and led him to Tintagel, where they bathed him, and washed him, and gave him hot food until he came to himself; but none of them knew who he was, or recognised him as Sir Tristan.

It so happened one day that the queen, Iseult the Fair, heard of the man who had run naked in the forest, and how the king had brought him home to the court. Then Iseult the Fair called Brangane and said: 'Come with me, for we will go and see the man that my lord brought from the forest.'

So they found the sick man in the garden taking his rest, and resting in the sun. So when the queen looked on Sir Tristan she did not remember him. But she said again and again to Brangane: 'I think I have seen him before, in many different places.' But as soon as Sir Tristan saw her he knew her well enough. And he turned his face away and wept.

The queen always had a little brachet with her which Sir Tristan gave her when she first came into Cornwall, and that brachet would never leave her unless Sir Tristan was nearby. And as soon as this little brachet scented Sir Tristan, she leapt on him and licked him all over, and then she whined and smelled his feet and his hands, and all over his body.

'Ah, my lady,' said Brangane to Iseult the Fair, 'alas, alas, I see it is my own lord, Sir Tristan.'

And thereupon Iseult fell down in a faint and lay there a great while. And when she could speak she said: 'My lord Sir Tristan, I bless God that you are still alive. But I am sure that this little brachet will lead to your being discovered, for she will never leave you. And I am sure as soon as my lord, King Mark, recognises you he will banish you from Cornwall, or destroy you; for God's sake, my own lord, grant King Mark his will, and go to the court of King Arthur, for there you are beloved; and I will write to you whenever I can; and when you wish you can come to me, and I will do whatever you wish, and live as poor a life as any queen or lady ever did.'

'My lady,' said Sir Tristan, 'leave me, for I have undergone much anger and danger for love of you.'

Then the queen left, but the brachet would not stir from him; and King Mark came, and the brachet set upon him, and bayed at them all. Sir Andred said: 'Sir, this is Sir Tristan, I can tell from the brachet.'

'No,' said the king, 'I cannot believe that.'

Then the king asked him on oath who he was.

'As God help me,' said he, 'my name is Sir Tristan of Lyonesse; do with me as you wish.'

'Ah,' said King Mark, 'I am sorry that you have recovered.'

And he summoned his barons to condemn Sir Tristan to death. Many of his barons would not agree to this, in particular Sir Dinas the seneschal, and Sir Fergus. And so by their advice Sir Tristan was banished from the country for ten years, and he took his oath to do so on a book before the king and his barons. And so he was made to leave Cornwall. Many barons brought him to his ship; some were his friends and some his foes.

SIR TRISTAN IN LOGRES

And so Sir Tristan sailed from Cornwall, vowing that he would revenge himself for Mark's ingratitude. When he came to Logres, he encountered Sir Dinadan, and rode on in his company. As they went on their way, they found Sir Lancelot, beset by thirty knights, and with Tristan's help, Lancelot drove them all off. The three knights sought adventures together, and met with Sir Gawain, who Sir Breuse sans Pité had overcome and had bound to his horse; they rescued him, but Sir Breuse fled so fast they could not overtake him. But Lancelot outrode Tristan, and they became separated. Tristan dismounted to rest; he pulled off his helm and washed his face and his hands, and so he fell asleep.

In the meanwhile Brangane had sought Sir Tristan many ways and days in that country. And when she came to the well she looked at him and did not recognise him as Sir Tristan, but she knew him by his horse, called Passe-Brewel, which he had had for many years; for when he was mad in the forest Sir Fergus kept him. She waited until he was awake, and greeted him, and told him how she had sought him far and wide, and that she had letters from Queen Iseult the Fair. Then Sir Tristan read them, and was glad; he said: 'Brangane, you shall ride with me till the tournament at the Castle of Maidens has finished, and then you shall take letters and news with you.'

Sir Tristan rode in search of lodging, and met a good ancient knight, Sir Pellounes, and begged to lodge with him. Sir Pellounes told him that at the great tournament to be held at the Castle of Maidens, Sir Lancelot and thirty-two knights of his blood had decided to fight using shields with the arms of Cornwall. And as they talked, a messenger came and told Pellounes that his son, Sir Persides de Bloise, had come home; and Pellounes thanked God that he had come, and told Sir Tristan that in two years he had not seen his son, Sir Persides.

'Sir,' said Sir Tristan, 'I know your son well enough for a good knight.'

So Sir Tristan and Sir Persides came to their lodging both at once, and unarmed and dressed. And then these two knights welcomed each other. And when Sir Persides understood that Sir Tristan was of Cornwall, he said he was once in Cornwall: 'And there I jousted before King Mark; and I overthrew ten knights, but Sir Tristan of Lyonesse overthrew me, and took my lady away from me, and I shall never forget that, but bide my time.'

'Ah,' said Sir Tristan, 'so you hate Sir Tristan. Do you think that Sir Tristan cannot resist you?'

'Yes,' said Sir Persides, 'I know that Sir Tristan is a noble knight and a much better knight than I, yet I owe him no goodwill.'

As they stood talking at a bay-window of the castle, they saw many knights riding to and fro toward the tournament. Sir Tristan noticed a fine knight riding on a great black horse, and a black-covered shield.

'Who is that,' said Sir Tristan, 'with the black horse and the black shield? He seems a good knight.'

'I know him well,' said Sir Persides, 'he is one of the best knights of the world.'

'Then it is Sir Lancelot,' said Tristan.

'No,' said Sir Persides, 'it is Sir Palamides, who is not yet christened.'

Then they saw many people of the country salute Sir Palamides. And later a squire told Sir Pellounes, the lord of that castle, that a knight with a black shield had struck down thirteen knights.

'Fair brother,' said Sir Tristan to Sir Persides, 'let us put on our cloaks, and let us go and see the fighting.'

'No,' said Sir Persides, 'we will ride like men and good knights.'

So they armed and took their horses and great spears, and went where many knights were practising before the tournament. When Sir Palamides saw Sir Persides, he sent his squire to require him to joust with him. And when Sir Persides heard this, he prepared to joust with Sir Palamides, but Sir Persides was unhorsed when they met. So Sir Tristan made ready to avenge Sir Persides, and Sir Palamides saw this: he was ready before Sir Tristan, and struck him before he had even got his spear in the rest, sending him over his horse's tail. Sir Tristan got up quickly and was very ashamed that he had fallen; he sent Gorvenal to Sir Palamides to ask him to joust, but Palamides refused to do so for the moment, saying that he knew his adversary better than he thought, and if he was angry he should have his revenge at the tournament the next day.

And it is written in the heralds' books, who keep high record of such matters, that at the Tournament of the Castle of Maidens, Tristan bore off the prize on the first day; on the second day he won no prize, but he and Sir Palamides fought fiercely, and Tristan overcame him. On the third day the prize was adjudged to Sir Lancelot, who declared that Tristan deserved it better than him.

But in the fighting Tristan received a great wound from Lancelot, and so he rode off with Dinadan before the jousts had ended to seek somewhere where he might rest and recover. And as he rested, Sir Palamides came to them; but before he could reprove Sir Tristan again, a knight and his men-at-arms appeared and seized all three of them because his sons had been killed by Tristan in the tournament, though Tristan had not meant them harm; and he threw them all three into a vile and stinking prison.

And there Sir Tristan nearly died of his wound; and every day Sir Palamides would reproach Sir Tristan, because of his old hatred for him.

But Tristan replied with fair words, and said little. When Sir Palamides saw how ill Tristan was, he abandoned his old hatred, and grieved for him, and comforted him as best he could. And Tristan was in great distress, for he was undermined by sickness, and that is the greatest pain a prisoner may have. For as long as a prisoner has his health, he may bear his imprisonment by God's mercy, in hope of being delivered; but when sickness attacks him, then for a prisoner all his wealth is gone, and he truly has cause for weeping. And Tristan was in such despair that he almost killed himself. But the knight who held them prisoner saw that they were noble knights indeed, and that it would be shame if they died because he had imprisoned them. So he made his peace with Tristan, and released them; and after a time Tristan recovered, and rode again in search of adventures; and each of them went his way.

Then Sir Tristan departed, and in every place he asked after Sir Lancelot, but he could not hear whether he was dead or alive; and therefore Sir Tristan was very sorrowful. So Sir Tristan rode along the edge of a forest, and saw a great tower by a marsh on one side, and on the other side a fair meadow, where ten knights were fighting together. When he came nearer, he saw that one knight was fighting against nine others, and he was doing so marvellously that Sir Tristan was amazed that a single knight might do such great deeds of arms. And in a little while he had slain half their horses and unhorsed them all, and the other horses ran loose in the fields and forest. Then Sir Tristan pitied the one knight who was fighting so hard; he thought it was Sir Palamides, from his shield. And so he rode to the knights and called to them, and told them to cease their battle, for they brought shame on themselves to fight so many knights against one. Then the master of those knights, Breuse sans Pité, the most mischievous knight living, answered: 'Sir knight, what business is it of yours? If you are wise, go back where you came from, for this knight shall not escape us.'

'That would be a pity,' said Sir Tristan, 'if such a good knight should be slain in so cowardly a fashion; and therefore I warn you I will help him with all my power.'

So Sir Tristan dismounted, because they were on foot and he did not want his horse killed. He raised his shield, with his sword in his hand, and he struck out fiercely on the right hand and on the left hand; at almost every stroke he struck down a knight. And when they saw how he fought, they all fled with Breuse sans Pité to the tower, and Sir Tristan followed close behind with his sword in his hand. But they escaped into the tower, and shut Sir Tristan out. And when Sir Tristan saw this he returned to Sir Palamides, and found him sitting under a tree badly wounded.

'Ah, fair knight,' said Sir Tristan, 'I am glad to have found you.'

'I thank you,' said Sir Palamides, 'for you have rescued me and saved me from my death.'

'What is your name?' said Sir Tristan. He said: 'My name is Sir Palamides.'

Sir Tristan said: 'I have done you a great favour today by rescuing you, when you are the man in the world that I most hate; but now prepare to fight me.'

'What is your name?' said Sir Palamides.

'My name is Sir Tristan, your mortal enemy.'

'If you are,' said Sir Palamides, 'you have done so much for me today that I cannot fight with you; for since you have saved my life it will be no honour for you to fight me, for you are fresh and I am badly wounded. If you want to challenge me, set a day and I will meet with you without fail.'

'That is well said,' said Sir Tristan, 'I will meet you in the meadow by the river of Camelot, where Merlin set the stone.'

Then Sir Tristan asked Sir Palamides why the ten knights did battle with him.

'For this reason,' said Sir Palamides; 'as I rode seeking adventures in a forest near here I caught sight of a dead knight, and a lady weeping beside him. And when I saw her, I asked her who slew her lord. "Sir," she said, "the falsest knight in the world, and the greatest villain that anyone heard of, and his name is Sir Breuse sans Pité." So I made the lady to mount her palfrey, and I promised her to protect her, and to help her to bury her lord. Suddenly, as I came riding by this tower, Sir Breuse sans Pité rode out, and struck me from my horse. Before I could remount, Sir Breuse slew the lady. I was much ashamed, and so the fight between us began: and this was the reason for the battle.'

'Well,' said Sir Tristan, 'now I understand why you fought. But remember that you have promised to fight with me; it shall be this day fortnight.'

'I shall not fail you,' said Sir Palamides.

'Well,' said Sir Tristan, 'I will go with you until you are out of danger from your enemies.'

So they mounted and rode together to that forest, and there they found a spring bubbling with clear water. Sir Tristan said: 'I would like to drink that water'. When they dismounted, they saw a great horse tied to a tree, which neighed all the time, and a knight armed, sleeping under a tree, fully armed except for his helm which lay under his head.

'By the good Lord,' said Sir Tristan, 'that is a fine-looking knight sleeping there; what shall we do?'

'Awake him,' said Sir Palamides. So Sir Tristan awakened him with the butt of his spear. The knight rose up quickly and put his helm on his head, and took a great spear in his hand; and without any more words he charged at Sir Tristan, and struck him clean out of his saddle to the ground, and hurt him on the left side, so that Sir Tristan lay in great danger. Then he galloped further, and turned, and came hurtling upon Sir Palamides, and struck him partly through the body, so that he fell from his horse to the ground. And then this strange knight left them there, and went on his way through the forest. Sir Palamides and Sir Tristan got up and caught their horses again, and asked each other what they should do.

'By my head,' said Sir Tristan, 'I will follow this strong knight who has shamed us.'

'Well,' said Sir Palamides, 'I will rest near by with a friend of mine.'

'Do not fail,' said Sir Tristan to Palamides, 'to meet me on the day set to do battle; I do not think you will be there, for I am much bigger than you.'

'I do not fear you,' said Sir Palamides, 'and if I am not sick nor a prisoner, I will not fail you. But I have more reason to think that you will not meet me, for you are going to ride after that strong knight, and if you meet with him you are unlikely to escape.'

So they went their separate ways.

And the tale tells us that after many adventures Tristan came to Arthur's court. But King Mark would not give up his enmity; for when he was accused before King Arthur by Sir Amant, of killing a knight treacherously, he came in answer to the summons, bringing with him two knights in the hope that he might serve Sir Tristan in the same fashion. And on the way King Mark encountered Sir Dagonet, Arthur's fool, who had dressed in Sir Mordred's arms and armour for a jest; and the king would not joust with him, but turned tail and fled as soon as he was challenged. By chance King Mark met Sir Palamides as he rode headlong; and Sir Palamides, hearing of his plight, unhorsed Dagonet and six of the seven knights who were with him. But Dinadan, the seventh knight, rode after Sir Palamides.

And as he came into a forest he met a knight hunting deer.

'Sir,' said Sir Dinadan, 'did you meet a knight with a shield of silver and lions' heads?'

'Yes,' said the other, 'I met that knight only a little while ago, and he went that way.'

'I thank you for that,' said Sir Dinadan, 'for if I can find the track of his horse I will not fail to find that knight.'

Late that evening, as Sir Dinadan rode on, he heard a noise that sounded like a man weeping. Sir Dinadan rode towards that noise; and when he came close to it he alighted from his horse, and went up to him on foot. He found a knight standing under a tree, and his horse tied by him, and the helm off his head; and he bemoaned his love for Iseult the Fair, the

Queen of Cornwall, and said: 'Ah, fair lady, why do I love you? You are the fairest of all, and yet you never show love to me, nor kindness. But I still must love you. And I may not blame you, fair lady, for my eyes are cause of this sorrow. And yet I am but a fool to love you, for the best knight in the world loves you, and you love him, that is Sir Tristan of Lyonesse. And the falsest king and knight is your husband, and the greatest coward and full of treason is your lord: King Mark is both. Alas, that so fair a lady should be matched with the most villainous knight of the world.'

King Mark heard everything that Sir Palamides said about him; and when he saw Sir Dinadan, he was afraid that if Dinadan saw him he would tell Sir Palamides that he was King Mark; and so he took his horse and rode to his men, where he commanded them to wait for him. And so he rode as fast as he could to Camelot; and the same day he found Amant ready to do battle, who had accused him of treason; The king commanded them to do battle, but by misadventure King Mark struck Amant through the body, even though Amant had right on his side. And King Mark left the court in haste, fearing that Sir Dinadan would tell Sir Tristan and Sir Palamides who he was.

When Sir Lancelot saw King Mark fleeing, he went at once to King Arthur, and said:'Sir, I pray you give me leave to go after to that false king and knight.'

'I beg you,' said King Arthur, 'bring him back, but do not kill him, for that would be dishonourable.'

Then Sir Lancelot armed himself quickly, and mounted a great horse, and took a spear in his hand and rode after King Mark. And in three miles Sir Lancelot overtook him, and called to him: 'Turn back, traitorous king and knight, for whether you will or not you shall go with me to King Arthur's court.'

King Mark halted and looked at Sir Lancelot, and said: 'Sir, what is your name?'

'My name is Sir Lancelot; defend yourself!' When King Mark learned that it was Sir Lancelot who was charging him with a spear, he cried: 'I yield to you, Sir Lancelot, honourable knight.'

But Sir Lancelot would not hear him, but charged at him. King Mark made no attempt to defend himself, but tumbled down out of his saddle to the ground like a sack, and there he lay still, and begged Sir Lancelot for mercy.

'Arise, traitor knight and king!'

'I will not fight,' said King Mark, 'but I will go with you wherever you want.'

'Alas, alas,' said Sir Lancelot, 'that I may not give you one blow for the love of Sir Tristan and of Iseult the Fair, and for the two knights that you have killed treacherously.' And so he brought him to King Arthur; and there King Mark alighted, and threw his helm from him upon the ground, and his sword, and fell flat on the ground at King Arthur's feet, and begged him for grace and mercy.

'God help me,' said Arthur, 'I suppose that I must welcome you, because you have come against your wishes.'

'That is true,' said King Mark, 'for my lord, Sir Lancelot, brought me here by force, and I yielded to him.'

'Well,' said Arthur, 'you know that you ought to do me service, homage, and fealty; but you have never done so, and have destroyed my knights. Will you do so now?'

'Sir,' said King Mark, 'whatever your lordship will require of me, I will make amends as best I can.'

For his speech was fair, and his deeds were false. But Arthur would not give him grace until he had been reconciled with Tristan.

THE TREASON OF KING MARK

Now the story tells of the treason of King Mark which he plotted against Sir Tristan. On the coasts of Cornwall a great tournament and jousts were proclaimed; this was done by Sir Galahaut the High Prince and King Bagdemagus, in order to kill Lancelot, or else utterly destroy and shame him, because Sir Lancelot had won the prize. Their plot was revealed to King Mark, and he was very glad to learn of it.

Then King Mark thought that he would get Sir Tristan to that tournament disguised so that no man should know him, intending that the High Prince should think that Sir Tristan was Sir Lancelot. So Sir Tristan rode into the lists in disguise. And at that time Sir Lancelot was not there, but when they saw a knight in disguise do such deeds of arms, they thought it was Sir Lancelot. And King Mark said to everyone that it was Sir Lancelot. Then they set upon him, both King Bagdemagus, and the High Prince, and their knights, so that it was a marvel that Sir Tristan could resist them. Notwithstanding all the pain that he had, Sir Tristan won the prize at that tournament, and there he hurt many knights and bruised them, and they hurt him and bruised him in return. So when the jousts were finished they found out that it was Sir Tristan of Lyonesse; and King Mark's party were glad that Sir Tristan was hurt, and the rest were sorry for it; for Sir Tristan was not so hated as was Sir Lancelot within the realm of England.

Then King Mark came to Sir Tristan and said: 'Nephew, I am sorry that you are hurt.'

'I thank you for that, my lord,' said Sir Tristan. Then King Mark had Sir Tristan put in an horse bier as a great sign of love, and said: 'Nephew, I shall be your doctor myself.'

And so he rode with Sir Tristan, and brought him to a castle by daylight. And King Mark made Sir Tristan eat, and gave him a drink; as soon as he had drunk it he fell asleep. That night King Mark had him carried to another castle, where he put him in a strong prison, and there he ordained a man and a woman to give him his meat and drink. And he was there a great while.

So Sir Tristan was missing, and no one learned where he had gone. When Iseult the Fair heard that he was missing, she went in secret to Sir Sadok, and begged him to find out where Sir Tristan was. Sadok discovered that he had been put in prison by King Mark; and he and two of his cousins laid an ambush close to the castle of Tintagel. When King Mark and four of his nephews rode past, Sir Sadok caught sight of them and he broke out of ambush and attacked them. And when King Mark saw Sir Sadok he fled as fast as he could, and Sir Sadok slew all four of King Mark's nephews. Then Sir Sadok rode until he and his companions came to a castle called Arbray, and there in the town they found Sir Dinas the seneschal. When Sir Sadok told Sir Dinas all the treason of King Mark, he defied such a king, and said he would give up the lands that he held of him; and many other knights did likewise. Then by his own advice, and Sir Sadok's, he garrisoned all the towns and castles within the country of Lyonesse, and assembled as many men as he could.

When King Mark escaped from Sir Sadok he rode to the castle of Tintagel, where he issued a summons to all who could bear arms, for he knew that he must fight. But when King Mark learned that Sir Sadok and Sir Dinas had rebelled in the country of Lyonesse, he turned to wiles and treason. He had counterfeit letters forged from the Pope, and found a strange clerk to bear them to him; the letters specified that King Mark was to make ready his army to come to the Pope, upon pain of cursing, to go to Jerusalem and make war on the Saracens.

When this clerk came, King Mark sent copies of the letters to Sir Tristan with a message that if he would go to war against the Saracens, he would be released, and would lead the king's army. When Sir Tristan had read the letter, he said to the clerk: 'Ah, King Mark, you have always been a traitor, and always will be; but, clerk,' said Sir Tristan, 'say this to King Mark: Since the Pope has sent for him, tell him to go there himself; for, traitor king as he is, I will not go at his command, even if I get out of prison, for I know how well he has rewarded me for my true service.'

Then the clerk returned to King Mark, and told him Sir Tristan's answer.

'Well,' said King Mark, 'we will trick him yet.'

So he went into his chamber, and forged more letters; and the letters specified that the Pope desired Sir Tristan to come himself, to make war on the miscreants.

When the clerk went back again to Sir Tristan and took him these letters, Sir Tristan looked at them and soon saw that they were forged by King Mark.'

'Ah,' said Sir Tristan, 'King Mark, you have always been false, and you will be so to the end.'

By then four wounded knights had come to Tintagel; one of them had his neck almost broken in two. Another had his arm cut off, the third had a spear through his body, the fourth had his teeth stricken in twain. And when they came to King Mark they cried: 'King, why do you not escape, for the whole country has arisen against you?' And King Mark was in a fury.

And in the meanwhile Sir Perceval came into the country to seek Sir Tristan. And when he heard that Sir Tristan was in prison, Sir Perceval rescued Sir Tristan by knightly means. And when he was rescued, Sir Tristan said to Sir Perceval: 'If you will stay in this region, I will ride with you.'

'No,' said Perceval, 'I must go into Wales.'

So Sir Perceval left Sir Tristan, and rode straight to King Mark, and told him how he had delivered Sir Tristan; and he told the king that he had done himself great shame by putting Sir Tristan in prison, 'And the noblest knights of the world love Sir Tristan, and if he will make war upon you, you will not be able to resist him.'

'That is true,' said King Mark, 'but I cannot love Sir Tristan, because he loves the queen my wife, Iseult the Fair.'

'For shame,' said Sir Perceval, 'do not say so. Are you not uncle to Sir Tristan, and he your nephew? You should never think that so noble a knight as Sir Tristan would do himself so great a villainy as to hold his uncle's wife,' said Sir Perceval, 'but he may love your queen innocently, because she is one of the fairest ladies in the world.'

Then Sir Perceval left King Mark. But when he had gone King Mark thought of new treason, even though he had promised Sir Perceval that he would never hurt Sir Tristan. So King Mark sent to Sir Dinas the seneschal that he should dismiss all the people that he had raised, for he sent him an oath that he would go himself to the Pope of Rome to make war on the heathen. When Sir Dinas heard this, he dismissed all his men; but as soon as they had gone home, King Mark found Sir Tristan with Iseult the Fair; and he treacherously captured him and put him in prison, contrary to his promise to Sir Perceval.

When Queen Iseult understood that Sir Tristan was in prison she was as sad as any lady or gentlewoman ever was. Then Sir Tristan sent a letter to Iseult the Fair, and begged her to be his good lady; and if it pleased her to make a vessel ready for her and him, he would go with her to the realm of Logres. When Iseult the Fair understood Sir Tristan's letter and his intent, she answered that she would have the vessel made ready, with everything that was needed.

Then Iseult the Fair sent to Sir Dinas, and to Sadok, and begged them somehow to capture King Mark and put him in prison, until she and Sir Tristan had departed for the realm of Logres. When Sir Dinas the sene-schal understood the treason of King Mark he promised that the king should be put in prison. And all their plans were carried out.

Then Sir Tristan was released from prison, and Iseult the Fair and Sir Tristan took ship, and came by water into this land. They had not been here for more than four days when there came a cry of a joust and tournament that King Arthur was holding. When Sir Tristan heard of that tournament he disguised himself and Iseult the Fair, and rode to that tournament. And when he came there he saw many knights joust and tourney; and so Sir Tristan joined in the lists, and to be brief, he overthrew fourteen knights of the Round Table. When Sir Lancelot saw these knights defeated, he prepared to attack Sir Tristan. Iseult the Fair saw that Sir Lancelot had come into the field, and sent him a ring, telling him that the disguised knight was Sir Tristan of Lyonesse. When Sir Lancelot heard that Sir Tristan was there he was very glad, and would not joust. Then Sir Lancelot caught sight of Sir Tristan, and rode after him; and they met joyfully. Sir Lancelot brought Sir Tristan and Iseult the Fair to Joyous Gard, his own castle, and told them to treat it as their own; that castle was garnished and furnished for a king and a queen to live there. And Sir Lancelot told all his people to honour them and love them as they would do himself.

So Sir Lancelot went to King Arthur; and he told Queen Guinevere that the knight who jousted so well at the last tournament was Sir Tristan, and that he had with him Iseult the Fair, despite King Mark. Queen Guinevere told all this to King Arthur, and he was very glad of Tristan's coming. So because of Sir Tristan King Arthur had it proclaimed that on May Day there should be a joust before the castle of Lonezep, close by Joyous Gard. And Arthur declared that all the knights of this land, and of Cornwall, and of North Wales, should joust against those of Ireland, Scotland, and the remnant of Wales, and the country of Gorre, and Surluse, and of Listinoise, and they of Northumberland, and all they that held lands of Arthur on this side of the sea.

When this proclamation was made many knights were glad; but others were unhappy. 'Sire,' said Lancelot to Arthur, 'these jousts will put those of us who are your companions in great jeopardy, for there are many knights envy us greatly; so we shall have to fight hard on the day.'

'As for that,' said Arthur, 'I do not care; we will show them who are the most skilful jousters.'

And when Sir Lancelot understood why King Arthur had called these jousts, then he arranged that Iseult the Fair should watch them in a secret place suitable for her rank.

And Sir Tristan and Iseult the Fair enjoyed themselves together each day with all kinds of entertainment that they devised; and every day Sir Tristan would go hunting, for he was at that time called the best chaser of the world, and the noblest blower of a horn in all manner of measures; for as books report, from Sir Tristan came all the good terms of venery and hunting, and all the sizes and measures of blowing of a horn; and of him we had first all the terms of hawking, and which were beasts of chase and beasts of venery, and which were vermin, and all the blasts that belong to the different kinds of game: first to the uncoupling, to the seeking, to the rechate, to the flight, to the death, and to strake, and many other blasts and terms, so that all kinds of gentlemen have cause to praise Sir Tristan to the world's end, and to pray for his soul.

SIR TRISTAN AND SIR DINADAN

And one day as Sir Tristan rode out hunting he met Sir Dinadan, who had come in search of him. Then Sir Dinadan told Sir Tristan his name, but Sir Tristan would not tell him his name, which made Sir Dinadan angry.

'I saw a foolish knight like you earlier today,' said Sir Dinadan, 'lying by a well, and he seemed to be asleep; and he lay there grinning like a fool, and would not speak, and his shield lay by him, and his horse stood by him; and I am certain he was a lover.'

'Sir,' said Sir Tristan, 'are you not a lover?'

'I have no time for that skill!' said Sir Dinadan.

'That is not well said,' said Sir Tristan, 'for a knight will never achieve prowess unless he is a lover.'

'That is well said,' said Sir Dinadan; 'now tell me your name, since you are a lover, or I shall do battle with you.'

'But,' said Sir Tristan, 'it is not reasonable to fight with me unless I tell you my name; and I shall not tell you for the moment.'

'You should be ashamed!' said Dinadan, 'Are you a knight and do not dare to tell me your name? So I will fight with you.'

'I will only fight if I want to. And if I do battle with you,' said Sir Tristan, 'you will not be able to resist me.'

'You are a coward,' said Sir Dinadan.

And as they argued, they saw a knight come riding towards them.

'Look,' said Sir Tristan, 'here comes a knight who will joust with you.'

Sir Dinadan looked at the knight and said: 'That is the same daft knight that I saw lying by the well, neither sleeping nor waking.'

'Well,' said Sir Tristan, 'I know that knight by his covered shield of azure; his name is Epinegris, and he is as great a lover as I know, and he loves the daughter of the king of Wales, a very beautiful lady. I expect, if you ask him, he will joust with you, and then you can prove whether a lover is a better knight than you, who will not love a lady.'

'Now you will see what I can do,' said Sir Dinadan. So he said in a loud voice: 'Knight, make ready to joust with me, for it is the custom of errant knights to joust with each other.'

'Sir,' said Epinegris, 'is the rule of you errant knights to make a knight to joust against his will?'

'No matter,' said Dinadan, 'make ready.'

And they spurred their horses and met so hard that Epinegris unhorsed Sir Dinadan. Then Sir Tristan rode to Sir Dinadan and said : 'It seems to me that the lover has done well.'

'Coward,' said Sir Dinadan, 'if you are a good knight revenge me.'

'No,' said Sir Tristan, 'I will not joust now, but take your horse and let us go on our way.'

'God save me,' said Sir Dinadan, 'from your company, for I have not prospered since I met you.'

'Well,' said Sir Tristan, 'perhaps I could tell you news of Sir Tristan.'

'Sir Tristan would be much the worse if he was in your company', said Dinadan: and so they parted.

'Sir,' said Sir Tristan, 'I may yet meet you in other places.'

And so Sir Tristan rode to Joyous Gard, and alighted and disarmed. And Sir Tristan told Iseult the Fair of Sir Dinadan.

'He is the best joker and jester, and a noble knight, and the best fellow that I know, and all good knights love his fellowship.'

'Alas,' she said, 'why did you not bring him with you?'

'Do not worry,' said Sir Tristan, 'he is riding through the countryside looking for me, and will not leave until he has met me.'

And he told Iseult the Fair how Sir Dinadan declaimed against all lovers. Just then a servant told Sir Tristan that a knight errant had come into the town, with certain colours upon his shield.

'That is Sir Dinadan,' said Sir Tristan: 'send for him, my lady Iseult, and I will keep out of the way; you will hear the merriest knight and the maddest talker that you ever spoke to; and I beg you with all my heart to make him welcome.'

So Iseult the Fair sent a messenger into the town, and asked Sir Dinadan to come to the castle and keep a lady company; he mounted his horse and rode into the castle where he alighted, and was unarmed. Iseult the Fair came to greet him and asked him where he came from.

'Madam,' said Dinadan, 'I am of the court of King Arthur, and knight of the Table Round, and my name is Sir Dinadan.'

'What are you doing in this country?' said Iseult the Fair.

'Madam,' said he, 'I seek the good knight Sir Tristan, for I was told that he was in this country.'

'It may well be so,' said Iseult the Fair, 'but I am not aware that he is here.'

'Madam,' said Dinadan, 'I marvel at Sir Tristan and other lovers; what is wrong with them, that they are so mad and so besotted about women.'

'Why,' said Iseult the Fair, 'are you a knight and not a lover? You should be ashamed; and no one will call you a good knight unless you fight for a lady's sake.'

'God keep me from it,' said Dinadan, 'for the joy of love is too short, and the sorrow of it lasts too long.'

'Ah,' said Iseult the Fair, 'do not say that; the good knight Sir Bleoberis was here lately, who fought with three knights at once for a girl's sake, and won her in the presence of the king of Northumberland.'

'It was indeed so,' said Sir Dinadan, 'I know him well for a good knight of noble blood, of the kin of Sir Lancelot du Lac.'

'I beg you,' said Iseult the Fair, 'will you fight for my love with three knights that do me great wrong? As you are a knight of King Arthur's, I demand that you do battle for me.'

Sir Dinadan said: 'I will tell you that you are as fair a lady as I ever saw, and much fairer than my lady Queen Guinevere, but, in a word, I will not fight for you with three knights!' Then Iseult laughed, and made fun of him.

And early in the morning Sir Tristan armed himself, and Iseult the Fair gave him a good helm; and then he promised her that he would meet with Sir Dinadan, and the two of them would ride together into Lonezep, where the tournament was to be held: 'And there I will prepare a place for you to see the tournament.' Then Sir Tristan set out with two squires who carried his shield and his spears.

And Dinadan left after him and rode at a great pace until he had overtaken Sir Tristan. And when Sir Dinadan had overtaken him he recognised him from the day before, and hated his company above that of all other knights.

'Ah,' said Sir Dinadan, 'are you the coward knight whom I met yesterday? Defend yourself, for you shall joust with me whether you want to or not.'

'Well,' said Sir Tristan, 'I have no desire to joust.'

And so they let their horses run at each other, and Sir Tristan missed him on purpose, and Sir Dinadan broke his spear on Sir Tristan. At this Sir Dinadan got ready to draw his sword.

'Do not do that,' said Sir Tristan; 'why are you so angry? I will not fight.'

'Coward,' said Dinadan, 'all knights would be ashamed of you.'

'Very well,' said Sir Tristan, 'I do not care, for I will follow you and be under your protection; because you are so good a knight you will save me from attack.'

'The devil deliver me from you,' said Sir Dinadan, 'for you are as good a man of arms as I ever saw, and the greatest coward as well. What are you going to do with those great spears that you are carrying with you?'

'I shall give them,' said Sir Tristan, 'to some good knight or other when I come to the tournament; and if I see you do best, I shall give them to you.'

And as they talked they saw a knight errant in front of them, who prepared to joust with them.

'Look,' said Sir Tristan, 'there is a knight who will joust; go and fight him.'

'Shame on you,' said Sir Dinadan, 'I will go.'

And so they made ready their shields and spears, and they came together so hard that the other knight struck Sir Dinadan from his horse. Sir Tristan said: 'You would have done better to leave him alone.'

'You are a coward as always,' said Sir Dinadan, and got up with his sword in his hand, to do battle on foot.

'Shall we fight in love or in anger?' said the other knight.

'Let us do battle in love,' said Sir Dinadan.

'What is your name,' said the knight.

'Sir Dinadan.'

'Ah, Dinadan,' he answered, 'my name is Gareth, youngest brother of Sir Gawain.'

Then they welcomed each other, for Gareth was the best knight of all his brothers. So they took their horses, and discussed Sir Tristan, saying what a coward he was; and Sir Tristan heard every word and laughed at them.

And again they saw a knight in front of them, well horsed and well armed, making ready to joust.

'Knights,' said Sir Tristan, 'decide between you who shall joust with the knight over there, for I warn you I will have nothing to do with him.'

'Then I will,' said Sir Gareth. And so they encountered each other, and the knight struck Sir Gareth over his horse's tail.

'Now,' said Sir Tristan to Sir Dinadan, 'get ready and revenge the good knight Gareth.'

'No, I will not,' said Sir Dinadan, 'for he has struck down a much bigger knight than me.'

'Ah,' said Sir Tristan, 'Sir Dinadan, I see that your heart fails you. Watch me, and see what I shall do.'

And then Sir Tristan charged that knight, and struck him clean from his horse. When Sir Dinadan saw that, he was much amazed; and he realised that it was Sir Tristan.

The other knight was on foot and drew his sword to do battle.

'What is your name?' said Sir Tristan.

'Sir Palamides.'

'Which knight do you hate most?' said Sir Tristan.

'I hate Sir Tristan to the death, for if I ever meet him, one of us shall die.'

'Well said,' said Sir Tristan, 'I am Sir Tristan of Lyonesse; do your worst.'

When Sir Palamides heard him say this, he was thunderstruck. And then he said: 'I beg you, Sir Tristan, forgive me my ill will, and while I live I shall serve you above all other knights alive. And I am very sorry that I have borne you ill will, for it seems to me that you are a good knight, and so, Sir Tristan, do not take offence at my unkind words.'

'Sir Palamides,' said Sir Tristan, 'that is well spoken; I know you are a good knight, for I have seen you put to the test. You have undertaken many great enterprises and achieved them, and so,' said Sir Tristan, 'if you bear me any evil will, you may attack me, for I am ready to fight.'

'Not so, my lord Sir Tristan: I will do you knightly service in all things as you command.'

'And I accept your offer,' said Sir Tristan. And so they rode on their way, talking of many things.

'My lord Sir Tristan,' said Dinadan, 'you have made fun of me, for I came into this country to find you, because my lord Sir Lancelot said you were here; but he would not tell me where to find you.'

'Sir Lancelot knew exactly where I was,' said Sir Tristan, 'for I was living in his own castle.'

'Well,' said Sir Tristan, 'we must set out tomorrow.'

And he arranged to send his two pavilions to be pitched close by the well of Lonezep, and that Iseult the Fair should be there. When Sir Palamides heard that she would be there, he was overcome with joy, but said little. So when they came to Joyous Gard Sir Palamides did not want to go into the castle, but Sir Tristan took him by the finger, and led him in. And when Sir Palamides saw Iseult the Fair he was so full of love that he could scarcely speak. So they went to dine, but Palamides could not eat. And the next day they prepared to ride towards Lonezep, and Tristan and his companions came to the well where his two pavilions were pitched; there they alighted, and saw many pavilions and a splendid display. Then Sir Tristan left Sir Palamides and Sir Gareth there with Iseult the Fair, and he and Sir Dinadan rode to Lonezep to hear the news; and Sir Tristan rode Sir Palamides' white horse. And when he came into the castle Sir Dinadan heard a great horn blow, and many knights gathered at the sound. Then Sir Tristan asked a knight: 'What does that horn call mean?'

'Sir,' said the knight, 'it is to gather all those who will fight against King Arthur at this tournament. The first is the king of Ireland, and the king of Surluse, the king of Listinoise, the king of Northumberland, and the king of the best part of Wales, with many other countries.'

And they discussed how they should be organised; and Marhalt, king of Ireland, said: 'Lords and fellows, we must defend ourselves well; King Arthur is sure of many good knights, or else he would not challenge us with so few knights. Every king must have a standard of his own, so that every knight can find their way to their natural lord, and every king and captain can help his knights if they have need.'

When Sir Tristan had heard them, he rode to King Arthur to see what he had to say.

THE TOURNAMENT AT LONEZEP

But as soon as Sir Tristan came to Arthur, Arthur called Sir Tristan and asked him what was his name.

'Sir,' said Sir Tristan, 'excuse me for now, for I will not tell you my name.'

With that Sir Tristan rode off.

'I am very surprised,' said Arthur, 'that that knight will not tell me his name', and he sent Sir Girflet to ride after him and say to him that King Arthur would like to speak with him privately.

'I will,' said Sir Tristan, 'on condition that no one asks me my name.'

'I undertake,' said Sir Girflet, 'that you will not be asked for your name.'

So they rode together back to King Arthur.

'Sir,' said King Arthur, 'why will you not tell me your name?'

'Sir,' said Sir Tristan, 'I have my reasons for not giving my name.'

'Which side will you fight on tomorrow?' said King Arthur.

'Truly, my lord,' said Sir Tristan, 'I do not know yet which side I will be on, until I come into the field, and then I will join whichever side I prefer; tomorrow you shall see which side I choose.' And with that he returned to his pavilions.

And the next day they armed themselves all in green, and came into the field; and young knights began to joust, and did many praiseworthy feats of arms. Then Gareth asked Sir Tristan for leave to break his spear, because he had not yet done so in the lists.

Sir Tristan laughed, and said: 'I pray you do your best.' Sir Gareth got a spear and offered to joust. A knight who was nephew to the king of the Hundred Knights, Sir Selises, prepared to oppose Sir Gareth, and they met together so hard that they each struck the other down, horse and all, to the ground, so they were both bruised and hurt; and they lay there till the king with the Hundred Knights helped Selises up, and Sir Tristan and Sir Palamides helped Gareth up again. And so they rode with Sir Gareth to their pavilions, where they pulled off his helm. And when Iseult the Fair saw Sir Gareth bruised in the face she asked him what had happened to him.

'Madam,' said Sir Gareth, 'I had a great blow, and gave one in return, but none of my fellows, God thank them, would rescue me.'

'Indeed,' said Palamides, 'it was not for us to joust today, for no proved knights have jousted today, and it was you who insisted on jousting. And when the other party saw you offer to joust they sent a very good knight against you; and you met him well, and neither of you are dishonoured. So rest yourself, so that you will be ready to joust tomorrow.'

'Which side,' said Tristan, 'would it be best to join tomorrow?'

'Sir,' said Palamides, 'I advise you to oppose King Arthur tomorrow, for Sir Lancelot and many good knights of his kindred will be on his side. And the better they are, the more praise we will win if we can challenge them.'

'That is said like a true knight,' said Sir Tristan.

The next day at dawn they were all arrayed in green trappings, shields and spears, and Iseult the Fair in the same colour, and her three ladies. And the three knights rode up and down the field, and led Iseult the Fair to where she could see all the jousts from a bay-window; but she kept her wimple on so that no one could see her face. And then the knights rode straight to the party of the king of Scots.

When King Arthur saw them do this, he asked Sir Lancelot who these knights and the queen were.

'Sir,' said Lancelot, 'I cannot say for certain, unless Sir Tristan is in this country, or Sir Palamides, in which case it is them, and Iseult the Fair.'

Then Arthur called Sir Kay and said: 'Go and read the names on the seats, and tell me how many of the knights of the Round Table are missing.'

When Sir Kay returned, he said: 'These knights are missing: Sir Tristan, Sir Palamides, Sir Perceval, Sir Gaheris, Sir Epinegris, Sir Mordred, Sir Dinadan, Sir La Cote Male Taile, and Sir Pelleas.'

'Well,' said Arthur, 'I expect some of them are fighting against us today.'

Then two brothers, cousins to Sir Gawain, Sir Edward and Sir Sadok, asked King Arthur to allow them to have the first jousts, for they were from Orkney.

'I am pleased,' said King Arthur. Then Sir Edward encountered the king of Scots, in whose party Sir Tristan and Sir Palamides were; and Sir Edward struck the king of Scots clean off his horse, and Sir Sadok struck down the king of North Wales, and gave him a great fall. At this there was a great cheer from King Arthur's side, and that made Sir Palamides very angry. So he made ready his shield and his spear, and with all his might he met Sir Edward of Orkney, striking him so hard that his horse could not stand the blow, and so they hurtled to the earth; and then with the same spear Sir Palamides struck down Sir Sadok over his horse's tail.

'Who is that knight in green?' said Arthur, 'He jousts very strongly.'

'Certainly,' said Sir Gawain, 'he is a good knight.'

As they stood talking there came into the lists Sir Tristan on a black horse, and before he drew rein, he struck down with one spear four good knights of Orkney that were kin to Sir Gawain; and Sir Gareth and Sir Dinadan each struck down a good knight.

'That knight on the black horse,' said Arthur, 'is doing great feats of arms.'

'Wait,' said Sir Gawain; 'the knight on the black horse has scarcely begun.'

Then Sir Tristan sent horses to the two kings whom Edward and Sadok had unhorsed at the beginning, so that they could remount. And then Sir Tristan drew his sword and rode into the thickest of the fighting against them of Orkney; and there he struck down knights, and knocked off helms, and pulled away their shields, and hurled down many knights: Arthur and all knights were amazed when they saw one knight do such great deeds of arms. And Sir Palamides did likewise. King Arthur compared Sir Tristan on the black horse to a mad lion, and Sir Palamides on the white horse to a mad leopard, and Sir Gareth and Sir Dinadan to eager wolves. But the four kings had agreed that none of them should help the other's men, but each king's company should aid their own fellows. So when Sir Tristan did such deeds of arms against the men of Orkney, they grew weary of him, and withdrew to Lonezep.

Then the heralds and the crowd proclaimed that the green knight had done marvellously, and beaten all the men of Orkney. By the heralds' reckoning, Sir Tristan had struck down with spear and sword thirty knights; and Sir Palamides had struck down twenty knights, and most of these fifty knights were King Arthur's men, and proved knights.

'God help me,' said Arthur to Sir Lancelot, 'shame on us to see four knights beat so many knights of ours; get ready, for we will go and fight them.'

'Sire,' said Lancelot, 'these are two good knights, and weary from their day's work; it will be no honour to overcome them now.'

'I do not care,' said Arthur, 'I will have my revenge; take with you Sir Bleoberis and Sir Ector, and I will be the fourth,' said Arthur. When they were ready on horseback, Arthur said: 'Choose which of them you will fight.'

'Sir,' said Lancelot, I will meet with the green knight on the black horse; my cousin Sir Bleoberis shall match the green knight on the white horse; and my brother Sir Ector shall encounter the other green knight on a white horse.'

'Then,' said Arthur, 'I must fight the green knight upon the grey horse.'

And so they rode on together. Sir Lancelot encountered Sir Tristan, and struck him so heavily on the shield that he threw horse and man to the ground; but Sir Lancelot thought he had defeated Sir Palamides, and went on his way. And then Sir Bleoberis encountered Sir Palamides, and he struck him so hard on the shield that Sir Palamides and his white horse collapsed to the ground. Then Sir Ector de Maris struck Sir Gareth so hard that he fell off his horse. And the noble King Arthur encountered with Sir Dinadan, and he struck him clean from his saddle. And then word went round that the green knights had been overthrown.

When the king of North Wales saw that Sir Tristan had a fall, he thought of the great deeds of arms Sir Tristan had done, and he made ready many knights. The custom was that if a knight could not be remounted by his fellows, he should be the prisoner of the side who had struck him down. So the king of North Wales rode straight to Sir Tristan; and when he came near him he dismounted quickly and led his horse to Sir Tristan, and said: 'Noble knight, I do not know you from what country you come, but for the noble deeds that you have done today take my horse, and leave me to do as well I may.'

'I thank you for that,' said Sir Tristan, 'and I will try to repay you: do not go far from us, and I think I shall win you another horse.'

Sir Tristan mounted the horse, and met King Arthur, and he gave him such a blow upon the helm with his sword that King Arthur could not sit in his saddle. And Sir Tristan gave the king of North Wales King Arthur's horse. There was much fighting round King Arthur as his men tried to remount him; but Sir Palamides would not allow King Arthur to be remounted, fighting fiercely to prevent his men from reaching him. Meanwhile Sir Tristan rode through the thickest of the fighting, and struck down knights on the right hand and on the left hand, and knocked off helms. Then he went to his pavilions, and left Sir Palamides on foot; and Sir Tristan changed his horse and disguised himself all in red, horse and harness.

And when Iseult the Fair saw that Sir Tristan was unhorsed, and could not find out where he was, then she wept greatly. But Sir Tristan, when he was ready, came riding cheerfully into the field, and then Iseult the Fair caught sight of him. And he did great deeds of arms; with one great spear, he struck down five knights without stopping. Then Sir Lancelot recognised him as Sir Tristan, and regretted that he had struck him down; so he went out of the fighting to rest. When Sir Tristan returned to the fray, he used his great strength to put Sir Palamides back on his horse, and likewise Sir Gareth and Sir Dinadan, and then they began to do great deeds. But neither Sir Palamides nor his two fellows knew who helped them to remount. But Sir Tristan stayed with them and helped them, and they did not recognise him, because he had changed into red armour.

So when Iseult the Fair saw that Sir Tristan had remounted, she was very glad, and laughed aloud. And as it happened, Sir Palamides looked up at her window, and he caught sight of her as she laughed; and he was so joyful that he struck down, either with his spear or his sword, whoever he met; for by catching sight of her, he was so enamoured of her that if both Sir Tristan and Sir Lancelot had been against him they would have met their match; and in his heart, as the book says, Sir Palamides wished that he could overcome Sir Tristan in front of everyone, because of Iseult the Fair. Then Sir Palamides began to double his strength, and everyone was astonished; and he kept looking up at Iseult the Fair. Sir Tristan saw how Sir Palamides was fighting so well, and he said to Sir Dinadan: 'Sir Palamides is a very good knight and has great stamina, but I never saw, nor heard anyone say, that he could do such deeds in one day.'

'It is his day,' said Dinadan; and he would say no more to Sir Tristan; but he said to himself: 'If you knew for whose love he does all these deeds of arms, you would soon cut short his courage.'

'I am sorry,' said Sir Tristan, 'that Sir Palamides is not christened'; and King Arthur and all those who watched him said the same. Then all the people gave him the prize as the best knight that day, better than Sir Lancelot or Sir Tristan.

'Well,' said Dinadan to himself, 'for all the honour that Sir Palamides has got here this day he should thank Queen Iseult, for if she had not been here today Sir Palamides would not have won the prize.'

At that moment Sir Lancelot du Lac came into the field, and heard Sir Palamides being acclaimed for his prowess. He made ready to ride against Sir Palamides with a mighty spear, hoping to unhorse him. And when Sir Palamides saw Sir Lancelot come at him so fast, he charged at Sir Lancelot as fast as he might with his sword; and at the moment when Sir Lancelot would have hit him he struck his spear aside, and cut it in two with his sword. And Sir Palamides rushed at Sir Lancelot, and hoped to overcome him; and with his sword he struck the neck of Sir Lancelot's horse, and Sir Lancelot fell to the ground. Then everyone cried: 'See how Sir Palamides the Saracen has struck down Sir Lancelot's horse!' Many knights were angry with Sir Palamides for this deed; but others said that it was not knightly to kill a horse wilfully in a tournament, but this had been done in plain battle, life for life.

When Sir Ector de Maris saw Sir Lancelot in trouble and forced to fight on foot, then he eagerly got a spear, and ran against Sir Palamides, striking him so hard that he unseated him completely. Sir Tristan saw this, and did the same in turn to Sir Ector de Maris. Then Sir Lancelot attacked Sir Palamides fiercely with his sword and said: 'You have done me the greatest harm that any knight ever did to me in a tournament and joust, so defend yourself!' 'Mercy, noble knight,' said Palamides, 'forgive what I did, for I have no power or might to withstand you, and I have done so much this day that I shall never be able to equal it all my life; spare me today, and I promise you I shall always be your knight while I live. If you take the praise from me today, you take the greatest praise that I ever had or ever will have all my life.'

'Well,' said Sir Lancelot, 'you have done marvellously well this day; I think I know for whose love you do it, and I know well that love is a great mistress. And if my lady were here,' said Sir Lancelot, 'you should not bear away the prize. But beware lest your love is discovered, for if Sir Tristan knows of it you will repent it.'

And with that Sir Lancelot allowed Sir Palamides to go.

Then Sir Lancelot recovered his horse through his great strength, in spite of twenty knights. And when Sir Lancelot was mounted he did many marvels, as did Sir Tristan and Sir Palamides. Then Sir Lancelot struck down with a spear Sir Dinadan, and the king of Scotland, and the king of Wales, and the king of Northumberland, and the king of Listinoise; and in all he and his fellows struck down well over forty knights. Then the king of Ireland and the king of the Straight Marches came to rescue Sir Tristan and Sir Palamides. A great mêlée began, and many knights were struck down on both sides; but Sir Lancelot and Sir Tristan spared each other, and Sir Palamides would not meddle with Sir Lancelot. And King Arthur sent out many knights of the Table Round; and Sir Palamides was always in the front of the affray, and Sir Tristan did so strongly and so well that the king and all the others were full of admiration. And then the king had the trumpets blown to signal that the knights should go to their lodgings; and because Sir Palamides began first, and never went or rode out of the field to rest, but fought excellently either on foot or on horseback for the longest time, King Arthur and all the kings gave Sir Palamides the honour and the prize as for that day.

Then Sir Tristan commanded Sir Dinadan to fetch Iseult the Fair, and bring her to his two pavilions that stood by the well. When Sir Palamides learned that Sir Tristan was in the red armour, and on a red horse, he was glad, and so were Sir Gareth and Sir Dinadan, for they all thought that Sir Tristan had been taken prisoner. And then every knight went to his inn. And when King Arthur and all the knights talked of the day's events, they wondered at Sir Palamides' deeds.

'Sir,' said Sir Lancelot to Arthur, 'if Sir Palamides was the green knight he fought best today, yet I know there was a better knight there than him, and I shall prove as much.'

And on the other side Sir Dinadan mocked Sir Tristan and said: 'What the devil is the matter with you today? Sir Palamides' strength never weakened today, but rather he doubled it. And you, Sir Tristan, went around all day as if you were asleep; I think you are a coward.'

'Well, Dinadan,' said Sir Tristan, 'I was never called a coward before; and even though Sir Lancelot gave me a fall, you have no right to call me coward.' And so Sir Tristan was very angry with Sir Dinadan. But Sir Dinadan said all this because he wanted to anger Sir Tristan, and awaken his spirits; for Sir Dinadan knew well that if Sir Tristan was really angry, Sir Palamides should not get the prize the next day.

'Truly,' said Sir Palamides, 'Sir Lancelot has no equal for noble knighthood, courtesy, prowess, and gentleness. I acted very uncourteously to him, and in an unknightly fashion, and he behaved courteously in return; for if he had been as unkind to me as I was to him, I would have won no praise today. And therefore,' said Palamides, I shall be Sir Lancelot's knight while my life lasts.'

The next day Sir Tristan was ready, and Iseult the Fair, with Sir Palamides and Sir Gareth. They rode all dressed in new green habits to the forest. And Sir Tristan left Sir Dinadan sleeping in his bed. And it so happened that the king and Lancelot stood at a window and saw Sir Tristan and Iseult ride past.

'Sir,' said Lancelot, 'there rides the fairest lady of the world, except for Queen Guinevere.'

'Who is that?' said Arthur.

'Sir, said he, 'it is Queen Iseult.'

'Take your horse,' said Arthur, 'and arm yourself; I will do the same, and I vow that I will see her.'

They were soon armed and horsed, and each took a spear and rode to the forest.

'Sir,' said Lancelot, 'do not go too near them, for they are two knights as good as anyone now living; do not be too hasty, for they may take offence if you ride to her without due formality.'

'I do not care,' said Arthur, 'I will see her, for I do not mind whom I grieve.'

'Sir,' said Lancelot, 'you put yourself in great danger.'

'All the same,' said the king, 'we will undertake the adventure.'

So the king rode straight to her, and greeted her.

'Sir,' she said, 'you are welcome.' Then the king looked at her, and admired her beauty.

At this Sir Palamides came to Arthur, and said: 'Uncourteous knight, what are you doing here? It is not courteous to come upon a lady so suddenly, so go back where you came from.' Arthur took no notice of Sir Palamides' words, but continued to gaze at Iseult.

Sir Palamides was angry and took a spear, and came charging at King Arthur, and struck him down with it. When Sir Lancelot saw the harm Sir Palamides had done, he said to himself: 'I am reluctant to attack that knight, because if I strike down Sir Palamides I will have to face Sir Tristan. I cannot match them both, for they are two noble knights; all the same, whether I live or I die, I must revenge my lord, and so I will, whatever happens.'

And Sir Lancelot cried to Sir Palamides: 'Keep from me!' Sir Lancelot and Sir Palamides rushed together with spears, but Sir Lancelot struck Sir Palamides so hard that he went clean out of his saddle, and had a great fall.

When Sir Tristan saw Sir Palamides fall, he said to Sir Lancelot: 'Sir knight, guard yourself, for I must joust with you.'

'As for jousting with me,' said Sir Lancelot, 'I will not fail you, for I am not afraid of you; but I would rather not fight you, for it was my duty to revenge my lord, who was unhorsed without warning and in unknightly fashion. So I revenged that fall, but that should not displease you, for he is such a friend to me that I may not see him put to shame.'

Sir Tristan at once understood by his person and by his knightly words that it was Sir Lancelot du Lac, and realised that it was King Arthur whom Sir Palamides had struck down. And then Sir Tristan put up his spear, and set Sir Palamides on his horse again. Sir Lancelot did likewise for King Arthur on horseback and they departed.

'God help me,' said Sir Tristan to Palamides, 'it was not honourable to strike down that knight as suddenly as you did. You should be ashamed, for the knights came here to see a fair lady; and every good knight may look at a fair lady. It will turn to anger, for he whom you struck down was King Arthur, and the other was the good knight Sir Lancelot. For if there had been five hundred knights in the meadow, he would not have refused them, and yet he said he would refuse me. From that I knew it was Sir Lancelot, for he always gives way to me, and shows me great kindness; and he bears the flower of all chivalry, without exception. If he is truly angry, and will not spare his opponent, I know of no knight alive whom Sir Lancelot cannot overcome, whether on horseback or on foot.'

'I cannot believe,' said Palamides, 'that King Arthur would ride like that, in secret, as a poor knight-errant.'

'Ah,' said Sir Tristan, 'you do not know my lord Arthur, for all knights may learn to be a knight from him. And so you should be sorry for your unkindly deeds to so noble a king.'

Then there was a proclamation, that when the knights heard a horn blow they should make jousts as they did the first day. And Sir Ywaine son of King Urien and Sir Lucan the butler began the jousts the second day. And at the first encounter Sir Ywaine struck down the son of the king of Scots; and Sir Lucan ran against the king of Wales, and they shattered their spears; and they were so fierce in their charge that both fell to the ground. Then the men of Orkney remounted Sir Lucan. And Sir Tristan came into the field and struck down Sir Uwaine and Sir Lucan; and Sir Palamides struck down two other knights; and Sir Gareth struck down two more knights. Then Arthur said to Sir Lancelot: 'Those three knights are doing exceedingly well, especially the first who jousted.'

'Sir,' said Lancelot, that knight has hardly started, but you will see him do marvels today.' And the duke of Orkney's son then came into the place, and they began to do many deeds of arms. When Sir Tristan saw them begin, he said to Palamides: 'How do you feel you? Will you do as well today as you did yesterday?'

'No,' said Palamides, 'I feel so weary, and so badly bruised from yesterday, that I cannot fight for as long as I did yesterday.'

'I am sorry for that,' said Sir Tristan, 'for I shall miss you today.'

Sir Palamides said: 'Do not rely on me, for I cannot do as well as I did yesterday.'

But Palamides only said this to deceive Sir Tristan.

'Sir,' said Sir Tristan to Sir Gareth, 'I must then rely on you; do not go far from me, and rescue me if need be.'

'I shall not fail you,' said Sir Gareth. Then Sir Palamides rode alone; and then out of envy of Sir Tristan he put himself in the thick of the fighting with the men of Orkney, and there he did such marvellous deeds of arms that all men wondered at him, for no one could withstand his blows. When Sir Tristan saw Sir Palamides do such deeds, he marvelled and said to himself: 'He is weary of my company.' So Sir Tristan watched him for a long time and did little else, for he was amazed at the strength of Sir Palamides as he fought.

'Sir,' said Sir Gareth to Sir Tristan, 'remember what Sir Dinadan said to you yesterday, when he called you a coward; he did not say so out of malice, for you are the man in the world that he most loves. He said it to guard your honour; show me what you can do today, and stop marvelling at Sir Palamides, for he is trying to win all the praise and honour from you.'

'I can well believe it,' said Sir Tristan. 'Now that I realise his ill will and envy, you shall see that if I do my utmost, the praise that is now his shall be mine.'

Then Sir Tristan rode into the thickest of the fighting, and did such great deeds of arms, that everyone said that Sir Tristan did twice as much as Sir Palamides had done before. And then the acclaim for Sir Palamides ended, and everyone praised Sir Tristan. 'See how Sir Tristan unhorses so many knights, and how many knights he smites down with his sword, and how many helms and shields he splits.'

And so Sir Tristan defeated all the men of Orkney.

'I told you,' said Sir Lancelot to King Arthur, 'that a knight would play his pageant today. That knight over there has strength and wind, and does the deeds of a true knight.'

'You speak truly,' said Arthur to Lancelot, 'for I never saw a better knight; he is far better than Sir Palamides.'

'Sir, that is right,' said Lancelot, 'for it is that noble knight Sir Tristan.'

'I believe it,' said Arthur.

But when Sir Palamides heard that the crowd no longer acclaimed him, he rode off to one side and watched Sir Tristan. And when Sir Palamides saw Sir Tristan do so marvellously well he wept bitterly out of envy, for he realised that he would get little praise that day if Sir Tristan used all his strength and manhood.

Then King Arthur, and the king of North Wales, and Sir Lancelot du Lac came into the field; and Sir Bleoberis, Sir Bors de Ganis and Sir Ector de Maris were with Sir Lancelot. And then Sir Lancelot with the three knights of his kin did such great deeds of arms that the crowd shouted for Sir Lancelot. They beat the king of Wales and the king of Scots, and made them leave the field; but Sir Tristan and Sir Gareth remained and endured all the attacks. But Sir Lancelot and his three kinsmen spared Sir Tristan. Then Arthur said: 'Is that Sir Palamides who holds out so well?'

'No,' said Sir Lancelot, 'it is the good knight Sir Tristan, for you can see Sir Palamides over there, watching and waiting, and doing little or nothing. Sir, you must realise that Sir Tristan hopes to beat us all out of the field today; but I shall not beat him, but let anyone else try to beat him. Look at Sir Palamides waiting over there, as though he were in a dream; he is very sad that Tristan is doing such deeds of arms.'

'He is a fool,' said Arthur, 'for he was never a match for Sir Tristan. If he envies Sir Tristan, and comes in on the same side as him, he is a false knight.'

As the king and Sir Lancelot talked, Sir Tristan rode in secret out of the fighting; no one saw him except Iseult the Fair and Sir Palamides, for those two would not take their eyes off Sir Tristan. And when Sir Tristan came to his pavilions he found Sir Dinadan in his bed asleep.

'Wake up,' said Tristan, 'you ought to be ashamed to sleep when knights are fighting in the field.'

Then Sir Dinadan got up quickly and said: 'What do you want me to do?'

'Get ready,' said Sir Tristan, 'to ride with me into the field.'

So when Sir Dinadan was armed he looked at Sir Tristan's helm and on his shield, and when he saw so many dents upon his helm and upon his shield, he said, 'It was just as well that I was asleep, for if I had been with you, I would have followed you out of shame rather than prowess; and looking at those dents I would have been as badly beaten as I was yesterday.'

'Enough of your jokes,' said Sir Tristan, 'and come on, so that we can get back in the field again.'

'What,' said Sir Dinadan, 'is your blood up? Yesterday you behaved as if you were dreaming.'

So Sir Tristan put on black armour.

'What is the matter with you today?' said Dinadan, 'You seem wilder than you were yesterday.'

Sir Tristan smiled and said to Dinadan: 'Follow me closely; if you see me outmatched, be behind me, and I shall get you clear.'

So Sir Tristan and Sir Dinadan took their horses. Sir Palamides caught sight of all this, as did Iseult the Fair, for she knew Sir Tristan from all the rest.

When Sir Palamides saw that Sir Tristan was disguised, he planned to harm him. He rode over to a knight who was badly wounded, who sat by a spring to one side of the field.

'Sir knight,' said Sir Palamides, 'lend me your armour and your shield, for mine is too well known in this field, which has done me great damage. You shall have my armour and my shield which are as good as yours.'

'You may have my armour and my shield,' said the knight, 'if they will help you.'

So Sir Palamides armed quickly in that knight's armour and his shield, which shone like crystal or silver, and rode back into the field. Neither Sir Tristan nor King Arthur's party knew Sir Palamides. Just as Sir Palamides came into the field Sir Tristan struck down three knights, as Sir Palamides watched. And then Sir Palamides rode against Sir Tristan, and they broke their great spears down to the handguards. And then they rushed together eagerly with swords. Then Sir Tristan wondered which knight it was who fought so well against him; and he was angry, for he felt that he was very strong, and that once he had defeated him he would not be able to deal with the other knights. So they slashed at each other and gave many heavy strokes, and many knights wondered who was fighting with Sir Tristan. But Iseult the Fair knew well that it was Sir Palamides who fought with Sir Tristan, for she had seen him change his harness with the wounded knight. And then she began to weep so bitterly because of Sir Palamides' treachery that there she swooned.

Then Sir Lancelot came in with the knights of Orkney. And when the other side caught sight of Sir Lancelot, they cried: 'Return, return, here comea Sir Lancelot du Lac.'

And knights came to him and said: 'Sir Lancelot, you must fight with the knight over there in the black armour, for he has almost overcome the knight who fights with him with the silver shield.'

Then Sir Lancelot rode between Sir Tristan. and Sir Palamides, and Sir Lancelot said to Palamides: 'Sir knight, let me have the battle, for you need to rest.' Sir Palamides knew Sir Lancelot well, and so did Sir Tristan, but because Sir Lancelot was a far stronger knight than himself he was glad, and allowed Sir Lancelot to fight with Sir Tristan. For he realised at once that Sir Lancelot had not recognised Sir Tristan, and hoped that Sir Lancelot should beat or shame him. And so Sir Lancelot gave Sir Tristan many heavy blows; if Sir Lancelot did not know Sir Tristan, Sir Tristan knew who Lancelot was. And they fought together for a long while, until Iseult the Fair was almost mad with anguish.

Then Sir Dinadan told Sir Gareth that the knight in the black harness was Sir Tristan: 'And Lancelot is fighting him, and he will have the better of him, for Sir Tristan has already done much this day.'

'Then let us strike him down,' said Sir Gareth.

'It is better that we do that,' said Sir Dinadan, 'than Sir Tristan should be shamed, for over there the strong knight with the silver shield is waiting to fall upon Sir Tristan if need be.'

Gareth rushed at Sir Lancelot, and gave him a great blow upon his helm so that he was dazed. And Sir Dinadan came with a spear, and he struck Sir Lancelot so hard that horse and all fell to the ground.

'For shame,' said Sir Tristan to Sir Gareth and Sir Dinadan, 'why did you smite down so good a knight as he is, when I was fighting him? I was holding him at bay without your help.'

Then Sir Palamides came and struck Sir Dinadan from his horse, and Sir Lancelot, because Sir Dinadan had struck him before, assailed Sir Dinadan very sorely, and Sir Dinadan defended himself mightily. Sir Tristan knew that Sir Dinadan could not hold out against Sir Lancelot, and was sorry. But Sir Palamides made a fresh attack on Sir Tristan. And when Sir Tristan saw him come, he decided to deal with him quickly, because he wanted to help Sir Dinadan, who was in great peril with Sir Lancelot. Sir Tristan galloped at Sir Palamides and gave him a great blow, and then seized him and pulled him down underneath him. The two of them fell, and Sir Tristan leapt up lightly and left Sir Palamides, and went between Sir Lancelot and Dinadan, and fought Lancelot.

At once Sir Dinadan seized Sir Tristan's horse, and said loudly, so that Sir Lancelot might hear it: 'My lord Sir Tristan, take your horse.'

And when Sir Lancelot heard him name Sir Tristan, he said: 'What have I done? I am dishonoured. Ah, my lord Sir Tristan,' said Lancelot, 'why were you disguised? You have put yourself in great peril this day; but I ask you to pardon me, for if I had known you we would not have fought this battle.'

'Sir,' said Sir Tristan, 'this is not the first kindness you showed me.' So they were both remounted.

Then all the people on one side gave Sir Lancelot the honour and the prize, and on the other side all the people gave Sir Tristan the honour and the prize; but Lancelot said: 'No, I am not worthy to have this honour, for I declare before all knights that Sir Tristan has been longer in the field than I, and he has struck down many more knights this day than I have done. And therefore I will give Sir Tristan my voice and my name, and I ask all my lords and fellows to do so.'

Then all the dukes and earls, barons and knights, agreed that Sir Tristan had proved the best knight that day.

Then they blew the trumpets to signal that the knights should go to their lodgings, and Queen Iseult was led to her pavilions. But she was furious with Sir Palamides, for she had seen his treason from beginning to end. And all this time neither Sir Tristan, Sir Gareth nor Dinadan knew of the treason of Sir Palamides.

So when the tournament was done, Sir Tristan, Gareth and Dinadan, rode with Iseult the Fair to their pavilions. And Sir Palamides rode with them in their company in his disguise. Sir Tristan saw him and recognised him as the same knight with the shield of silver who had fought him so hotly that day.

'Sir knight,' said Sir Tristan, 'we do not need your company.'

Sir Palamides answered as if he did not know Sir Tristan: 'One of the best knights of the world commanded me to be in this company, and until he dismisses me from his service I will not be discharged.'

And Sir Tristan knew that it was Sir Palamides.

'Ah, Sir Palamides,' he said, 'you have long been called a gentle knight, but you do not deserve that name; you have showed me great ungentleness today, for you almost brought me to my death. I would have done well enough against you, but Sir Lancelot and you together were too much for me; for I know no knight living for whom Sir Lancelot is not too strong, if he uses all his strength.'

'Alas,' said Sir Palamides, 'are you my lord Sir Tristan?'

'You know me well enough.'

'By my knighthood,' said Palamides, 'until now I did not recognise you; I thought that you were the king of Ireland, for you bore his arms.'

'Indeed I did,' said Sir Tristan, 'and I have that right, for I won them in fair fight from the Morholt.'

'Sir,' said Palamides, 'I thought you had joined Sir Lancelot's side, which was why I joined him.'

'I believe you,' said Sir Tristan, 'and so I forgive you.'

So they rode on to their pavilions; and when they dismounted they unarmed themselves and washed their faces and hands, and went to dine. But when Iseult saw Sir Palamides she flushed, and could not speak for anger. Sir Tristan saw this and said: 'Lady, why are you so angry with us? We have had our work cut out today.'

'My dearest lord,' said Iseult the Fair, 'for God's sake do not be displeased with me, for I saw how you were betrayed and almost brought to your death. I saw exactly how the treachery was done; why should I tolerate such a felon and traitor as Sir Palamides in my presence? I saw him watch you when you went out of the field, and wait on horseback until he saw you come back. Then I saw him ride to the wounded knight, and change armour with him. When he rode back into the field, he looked for you, and deliberately fought with you. I was not greatly afraid of what he might do, but I dreaded Lancelot's attack, who did not recognise you.'

'Lady,' said Palamides, 'say what you will, I must not contradict you; but by my knighthood I did not know Sir Tristan.'

'Sir Palamides,' said Sir Tristan, 'I accept your excuse, even though you attacked me fiercely, and all is pardoned for my part.'

Then Iseult the Fair lowered her head and said no more for the time being.

And then two knights came to the pavilion, where they dismounted and came in fully armed.

'Fair knights,' said Sir Tristan, 'you should not come to me armed while we are at dinner; if you wanted to challenge me when we were in the field, I would have satisfied you.'

'No,' said one of the knights, 'we have not come to fight, but as your friends. I have come to see you, and this knight has come to see Iseult the Fair.'

'Then take off your helms,' said Sir Tristan, 'so that I can see you.'

'We will do so,' said the knights.

While they were unlacing their helms, Sir Dinadan whispered to Sir Tristan: 'Sir, that is Sir Lancelot du Lac who spoke, and the other is my lord King Arthur.'

Sir Tristan said to Iseult the Fair, 'Lady, arise, for here is my lord, King Arthur.'

Then the king and the queen kissed, and Sir Lancelot and Sir Tristan embraced each other; and at the request of Iseult the Fair, King Arthur and Lancelot were unarmed, and there was much merry talk.

'Lady,' said Arthur, 'it is many a day since I first desired to see you, for you have been praised far and wide; and I declare that you are the fairest that ever I saw, and Sir Tristan is as fair and as good a knight as any I know; it seems to me that you are well matched.'

'Sir, God thank you,' said Sir Tristan and Iseult. They talked of many things and of all that had happened in jousts.

'But why,' said King Arthur, 'Sir Tristan, did you fight against us? You are a knight of the Table Round; by right you should have been with us.'

'Sir,' said Sir Tristan, 'here is Dinadan, and Sir Gareth, your own nephew, who persuaded me to be against you.'

'My lord Arthur,' said Gareth, 'I may well bear the blame, but Sir Tristan's deeds are his own.'

'I am sorry for it,' said Dinadan, 'for this wretched Sir Tristan brought us to this tournament, and he caused us to have many great blows.'

At this the king and Lancelot laughed so that they could not stay seated.

'Which knight was it,' said Arthur, 'who pressed you so hard, with the shield of silver?'

'Sir,' said Sir Tristan, 'he is sitting here at table.'

'What,' said Arthur, 'was it Sir Palamides?'

'Indeed it was him,' said Iseult the Fair.

'That was not a knightly deed,' said Arthur, 'and not fitting, for I have heard many people call you a courteous knight.'

'Sir,' said Palamides, 'I did not know Sir Tristan, because he was so disguised.'

'It may well be true,' said Lancelot, 'for I did not know Sir Tristan either; why you did turn on our party?'

'I have pardoned him,' said Sir Tristan, 'and I would be very sorry to leave his fellowship, for I love his company.' So they talked of other things.

And in the evening King Arthur and Sir Lancelot departed to their lodging; but Sir Palamides could not rest all night, but wept bitterly. The next day Sir Tristan, Gareth and Dinadan arose early, and went to Sir Palamides' chamber, where they found him fast asleep, for he had been awake all night, and they could see from his cheeks that he had been weeping. 'Say nothing,' said Sir Tristan, 'for I am sure he is angry and sorry because both I and Iseult the Fair rebuked him.'

Then Sir Tristan had Sir Palamides woken, and told him to get ready, for it was time to go to the field. When they were ready they were armed, and clothed all in red, as was Iseult; and so they led her at a canter through the field to the priory which was her lodging. And then they heard three blasts blow, and every king and knight prepared for the field. And the first two who were ready to joust were Sir Palamides and Sir Kainus le Strange, a knight of the Table Round. And so they met: Sir Palamides struck Sir Kainus so hard that he fell. And at once Sir Palamides struck down another knight, and broke his spear; he pulled out his sword and did extraordinarily well. And everyone acclaimed Sir Palamides. 'Palamides is beginning to play his pageant,' said King Arthur, 'he is a very good knight.'

But as they spoke, Sir Tristan came in like thunder, and he charged at Sir Kay the seneschal, whom he struck clean off his horse; with that same spear Sir Tristan struck down three more knights, and then he drew his sword and did marvellously. Then the acclaim changed from Sir Palamides to Sir Tristan, and everyone cried: 'Tristan, Tristan.' And Sir Palamides was clean forgotten.

'That knight too is playing his pageant,' said Lancelot to Arthur.

'You will see those two knights do wonders today,' said Arthur to Lancelot.

'Sir,' said Lancelot, 'Palamides is jealous of Tristan and is trying to outdo him; but Sir Tristan does not know of the secret envy which Sir Palamides has for him. Everything that Sir Tristan does is for the sake of knighthood.'

And then Sir Gareth and Dinadan did wonderful deeds of arms, so that King Arthur praised them greatly; and the kings and knights of Sir Tristan's side did exceedingly well, and held fast together. Then Arthur and Sir Lancelot took their horses and rode into the thickest of the fighting. And there Sir Tristan unhorsed King Arthur without recognising him; Sir Lancelot would have rescued him, but there were so many against Sir Lancelot that they pulled him down from his horse. And then the king of Ireland and the king of Scots with their knights did their best to take King Arthur and Sir Lancelot prisoner. When Sir Lancelot heard them say this, he fought like a hungry lion, so that no knight dared approach him.

Sir Ector de Maris rode against Sir Palamides, and shivered his spear on him. And then Sir Ector wheeled round and gave Sir Palamides such a slash with a sword that he bent over his saddle-bow; at this Sir Ector pulled down Sir Palamides under his feet. Then Sir Ector de Maris brought Sir Lancelot du Lac a horse, and told him to mount; but Sir Palamides leapt in front of him, caught the horse by the bridle, and jumped into the saddle. So Sir Ector brought Sir Lancelot another horse, and when he was mounted again, he struck down four knights with one spear. Sir Lancelot brought to King Arthur one of the best horses he could find, and then Sir Lancelot with King Arthur and a few of his knights did marvellous deeds; Sir Lancelot alone struck down and pulled down thirty knights. Nonetheless the other party stood so fast that King Arthur and his knights were defeated.

Then Sir Tristan called Sir Palamides, Sir Gareth and Sir Dinadan, and said: 'Friends, I shall fight on King Arthur's side, for I never saw so few men do so well, and as knights of the Round Table we will be disgraced if we watch our lord King Arthur, and that noble knight Sir Lancelot, being defeated.'

'It would be a good deed,' said Sir Gareth and Sir Dinadan.

'Do your best,' said Palamides, 'for I will not change from the side I came into the field with.'

'You are doing that because of me,' said Sir Tristan; 'God speed you in your journey.'

And so Sir Palamides left them. Then Sir Tristan, Gareth, and Dinadan joined Sir Lancelot. Sir Lancelot struck down the king of Ireland from his horse, and the king of Scots, and the king of Wales; and then Arthur ran to Sir Palamides and unhorsed him; and Sir Tristan overcame everyone he met. Sir Gareth and Sir Dinadan did noble deeds; and all the other parties began to flee.

'Alas,' said Palamides, 'I have lost all the honour that I won'; and he went his way weeping, and rode until he came to a well, where he turned his horse loose, and took off his armour, and wept like a madman. Then many knights gave the prize to Sir Tristan, and many gave the prize to Sir Lancelot.

'Fair lords,' said Sir Tristan, 'I thank you for the honour you would give me, but I ask with all my heart that you should give your voice to Sir Lancelot, for that is what I will do.'

But Sir Lancelot would not have it, and so the prize was given to them both. Then every man rode to his lodging, and Sir Bleoberis and Sir Ector rode with Sir Tristan and Iseult the Fair to their pavilions. Then as Sir Palamides was at the well weeping, the kings of Wales and of Scotland rode hurriedly past, and they saw Sir Palamides in his distress. So they caught Sir Palamides' horse for him, and made him arm himself and mount his horse; and so he rode with them, weeping pitifully. So when Sir Palamides came to the pavilions of Sir Tristan and Iseult the Fair, he asked the kings to wait for him while he spoke to Sir Tristan. And when he came to the door of the pavilions, Sir Palamides said in a loud voice: 'Where are you, Sir Tristan of Lyonesse?'

'Sir,' said Dinadan, 'that is Palamides.'

'What, Sir Palamides, will you not come in here among us?'

'Shame on you, traitor,' said Palamides, 'if it was daylight I would kill you with my own hands. If I can ever get you alone, you shall die for today's deed.'

'Sir Palamides,' said Sir Tristan, 'you blame me wrongly, for if you had done as I did you would have won honour. But since you warn me so clearly, I shall be very wary of you.'

'Shame on you, traitor,' said Palamides, and with that he left.

The next day Sir Tristan, Sir Bleoberis, Sir Ector de Maris, Sir Gareth, and Sir Dinadan journeyed by sea and land and brought Iseult the Fair to Joyous Gard, where they rested for a week, with all the mirth and sport they could devise. And King Arthur and his knights went to Camelot, and Sir Palamides rode with the two kings; and he grieved as much as a man could, for he was not only in despair at parting from Iseult the Fair, but he was also full of sorrow at leaving the fellowship of Sir Tristan; when Sir Palamides remembered how kind and gentle Sir Tristan was, he could never be cheerful. And Palamides had killed a knight in the tournament at Lonezep, and it chanced that he rode through that knight's lands, where his vassals seized him, and condemned him to death. But as they took him to judgement, Sir Lancelot came up and recognised him; and he rescued him, though Palamides did not know him, for he was disguised. The two knights rode to Joyous Gard, and outside the castle they met with Sir Tristan.

'Fair knight,' said Sir Tristan to Sir Lancelot, 'where are you from?'

'I am a knight errant,' said Sir Lancelot, 'riding to seek adventures.'

'What is your name? said Sir Tristan. 'Sir, at this time I will not tell you.'

Then Sir Lancelot said to Sir Tristan and to Palamides: 'Now you have met, I will leave you.'

'Not so,' said Sir Tristan; 'for knighthood's sake, ride with me to my castle.'

'I cannot ride with you, for I have many deeds to do in other places, and for now I cannot stay with you.'

'As you are a true knight,' said Sir Tristan, 'let me entertain you tonight.' Then Sir Lancelot agreed: for in truth he had only come into that country to see Sir Tristan.

When they came into Joyous Gard they alighted, and their horses were led into a stable; and then they unarmed themselves. And when Sir Lancelot was unhelmed, Sir Tristan and Sir Palamides knew him. Then Sir Tristan embraced Sir Lancelot, and so did Iseult the Fair; and Palamides kneeled before Sir Lancelot and thanked him. When Sir Lancelot saw Sir Palamides kneel, he quickly took him up and said: 'Sir Palamides, I and any knight in this land would be bound to rescue so noble a knight as you, anywhere in the length and breadth of this realm.' And they were all joyful; but the more often Sir Palamides saw Iseult the Fair, the sadder he became each day.

Then Sir Lancelot left within three or four days, and Sir Ector de Maris rode with him; and Dinadan and Sir Palamides were left there with Sir Tristan for two months and more. But Sir Palamides faded and mourned, to everyone's amazement. One day, at dawn, Sir Palamides went into the forest by himself alone; and there he found a well. He looked into it, and in the water he saw his own face, disturbed and faded, not at all as he used to be. 'What does this mean?' said Sir Palamides, and he said to himself: 'Ah, Palamides, Palamides, why are you so faded, when you were once called one of the fairest knights of the world? I will not lead this life any more, for I may never get her whom I love.' And he lay down by the well, and began to make a poem about Iseult the Fair and himself.

And the same day Sir Tristan had ridden into the forest to hunt deer; but he would never go hunting unarmed, because of Sir Breuse sans Pité. And as Sir Tristan rode past, he heard someone singing in a loud voice, and it was Sir Palamides lying by the well. Sir Tristan rode softly thither, for he thought it was some knight errant. And when Sir Tristan came near him he dismounted and tied his horse fast to a tree, and then approached on foot; and he saw Sir Palamides by the well, singing a sad song of Iseult the Fair, which was both marvellously well written, and full of the deepest sorrow. Sir Tristan heard the whole song from beginning to end, and it troubled him greatly.

When Sir Tristan had heard all Sir Palamides' complaints, he was furiously angry, and thought of killing him as he lay there. Then Sir Tristan remembered that Sir Palamides was unarmed, and restrained his anger. He went quietly to Sir Palamides, and said: 'Sir Palamides, I have heard your complaint, and now I know of your treason towards me, for which you shall die; but I cannot kill you unarmed. What have you to say in your defence?'

'Sir,' said Palamides, 'my defence is this: as for Queen Iseult the Fair, I assure you that I love her above all other ladies in this world; and I shall share the fate of that noble knight Sir Kaherdin, who died for the love of Iseult the Fair. For I have loved Iseult the Fair many a day, and she has been the cause of my reputation, for else I had been the most ordinary knight in the world. Because of her, I have won such fame as I have; for when I thought of Iseult the Fair I won fame wherever I went. But I never had any reward from her all the days of my life, and I have still been her true knight. Sir Tristan, I do not fear death, for I do not care whether I live or die. And if I were armed as you are, I should at once do battle with you. I have done you no treason, for love is free for all men, and though I have loved your lady, she is my lady as well as yours; if either of us is wronged, it is I, for you have your desire of her, and I will never do so; and yet I shall love her to the last days of my life as well as you.'

Then Sir Tristan said: 'I will fight with you to the death.'

'I grant you that,' said Palamides, 'for I shall never fight in a better quarrel, and if I die at your hands, I cannot be killed by a better knight. And since I know that I shall never be loved by Iseult the Fair, I am as ready to die as to live.'

'Then set a day,' said Sir Tristan, 'when we shall do battle.'

'In a fortnight,' said Palamides, 'I will meet with you in the meadow in front of Joyous Gard.'

'For shame,' said Sir Tristan, 'will you set a day so far off? Let us fight tomorrow.'

'No,' said Palamides, 'for I am weak, and have been long sick for the love of Iseult the Fair, and so I will rest till I have my strength again.'

So then Sir Tristan and Sir Palamides promised faithfully to meet at the well in a fortnight. 'I remember,' said Sir Tristan to Palamides, 'that you once broke a promise when I rescued you from Breuse sans Pité and nine knights; you promised to meet me at the stone near the grave beside Camelot, and you failed to do so.'

'I was in prison that day,' said Palamides to Sir Tristan, 'so I could not keep my promise.'

'If you had kept your promise,' said Sir Tristan, 'we would not have to fight now.'

And they went their ways. Sir Palamides took his horse and his harness, and rode to King Arthur's court, where he got four knights and four sergeants-of-arms, and returned to Joyous Gard. And in the meanwhile Sir Tristan hunted every day; and about three days before the battle was to take place, as Sir Tristan hunted a deer, an archer shot at the same deer, and by misfortune he struck Sir Tristan in the thigh, and the arrow killed Sir Tristan's horse. When Sir Tristan was hurt he was very grieved, for he bled badly; he took another horse, and rode sadly to Joyous Gard, sorrowing more for the promise that he had made with Sir Palamides to do battle with him within three days, than for the wound in his thigh. And no one could cheer him with anything that they could suggest, not even Queen Iseult the Fair; for he believed that Sir Palamides had shot him so that he should not be able to do battle with him on the day set.

But none of Tristan's knights believed that Sir Palamides would hurt Sir Tristan in this way, either by his own hands or by plotting with others. Then when the fortnight was up, Sir Palamides came to the well with four knights from Arthur's court, and four sergeants-of-arms, whom he had brought to keep a record of his battle with Sir Tristan. He came into the field, and waited nearly two hours; and then he sent a squire to Sir Tristan, and asked him to come into the field to keep his promise.

When the squire came to Joyous Gard, as soon as Sir Tristan heard of his arrival he ordered that the squire should come to his presence even though he was in bed. 'My lord Sir Tristan,' said Palamides' squire, 'my lord Palamides is waiting for you in the field, and he wants to know whether you will fight or not.'

'I am very grieved by this news,' said Sir Tristan, 'tell Sir Palamides that if I were in good health, I would not lie here, and he would have no need to send for me if I could either ride or walk.' And to prove that he was not lying, Sir Tristan showed him his thigh with a wound six inches deep.

'Now you have seen my wound, tell your lord that this is no feigned matter; as soon as I am whole I shall seek him endlong and overthwart, and that I promise you as I am true knight. If I can ever find him, he shall have his fill of fighting from me.'

So the squire departed; and when Palamides learned that Tristan was hurt he was glad and said: 'Now I am sure I shall have no shame, for I know that I would have been hard pressed by him, and probably have been defeated, for he is the hardest knight alive in battle except Sir Lancelot.'

So Sir Palamides rode where fortune led him, and within a month Sir Tristan was healed. And then he took his horse, and rode from country to country, achieving strange adventures wherever he rode; and he asked after Sir Palamides all the time, but all that summer Sir Tristan could never find Sir Palamides. But as Tristan went in search of Palamides, he won many great battles, so that everyone praised Sir Tristan, and said nothing of Sir Lancelot. For this Sir Lancelot's brothers and kinsmen would have slain Sir Tristan because of his fame. But when Sir Lancelot learned of this, he said to them openly: 'If out of envy any of you are so bold as to harm my lord, Sir Tristan, I will kill the best of you with my own hands. You should be ashamed for thinking of killing him because of his noble deeds. God prevent that ever any knight as noble as Sir Tristan should be destroyed by treason.'

When Sir Tristan came home to Joyous Gard from his adventures, Iseult the Fair told him of the great feast that was to be held the next Whitsunday; and she told him how Sir Lancelot had been missing for two years, and how all that time he had been out of his mind, and had been cured by the Holy Grail. 'Sir,' said Iseult, I know it all, for Queen Guinevere sent me a letter in which she told me all this, and asked you to search for him. And now, blessed be God,' said Iseult the Fair, 'he is whole and sound and has come back to the court.'

'I am glad of that,' said Sir Tristan, 'and now you and I will prepare to go to the feast.'

'I shall not go,' said Iseult, 'for because of me, many knights are against you, and you will be challenged by them if I am with you.'

'But I will not go,' said Sir Tristan, 'unless you are there.'

'If that is how things stand,' said Iseult the Fair, 'I shall be blamed by all queens and ladies of estate; for how can you, one of the noblest knights of the world, and a knight of the Round Table, miss that feast? What will the knights say among themselves? "See how Sir Tristan hunts and hawks, and cowers within a castle with his lady, and forsakes honour.""Alas," some will say, "it is a pity that he was ever made a knight, or that he should ever have had the love of a lady."And what will queens and ladies say of me? "It is a pity that I hold such a noble knight as you from winning fame."' 'That is well said,' said Sir Tristan to Iseult the Fair, 'and it is noble counsel; you have truly shown your love for me. I will in part do as you advise. But no man or child shall ride with me: I will go alone. And I will ride there on Tuesday next coming, with only my spear and my sword.'

And so when the day came Sir Tristan took his leave of Iseult the Fair; she sent with him four knights, and within half a mile he sent them back again. But a mile after that Sir Tristan saw Sir Palamides, who had struck down a knight, and almost wounded him to death. Then Sir Tristan regretted that he had no armour on, and held back from going to meet him. Sir Palamides recognised Sir Tristan, and shouted to him: 'Sir Tristan, now we have met, and before we part we will redress our old scores.'

'As for that,' said Sir Tristan, 'no Christian man can boast that I fled from him; you are a Saracen, Sir Palamides, and you too shall never boast that Sir Tristan of Lyonesse fled from you.'

Sir Tristan spurred his horse to a gallop, and came straight upon Sir Palamides with all his might, breaking his spear on him in a hundred pieces. At once Sir Tristan drew his sword, and he turned his horse and struck at Palamides, giving him six great strokes upon his helm. At this Sir Palamides stood still, and looked at Sir Tristan, and marvelled at his madness; and he said to himself: 'If Sir Tristan had his armour on, it would be hard to make him end this battle, but if I turn round and kill him, I shall be dishonoured wherever I go.'

Then Sir Tristan said: 'You coward knight, what do you want to do; why will you not fight with me? I shall withstand all your malice.'

'Ah, Sir Tristan,' said Palamides, 'you know perfectly well I cannot fight with you, for you are here naked and I am armed, and if I kill you, dishonour shall be mine. I know your strength and your hardiness and that you can withstand a good knight.'

'That is true,' said Sir Tristan.

'Then answer a question for me,' said Sir Palamides.

'Tell me what it is,' said Sir Tristan.

'Suppose,' said Sir Palamides, 'that you were fully armed as I am now, and I was as naked as you are now, what would you do to me?'

'Ah,' said Sir Tristan, 'now I see your purpose, Sir Palamides, for I have to pronounce my own doom; but what I shall say is not spoken out of fear of you. It is this: Sir Palamides, you must leave me, for I would not fight you if matters were as you have described.'

'Nor will I,' said Palamides, 'so ride on your way.'

'That is for me to choose,' said Sir Tristan, 'whether I ride on or stay. But Sir Palamides, I marvel that you who are so good a knight, will not be christened, when your brother, Sir Safere, was christened long ago.'

'I may not yet be christened,' said Sir Palamides, 'because of a vow that I made many years ago; in my heart I believe in Jesu Christ and his mild mother Mary; but I have one battle to fight, and when that is done I will be baptised with a good will.'

'You shall not seek that battle for long,' said Tristan, 'for God forbid that through my failing you should live a Saracen any longer. Over there is a knight whom you, Sir Palamides, have hurt and struck down. Let me be armed in his armour, and I shall soon fulfil your vow.'

'As you will,' said Palamides. So they rode over to the knight who sat on a bank, and Sir Tristan greeted him, and he weakly returned his greeting.

'Sir knight,' said Sir Tristan, 'tell me your name.'

'Sir, he said, 'my name is Sir Galleron of Galway, a knight of the Round Table.'

'I am sorry that you are wounded,' said Sir Tristan, 'but I must ask you to lend me all your armour, for as you see I am unarmed, and I must do battle with this knight.'

'Sir,' said the wounded knight, 'you shall have it with a good will; but you must beware, for I warn you that knight is formidable. I beg you, tell me your name, and the name of the knight who has beaten me.'

'Sir, I am Sir Tristan of Lyonesse, and the knight who has hurt you is Sir Palamides, brother to the good knight Sir Safere; he is still unchristened. And either he shall kill me or I him, or he shall be christened before we take leave of each other.'

'My lord Sir Tristan,' said Sir Galleron, 'your renown and worship are well known through many realms; God save you this day from shame.'

Then Sir Tristan unarmed Galleron, who was a noble knight, and had done many deeds of arms, and he was a large and well-built knight. And when he was unarmed he stood up, even though he was bruised in the back with a spear; and Sir Galleron armed Sir Tristan as best he could. And then Sir Tristan mounted his own horse, and got Sir Galleron's spear in his hand; and at the same time Sir Palamides was ready. And so they came hurtling together, and each struck theother in the middle of their shields. Sir Palamides' spear broke, and Sir Tristan brought down Palamides' horse; and Sir Palamides, as soon as he could, got clear of his horse, and made ready his shield, and pulled out his sword. At this Sir Tristan dismounted and tied his horse to a tree.

And then they came together like two wild boars, lashing together, tracing and traversing like noble men who had been well tried and tested in battle; but Sir Palamides dreaded the strength of Sir Tristan, and tried to keep him at a distance. Thus they fought for more than two hours, but often Sir Tristan struck such strokes at Sir Palamides that he forced him to his knees; and Sir Palamides cut away many pieces of Sir Tristan's shield; and then Sir Palamides wounded Sir Tristan, for he was a skilled fighting man. Then Sir Tristan was mad with anger, and rushed upon Sir Palamides with such force that Sir Palamides fell to the ground; and as he leapt to his feet, Sir Tristan wounded Palamides badly through the shoulder. Sir Tristan still fought as hard as ever, nor did Sir Palamides falter, but gave him many heavy blows. At last Sir Tristan redoubled his blows and struck Sir Palamides' sword out of his hand; if Sir Palamides had stooped for his sword he would have been killed.

Then Palamides stood still and looked at his sword very sorrowfully.

'Palamides,' said Sir Tristan, 'now have I you at my mercy just as you had me earlier today; but it shall never be said among good knights, that Sir Tristan killed a knight who was weaponless; so pick up the sword, and let us make an end of this battle.'

'I could fight on if I wished,' said Palamides, 'but I have no great desire to fight any more, because I have not offended you so gravely that we may not be friends again. If I have wronged you, it was for the love of Iseult the Fair. She is peerless above all other ladies, and I never did her any dishonour; through her I have earned much of my reputation. And I never wronged her own person, and any offence I have committed was against you. For that you have given me this day many heavy blows, and I have given you some in return; and I have never met your match, except for Sir

Lancelot du Lac. Therefore my lord, I ask you to forgive me for my offences; and this very day take me to the nearest church, where I will confess, and have me baptised. Then we will ride to Arthur's court for the Whitsun feast.'

'Take your horse,' said Sir Tristan, 'and it shall be as you say; may God forgive all your envy, for I do so. And within a mile of here is the bishop of Carlisle, who shall give you the sacrament of baptism.'

Then they took their horses and Sir Galleron rode with them. And when they came to the bishop Sir Tristan told him what they desired. Then the bishop had a great vessel filled with water, and when he had consecrated it he heard Sir Palamides' confession, and baptised him, and Sir Tristan and Sir Galleron were his godfathers. And then soon after they departed, riding toward Camelot, where King Arthur and Queen Guinevere and most of the knights of the Round Table were. And so the king and all the court were glad that Sir Palamides was christened. And after the feast Sir Tristan went back to Joyous Gard, and Sir Palamides followed the adventure of the Questing Beast.

KING MARK SLAYS TRISTAN, AND ISEULT DIES OF GRIEF

Mark, traitor to his race, had in the meantime enlisted the aid of the Saxons, and invaded Logres, for he hated Arthur as much as Tristan. He came unexpectedly to Joyous Gard, where the gates stood open, for no one had warned those who lived there that there was war in the land; and Tristan was lying wounded at an abbey far away. Mark seized Iseult, and fled back to Cornwall.

When Tristan recovered, he followed Iseult to Tintagel, and Dinas the seneschal gave him shelter. Tristan found means to meet Iseult in secret in her chamber in the castle; but one day, as he sat at Iseult's feet, playing his harp, and singing a new song he had composed in her honour, the jealous Andred heard him, and went to summon Mark. The king, traitor that he was, came with a poisoned spear which Morgan le Fay had given him, and gave him a great wound. Tristan was too weak to strike back at the king, who fled, and he was taken back to the castle of Dinas the seneschal. There he lay in increasing agony, and no doctor could help him. Mark, at first overjoyed that he had at last avenged himself, heard Iseult's grief, and little by little realised what he had done. Learning that Tristan was not expected to live for more than two or three days, he repented of his misdeeds, and when Tristan asked to see him, he and his household, in deepest mourning, went to Dinas' castle. Here they found Tristan too weak to sit up.

Tristan said to Mark: 'Lord, you may well rejoice, for Tristan has come to the end of his life. But the day will come when you would give half your kingdom not to have been his murderer.'

The king wept silently, and Tristan forgave him: 'Do not weep, my lord and uncle. This is Andred's doing more than yours. I ask only this, that Iseult may see me once more.'

And the king consented.

When Iseult came, Tristan said: 'Alas, your coming cannot cure me: Tristan who loved you is dead.'

Iseult wept and sighed, and asked, 'Is this the truth?'

And Tristan answered, holding out his arms: 'Are these the arms of Tristan that once held you? Look, they are not Tristan's, but those of a dead man.'

The next day, he pardoned Mark, and then turned to Iseult, saying: 'What will you do after my death? Is it possible that Iseult can live without Tristan?'

Iseult answered, weak with grief and anguish: 'I am so faint with suffering that I cannot survive your death. Come, hold me in your arms.'

She lay down beside him, and Tristan said: 'Now that I hold you, death has no terrors for me.'

And as Tristan embraced her, she died in his arms; and Tristan, who might have lived another hour, saw that she was dead, and yielded up the ghost. At first those around them thought that they had fainted, but they soon knew that they were both dead, dead of the great love that they bore one another.

And Mark interred them with great pomp, honouring them in death as he had dishonoured them in life; he laid them in the richest tomb that had ever been seen, golden, set with precious stones; on it gleamed sapphires and rubies and emeralds. It stood in the midst of the church, with two statues above it, cast in copper, living images of the two lovers, a shrine at which all those who loved truly and knew love's high secrets came to worship.

ACKNOWLEDGEMENTS

This book is based on the work of the great translators of Arthurian legend, and follows their texts with varying degrees of fidelity. In the case of the master of Arthurian translation, Sir Thomas Malory, his version has been put into modern English (and particularly into modern English word order!) while retaining as much as possible of the original; but inevitably it is a pale shadow of his rich and often idiosyncratic language. His work is the basis for parts of *Arthur and the Round Table* and *Tristan the Courtier*, and for most of *Galahad*. Another great translator, Hilaire Belloc, working from the French of Joseph Bedier, is the source for much of *Tristan and Iseult*. Here I have – reluctantly – modified his more archaic poetic phrases, while happily borrowing the strong and simple lines which make this a classic retelling. I am most grateful to Peters, Fraser and Dunlop and the Estate of Hilaire Belloc for granting me permission to do this.

Nigel Bryant's excellent version of the *Perlesvaus* or *High Book of the Grail* is the basis for the St Augustine's Chapel episode in *Arthur the Emperor*; my thanks to the author for permission to use this.

I am grateful to Penguin Books for permission to use excerpts from Geoffrey of Monmouth's *History of the Kings of Britain* translated by Lewis Thorpe; Gottfried von Strassburg's *Tristan*, translated by A. T. Hatto; and *The Death of King Arthur* translated by James Cable. These form the basis, respectively, for *Arthur the Emperor*, parts of *Tristan and Iseult*, the second part of *Perceval*, and the end of *Arthur and the Round Table*. The translations of the *True History of the Death of Arthur* (at the end of *Arthur the Emperor*) and the *Elucidation Prologue* (at the beginning of *Perceval*) are my own.

The text from the four editions published by Penguin has been slightly modified to harmonise spelling of names, and to avoid abrupt changes of style and vocabulary; the same applies to the versions by Nigel Bryant. In these cases, changes have been kept to the minimum required to ensure that the text reads easily.

In particular, names have been standardised throughout, to ensure that the reader is not distracted by discontinuities; the spellings finally selected have largely been determined by familiarity rather than any scholarly logic.

FURTHER READING

The major Arthurian romances are all available in translation, but Sir Thomas Malory is probably the best starting point for further explorations: he offers a version of most of the main themes of the medieval romances, and the most accessible edition is that by Janet Cowan in Penguin Classics.

For the individual romances, working in chronological order, there is an Everyman collection of the works of Chretien de Troyes, translated by D. D. R. Owen. However, the best source for Chretien's *Perceval* is the version by Nigel Bryant, published by Boydell, because it includes the work of the three writers who continued the unfinished romance, and eventually completed it. Nigel Bryant has also translated the *Perlesvaus* as *The High Book of the Grail* (Boydell), which is the first alternative version of the Grail story. Wolfram von Eschenbach's *Parzival* is available in Penguin Classics, translated by A. T. Hatto, as is his version of Gottfried von Strassburg's *Tristan*, together with fragments of the earlier French romances. There is also a version of *Parzival* by Charles E. Passage and Helen Mustard published by Vintage; neither of the existing translations of this very difficult romance are really satisfactory, and a new version by Cyril Edwards is in preparation. The Hilaire Belloc translation of Joseph Bedier's compilation of the early Tristan romances is available as a Vintage paperback.

The romances of the so-called 'Vulgate Cycle', the main texts of the Arthurian story in the Middle Ages, are available complete in a version by several hands under the editorship of Norris Lacy; it is in five large volumes, and is published by Garland, New York. Two branches are available in Penguin Classics: *The Quest for the Holy Grail* translated by Pauline Matarasso, and *The Death of Arthur* translated by James Cable. For the less well-known romances, see the *Arthurian Archives* series published by Boydell, which so far cover Norse and Dutch romances.